FAMILY LAW: PROCESSES, PRACTICES AND PRESSURES

Family Law
Processes, Practices and Pressures

Proceedings of the Tenth World Conference of the International Society of Family Law, July 2000, Brisbane, Australia

Edited by

John Dewar

and

Stephen Parker

HART PUBLISHING
OXFORD AND PORTLAND, OREGON
2003

Published in North America (US and Canada) by
Hart Publishing
c/o International Specialized Book Services
5804 NE Hassalo Street
Portland, Oregon
97213-3644
USA

Hart Publishing is a specialist legal publisher based in Oxford, England. To order further copies of this book or to request a list of other publications please write to:

Hart Publishing, Salters Boatyard, Folly Bridge, Abingdon Rd, Oxford, OX1 4LB
Telephone: +44 (0)1865 245533 Fax: +44 (0) 1865 794882
email: mail@hartpub.co.uk
WEBSITE: http//:www.hartpub.co.uk

British Library Cataloguing in Publication Data
Data Available

ISBN 1-84113-308-6 (paperback)

Typeset by SNP Best-set Typesetter Ltd., Hong Kong
Printed and bound in Great Britain by
Biddles Ltd, www.biddles.co.uk

Contents

Part II: Practices

Part III: Pressures

Introduction

John Dewar and Stephen Parker*

The environment in which family law systems operate around the world is, it seems, becoming more complex. There is growing pressure on legislators to 'do something' about family law and its administration (although what that 'something' is varies according to taste—to arrest a perceived decline in family life, to implement international human rights norms, to advance someone's rights, to improve the protection of vulnerable groups, to protect the public purse). Courts are increasingly under pressure to deploy diminishing resources cost-effectively in the face of a seemingly inexorable increase in demand for their services. Legal practitioners find they have to adapt to these changes, and adjust their practices to a world in which it is unclear whether there is a role for lawyers at all. At the same time, people's lives change—family life is lived in more diverse forms and family practices are becoming more subtle, attenuated and diverse than ever before.

This volume is a collection of papers from the tenth World Conference of the International Society of Family Law, held in July 2000 in Brisbane, Australia. The conference's theme, 'Processes, Practices and Pressures', was designed to capture some of these trends. The theme was designed to permit an exploration of the complexities of the family law environment—whether top-down pressures coming from international or domestic legislators, or bottom-up changes in social and professional practices. The resulting collection of papers is broad-ranging, but reveals a number of consistent threads.

THE IMPACT OF CONSTITUTIONAL AND HUMAN RIGHTS NORMS

Postwar family law has been characterised in many jurisdictions by wide-ranging discretionary decision-making vested in courts. This has been thought necessary to enable courts to tailor solutions to individual circumstances, and expresses a belief that family law outcomes are better if tailored rather than prescribed in advance. One consequence of this is that family law has not, on the whole, been

* John Dewar is Professor and Dean of Law, Griffith Law School, Queensland, Australia; Stephen Parker is Professor and Dean of Law, Faculty of Law, Monash University, Melbourne.

thought of as conferring rights on family members, in the sense of claims to specific outcomes. This is changing, however, as international human rights conventions are perceived as having implications for state family laws; and as lawyers become more creative in their use of constitutional argument to advance the claims of groups hitherto excluded from the mainstream of family law procedures and remedies, and from the public law entitlements associated with 'family' membership. The chapters by Sutherland and by Roca and Morales explore the implications of human rights arguments in a family law context.

THE CULTURAL CONTEXT

At an international level, the universalising tendencies of human rights frequently brush up against local cultural or religious norms and pose the question of which is to prevail. At the same time, within each legal system, the constitutional norms of the state, or the assumptions underlying state family law itself, may sit uneasily with the practices of religious or ethnic groups. This is often a fruitful source of tension for family law, and is the subject of the chapters by Jessep, who explores the relationship between customary law and constitutional law in Papua New Guinea; Knoetze, who considers the relationship between customary inheritance practices and state law in South Africa; and Freeman, who looks at some recent English cases involving questions of race or religion. If there is a pattern detectable in all this, it seems to be that there is a convergence between countries in which Western legal principles have been superimposed on pre-existing customary law (where there is a rolling back of recognition of customary law) and Western countries such as the United Kingdom, which have a large ethnic or religious minorities (to whom legal principles are being slowly accommodated).

GIVING CHILDREN AN EFFECTIVE VOICE

Article 12 of the UN Convention on the Rights of the Child states that children have a right to an opportunity to be heard in judicial or administrative proceedings affecting them, and that children capable of forming views should be able to express them. Yet, in many jurisdictions, the means by which children's views are ascertained and taken into account falls some way short of the standard set by the Convention. The presentation of a child's view to a decision-maker is often heavily dependent on, or mediated by, an adult; and the shift towards mediation and other forms of non-judicial dispute resolution may mean that there is no formal process for bringing children's views to light at all. All of this means that giving full and effective force to Article 12 requires a more thorough-going examination of the processes and practices of family dispute resolution than has occurred hitherto. The chapters by Chisholm, Lowe and Murch, Masson, and Tapp et al. address the issue of the extent to which children are currently seen as autonomous agents in the family law system, with views to be respected and properly taken into account and, to the extent that they are not, how things can be changed so as to give better effect to the spirit of Article 12. The radical implications of adopting a child-centred approach to decision-making are illustrated by Carol Smart's chapter, which offers a clue to what children might really want if asked. Smart's work offers a powerful challenge to some of the assumptions made about how best to resolve parental disagreement over living arrangements for children.

POST-SEPARATION PARENTING

A striking feature of family law policy during the final decade of the twentieth century has been the increased emphasis on the sustenance and management of post-separation parenting. The rise of parenthood as a significant legal status, coupled with increasingly insistent demands that men be treated 'equally' as parents after divorce, has led to new legal frameworks and practices for managing shared parenting over time. Richard Collier's chapter offers a subtle and cogently argued reading of the cultural-legal context of these developments; and Reg Graycar shows how law reform in this area can be driven by anecdote rather than by a consideration of research data. The UK *Children Act* 1989, which introduced the notion of joint but independent parental responsibility, has been copied more or less directly in many countries around the world. The Portuguese experience of such legislation described by Sottomayor will have resonance in those jurisdictions that have followed the path of the *Children Act.* Yet making shared parenting after separation a reality for many families requires more than just a legislative prescription. The sustaining of parental relationships over time, between adults who no longer wish to live with each other, requires innovative service delivery of the sorts described by Bastard and Kelly in their chapters, dealing respectively with contact centres and special Masters programmes for high-conflict couples. Bastard's chapter, however, highlights some of the potential contradictions and uncertainties entailed in attempting to maintain parent–child relationships in these circumstances—in particular, whether post-separation parent–child relations should be regarded as dyadic (ie as existing between the child and each parent individually) or triadic (so that the relation between the child and parents hinges on the relationship *between the parents*).

SHIFTING FINANCES

It is widely acknowledged that family laws have only a limited capacity to control the financial circumstances of divorcing couples after separation. In part, this is because of the rapidly changing economic and financial environment in which family law must operate. The composition of family wealth has changed significantly in the last 25 years—in particular, employment-related assets such as superannuation and stock or share options have, for some families, dwarfed more traditional forms of family investment. Rosettenstein's chapter considers the implications of the latter for law reform and highlights the complexities entailed in dealing with assets acquired during a marriage but which materialise, if at all, at some point in the future. Bissett-Johnson similarly highlights the broader economic context in which family law functions and argues for a more coherent government approach to macro-economic management that puts greater weight on the needs of family members, especially those divorced or separated.

CHANGING FAMILIES, CHANGING NORMS

The diversity of family life, especially as lived after separation or divorce, and the pressure for legal recognition of gay and lesbian relationships has raised acutely the question of how relationships should be defined for legal purposes and with what consequences. Legislators around the world are grappling with this in a range of constitutional and normative contexts. In her chapter, Mazzotta shows how Italian law has struggled to provide a coherent legal framework for families reconstituted after divorce and separation; and Van Der Burght is critical of the way in which the Dutch legislature has introduced the concept of registered partnership. His chapter is a good illustration of the complexities arising from creating and maintaining a status parallel to marriage within one legal system—let alone in the context of an international community of legal systems. Similarly, Parker and Atkins' account of the history of property legislation for unmarried couples highlights some of the complexities confronting legislators in this area.

LAWYERS AND COURTS

There is a near-universal trend in legal systems away from court-based dispute-resolution towards out-of-court alternatives. At the same time, it is recognised that these alternatives are not well suited to dealing with cases involving family violence or child abuse, and there is a growing trend towards developing specialist interventions or pathways to deal with such cases. Muller-Petersen et al. describe such an intervention in Pennsylvania in the United States; and Field et al. examine the use by magistrates in Queensland, Australia of their powers to make ouster orders under state legislation. The funding environment for family law grows increasingly bleak, and some of the papers examine court-centred and legal professional services in the context of shrinking public resources. Burman et al. provide a history of the development of a specialist Family Court in South Africa, and consider its chances of achieving its objectives in a tight funding environment. Hunter provides a summary of her work on measuring the quality of legally aided services in family law—a body of work that, incidentally, amounts to the most comprehensive survey yet undertaken of the work of family lawyers in Australia.

This summary of themes does not account for all the papers appearing in this collection—others cover adoption, actions in tort, matrimonial property systems, the role of fault and research in children's issues. Even so, the themes listed above will, we hope, assist readers to make sense of the collection.

The papers are divided into three sections: Processes, Practices and Pressures. The section on processes considers legal processes and the institutional structures in which they take place, chiefly the courts; the section on practices looks at changing social behaviour and professional or institutional responses to them; and the section on pressures considers the factors driving change in the law or legal system. Inevitably, these three categories are not watertight, and some papers could have appeared under more than one heading. Nevertheless, the arrangement reflects the manner in which the papers were grouped at the conference itself—a conference widely regarded, like the Sydney Olympics held later in the same year, as the 'best ever' ISFL World Conference!

The editors wish to record their thanks to all the contributors, and to all those who gave papers at the conference but which, for whatever reason, do not appear here; to Richard Hart and Hart Publishing for taking the project on for a second time; and to Susan Jarvis for her hard work in producing a manuscript fit to send to the publishers.

John Dewar
Stephen Parker

Brisbane and Melbourne
July 2002

PART I
Processes

1

Children's Participation in the Family Justice System: Translating Principles into Practice

Nigel Lowe and Mervyn Murch*

INTRODUCTION

This paper examines the increasingly important issue of children's participation in the family justice system, focusing on two key questions.[1] Firstly, what are the value positions underlying the concept of children's participation? Secondly, how might the concept be translated into practice? In considering these issues, particular reference will be made to two recent Cardiff studies, one concerned with adoption[2] and the other with divorce.[3]

New Focus on Children's Participation in the Legal Process

Historically, the great shift in English law governing parent and child was the move from the position where children were of no concern at all to one where their welfare was regarded as the court's paramount concern. This fascinating devel-

* Nigel Lowe is Professor of Law and Director of the Centre of International Family Law Studies, Cardiff Law School, and Chair of the Family Studies Research Centre, Cardiff University, Wales. Mervyn Murch is Professor of Law, Cardiff Law School, Wales.

[1] It should be noted that the questions about whether children should participate and how to weigh children's views when they conflict with those of parents and other adults will *not* be discussed since these have been considered extensively elsewhere—see, eg C Piper, 'Ascertaining the Wishes and Feelings of the Child: A Requirement Honoured Largely in the Breach?' [1997] *Fam Law* 796; C Piper 'The Wishes and Feelings of the Child', and J Roche 'Children and Divorce: A Private Affair' in S Day Sclater and C Piper (eds) *Undercurrents of Divorce* (Dartmouth, 1999), pp 55–98.

[2] 'Adopted Children Speaking' (co-directed by Professors Lowe and Murch). A book entitled *Adopted Children Speaking* by C Thomas and V Beckford with N Lowe and M Murch was published by BAAF in 1999.

[3] 'Children's Perspectives and Experience of the Divorce Process', co-directed by Professors I Butler, G Douglas, FL Fincham and M Murch. This project, known by its acronym 'KIDs' (KIDs in Divorce), was completed in June 2000. The first report was submitted to the Economic and Social Research Council and published in Dec 2000 as *Children 5–16 A Research Briefing No 21*. See n 60 below. See also G Douglas, M Murch, M Robinson, L Scanlan and I Butler, 'Children's Perspectives and Experience of the Divorce Process' [2001] *Fam Law* 373.

opment has been well charted and needs no further elaboration here.[4] Notwithstanding the entrenchment of the welfare principle,[5] traditionally under English law children's futures have been decided upon the views of adults—that is, of parents and professionals. In other words, the welfare principle itself is adult-centred and paternalistic.[6] Even so, what we have been witnessing over the last decade or so is an equally significant cultural shift in which children are no longer simply seen as passive victims of family breakdown but increasingly as participants and actors in the family justice process. In consequence, in various family proceedings it is incumbent upon the courts to ascertain and to take duly into account children's own wishes and views.

Internationally, impetus for this new focus has been given by Article 12 of the United Nations Convention on the Rights of the Child 1989, under which:

> States Parties shall assure to the child who is capable of forming his or her own views the right to express those views freely in all matters affecting the child, the views of the child being given due weight in accordance with the age and maturity of the child . . . The child shall in particular be provided the opportunity to be heard in any judicial and administrative proceedings affecting the child, either directly, or through a representative or appropriate body, in a manner consistent with procedural rules of national law.

In Europe, the European Convention on the Exercise of Children's Rights 1996[7] aims to supplement the UN Convention, inter alia, by providing procedural mechanisms by which the voices of children can be heard in legal proceedings concerning them. In particular, Article 3 provides that a child 'considered by internal law as having sufficient understanding' shall, in the case of judicial proceedings affecting him or her, be granted and entitled to request the following rights:

(a) to receive all relevant information;
(b) to be consulted and express his or her views;

[4] See, eg J Hall, 'The Waning of Parental Rights' [1972 B] CLJ 248, S Maidment, *Child Custody and Divorce* (Croom Helm, 1984), Ch 4, N Lowe, 'The Legal Position of Parents and Children in English Law' [1994] *Singapore Journal of Legal Studies* 332, and N Lowe and G Douglas, *Bromley's Family Law* (Butterworths, 9th edn, 1998), pp 300 *et seq*, and the authorities there cited.

[5] In particular, by the House of Lords' decision in *J v C* [1970] AC 668 and, to a lesser extent, *Re KD (A Minor)(Ward: Termination of Access)* [1988] AC 806. But note the much earlier decision in *Ward v Laverty* [1925] AC 101. For an extensive analysis of these and other House of Lords decisions on the development and application of the welfare principle, see N Lowe, 'The House of Lords and the Welfare Principle', in C Bridge (ed), *Family Law Towards the Millennium—Essays for PM Bromley* (Butterworths, 1997), p 125 *et seq*. But see further below for discussion of whether the paramountcy principle is human rights compliant.

[6] As Maidment, n 4, p 149 commented in 1984: 'The welfare principle, ostensibly child-centered, has also been and probably always will be a code for decisions based on religious, moral, social and perhaps now social science-based beliefs about child rearing . . .' However, she adds that: 'These decisions were in the past and are for the present made by adults for adults about adults. When a court makes a custody decision it may attempt to heed the child's needs, but it is essentially making a decision as to which available adult . . . is to care for the child.'

[7] This convention came into force on 1 July 2000, following ratification by Greece, Poland and Slovenia.

(c) to be informed of the possible consequences of compliance with these views and the possible consequences of any decision.

While Article 4 further provides for children to have the right:[8]

> to apply, in person or through other persons or bodies, for a special representative in proceedings before a judicial authority affecting the child where internal law precludes the holders of parental responsibilities from representing the child as a result of a conflict of interest with the latter.

Another international instrument of importance is the European Convention on Human Rights which, as a result of the *Human Rights Act* 1998, became internally binding in English courts as and from 2 October 2000. Of particular interest in this context is Article 6, which provides, inter alia, that: 'In the determination of his civil rights and obligations . . . *everyone* is entitled to a fair and public hearing within a reasonable time by an independent and impartial tribunal established by law.' (emphasis added) As Fortin[9] has observed: 'On the face of it, Article 6 delivers a great deal. It guarantees the right of access to a court or tribunal, and, once there, the right of a fair hearing. It might therefore provide the means for challenging the law relating to children and their families . . .' Notwithstanding the hitherto restrictive interpretation of this Article, Fortin nevertheless suggests that Article 6 could be thought to vest a right in a child to have separate legal representation in proceedings brought by or concerning him or her. Lyon has gone further by suggesting[10] that the way in which children are currently treated in private family proceedings is in breach of Article 6 when read in conjunction with Article 14 (which prohibits discrimination on any ground), which she contends could be wide enough to include a child's or young person's age.

Another issue highlighted[11] by the implementation of the *Human Rights Act* 1998 is the compatibility of the paramountcy principle with Article 8. Although the judicial view is that it is compatible,[12] it has been argued by

[8] This is subject to Art 9 which empowers the judicial authority to appoint a special representative for children (irrespective of their capacity or understanding) in cases of a conflict of interest between a child and the holders of parental responsibility. See further the Explanatory Report on the Convention published in 1997 by the Council of Europe.

[9] J Fortin, 'The HRA's Impact on Litigation Involving Children and their Families' (1999) 11 *CFLQ* 237 at 244.

[10] See C Lyon, 'Children's Participation in Private Law Proceedings' in M Thorpe and E Clarke *No Fault or Flaw: The Future of the Family Law Act 1996* (Family Law, 2000), p 70—Query whether this argument would be accepted since the courts might well say that there are good reasons for differentiating between children and adults in the matter of participating in legal proceedings, with the former needing more protection from, for example, the rigours of cross-examination, than the latter.

[11] It should be pointed out that, long before the *Human Rights Act* 1998 was ever enacted, the House of Lords had ruled in *Re KD (A Minor) (Ward: Termination of Access)* (see n 5) that the paramountcy of the child's welfare was compatible with the European Convention on Human Rights.

[12] See *Re L (Contact: Domestic Violence); Re V (Contact: Domestic Violence; Re M (Contact: Domestic Violence); Re H (Contact: Domestic Violence)* [2000] 2 FLR 334 at 346, in which Butler-Sloss P observed that the European Court on Human Rights has long accepted that 'where there was a serious conflict between the interests of a child and one of its parents which could only be resolved to the disadvantage of one of them, the interests of the child had to prevail under Art 8(2)'. For this, she relied

Herring[13] and others[14] that, insofar as the courts apply a purely individualistic approach based solely on weighing the child's interests, they are acting in breach of the Convention because too little attention is paid to parents' rights. Herring suggests that the courts should instead apply what he calls a 'relationship-based welfare approach' and 'move away from conceiving the problem as a clash between children and parents and in terms of weighing two conflicting interests and towards seeing it rather as deciding what is a proper parent–child relationship'. While it remains to be seen whether the courts will apply this somewhat sophisticated approach, there seems little doubt that they will have to give more attention to the parents' position than they have done in the past.

Nevertheless, whatever attention is paid to parents' interests, the child's welfare must remain the court's paramount consideration, and consequently it seems clear that the international obligation to listen to the child can in no way be diminished by the implementation of the *Human Rights Act*.

The Place of the Child in English Domestic Proceedings

Substantively, English domestic law arguably cautiously complies with the essential requirements of Article 12 of the UN Convention.

The Position in Adoption Proceedings

So far as adoption law is concerned, it has—perhaps surprisingly—always been incumbent upon the court to give due consideration to the wishes of the children concerned having regard to their age and understanding.[15] Currently, section 6 of the *Adoption Act* 1976 obliges both a court and an adoption agency when 'reaching any decision relating to the adoption of a child' to 'so far as practicable ascertain the wishes and feelings of the child regarding the decision and give due consideration to them, having regard to his age and understanding'. On the other hand, children are only made parties to adoption proceedings where they are in the High Court or County Court,[16] and consequently it is only at that level that

upon, inter alia, *Johansen v Norway* (1996) 23 EHRR 33. See also *Payne v Payne* [2001] EWCA Civ 166 at [38], [2001] 1 FLR 1052, per Thorpe LJ.

[13] In 'The *Human Rights Act* and the Welfare Principle in Family Law—Conflicting or Complementary?' (1999) 11 CFLQ 223.

[14] See, eg H Reece, 'The Paramountcy Principle: Consensus or Construct?' (1996) 49 *Current Legal Problems* 267 and A Vine, 'Is the Paramountcy Principle Compatible with Article 8?' [2000] *Fam Law* 826.

[15] See the *Adoption of Children Act* 1926, s 3(b). This was subsequently re-enacted in the *Adoption Acts* of 1950, s 5(1)(b) and 1958, s 7(2).

[16] See the Adoption Rules 1984, r 15(2), as amended by the Adoption Amendment Rules 2001 (SI 2001/819). It might be noted that it was only from April 2001 that children could be made parties to adoption proceedings in the County Court.

they are separately represented.[17] Moreover, unlike Scottish Law,[18] English Law makes no provision for requiring even older children's agreement to their adoption.[19]

The Position in Private Law Proceedings Other than Adoption

So far as private law proceedings concerning children other than adoption are concerned, it was only under the *Children Act* 1989 that the courts became formally obliged to consider the child's wishes and feelings, although in practice this had long been the position.[20]

The *Children Act* obligation derives from the opening part of the so-called 'statutory checklist'—namely section 1(3)(a), under which the court must have regard to 'the ascertainable wishes and feelings of the child concerned (considered in the light of his age and understanding)'.

However, the *obligation* to apply the checklist in private law proceedings only arises in *contested* applications.[21] In other words, even where private law orders are sought under the *Children Act*,[22] if the *adults* are agreed, there is no obligation to consult these children. Indeed, one of the reasons for limiting the application of the checklist to contested cases was to protect family autonomy. This non-interventionist standpoint is particularly evident in divorce proceedings. Before the *Children Act*, section 41 of the *Matrimonial Causes Act* 1973 required the divorce court to be satisfied that the proposed arrangements for the welfare of any child of the family were 'satisfactory' or 'the best that can be devised in the circumstances' or that 'it is impracticable for the party or parties appearing before the court to make any such arrangements'. The *Children Act*,[23] however, amended section 41 so as to require the courts instead merely to '*consider* . . . whether it

[17] Under English Law, adoption applications may be made to a Magistrates' Court, County Court or High Court. In practice, most are made in the County Court. There is also provision allowing proceedings to be transferred from one court level to another. For details, see Lowe and Douglas n 4, p 665.

[18] Originally provided for by s 2(3) of the *Adoption of Children (Scotland) Act* 1930, it is currently required by s 6 (2) of the *Adoption (Scotland) Act* 1978.

[19] Under the 'proposed' Adoption Bill 1996 cl 41(7) it would not have been possible to make an adoption order in relation to a child aged twelve or over unless the court was satisfied that the child consented or was incapable of giving such consent. Interestingly, however, no such provision was contained in the Adoption and Children Bill 2001, introduced on 15 March.

[20] As Butler-Sloss LJ said in the pre-*Children Act* decision, *Re P (A Minor) (Education)* [1992] 1 FLR 316 at 321: 'The courts over the last few years, have become increasingly aware of the importance of listening to the views of older children and taking into account what children say, not necessarily agreeing with what they want nor, indeed, doing what they want, but paying proper respect to older children who are of an age and maturity to make their minds up as to what they think is best for them.'

[21] *Children Act* 1989, s 1(4)(a).

[22] Viz under s 8, namely, residence, contact, specific issue or prohibited steps orders.

[23] Sch 12, para 31. As Cretney has commented (see 'Defining the Limits of State Intervention' in D Freestone (ed), *Children and the Law* (Hull University Press, 1988), p 61, it was with 'an astonishing stroke of tactical boldness' that this crucial change was contained in a Schedule entitled 'Minor Amendments'.

should exercise any of its powers under the *Children Act* 1989 with respect to [any children of the family]' (emphasis added) and only in exceptional cases delay the granting of the divorce decree. In so doing, the legislation has, in the words of Douglas et al.,[24] shifted the focus of the court's attention:

> away from having to be satisfied that the divorce may proceed in the interests of the children, to finding some exceptional reason why the divorce should not go ahead. The assumption which lies behind this approach is that parents may be trusted in most cases, to plan what is best for their children's futures, and that, where they are in agreement on this, it is unnecessary and potentially damaging for the state, in the guise of the court, to intervene.

Since the implementation of the *Children Act*, parliament has had cause to rethink the wisdom of this non interventionist strategy; indeed, during the passage of the Family Law Bill 1996, concern was expressed about insufficient attention being paid to children's interests in the divorce process.[25] Reflecting this concern, the *Family Law Act* 1996 would have strengthened the emphasis on the children's welfare, first by setting out in section 1 the basic principles to which the court should have regard—namely, the need to bring to an end an irretrievably broken down marriage:

> (i) with the minimum distress to the parties and the children affected;
> (ii) with questions dealt with in a manner designed to promote as good a continuing relationship between the parties and any children affected as is possible in the circumstances.

Secondly, it was intended to replace section 41 of the *Matrimonial Causes Act* 1973 with section 11 of the 1996 Act. This, whilst not changing the fundamental standpoint established by the *Children Act* 1989, was to have obliged a divorce court, when deciding whether it should exercise its powers under the *Children Act*, to: (a) treat the child's welfare as the paramount consideration; and (b) have particular regard to a checklist of factors including 'the wishes and feelings of the child considered in the light of his age and understanding and the circumstances in which those wishes were expressed'. Commenting on this provision, the Lord Chancellor (Lord Irvine) said it:

> is fully in tune with the new and increasing contemporary awareness that a child is a person in his or her own right . . . the divorce process must now have regard to the interests and views of the children. They will now have a right to be consulted about the proposals which parents are making for the future in which they have a vital interest.[26]

[24] Douglas, Murch, Scanlan and Perry, 'Safeguarding Children's Welfare in Non-Contentious Divorce: Towards a New Conception of Legal Process?' (2000) 63 *MLR* 177 at 183–84. As the authors point out, contrary to the Law Commission's recommendation, under r 2.39 of the Family Proceedings Rules 1991, this scrutiny is not carried out until after the district judge has determined that the petition is made out.

[25] The Lord Chancellor's Department is currently reviewing the working of the *Children Act* 1989.

[26] *Hansard*, HL Debs Vol 573, Col 1076 (June 1996).

The Effect of Abandoning Part II of the Family Law Act 1996

Despite the obvious importance of these provisions, the government announced in January 2001 that, in the light of disappointing findings from the research at Newcastle University into the proposed scheme for information sessions for divorcing parents, the whole of Part II of the 1996 Act would not be implemented and indeed in due course would be repealed.[27]

Even where their views, wishes and feelings have to be taken into account, children are not normally made parties to the proceedings, though there is power to do so in proceedings before the High Court and County Court,[28] though not the Magistrates' Court. The normal process through which the court will learn of the child's views is through a court welfare report,[29] although a judge does have power to interview a child in private.[30] The current practice is to use this power sparingly.[31]

The use of what are now called Children and Family Reporters[32] means, of course, the involvement of yet another *adult* in the judicial process. Moreover, valuable though the system undoubtedly is, it is to be noted that the Reporter's function is to provide an independent report on the family's circumstances for the court. It is *not* to represent the child.[33]

The Position in Public Law Proceedings

In contrast to private law proceedings, the child's voice is much better served in public law proceedings. First, it is incumbent on the court to have regard to the child's ascertainable wishes and feelings in all proceedings (ie whether or not contested) under Part IV of the *Children Act* 1989.[34] Secondly, under section 41 of the

[27] See the Lord Chancellor's announcement on 16 Jan 2001 HL Official Report col WA 126. For discussion of the many issues and implications of non-implementation, see Thorpe and Clarke, n 10.

[28] Under the Family Proceedings Rules 1991, r 9.5 see, for example, *Re A (Contact: Separate Representation)* [2001] 1 FLR 715, CA. Fortin, n 9, has commented that it is 'questionable whether the existing system denying legal representation to mature children in private law disputes over their upbringing can continue without challenge under the European Convention on Human Rights'. Normally, where a child is made a party to proceedings, the court will appoint the Official Solicitor (subject to his consent) or some other proper person to represent the child: Family Proceedings Rules 1991, r 9.5. However, if the child is of sufficient understanding, he or she may defend proceedings without a next friend: r 9.2A, discussed further below.

[29] The power to order a report is through s 7 of the *Children Act.*

[30] See Lowe and Douglas, n 4, p 462.

[31] For critical analysis of current judicial practice, see Lyon, n 10, pp 67–79.

[32] Formally known as welfare officers. This change of designation came into effect on 1 April 2001 following the establishment of the new Children and Family Court Advisory and Support Service (CAFCASS) which amalgamated the former court welfare service with the former guardian *ad litem* service under the *Criminal Justice and Court Services Act* 2000.

[33] For further discussion of the role of what were then the welfare officers under English Law, see Lowe and Douglas, n 4, p 455 *at seq.*

[34] Ss 1 (3)(a) and (4)(b) of the 1989 Act.

Children Act, courts are required in public law proceedings[35] to appoint what are now called Children's Guardians[36] for the child, 'unless satisfied that it is not necessary to do so in order to safeguard his [sic] interests'. Furthermore, unlike Children and Family Reporters, Children's Guardians represent children in the proceedings and are therefore parties to them. They also have the power to instruct legal representation for the child.[37] Notwithstanding their party status, children do not have a right to attend the hearing,[38] and indeed there is a general feeling that it is commonly not in a child's interest to do so.[39]

Children's Ability to Bring their Own Proceedings

One innovation of the *Children Act* was to make clear provision[40] for children to bring their own proceedings. The scheme is that children wishing to seek a section 8 order must first obtain leave of the court. It is established that leave must be sought in the High Court[41] and, before it can be given, the court must be satisfied that the child has sufficient age and understanding.[42] Where the child is of sufficient understanding, the normal rule of having to bring proceedings through a Next Friend does not apply[43] and instead the child may instruct a solicitor in his or her own right. In practice, very little use is made of this provision because it takes an extremely confident, knowledgeable, resourceful and determined child or young person to commence such proceedings.

[35] Technically the power arises in 'specified proceedings', which include care and supervision proceedings, emergency proceedings brought by a local authority, contact in care proceedings and those concerned with discharge from care applications.

[36] Formerly guardians *ad litem*. These changes were made following the establishment of CAFCASS (see above).

[37] See eg *Re S (A Minor) (Guardian Ad Litem/Welfare Officer)* [1993] 1 FLR 110, 114–15, per Butler-Sloss LJ.

[38] Under the Family Proceedings Rules 1991, r 4.16 (2) and the Family Proceedings Courts (*Children Act* 1989) Rules 1991, r 16 (2), (7), the court has a discretion to hear the case in the child's absence if it considers it in the interest of the child.

[39] See, eg *Re C (A Minor) (Care: Child's Wishes)* [1993] 1 FLR 832, in which it was held that guardians *ad litem* should think carefully about the arrangements for children who are to be present in court. Fortin, n 9, questions whether this reluctance to allow children to attend care proceedings is consistent with Art 6 of the European Convention on Human Rights.

[40] Before the Act, wardship offered a limited means by which children could initiate legal proceedings, see N Lowe and R White, *Wards of Court* (Barry Rose, 2nd edn, 1986), paras 3–4.

[41] *Practice Direction (applications by children: leave)* [1993] 1 All ER 820.

[42] Viz under s 10 (8) of the 1989 Act. As established by the leading decision, *Re S (A Minor) (Independent Representation)* [1993] 2 FLR 437, there is no hard and fast rule in determining whether a child is of sufficient age and understanding. As Sir Thomas Bingham MR put it: 'Different children have differing levels of understanding at the same age. And understanding is not absolute. It has to be assessed relatively to the issues in the proceedings.' His Lordship added, however, the following caveat: 'Where any sound judgment in these issues calls for insight and imagination which only maturity and experience can bring, both the court and the solicitor will be slow to conclude that the child's understanding is sufficient.'

[43] Family Proceedings Rules 1991, r 9.2A, for the application of which, see *Re T (A Minor) (Child:Representation)* [1994] Fam 49.

The Children's Commissioner for Wales[44]

One important development has been the creation of a Children's Commissioner for Wales (but not for the rest of the United Kingdom). That office was established in 2001 following the recommendations of the Waterhouse Report[45] and through the *Care Standards Act* 2000 and the *Children's Commissioner of Wales Act* 2001. The Commissioner is the first children's 'ombudsman' to be established within the United Kingdom.[46] It is also the first time in this country, and possibly the world, that children have been formally involved in the appointment process of such a public-sector officer.[47] Space forbids detailed discussion of this office save to say that the Commissioner's remit includes considering and making representations to the Welsh Assembly about 'any matter affecting the rights or welfare of children in Wales'.[48] More specifically, the Commissioner has the power to review and monitor the operation of arrangements for dealing, inter alia, with complaints and advocacy for children.[49] He or she also has power to examine the cases of individual children—including, inter alia, assisting them in pursuing a complaint.[50] The Commissioner also has the more general power to review the effect on children of the exercise, or proposed exercise, by the Assembly of any function including the making or proposed making of subordinate legislation.[51]

Clearly, this is an important office which has the potential to significantly improve the protection of children's interests at an important level; however, time will tell whether the Commissioner will prove to be a 'champion' for children in Wales, as its First Minister intends.[52]

Translating Principles into Practice

It is one thing to accept that children's voices should be listened to when legal and administrative authorities are taking decisions about them, but quite another to

[44] We are indebted to our colleagues, Professor Gillian Douglas and Kathryn Hollingsworth, for giving us sight of their draft article 'Creating a Children's Champion for Wales'.

[45] 'Lost in Care: Report of the Tribunal of Inquiry into the Abuse of Children in Care in the Former County Councils of Gwynedd and Clwyd Since 1974' (HC 201, 2000).

[46] Though note that there have been moves to establish Commissioners both in Northern Ireland and Scotland. There is also a London Children's Right Commissioner established by the Mayor of London. There is also a Minister for Children in the Westminster Parliament.

[47] See the Children's Commissioner for Wales (Appointment) Regulations 2001 (SI 2001/3121-W 199).

[48] *Care Standards Act* 2000, s 75A. It might also be noted that the Regulations provide that in exercising his functions the Commissioner should 'have regard' to the UN Convention on the Rights of the Child which is the first such reference in UK legislation.

[49] *Ibid.*, s 74.

[50] *Ibid.*, s 76. In practice investigation of individual complaints are likely to be aimed at highlighting prejudicial practices affecting children more generally.

[51] *Ibid.*, s 72B.

[52] Viz Rhodri Morgan. See Assembly *Record*, 7 Dec 2000.

get beyond the rhetoric of legislative aspiration, so as to genuinely enable children to have a greater say in the processes which shape their futures. Indeed, there is a growing body of research[53] to suggest that most practitioners in the family justice system—court welfare officers, guardians *ad litem*, solicitors and judges, and so on—lack the necessary skills and understanding for effective direct face-to-face work with children.

These studies highlight three areas of concern:

(1) Historically, in our culture, children are not used to being listened to. For example, as Schofield and Thoburn have commented:[54] 'Children in our society are not accustomed to having their views taken into account in their everyday lives at home or at school. We do not live in a culture which supports participation by children.'

(2) Many adults seem to have difficulties in listening to children. A number of reasons have been advanced for this. For example, Neale has commented:[55] 'Adults view children as essentially other. They are seen as less important and they are dependent and less powerful. Language is a tool used communally or on the basis of shared understandings. Adults interpret what children say. Welfare professionals do so on the basis of their understanding of what is in the child's best interest.' Smith[56] postulates that adults fear they will upset children by talking about difficult experiences such as separation and divorce. Hunt and Lawson[57] comment that many professionals are aware of their lack of training and experience in talking to and listening to children. Even more challengingly, Day, Sclater and Piper assert[58] that adults protect themselves from their own vulnerabilities by projecting them (unconsciously) on to the children. They suggest that, in order to keep that anxiety contained, adults rationalise that it is vital *not* to listen to children's own constructions of their needs but instead to act as if they know children's best interests better than the children do. Finally,

[53] Much of which is summarised by A O'Quigley, *Listening to Children's Views and Representing their Best Interests—A Summary of Current Research* (Joseph Rowntree Foundation, 1999), pp 35–36. Note also C Sawyer's work, particularly on solicitors' ability in assessing children's competence—see, eg 'The Competence of Children to Participate in Family Proceedings' (1995) 7 *CFLQ* 180 and the study for the Calouste Gulbenkian Foundation by C Lyon, E Surrey and J Timms, *Effective Support Services for Children and Young People when Parental Relationships Break Down* (Liverpool University Press, 1998).

[54] G Schofield and J Thoburn, *Child Protection: The Voice of the Child in Decision Making* (Institute for Public Policy Research, 1996), p 62. Note also the comment by AL James and A James 'Pump up the Volume: Listening to Children' in (1999) 6 *Separation and Divorce in Childhood* 206: 'Ours is a culture that does not particularly like children. The adage that "children should be seen and not heard" has an authentically English ring about it.'

[55] B Neale, 'Dialogues with Children in Participation and Choice in Family Decision Making' (unpublished paper, 1999).

[56] N Smith, 'All Change' (1999) *UK Youth* (Spring) 12.

[57] J Hunt and J Lawson, *Crossing the Boundaries—The Views of Practitioners of Family Court Welfare and Guardian Ad Litem Work on the Proposal to Create a Unified Court Welfare Service* (National Council for Family Proceedings, 1999), p 38.

[58] Day Sclater and Piper, n 1, p 8.

Murch et al. believe[59] that many adults (including welfare professionals, solicitors and judges) confuse 'participation' with decision-making. They are reluctant to even speak or to listen to children because they see this as inappropriately asking the child to decide.

(3) Children can have disturbing experiences when talking to professionals. In this respect, the Joseph Rowntree Research Review[60] makes five important and troubling points:

- (a) Children were generally reluctant to talk to outsiders about family issues, as this was seen as disloyal and liable to lead to an escalation of problems.
- (b) Professionals were seen as having been interventionist rather than supportive.
- (c) The discussions that children had with professionals often felt like interrogations.
- (d) Adults were frequently experienced as judgmental and intrusive in their approach.
- (e) Discussions were often not treated as confidential.

Neale and Smart concluded their study thus:[61] 'Professionals may be perceived as inflexible, intrusive, condescending, deceitful, untrustworthy, disrespectful and reinforcing in a myriad of ways their superiority to the child.'

We would add that children in certain respects inhabit different cultural worlds from adults. They can be baffled by the language of adults, especially by professional jargon. Equally, adults are often unfamiliar with children's language codes which, in any event, can differ from age group to age group. In the family justice system, there are emerging practice debates on how to develop the communication skills required by children's representatives and about whether, and if so how, judges should see and listen to children when taking decisions about them. The prevailing practice in England and Wales, as we have seen, is that they should not—in part because with the adversarial culture it is not possible to promise children that what they say to the judge will be treated in confidence.[62] But in this respect, as Lyon has pointed out, judges are not in a substantially different position from Children and Family Reporters or Children's Guardians.[63]

[59] M Murch, G Douglas, L Scanlan, A Perry, C Lisles, K Bader and M Borkowski, *Safeguarding Children's Welfare in Uncontentious Divorce: A Study of section 41 of the Matrimonial Causes Act 1973* (Lord Chancellor's Department, Research Series No 7/99, 1999), pp 178–85.

[60] At p 44. This report draws upon studies by B Neale and C Smart, *Agents or Dependants? Struggling to Listen to Children in Family Law and Family Research*, Working Paper No 3 (Centre for Research on Family, Kinship and Childhood Leeds University, 1999), L Trinder, 'Competing Constructions of Childhood: Children's Rights and Children's Wishes in Divorce' (1999) 19 JSWFL 291.

[61] See p 33.

[62] See *B v B (Interviews and Listing Arrangements)* [1994] 2 FLR 489, 496, per Wall J, sitting in the Court of Appeal.

[63] Lyon, n 10, p 74.

Ascertaining the Wishes and Feelings of the Child: Do Differences of Principle Lead to Differences in Practice?

One possible reason why the government has abandoned Part II of the *Family Law Act* 1996 is that there are divergent views about the assumptions underlying provisions relating to children. For example, in much socio-legal writing the theoretical debate is assumed to revolve around the potentially conflicting paradigms—a welfare best-interest approach on the one hand and a rights approach on the other.[64]

The Traditional 'Best Interest' Approach

Piper (1999)[65] takes the view that both the *Children Act* 1989 and the *Family Law Act* 1996 (which she anticipated being fully implemented) provide a framework which means that children's views are ascertained:

> as part of a process in which adults decide what is best for the child and within the context of divorce try to protect the child from a particular set of perceived risks of harm. These risks, predicated on the influential image of the child as a vulnerable victim of divorce whose present happiness and future stability is deemed to depend upon harmonious joint parenting, can be removed only by the encouragement of parental decision making and control.

Such a view places section 11 of the *Family Law Act* 1996 firmly within a traditional paternalistic child-saving model and is consistent with much of the research material concerning practitioners' approach to children which was reported in the Cardiff study of section 41 of the *Matrimonial Causes Act* 1973 carried out for the Lord Chancellor's Department.[66] In our opinion, one unfortunate consequence of this approach is that most children of divorcing parents are badly informed about the processes involved and are left feeling excluded from and unrecognised by the system.

A Children's 'Rights' Approach

The 'rights of the child' approach is sometimes referred to as being constructed on a liberationist position.[67] This takes the view that children should have similar basic rights to adults, that the distinction between childhood and adulthood is arbitrary,[68] and that to apply the traditional best-interest approach is to label

[64] For fuller discussion of the interaction of these two approaches, see Roche and Piper in Day Sclater and Piper, n 1. Also H Hendrick *Children, Childhood and English Society (1880–1990)* (Cambridge University Press, 1997), pp 97–99. Also K Marshall, *Children's Rights in the Balance: The Participation–Protection Debate* (The Stationery Office, Edinburgh, 1997).

[65] See p 88.

[66] See n 50, p 42.

[67] See Roche, n 1, p 56.

[68] See D Archand, *Children, Rights and Childhood* (Routledge, 1993).

children as objects of welfare rather than as young citizens who are the subject of rights.[69] This young citizen approach was endorsed by Giddens in his 1999 Reith lectures on the family, in which he advanced the view that modern Western family life is increasingly based on a participant democratic approach in which parents consult children when taking important decisions about them.

In addition to these two contrasting approaches, which have largely dominated social-legal discourse on the subject of children, there are signs that two more distinct approaches are emerging from the theoretical worlds of the sociology of childhood and the behavioural sciences. The former views children as social actors in their own terms; the latter adopts the community mental health approach.

The Child as Social Actor

This third approach, assuming increasing significance in the developing social research literature of modern childhood,[70] sets out to understand children's experiences 'in their own terms' and to take their words at face value as the primary source of knowledge about their experience.[71] This approach—endorsed, incidentally, by the Scottish Law Commission[72]—is concerned, as Butler and Williamson[73] point out, with 'hearing the voice of the child, untrammelled by professional discretion or interpretation'. It could therefore be argued that, if a court is to understand children's perceptions in their own terms and to appreciate what the experience of divorce and family change means to them, a similar approach should be applied. Yet, as Roche points out,[74] to move from the current position, in which the words of the child are 'filtered through the lens of concern of

[69] See K Marshall, n 55. Marshall's small interdisciplinary study of how children's participation was viewed by various practitioners concluded: 'If children are truly to be regarded as human beings and citizens in their own right, the professionals who provide the framework within which the system operates must become accustomed to considering children of all ages as consumers and clients.'

[70] See, for example, many of the studies in the recent Economic Social and Research Council research programme, 'Children 5–16: Growing into the Twenty first Century'. Its twenty-two different projects have a common theme: looking at children as social actors. Its findings about children's experience of and response to contemporary society have wide-ranging implications for policy and practice. Other studies within this program include DP Alderson and S Arnold, *Children's Rights in Schools* (London Institute of Education); *Children;* M Candappa, I Egharerba, M Grenier and P Moss, *Extraordinary Childhoods: Social Roles and Social Networks of Refugee* (Thomas Coram Research Unit, London); A James, C Jenks and P Christiensen, *Changing Times: Children's Understanding and Perception of Social Organisation* (Hull University and Goldsmith College, London); C Smart, B Neale and A Wade, *New Childhoods: Children and Co-Parenting after Divorce* (University of Leeds); and GM Valentine, SI Holloway and N Bingham, *Cyberkids, Children's Social Networks, Virtual Communities, and Online Spaces* (Sheffield University and Loughborough University).

[71] See, eg L Marrow and M Richards, 'The Ethics of Social Research with Children' (1996) 10 *Children and Society* 90.

[72] The Scottish Law Commission (1992) *Report on Family Law* explores the meaning of terms and such as 'wishes and feelings' 'maturity' and the general concepts of competence, paras 260–64, and takes the view that a child's own view ought to be taken into account and not just as an aspect of welfare.

[73] I Butler and H Williamson, *Children Speak: Children, Trauma and Social Work* (Longman, 1994).

[74] See p 71.

mediators and other welfare professionals, operating the current family justice system', to one in which the child's concerns are considered in their own terms will involve a major cultural shift in family law practice. Even so, Roche is an optimist. His plea is that we 'need to be able to hear the unfamiliar and the law could provide one framework in which many voices of childhood can be heard on matters that move and concern them'.

The Community Mental Health Approach

This approach starts from the position that the practices and procedures of the family justice system (like other state social care and educational systems) impact on children's lives, whether or not their wishes and feelings are ascertained. This is acknowledged, for example, in section 1(2) of the *Children Act* 1989, which states that delay is normally to be regarded as detrimental to the child. The underlying thinking behind this principle is that a young person's sense of time is different from that of an adult, and that delay in reaching decisions about a child's future care can add to stress and anxiety—particularly if the child experiences a threat, actual or imagined, of separation from those with whom he or she is attached. In this sense, therefore, avoidable delay can be described, to use a medical metaphor, as iatrogenic (ie system-induced harm). But the converse is also true: practice and procedures can be designed and operated positively to promote a child's well-being, to buffer the impact of stressful events and even to increase a child's capacity to cope with stressful, critical situations. In adoption, both the recent review by the Prime Minister's Performance and Innovation Unit (PIU)[75] and the White Paper[76] have highlighted the serious problem of delay, particularly for children who are to be adopted out of care. One of the intractable weaknesses of our current child care system and the slow moving nature of court proceedings is that, following their removal from often dangerous and neglectful families, children can be placed in a series of short-term foster homes before permanent adoptive homes can be found for them. The stress involved in moving from one placement to another and the adverse effects on a child's behaviour, concentration levels, educational attainment and above all capacity to form secure attachment may well be cumulative.[77] Of seminal importance in this approach is the work of Rutter,[78] Hetherington, Cox and Cox,[79] and Caplan and

[75] Cabinet Office, *Report of the Performance and Innovation Unit Concerning Adoption* (2000).

[76] Department of Health (Cm 5017, 2000) *Adoption: A New Approach* (Stationery Office, London), p 15.

[77] See H Rudolf Schaffer, *Making Decisions about Children: Psychological Questions and Answers* (Blackwell, 1999), p 231. Schaffer, a leading developmental child psychologist, observes: 'Isolated crises need not lead to later disorder. Specific stresses are only of long-term significance if they are the first link in a chain of unfortunate events . . . It is the totality of experience as it impinges on the child throughout the formative years, rather than a specific event, that accounts for the end result.'

[78] M Rutter, 'Resilience in the Face of Adversity: Protective Factors and Resistance to Psychiatric Disorder' (1985) 47 *British Journal of Psychiatry* 606.

[79] EM Hetherington, M Cox and R Cox, 'Long-term Effects of Divorce and Remarriage on Children' (1995) 245 *Journal of the American Academy of Child Psychiatry* 518.

Caplan.[80] Such an approach would justify, for example, giving children reliable information about the processes of divorce, enabling them not to feel excluded if they wish to participate in certain aspects of proceedings themselves, and providing them with support if they need it at critical times in the divorce process.[81] Moreover, it seems to us that any support which reduces child suffering at the time is justification in itself. Note that this approach is less paternalistic than the conventional child-saving welfare approach, and can be used to make a supporting behavioural science case for both the children's rights and the child as social actor approaches which are outlined above.

Variable Competence in Children: How Can the Family Justice System Respond?

The four approaches outlined above in practice represent a spectrum of opinion. As Hendrick observes: 'There are many gradations of perspectives amongst scholars and activists.'[82] The issue of assessing a child's competence to participate is central to the whole debate. As Lord Scarman observed in the *Gillick* case:

> The underlying principle of the law . . . is that parental right yield to the child's right to make his own decisions when he reaches a sufficient understanding and intelligence to be capable of making up his own mind on the matter requiring decision.[83]

In practice, the crucial questions that follow from this are, first, how do courts assess when a child has reached sufficient understanding and intelligence; and second, how best can a child's capacity to participate in proceedings be facilitated to the extent that they might wish to express their wishes and feelings? Although children's social competence and capacity to understand generally increase as they get older, children vary widely in their developmental levels. Some as young as five can have a command of language as good as others of ten years of age or more. Some are emotionally resilient and others are very vulnerable. Some are extrovertedly confident, others introvertedly inhibited and shy. Some children have learning difficulties and are unable to read—for example, information leaflets—and can easily be confused by articulate practitioners who lack the responsive skills to communicate appropriately. The challenge, therefore, is for the family justice system to develop both practices and procedures to enable children to participate to the extent that they might wish and to find practitioners equipped

[80] C Caplan and R Caplan, 'Primary Prevention of Psycho-Social Disorders in Children of Divorce', Lecture given to the 5th World Conference on Innovations in Psychiatry, Central Hall, Westminster (Institute for the Study of Psychological Stress, Jerusalem 1995).

[81] G Douglas, M Murch and A Perry, 'Supporting Children when Parents Separate—A Neglected Family Justice or Mental Health Issue? (1996) 8 CFLQ 121 and G Douglas, M Murch, L Scanlan and A Perry, 'Safeguarding Children's Welfare in Non-contentious Divorce: Towards a New Conception of the Legal Process' (2000) 63 MLR 177.

[82] See p 77.

[83] *Gillick v West Norfolk and Wisbech Area Health Authority* [1986] AC 112 at 186D.

with the necessary skills for direct face-to-face work with children—listening to them and seeking to understand their at times unexpected and unfamiliar messages. Marshall rightly argues that:

> those charged with assessing the child's maturity . . . should be mature themselves and trained in child development and in communication with children and young people, including particular groups such as adolescents and those with special needs who present difficulties with some adults.[84]

ABOUT THE CARDIFF PROJECTS

At this point we turn to our own two Cardiff studies to explore further the issue of how best to communicate with children and engage them in the legal process. We go into some detail about the method of approach in order to illustrate the care which we think needs to be taken when approaching children.

Adopted Children Speaking: The Structure of the Samples

This was a qualitative study funded by the Department of Health and based on interviews with 41 adopted children aimed at contributing to the development of knowledge and understanding of children's views and experience of the adoption process and the support they need. It was the final—albeit distinct—phase of a larger study entitled 'Supporting Adoption' (also co-directed by Professors Lowe and Murch).[85]

This latter study conducted a postal questionnaire responded to by 226 adoptive families and followed up by 48 interviews with adoptive parents (couples or single adopters). At the end of these interviews, the parents were asked if they were willing for their adopted children to be interviewed at a later date. The majority (40 out of the 48) agreed, and 20 of these families, including 27 children, participated in this children study. An additional 17 adoptive parents were contacted from the 226 families who had responded to the questionnaire who had indicated a willingness to be interviewed, but who were not. Eight families from this additional sample, including 14 children, took part in this study.

The final sample of 41 children comprised 25 girls and 16 boys. The bias in favour of girls was due to parents passing more invitations to participate in the projects to girls rather than to boys. Most of the children were white and placed with white families. Four children were of mixed heritage—one was in a same-race placement and the other three were placed trans-racially. Some of the children had special needs. The parents indicated that eight had learning difficulties,

[84] Marshall, n 55.

[85] N Lowe and M Murch, M Borkowski, A Weaver, V Beckford with C Thomas, *Supporting Adoption—Reframing the Approach* (BAAF, 1999).

that the same number had behavioural difficulties and that nine had emotional special needs. Two of the children had physical disabilities.

Adoption was the original purpose of the placement for 32 of the 41 children. Six had been placed with long-term foster carers who subsequently applied for adoption and there were three children whose short-term foster placements evolved into long-term arrangements and then into adoption.

Twenty of the children were placed singly, although ten of these had siblings placed in other adoptive and foster families. The other 21 were placed in sibling groups—nine pairs and one group of three. Twelve children were adopted by families with other adopted children. Only six became part of families which included birth children.

The mean age of placement of the group was five years (ranging from two months to ten years and four months). Once in placement, the children waited on average two years and four months before their adoption orders were made. At the time of the interview, the children were aged between eight and fifteen, but most of them (83 per cent) were between eight and twelve. On average, they had been in the family for five years and eight months. All 41 children were interviewed after their adoption orders had been made. The average length of time between the making of that order and the interview was two years and ten months.

The KIDs Project

The KIDs study, funded by the ESRC, aimed to explore through children's first-hand accounts how they experience and live through their parents' separation and divorce, how they engage with and seek support from the family justice system, and how they construct and use their own networks. The population comprised 51 girls and 53 boys (their average age at time of interview was eleven years six months) for whom divorce was a recent experience (on average, children were interviewed within fifteen months of the petitioner parent obtaining a decree nisi). This population was derived from an initial sample of 315 cases/families drawn at random from the records of three courts in South Wales and three in the South West of England. The courts served a mix of city, town and country, thereby increasing the likelihood that the final population would be representative of divorce cases in England and Wales. Each case involved at least one child aged between eight and fourteen years, whose parents had been granted a decree nisi between January and August 1997. In 38 families, one child was interviewed, in 30, two children were interviewed, and in two families, three children were interviewed. In ten cases, the child interviewed was an only child. In 14 cases, the divorce was between the child's birth mother and stepfather. Seventy-one children were living with a lone mother, six with a lone father and 25 with a parent and the parent's new partner. Two children were still living with both divorcing parents.

Approaching the Children

Consent of Parents

In both studies, initial contact with children was made through the parents. In the case of the Adopted Children Speaking project, the adoptive parents were sent a pack containing, among other things, a fact-sheet outlining the project's aims and researchers' approach and describing the arrangements and format for interviews. It also indicated which stages of the adoption process were of interest. The sheet also described the contents of the enclosed *Children's Invitation Pack* and offered reassurance about consent and confidentiality. The fact sheet provided essential background information to enable parents to come to an informed decision about their children's participation. Parents were invited to contact the researchers if they had any questions about the research. About half the parents who received the packs passed them on to the children.[86]

In the KIDs project, initial contact was made by a letter sent to parents through the Court Service and, provided they did not opt out at that stage,[87] parents with residence were sent a KIDs newsletter and then were contacted by telephone or letter. At each of the stages, the child-focused nature of the research was stressed, as was the requirement that children as well as parents had to agree to participate: 30 per cent of the families sampled agreed to participate.

In the adoption project, it was the team's belief that the care taken in introducing the researcher, the child-friendly tools used during the interview, the assurances about confidentiality and safe storage of the information, and efforts to allow children to influence important aspects of the interview had a positive effect on the children's openness. The KIDs project was no less successful in communicating with children, though in some respects the methodology was different. The key to both projects was gaining the children's trust and confidence. It must be acknowledged immediately that the researchers in both projects had the advantage of being solely interested in the children and having no other investigative role. Professionals are more likely to be identified by the children as having some official role and moreover are not in a position to promise confidentiality. Nevertheless, as *Adopted Children Speaking*[88] concluded:

> It seems vital that professionals have or learn the skills to communicate effectively with children, not just in relation to adoption work but in respect of the whole range of child-related legal and social work practice. Indeed, unless they do acquire and use these skills, the legal requirement . . . to 'ascertain (so far as practicable) the wishes and feelings of the child . . . and give due consideration to them, having regard to his age and understanding' cannot really be complied with.

[86] A variety of reasons were given for not participating, including the surprising explanation that the placements were going very well! See the comments in *Adopted Children Speaking*, n 2, p 9.

[87] That is, parents who did not wish to participate had expressly to opt out and 30% did so.

[88] *Adopted Children Speaking*, n 2, pp 132–33.

The Findings

Although the subject matter of the two projects—the child's own adoption, and the parents' divorce—are quite different, both represent critical and often stressful transitions in the child's life which it seems incumbent upon the state to make as smooth as possible for its citizen children. Strikingly, notwithstanding their different backgrounds, the projects revealed common findings in particular about the children's misconceptions about the court and legal process, their feelings of isolation and ignorance of what was going on and their need for support. We summarise these here to give an impression of the kind of findings which have already been reported, or will be reported, more fully elsewhere. In doing so, we have chosen some representative individual quotes to illustrate general themes. Other important subject areas not considered here include the thorny question of contact.

Misconceptions about the Court and the Legal Process

A common misconception among children is to associate courts with criminal wrongdoing. One eight-year-old girl in the adoption project, when asked whether she had been to court, replied indignantly that she had not. However, her older sister, who was being interviewed with her, told her that she had in fact been to court. For a moment, the younger girl was adamant that she had not, adding 'I wasn't bad', but later said: 'Oh yes I did', adding that it was 'not like going to court for being naughty'. A number of the adopted children sample expected their adoption hearing to be in a criminal court, imagining that there would be a jury and many other people present, including the police and MPs, and that they would have to swear an oath. Similar misconceptions were evident in the KIDs project. One ten-year-old boy, when told by his father 'they were going to court', thought 'they were gonna get like, arrested'. An eight-year-old girl, when told by her father that he was going to court, explained that she thought she would 'have to go with him, and stand up in one of those boxes, and say who we wanted to live with and who we wanted to put down as guilty'.

The *fear* of having to go to court is another recurring theme and is graphically illustrated by a nine-year-old adopted boy's recollection of his fears (still palpable at the interview) the night before his adoption hearing. He explained how, because he was frightened, he hid his pretend sword under his duvet. When asked what he was scared about, he replied that he thought the judge 'was going to be all mean and hammer the hammer down . . . that sort of wooden thing . . . when they go 'Order in the Courts'. He added: 'I was scared because I had never seen a judge before—that's the first time I ever did and I never knew what it was going to be like. So I was scared.'

Yet, ironically, most of the adopted children had positive memories of meeting the judge. One boy commented: 'He wasn't like a boring old judge who's always going "Sit up straight" and all that. He was pretty funny.'

Perhaps not surprisingly, the children knew relatively little about the legal process. This was particularly evident in the KIDs study. Many of the children recalled being told very little about the process. As one put it: 'I know it is something to do with lawyers and everything, but I haven't really been told. I've had to suss it out for myself.' Another explained how he had worked it out from a TV soap opera (*Eastenders*). One perception of the legal side of divorce was that it was something for adults to know about, something 'private' or 'secret'. Although children were less interested in this than in other aspects of divorce (understandably so, as for the most part it was rather incidental to other changes they were having to cope with), they nevertheless did generally want to be better informed about the process.

Although no doubt no more knowledgeable about the legal process, the adopted children did generally seem to have a good grasp of what adoption meant, although some needed repeated explanations. One particularly perceptive comment came from a thirteen-year-old girl who summed up the adoption hearing, saying: 'I love reading the end of a book because of the feeling of triumph that you've finished it . . . And I guess that was the same feeling in court, watching them close the book, really shutting it . . . knowing that nothing else was going to happen. It was just going to be an ordinary life from now on . . .'

Feelings of Isolation and Ignorance of What is Happening: The Need for Reliable Information[89]

Many children found their parents' separation constituted the worst or hardest part of their experience of divorce; being told or finding out about the separation was often recalled as a time of shock, worry, confusion and upset. As one thirteen-year-old girl put it: 'It feels normal that other people are splitting up but not *your* Mum and Dad. I mean you think your Mum and Dad are going to be together forever and you can't believe it's happened.'

Children frequently felt excluded from decisions which directly affected them and expressed a wish to be kept informed and actively considered and consulted throughout the process. Few children felt actively 'prepared' by their parents for the separation, even where parents themselves were planning the split. Where explanations were offered, children reported that limited information was given to them. One finding was that, although 99 per cent of parents reported that they *had* told their child about the divorce, only 71 per cent of the children agreed. Over a third of the children (44 per cent) recalled nothing being said about divorce at the time of their parents' separation. Some children thought that their parents

[89] In their review of the impact on children of their parents' divorce and separation, B Rogers and J Prior in *Divorce and Separation—The Outcomes for Children* (Joseph Rowntree Foundation, 1998), pp 15–17 observed that 'numerous studies have documented the stress experienced by children and their families in these circumstances' and have shown 'the importance of communicating with children, both in the sense of listening and being sensitive to their needs, and in terms of clearly explaining what is happening'.

were trying to shield them from some of the unpleasantness of what was happening, but would have preferred almost any dialogue to the resulting uncertainty. Some children found it difficult to ask parents for information and advice. Most wanted their parents to take responsibility for keeping them informed and involved in what was going on, and expressed a wish for more 'whole family' discussions about the divorce. Initially, many of the children were concerned that they would have to move home, change schools or that they would lose contact with their friends, some of whom were important sources of support.

A similar feeling of isolation and exclusion was evident in the adoption study. With few exceptions, children felt excluded from the general process of being matched and introduced to their adoptive family. In particular, they did not feel included in the preparation or presentation about themselves for their families. In one case, a thirteen-year-old girl remembered having been told by social workers that they were looking for an adoptive family for her and then spending a least two years with foster carers before moving to her adoptive home. During that time, she was aware of being advertised for adoption in a catalogue or magazine and commented in relation to the wait that 'it didn't feel very nice, that you weren't being chosen'. The children wanted their prospective parents to know something about their needs, likes, dislikes and personal qualities, and some had reservations about the ways in which the advertisement portrayed them. Over half the sample had painfully long periods (some as long as four years) before being matched with their new families.

Need for Support

Mention has already been made of the shock and worry experienced by the children on hearing of their parents' separation; this was one time when they needed support. However, although most sought out someone with whom they could share their feelings, there was also a strong concern to retain control over who found out and when. Indeed, 59 per cent of children said that they had kept the divorce a secret from certain people. One ten-year-old boy simply said: 'I just wanted people not to know 'cos they would all ask me questions.' Another ten-year-old boy said: 'Well I've kept it a secret from my worst friend, 'cos he'll probably tease me and all that. I told one of my friends and he called me "Dad-less".' A few parents themselves asked children to keep things 'secret', although most left it to children to decide whom and when to tell.

Commonly, parents, other family members, friends, pets and toys were turned to as sources of support and comfort. Frequently children sought to distract themselves from what was happening by having fun with friends or taking part in sport, watching TV or sleeping—or simply 'keeping out of the way'. A few turned to more aggressive means, including tantrums or causing minor damage to property. A minority took refuge in habitual behaviours such as nail biting or smoking. Most reported some difficulties in talking about what had happened: it was upsetting; they could not 'explain' why it had happened; and they lacked the experience and emotional vocabulary to express how they felt.

These findings sound a striking parallel with those in the adoption study. The children's comments about their move to their adoptive homes are particularly poignant and conveyed a deep sense of isolation and loneliness. They described how these moves meant significant, simultaneous changes in almost every aspect of their lives—a new family, home, neighbourhood, school and friends. Though clearly needing the greatest of support at this stage, as with divorce, the children were generally reluctant to let it be known to any but trusted friends that they were adopted, particularly at school. Indeed, for many it was a big decision whether even to tell a trusted friend. This fear of being teased or bullied, if it were known that they were adopted, was well founded. Thirteen out of our 41 sample children described being verbally harassed and even physically attacked (one had been stoned by two boys in the school playground). The overwhelming message from the children was that, as adopted children, they were 'different'.

As against these depressing findings, we more encouragingly found that 78 per cent of the children identified their adoptive parents as sources of support. Twenty per cent found their adoptive siblings and extended adoptive family members helpful, but they were more commonly spoken of as people with whom to have fun and fights.

CONCLUSIONS

The Overarching Messages of the Cardiff Studies

The overarching message of the 'Adopted Children Speaking' study is that the adults involved in the adoption process need to be sensitive to children's individual needs, particularly by involving them and keeping them informed in a way which takes account of their age, understanding and sense of time. The support offered needs to be underpinned by good adult–child and child–adult communication, but the responsibility for establishing the effective communication lies with the adults.

But such a message would not have been out of place in the KIDs study. Equally, one of the points to emerge from KIDs is that many of the children's concerns are not being picked up and responded to, which is no less true of the adoption study.

Both adoption and divorce of the parents represent critical initial life-changing events for the children. A number of children are confused and have poor information about the process (be it adoption or divorce) and about what to expect. That in turn contributes to their understandable anxiety, stress and sense of isolation, which consequently makes the process of adjustment more difficult. In the case of children of divorcing parents, the children's confusion and lack of information can result from one or both of the parents finding it difficult to talk to their children, though as often as not the parents themselves many be confused or uncertain about the future. Moreover, since most divorces and related children's issues are uncontested, the professionals involved in the process (solicitors, welfare officers, mediators, judges) hardly ever see them, and because there are no other obvious sources of support and information, children are frequently left to find their own ways of coping.

In contrast to children of divorcing parents, children involved in the adoption process will have been seen by a number of professionals, yet all too frequently they are also left uninformed about the legal process and sometimes bewildered and confused as to what is happening. In this, they share the experience of many adopters who are also left uninformed about the adoption process.[90] Indeed, the message from the adoption study is that, while professionals work hard *for* children, they do not necessarily work *with* children. Certain obvious things need to be addressed—for example, the ignorance and fear about the court. Here there is a crying need to develop ways and means to explain the court process and to familiarise children with the court room and judge before any hearing. Practitioners also need to remember not to talk about the children in their hearing unless they address them directly. Children, just like adults, need to be fully informed as to what is going on. It is unacceptable to make children wait many months for an adoptive placement without even attempting to inform them about what is happening.

Being able to communicate with children and being sensitive to their needs are the absolute minimum requirements of putting into practice legal obligations to ascertain and have regard to children's wishes and feelings. It is evident from these two studies that there is a long way to go even for professionals, let alone parents, to achieve this.

Towards a New Conception of Support Services for Children in the Family Justice System

The challenge facing those responsible for developing the family justice system is how to take on board the important messages from the growing body of recent empirical studies, including the Cardiff research summarised in this paper, which has sought to ascertain how children themselves view the practice and processes of the family justice system and child protection services. Ironically, whilst the abandonment of Part II of the *Family Law Act* 1996 is in many respects to be regretted, it at least gives more time to consider how best to translate the findings of research into practice.

[90] See, generally, Lowe and Murch et al, *Supporting Adoption* n 85, who recommend (see pp 434–36) that adopters should be treated as working in partnership with the adoption agency and with whom there should be an adoption agreement through which applicants would be fully informed about the process.

The Need for Cultural and Organisational Change

As Piper[91] points out, at a rhetorical level—that of professional and political aspiration—a great deal of emphasis is given to the child's rights and to hearing the voice of the child, but that is still largely framed in a traditional child-saving paternalistic approach. There remains 'an undercurrent of non-engagement with children which must be brought to the surface before there can be any real hope that more than a very small minority of children feel that they have been heard'. Fundamentally, therefore, what is required is nothing less than a major shift in the culture of family law practice—namely, to take much more seriously children's rights to information and participation in decisions which directly affect them.[92] The movement towards this is, of course, well underway throughout the developed Western industrialised world, reinforced as it is by the UN Convention of the Rights of the Child 1989 and, though this has still to be ratified by the United Kingdom, the European Convention on the Exercise of Children's Rights 1996.

Yet some idea of the ambivalent way in which the government is approaching this issue can be seen by comparing the proposals for reforming adoption with those for divorce law. Thus, in the context of adoption, the White Paper issued in December 2000 states:

> Children have a right to have their views listened to, recorded and acted upon, subject to their age and understanding, in the process of planning and making decisions about their future.[93]

Whilst the subsequent Draft National Adoption Standards issued for consultation reinforces this approach by adding that:

> Where the views of the child are not acted upon, the reasons for not doing so will be explained to the child and properly recorded.[94]

In contrast, in the so-called 'private' realm of divorce, by abandoning Part II of the *Family Law Act* 1996, the government has shied away from those provisions which would have made it obligatory to ascertain the wishes and feelings of the children. For the time being at least, until it becomes clear whether these provisions can be salvaged and incorporated in any subsequent divorce legislation, English family law will therefore manifest an ambivalent approach to the participation of children: involving them in the adoption process but, whilst not overtly

[91] Piper, n 1.

[92] K Marshall, n 56, p 103. In offering a possible framework for children's participation based on what she refers to as a 'child-centred system', she asserts that 'a child's right to participate should not be qualified by considerations of the child's interests. Adults cannot deny children the possibility of participation on the ground that involvement in existing decision-making processes would be damaging to a child. It is the task of adults to devise a system which facilitates appropriate participation of children.'

[93] Department of Health, n 76, para 5.16.

[94] Department of Health, *Draft National Adoption Standards for England, Scotland and Wales* (2000), p 4, para 3. See n 97.

keeping them out, by no means being so ready to include them in the divorce process, even where their interests are directly involved.

Of course, it could be argued that one reason for the abandonment of section 11 of the *Family Law Act* 1996 was that the government saw clearly that, as far as support services for the family justice system were concerned, there would be little point in introducing its provisions in private family law if the court welfare service had little experience of direct work with children.[95] The study by Hunt and Lawson[96] showed clearly that the needs of children and families in private law cannot always be adequately met under current arrangements; improvements in the standard of court welfare practice depended on developing certain skills, 'particularly working with children and understanding child care and child protection;' and there was a widespread perception that the court welfare service would not be able to develop in these respects until the organisational link with the Probation Service (predominantly an adult-focused community crime treatment service) was severed. That major policy step has now been taken with the decision to create the new Children and Family Court Advisory and Support Service (CAFCASS) which became operational on 1 April 2001.[97]

The Need for Specialist Training

Nevertheless, organisational change will not necessarily in itself enable practitioners to acquire the necessary skills and understanding to communicate better with children in ways that are acceptable to and supportive of them. Professional and post-professional education and training will have to change too, in order to equip staff of the new service to take on more appropriate roles to support children and families, to listen properly to children, to meet their information needs when their lives are undergoing major change, and to enable them to participate more effectively in the family justice process.[98]

Currently, arrangements for this type of training in the family justice system are woefully deficient. The problem is the more bizarre because judges commonly assume—mistakenly—that court welfare officers and guardians *ad litem*, as trained social workers, have the necessary skills and understanding. It may well be the case that, in comparison to court welfare officers, guardians *ad litem*, who are usually selected for their experience of local authority childcare work, have much more experience of direct work with children. However, this does not

[95] Similar research-based concerns are expressed by Piper, n 1, pp 87–88.

[96] Hunt and Lawson, n 57, p 104.

[97] Note the Adoption White Paper at para 8.19 indicates the government's intention to develop national standards for this new service. It will also be noted that following amendments introduced by the Family Proceedings Courts (*Children Act* 1989) (Amendment) Rules 2001, r 4.11B require the Children and Family Reporter, inter alia, to notify the child of the contents of his report as he considers appropriate to the child's age and understanding.

[98] The Adoption White Paper (2000) at para 8.20 also acknowledges that the creation of CAFCASS presents an opportunity to develop more specific training and development for its officers.

necessarily mean that they have received special training in this area of work. As the Prime Minister's Review of Adoption[99] points out:

> Professional social work training has become ever more generic, meaning that social workers entering children and families work have limited specialist skill and are likely to have received little training on fostering and adoption issues.

In practice, experience counts for a good deal. Some professionals pick up the necessary skills on the job by trial and error. A small exploratory study by Masson and Oakley[100] on the representation of children by guardians *ad litem* and solicitors in public law proceedings found that most guardians were skilled at establishing rapport with children but often felt constrained by the limited time they had. With respect to children's solicitors,[101] the study observed:

> Solicitors representing children receive little training about how to relate to children, yet children involved in care proceedings are often the most vulnerable of all children. Many solicitors learn to relate to children by experience but some solicitors in the study indicated they had little confidence in their ability to speak to children.[102]

One Way Forward?

All the available evidence therefore suggests that, in England and Wales, the professional educational task of learning the art and skills of communicating successfully with children as far as family justice practitioners are concerned has barely begun. This is in part because the necessary educational provision at both the professional and post-professional levels does not yet exist. As the Rowntree Report observes:[103]

> Professionals very often do not have the skills to help children to talk . . . there is at present no training course teaching the skills needed by people working in this way with children.

Now that the President of Family Division has established an Interdisciplinary Committee with a special Education and Training Subcommittee, the opportunity exists to review all the core competencies of family justice practitioners, including their skill levels in working with children (ie judges, solicitors, barris-

[99] See p 16. Note also the comment by P Marsh and J Trisiliotis, *Ready to Practise?: Social Workers and Probation Officers—Their Training and Their First Year of Work* (Avebury, 1996), p 183: 'In spite of the fact that the majority of children entering local authority care or who are placed on supervision are now adolescents and young people, there were almost no references to courses targeting the skills and knowledge required to work with this age group and their families.'

[100] J Masson and A Oakley, *Out of Hearing: Representing Children in Care Proceedings* (Wiley, 1999). This was based on interview sample of 20 children and young people (six girls and fourteen boys) aged between nine and sixteen years.

[101] *Ibid.*, p 71. See also findings by Sawyer, n 44.

[102] *Ibid.*, pp 74–75. See also C Piper, 'Norms and Negotiation in Mediation and Divorce' in M Freeman (ed), *Divorce, What Next?* (Dartmouth, 1996) for a review of research on divorce solicitors generally.

[103] See pp 50–52.

ters and staff of the new CAFCASS) and the available educational provision for post-professional development.[104] It is to be hoped that the development of the special skills and understanding needed to work with children to enable them to participate more appropriately in proceedings will be high on the agenda of this subcommittee and that the government will acknowledge the issue and provide appropriate funding for the necessary training. If this were to happen, then some of the research experience about the best ways of approaching children and listening to their views which research teams, including those at Cardiff, have developed and which have been explained in this article, may have wider application.

[104] The Education and Training Sub Committee (ETSC) advises the President's Interdisciplinary Committee on:

(a) the continuing need for interdisciplinary education and training within and across the family justice system;
(b) the opportunities to develop and deliver such education and training;
(c) the potential for financial underpinning for such education and training;
(d) the ways in which relevant organisations professional bodies and government department might best be involved to support the strategic aims of the ETSC.

2

Children's Participation in Family Court Litigation

Richard Chisholm*

INTRODUCTION

When it comes to children's rights in family law, I would like to propose a simple concept: we need to think about a wide range of possible ways in which children might participate in family law, and we should consider how those varied forms of participation might be good for them, or bad for them.

It may not be obvious why this simple idea is of any interest, but it seems to me that the discussions of the role of children in family litigation with which I am familiar tend not to explore all the relevant territory. For example, most judicial discussions about whether children should give evidence discuss the potential *disadvantages* for the child, but not the potential *advantages*. And children's participation in what is now known as primary dispute resolution seems to have been rather unexplored. So I thought it would be useful to draw up lists of ways in which children might participate, and ways in which participation might be good for them or bad for them. The results of that structured consideration should inform particular decisions we make about each case, on issues such as whether children should give evidence, or should be represented, or should be told what is happening. The results should also be useful in formulating any rules or guidelines relating to these matters.

Who Decides How Children Participate and on What Basis?

Before embarking on the main topic, I want to consider briefly the decision-making process: who decides whether and how children might participate in Family Court proceedings, and on what principles should that decision be made? For convenience, I will assume that the proceedings involve competing claims for residence, and issues about contact, between a child's parents. Ultimately, the basic

* Judge of the Family Court of Australia. The paper draws on an article published in (1999) 13(3) *Australian Journal of Family Law* 197.

principle is that the court's final orders should reflect its findings, on the evidence about what is most likely to promote the child's best interests, which are to be considered the paramount consideration. But the issue here is about questions that must be resolved *before* that final conclusion—namely the extent to which the child should be an active participant in the proceedings (before and during the trial) as distinct from merely the subject of the litigation. Who decides this, and how?

The starting point, I think, is that each parent has 'parental responsibility' for the child. This term has replaced terms such as custody and guardianship. It means, roughly, that the parents have legal authority to make decisions about their children. Assume that, at the start of the proceedings, no earlier contrary orders have been made, and thus each parent has parental responsibility. Initially, each of them has the task of considering how the children might be involved. Should the children be told that the case is going to court? What should each parent say to them? Ideally, of course, the parents should consult about this, and work out how best to present the situation to the children. Some may be able to do so. But in many cases—and particularly those that cannot be settled and must ultimately be decided by the court—the parents' relationship is too hostile and fraught for such discussions. Each may have taken what seemed at the time to be the appropriate action. The children may thus have been treated very differently by each parent.

Each parent will normally become involved with professional people, most obviously lawyers and perhaps counsellors and other people associated with the family or the children. In due course, they will encounter registrars and counsellors attached to the court. These people will be involved in the pre-trial processes. Their task, in a word, will be to assist the parties at every point to resolve the matter if they can, and also to 'case manage' the litigation. Orders will be made about the filing of documents and the like, and there will be preliminary meetings and conferences during which documents will be filed and cases prepared for the final hearing. There may be early interim proceedings, and a brief early hearing to determine what arrangements should be made pending the final hearing. There is likely to be a delay of at least several months between the initial filing of the application and the final hearing. Much will have happened during this period.

In essence, I think, the decisions about the children's involvement during these pre-trial processes involve a number of people. The parents have parental responsibility. But in the course of the proceedings, others will be involved in advisory and consultative capacities, notably lawyers and counsellors. Some will be involved in decision-making roles, notably registrars. They decide various matters relating to the preparation of the case. These decisions include whether the child will be separately represented, whether a family report will be prepared, and so on.

It would not advance my argument to describe the detail of all this. I simply make the point that the parents, lawyers, counsellors, registrars and others are involved along the way, and participate variously in making the many decisions that are made in preparation for the trial. It is probably fair to say that the main focus of much of the activity, at least for the professionals, is firstly in assisting settlement, and secondly in preparing for the trial. Part of the second issue is, of course, whether children should be separately represented.

But the period of preparation for the trial is itself part of the children's lives. They probably know something troubling is going on. They will need to work out for themselves, or guess, or be told, what is going to happen, and when, and how. I imagine that in many cases this period is very stressful for many children. They may have all sorts of anxieties about the ultimate result and about the process, and their role in it.

I suggest that how the children are treated, what they are told and how their concerns are addressed are all important issues, highly relevant to their best interests. If so, it follows that making decisions about these things, or advising about them, are an important part of the responsibilities of all those involved, whether making decisions or giving advice. These decisions along the way seldom emerge for lawyers in the form of reported or even unreported judgments. They have all been made, for better or worse, by the time the case comes up for trial. While important issues can arise for the judge to determine at the trial, many of the important questions about children's participation have effectively been determined by the time the final trial starts.

On what basis or principles should these issues be decided? A possible answer is that the principle that the child's best interests are paramount should apply to these pre-trial decisions as much as to the final decision the court should make. To the extent that they are made by the parents in exercise of parental responsibility, there is authority to the effect that those responsibilities should be exercised according to this principle.[1] To the extent that they are made by lawyers advising their clients, or counsellors, they will no doubt be determined by professional values, but these will no doubt, at a minimum, treat the interests of the child as 'a primary consideration'.[2] Whether or not the 'paramount consideration' principle strictly applies in this area, it is appropriate to give the children's interests great weight, given that ultimately, when the final decision is to be made, those interests must be treated as paramount.

What do the child's interests require? Identifying the choices, and the pros and cons of each, is the topic of this article, but I would make two more general points at this stage. First, a focus on the children's interests requires consideration of both short-term and long-term aspects. It is appropriate to give consideration to whether particular measures will immediately cause anxiety, or reduce anxiety, in the child, but also to consider, for example, whether particular measures are likely to assist the court in its ultimate determination, and thus advance the child's interests in the future.

[1] *Secretary, Dept Health and Community Services v JMB and SMB* ('Re Marion') (1992) 175 CLR 218; (1992) 15 Fam LR 392.

[2] United Nations Convention on the Rights of the Child, Art 3.

The second point relates to the nature of children's rights. There is a vast literature on the nature of children's rights, and I do not intend to add to it here. However, I would like to indicate briefly the position that underlies the discussion to follow. In my view, it is unsatisfactory to simply transpose adult rights to children, and assert that they are entitled to freedom of expression, freedom of association and all the other rights that adults are supposed to have. This ignores the special position of children. It follows that providing children with less than *adult* autonomy rights does not necessarily infringe their rights. It is equally unsatisfactory to say that children have *no* rights of this kind, and that such matters are irrelevant to the task of adults in determining what is best for children. This ignores the claim of children to be treated with respect and dignity, rather than as objects. It is very easy to overlook the importance of consulting children and thinking about their understanding of what is going on, and failing to do so can be very distressing to children, and a violation of their rights.

I think it is helpful to consider that those making decisions within the legal framework face the same challenge as parents. They need to respond to the distinctive needs and interests of children, *including their need to exercise and develop their capacity to understand what is happening, express their wishes, and make decisions about aspects of their own lives.* This response will often entail difficult judgments and assessments. The challenge of making them cannot be avoided either by ignoring children's need for autonomy (the error of saying 'children should be seen and not heard') or ignoring their need to be protected against a degree of responsibility that is inappropriate for them (the error of routinely treating children as adults).

Discarding each of these simplistic and extreme approaches makes life more difficult for the decision-makers. But it is necessary to think through the various options, and their advantages and disadvantages, in order to make wise decisions, especially fine-grain decisions about the involvement of children prior to the trial. It is necessary to discriminate, to agonise. It might be appropriate to provide some information to some children but not to others. It might be best to encourage one child, but not another, to discuss the issues. The age of the child will be an important matter, but it is by no means the only one to be considered. The decision may, for example, be influenced by the way a child has been treated in the past. It might be appropriate to take one approach with a child whose parents have always discussed issues openly, and another with a child whose parents have sought to protect the child from any exposure to family conflict.

PRESENT LAW AND PRACTICE

Legislative Principles

I start with a look at what *principles* are articulated in the legislation—first in provisions that apply to litigation, and then in provisions dealing specifically with 'primary dispute resolution'. I will limit the discussion to proceedings governed by the *Family Law Act* 1975, although many of the principles and practices can be found in the laws of other jurisdictions.

Principles for Litigation

The fundamental principle is that the child's best interests must be regarded as the paramount consideration when the court comes to consider what parenting order to make.[3] This principle, however, does not specify whether or how children might *participate* in the proceedings. It is also reasonably clear that the principle does not strictly apply to procedural and other decisions leading up to the final parenting orders, such as the decision about whether or not to appoint a child's representative.[4]

There were some principles in the original 1975 *Family Law Act*, tucked away in section 43, but as a result of recent amendments in family law,[5] there seems no end to statements of principles, objectives, goals and the like. These are well known and do not need to be discussed.[6] Here it is only relevant to consider what principles the Act contains about children's *participation*. The answer is easy. The topic does not rate a mention among the principles—for example, in section 43 or section 60B. On the other hand, the child's *wishes* are first in the list of things the court must take into account;[7] and nothing in the Act permits the court or any person to require the child to express his or her wishes in relation to any matter.[8]

Article 12 of the Convention on the Rights of the Child provides (emphasis added):

> (1) State Parties shall assure to the child who is capable of forming his or her own views *the right to express those views* freely in all matters affecting the child, the views of the child being given due weight in accordance with the age and maturity of the child.
> (2) For this purpose, the child shall in particular be provided with *the opportunity to be heard* in any judicial and administrative proceedings affecting the child, either directly or through a representative or an appropriate body, in a manner consistent with the procedural rules of national law.

[3] S 65E.

[4] See especially the High Court decisions *CDJ v VAJ* (1998) 23 Fam LR 755; FLC92–828, *ZP v PS* (1994) 181 CLR 639; 17 Fam LR 600 and *Northern Territory of Australia v GPAO* (1999) 161 ALR 318; (1999) *24 Fam LR* 253. The matter is discussed in the commentary to section 65E in vol 1 of the Butterworths *Family Law Service.*

[5] Including child support.

[6] The leading authority is *B and B: Family Law Reform Act 1995* (1997) 21 Fam LR 676 (FC).

[7] S 68F(2)(a); substantially identical in this respect to former s 64(1)(b).

[8] S 68H. The Full Court has emphasised the importance of giving appropriate weight to children's wishes: *H v W* (1994) Fam LR 788; (1995) FLC 92–598.

Article 12(1) of the Convention could be seen as reflected in sections 68F and 68H, although perhaps the Act does not give it as much emphasis as if it had been included in the sections articulating principles. Article 12(2) does not seem to be reflected in any statement of principle, although the 1995 amendments leave intact an array of provisions which enable children to participate in various ways (to be considered shortly).

Principles in Primary Dispute Resolution

When we turn to the legislation on primary dispute resolution, the cupboard is even barer. There is much about the desirability of parents agreeing, and a number of provisions to that end, but not a word about the relevance of children's wishes, or their participation. The legislative silence on the topic is carried through (appropriately) to the delegated legislation: one searches the rules in vain for any reference to children participating in primary dispute resolution. For example, the form of application for a parenting plan[9] sets out numerous categories of relevant information: names, ages, who lives with whom, criminal convictions, proposed arrangements for the child, and much else. But there is nothing about what the child wants, what information the child has about what is going on, whether the child wants to be consulted. This is consistent with the 1995 amendments, which have nothing new to say about children's rights to be heard, and do not refer to these rights in places where one might expect to find them.

Thus, in connection with parenting plans, parents are 'encouraged to agree' about matters concerning the child,[10] but not encouraged, for example, to consider what explanation should be given to the children, or to consider to what extent if at all the children should participate in the process. In the parenting plan form, as in the law long ago, the child is neither seen nor heard.

Summary

In terms of principles, therefore, the legislation provides, in summary, that the children's best interests are paramount, and that their wishes, if freely given, should be taken into account in litigation. The legislation provides mechanisms for discovering their wishes. But it says nothing else about involving them—no statement of principle that implements Article 12(2) of the Convention. And in relation to primary dispute resolution, the Act does not even suggest that it is a good idea for anyone to pay attention to the children's wishes. It is an important question whether the legislation, especially combined with the recent cuts in legal aid, is compatible with Australia's obligations under the Convention.

[9] Form 26A.

[10] S 63B.

Mechanisms

We now turn from principles to mechanisms, and practice. The Act provides various mechanisms for children to participate in parenting matters. First and most remarkably, children can be *parties* to proceedings.[11] However, this provision is virtually a dead letter: one scratches around for examples of its actual use.[12]

Children can be separately represented.[13] And lots of them are: in Australia, well over 2,500 such appointments were made in 1995–1996, nearly three times as many as in 1992–1993. The increase seems largely attributable to the guidelines issued by the Full Court in *Re K* (1994).[14] The role of the child representative is discussed further below.

The Act makes provision for a number of ways in which the court may learn what a child's wishes are, notably by means of a family report or an Order 30A report.[15] It is common for reports to convey the wishes of children, and the independent report is 'one of the recognised ways of obtaining information about the children's wishes'.[16] In practice, what is conveyed is richer than the word 'wishes' suggests, and includes perceptions and feelings.[17]

The rules expressly provide for a practice of long (though not necessarily *good*) standing, namely that the judge interviews the children privately.[18] The practice finds few adherents today, and is (to my knowledge) rare.[19] Commentators usually refer to two problems. First, that judges have no special training or skills in conducting such interviews. Secondly—and for many commentators this is the decisive matter—if the interview is to be confidential, as the rules provide, the result would be hard to reconcile with natural justice, for the judge would act on material unknown to and untestable by the parties. However, nobody seems to want to ban the practice: most people say there is no harm in keeping it as an available option, just in case.[20]

There is provision for judges to be assisted by assessors.[21] The Australian Law Reform Commission (ALRC) writes that assessors 'have not been widely used'. This is an understatement in my experience: I have never heard of the section

[11] S 65C(b).

[12] Usually such research begins and ends with *Pagliarella* (1993) FLC 92–400.

[13] *Family Law Act* 1975, s 68L.

[14] *Re K* (1994) 17 Fam LR 537; [1994] FLC 92–461.

[15] *Family Law Act* 1975, s 62G. See Family Court of Australia, *Guidelines for the Ordering and Preparation of Family Reports*, Feb 1993. The Australian Law Reform Commission found that family reports were used in about 60% of contested cases: *ALRC 84*, 16.35.

[16] *Marriage of N* (1977) 30 FLR 516; [1977] FLC 90–208; *Marriage of Curr* [1979] FLC 90–611.

[17] A point made in a seminal early article by Audrey Marshall, Joyce Grant and Jill Nasser, 'Children's wishes in Custody and Access Disputes' (1980) *Law Soc Jl* 49.

[18] See Order 23, r 5(1).

[19] The child's representative, where there is one, must consent: O23 r 5(4).

[20] For example, *ALRC 84*, Rec 153.

[21] *Family Law Act* 1975, s 102B.

being used. The ALRC says that the court 'could benefit from exploring the greater use of assessors in children's cases',[22] but does not say how, or who would pay for the assessors.

Children can give evidence, although the rules provide that (except where they are *parties*—rare, as previously noted) they cannot be called as a witness, or swear an affidavit, unless the court so orders.[23] Both the authorities and practice suggest that courts rarely so order. I return to this topic later. I note here, however, that the few reported judicial discussions of when children should be permitted to give evidence generally assume that, while the process might assist the decision-maker, it might harm the child.[24] The remarks do not embody the outdated assumption that children are *incapable* of giving evidence,[25] but neither do they contemplate the possibility that there might be cases in which children could *benefit* from giving evidence, a matter to be considered later.

Children's Involvement in Primary Dispute Resolution

My impression is that, internationally and locally,[26] it has been more the exception than the rule to involve children in primary dispute resolution. Reviewing the literature, Carole Brown writes:[27]

> In litigated cases children are interviewed and assessed by professionals who specialise in child development and the dynamics of family relationships. Hence in the case going to trial the child is very involved, perhaps too involved, in the decision making process.
>
> However, between 90 and 95 per cent of custody and access disputes are resolved without going to trial and many of those are resolved through mediation and conciliation. In spite of the huge number of out of court settlements in children's disputes, it is unlikely that the children will be involved in the decision making process where those settlements are assisted by a mediator or conciliator be they in the United Kingdom, Australia, Canada or the United States.

However, at least in recent years, there has been a continuing debate about the topic. Brown sums up the arguments pro and con as follows:[28]

[22] *ALRC 84*, 16.44.

[23] Family Law Rules, Order 23 r 5(5) and (6).

[24] *Marriage of Borzak* (1979) 5 Fam LR 571, 575; *Marriage of Cooper* (1980) 6 Fam LR 288; *Marriage of Foley* (1978) 4 Fam LR 430 at 432; (1978) FLC 90–511.

[25] A matter canvassed extensively in JR Spencer and R Flin, *The Evidence of Children: the Law and the Psychology* (2nd edn, Blackstone).

[26] I was told this when I gave a talk on the subject some years ago for the Australian Dispute Resolution Association.

[27] Carole Brown, 'Involving Children in Decision Making Without Making them the Decision Makers': Paper presented at a Seminar for Directors of Court Counselling and Casework Supervisors, Victor Harbour, SA, Feb 1996 ('Brown, 1996'). I have omitted the extensive citations.

[28] *Ibid.*

Those who say that children should rarely be included in mediation claim that:

- — it places responsibility on the child for making decisions that their parents are unable to make;
- — it erodes parental rights and responsibilities and undermines their authority;
- — it places the child in a powerful position and consequently can erode parent child relationships;
- — it creates further stress for the child who may have divided loyalties;
- — it places the child at risk of retribution from a disappointed parent;
- — it further exposes the child to the parental conflict; and furthermore
- — mediators may not have appropriate training and skills in child development and family dynamics, nor adequate knowledge of the impact of divorce on children to allow them to interpret the child's actions, statements and preferences in context.

Those in favour of involving chidden more in mediation maintain that including the child is important for the following reasons:

- — Including input from the child helps parents maintain the focus on the needs of the child as the paramount consideration.
- — Children have a right to know what is happening.
- — The mediator, having assessed the child, can act in the interests of the child and advocate for the child where the parents have a diminished capacity to do so.
- — Children frequently reveal their feelings to a neutral third party where they are reluctant to disclose them to their parents.
- — The mediator can help reduce a child's fears and anxieties about divorce and address guilt feelings where they occur.
- — When they are given an opportunity to discuss their parent's separation children get a sense that their feelings are important and that they are being listened to.
- — Though parents may be able to negotiate an agreement in the absence of input from the child, this does not always take account of the child's needs, attachments and wishes, hence involving the child can be a way of validating the agreement with the child and increasing the likelihood of it working.
- — It helps keep the lines of communication open between the parents and the parents and the child.
- — If parents are unable to comprehend the impact of their continued conflict on their child this can be reflected back to them by the mediator or the child with the mediator's assistance.

The approach to involving children in primary dispute resolution in the Family Court is the topic of a recent Guideline for court counsellors.[29]

[29] Kindly supplied by Dr Carole Brown.

SOME REFORM PROPOSALS

Principles

I have noted the absence of legislative statements of principle about children's participation, especially in primary dispute resolution. It would be possible—and may be desirable if the legislation is to continue to include statements of principle—to remedy this lack. The ALRC report is interesting in this context, and will no doubt be much discussed.

The new child welfare legislation in New South Wales, reflecting the recommendations of a thorough review,[30] contains such a statement of principle. Section 10 provides:[31]

> *10 The principle of participation*
>
> (1) To ensure that a child or young person is able to participate in decisions made under or pursuant to this Act that have a significant impact on his or her life, the Director-General is responsible for providing the child or young person with the following:
>
> (a) adequate information, in a manner and language that he or she can understand, concerning the decisions to be made, the reasons for the Department's intervention, the ways in which the child or young person can participate in decision-making and any relevant complaint mechanisms;
> (b) the opportunity to express his or her views freely, according to his or her abilities;
> (c) any assistance that is necessary for the child or young person to express those views;
> (d) information as to how his or her views will be recorded and taken into account;
> (e) information about the outcome of any decision concerning the child or young person and a full explanation of the reasons for the decision;
> (f) an opportunity to respond to a decision made under this Act concerning the child or young person.
>
> (2) In the application of this principle, due regard must be had to the age and developmental capacity of the child or young person.
> (3) Decisions that are likely to have a significant impact on the life of a child or young person include, but are not limited to, the following:
>
> (a) plans for emergency or ongoing care, including placement;
> (b) the development of care plans concerning the child or young person;

[30] NSW Dept of Community Services, Legislation Review Unit, *Review of the Children (Care and Protection) Act 1987: Recommendations for Law Reform* (December 1997), p. 16.

[31] *Children and Young Persons (Care and Protection) Act* 1999 (NSW), s 10.

(c) Children's Court applications concerning the child or young person;
(d) reviews of care plans concerning the child or young person;
(e) provision of counselling or treatment services;
(f) contact with family or others connected with the child or young person.

The Role of the Children's Representative

The law on the role of children's representatives is relatively well settled.[32] I need not repeat the various authoritative statements about the role of the child's representative, but merely note that it is clear that he or she is not bound to advocate for the child's wishes in the way a lawyer is bound to follow the instructions of an adult client. However, there is a continuing debate, in various jurisdictions, about what role children's representatives *should* perform in court proceedings.[33] In particular, there is a debate about the extent to which the child's representative should treat the child as autonomous. At one extreme is the position that the child should be regarded as the client, able to give instructions to the lawyer. I will call this the 'lawyer–client' model. At the other would be what the ALRC calls the 'best interests' model, which probably reflects the Family Court authorities, that the child representative should make submissions based on what he or she considers best for the child (while being under an obligation to ensure that the court knows about the child's wishes). The different positions taken in this topic reflect different positions taken on children's rights and autonomy: this is why I discussed this briefly earlier in this paper.

A number of recent discussions of reform favour the adoption of something like the ordinary solicitor–client model in cases where the child has a capacity to give instructions; and use of the 'best interests' model representation where children lack this ability. This approach of course requires a judgment to be made about the child's capacity. The New South Wales Review proposes an age-based starting point, that 'there should be a rebuttable presumption that children ten years and older can instruct their legal representative'.[34] The ALRC's detailed recommendations are too long to reproduce here, but they are interesting and deserve careful consideration.[35] Among other things, the ALRC recommends that there should be a rebuttable presumption that a child over the age of sixteen years living independently is competent to initiate or defend litigation; and 'in all cases where a representative is appointed and the child is able and willing to express views or provide instructions, the representative should allow the child to direct the litigation as an adult client would. In determining the basis of representation,

[32] *Marriage of Bennett* (1991) 14 Fam LR 397, 404; [1991] FLC 92–191; *P & P* (1995) FLC 92–625.
[33] There is a very detailed discussion, with extensive citations, in ALRC 84, ch 13.
[34] NSW Dept of Community Services, Legislation Review Unit, *Review of the Children (Care and Protection) Act 1987: Recommendations for Law Reform* (December 1997), p 68.
[35] I have omitted the passages dealing with the manner of implementation.

the child's willingness to participate and ability to communicate should guide the representative rather than any assessment of the "good judgment" or level of maturity of the child.' It stresses the need for representatives to meet with the children they represent.

I do not want to enter into this interesting and complex debate, except to make two points. First, determining children's capacity may be a little tricky. As the American Bar Association rather finely put it:[36]

> disability is contextual, incremental, and may be intermittent . . . A child may be able to determine some positions in the case but not others. Similarly, a child may be able to direct a lawyer with respect to a particular issue at one time but not at another.

The second point is that the tension between the 'best interests' model of representation and the lawyer–client model is closely connected to the view one takes about children's rights and autonomy, a topic mentioned earlier. Those who would defend a more paternalistic ('best interests') model do not mainly argue that children lack *capacity* to instruct lawyers. Their main argument is that it is not *desirable* for children to do so—or, more accurately, that somebody should decide whether it is desirable for children in a particular case to do so.

The strength of the lawyer–client model, I think, is the difficulty in finding anyone suitable to make informed and qualified decisions about the desirability of children's participation. Given this problem, there is some attraction in reliance on age-based or other presumptions of capacity. The weakness is that this focus on children's capacity may lead to their being involved in ways that are within their capacity, but bad for them.

For these reasons, I think this a difficult problem. While I don't suggest that we give up the attempt to clarify the role of those who represent children, I wonder what the limits are to which we can realistically define the role. I was impressed in this connection with a nice line quoted by the ALRC that the representation of children 'requires thoughtful improvisation rather than adherence to a script'.[37]

Children Giving Evidence

In proceedings under the *Family Law Act*, it is very rare for children to give evidence. In my experience, it is unusual for any party, or for the child's representative, to suggest that the children themselves should give evidence.

The rules provide that (except where they are *parties*—rare, as previously noted) children cannot be called as a witness, or swear an affidavit, unless the court so orders.[38] Both the authorities and practice suggest that courts rarely so order.

[36] ABA, Standards of Practice of Lawyers Who Represent Children in Abuse and Neglect Cases (1996), B–3; cited in ALRC 84, 269.

[37] LE Shear, 'Children's Lawyers in Californian Courts: Balancing Competing Policies and Values Regarding Questions of Ethics' (1996) 34 *Family and Conciliation Courts Review* 275 at 294, quoted in ALRC 84 at 269.

[38] Family Law Rules, Order 23 r 5(5) and (6).

The Full Court has suggested that, in the light of the decision in *Harrington* v. *Lowe*,[39] the rule restricting children giving evidence might be invalid as extending beyond 'practice and procedure'.[40] If the rule is invalid, the question would then arise whether the trial judge would have the power to make an order preventing a child from swearing an affidavit, or giving evidence, in a particular case. If there is to be a technical problem in this area, I would expect the legislation to be amended to create rules along the lines of Order 23, since everyone seems to agree that the court should be able to prevent children giving evidence. I will not pursue this discussion, since my concern is with the policy and principle, not with the validity of the rules or even the court's present powers.

There are few reported judicial discussions of this provision. Wood SJ once remarked briefly that 'the prohibition against calling a child as a witness is designed to prevent a child under 18 from giving evidence for or against either of his parents'.[41] Watson J, referring to the equivalent provision of the regulations, once said it was 'obviously designed for the protection of children and for their removal as far as possible from forensic partisanship in spousal conflict'.[42]

The question of whether a child should be allowed to give evidence was considered in more detail in *Foley*,[43] where Lambert J said:

> The objection, however, raises the questions of the principles which should be applied in the exercise of the discretion to admit or refuse evidence by affidavit or orally from a child under 18, and the procedures for ascertaining the relevant facts upon which those principles should be applied.
>
> In my view some of the factors which are relevant for consideration in the exercise of the discretion are:
>
> 1) The nature and degree of cogency of the evidence it is sought to adduce through the child.
> 2) Whether such evidence is reasonably available from an alternative source.
> 3) The maturity of the child.
> 4) The nature of the proceedings, and the relationship of the child to persons affected by those proceedings.
>
> As well the court should weigh the value of the evidence to the determination of the issues between the parties against the possible detriment to the child in being thus involved in the adversary procedures between the parties. This necessarily involves some consideration of the prospects of a continuing relationship between the child and the parties following the necessary determination of the issues between the parties.

I underline the point that these remarks have to do primarily with ensuring that the child's involvement as a witness is not harmful to the child. They do not

[39] *Harrington v Lowe* (1996) 20 Fam LR 145 (HC).
[40] *Marriage of Renshaw and Renschke* (1997) 22 Fam LR 354.
[41] *Marriage of Borzak* (1979) 5 Fam LR 571, 575.
[42] *Marriage of Cooper* (1980) 6 Fam LR 288.
[43] *Marriage of Foley* (1978) 4 Fam LR 430 at 432; (1978) FLC 90–511.

embody at all, I think, outdated views that children are *incapable* of giving evidence.

The approach to date has possibly been unduly protective. Perhaps there are cases where children have been much involved, and really want to talk to the judge. If so, there are advantages in having the talk out in the open, in court, rather than in a private session with the judge, after which the losing party may well feel unjustly treated (not having the chance to know what was said, or to contest it). On the other hand, this approach would obviously put pressure on the child, and would often be undesirable. The idea of children giving evidence is probably most palatable in the case of older children. But in the case of older children of sufficient maturity, to warrant consideration of their giving evidence, their wishes (which can be conveyed through a family report) are likely to be very influential in any case, so the outcome of the case may not be much affected by putting them through the experience of giving evidence.

My own experience has been limited. In one case, the question was whether the children should have contact with the father, who had killed their mother. I was told the older child wanted to speak to the judge. The father was unrepresented, so that if the child were to give evidence he could have been cross-examined by his father, who had stabbed his mother. It was not an appealing prospect. After discussion with the parties and the children's representative, and in the end with the agreement of everyone, a video tape was made in which the child responded to questions (formulated in court) asked by a counsellor. The video was shown in court. The child (who did not want to see his father) was told that the video would be shown in court.

In the other case, a contest between a grandmother and a mother, involving international elements and child sexual abuse, one party submitted that the children should give evidence. The children's representative did not support the application. I did not allow the children to give evidence, mainly because there was a vast amount of evidence—from counsellors, a child psychiatrist and others—about their wishes, which had been firmly expressed on many occasions. I thought that having them give evidence would not provide anything new, and could have adverse effects on them.

I only wish to make two further comments. First, it may be useful to state in the Act whether trial judges have power to limit or dispense with cross-examination of child witnesses. On the face of it, having them give evidence includes exposing them to cross-examination by, or on behalf of, at least one parent. If we are to move in the direction of children giving evidence more frequently, this question needs to be considered. While ordinary principles of the adversary system would presumably require the child, like any witness, to be available for cross-examination, it might be arguable—especially if the proceedings are to be considered as more in the nature of an inquiry than an adversary process—that this matter could be reconsidered.

Secondly, if we are to have children give evidence in a larger proportion of cases, we should take the opportunity to learn from developments in other jurisdictions in which they routinely do so. I have in mind especially the jurisdiction of the Children's Court, both in relation to care and protection and juvenile justice, and the jurisdiction of the ordinary criminal courts, which deal among other things with prosecutions for sexual abuse of children. In this area there has been considerable research and experience using various techniques including closed-circuit video. Clearly we should learn from our colleagues in these other jurisdictions if we are to explore this territory.

MAKING CHOICES ABOUT CHILDREN'S PARTICIPATION

What Children Want

There have been surveys in which people have asked children who have been involved in legal proceedings what they wanted, or how they saw things. Such literature as I am familiar with suggests two things:

1. Children often want to know what is going on and want to have their views taken into account.
2. This does not much happen.

I mention some examples. In Margaret McDonald's research on a sample of separated families, three-quarters of the children said that they were not consulted by their parents about when and for how long they wanted visits, and 81 per cent said they were not consulted about any changes to arrangements, even though changes occurred in about one-third of cases.[44] Most parents (over 90 per cent) did not talk to their children about matters being disputed in the Family Court. Carole Brown summarises survey results of children who were involved in mediation:[45]

> In Garwood's study (1989, 1990) she asked children about their experiences in conciliation. Twenty-four of the 28 children interviewed said they had benefited from their attendance at conciliation and most of them mentioned a definite improvement in communication, especially with the non-custodial parent. Some children also said that conciliation had helped them by allowing them to express their feelings with someone who knew how they felt.
>
> The children were also asked about the possibility of attending a children's group to meet and talk with other children of their own age whose parents were also separated or divorced. Three quarters welcomed the idea, the rest were uncertain or not in favour.

[44] Margaret McDonald, *Children's Perceptions of Access and Their Adjustment in the Post-Separation Period* (Family Court of Australia, Research Report No 9, 1990). The information in the text is drawn from pp 25–27.

[45] Brown, 1996, n 27.

> There were some areas, however, that needed attention. For example, some of the children interviewed said that they had wanted to know more about the format to the appointment ahead of time. They reported that they were nervous and this was partly attributable to the uncertainty about what was going to happen. They suggested that there should be more information to prepare them for the appointment and that they should know in advance whether one or both parents would be present at the meeting and whether they would be seen separately or with other family members.
>
> Some of the younger children reported that they did not always understand what the conciliator was saying. This has a clear message about the choice of language and the concepts used when dealing with children.

There are startling statements in ALRC 84 about children not being spoken to by their legal representatives.[46] The Australian Law Reform Commission gives a number of examples of children in detention complaining that their lawyers (in juvenile justice cases) did not listen to them. It goes on to say:[47]

> 4.25 These perceptions reflect children's real experiences of legal processes. They were confirmed by other participants in these legal processes. In the public hearings and in private meetings, the Inquiry heard many examples of representatives in family law proceedings refusing to speak with their child clients or of children who were distraught after hearings because their legal representative had not done what the child had instructed. One young girl, aged 12, even telephoned the Inquiry to seek our intervention in Family Court proceedings on her behalf. She was caught up in a long running Family Court case, and although she had been interviewed by various social workers, counsellors, psychologists and police officers she had never been interviewed by the legal representative appointed to her case. She believed that no one had told the judge what her wishes were. Some children may also feel marginalised by the court system because it is:
>
> '[an] adversarial system . . . dominated by legal strategising by competing parties to maximise their chances of winning the case . . . The interests of the child often get lost between the warring parties.'
>
> 4.26 Court processes were not the only legal processes to receive scathing criticism from young people. Service delivery agencies and schools were also seen by young people as uncaring bureaucracies in which the child's voice was often ignored. For example, one young person described a situation in which he had applied for Abstudy's living away from home allowance after he moved out of his house. He felt that there was no one to talk to at the relevant department about the problems he was experiencing in this application process.
>
> 'I was passed from person to person when I telephoned. No one took responsibility for my case.'

[46] *ALRC 48.*

[47] *ALRC 48*, paras 4.25–4.27 (citations omitted).

4.27 Another young man who had experienced the care and protection system said that he was not allowed any involvement in decisions regarding his placement with various foster parents. Sometimes he did not even know the reasons why his placement was being changed. Another young person described a social worker's refusal of his request to meet prospective foster parents before being moved. Other young people confirmed that lack of consultation by child welfare workers was a consistent problem in all care and protection systems.

'Kids don't have any rights when dealing with the Department of Family, Youth and Children's Services. Kids are told what to do rather than consulted. Social workers don't listen to kids' wishes.'

The Inquiry's survey of young people found that of the young people in detention facilities who had also had some involvement with care and protection systems, 72 per cent felt that they did not have enough say in decisions made.

Some Forms of Participation

In considering whether a child should participate, one important factor is the kind of participation. Thoughtful commentators often make the point that whether participation is a good idea for children depends on what kind of participation it is. Thus Carole Brown, speaking of involving children in mediation, writes:[48]

> There is a distinct difference between involving children *so that they have a better understanding of what is happening in their lives and allowing them to express their feelings* to someone who understands what it is like to be in their position as against involving the child *as a tie breaker or a fall back decision-maker* for parents who are unable to resolve their differences and cannot see beyond their own needs. What is being advocated in this paper is the former approach rather than the latter.[49]

Again, dealing with litigation, the ALRC writes:[50]

> 8.15 It is generally assumed that children would be unduly traumatised by giving direct evidence in litigation concerning the breakdown of their parents' relationship, that they may be manipulated into giving evidence favourable to one parent or may even manipulate parents to achieve their own ends. These remain factors for concern.
>
> 8.16 However, there is a difference between asking a child *to give evidence in relation to disputes of fact* (which should generally be avoided) and allowing a child the opportunity to *express his or her wishes as to the outcome of a matter.* Children should not be required or pressured to do so but it may be appropriate for mature children to give evidence of their wishes where they freely indicate a desire to do so. In those

[48] Brown, 1996, n 27.
[49] *Ibid.*
[50] ALRC, *DRP* 3, May 1997.

> cases, the voluntary involvement of children in the family decision making process can be a real benefit to children, to the Court and to the ultimate decision.

In these two quotations I have underlined the phrases capturing the distinction drawn in each extract. Note that in each case there are two main categories of activities. A larger number of types of participation emerges from the following, by a mediator with acknowledged expertise in children's involvement:[51]

> —Children have a right to give their input into decisions that will affect their lives.
> —Children can provide useful information.
> —Children are often excellent creative problem-solvers.
> —Children often need an opportunity to express their feelings . . .

I think it is possible to expand on these ideas, and set out a larger variety of ways in which children could participate. Here are some:

1. They might tell someone how they understand and experience the situation—for example, that they hope their parents will live together again; or that they feel it is their fault.
2. They might describe particular incidents.
3. They might express their wishes about outcomes. These might be wishes as to what others see as the main issue (to live with one parent or the other) or some other issue, for example, to stay at the same school, or to stay with a sibling; or to *leave* a school or a sibling.
4. They might want to express their feelings. For example, they might want to tell a parent who has left home that they miss that parent; or that they feel angry at having been abandoned by the parent.
5. They might want to discover information: why don't we eat out at restaurants any more? Why do we stay with grandma every Sunday? Why does Mum cry all the time? Will I really be sent to a children's home if I misbehave?
6. They might want to bargain: I'll go to visit Dad, but only if I can stay in the basketball team and play on Saturdays.
7. They might seek reassurances or promises: that they won't be abandoned by one parent, or that they will be able to stay at the same school next year, or that they will be told in advance before anything *else* happens.

You could no doubt amplify and expand this list, but it will do for now. Its value, even in its present form, is to emphasise the wide range of possibilities. Let me develop some of the ideas that stem from the list.

Participation Over a Period of Change

Much of the participation described will not occur on one occasion only. Much of it will occur over a period of time. It involves, for the child, *managing a period*

[51] Bernard Mayer, 'Working with Children in Mediation' (CDR Associates, 1988), p 31.

of change. This fits in with the point made by Carole Brown and others that family breakdown is better regarded as a *process* than an event. In this respect, the legal framework does not fit the reality very well. The legal framework presupposes a set of procedures directed towards and culminating in the *trial*, a single period of oral evidence and argument followed by a judgment: end of story. But for the family members, the reality is more a matter of a process of adjustment that may take months or years, and in which the trial will be an important episode, but by no means the end of the story. We must think in terms of children's participation at various stages in the story. At different stages, different people will be in a position to consider the question. Initially it will be a matter for parents and other family members: what do we tell the children? Once counsellors, lawyers and others are involved, they will have an opportunity to consider the question. It may be of particular importance to make wise decisions early on about how children are to be involved; if they are left out, or inappropriately involved, at the early stages this may create problems that will be difficult to undo later on. When the question is being considered later on, one of the key questions will be the extent to which children have *already* been involved.

Learning What is Going On

This seems a very important and valuable kind of participation for many children. Children often want to know what is going on, and can be greatly upset if they don't know, and can make their own assumptions (eg 'It must be something *I* did').[52] This form of participation does not run into most of the problems associated with other forms of participation—for example, the child does not express a preference between parents.

Expressing Emotions

It may be important for children to express their emotions, and perhaps go through the process of grieving. This might be a part of coming to terms with what is happening to them. Doing this may require them to talk through the issues with their parents, or perhaps with others, such as the child representative. They should be given the opportunity to do this.

Expressing Preferences about What Should Happen

The preferences might be about the main outcome—for example, to live with one parent—or a subsidiary one—for example, staying at the same school, whatever the outcome of the residence question. This is the most obvious type of participation, the focus of much of the law previously discussed. But I suspect that there are many children who would not want to do this, but would still want the

[52] This point is repeatedly stressed in *ALRC 48* and the Family Law Council's 1996 Report.

decision-maker to know their preferences about other matters, such as school attendance, continuing activities and friendships.

Contributing to the Consideration of Outcomes through Discussion or Bargaining

This is perhaps a less obvious form of participation, at least for lawyers. But in primary dispute resolution, and in the case of older children, this can be very important.

I know of a case[53] in which the parents had encountered an impasse: should their two children, aged eleven and nine, live with parent A, or with parent B, or alternate between parents? Each of the three options seemed unacceptable to at least one parent, though they lived near each other. In mediation, the children had a session with the mediator in the absence of their parents. They had discussed it between themselves and had worked out a solution. They said they knew each parent was sad when they were not with the children, and that they too missed that parent. The children said that they did not need to be together all the time. And so they suggested a regime in which for some periods one child would be alone with each parent and at other times the children would be together. This proposal was greeted with relief and high emotion, and formed the basis of the eventual solution finalised by the parents. The point is that the kids thought of it and the parents had not been able to. And perhaps the fact that the proposal came from the children made it easier for each parent to accept it without loss of face.

Stating Observations about Fact

This is perhaps the simplest and most obvious kind of participation, the kind most relevant to litigation. Children can state observations about matters of fact: whether they were left alone at night, whether a parent hit them with a stick, and so on. Their statements could be important in helping the court determine disputed questions of fact. It seems important to distinguish between situations where the child *wants* to make statements to the court from those where someone else thinks that the child's evidence could help the decision-maker determine an important issue.

Reasons Why Children's Participation Might be Desirable

I now want to identify some reasons why it might be good for children to participate. Some reasons will apply more to some forms of participation than to others.

[53] Communication from Elizabeth Chisholm.

—Children's participation might help parents understand their needs.[54]
—Children's participation might help parents realise what consequences their actions have had, and what consequences their contemplated actions might have, on the children. For example, a parent who has somewhat withdrawn from family conflict, and feels like getting away from it all overseas for a few weeks, might reconsider, or explain, or write or telephone the child frequently, if the child has told the parent she feels angry at being abandoned.
—Children's participation might help the parents to work out an arrangement they would not otherwise have thought of.
—Children's participation might give them a sense of having some control over their lives and affairs, which might be good for their psychological well-being.[55]
—Children's participation might provide them with information or reassurance that will make them happier, or less anxious.
—Children's participation might have the consequence that they are treated as persons and not as objects.
—Children's participation might involve complying with Australia's human rights obligations—for example, under Article 12(2) of the Convention on the Rights of the Child.
—Children's participation might provide useful corroborative evidence to help the decision-maker decide a relevant matter, such as whether a parent left the children alone at night, or hit them with a stick.
—Children's participation might reduce the amount of inflammatory material in affidavits and exchanges, since the parents will know the children will be exposed to it.

Why Children's Participation Might be Undesirable

By contrast, here is a list of some of the reasons why children's participation might be *undesirable.*

—Children might be stressed by the process of participation—for example, by multiple interviews where child abuse is alleged.
—Children might be required to behave in adult ways, or take adult decisions, and thus to a greater or lesser extent be 'deprived of their childhood'.

[54] McDonald writes that: 'Children's wishes regarding future relationships with both separated parents are often disregarded by adults who conclude that they are cognisant of their children's feelings. Research to date does not support that view. Parents and professional alike need to be reminded that children are able to express their needs in a logical and insightful manner.': quoted in Moloney, 'Beyond custody and access: A children's rights approach to post separation parenting' (1993) 7 *AJFL* 249 at 256.

[55] This important point is emphasised by the Family Law Council, *Involving and Representing Children in Family Law* (1996), especially at paragraphs 3.14–3.17.

—Children might be coached, bribed, threatened or otherwise interfered with by adults who want the children to participate in ways that the adult wants. (If the children were unable to participate, they may not be subjected to such behaviour.)
—Children might be put in a position of having to betray or condemn one parent by expressing affection or loyalty to the other.
—Children might find themselves in a situation of being able to manipulate adults who are supposed to have responsibility for them.
—Children might lack competence, or information, relevant to the way they are participating. Thus a child who has received many presents and much affection from a parent who leaves the home following separation might want to go to live with that parent, not knowing the difficulties that parent would have in providing full-time care (eg because the parent's new partner can't stand children).
—Children's wishes might reflect a distorted parent–child relationship. A child might want to stay with a parent, and look after them, because the child has become identified with that parent's grief and helplessness. In extreme cases, the parent–child relationship can be reversed in emotional and other areas: child psychiatrists sometimes refer to these situations as involving 'parentified' children.
—Children might say things that have multiple adverse consequences which the child cannot predict. For example, a child might reveal that a parent had said highly offensive things about a grandparent, who might tend to withdraw or retaliate, polarising family feelings.
—Children's participation might *increase* the amount of inflammatory material in affidavits and exchanges, since the parents will know the children will be exposed to it.

CONCLUSIONS: DETERMINING CHILDREN'S PARTICIPATION IN PARTICULAR CASES

I agree with the Australian Law Reform Commission that 'the degree of children's involvement should be determined in each case on the basis of the wishes and needs of the child involved. Ensuring that in each case the child's participation in these processes is appropriate may be difficult but the challenge should not be avoided.'[56] I also agree that appropriate training should be provided.[57] I have tried to identify some ideas that might assist in achieving this objective. I will conclude by highlighting some main points of the argument.

[56] This important point is emphasised by the Family Law Council, *Involving and Representing Children in Family Law* (1996), especially at paragraphs 3.14–3.17. See to the same effect the submission by Relationships Australia.

[57] Australian Law Reform Commission, para 16.25.

It seems desirable, if we are to have legislative principles, to given an honourable place to children's rights to participate in proceedings, and to ensure that the legal aid system and our courts work so that we comply with Article 12 of the Convention on the Rights of the Child. The New South Wales legislation, quoted above, provides one valuable model.

Children should be able to participate in *negotiated* outcomes through the primary dispute resolution system.[58] There are many barriers to their doing so.[59] With the honourable exception of the new Family Court guidelines, there seems much more conscious and explicit attention to children's participation in litigation than in primary dispute resolution. This seems both curious and unfortunate. There are many reasons why they might be *more* easily and more fruitfully involved in primary dispute resolution than in litigation. In comparison to litigation, primary dispute resolution handles families where the parties have more capacity to work things out. Those that go to litigation are generally the most difficult, high-conflict cases. If one reconsiders the list of advantages and disadvantages, I would think that in general the advantages would be more likely to outweigh the disadvantages in primary dispute resolution than in litigation. And the forms of participation for children could in some ways be more flexible.

In deciding what involvement, if any, children should have in litigation, it is difficult to overstate the importance of taking into account the age and characteristics of each child. Children vary as much as adults in their personalities, talents, vulnerabilities, and so on. Some children will be outraged if they don't get to say their piece; others would shrink from the prospect. And there will be endless variation in their capacities to participate, their insight, their honesty, and the like. In my view, the great differences between individual children are sometimes lost sight of as we try to find patterns and guidelines for our decisions and policies. But among the things we should take into account, the individual characteristics of the child are among the most important. They include the age and maturity of the child; the extent to which the child has *previously* been involved in the family dispute; the level of conflict between the parents; the area of dispute (is there a contest for residence, or does the dispute relate to some narrower issue, such as choice of school?); and many others.

It is said that we should not 'put adult responsibility for adult decision-making on children',[60] and that is no doubt correct; but there many types of involvement that do not do that, and also do not ignore the children. Providing children with information about what is going on has much to commend it. Children, after all, have to live with the result of whatever is decided, and only if they know what is going on can they make informed decisions about what sort of involvement they want to have. It seems likely in many cases that children will have gleaned that

[58] Moloney (cited in n 2, above): 'listening carefully to children would mean that children would have the right to be present at counselling, mediation or a court hearing when their future was being discussed' (p 256).

[59] This is a big theme of *ALRC 84*, for example, at para 4.11 and following.

[60] Attorney-General's submission to the Australian Law Reform Commission, quoted at para 16.19.

something is going on, from such events as arguments, or a parent leaving home, or surprisingly sleeping in the garage. And often parents will have sought support or sympathy from the children, or sought to recruit them to their side. I suspect that in the case of children, as in the case of adults, a great deal of stress would flow from uncertainty and lack of a sense of being able to control the situation. In many cases, I would guess, keeping the children out of the conflict is not an option, because they are already in it; but making them better informed might well be an option.

Next, I suspect it is easy to underestimate the importance for children (as for adults) of giving them a chance, if they wish, to make their views and feelings known—to the parents, to the court, and perhaps to others. This seems to me quite different from putting on them the responsibility for making the decision, the usual rationale for ignoring children. Many children, surely, would appreciate the chance to make their views and feelings known, while realising perfectly well that the decision was up to the adults.

If these views are accepted, it seems necessary to reconsider all aspects of the system: primary dispute resolution and litigation. The legislature needs to consider what principles might be appropriately put into the legislation to provide guidance. Whether assisted by legislative principles or not, a series of decisions needs to be made at each stage in every case about what type of participation the children should have.

In each case, the question arises, *how are these children to participate in these proceedings*? Addressing this question should be a normal part of what *parents* do when the family breaks down, what *lawyers* do when they talk to clients, what *child representatives* do when they prepare their cases, what *counsellors* and O30A experts do when they prepare their reports; what *registrars and judges* do when they make procedural and final determinations. Perhaps we have all given too little attention to this question. If we address it systematically, so that each case proceeds on the basis of thoughtful decisions about how the children themselves should be involved, we might make a real advance towards a more child-centred family law.

3

Delivery Systems for Protective Services and Related Legal Services for Victims of Domestic Violence Within a Major American State

Jane Muller-Peterson, Robert E Rains and Andrea C Jacobsen*

INTRODUCTION

The purpose of our research has been to examine the processes, practices and pressures affecting the delivery of legal services to victims of domestic violence, using as a model a major American state, Pennsylvania. Pennsylvania is a large state with an estimated population of over twelve million individuals distributed among two major metropolitan areas (Philadelphia and Pittsburgh), several smaller metropolitan areas and extensive rural regions.[1] This large state comprises over 46,000 square miles (119,000 square kilometres).[2]

Like all American states,[3] Pennsylvania has a statute providing for civil injunctive relief for victims of domestic violence;[4] indeed, Pennsylvania enacted the first such law in the United States.[5] The *Protection From Abuse Act* (PFA) authorises a victim of domestic violence on behalf of herself and/or minor children to file in county court[6] for an immediate *ex parte* order[7] enjoining the abuser from further violence and also allowing for a range of further relief including such matters as evicting the abuser from the residence, entering a temporary order of support

* Professors Jane Muller-Peterson and Robert E Rains teach at the The Dickinson School of Law, The Pennsylvania State University. Andrea C Jacobsen is an attorney in Carlisle, Pennsylvania. At the time of writing, she was a partner in the law firm of Jacobsen and Milkes. She is now in solo practice.

[1] Statistical Abstract of the United States, 119th edn, 1999, Table No 26, p 28, Table 46, p 46.

[2] *Ibid.*, Table 393, p 239.

[3] Toni L Harvey, 'Batterers Beware: West Virginia Responds to Domestic Violence', (1994) 97 *W Va L Rev* 181 at 185.

[4] 23 Pa Consolidated Statutes (PaCS), ch 61.

[5] Act of 7 Oct 1976, PL 1090, No 218.

[6] 23 Pa CS § 6106. NB Although the statute is gender-neutral, we use the female article and pronoun throughout this paper when referring to victims, and the male article and pronoun when referring to abusers, because by far the greatest number of plaintiffs are female.

[7] 23 Pa CS § 6107(b).

(maintenance), entering a temporary custody and visitation (access) order, prohibiting further contact, ordering the abuser to relinquish weapons, ordering him to pay the plaintiff's reasonable losses resulting from the abuse, and prohibiting stalking or harassment.[8] Unless the matter is resolved by the parties or dropped by the plaintiff, the court must hold a bench trial within ten days, at which the plaintiff has the burden of proof by a preponderance of the evidence that abuse has occurred.[9] If she meets that burden, the court will enter a protective order for up to eighteen months which may impose any or all of the remedies set forth above.[10] If the defendant violates a PFA order, he may be found guilty in a subsequent proceeding of indirect criminal contempt and may be fined up to $1,000 or incarcerated for up to six months, or both.[11]

In addition to state remedies, a federal statute, the *Violence Against Women Act* of 1994 (VAWA),[12] has provided a number of remedies to address domestic violence at the national level. Particularly pertinent here is a provision requiring each state to give 'full faith and credit'[13] to protective orders issued by the court of another state (subject to certain due process[14] conditions).[15] Also relevant is a provision in another federal statute, colloquially known as the Brady Bill,[16] which makes it illegal for any person who is subject to a state domestic violence protective order (entered under certain conditions) to possess a firearm or ammunition.[17]

Because of the prevalence of domestic violence, statutory mandates placed upon the courts, and the difficulties generally experienced by poor people—especially women—in accessing the legal system, there has been significant interaction in the last two decades among the courts, legal services organisations which are funded to provide free legal services to the poor (sometimes known as legal aid or legal assistance programmes) and entities that provide social services to aid victims of domestic violence. Pennsylvania is divided into 67 counties[18] with greatly varying demographics and economics. For reasons which we will describe below, there is great diversity from county to county in how these entities interact.

In the latter part of the 1990s, a committee made up of representatives from legal services and domestic violence services programmes undertook a survey to

[8] 23 Pa CS § 6108.

[9] 23 Pa CS § 6107(a).

[10] 23 Pa CS § 6108(d). Until May 2000, the maximum length of an initial order was one year.

[11] 23 Pa CS § 6114.

[12] Pub. L 103–322. NB. Although one provision of VAWA was ruled unconstitutional by the US Supreme Court in *United States v Morrison*, 120 S Ct 1740 (2000), most of the Act remains intact. VAWA was 'reauthorised' by Congress in Oct 2000.

[13] US Constitution, Art IV, S 1.

[14] US Constitution, Amendment XIV, S 1.

[15] 18 USC § 2265.

[16] Named for James Brady, Press Secretary to President Reagan, who received a severe brain injury in the shooting assassination attempt on the President by John W Hinkley, Jr on 30 March 1981.

[17] 18 USC § 922(g)(8). One of these conditions, related to hearings, will be discussed in the text below.

[18] *The Pennsylvania Manual*, Vol 114, nos 6–4 (Dec 1999).

examine how the legal and related services were actually being rendered throughout the state. This resulted in a report, published in 1998, describing five legal service delivery systems.[19]

During 2000, we followed up the 1998 Systems Survey to attempt to reach conclusions about what features make up a good service delivery system and what kinds of coordination among the courts, legal services provider and domestic violence services providers can offer those features. We believe that the Pennsylvania experience will provide useful insights not only for Pennsylvania, but for the entire United States and perhaps for other countries.

BACKGROUND AND DESCRIPTION OF PRIOR STUDY IN PENNSYLVANIA

The 1998 Systems Survey was the result of a collaboration between the Pennsylvania Project Directors Corporation, a coordinating body of legal services programs in the state, and the Pennsylvania Coalition Against Domestic Violence (PCADV), the statewide network of 65 domestic violence programmes.[20] For more than twenty years, these two communities of service providers had collaborated to various degrees at the local and state level to provide services to victims of domestic violence and to advocate on their behalf. They undertook the survey to examine the status of legal services delivery to victims of domestic violence in Pennsylvania with the hope that the information provided would improve services, strengthen collaboration, and lead to the development of new resources for legal assistance to victims of domestic violence.[21]

Because of the involvement of the two communities, and the many different organisations within each, in the creation of services for victims, different services and differing degrees of collaboration had emerged. In 1988, amendments to the *Protection From Abuse Act* resulted in the addition of the courts as another primary player in the development of services for victims.[22] One of the amendments expanded the Act to include all 'intimate partners', in addition to family or household members. Until 1988, legal services programs, designed to serve low-income people in a variety of civil matters, had also provided assistance to nearly all victims of domestic violence, often with the assistance of staff members from the domestic violence services programme. The funds utilised for this special service were primarily federal Title XX Social Services block grant funds,[23] allocated

[19] Pennsylvania Project Directors Corporation and Pennsylvania Coalition Against Domestic Violence, Partners in the Protection From Abuse Process: Systems of Legal Advocacy and Representation in Pennsylvania(1998). (Hereinafter the 1998 Systems Survey or the 1998 Survey).

[20] 1998 System Survey, See n 19, Introduction, at v.

[21] *Ibid.*, at v–vi.

[22] Act of 20 April 1988, PL 355, No 56.

[23] Title XX of the *Social Security Act*, Block Grants to States for Social Services, 42 USCS § 1397 *et seq.*

to the states to use for a variety of social service programmes. Because it was apparent to those amending *the Protection From Abuse* statute that the funds allocated to legal services programmes were insufficient to handle the expanded caseload, the authors of the amendments included a provision requiring that the courts provide simplified forms and clerical assistance to help plaintiffs with the writing and filing of petitions for a protection order when they were not represented by counsel.[24] That meant courts and service providers had to decide the role each would play in the new system and the extent to which litigants would receive assistance at each stage of the proceeding. The major players in the systems which developed are therefore the courts, domestic violence services providers, and legal services organisations.

To some degree, the systems were determined by who took the initiative to obtain funds. The courts were going to have to expend funds anyway, and when legal services or domestic violence services organisations applied to the county court systems to assume the courts' new obligations, they were often funded by the court system to provide the statutorily mandated services in conjunction with the services they were already providing. In some counties, the organisations which obtained this funding obtained additional funds from other government sources, foundations or other non-governmental sources to provide still more services. In other counties, the courts hired new staff members to assume the new obligations, and in still others they assigned these duties to existing staff members. The variety of responses to the new legal mandate, coupled with the variety of delivery systems already in existence at the time the 1988 amendments took effect, led to significant diversity in delivery systems around the state.

The 1998 Systems Survey examined the services provided to victims at different stages of the legal proceedings, the type of organisation that was providing each of the services, and the extent to which victims proceeded without assistance.[25] Questionnaires were sent to each of the 138 domestic violence and legal services providers in the state to obtain information about the local legal services delivery system for victims of domestic violence. Based on the responses, five types of service delivery systems were identified, and the common features of each were described.

In System One, which was utilised in 28 counties at the time the 1998 Survey was completed, *pro se* petitioners are assisted at the initiation of PFA cases by lay legal advocates employed by domestic violence services programs. Once temporary orders are granted, victims receive representation throughout the remainder of the legal proceedings by attorneys, primarily employed by legal services programmes. In many of the counties utilising this system, the court requires petitioners to go to the domestic violence services organisation as the first step in the process to obtain a Protection Order. Cooperative working relationships are critical to the success of this system. Some of the areas of concern noted were that, in

[24] 23 Pa CS § 6106(h).

[25] 1998 Systems Survey, n 13, *supra*, Executive Summary, at vii.

this system, PFA orders often do not provide the full range of relief possible under the statute. In a number of the counties employing this system, custody issues are never addressed in the PFA process and in others, child or spousal support, victim restitution and other specific forms of relief are not regularly requested or obtained. Further concerns were the infrequent entry of temporary orders in many of the counties with this system, the lack of availability of warning letters as an alternative to filing for a protective order, and the lack of representation in related legal matters.

In System Two, utilised by 12 counties at the time of the 1998 Survey, petitioners file at the court without the assistance of even lay legal advocates. In most System Two counties, legal services attorneys or *pro bono* attorneys participating in a programme coordinated by legal services or the county bar association provide representation for obtaining a final order. The study noted that women in many of these counties report feelings of fear, confusion and frustration as they struggle to begin the PFA process. It also noted that they may be deprived of the opportunity to consider and request all appropriate forms of relief afforded by the Act or to learn of alternative forms of relief, and they may inadvertently provide information to their abusers which could place them at risk of escalating violence.[26]

In System Three, utilised by 11 counties at the time of the 1998 Systems Survey, attorney representation is available to victims who wish to have it throughout the proceedings. In some System Three counties, a petitioner must first go to the domestic violence services organisation, and in others the petitioner may initiate the process at the legal services office. But in all of the counties with this system, there is an opportunity for legal consultation prior to filing a petition, and there is an opportunity to discuss options other than filing a petition for protection from abuse, such as counsel sending a warning letter to the abuser. In many of these counties, the legal services office which handles the protection from abuse case also handles other related matters, such as child support, long-term custody, housing and employment matters, and divorce.

In System Four, utilised by five counties, almost no legal representation is available, and in most of the counties utilising this system, the victim receives no advice regarding legal options prior to the filing of a petition.

Finally, in System Five, utilised in three primarily urban counties, legal services to victims of domestic violence are provided through specialised centres. At least one of these centres provides assistance in criminal as well as civil matters. Staff members assist battered women throughout the entire PFA process and often provide assistance with related matters. The 1990 Survey raised the question of the practicality of establishing such specialised units when similar or identical

[26] The *PFA Act* provides that the court may consider whether the plaintiff or her family is endangered by disclosure of the permanent or temporary address of the plaintiff or minor children: 23 Pa CS § 6112. An uncounselled petitioner may not be aware of this provision. See 1998 Systems Survey, n 13, p 20.

services can be provided through legal services offices with broader missions, and such specialised units might compete against legal services programs for funds.

Ironically, the 1998 Survey had an opposite effect to that intended in some parts of the state. It was designed as a tool to help service providers improve legal assistance to victims of domestic violence, to strengthen collaboration among domestic violence programmes, legal services programmes and other partners in the delivery system, and to generate new resources for legal assistance to victims of domestic violence.[27] In some counties, the improvements envisioned did occur, but in others high-quality services were eliminated or reduced when it was learned that some counties provided far less. Cost appeared to be the motivating factor, and without information about the advantages and disadvantages of the different service delivery models, there was little to balance against savings. It became evident that a new study *evaluating* the systems was necessary to provide guidance to court systems contemplating change; hence we undertook that evaluation.

ASSESSMENT OF CURRENT DELIVERY SERVICES

Goals

Our primary goal in undertaking the current study was to assess the systems described in the earlier study. A second goal was to examine changes and innovations in the county systems which occurred after the 1998 Survey was completed. Of particular interest to us was to assess the importance of attorney involvement at various stages of the proceedings. Finally, it was our goal to find out about particularly effective practices in individual counties which have not been widely adopted throughout the state and to disseminate information about them.

Method and Scope of the Inquiry

We began our research by sending a preliminary questionnaire to each organisation which had been contacted for the 1998 Survey, each domestic violence services office and each legal services office in the state of Pennsylvania. In addition to asking that a contact person be identified in each office, we asked respondents[28] to tell us if they thought their system had been accurately described in the original study and, if it had not, to indicate which system description would have been

[27] 1998 Systems Survey, n 13, Introduction, p v.

[28] As used in this article, the term 'respondents' refers to entities and individuals that responded to our surveys and follow-up interviews, not to defendants accused of abuse.

more accurate. We also asked them to inform us if their county's system had changed in the last two years and, if so, what the changes were and why they were made. Finally, we asked them to address whether any changes made had increased or decreased the effectiveness of the system for victims of domestic violence or had an impact on the efficiency of the court system.

We received information from 74 respondents working with victims of domestic violence in 61 of Pennsylvania's 67 counties. Based on the information we received, we divided respondents into groups to be asked follow-up questions on specific issues. For example, one questionnaire was designed for those in counties with partial *pro se* systems and another for those in counties providing attorney representation at all stages. Some of the questions had been raised in the 1998 survey as 'issues to consider' at the end of the descriptions of each delivery model. Others emerged from answers to the preliminary questionnaire in our follow-up study, as respondents described changes and innovations in their systems. For example, because a large number of respondents described the new PFA Database, PFAD,[29] as having a significant impact on their systems, we designed a separate questionnaire for counties implementing it. Still other questions were designed to elicit information about unusual or particularly effective practices which others might benefit from adopting.

The questions covered a wide variety of topics, including coordination of services among the players in the system, the extent to which information is provided to victims at various stages of the proceedings, the kinds of help or representation which are provided before and after the initial filing, whether and how cases are settled, the types of relief clients obtain in temporary and final orders, how custody is handled, whether the attorneys handling PFAs also handle other matters, how contempt is handled, whether there is an alternative to gaol or fines, such as court-ordered counselling for batterers, and whether there are special court procedures for handling PFA cases, such as specially assigned judges or special PFA days.

In addition to providing information about how services to victims are provided in their counties, respondents were asked to state what was good and bad about their procedures, what would improve the way services were provided, and what they would change if money were no object. Respondents were generally given the option of responding in writing or in an interview format. In a county which had recently experienced a significant change in how services were being provided, we scheduled a series of interviews. It was our view that the players in that system would bring an unusual and insightful perspective to the task of assessing services because of their experience in two significantly different service models. In that county, we also personally interviewed the judge who had been assigned to handle the county's entire caseload of Protection From Abuse cases.

[29] 'PFAD' refers to the Protection From Abuse Database, a computerised system which is discussed below.

Focus on the Availability of Information and Legal Advice

Instead of assessing each of the five types of system which the 1998 Survey described, this paper will focus on the extent to which information and advice must be provided in an effective system, regardless of which of the three primary players has assumed particular functions within the system. Because there are so many variations in how services are provided, and because as systems evolve they incorporate to greater or lesser degrees features of another system, it is difficult to place counties definitively in one system or another, and it is therefore more useful to describe the problems and benefits connected with particular practices. It is our conclusion that, whatever the system and whichever organisation has taken on the job of starting the process, the system can be effective if services are coordinated so that adequate information and advice to clients are incorporated into it. We were gratified to note—particularly in light of our initial observation that in some counties the 1998 survey was used as a justification to cut services—that in others there has been a trend to enhance services to victims. These counties have incorporated into their existing systems—often through collaboration and coordination with other entities—features from a different service model. For example, there is a trend in System Two counties, where petitioners file at the court, for the court staff to encourage or even require victims to contact a domestic violence services organisation, so that they are better informed and learn of all available options before filing. There is likewise a trend among domestic violence services organisations to collaborate more closely with legal services organisations or to contract with or hire a lawyer so that legal assistance can be provided to victims earlier in the proceedings. Interviews with respondents in domestic violence services organisations revealed that, in many of those cases where victims have not yet established a close relationship with a lawyer, various options for doing so are under consideration.

Problems when Information and Advice are Delayed

The responses from advocates in counties in which legal assistance is not available at the outset of the process to obtain an order of protection from abuse—still perhaps the majority of counties in Pennsylvania—demonstrate why there is a growing trend away from this model. Respondents from these counties consistently described problems resulting from the lack of information and representation provided to victims, and the most common response to the survey question asking what respondents would change if money were no object was that clients should have more and earlier access to legal advocates and lawyers.

Respondents described four problems which arise when legal assistance is unavailable at the outset of the proceeding: the screening burden on the court; the lack of alternatives for victims of domestic violence; the dismissal of meritorious cases; and a lack of settlement mechanisms.

Screening Burden on the Court

The court is burdened with screening out cases lacking merit, costing enormous amounts of judicial time. A judge we interviewed in a county whose system changed from a system in which legal services were available from the beginning to the end of the process to a system in which court staff provide clerical assistance but no advice to petitioners stated that the county's caseload of Protection From Abuse cases increased 40 per cent after the change, and that she spent large amounts of time determining which cases warranted entry of a temporary order and which cases did not.[30] In another county, the judge conducts an in-person interview with each petitioner to make that determination.

In trying to solve this problem, court systems have come up with a variety of solutions. Some counties have court staff do limited screening, such as determining whether the relationship of the victim to the defendant is that required by the *Protection From Abuse Act.*[31] This reduces the burden on the judiciary somewhat, but most of the screening must still be done by a judge. Other counties hire a lawyer to be a hearing officer and to screen out petitions which are not sufficient under the Act. This solution costs money which could perhaps be better spent on attorneys for plaintiffs. When a hearing officer determines that a case has insufficient merit under the law, the victim has no access to an advocate who might help her to plead her case successfully or who might advise her about alternative remedies. One court, not wishing to sort out cases before the client has obtained legal advice, gives no relief in the temporary *ex parte* order at all, but simply sets a hearing date. This practice diverges from the statutory mandate which provides: 'If a plaintiff petitions for a temporary order for protection from abuse and alleges immediate and present danger of abuse to the plaintiff or minor children, the court *shall* conduct an ex parte proceeding.'[32] The statute contemplates that courts will consider the circumstances of plaintiffs who may be in immediate danger of abuse and provides that: 'The court may enter such temporary order as it deems necessary to protect the plaintiff or minor children when it finds they are in immediate and present danger of abuse.'[33] A court which declines to have *any* process for the issuance of temporary orders violates at least the spirit, if not the letter, of this provision. Furthermore, by scheduling every case for hearing, regardless of its legal merit, the court has not taken advantage of the opportunity to free itself from the burden of hearing cases which do not meet the requirements of the Act; in addition, the court has imposed unnecessary burdens on others. The time of defendants, witnesses and plaintiffs is spent needlessly. Even more problematic,

[30] Interview with Hon. Jeanine Turgeon, CP Dauph., 30 May 2000.

[31] Under the Act, to be covered, abuse must be 'between family or household members, sexual or intimate partners or persons who share biological parenthood'. 'Family or household members' are defined as 'spouses or persons who have been spouses, parents and children, other persons related by consanguinity or affinity, current or former sexual or intimate partners or persons who share biological parenthood': 23 Pa CS § 6102.

[32] 23 Pa CS § 6107 (b) (emphasis added).

[33] *Ibid.*

when relief is denied in cases which are not legally sufficient, the message sent to defendants may be that they are doing nothing wrong, and victims may be placed in more danger than they were in before proceeding.

In other counties, the problem of screening *pro se* cases has been solved, at least to some degree, by a strong collaboration between the court and the domestic violence services organisation. In some counties, this is accomplished by a court rule requiring that all those who wish to file petitions go first to the county's domestic violence services organisation. In others, domestic violence services organisations have a presence at the courthouse to explain the law and options to those filing. Some courts provide office space to these organisations free of charge. In one county, the domestic violence services organisation describes its work at the court as 'volunteering'. In another, the court's PFA coordinator calls the domestic violence services organisation to come to assist each time a *pro se* plaintiff comes to file a petition, and a domestic violence services staff member goes to the courthouse to talk to *pro se* plaintiffs before they file, whenever possible. Whether meeting with victims at their own offices or at the courthouse, legal advocates from domestic violence services organisations point out to victims facts which should go into their pleadings and avenues for relief they should consider. They talk to victims about their options, and help them with safety planning. When the domestic violence services organisation has a relationship with the local legal services program or an attorney, victims with borderline or complex cases can obtain advice from an attorney in person or by telephone.

Lack of Alternatives for Victims of Domestic Violence

A second problem which arises when legal assistance is unavailable at the outset of a proceeding is the lack of alternative remedies available to those seeking orders. In systems in which a lawyer is available to screen the case for merit, victims with weak cases, or cases which do not yet rise to the level of abuse required by the Act, are presented with the option of having the lawyer send a warning letter to the abuser. That letter informs the person who has placed the victim in fear of abuse of the legal actions available to the victim—both criminal and civil—if the threatening or abusive behaviour continues. The warning from a lawyer of future legal action which may be initiated if threatening or violent acts continue is sometimes enough to stop a slowly escalating domestic violence situation. In counties in which there is no involvement of legal services or any other attorney at the outset of the process, but there is some screening by domestic violence services staff, victims are given sample letters they can write themselves describing actions they will take in the future if threats and violence continue or escalate. When no initial screening of cases takes place, neither of these alternatives is available. Instead, the victim is likely to bring an action which will fail, sending the message to the defendant that his behaviour can continue with impunity.

Dismissal of Meritorious Cases

A third consequence of the lack of legal assistance at the outset of a case is that cases which warrant entry of an order may be thrown out. The victim of abuse is simply lacking the knowledge and skills necessary to include in her petition the legal basis for entry of an order. A petitioner may, for example, write that her ex-boyfriend broke the windshield on her car without mentioning that he made threats to harm her or that he confined her against her will, which would provide a stronger basis for the entry of an order. As noted, in one county the judge does an in-person interview with each petitioner to determine whether there is a basis for entering an order. Most courts cannot or will not go to the effort of doing an in-person interview with each petitioner to determine whether there is a basis for an order and may dismiss cases that appear on paper to lack merit. In some counties, courts grant no temporary relief in cases which appear weak, but do schedule them for hearing. When courts rely upon a *pro se* pleading written without the benefit of advice, relief can be denied to plaintiffs who may genuinely be in immediate danger but who do not have an understanding of the law or sufficient skill in drafting the petition to convey the relevant circumstances.

Lack of Settlement Mechanisms

A final problem in systems in which no legal assistance is available before the initial filing is the lack of opportunity to settle cases efficiently. The consequence for lawyers, who get involved after the initial filing in such systems, is that they must prepare each case for hearing, even when there is a high probability that the case will ultimately settle. Attorneys with several cases scheduled on one day—which is frequently the situation because many courts have special PFA days—must move from case to case at the courthouse trying to obtain settlements, and cannot give each case the time it deserves. The consequence for the court is that time must be spent hearing cases that would have been settled had the defendant had the opportunity to contact the lawyer before the hearing date, or that judges must wait around while settlement talks occur which otherwise could have taken place before the scheduled court date. By contrast, in counties where a legal services programme is listed as the attorney on the petition and the defendant is made aware of the opportunity to settle the case, approximately 90 per cent of the cases settle prior to hearing. Defendants know who is handling the case for the petitioner and are sometimes provided with instructions for settling the case at the time the papers are served.[34]

[34] The legal services office located in Cumberland County informs defendants in a document entitled 'Instructions to the Defendant', which is served on defendants with the Petition for Protection From Abuse, that they may consent to entry of a Protection Order as an alternative to having the matter heard. These instructions provide information about how to do so and inform defendants that the Consent Agreement should be prepared before the date and time scheduled for the hearing. They

In trying to address the problem of a system's lack of settlement opportunities prior to the hearing date, some courts have developed procedures which, once again, diverge from those delineated in the *Protection From Abuse Act*. The hearing, which under the Act is intended to result in a final order,[35] is treated instead as a settlement conference. A second hearing is set for those cases which do not settle. This means that any temporary relief granted is in effect for longer than the ten days anticipated by the statute. Some courts schedule the second hearing as much as two or even three months after the originally scheduled hearing, burdening defendants for a time period significantly longer than that envisioned in the statute as acceptable for *ex parte* relief to remain in effect. Holding a second hearing in cases which do not settle also means that parties and witnesses must make arrangements to come to court again. Survey respondents reported that this leads some plaintiffs to drop their cases, particularly when employers are unsympathetic to missed work for court proceedings and the plaintiff's job is at risk. In still another variation of procedures different from those described in the statute, which have evolved because of the problem of obtaining settlements in *pro se* cases, some counties have hired lawyers to act as hearing officers to try to obtain settlements. Their orders are appealable to a judge within ten days. This again raises the question of how limited funds can most effectively be used. The same funds spent on a legal services or other attorney to handle plaintiffs' cases would probably achieve the objective of obtaining settlements while also achieving additional objectives such as early merit screening and a holistic approach to the clients' legal problems, which often include issues related to child support, custody, housing and monetary losses such as lost wages due to missed work or medical expenses, or other damages caused by the abuse.

In one county, on the day scheduled for the final hearing, the judge reduces the number of cases which go to hearing by having his law clerk go to the parties to try to obtain settlements. The survey respondent in that county noted, however, that the primary reason for this procedure is not to save valuable judicial time but to avoid the federal mandate contained in the Brady Bill,[36] which prevents those subject to protective orders from possessing or receiving firearms. A precondition to issuance of a 'Brady indicator' is that the protective order be 'issued after a hearing of which such person received actual notice, and at which such person had an opportunity to participate'.[37] There is an ongoing dispute as to whether entry of an agreed order, when a formal hearing has been scheduled but not held,

further notify defendants of a $25.00 surcharge which is assessed against them if the case goes to a hearing and the judge grants a Protection Order, and informs them that if that occurs, they may also be required to pay the equivalent of the plaintiff's attorney fees to an entity which funds legal services: 23 Pa CS § 6106 (c) and (d).

[35] 23 Pa CS § 6107(a) provides that: 'Within ten days of the filing of a petition under this chapter, a hearing shall be held before the court, at which the plaintiff must prove the allegation of abuse by a preponderance of the evidence. The court shall advise the defendant of the right to be represented by counsel.'

[36] 18 USC § 922(g). See n 17.

[37] 18 USC § 922(g)(8)(A).

compels the firearms prohibition. Given the very high value placed in American society in general, and in parts of Pennsylvania in particular, on the right to bear arms,[38] it should not be surprising (although potentially tragic) that some local judges attempt to arrange PFA proceedings so that abusers can keep their weapons.

In at least one county where representation is assigned only after entry of a temporary order, the problem of achieving settlements has been reduced by a procedure which enables the court administrator to provide to defendants the name of the attorney who is representing the plaintiff and how to contact the attorney. A notice to defendants similar to that used in Cumberland County,[39] combined with this procedure, would be likely to facilitate additional settlement negotiations.

Weighing the Costs and Benefits of Providing Information and Legal Advice from the Outset of Proceedings

The problems encountered in systems which do not provide legal advice from the outset of the proceedings suggest that the expenditure of funds for legal assistance to victims of domestic violence is not only warranted, but may actually be cost-effective. The increased time judges must spend sorting out cases and the development of courthouse attorney positions or law clerk positions to relieve the pressure on judges are costs which must be weighed against the cost of legal advice to clients early in the process. Whether or not the provision of early legal assistance is more cost effective than the provision of clerical assistance with the resulting additional burdens on the court system, the systems which provide early legal advice and assistance operate more efficiently and provide better services to victims—which justifies at least some additional expenditure of funds.

It is our recommendation, therefore, that any system which attempts to provide free access to the courts for victims of domestic violence should include some degree of legal assistance for them at the outset of the proceeding. This might be provided directly by an attorney or paralegal in a legal services office, or it might be provided through a partnership of domestic violence services advocates and lawyers or legal services organisations, each of which would provide specialised and complementary services, so that attorneys' services as compared to those of lay advocates or paralegals could be used in the most cost-effective manner. For example, in a few counties, the domestic violence services organisation has a contract with legal services to have an attorney supervise their legal advocates. In other counties, the domestic violence services legal advocates have office space at a legal services office so victims can easily be referred to a legal staff member. In others, the domestic violence services organisation and the legal services organi-

[38] US Const Amend II.
[39] See n 35.

sation have formed a new entity in which they collaborate to ensure coordinated services and free representation to victims; and in still others, the legal services organisation requests that all clients start the PFA process at the domestic violence services organisation, which both provides and gathers information. The legal services staff then make themselves available to discuss any difficult legal issues with the domestic violence services staff member or the victim. When the client decides to go forward with a petition for a protective order, the domestic violence services organisation transmits the information, and sometimes a draft petition, electronically to the legal services staff for review. These sorts of close relationships allow for a significant expansion of the advice and assistance which can be provided to *pro se* plaintiffs without disturbing significantly the roles each organisation has assumed within the system and without greatly increasing costs. At a minimum, any system which provides free access to the courts for victims of domestic violence should at least include 'options counselling'[40] by a lay advocate and access to legal advice and assistance throughout the proceedings, even when petitions are filed *pro se*.

COMPUTERISED INNOVATIONS: PFAD

At the time we undertook the 2000 study, a new statewide computer system, PFAD—the Protection From Abuse Database—was beginning to come online in some Pennsylvania counties. The 1994 amendments to the *Protection From Abuse Act*[41] mandated registration at the state level of each PFA order entered by the courts of Pennsylvania.[42] The amendments required the Pennsylvania State Police (PSP) to establish and maintain a statewide registry of protection orders and a complete and systematic record and index of all valid temporary and final court orders of protection or court-approved agreements entered anywhere in the state. The PSP Registry must include the following information: the names of the litigants and any protected parties; the address of the defendant; the date an order was entered; the date it expires; the relief granted under the order; the judicial district where the order was entered; and, if furnished, the Social Security number and date of birth of the defendant.[43]

Within twenty-four hours after entry of any PFA order, the Prothonotary (clerk) of the court must send a copy of the order to the registry, and subsequently a copy of any later amendment or modification or revocation of the order. The Pennsylvania State Police must enter the orders, amendments or revocations into the registry within eight hours of receipt. The registry is to be available at all times

[40] This term is used by domestic violence services organisations to describe the information they provide to victims of domestic violence so that they can make informed choices. It is also called 'empowerment counselling'. See 1998 Systems Survey, p 20.

[41] Act of 6 Oct 1994, PL 574, No 85.

[42] 23 Pa CS § 6105(e).

[43] *Ibid.*

to inform courts, dispatchers and law enforcement officers of any valid protection order involving any defendant and to enable the PSP to conduct a criminal history check in connection with the provisions of the *Uniform Firearms Act*.[44]

The law enforcement agencies of Pennsylvania are also required to transmit to the registry information related to crimes of violence between family or household members. The PSP is required under the statute to compile and analyse the data received, including aggregate county and department-based statistical profiles.

Several years after the implementation of the registry, the need for a complementary database was identified. The Protection From Abuse Database (PFAD)[45] is a project of the Pennsylvania Coalition Against Domestic Violence (PCADV), a non-profit organisation of local and state-wide domestic violence shelters and service providers which oversees the funding and delivery of domestic violence services in the state.

PFAD is a computer archival system that operates in conjunction with the PSP Protection Order Registry. The mission of the PFAD database is to identify and track all PFA proceedings in the state. It is *not* a public database. Rather, it is a secure system that only authorised users can access via a secure internet website. The database is intended to:

—automate the PFA process in the courts;
—create and disseminate the PSP Protection From Abuse Summary Data Sheet, which identifies and standardises the information necessary for inclusion in the PSP Protection Order Registry;
—provide critical statewide data for analysis by the courts and law enforcement agencies in the state; and
—contain all standardised PFA forms approved by the Pennsylvania Supreme Court, as well as other forms necessary for a typical protection order case.

Access to the system is available to court personnel, law enforcement agencies, domestic violence advocates and legal practitioners who have applied for access and whose account information has been reviewed and authorised by the PFAD System Administrator.

PFAD was established through the cooperation of PCADV and the Administrative Office of the Pennsylvania Courts (AOPC). It has been a project of particular interest to the Pennsylvania Supreme Court because it offers the opportunity to review how electronic pleading and court order issuance might work in the eventual context of all court business. For PFA matters, the database originally went online in 1999 for pilot testing in nine of the sixty-seven Pennsylvania counties. Training was provided to court personnel, law enforcement agencies and domestic violence advocates in each of those counties. The initial implementation of the system allowed some tinkering as 'bugs' were identified and correc-

[44] *Ibid.*; see also 18 Pa CS ch 61, Subch A.
[45] www.pfad.org

tions were attempted. Now, a majority of the counties in the state have had their personnel trained and are online. Resistance to the technology continues in some of the smaller and more remote counties, but this is expected to dissipate as the advantages of the system are demonstrated and the availability of computers to local law enforcement agencies becomes universal.

Among the significant advantages of the system have been the speed and accessibility it has brought to the PFA system in those counties in the state which are online. With PFAD, PFA petitions can be drafted and transmitted to the court electronically. Physical filing of the pleadings is still required in most courts. In some counties, relief can be granted, and a protective order will actually be immediately printed and signed by the judge and entered on the system in the courtroom before the parties walk out the door of the courthouse. Indeed, in at least one county, the judge will not allow the parties and counsel to leave the courtroom without certified copies of the protective order in hand.[46]

The immediate availability of orders has eliminated the worry often present immediately after the judge agrees that a protective order is needed and before the order is signed, transmitted to the Prothonotary, forwarded to the Pennsylvania State Police and local law enforcement officials and served on the defendant. The victim seeking protection from a defendant waiting outside the courthouse will at least have the advantage of a valid order, which can be immediately enforced in the event of further harassment or abuse. Until the defendant has actually been served with a protective order, it is questionable whether he can be held in contempt for violating it, even if he has actual notice of its terms.

The PFA database can be searched by county, by surname or first name, or other indicia to find whether current or prior orders exist.[47] PFAD has enhanced the ability of local law enforcement officials to access the stored information quickly because it is available to authorised users from the World Wide Web, rather than from the limited Pennsylvania State Police registry system. It has also facilitated the preparation of petitions for contempt, and requests for modification or extension, because the terms of the existing order can be immediately accessed and copied in the authorised advocate's word processing system.

PFAD can provide a great benefit with regard to the distribution of PFA orders. In our large and geographically diverse state, law enforcement is provided by a multitude of state, county and municipal agencies, including the Pennsylvania State Police, county sheriffs' offices, and city, borough and township police forces. Many victims work, live and commute through areas served by various law enforcement agencies. If an advocate wanted to assure that each local police force would enforce a PFA order, it was traditionally necessary to obtain several certified orders and distribute them to a number of agencies that might be charged

[46] Interview with Hon Jeannine Turgeon, CP Dauph, 30 May 2000, n 31.

[47] In the interview referenced in n 31, Judge Turgeon voiced her unhappiness that the PFAD does not allow access to the initial petition, thus depriving the judge of knowledge of the initial allegations, especially where the petition was filed in a different county.

with enforcement. Every local police force agency would be served to alert them to the existence of the order and the possible need for prompt action in the event of a violation. Now, any of several jurisdictions in the state that might be traversed by a plaintiff during the course of her daily life can immediately confirm the existence of a current order online, as needed.

The PFAD system can also be used for the preparation and negotiation of terms of final orders by advocates on behalf of victims of domestic violence. As individual counties have come online, modifications to forms have been developed to meet local concerns and needs within the context of the uniform form system. Currently, PFAD forms online include the original petition (in English and in Spanish), Temporary Order, Continued Temporary Order, Amended/Modified Temporary Order, Notice of Hearing, Order Assessing Costs, Order to Dismiss, Order to Vacate, Final Order, Amended/Modified Final Order, Extended Final Order and Affidavit of Service.

Survey responses about PFAD were generally very positive. Respondents noted that in counties where the domestic violence services advocates or legal services lawyers put the orders into the system, they are able to make sure orders are complete and correct. They also noted that implementation of PFAD has brought about increased collaboration among the court staff, legal advocates and legal services providers. One respondent praised its efficiency and noted that it also provided a bond with the courthouse staff. Another stated that it had opened the doors to the judges' chambers, which were difficult to access before.

The main complaint about PFAD has been that it is time consuming. When orders are prepared in the courtroom, advocates and parties must often wait significant periods of time for their orders to be processed, particularly when several cases are heard consecutively. Another complaint has been about the limitation on who may have access to PFAD. For example, the judge we interviewed would like professionals providing counselling to batterers to have access to their court papers online.[48]

CONCLUSION

Systems in which victims of domestic violence have early access to legal advice provide many advantages over those that do not. When victims have access to lawyers, they have more options. Instead of filing a petition for protection from abuse, they may ask a lawyer to send a warning letter informing the person who has placed them in fear of abuse of the potential criminal and civil legal consequences of their actions. The availability of this alternative may prevent victims from filing an unsuccessful petition in which their partners' acts, while alarming to them, do not rise to the statutory standard of abuse; such unsuccessful petitions may increase the risk of harm. Whether or not the circumstances of the case

[48] Interview with Hon Jeanine Turgeon, n 31.

meet the requirements of the *Protection From Abuse Act*, such a letter may put a stop to escalating threats or acts of violence. A warning letter in lieu of a formal filing may defuse a volatile situation, and prevent an abuser from crossing the line into criminal activity and its potential consequences.

Early legal involvement may also make future violence less likely because more matters which could lead to future conflict get resolved. If victims wish to separate from the person they fear, they may decide—after consultation with a lawyer—to proceed with divorce, custody (residence and access) and child support (maintenance), or a combination of legal actions, including a petition for protection from abuse. A lawyer may also be able to assist the client with such related legal matters as housing, employment or financial affairs. To the extent that lawyer involvement results in ancillary relief, it may eliminate or resolve potential points of conflict between the parties which could lead to further violence.

Another advantage of early representation to victims is that, when they are represented, they are often spared the stress of facing the abuser in court. The intervention, whether in the form of a warning letter or a settlement, may even preserve the relationship between the spouses or intimate partners, which is sometimes a victim's primary or secondary goal. Finally, early legal assistance enables victims who lack the knowledge and skills to submit legally sufficient petitions to do so, so that all victims genuinely in need of protection will be able to obtain it.

Early legal involvement benefits not only victims, but also the courts and even abusers or those accused of abuse. When attorneys sort out the cases which are appropriately brought as protection from abuse cases from those which are not, courts are spared the burdensome task of doing so. In addition, because cases handled by lawyers are far more likely to settle before the scheduled court date, courts are spared spending time on needless hearings or waiting for parties to settle a case at the time scheduled for hearing. Abusers or those accused of abuse are also spared needless court appearances.

Because of the benefits to the courts and to the parties of legal representation from the outset of the proceedings to obtain a protective order, the best service delivery system for victims of domestic violence will include legal representation from the outset of the process. When that is not possible, the system should at least provide options counselling by a lay advocate who has access through close collaboration among the players in the system to legal advice from an attorney and who is able to refer victims to a lawyer in the many circumstances in which they could benefit from prompt advice or representation.

4

Paternalism, Participation and Placation: Young People's Experiences of Representation in Child Protection Proceedings in England and Wales

Judith Masson*

INTRODUCTION

Article 12 of the UNCRC requires states to provide children with 'the opportunity to be heard' in judicial or administrative proceedings affecting them on the basis that children capable of forming views have a right to express these freely. However, unlike some other parts of the Convention, Article 12 is not merely recording the existing practices of those who drafted it or have ratified it.[1] Rather, it seeks to challenge children's exclusion from the public arena, and by so doing facilitate their development and improve decisions which are taken about them. Children's right to participate is a recognition of their status as persons and an acknowledgement of the importance of their views—they are *experts in their own lives.* It forms the basis of a different compact between adults and children based on involvement in decision-making rather than exclusion from it.

Implementing the ideals of the UNCRC is proving a more problematic process than its enactment; achieving real change for children will challenge the vested interests of adults, institutions and corporations. Drawing on research,[2] this paper explores the barriers to children being heard in legal proceedings through a study of their representation in care proceedings in England and Wales. In particular, it demonstrates how professional relationships (between children, their representa-

* School of Law, Warwick University, Coventry, England.

[1] One illustration of this is the Council of Europe's adoption of a Convention on the Exercise of Children's Rights in 1995 with the aim of implementing rights in the UN Convention: see C Sawyer, 'One Step Forward, Two Steps Back—the European Convention on the Exercise of Children's Rights' [2000] *CFLQ* 151.

[2] J Masson and M Winn Oakley, *Out of Hearing* (Wiley, 1999); A Clark and R Sinclair, *The Focus on the Child* (National Children's Bureau, 1999); J McCausland, *Guarding Children's Interests* (The Children's Society, 2000); M Ruegger, 'Seen and Heard but How Well Informed? Children's Perceptions of the Guardian *Ad Litem* Service' (2001) 15 *Children and Society* 133.

tives and the judiciary), attitudes to children, the role of the court and court processes interact to discourage children's participation and muffle their voices. Despite the provision of two representatives for children in these proceedings—a specialist social worker to act as children's guardian (formerly known as a guardian *ad litem*)[3] and a lawyer trained to act for children—their representation is focused on paternalism and placation rather than their participation.

English law's willingness to engage with children as children in judicial processes is a relatively recent phenomenon. Although juvenile courts were established in the eighteenth century, children accused of the most serious offences are still tried in adult courts, a process which can lead to unfairness because it is hard for children to cope with the rigors of crown court proceedings, to follow what is going on and to take part.[4] Until the end of the twentieth century, there were barriers to children acting as witnesses. Evidence law was constructed on the basis of children's supposed unreliability and incredibility;[5] those 'of tender years' could not be witnesses in criminal trials and older children's statements required corroboration. Concerns about the difficulty of convicting those who had sexually abused children led to reforms which allowed children's evidence to be heard and took limited account of their greater vulnerability but failed to make structural changes to the adversarial system for children's benefit.[6] These changes do not reflect beliefs that children should be involved with the courts or that legal process should change to accommodate children; rather, they are reactive and instrumental—based on a need to comply with international standards[7] and the realisation that children's evidence is essential for convictions. Rather than leading to the development of a more child-friendly legal process, the impact of hostile cross-examination on children has reinforced views that court is no place for them.

Children are also involved in civil proceedings, almost always as plaintiffs seeking compensation for personal injury.[8] The court rules presume that they are incompetent to act alone and require them to be represented by a litigation friend, a role generally performed by their mother. Children are given added protection by requirements for the litigation friend to instruct a solicitor and for any settlement to be approved by the court.[9] These provisions may help ensure that children's cases are not inappropriately compromised, but they may make justice

[3] The changes in terminology were introduced in the Family Proceedings (Amendment) Rules 2001 (2001 SI 821), following the introduction of the new Children and Families Court Advisory and Support Service (CAFCASS).

[4] *T and V v UK* (2000) 30 EHRR 121; a *Practice Direction* [2000] 2 All ER 285 has introduced pre-trial familiarisation visits for children tried in the Crown Court.

[5] See generally J Spencer and R Flin, *The Evidence of Children* (2nd edn, Blackstone Press, 1993).

[6] *Criminal Justice Acts* 1988, 1991; *Youth Justice and Criminal Evidence Act* 1999.

[7] See also *McKerry v Teesdale and Wear Valley Justices* in *The Times*, 29 Feb 2000, where young defendants' need for privacy was discussed in the light of international law and practice.

[8] For a discussion of the law and practice of children's litigation, see J Masson and A Orchard, *Children and Civil Litigation*, Lord Chancellor's Department Research Series 10/99 (1999) available from www.lcd.gov.uk/research.

[9] Ord 80 rr 2, 10; CPR r 36.

for children less accessible, more bureaucratic and more expensive. Children are generally neither parties nor witnesses in family proceedings between their parents, even when their residence or contact is in issue.[10] The courts have generally taken the view that these are adults' disputes from which children should be shielded.[11] However, if a welfare report is commissioned, a child may have the opportunity to tell the court their wishes and feelings, via the children and family reporter (formally known as the court welfare officer).

CHILDREN'S REPRESENTATION IN CARE PROCEEDINGS IN ENGLAND AND WALES: HISTORY AND DEVELOPMENT

Care proceedings have been modelled on criminal proceedings with the child as the respondent to a claim by the local authority that he or she is being ill-treated[12] or suffering significant harm.[13] Children have party status and legal representation, but there is no tradition of their active involvement in the proceedings. Before 1979 (when the Law Society issued guidance against the practice), lawyers routinely obtained their instructions from the child's parents.[14] Thereafter, solicitors were left to represent children without adults' instructions and parents were unrepresented.[15] Solicitors reported being unsure about their role; some obviously provided moral support to children attending the hearing, while others appeared to ignore their client. Where they represented younger children, solicitors rarely attempted to relay the child's wishes to the court, but they might test the local authority's evidence or seek to present an alternative view from an independent social worker. Where children were older, there were two distinct approaches to representation: presenting children's views, often with a qualification; or reporting them, but arguing that they were contrary to their client's best interests.[16]

In response to concerns that courts had insufficient information to make appropriate decisions in care cases,[17] the *Children Act* 1975[18] established a system

[10] There are exceptions: see *Re A. (contact: separate representation)* [2001] 1 FLR 715 and *Re K. (replacement guardian ad litem)* [2001] 1 FLR 663, where children were made parties in disputes between parents to ensure that their interests were fully represented.

[11] See J Masson, 'Representations of Children' [1996] CLP 245.

[12] *Children and Young Persons Act* 1969, s 1. It was the original intention of this Act to raise the age of criminal responsibility and deal with 'young offenders' as children in need of care and protection.

[13] *Children Act* 1989, s 31.

[14] Since they were not parties, had only limited rights to participate in these proceedings and had no access to legally aided representation, instructing the child's representative enabled the parents to participate.

[15] Parents were given full rights to participate and access to legal aid in 1988 by the *Children and Young Persons (Amendment) Act* 1986.

[16] A Macleod and E Malos, *Representation of Children and Parents in Care Proceedings* (Family Law Research Unit, University of Bristol, 1984).

[17] It was a response to the death of Maria Colwell who was killed by her stepfather following a court decision at the request of her mother to discharge the order committing her to local authority care: *Report of the Committee of Inquiry into the care and supervision provided in relation to Maria Colwell* (HMSO, London, 1974).

[18] ss 64, 65.

where children could be represented by a guardian *ad litem* (usually an experienced child care social worker) *and* a solicitor. Guardian *ad litem* appointments were initially restricted to uncontested applications for the discharge of care orders because these were the cases where the court was most likely to have partial information. In 1984, they were extended to all care cases (and proceedings relating to the termination of contact with children in care), but the appointment of a guardian *ad litem* for the child was subject to the court's discretion; appointment rates varied widely depending on the availability of guardians.[19]

The appointment of a guardian *ad litem* provided the child's solicitor with a professional social worker who could form a view about what was in the child's best interests and give instructions. Lawyers generally welcomed this and relied heavily on the guardian; although the lawyer technically remained the child's lawyer, effectively he or she took on the guardian's case. The court rules required the solicitor to follow the guardian's instructions except where the child was competent and wished to give instructions which conflicted with those of the guardian. However, lawyers remained reluctant to take instructions from their child clients. Murch and colleagues noted that there were 'understandable' occasions where lawyers reported, but did not advocate, children's views which they considered damaging.[20]

The *Children Act* 1989 developed this tandem system of representation, creating a presumption of appointment and extending the range of cases where it applied.[21] The system has also matured with the expertise of the lawyers and guardians who act as representatives, most of whom have been involved since the implementation of the Act in 1991. The lawyers are usually members of the Law Society's Children Panel.[22] Children's guardians were members of local GALRO Panels[23] mostly run by—but independent of—local authority Social Services departments.[24] Many guardians were self-employed but all were required to provide a service in accordance with the National Standards[25] and their panel's service agreement. In April 2001, a new organisation—the Children and Family Court Advisory and Support Service (CAFCASS)—was established to take over responsibilities for providing children's guardians and reporting in family cases.[26]

[19] M Murch, J Hunt and A Macleod, *Representing the Child in Civil Proceedings Research Project 1985–1989: Summary of Conclusions and Recommendations* (Socio-legal Centre for Family Studies, University of Bristol, 1990).

[20] See n 19, p 12.

[21] *Children Act* 1989, s 41; Family Proceedings Rules 1991 (1991 SI 1247). The tandem system applies to proceedings specified in r 4.2(2).

[22] Panel membership is dependent on training, experience and a selection interview. Panel members must give an undertaking that they will handle cases personally rather than pass them to colleagues: see C Liddle, *Acting for Children* (Law Society, 1992).

[23] The Guardians *Ad Litem* and Reporting Officers (Panels) Regulations 1991 (1991 SI 2051); see also Department of Health, *Children Act 1989 Guidance and Regulations vol 7* (HMSO, London, 1991).

[24] GALRO services have been provided in some areas by one of three voluntary organisations: the NSPCC, the Children's Society and NCH Action for Children.

[25] *National Standards for the Guardian Ad Litem and Reporting Officer Service* (Department of Health, 1995).

[26] *Criminal Justice and Court Services Act* 2000, s 11.

Children's guardians and children and family reporters will all be employed by the new service.

CHILDREN'S REPRESENTATION IN CARE PROCEEDINGS: CURRENT PRACTICE

Despite the work of the *Children Act* Advisory Committee to establish good practice in the courts,[27] a code of practice for solicitors[28] and National Standards for guardians *ad litem*, there are considerable variations in practice in care cases.[29] Judges retain discretion over the conduct of cases in their courts.[30] For example, some judges have expected the local authority to provide full details of the child's future care, including the address of foster parents and arrangements for schooling, whilst others have been content that the plan stated that the child was to be fostered.[31] Although variability may be beneficial by allowing the process to be tailored to the circumstances of the case (for instance, in the above example, either putting pressure on the local authority to find a placement or allowing proceedings to be ended so that the local authority can focus on the social work tasks), the uncertainty it creates may be detrimental. The children's guardian cannot know whether a request for an adjournment 'until details of the child's care are finalised' will succeed, how long the hearing will last or whether a care order will be made that day, and consequently cannot prepare the child.

Both children's guardians and solicitors have worked as independent professionals without supervision or management of their actions.[32] Solicitors' practices vary because of their own approach to issues such as the child's competence,[33] their need to accommodate the idiosyncrasies of the court and their willingness to act independently of the guardian.[34] As one solicitor succinctly put it: 'You can't say boo to your guardian else you won't get any more work.'—a view that has been endorsed by some guardians.[35] Guardians' practice has differed both within panels

[27] *Children Act* Advisory Committee, *Good Practice Guidance* (Lord Chancellor's Department, 1997).

[28] Solicitors' Family Law Association, *Guide to Good Practice for Solicitors Acting for Children* (4th edn, Solicitors' Family Law Association, 1997).

[29] Masson and Winn Oakley, n 2, ch 9.

[30] It should be noted that most cases are not reserved to a particular judge and will be heard by different judges at different stages before the final hearing.

[31] The Department of Health has recently issued circular LAC 99/29, setting out what it considers should be included in the care plan. This largely repeats guidance issued in 1991 and endorsed in *Re J (care: care plan)* [1994] 1 FLR 253. The implementation of the *Human Rights Act* 1998 has provided the basis for further monitoring of care plans, see below nn 54, 102 and accompanying text.

[32] The establishment of CAFCASS is likely to lead to more control of guardians; the system of franchising legal aid practitioners is also intended to ensure minimum practice standards.

[33] C Sawyer, *The Rise and Fall of the Third Party* (Oxford Centre for Socio-legal Studies, 1995); C Sawyer, *Rules, Roles and Relationships* (Oxford Centre for Socio-legal Studies, 1999).

[34] Masson and Winn Oakley, n 2, pp 58, 61, 98.

[35] C Sawyer 'Professional Practices in Public Law' [2000] *Fam Law* 109.

and between them. There are wide variations in the amount of time spent, and how that time is used, by different guardians on similar cases,[36] but CAFCASS is likely to bring more standardisation.

The court rules place the solicitor in the position of advocate for the child and require him or her to take instructions from the guardian in the majority of cases. Only where the child is competent to give instructions, wants to do so and has instructions which conflict with those of the guardian is the solicitor empowered to take the child's instructions rather than those of the guardian.[37] The guardian's role is to instruct the child's solicitor, to investigate the case, to advise the court about various matters including the child's wishes and to prepare a written report on the interests of the child for the court.[38] Theoretically, tandem representation always provides the court with a professional view about the child's welfare and the child's own view about their wishes. The solicitor, acting on the guardian's instructions, generally advocates for the child's welfare but the provision for separate representation ensures that a mature child can have an advocate. The guardian has to appoint another solicitor or put their view through another party, usually the local authority. In practice, separate representation is rare and the child's view is often eclipsed by welfare arguments or by a *fait accompli.*

Courts try to appoint a guardian as soon as specified proceedings are started. The court contacts the local CAFCASS administrator, who will identify a guardian who is able to take on a new case; most guardians take any type of case but there is some specialisation, particularly in less common applications such as secure accommodation cases. The guardian's availability and skills are not the only criteria for appointment; where there have been previous proceedings the court will usually seek the reappointment of the guardian who knows the case and has an established relationship with the child.[39] Once the guardian has been appointed, he or she will usually appoint the child's solicitor. Most guardians work with a small number of solicitors and select who to appoint according to their knowledge of the case (which at this point is limited to the information on the application).[40] Thus a guardian would not select a male solicitor for a girl who had been sexually abused. In some areas, particularly London, a shortage of guardians means that it may take over a month to make an appointment. In such cases, the court usually appoints the solicitor so that the child is represented at the first hearing.

[36] A Clark and R Sinclair, *The Focus on the Child* (National Children's Bureau, 1999); *Panel Managers Annual Workshop 1999* (Department of Health, 1999).

[37] Family Proceedings Rules 1991, r 4.12.

[38] Family Proceedings Rules 1991, r 4.11.

[39] A mother's challenge to such a reappointment on the basis that the guardian's recommendations amounted to bias has been rejected: *Re J (adoption: appointment of guardian ad litem)* [1999] 2 FLR 86.

[40] The child's ethnicity and language are not recorded on the application, so it is generally not possible for the guardian to consider this unless he or she meets the child or reads their Social Services file before appointing the solicitor.

Guardians generally visit the child between six and ten times during the proceedings.[41] Most children in the studies had some understanding of the guardian's role—'to say what you are feeling . . .'; 'He writes and sends it to the court.' Most were satisfied with what their guardian did for them, reporting that they trusted their guardian and would not have wanted a change.[42] A few children were dissatisfied, feeling that their guardian had not visited enough times, or had not talked or listened to them adequately. Others said that the guardian had come too often and wasted their time by repeating things. Solicitors usually saw their child clients less frequently than the guardian—half saw them no more than twice. Children's views about solicitors were generally more hazy and less positive:[43] '[She was] quick'; 'I don't really know 'cause I didn't see her much.'[44] Some children could not remember their solicitor and did not really distinguish between their solicitor and guardian. Only those who had attended a hearing could give a clear account: 'Solicitors are more to do with the paperwork and the legal side of it . . . they speak for you at court.'[45]

Working directly with the children to establish their best interests, wishes and feelings is only one aspect of the guardian's work, and takes up about 5 per cent of the time spent on a case.[46] Guardians usually see the main adults in the child's family, the professionals who work with the child (teachers, doctors, health visitors, carers and social workers) and read social services files concerning the child and family. Guardians mediate and negotiate with social workers, perhaps seeking agreement about a placement or contact arrangements.[47] They also have responsibilities to ensure that necessary expert evidence is obtained, that experts meet before the hearing (and, where possible, identify areas of agreement),[48] to provide advice on timetabling and case management, and to prepare a report to the court.[49]

The report to court is the main mechanism whereby the guardian presents to the court their views of the child's interests and an account of the child's wishes and feelings. The report is sent to all the adult parties and can have a major impact on the proceedings and outcome. If, for example, the guardian indicates that future contact with a parent is contrary to both the child's interests and their wishes, it is most unlikely that public funding would be continued to cover the

41 Clark and Sinclair, n 2, p 23; The number of visits in Masson and Winn Oakley's study was smaller (average four to five): p 70.

42 Masson and Winn Oakley, n 2, p 71; Ruegger, n 2, p 138.

43 Masson and Winn Oakley, n 2, pp 72–76; McCausland, n 2, p 89.

44 Masson and Winn Oakley, n 2, p 74.

45 *Ibid.*, p 72.

46 Clark and Sinclair, n 2, p 27. On average, guardians spend over 150 hours on each care case.

47 Clark and Sinclair, n 2, ch 6; Masson and Winn Oakley, n 2, p 142.

48 J Brophy, C Wale, and P Bates, *Myths and Practices* (BAAF, London, 1999); *Re C (expert evidence: disclosure: practice)* [1995] 1 FLR 204.

49 FPR 1991, r 4.11A(4),(6)–(10); J Timms, *Children's Representation* (Sweet & Maxwell, 1995); DH, *Guide for Guardians Ad Litem in Public Law Proceedings Under the Children Act 1989* (HMSO, 1995). Almost 20% of guardian time is spent writing the report: Clark and Sinclair, n 2, p 35.

parent's representation at a hearing.[50] Although courts are not required to follow the guardian's recommendations, both solicitors and guardians view the report as very influential. Social workers ascribe less weight to the guardian's report, but recognise that the guardian does influence the local authority's thinking.[51] The outcome in the majority of cases accords with the local authority's proposals.[52]

There are two issues for the court to decide in care proceedings: whether the local authority has proved the threshold condition—the significant harm test; and, if so, what order should be made. The court can commit the child to the care of the local authority (giving it parental responsibility and the right to make decisions about the child's future care), make an order for the child's supervision, make any section 8 order—for example, a residence order so that a relative has parental responsibility—or make no order.[53] The court does not determine how the local authority looks after a child in its care; it has no further involvement in the arrangements unless there is a dispute about contact, an adoption order is sought or there is an application to discharge an order.[54] Although a small minority of cases are heavily contested on both issues and have hearings which last for weeks, the majority of cases are largely agreed by the time of the final hearing. Outstanding areas of disagreement are mainly about what should happen to the child in the future, but in the case of older children parents are less likely to claim that they should continue to care for their child.[55] Hearings take place in courts to which the public have no access; in uncontested cases they are short. It is unusual for children to be present.

PATERNALISM

From the setting up of Children's Departments in 1948, child care practice in England and Wales has been paternalistic.[56] The state could provide better care than many parents and social workers knew what was best for children. The welfare of children who could not be looked after by their parents was best pro-

[50] Legal Aid Board, 'Matrimonial Family Guidance Revision' (1997) 19 *Legal Aid Focus* 4; Legal Services Commission, *Funding Code* (2001), p 20.17.4.

[51] Clark and Sinclair, n 2, pp 80–81 and ch 8.

[52] J Hunt and A Macleod, *The Last Resort*, TSO (1999).

[53] *Children Act* 1989, ss. 8, 10, 33, 35 for an explanation of the orders: see S Cretney, and J Masson, *Principles of Family Law* (6th edn, Sweet & Maxwell, 1997), p 811.

[54] J Dewar, 'The Courts and Local Authority Autonomy' 7 *Child and Family Law Quarterly* 15; M Hayes 'The Proper Role of Courts in Care Cases' 8 *Child and Family Law Quarterly* 201. Before the *Children Act* 1989, the court exercising its wardship jurisdiction (under which at least half of child care cases were considered) had the power to supervise the local authority's care, but lacked a system for monitoring local authority action and largely relied on the parties to bring matters before the court: see J Masson and S Morton, 'The Use of Wardship by Local Authorities' (1989) 52 *Modern Law Review* 762. However, in *Re W and B; Re W(care plan)* [2001] 2 FLR 582, the Court of Appeal accepted that where fundamental elements of a care plan were not provided and this impacted on a parent's or child's rights under the European Convention on Human Rights, the case could be referred back to the court under the *Human Rights Act* 1998, s 7(1).

[55] In Masson and Winn Oakley's study, none of the parents opposed the making of a care order.

[56] See J Masson, 'From Curtis to Waterhouse: State Care and Child Protection in the UK, 1945–2000' J in Eekelaar and S Katz (eds), *Crosscurrents* (Oxford University Press, 2000), pp 565–87.

tected through whatever arrangements the local authority chose to make. Although from the 1970s well-publicised failings[57] of the system meant that both the public and social workers lost confidence in the state's ability to provide care, it was only after the enactment of the *Children Act* 1989 that there were moves towards an ethos of partnership and the acceptance that parents and children should be consulted when children were in care.[58]

Judicial attitudes to welfare were similarly paternalistic; courts readily endorsed local authority plans for children and paid little attention to claims that children had rights.[59] In the rare cases where children were involved in private law litigation, the court appointed the Official Solicitor to act as the child's guardian *ad litem*; the case presented on behalf of the child focused on the child's welfare, not their wishes and feelings.[60] Judges in the Family Division expressed the view it was not in children's interests to be involved in proceedings: 'To sit for hours or even days listening to lawyers debating one's future is not an experience which should be wished on any child.'[61] Attending court could be intimidating and frightening, and children might hear sexually explicit evidence:[62] 'The court must always bear in mind that attendance at court is likely to be harmful to the child.'[63]

Following on from this, guidance from the *Children Act* Advisory Committee strongly discouraged children's attendance at their care proceedings; only where some clear benefit could be identified should children attend.[64] The combination of judicial statement and committee guidance ensured wide dissemination of these views, which were then reflected in the approach taken in the lower courts and by many representatives.

Although guardians were advised in 1992 that the 'direct involvement in the determination of the case can help enhance a child's sense of worth and of being believed, and provide reassurance that the adult world is taking their distress seriously',[65] many of their practices have sought to distance children from the proceedings rather than involve them. Guardians interviewed for *Out of Hearing* were generally uneasy about children attending court, accepted the judicial view that attending the proceedings was not good for children and supported their attendance only if it was a 'happy case'—for example, where the foster carers were

[57] Inadequate investigations leading to deaths of placed with parents or the inappropriate separation of child and parent, and wide-scale abuse in children's homes, see above n 56.

[58] *Children Act* 1989, s 22(4)(5).

[59] Some of the best examples are the cases concerning medical treatment: *Re R* [1992] Fam 11; *Re E* [1993] 1 FLR 386; *Re W* [1993] Fam 64; *Re S.* [1994] 2 FLR 1065.

[60] *Re S (a minor)(independent representation)* [1993] Fam 263; Masson [1996] CLP 245. The Family Proceedings Rules 1991, r 9.2A clarified that mature children could participate in private family law proceedings without a guardian *ad litem* but a *Practice Direction* required these cases to be transferred to the High Court.

[61] *Re C (a minor)(child's wishes)* [1993] 1 FLR 832 per Waite J.

[62] *Nottingham v P* [1993] 1 FLR 514 at 520.

[63] *Re W (secure accommodation order: attendance at court)* [1994] 2 FLR 1092.

[64] *Children Act* Advisory Committee *Annual Report 1993–94* (Lord Chancellor's Department, 1994), p 45. These views were repeated in the CAAC *Final Report* (1997) p 36, where practitioners were also warned not to mislead children into thinking they could attend.

[65] DH, *The Manual of Practice Guidance for Guardians Ad Litem and Reporting Officers* (1992) p 52.

applying for a residence order—or 'a nice occasion' where a care order was being discharged.[66] Paternalism was not the only reason for guardian's concern about children's attendance. Guardians were aware that judges did not want children to be there, and they knew it was difficult to ensure the child was being looked after whilst finalising negotiations with the other parties. Although solicitors viewed children's attendance at hearings more positively, they were also concerned about seeking permission for the child's attendance. They did not want to give them the impression that the court would readily agree and were also concerned that some judges did not have 'the added compassion' required for care proceedings.[67]

Children were also distanced from the proceedings in other ways. They were rarely shown any of the case papers, witness statements and so on. Children's solicitors often did not continue to see them (relying on the guardian for any contact) because they were concerned that the proceedings brought too many strangers into the child's life or felt that they were no good at communicating with children and might upset them. It was the exception for children to be shown the whole of the guardian's report; guardians preferred to print out a short extract or read excepts to the child.[68] Partly because of their short-term involvement, they were anxious that children should not learn from their report information which social workers or parents had withheld. Guardians were also concerned not to upset children with unpleasant facts or criticism of their parents: 'My heart sank a bit, because there were these things in there that I felt would be quite hurtful. And I was trying to skip pages, just to protect her feelings really.' Only if the guardian believed that more damage would be caused by withholding the report, or children demanded to see it, were children allowed to see a copy, and even then details such as addresses might be blanked out. In contrast, children did not specifically mention being upset by what they might read; some felt they had 'a right to see [the report]' because it was about them and it was better 'to know the truth now rather than find out later'.

However, not every child said they wanted to see or be read the report. In one case, the solicitor's concern for a girl's welfare led her to avoid making an application that the girl should have contact with the father convicted of sexually abusing her. The lawyer (incorrectly) told Sylvia , aged fourteen years, that contact could not be raised in care proceedings, but that she could bring contact proceedings later. The lawyer subsequently explained to the researcher that she opposed contact and knew that the guardian and local authority agreed with this. She said Sylvia was not competent to give instructions—a view with which the guardian disagreed. Sylvia was subsequently told that the court had said she could not see her father until she was eighteen. Given the strength of Sylvia's wishes and her attempts to find her father's address, it seemed unlikely that the court's view would control contact, but rather make it secret and more risky for Sylvia.

[66] Masson and Winn Oakley, n 2, p 111.

[67] *Ibid.*, p 113. One solicitor recalled a case where an entire discharge application had been conducted in silence.

[68] Clark and Sinclair, n 2, p 39; Masson and Winn Oakley, n 2, p 104; McCausland, n 2, p 77.

PARTICIPATION

Not all children wanted to participate in legal proceedings concerning them; those who did wanted different degrees of participation. Children who have spoken to researchers wanted an opportunity to have their views listened to and some wanted to read the report.[69] In the *Out of Hearing* study, half the children wanted to go to court but some said they felt too anxious, were not bothered or that the proceedings were a waste of time.[70]

There are both ethical and practical reasons why the manner and extent of their participation in care proceedings should be a matter of choice for children. Children's vulnerability and relative powerlessness are the basis for state involvement; in taking action to protect children, the state should take particular care that it does not compound children's adversity by failing to recognise their individuality. Before the *Children Act* 1989, children over the age of five years had to be brought before the court in care proceedings.[71] Attendance in these circumstances was not about the child's involvement, but to establish their identity for the court. This practice was severely criticised because of its damaging and disruptive effect on children who were brought from distant placements to courts which completely lacked facilities for them.[72] Similarly, attendance in secure accommodation proceedings[73] appeared to be part of the child's social disciplining, providing an opportunity for the magistrates to lecture the child and to encourage better behaviour.[74] Any assessment of the child's welfare requires some degree of cooperation from the child; it may be easier to gain this where matters are explained and negotiated rather than imposed.

Children, like adult clients, cannot participate in the legal process without some knowledge of the way it works and the options available to them. Representation in legal proceedings involves ensuring the client understands the process and their rights within it so that they can give instructions, and following those instructions so as to achieve the client's goals. Good communication between client and representative is essential: the client needs to know what to tell the representative; the representative must be clear that he or she has understood the client's instructions and all the facts relevant to the client's case. Representation by guardians

[69] Masson and Winn Oakley, n 2; Ruegger, n 2, pp 140, 143; McCausland, n 2, ch 6.

[70] Masson and Winn Oakley, n 2, pp 114–15; Ruegger, n 2, p 142; see also McCausland, n 2, pp 77–80. In Ruegger's study, over one-third of children wanted to go to court, but two-thirds reported that they had not been consulted about this and only one was permitted to attend.

[71] *Children and Young Persons Act* 1969, ss 2(9), 22(1).

[72] Association of British Adoption Agencies, *Care Proceedings* (ABAFA, 1979).

[73] *Children Act* 1989, s 25(1); although the courts claim discretion over the child's attendance: *Re W (secure accommodation: attendance at court)*[1994] 2 FLR 1092. *Re K (secure accommodation: right to liberty)* [2001] 1 FLR 485 C.C. provides a good example of how a young person can be involved in proceedings. The four children subject to these proceedings in the *Out of Hearing Study* all attended their hearings.

[74] The right to attend is protected by ECHR, Art 6; unless a mature child has the opportunity to instruct their lawyer on points raised at the hearing he or she does not receive a fair trial: *Re C (secure accommodation order: representation)* [2001] 2 FLR 169 CA.

focuses on getting information from the child about their experiences, feelings and expectations in order to provide an assessment for the court. Guardians have given less attention to explaining what was happening in the proceedings and when matters might be finalised.[75]

Before the creation of CAFCASS, many GALRO panels had prepared leaflets for children about the role of the guardian in care proceedings, but there was no standard practice of using them. Some guardians specifically stated that they thought it was better to explain things personally, but this left children dependent on their own memories and understanding and they could not easily seek clarification from their carers or social workers. The leaflets and other written materials to explain the process varied: some were clear but most provided little information and some were misleading—for example, showing a police officer in the picture of the court.[76]

A new approach to providing written information is being established by CAFCASS. It agreed to support work by the NSPCC to prepare packs of written material for children involved in proceedings. A group was established including young people in care and professionals involved in the proceedings to design and write two sets of leaflets suitable for younger and older children. Particular attention has been paid in development to present the information children and young people need or want in ways that they find helpful. These 'Power Packs' are to be given to children and young people subject to proceedings, and used by children's guardians to explain the process.[77]

Children who are separately represented in care proceedings have the greatest degree of participation. They are the lawyer's direct client and will usually have access to all the court papers, although the solicitor may explain the contents and seek comments rather than allow children to read them and prepare their own response. Although there are solicitors who take a robust view of their responsibilities towards child clients, routinely taking instructions from older children or writing to all the other parties warning that they might have to take the child's instructions rather than the guardian's,[78] such practices are not common. Few children are separately represented;[79] the participation of the majority is circumscribed by the relationship between their guardian and their solicitor. In most cases, the solicitor will have been selected by the guardian.

[75] Masson and Winn Oakley, n 2, ch 6; McCausland, n 2, p 96. Clark and Sinclair (n 2) do not include 'adviser to the child' as an aspect of the guardian's role and identify the purpose of the guardian's visits to the child as 'getting to know the child': p 27.

[76] Masson and Winn Oakley, n 2, ch 6. Before the *Children Act* 1989, care cases were heard in juvenile courts and police officers might be present. Children were often particularly anxious that they had done wrong, so this picture could add to rather than allay their fears.

[77] Further details can be seen on the NSPCC website: www.nspcc.org.uk The development work for the Power Pack was led by Dr Maureen Winn Oakley and followed on from the research undertaken with the author for *Out of Hearing*.

[78] Masson and Winn Oakley, n 2, p 137.

[79] None of the research studies has included any child separately represented. Some idea of the extent of separate representation comes from the amount expended by guardian panels to provide lawyers for guardians who cannot use the child's lawyer. These suggest that half the panels had no case of separate representation in 1996.

A few guardians may sometimes consult the child about the solicitor's appointment, but this is not a common practice.[80] Barbara, who was given this choice, immediately formed a positive impression of her lawyer: 'Someone got a list and we chose her. I went and met her . . . I just liked her attitude . . . She is more than a friend.'

Most solicitors meet their child clients;[81] guardians usually require this. Solicitors usually rely on the guardian to provide them with information about the child and to introduce them to the child. They recognise that guardians are skilled at establishing rapport with children and find the guardian's practical assistance (eg identifying the child's favourite football team) and moral support helpful. Solicitors rarely form strong professional relationships with children and many stop seeing them after initial visits. Where they do continue to see the child, they usually accompany the guardian and play a lesser role in the discussions.[82] Although a few solicitors maintain a direct relationship with their child client throughout the proceedings, there are guardians who object to this.[83]

Although some guardians send a card to let children know when they are visiting, visits even to older children are arranged with carers. Consequently, children do not always have the opportunity to prepare for them. Visits generally take place where children are currently living, but sometimes guardians take children out, particularly to fast-food restaurants. Children clearly enjoy these treats, but do not necessarily want to talk seriously in them. Privacy, and not being overheard or interrupted, are important to children when confiding in their guardians.[84] Carl's guardian spoke to him about staying with his mother in her presence. He said very little, but later ran away to a relative. Later he told the researcher that if he had been able to see his solicitor he would have told her 'why I had run off and all that'. Children are usually seen alone or with siblings; the presence of brother and sisters makes it easier for some children to talk, but others are distracted or feel unable to express their own (different) views. Guardians do not always pick up the obvious cues: 'It would have been better [to talk to me on my own] because [my brother] is always leaping about making noises.'

Although some solicitors make sure children know the firm's telephone number so they can contact them if necessary,[85] they do not generally write to their child clients. When this issue was discussed with solicitors at a workshop at the Association of Lawyers for Children Annual Conference in 1998, only a few stated it

[80] Only one guardian mentioned it in the *Out of Hearing* study: Masson and Winn Oakley, n 2, p 58.

[81] A study by Clark in 1993 found that one-third of older children had not seen their solicitor and nine of the twenty-one children in McCausland's study could not remember doing so: McCausland, n 2, p 89.

[82] Masson and Winn Oakley, n 2, pp 72–75.

[83] *Ibid.*, p 99. The guardian could avoid conflict over the approach to the work by careful selection of the solicitor, see above.

[84] Ruegger, n 2, pp 139–40.

[85] This practice was more related to developing their practice (particularly in juvenile justice work) than in maintaining contact in the current proceedings. It also assumed that children had access to the phone, which for children living with parents or in foster care is not guaranteed.

was their usual practice to write to older child clients. More common were views such as: 'Most of my child clients can't read anyway'; and 'It's demeaning for the child to receive a letter they can't understand.' These solicitors took quite a different approach when acting for parents who might also be illiterate. When acting for children they assumed that they had neither the right nor the need to know what was happening in the proceedings, or believed that their oral explanations were adequate. Given these attitudes to children, it is perhaps unsurprising that one of the children in the *Out of Hearing* study defined a solicitor as 'someone who writes letters to other people'. The solicitors' views contrasted with the views and actions of children who had received letters from their representatives. Letters were very significant to them; most had kept their letters, even though they might not understand all that had been written and one child recalled when he had received his letter.

The documents for the proceedings are served on the guardian or the solicitor rather than the child. The representative has the responsibility of informing the child about their contents, but only where the child has sufficient understanding.[86] The Solicitors Family Law Association cautions solicitors against allowing children to become too involved in the proceedings.[87] In practice, guardians and solicitors rarely feel it to be necessary to show children any of the court papers, but solicitors are willing to show them to older children *if they ask*. However, it is far from clear that children know there are documents which they can ask to see.

Most children's participation is limited to talking to their guardian and attending for assessment by experts. However, some children are asked to write their views for the guardian's report or make drawings which are shown to the court. Although children have contributed to the report, most have only limited access to it. It is more usual to allow children to see only the part of the report which recounts their views. Some children are dissatisfied and feel let down when they do not see the whole report: 'She told us that she'd definitely tell us and she would show us her report. First she only showed us the part mentioning us. I would have like to see it all.'

It is not clear that children are given adequate explanations about the report or that they all understand that the report is available to all the other parties. Guardians usually state that the report is 'for the court' or 'for the judge', and some children in Ruegger's study spoke of their 'shock, shame, distress or anger' at learning that their views or remarks had been relayed (via the report) to their parents.[88] Some children were unaware that the guardian also gave the court a recommendation based on his or her own view of the child's welfare.[89] Without this knowledge, they could have no opportunity of challenging the guardian's recommendations.

[86] FPR 1991, r 4.11A(8).
[87] See n 28, para D3.
[88] Ruegger, n 2, p 140; see also McCausland, n 2, p 69.
[89] McCausland, n 2, p 71; Ruegger, n 2, pp 140–41.

Half of the children in the *Out of Hearing* study expressed an interest in attending court. They wanted 'to see where the judge sits', 'to speak to the judge', 'to hear the decision' or did not like people talking about them behind their backs.[90] Apart from those involved in secure accommodation proceedings, only one child, a fifteen-year-old boy, attended the final hearing. One solicitor who made (but did not press) an application for a fourteen-year-old client's attendance had it refused and a ten-year-old whose application was granted decided not to go because the hearing clashed with a special event at his school.

Children's limited participation caused some children to became alienated from the process and cease to take much interest; they became distanced from the guardian. Even where they remained involved, their agenda was not addressed. Their anxieties were not assuaged and opportunities to contribute positively to their lives were lost. However, these failings were not solely related to the way children were represented but also to the limitations of the court's powers over day-to-day arrangements for their care and of the guardian's role to the court proceedings. Not being present could also mean having to wait to find out what had happened. The representatives and the child's solicitor did not always make clear arrangements for the child to be told as soon as the hearing was over. This failing has been dealt with by a new rule requiring the children's guardian to ensure the child is informed about the outcome.[91]

PLACATION

Guardian and solicitor practice from the appointment of the solicitor to the presentation of the report is structured to avoid conflict between them.[92] Solicitors rely on guardians for their appointments, generally accept that they should follow the guardian's lead and know that taking an opposing view will reduce their chances of future appointments. Outside the major conurbations, the small size of panels gives guardians considerable patronage and power. Teamwork by representatives—for example, joint visits or division of responsibilities—rarely leads to the lawyer establishing a professional relationship with the child and also reduces children's opportunities to get independent advice from the solicitor—or, as one guardian put it, 'play one off against the other'. Solicitors' general lack of confidence in communicating with children contributes to their reluctance to work directly with them. Their reliance on the guardian means that, despite increasing experience in care cases, they do not develop these communication skills.

Both solicitors and guardians tend to rely on children raising issues or asking questions before they provide them with information. Tom, who opposed his mother's application for contact, was not told he might apply to have it dismissed

[90] Masson and Winn Oakley, n 2, p 115.
[91] Family Proceedings (Amendment) Rules 2001 (2001 SI 821) adding new rule 4.11A (10).
[92] Masson and Winn Oakley, n 2, pp 77, 146.

without a hearing, nor that future applications could be restricted, although he clearly wanted the process to end as soon as possible and not be repeated.[93] Although lawyers have expressed unease about withholding documents from older children, they seem less concerned with the fact they might be unaware of their existence. Representatives often wait for children to ask about going to court. If they do, they are sometimes offered a visit to the court building on the basis that 'children are more interested in seeing the cells'. Such visits may be 'therapeutically advantageous' in helping the child to understand the process and prepare for the final hearing,[94] and have been endorsed by the *Children Act* Advisory Committee.[95] They satisfy some children's curiosity, but may contribute to some children's anxieties. Tom told his guardian: 'I'm not really interested in the architecture'. Arranging visits to empty courts avoids conflict with the judge.

Although guardians sometimes show children the whole of their report, this is not always done in a way which children find helpful: 'I haven't had a chance to read it, I read it at court . . . but you know what I mean'; 'I would have like to read it . . . all of it, but [my guardian] had to go.' Few solicitors discuss the guardian's report with the child. There are a number of reasons for this. Some solicitors cease any direct involvement with the child long before the report is written. Others, who relied on the guardian, expressed the view that it was the guardian's job to discuss their own report. Solicitors also commented that they lacked the necessary skills to communicate very sensitive material; like guardians, they were anxious about giving children new information. However, unless children have an opportunity to learn what the guardian recommends, they cannot know whether this conflicts with their wishes. The practice of not disclosing the report and the withdrawal of the solicitor prevent children exercising their right to be separately represented.

Solicitors acknowledged that guardians' high status in the court made it difficult for children to challenge them. If conflict arose, it was better to try to negotiate—to get the guardian to recognise that the strength of the child's feelings made their recommendation unachievable or, more likely, to explain to the child that there were no practical alternatives to the guardian's recommended order. Given that the court's power is limited, lawyers taking this approach could be seen as being realistic about the outcome for the child. As one lawyer commented:

> I have had one . . . she was clearly competent . . . And we managed to get round it. [I said] 'Well, although you're not happy with how [the guardian's] reached her conclusions, you agree at the end of the day, you've still got the guardian but I will tell the court you don't agree with this, you don't agree with that, but you are happy an order should be made.' That's the thing to find out, what's the child's objection? Is it actually against the order?

[93] *Children Act* 1989, s 91(14).

[94] DH, *Guide for Guardians Ad Litem in Public Law Proceedings under the Children Act 1989* (HMSO, 1995), p 75.

[95] *Children Act* Advisory Committee, *Final Report* (1997), p 36.

Children could feel pressured to follow their lawyer's view: 'I didn't want an order . . . my solicitor thought there should be an order . . . he said it would be best and in the end I agreed . . . I will oppose next time.'

Conflict could also be avoided by concluding that the child was not competent to give instructions. There is no presumption of competence at any particular age and the courts have rejected such a presumption even where children approach the age of sixteen years.[96] It appears that children (like Sylvia) who wish to continue abusive relationships or dangerous lifestyles are unlikely to be considered competent and therefore unable to give instructions. Solicitors making such assessments are doing so within a context where welfare has traditionally predominated over rights and where they could face censure from the guardian and the court for advocating for the child a position which is viewed as damaging.[97]

Although guardians are sometimes dissatisfied with the care plan, it is often not possible to oppose the making of the order the local authority has sought. They might point out concerns to the court, but unless there are other potential carers there is no alternative for the court. Similarly, guardians and solicitors felt there was little they could do about social services' failures—for example, delays in finding suitable placements, unsatisfactory arrangements for contact or poor social work. They were generally reluctant to make complaints. They might try to encourage particular action but were concerned to maintain good relationships with the local authority and also empathised with social workers who carried large case loads and lacked resources. Such an approach may avoid difficulties for the guardian, but does not help to ensure the best solution for the child.[98]

THE IMPACT OF REPRESENTATION

Recent writing about the guardian service has stressed the 'added value' which guardians provide. All but two of the professionals (guardians, solicitors, social workers, magistrates, etc) who responded to Clark and Sinclair thought that the guardian 'had made a noticeable difference to the case'.[99] Similarly, professionals in McCausland's study valued the contribution guardians made to the process, particularly making the proceedings 'less contentious, shorter, more comprehensive and more child-focused'.[100] This emphasis on process also acknowledges that it is relatively rare for guardians to have major impact on outcome.[101] It is less

96 *Re H (a minor)(care proceedings: child's wishes)* [1993] 1 FLR 440.

97 This is one explanation for the refusal of a solicitor in the *Out of Hearing* study to accept as competent a fourteen-year-old girl who wanted contact with her sexually abusing father. The responses to this case from solicitors with whom it was discussed were uniformly critical: Masson and Winn Oakley, n 2, pp 36, 137.

98 The majority of complaints against guardians have been made by social workers.

99 Clark and Sinclair, n 2, p 84.

100 McCausland, n 2, p 95.

101 Clark and Sinclair, n 2, p 86; McCausland, n 2, p 94.

clear that the guardians and solicitors made much difference to children's experiences of their cases.

For lawyers practising in child care, court proceedings are central; for the children concerned, they are peripheral. Children's opportunities to participate are limited: they do not have access to the report and are kept out of court because adults believe that this is better for them. The court is also peripheral to children's concerns. In the *Out of Hearing* study, there were significant issues on the child's agenda which remained unaddressed at the end of the proceedings for eight out of the twenty children. What matters to children, both objectively and subjectively, is where they are living, their quality of life and their relationships, not their legal status. These are largely matters over which the court has almost no control. Until the recent intervention of the Court of Appeal, it was possible for the care plan to remain unimplemented or be altered without reference to the court.[102] Placement decisions are for the local authority alone. The court is required to consider the local authority's actual or proposed arrangements for contact and to invite comments from the parties, but can only respond to requests to make or vary orders; it cannot ensure that resources are provided to promote contact which has been proposed. Moreover, there is no duty on the local authority to allow children reasonable contact with brothers and sisters, or to help child to maintain friendships. Such contacts, which are so important to children,[103] have been given little attention by social workers and this neglect has not been challenged in the courts.[104]

Some children fail to engage with the process; others, like Sylvia, are seen to withdraw when the issues which concerned them are ignored. One child, asked if he had wanted to attend the care proceedings, answered: 'I can't go—it's not about me.'[105] Boredom was a major element in some children's response to the process, but guardians sometimes presumed that a child would not be interested.[106] Appearing disinterested is a common response from children and young people to a variety of situations. That it would be boring to attend their care proceedings was an idea which was frequently introduced or encouraged by representatives. Solicitors and guardians told children that they would find the hearing boring, and representatives and children told the researcher that hearings they had not attended *were* boring.[107] Representatives did not seem to realise the confusing message that this gave to children. If the hearing was boring, how could their views be interesting? And how could a bored court be interested in making important decisions about them? Overall, the process is alienating for children and young

[102] In *Re W and B; Re W (care plan)* [2001] 2 FLR 582 and see above n 54.

[103] A Mullender, *We are Family* (BAAF, 1999); J Masson, et al. (eds), *Lost and Found* (Ashgate, 1999).

[104] *Ibid.*; for a case example see *Re S (contact: application by sibling)* [1998] 2 FLR 897 where a child's short-term foster carer, who later became his adoptive parent, decided that there should be no contact between him and his siblings.

[105] Masson and Winn Oakley, n 2, p 114.

[106] *Ibid.*, p 104.

[107] *Ibid.*, p 112.

people. They are often isolated from their families and, because of the stigma associated with being in care, are unable or unwilling to talk to friends about what is happening. The process in which they were caught up is confusing and gives out mixed—but mostly negative—messages about their involvement.

IMPROVING CHILDREN'S REPRESENTATION

Children who have participated in four studies of the guardian system agree that their representatives should listen to them more, provide more and better information about the system and not make assumptions about the extent of their involvement in the proceedings. Researchers have noted with concern the variations in representatives' practices—particularly how much they tell children about their role and about the court process. Representatives have themselves noted how local authority and judicial practice influence their work, and how variations in practice can make it difficult for them to know what will happen.

Without greater standardisation of the process, there is a risk that written information provided for children (and parents) will not reflect the system applied to them. However, standardisation based on the current paternalistic attitudes is likely to exclude children from the process when many have said they want greater involvement in it. Standardisation of practice by children's guardians could also mean losing some of the best aspects of the service of committed professionals.

Children in the *Out of Hearing* study were generally dissatisfied with the access they had to the guardian's report. One girl suggested that the report should include a place for the child to sign that they agree with it, rather than assuming that where objections are not raised the child is content with it. Reports provide a clear account of the reasons which led to the local authority bringing proceedings and of the child's circumstances at that time. This is crucial information which needs to be understood by children. Not only should the contents be discussed with children, but a copy should be provided for them (probably on their social services file) so that they can consult it or discuss it with their social worker in the future.

Rather than exclude children from proceedings on the basis that attendance is harmful to them, procedures need to be changed to facilitate children's attendance and participation. If court arrangements can be changed to provide support for children who have to attend as witnesses, this could also be done for those who are parties and want to attend. Changing the process, particularly simplifying the language used, would also be helpful for parents and others, including professional witnesses, who are rarely involved in such proceedings and find them confusing.

In practice, children's lawyers generally act *for* the guardian. If they are to represent children *directly* they need to gain more skills and confidence in communicating with children and to be free from pressure by guardians to maintain partnership with them. One possible approach would be to presume that children of a specific age are competent to give instructions and for a solicitor to be appointed for them on that basis. In some cases guardians would need legal advice but this could be provided though the new service CAFCASS which should also promote standardisation of practice.

Whilst the court's powers over what happens to children remain very limited, improving children's representation will not ensure that their concerns are heard and addressed in the court process. The ideology of welfare which carries with it paternalistic ideas that professionals know best and the state can deliver good-quality care is scarcely credible. Identifying rights for children in the care system relevant to their experiences, based on the UNCRC, informing children of their rights and ensuring professionals use their skills to deliver these rights may provide a better way forward in the twenty-first century.

5

Issues in the Making of Ouster Orders Under the Domestic Violence (Family Protection) Act 1989 (Qld)

Rachael Field, Belinda Carpenter and Susan Currie*

INTRODUCTION

Ouster orders—also known as sole occupancy or exclusion orders—under domestic violence legislation ensure that a perpetrator of violence is removed from the family home, and that the victim and her children are able to avoid the cost and dislocation of escaping to alternative accommodation.[1] The *Domestic Violence (Family Protection) Act* 1989 (Qld)[2] (the Act) provides that a condition can be placed on a protection order made under the Act which prohibits a perpetrator of domestic violence from remaining in, entering (or attempting to enter) or approaching within a stated distance of a particular premises.[3] A protection order with such a condition attached to it works to override any legal or equitable interest the perpetrator may have in the property.[4]

* Rachael Field is a Lecturer in the School of Justice Studies, Faculty of Law, Queensland University of Technology (QUT). Belinda Carpenter and Susan Currie are Senior Lecturers in the School of Justice Studies at QUT. Thanks to Dr Ian Wells for comments on earlier drafts.

[1] Throughout this article, victims of violence are consistently referred to as being women. This is because it has long been acknowledged, both by Australian and international research, that 'women constitute the large majority of domestic violence victims'—Queensland Domestic Violence Task Force, *Beyond These Walls* (Queensland Government, 1988), p 13. *Beyond These Walls* refers to research pre-1988. Further confirmation that women continue to make up the majority of victims of violence can be found in, for example, National Committee on Violence Against Women, *National Strategy on Violence Against Women* (Department of the Prime Minister and Cabinet (Office of the Status of Women), 1992) and *Community Attitudes to Violence Against Women—Detailed Report* (AGPS, 1995). This is not to deny, however, that men are sometimes victims of violence.

[2] Other domestic violence legislation around Australia containing ouster order provisions includes: the *Domestic Violence Act* 1992 (NT), *Crimes Act* 1900 Part 15A—Apprehended Violence Orders (NSW), *Crimes (Family Violence) Act* 1987 (Vic), *Justice Act* 1902 (WA), *Justices Act* 1959 Part XA (Tas), and *Domestic Violence Act* 1986 (ACT).

[3] S 25, *Domestic Violence (Family Protection) Act* 1989 (Qld).

[4] S 25(3)(b), *Domestic Violence (Family Protection) Act* 1989 (Qld). The federal draft model domestic violence legislation includes a section almost identical to the Queensland provision indicating national support for the ouster condition and its consistent availability for all Australian victims of domestic violence: Domestic Violence Legislation Working Group, *Model Domestic Violence Laws—Report* (AGPS, 1999), s 16(2)(b), p 74.

The making of ouster orders is controversial,[5] notwithstanding the fact that 'the number of women and children made homeless by domestic violence is a disgrace.'[6] Ouster orders involve superordinating and prioritising the housing, support, social and familial needs of women and their children in a situation where in the past they have been subordinated to a societal assumption that it is the woman's responsibility to escape domestic violence.[7]

Ouster orders raise the issue of increased requirements for funding of men's emergency accommodation—and there is concern that this may be at the risk of funding for victim's services.[8] They challenge legal notions of proprietorial rights—that a 'man's home is his castle'.[9] Yet they also offer one of the most legally and socially significant ways to ensure that a perpetrator of domestic violence is held responsible for his actions, as well as providing some sense of normalcy for women and children whose lives are otherwise in chaos. In addition, ouster orders address the inevitable 'poverty and dislocation caused by [women and children] having to leave the family home.'[10]

Until recently, there was relatively little written about the jurisdiction of magistrates in the making of ouster orders, particularly in Queensland.[11] We do

[5] The issue was acknowledged by the Australian Law Reform Commission in 1986 as 'controversial': Australian Law Reform Commission, *Report (No 30) Domestic Violence* (AGPS, 1986), p 44.

[6] J Earle for WESNET, *Women's Services Network Submission on Model Domestic Violence Laws* (AGPS, 1998), p 6. The submission cites data from the Supported Accommodation Assistance programme which show that, in 38% of cases, domestic violence was the reason behind women seeking assistance from the programme (SAAP National Data Collection, Annual Report 1996–1997), *ibid.*; p 33.

[7] 'There is a need to diversify models [of services] to fit the needs of women rather than women attempting to fit the [current] model. This is very much needed in an environment where funding is limited for services responding to domestic and family violence and the societal expectation for women to leave a violent situation still exists.'—Partnerships Against Domestic Violence, *Home Safe Home—The Link Between Domestic and Family Violence and Women's Homelessness* (AGPS, 2000), p 31, referring to N Stanes, 'Meeting Women's Needs—Innovative Service Models Responding to Women Escaping Violence', (1998) 5 *Women Against Violence* 44.

[8] See further discussion on this below and nn 61–8.

[9] 'Workers and survivors often comment that the courts appear reluctant to limit the perpetrator's access to "his castle".' J Nunn, '"Sole Occupancy" Orders' in NSW Women's Refuge Movement, Domestic Violence and Incest Resource Centre, Council to Homeless Persons (eds), *Out of the Fire: Domestic Violence and Homelessness* (2001), p 35.

[10] Department of Families, Youth and Community Care (Qld), *Where to From Here?—Report on the Needs of Women Who have Experienced Domestic Violence* (Queensland Government, 1996), p 11. See also Earle, n 6, p 6.

[11] For example, the National Committee on Violence Against Women has noted that 'little is known about the extent to which protection orders are being made which exclude an offender from living in specified premises': National Committee on Violence Against Women *The Effectiveness of Protection Orders in Australian Jurisdictions* (AGPS, (1993), p 53. There is certainly very little academic writing in Australia specifically on the issue of ouster orders *per se.* There is, however, an increasing body of literature on connections between domestic violence and homelessness—a context in which the idea of ouster orders is becoming increasingly important. See, in particular, *Out of the Fire*, n 8 (14(2) Parity) and the *Home Safe Home* report, n 7. Writing on the use of ouster injunctions in the United Kingdom is also limited, but includes R Harper, 'Ouster Injunctions—A Guide to the Way Out' (1980) 77 *Guardian Gazette* 1276, SJ Parker, 'Towards an Adjustive Jurisdiction for Cohabitees?' (1980) 124 *Solicitors' Journal* 471, P Glover, 'Domestic Violence—The Choice of Emergency Procedures' (1981) 78 *Law Society's Gazette* 1268, JC Hall, 'Eviction of a Husband' (1984) 43 *Cambridge Law Journal* 38, and P Parkinson, 'The *Domestic Violence Act* and *Richards v Richards*' (1986) 16 *Family Law* 70. It

know, however, that magistrates in Tasmania[12] and Victoria[13] have been reluctant to make such orders,[14] and that in 1987 only 3.2 per cent of orders made in New South Wales included a requirement that the offender no longer reside in the family home.[15] We know that the reluctance of some magistrates to issue ouster orders relates to concern about preventing a man from attending his own premises.[16] We also know that, in some jurisdictions, the likelihood of obtaining an ouster order *ex parte* is low unless the magistrate is able to see physical injury.[17] And we know that police seem reluctant to assist with excluding perpetrators, as very few police initiate applications including a request for such a condition.[18] Finally, it has been suggested that many self-representing women do not know that the ouster option exists.[19]

We still do not know enough, however, about the making of ouster orders. This chapter aims to contribute to increasing our understanding in the area by first canvassing some of the current key political, legal and social issues relating to ouster orders, and then presenting the results of a survey of Queensland magistrates' attitudes on domestic violence, conducted in 2000, which asked whether Queensland magistrates felt comfortable ousting a violent person from their home.[20]

LEGAL, POLITICAL AND SOCIAL ISSUES RELATING TO OUSTER ORDERS

Domestic violence incontrovertibly results in the homelessness of many women and children.[21] Ouster orders have the potential to 'prevent some level of

should also be noted that the ouster jurisdiction of the Family Court exists under s 114 of the *Family Law Act* 1975 (Cth), whereby the court has the power to exclude a party to a marriage from 'entering or remaining in the matrimonial home or the premises in which the other party to the marriage resides'. This jurisdiction is far more widely explored in the literature and there is a significant amount of case law on the subject. See, for example, discussion on injunctions relating to the use and occupation of the matrimonial home in HA Finlay and RJ Bailey-Harris, *Family Law in Australia* (Butterworths, 4th edn, 1989), p 451. Of course, injunctions under the *Family Law Act* are limited in their availability to parties involved in proceedings arising out of a marital relationship. These injunctions are therefore not available to victims of violence who are not married to the perpetrator of violence against them. There are also cost and time issues involved in applications to the Family Court.

12 J Stewart, *Report to the Department of Community Services on Responses to Domestic Violence in Tasmania* (1990).

13 R Wearing, 'Family Violence: Has Anything Changed in Four Years?' (1991) 5 *Socio-Legal Bulletin* 4.

14 National Committee on Violence Against Women, n 11, p 53.

15 J Stubbs and D Powell, *Domestic Violence: The Impact of Legal Reform in NSW* (NSW Bureau of Crime Statistics and Research, 1989), p 31.

16 Wearing, n 13, pp 4–5.

17 J Nunn, '"Sole Occupancy" Orders' in *Out of the Fire*, n 9, p 35.

18 Nunn, n 17, p 35. WESNET also refers to police rarely seeking orders containing non-standard conditions—see Earle above n 6, p 6.

19 *Ibid.*

20 The full report will be available in 2002.

21 See SAAP data referred to above n 6.

homelessness'[22] by ensuring that it is the perpetrator of violence who is removed from the family home and forced to find alternative accommodation.

While a resistance to ousting perpetrators remains, however, the responsibility for escaping domestic violence will continue to lie with women and their children. A key legal dilemma that contributes to the perpetuation of this situation is that the legal system is not able to guarantee the safety or protection of women inside their own home if they remain with a violent partner.[23] More endemic and hard to overcome is the fact that 'society has accepted that the onus is on women to escape violence and services have been developed based on this principle.'[24]

Yet, as a result of leaving the home, women (and their children) experience 'considerable social and personal disruption and financial disadvantage.'[25] For example, they are often forced to leave their local area and move to much lower standard accommodation, 'with little or none of their furniture, clothes or possessions.'[26] As a result, the children are often forced to change schools and leave behind, amongst other things, connections to friends and sporting clubs.[27]

With little choice but to uproot their lives and escape, notwithstanding their economic and social vulnerability,[28] where do women and their children go? Keys Young have reported that refuges are the essential service for women who experience domestic violence because they provide a safe place to go in crisis.[29] A survey conducted in 1996 in Queensland confirms that the most frequently identified first need of women who experience domestic violence is 'a safe place to

[22] *Home Safe Home* report, n 7, p 27.

[23] J Macklin, 'Providing Protection, Choices and Opportunities for Women and Children Escaping Violence' (1998) 4 *Women Against Violence* 55, quoted in the *Home Safe Home* report, n 7, p 31.

[24] *Ibid.* The *Home Safe Home* report also comments that an increased use of ouster orders will require 'changes to the law in some areas, changes to police practices both at the time of crisis and at later stages and attitudinal changes at a broader social level'—see n 7, p 56.

[25] D Chung, R Kennedy, B O'Brien and S Wendt, 'The Impact of Domestic and Family Violence on Women and Homelessness: Findings from a National Research Project' in *Out of the Fire*, n 9, p 21. Partnerships Against Domestic Violence note also 'the problem of women and children having to leave the family home and live in temporary and often sub-standard accommodation while the perpetrator remains in the home': Partnerships Against Domestic Violence, *Current Perspectives on Domestic Violence—A Review of National and International Literature* (Commonwealth of Australia, 1999), p 21. Further, for example, the *Beyond These Walls Report* states that, whilst the perpetrator remains in the home, 'he continues to enjoy the comforts and benefits of remaining in a familiar environment while his wife [sic] and children must adjust to new, and often unsatisfactory circumstances and may be faced with the prospect of multiple moves'—see n 7, p 225.

[26] Department of Families, Youth and Community Care (Qld), n 10, p 89.

[27] *Ibid.*

[28] Macklin, n 23. Note also the National Committee on Violence's comment that 'The Committee's publication *Victims of Violence* (Grabosky 1989) described the particular vulnerability of victims of domestic violence. These victims, virtually all female, many with reduced earning capacity and having assumed primary responsibility for child care, are forced to choose between submitting to continued abuse and securing alternative accommodation which lies increasingly beyond their means.'—National Committee on Violence, *Violence: Directions for Australia* (Australian Institute of Criminology, 1990), p 156.

[29] Keys Young, *Against the Odds: How Women Survive Domestic Violence* (Partnerships Against Domestic Violence, 1998), p 78.

go.'[30] This is because, when women are forced to flee their home, 'only the most fortunate are able to afford alternative accommodation; [and] not all the remainder are able to impose on family or friends.'[31]

In 1996, there were 45 refuges and safe houses in Queensland, with other housing assistance being provided through the Crisis Accommodation Program (CAP), the Community Rent Scheme (CRS) and bond loans.[32] At federal level, the Supported Accommodation Assistance Program (SAAP) and Women's Emergency Services Program (WESP) exist 'to assist homeless people to achieve the maximum possible degree of self-reliance, gain access to a range of services and reintegrate into mainstream society.'[33]

For women escaping violence, refuges offer support, understanding, information and assistance, as well as providing accommodation and a safe place to be.[34] They also offer an opportunity to talk with other women who have experienced violence, assistance with working out what to do in the immediate and long-term future, and counselling.[35] Refuges positively validate women and their decision to escape violence, they reduce survivors' feelings of isolation, and they provide a sense of community where children can interact with each other, and where a culture of change and personal development is created.[36] Thirty-one per cent of respondents in the 1996 Queensland survey said that refuges were the most helpful domestic violence service they had contact with.[37]

Notwithstanding these important aspects of refuges, McGregor and Hopkins argue that refuges amount 'only to a Band-Aid approach to the problem of domestic violence, failing to tackle the root cause.'[38] Further to this argument is the reality that refuges are simply not accessible to everyone.

In terms of access to refuges, there are a number of key issues. Firstly, there are continuing problems with refuges simply keeping up with demands for emergency housing for survivors of violence.[39] The National Committee on Violence wrote

[30] Department of Families, Youth and Community Care (Qld), n 10, p 69.

[31] National Committee on Violence, n 28, p 156.

[32] Department of Families, Youth and Community Care (Qld), n 10, pp 12–13.

[33] *Home Safe Home* report, n 7, p 20.

[34] Department of Families, Youth and Community Care (Qld), n 10, p 43. The *Home Safe Home* report confirms that 'refuges/shelters remain an essential part of the domestic violence service system that enable women and children to access safe accommodation in escaping domestic and family violence. Refuges/shelters also provide women with support and are an important entry point to legal services and longer term accommodation for many women.'—see n 7, p 81.

[35] See n 7, p 63.

[36] See n 7, pp 64–65.

[37] Department of Families, Youth and Community Care (Qld), n 10, p 60.

[38] H McGregor and A Hopkins, *Working for Change—The Movement Against Domestic Violence* (Allen & Unwin, 1991), p 15. The issue of increasing perpetrators' programmes is canvassed further below.

[39] For example, the National Committee on Violence has stated that 'accommodation problems faced by victims of domestic violence include a dearth of acute crisis accommodation, insufficient "bridging" shelter pending the location of permanent residence, and lack of access to long-term housing, whether publicly provided or purchasable on the private housing market.'—see n 28, p 156. The *Home Safe Home* report also acknowledges the impact of the extent of demand on availability of refuge accommodation for women—see n 7, pp 21–22.

ten years ago that 'thousands seek emergency shelter accommodation each year. Many must be turned away for want of space.'[40] And it was documented in 1988 that 23,000 women and children in New South Wales were denied accommodation in the state's refuges.[41] In 1998, service providers were still commenting to government that 'access to domestic violence crisis services is often limited due to the level of demand (eg refuges are frequently full) and geographic factors (eg the nearest refuge may be literally hundreds of kilometres away).'[42] An associated problem is that refuges 'are often unable to provide lodging for more than a few days at a time.'[43]

Secondly, 'certain aspects of refuge service delivery may currently be deterring some women from using [refuges].'[44] That is, living in a refuge—whilst it offers safety and support—is temporary and can be extremely difficult. For example, some women feel that the strict security rules in refuges are not appropriate for their individual circumstances,[45] whilst others may be concerned about the lack of privacy that accompanies communal living[46]—although it should be noted that in many areas of Australia there is now a move to cluster units.[47] Women have also commented that refuge living can be confronting in that many of the families in the refuge are facing a multiple range of complex problems.[48] But even smaller issues, such as 'having to leave pets behind',[49] and differences over child discipline matters, can add significantly to the dislocation that is being suffered by women and their children.

Key areas where women experiencing domestic violence feel that refuges could respond better to their needs are the provision of better quality accommodation, more privacy[50] and more staff (especially at night).[51] The ability of refuges to

[40] National Committee on Violence, n 28, p 156.

[41] *Ibid.*

[42] Keys Young, n 29, p xiv.

[43] See n 29, pp 156–57.

[44] The *Home Safe Home* report, n 7, p 21.

[45] For example, the *Home Safe Home* report states that feedback from victims of violence who had used refuge accommodation indicated that 'high security requirements were 'out of sync' with the needs of some women and children who did not require such arrangements.'—see n 7, p 65.

[46] See n 7, pp 21–22 and 63–65, where the report states, for example, that 'those refuges/shelters only with communal living arrangements were seen as less able to meet the diverse needs of women and children' (p 65); that 'indigenous and culturally and linguistically diverse women could have difficulties in communication, customs, food preparation and cultural isolation in a communal living environment' (p 65); and that 'some women would not access a refuge/shelter because they assumed it was a communal living model and they did not feel able to live in such an environment' (p 64). The research of Chung, Kennedy, O'Brien and Wendt confirms difficulties in refuges for women related to communal living—see n 25, p 22.

[47] The *Home Safe Home* report, n 7, p 63.

[48] See n 7, p 64.

[49] *Ibid.*

[50] The research of Malos and Hague, which involved interviews of victims of violence in England and Wales, confirms that, although women feel safe in refuges, pressure on space and the resultant lack of privacy mean that the experience is sometimes intolerable. Further, this meant that some women feel compelled to return to their partner to avoid these difficulties: E Malos and G Hague, 'Women, Housing, Homelessness and Domestic Violence' (1997) 20 *Women's Studies International Forum* 397 at 403–4.

[51] Department of Families, Youth and Community Care (Qld), n 10, pp 44 and 45.

respond to these concerns is clearly dependent on the funding and resource limitations imposed by government.[52] Funding is also an issue in terms of strategies such as further research to assess the unmet accommodation needs of survivors of violence,[53] and developing, in 'close consultation with users of the services',[54] upgrades to existing refuges 'to ensure more private living arrangements'.[55]

An alternative option for policy development in responding to the housing needs of survivors of violence is to recognise and act on the notion that 'ultimately, the ideal outcome is that women who want to should be able to stay or return in the long term, to the family home'.[56] This option is based on the idea that women deserve to have their familiar surroundings and possessions, and that they should not be forced to move to refuge and then on to other accommodation because violence has been perpetrated against them.[57] Ouster orders are the key to putting this option into effect.

At the first Annual Meeting of Ministers on Women's Safety held in December 2000, it was agreed that one of the four priority areas would be 'increasing options for women who have experienced family violence'—particular reference was made in this context to the option of women and children being able to remain in the family home.[58]

It is possible to take the view that government may wish to push an increased use of ouster orders on the basis that this will relieve some of the funding and resource implications of improving services for survivors of violence. As Stanes points out, 'the current political and economic climate poses a threat for existing services ... Funding is being threatened by existing governments, which inevitably means that services will need to begin to compete for funding rather than present a united front.'[59]

An increased use of ouster orders would create new funding dilemmas for government, however. Firstly, it would result in a need for measures which will more adequately protect women and children in their home after the perpetrator has been ousted.[60] This protection requires 'rigorous and enforced legal sanctions'[61]

[52] The *Home Safe Home* report, n 7, p 65.

[53] The results of the Queensland Domestic Violence Client Needs Survey conducted in 1996 by the Department of Families, Youth and Community Care (Qld) resulted in the recommendation that 'the extent to which refuges, safe houses, and other crisis accommodation services are able to meet requests for assistance be assessed and that strategies be developed to meet the unmet need': Department of Families, Youth and Community Care (Qld), n 10. p 4.

[54] *Ibid.*

[55] *Ibid.*

[56] See n 10, p 89.

[57] Nunn, n 10, p 35.

[58] P Drysdale (Office of Women's Policy, Victoria), 'Women's Safety Strategy: A Whole-of-Government Response to Violence Against Women' in *Out of the Fire*, n 9, p 7.

[59] Stanes, n 7, p 48.

[60] Stanes refers to an ouster model which has the support of domestic violence workers, which includes legal protection by the police and courts—see n 7, p 49. The *Home Safe Home* report refers to Hughes (1999, p 8) as advocating ouster orders and suggesting that there is also a need for an expansion of outreach support programs which assist women and children to maintain their safety and security in the home after the perpetrator has left: see n 7, p 32.

[61] See n 7, p 27.

which necessarily involve resource implications for police and the courts, as well as other services. Secondly, it would result in a need for expanded emergency accommodation services for men.[62] This latter issue is controversial and difficult because it challenges some of the 'orthodoxies in the prevailing paradigm of service provision'[63] which are based on supporting women and children needing to escape domestic violence.

Men's crisis accommodation services are currently limited,[64] and there is general recognition that perpetrator programs need to be expanded.[65] It is crucial, if ouster orders are to be more frequently issued, that perpetrators' services are improved. This is because 'one of the reasons which has been cited for not removing men from the home in domestic and family violence situations is that they have nowhere to go, unlike women and children who have refuges/shelters.'[66]

For this reason, the Home Safe Home Report has recommended that there be 'a reorientation of men's emergency accommodation services to accommodate men removed from the home as a result of domestic and family violence.'[67] However, support for this notion is qualified by a number of important provisos. For example, resources for perpetrators 'must never be at the expense of, or diminish resources available for, victims'.[68] Further, such resources must be devel-

[62] 'To prevent the homelessness of women and children following domestic and family violence requires the removal of the perpetrator while there is the continuing use of violence. This requires the availability of appropriate accommodation for the man following domestic and family violence and the need for intervention that will aim to stop the use of violence.' See n 7, p 80.

[63] See n 7, p 78.

[64] Research of the Brisbane City Council in 1995 identified gaps in domestic violence services as including 'a lack of accommodation options for men to move to when violent [which] often results in women and children being penalised by moving from their support networks. There are few options when the perpetrator is prepared to move, so the woman often leaves instead.'—Brisbane City Council, *Brisbane City Council Domestic Violence Project Report: Creating A Safer and More Livable Brisbane* (1995), pp 63–64.

[65] Dr Carmen Lawrence advocates policies that more directly treat perpetrators for what they are and that intervene to change the behaviour of those who are the problem: C Lawrence (Shadow Federal Minister for the Status of Women), 'Challenging Orthodoxies: the Next Step' in *Out of the Fire*, n 9, p 10. Lawrence also identifies that there has been a shift in policy from tending to emergency needs of victims to addressing behaviour of perpetrators, commenting that 'the policy making challenge of responding to the problem rather than just trying to tend the victims of violence is a large one. It is much easier to remove those hurt by family violence from the home and assist them to re-build their lives than tackle the behaviour of perpetrators. But this is an inefficient response, up-ending the lives of families by removal and resettling; it is frequently an unsuccessful response, as a third of those who leave return to more abuse; and it does little to remove the risk of abuse recurring because it does not address the cause of the problem.'—*ibid.* The *Home Safe Home* report also supports better perpetrator programs (particularly for situations where women would like the relationship to continue if the violence stops)—see n 7, p 56. And the Brisbane City Council has noted 'a need for more work with men in the prevention of violence': Brisbane City Council, n 64, pp 63–64.

[66] The *Home Safe Home* report even acknowledges the issue that 'domestic violence activists who fought for safe accommodation for women and children so many years ago could not have foreseen that it would inadvertently have led to being a reason for removing and disrupting women and children leaving men in the home'—see n 7, p 57.

[67] Recommendation 20—n 7, p 80.

[68] V Wensing (WESNET), 'Why We Still Need Women's Services in the Twenty First Century' in *Out of the Fire*, n 9. p 18. 'It was clearly stated by stakeholders that any reorientation of men's emer-

oped with the central focus on the fact that they result in 'greater advocacy and support for women and children to remain in the home.'[69] As Carmen Lawrence has commented:

> Those involved in the area, mostly refuge-based workers, are understandably worried about the potential shifting of resources from safe harbours to the treatment of perpetrators or even more law enforcement. They are correct to seek undertakings from government that a shift in policy not be accompanied by the removal of resources. However, these concerns should not prevent consideration of reforms that might work to remove perpetrators from the family home rather than the victims.[70]

In addition to the political and philosophical difficulties with increasing the use of ouster orders, there are a number of practical problems. For example, there is an inherent danger for women and children who remain in the home in that the perpetrator knows exactly where they are, and also possibly knows ways into the property that don't require a key. Earle comments that ouster orders are 'not always appropriate—women are sometimes too fearful and at risk to remain in the home.'[71] There is also the issue that 'women fear that [ouster] orders might escalate perpetrator violence.'[72]

Further, WESNET notes that 'an exclusion order is not a permanent housing solution for women and children escaping violence'[73] and that other housing and property law reform—for example, in the area of residential tenancies—is also required.[74] This is because there are practical financial difficulties associated with women remaining in the home when there is 'only one income, especially when it is a Centrelink payment'.[75] That is, many women are unable to take over the rent[76] or mortgage payments on their own, although 'for women renting public housing the financial burden could be more manageable.'[77]

gency accommodation services to engage male perpetrators should not involve the transfer of funds from women's domestic violence services for such re-orientation.'—*Home Safe Home* report, n 7, p 57.

[69] See n 7, p 59.

[70] Lawrence, n 65, p 10.

[71] Earle, n 6, p 6. Women also see themselves as being an easy and inadequately protected target in their home—Chung et al., n 25, p 22.

[72] *Ibid.* Another issue is that women who leave temporarily and return once the perpetrator has been ousted find often that 'the home has been significantly damaged and household goods have been removed.'—*Ibid.* 'At times women have stated they will not try to get violent men out of their houses, because to do so would inflame them further and they had been hurt enough.'—Nunn, n 9, p 35.

[73] Earle, n 6, p 7.

[74] See, for example, Earle's reference to R Kennedy, P See and P Sutherland, *Minimum Standards for Residential Tenancies in Australia* (1995) and the need for laws across Australia that facilitate 'the exclusion of a tenant and transfer of tenancy in situations of domestic violence'—Earle, n 6, p 7.

[75] Chung et al., n 25, p 23.

[76] *Ibid.* Further, 'women in private rental are often forced to give up their house due to property damage by the perpetrator and/or overdue rent and other bills'—*Ibid.* As the *Beyond These Walls* report has put it, 'many victims of domestic violence experience difficulties as sole parents dependent on pensions or benefits, in competing in the private rental market . . . Public housing consequently has an important role to play in assisting the victims of domestic violence.'—see n 1, p 226. See also the entire chapter on Housing (pp 225ff.) for further discussion of these issues.

[77] Chung et al., n 25, p 23.

These difficulties are significant but, as with the political issues mentioned above, they should not deter us from pursuing the ouster order option. And certainly there are many benefits for women and their children that result from ousting the perpetrator of violence from the family home.

First, the lives of women and children who are survivors of violence are indisputably chaotic and ouster orders can provide in this chaos at least one important constant—that of the familiar home environment. Women who can remain in their own home are:

> more easily able to access their existing supports and networks, they may be able to continue employment or education more easily, they are more likely to have access to their furniture and other household goods and possessions. Their children are also likely to be able to continue existing friendships and supports and to maintain their school, sporting club and community associations.[78]

Secondly, many women have recounted how empowered they have felt through pursuing the option of remaining in the home.[79]

Thirdly, most women simply prefer to stay in their own home.[80] As WESNET points out: 'Eighty-seven per cent of women who experience violence do not approach a crisis service for assistance, they stay at home or other accommodation.'[81] Further, 'national SAAP data has shown that, of the women who have left the family home after experiencing violence, approximately 30 per cent return, and in remote areas almost 60 per cent.'[82] Often this means returning to the violence they tried to escape. Ouster orders can help prevent this.

Fourthly, ouster orders hold the perpetrator accountable for his violence.[83] As the Home Safe Home Report puts it: 'Homelessness for women and children who have experienced domestic and family violence is the result of social failure to

[78] See n 25, p 21. Further, Macklin comments that leaving the woman in the family home has particular benefits for the children, who can remain at school and close to their friends and family—see Macklin, n 23, p 57.

[79] For example, one woman has said: 'I gained strength by being in the home and remaining.'—the *Home Safe Home* report, n 7, p 56. Some women involved in the *Home Safe Home* report research stated that they 'did remain in the home and the perpetrator left, one woman reported that she stayed in the home for ten months but after constant harassment by the perpetrator and his relatives she reluctantly went to a refuge. When other women were asked what they would do differently if it happened again, a number said that they would fight to stay in their homes had they known the level of disruption, displacement and disadvantage they would face from having to flee. For those women who were able to remain they felt a strong sense of justice, even if they had difficulty in remaining.'—see n 7, p 57.

[80] The *Beyond These Walls* report stated that 'many victims of violence, given a choice, would prefer to remain in their own homes'—see n 1, p 225.

[81] The *Home Safe Home* report, n 7, p 32.

[82] *Ibid.*

[83] 'Men should take responsibility for the violence they inflict': Wensing, n 67, p 18. The principle that those who commit domestic violence must be held accountable for their behaviour was included in the Statement of Principles Agreed by Heads of Government at the National Domestic Violence Summit—Partnerships Against Domestic Violence, *First Report of the Taskforce 1998–1999* (Commonwealth of Australia, 1999), p 2. See also National Committee on Violence, n 28, p 156.

fully accept and deal with the criminality of the perpetrator's behaviour.'[84] It is 'ironic and unjust that it is the victims, and not the perpetrators, who are often effectively condemned to eviction,'[85] whilst the guilty party remains in full possession of the home, its contents and all the accompanying comforts.[86] Rather, it should be the perpetrator of violence who is made to bear the burden of the disruption of the family.[87] It is his responsibility, his violence.

Problematically, however, it will remain difficult to get men to take responsibility for their violence, as long as the adversarial legal process supports their denial or mitigation of responsibility for their behaviour when they are in court.[88] The next section of this chapter reports the findings of a survey on the attitudes of Queensland magistrates in the year 2000 to the making of ouster orders. It makes some connections between the magistrates' attitudes and what has been said earlier in the chapter, and draws some conclusions on directions for law reform in this area.

A SURVEY OF QUEENSLAND MAGISTRATES' ATTITUDES ON THE MAKING OF OUSTER ORDERS

A survey of Queensland magistrates' attitudes to domestic violence was conducted in May and June 2000. All 96 magistrates and acting magistrates in both urban and regional areas in Queensland were invited to respond to the survey.[89] Of the ninety-six surveys sent out, 38 responses were received, representing a response rate of 40 per cent.[90]

The survey instrument used was a modified version of the New South Wales Judicial Commission's survey of New South Wales magistrates conducted in 1998.[91] The Judicial Commission's survey did not ask a question about ouster

[84] The *Home Safe Home* report, n 7, p 78.

[85] See n 7, p 57. 'Some women felt strongly that they should be able to remain in the home with their children, as they had not committed the offences, yet they were paying the price by losing their home.'—n 7, p 78.

[86] Department of Families, Youth and Community Care (Qld), n 10, p 89.

[87] Macklin, n 23, p 57.

[88] The *Home Safe Home* report, n 7, p 57.

[89] Both through an initial mail-out and then a follow-up invitation which was made personally in June 2000 at the Magistrates' Conference in Brisbane.

[90] The New South Wales Judicial Commission's response rate was 56%. Nine of the twelve female magistrates in Queensland responded (a response rate of 75%) and 28 of the 84 male magistrates and acting magistrates responded (a response rate of 33.33%). Fourteen of the respondents had fewer than five years' experience as a magistrate, five had between five and ten years' experience, six had between ten and fifteen years' experience and eleven respondents had over fifteen years' of experience. Two respondents failed to enter their years of service as they felt that it was an identifying factor. Eighteen of the respondents were in the 51–60 age group, fourteen were in the 41–50 age group and five respondents were between 30 and 40. Eight of the respondents sat in city courts, eleven in country courts and seventeen sat in both city and regional areas.

[91] J Hickey and S Cumines, *Apprehended Violence Orders: A Survey of Magistrates*, Monograph Series Number 20 (Judicial Commission of New South Wales., 1999). The survey instrument was quite lengthy and searching in the questions it posed. All questions were of an open-ended nature.

orders. For the following reasons, we included a question on whether magistrates felt comfortable ousting a violent person from their home.

First, the issue that magistrates are reluctant to make such orders was raised anecdotally with us by a number of workers in the domestic violence field in Queensland. Secondly, as we said above, there are indications that ouster orders are currently significantly under-used,[92] that magistrates consider that a woman's accommodation needs are adequately met if she has access to a refuge,[93] and that 'women are discouraged from seeking ouster orders on the basis that they are rarely granted.'[94] Thirdly—again as has been indicated above—a number of recent publications on domestic violence and homelessness have confirmed the importance of reconsidering how ouster orders might address homelessness issues for woman and children resulting from domestic violence.[95] Finally, we were concerned by statements—for example, in the Australian Law Reform Commission's Report on Domestic Violence—that labelled removing a perpetrator of violence from his home as 'particularly restrictive'.[96] These issues, we felt, required testing with the Queensland magistrates.

Questions ranged from ones relating to magistrates' views on the causes of domestic violence to questions concerning specific issues to do with the operation of the *Domestic Violence (Family Protection) Act* 1989 (Qld). There were a number of research rationales behind the survey. The first was the paucity of empirical qualitative research on domestic violence in Queensland. In particular, there has been no research to date on the views of Queensland magistrates about domestic violence issues. Secondly, the Australian Law Reform Commission (ALRC) reported in 1994 that 'all over Australia women came to the Commission to explain how the legal system had failed them . . . How the horror of the violence against them . . . had been compounded by the law's failure to protect them. They complained of . . . their humiliation by a system of justice that they perceived as trivialising their injuries and disbelieving them.'—Australian Law Reform Commission, *Report (No. 67) on Equality Before the Law: Women's Access to the Legal System* (AGPS, 1994). The survey aimed to test magistrates' views on this perspective. Thirdly, Queensland statistics indicate that there has been an increase in the number of applications for domestic violence orders from 11,082 in 1994 to 14,041 in 1999. This might reflect an increased confidence in using the legal system on the part of survivors of violence, a possibility that the research aimed query in terms of magistrates' understandings. Fourthly, although research and writing in the field of domestic violence are increasing, there is generally a great need to expedite the development of the legal discourse on domestic violence. The ALRC, again in its 1994 Report, called for more research and better data on women and the legal system—see p 62. This research aims to be a contribution in responding to that call. Further, the ALRC was concerned in the 1994 report that much of the legal research that had been undertaken in areas such as domestic violence was not comparable due to different methodologies used in different projects and in different jurisdictions. By replicating the Judicial Commission of New South Wales' survey, our project has produced knowledge which is comparable, although unfortunately not on the issue of ouster orders.

92 Earle, n 7, p 6.

93 *Ibid.*

94 *Ibid.*

95 For example, see Partnerships Against Domestic Violence, n 25, the *Home Safe Home* report n 7, Earle, n 6, and *Out of the Fire*, n 9.

96 Australian Law Reform Commission, n 5, p 44. The ALRC also commented that 'whilst it is correct to say that property rights and freedom of movement are less important human rights than is the right of the victim to be free from violence and molestation, there is no doubt that the exclusion of the respondent from the home is a step which is fraught with high emotion and may have repercussions beyond the respondent's own feelings—*ibid.* The report made three recommendations in relation to ouster orders: first, that a respondent should be given notice that such an order is going to be applied for; second, that magistrates should be required to consider the effect of such an order

TABLE 1

	Male	*Female*	*Unknown*	*Total*	*%*
Yes	20	9	1	30	79
No	8	—	—	8	21

Queensland Magistrates' Responses to the Question: 'Do you feel comfortable ousting a violent person from their home?'

Magistrates around Queensland are making orders under the *Domestic Violence (Family Protection) Act* on a daily basis. They are key players in ensuring that victims of violence achieve justice through the legal system, and as such their understanding of issues relating to ouster orders is very important.[97]

Table 1 reflects that a total of 79 per cent of Queensland magistrates surveyed agreed that they feel comfortable ousting a violent person from their home, with 21 per cent of magistrates not feeling comfortable about making an ouster order. Those magistrates who felt uncomfortable were all male.

This result would seem, on the face of it, to belie the concerns on which the question was based. However, we have taken the view that, although many magistrates may assert that they feel 'comfortable' making such an order (because that was the word we used in the question) this 'comfort' may not necessarily translate into an appropriate issuing of orders. Certainly, an analysis of the comments provided by magistrates (in addition to their yes or no answer) confirms some of the concerns raised above, providing an important indication of magistrates' understanding of issues relating to ouster orders, and suggesting a possible need for specific training in this area. Some examples of these comments are as follows:

on the accommodation needs of the parties and the children; and third, that if *ex parte* orders are made they should not become effective until the respondent has been personally served with the order: *Ibid.*

97 The following commentary has been made on how Queensland magistrates approach the making of ouster orders—'Magistrates will take into account whether the house is in both names or one name only. Even if the house is in both names, some magistrates will make an *ex parte* order with the ouster condition but giving an early return date to the court. If the house is in the aggrieved's name only, the ouster condition is easier to obtain, although the magistrate may take into account the duration of the relationship and the needs of the children.' 'If an ex-parte order is not made, a short adjournment is made (usually from two days to a week) to allow for service of the application and to allow the matter to be brought before the court as soon as possible and to hear from the respondent. The magistrate will then make an ouster condition if he[sic] is satisfied that the aforementioned criteria have been fulfilled. The magistrate may include in the condition a time limit that the respondent can remain in the house to pack his/her belongings and/or to give him/her time to seek alternative suitable accommodation. Also, the magistrate may add to this condition that the respondent can return to the house at a certain time in the company of the police to collect his belongings.' 'Often the magistrate can forget to turn the page to see that your client has asked for other conditions'—C Steiner, 'Working Practically with the Legislation and Potential Issues for Practitioners', in *Domestic Violence—Queensland Law Society Continuing Legal Education Seminar Papers* (25 Sept 2001), pp 2–3.

—Women magistrates (all of whom felt comfortable making ouster orders) said that they felt comfortable making such orders—for example, 'provided that the [violent] person has been heard by the court and [is] present when the order is made,' and 'provided the circumstances warrant it.' One female magistrate was concerned to ensure that the respondent was heard in case 'they may set fire to the dwelling.' Another commented that 'my comfort is not relevant. If the circumstances of the case require that I do, then I do.'

—Male magistrates who responded that they felt comfortable making ouster orders said that this was 'providing there are sufficient grounds in the application,' 'if there is physical violence' and 'when the circumstances are bad enough' or 'if the aggrieved has no suitable alternative accommodation for herself and/or the children.' One male magistrate made the comment that 'the issue seldom is raised in court which is surprising!', whilst another commented that the 'protection of the aggrieved and other members of the family is the primary concern.' Finally, a male magistrate commented that 'if it is found that a person has committed an act of domestic violence to the extent that such an order had to be made then I will make it.'

—Only eight magistrates in Queensland said they did not feel comfortable making ouster orders—they were all male. However, five of these magistrates qualified their response by saying that, although they didn't feel comfortable ousting a violent person from their home, they would do it 'when necessary,' 'if there is some temporary accommodation for this person to attend' and 'on appropriate occasions.' One magistrate said he felt particularly uncomfortable making the order 'if the respondent spouse has a legal title to the premises'. Another commented that, whilst he doesn't like to make the orders, they are nevertheless 'short term and beneficial to both parties in ironing out their problems.' Finally, a comment was made to the effect that 'the circumstances of *both* parties must first be taken into account—for example, whether children are also involved.'

From these responses some key issues can be identified.

First, in order for many magistrates to feel comfortable ousting a violent person from their home, the violence must be seen to be relatively severe. For example, reference was made to a need for physical violence to have occurred. This finding concurs with research on magistrates and the making of orders under domestic violence legislation in Victoria conducted by Ingrid Wilson, which also indicated the priority of importance placed on physical violence.[98] It can also be linked to

[98] IM Wilson, 'Were these Serious Assaults?': An Analysis of Magistrates' Dialogue During Proceedings for Intervention Orders Under the *Crimes (Family Violence) Act* 1987—thesis completed in satisfaction of requirements of the BA (Hons) in Criminology at the University of Melbourne. Steiner confirms that 'most magistrates will grant (an ouster) condition when the application has not been served only if serious domestic violence is alleged, the aggrieved has children in her care and they are also at risk if the respondent is permitted to remain in the matrimonial home, and the aggrieved is able to indicate to the magistrate that the respondent has alternative accommodation available to him/her'—Steiner, n 97, p 2.

the notion that ouster orders are 'justified' only as a last resort measure, and this connects to magistrates' comments to the effect that orders are made 'provided the circumstances warrant it' and 'when the circumstances are bad enough'.

However, circumstances where there is severe physical violence, for example, are (as we discussed above) precisely the circumstances where ouster orders are likely to be most inappropriate.[99] That is, where a woman is frightened for her physical safety, and also for her children, she is least likely to want to remain in the family home and most likely to need the security of refuge accommodation. Magistrates should therefore not rely on the criterion of circumstances being 'bad enough' for the issuing of ouster orders because it is more appropriately where the circumstances are 'good enough' that such orders should be made.

Secondly, for many magistrates to feel comfortable making an ouster order, the respondent must be given the opportunity to be heard. That is, magistrates are reluctant to make ouster orders *ex parte*.[100] Whilst liberal legal notions of natural justice are satisfied by this requirement, it also plays directly into the problem, noted above, that perpetrators of violence are encouraged by the adversarial legal system to deny or mitigate their behaviour rather than take responsibility for the violence they have perpetrated. That is, if magistrates require that a perpetrator must always be heard by the court on an ouster condition, but then rarely oust him, legal process itself results in his being effectively rewarded for denying or mitigating responsibility for his violent behaviour.

Further, where a woman is seeking an ouster condition under a protection order, she is indicating to the court that she feels safe to remain in the home if the perpetrator is removed. If the magistrate is satisfied that a protection order should be issued under the legislation, then the requested ouster condition should be included in that order, whether or not the perpetrator is present in court at the time it was made.

Another issue in this context is that it is open to defence lawyers to make it particularly difficult for women to obtain an ouster order by simply advising the perpetrator not to be present in court.

Thirdly, only one out of 28 magistrates mentioned the issue of the respondent's proprietorial rights in relation to the premises from which he was being ousted. Our results may in fact represent a true lack of concern about this issue amongst Queensland magistrates. However, as research from other jurisdictions[101] suggests

[99] 'Obviously there are women and children for whom this is not an option where the perpetrator is particularly violent and relentless in his pursuit of the woman. As violence often increases following separation this is an important consideration in pursuing such a shift in practice. This is not a suitable choice either for women and children who do not wish to remain in the house where they experienced the trauma of domestic or family violence. Where there have been high levels of violence and the perpetrator is relentless in continuing to pursue the woman it is unlikely the woman would choose to remain in the home with such a high risk to safety. In essence where the woman and children consider their safety to be a major risk this is not an option at the point of crisis. For some of these women it could be an option at a later stage.'—the *Home Safe Home* report, n 7, p 56.

[100] See n 16.

[101] See n 15.

otherwise, it is possible either that the wording of our question failed to draw out a full response from magistrates on this point, or that for some other reason magistrates were reluctant to identify it as an issue.

It is also possible that the concern of magistrates that the respondent be heard before an ouster order is made is linked to concern about respecting the respondent's legal or equitable interests in the property. On this basis, it is important to reiterate that whatever a perpetrator's proprietorial rights are in relation to the property in question, they must always be overtly subordinated to the human right of women and children to live free of violence in their own home.

Fourthly, there was mention from both male and female magistrates that whether or not they feel comfortable making such orders is irrelevant. These magistrates maintain that if the order must be made, then it is made. This indicates a commitment to notions of objective justice which perhaps belies the subjective nature of the exercise of a magistrate's discretion in responding to applications for ouster orders. We would argue that a magistrate's feelings about the idea of ousting a person from their home certainly are relevant to whether these orders are being made. In order for justice to be served in the exercise of a magistrate's discretion in making ouster orders, it may be necessary for magistrates to more openly acknowledge the part their own feelings on the issue play in the making of such orders.

Fifthly, magistrates mentioned that information as to whether children are involved or whether the applicant has suitable alternative accommodation is relevant to their making of ouster orders. It is important, therefore, that lawyers advising or representing applicants for ouster orders ensure that this sort of information is always presented to the court when it is relevant.

Finally, one magistrate mentioned that 'the pre-printed order form we use makes no mention of the possibility (of making an ouster order). Consequently drafting such an order AFTER you have considered its possibility in the absence/reminder of a guideline is a difficult exercise. All indicates these orders are not for the feint-hearted.' This comment reflects a practical difficulty magistrates face in dealing with the making ouster orders. It is important, therefore, that any pre-printed order form used by magistrates in the making or domestic violence protection orders includes a possible ouster order.

WHERE TO NEXT?

While magistrates in Queensland assert that they feel comfortable ousting a perpetrator from his home, they have also shown us that they are most comfortable making such orders in circumstances where the orders themselves are most inappropriate (where the violence is severe, for example). The survey results certainly indicate that there is scope for magistrates to be better informed about issues for women and children in this context.

Interestingly, the qualitative comments from the magistrates reflect quite accurately a number of issues mentioned at the beginning of this chapter. This leads us to consider two key reform possibilities in this context. Both reform options are based on the fundamental principle that legal practice and procedure in relation to ouster orders should 'encourage women to make their own decisions, empowering them to take control of and rebuild their lives.'[102]

The first reform possibility is, as WESNET has recommended, that there should be 'a presumption in favour of an exclusion order where one has been requested and where the safety of the protected person/children would not be compromised by remaining in the family home.'[103] It has also been suggested that there be an obligation on the court—at least where children are involved—to consider making an ouster order, whether or not it has been requested.[104]

The Home Safe Home Report takes the idea even further by suggesting that legislative change for ouster orders could involve making such orders presumptive standard conditions to all protection orders unless there are reasons why this is not possible or appropriate—for example, where the violence is too severe.[105]

Secondly, the South Australian Domestic Violence Council (SADVC), in its Report on Legal Issues,[106] recommended a new 'cooling off period' for expedited *ex parte* ouster conditions. This proposal involves a '12 hour ouster order whereby the police, by telephone, can call a rostered magistrate for an order to remove and detain the defendant for a period of 12 hours. At the end of the time the defendant is released and no further action is taken.'[107] The idea is based on an understanding that 'many women express the view that they do not want the perpetrator charged with assault and do not want to add to their longer-term risk by applying for a restraining order, but they do want him removed and cooled off.'[108]

Certainly, there are issues in relation to this proposal concerning civil liberties and arbitrary arrest. Conversely, however, it is a central democratic right for women and children to be safe in their home. It has also been acknowledged that such a system may increase risks for women by inflaming perpetrators. However, the SADVC responds to this issue by saying that any action taken by a victim is likely to be inflammatory and that this proposal may at least give them some breathing space to consider their options.[109]

Finally, a recommendation has been made that 'legislation be introduced whereby the perpetrator is made to compensate the woman or the service for the expenses incurred when a woman is forced to leave the home to escape domestic violence.'[110]

[102] Wensing, n 68, p 18.

[103] Earle, n 6, pp 6–7. This reflects current laws in New South Wales, which require 'magistrates to give reasons if they decline to make an exclusion order'—see p 6.

[104] See n 6, pp 6–7.

[105] The *Home Safe Home* report, n 7, p 58.

[106] South Australian Domestic Violence Council, (198?) *Report—Legal Issues Task Force.*

[107] See n 7, p 102.

[108] *Ibid.*

[109] See n 7, p 103.

[110] Department of Families, Youth and Community Care (Qld), n 10, p 6.

CONCLUSION

Issues in relation to the making of ouster orders by magistrates have largely escaped academic scrutiny in Australia to date. The results of the survey conducted in Queensland prima facie reflect a generally positive approach on the part of magistrates to an issue which, as this chapter has shown, is fraught with difficulty. The comments of magistrates indicate, however, that much of their consideration of this issue is focused on ouster orders as an extreme response to physical violence. In order for social justice to be served for survivors of violence, ouster orders should in fact be issued far more frequently and in circumstances where the violence is not severe. This use of ouster orders is dependent not only on magistrates' development of a better understanding of issues for women in this context, but also on legal, social, policy and service developments that challenge past and current orthodoxies in terms of responses to domestic violence in Australia.[111]

[111] 'The challenge in rethinking both theoretical and policy considerations in family violence in Australia is to do so in a way which is adequate to the task of acknowledging difference in experience, difference in perspective, difference in need, and in developing policy which is responsive to those differences.'—J Stubbs, 'Introduction' in J Stubbs (ed) *Women, Male Violence and the Law*, Institute of Criminology Monograph Series No 6 (Federation Press, 1994), p 4.

6

The South African Family Court: A First World Ideal in a Second World Country

Sandra Burman, Emma Dingle and Nichola Glasser*

In the classification by income of the world's countries, South Africa is a middle-range, or 'Second World', country, with a far lower income or proportion of professional skills per capita than those ranked as First World countries. Yet it has ambitiously embarked on setting up a Family Court, an institution which is generally acknowledged to be very expensive even for First World countries. The first stage of its existence has just drawn to a close, making this a useful point at which to evaluate both its performance to date and desirable future developments. This paper explains how the Family Court came to be set up in its present form, describes its operation, and discusses the implications.[1] It then attempts to assess whether the court's current format and operation indicate delusions of grandeur, hypocritical window-dressing, dedicated idealism—or all three.

THE TORTUOUS PATH TOWARDS A FAMILY COURT

With statistics in the 1970s reflecting a rapid rise in the divorce rate, focus fell on the possibility of establishing a Family Court as a means of stabilising family life. Commissions were established and reports produced on the matter during the period 1974–1979, with the same conclusion being reached by all: the establishment of such an institution was not recommended.[2] In 1983, however—for a

* Centre for Socio-Legal Research, University of Cape Town, South Africa. The research was sponsored by the National Research Foundation and the University of Cape Town Research Committee, which we acknowledge with thanks. The views expressed in this work and the conclusions drawn are those of the authors and should not be regarded as those of the sponsors.

[1] As this paper was prepared for presentation in July 2000, the findings reflect a snapshot of the court at that stage. Inevitably there have been changes, and the Centre continues to monitor the court on an ongoing basis.

[2] Internal Report submitted on 21 Oct 1974 by Mr Thompson on his study tour of Family Courts in various cities in the United States and Canada; South African Law Commission Report on the law of divorce and matters incidental thereto, Report 57 of 1978; and the 1979 Galgut Commission of Enquiry into Civil Proceedings in the Supreme Court of South Africa. This last report was never tabled.

variety of political as well as legal reasons—the idea of creating such a court was finally accepted by the Hoexter Commission of Inquiry into the Structure and Functioning of the Courts.[3]

The Commission's recommendations on the Family Court were contained in a 1985 Bill, but the majority of them were subsequently rejected by a parliamentary sub-committee on the grounds that the projected expense would be too great.[4] The recommendations pertaining to the establishment of the office of 'Children's Friend' were, however, embodied in a statute—the 1990 *Mediation in Certain Divorce Matters Act.*[5] This Act established the Office of the Family Advocate with the stated aim of reviewing every divorce case in the High Court where minor children were involved, in order to safeguard the best interests of the child.[6]

In 1993, the *Magistrate's Court Amendment Act* was passed, providing for the minister at some future date to establish 'family courts for the adjudication of divorce actions and the appointment of family magistrates for the said courts.'[7] In order for family courts to be set up, it is necessary, in terms of section 2(k), for the minister to formally place a notice in the *Government Gazette.* The date for the establishment of these courts has thus far not been gazetted.

In 1995, a further Hoexter Commission was established and mandated to investigate, inter alia, the need for specialist courts. The report was finalised on 17 December 1997.[8] Many of the recommendations regarding the Family Court which were contained in it differed substantially from those of 1983. One salient difference was the suggestion that the court enjoy Superior Court status, presided over by judges appointed on the same terms as all High Court judges.[9] It was suggested that a Family Court be established in each provincial division of the High Court in which there was an Office of the Family Advocate. The repeal of

[3] Fifth and Final Report No RP 78/1983. Regarding reasons for the Family Court, see S Burman and M Huvers, 'Church versus State? Divorce Legislation and Divided South Africa' (1985) 12 *Journal of Southern African Studies* 116.

[4] Family Court Bill 62 of 1985 as discussed in B Goldblatt, 'A Feminist Perspective on the Law Reform Process: An Evaluation of Attempts to Establish a Family Court in South Africa' (1997) 13 *South African Journal on Human Rights* 382 and 1997 Hoexter Commission Report at 41. Goldblatt's article provides a comprehensive and useful overview of the attempts to establish a Family Court in South Africa.

[5] Act 24 of 1984.

[6] All civil law divorces were heard in the High Court except those of blacks, who could go to either the High Court or the cheaper Black Divorce Court, which had three divisions and a status analogous to a Regional Magistrate's Court. The Black Divorce Court left much to be desired: see S Burman, 'Roman Dutch Law for Africans: The Black Divorce Court in Action' (1984) *Acta Juridica* 171.

[7] Act 120 of 1993 at preamble.

[8] Commission of Inquiry into the Rationalisation of the Provincial and Local Divisions of the Supreme Court Third and Final Report No RP 200/1997.

[9] The Commission recommended the passing of a new statute entitled 'The Family Court Act' which would provide for 'the establishment of a Family Court of comprehensive jurisdiction which will be an independent Superior Court with its own specialised structure and functions': para 9.2 at 130. The reasons for this recommendation were primarily to ensure that family law was dealt with by the most highly trained judiciary and because public perceptions of the Magistrates' Courts linked them too closely to criminal law. The recommendation was in contrast to the 1983 Hoexter Report which suggested that the court be located at Regional Court level.

the *Mediation in Certain Divorce Matters Act* was recommended, with a proposed new Act establishing, as part of the Family Advocate's Office, a Family Counselling Service to be attached to the Family Court.[10] This service would be free of charge to all members of the public, regardless of whether or not they were involved in divorce or other family litigation.[11]

While the Commission was still deliberating, a further important legislative step occurred when early in 1997 the *Administration Amendment Act*[12] was amended to open the previously exclusive Black Divorce Courts to all races.[13] These courts had originally been set up to provide a cheap and speedy forum for divorces for the poorest section of the population where its members resorted to civil law marriages. As was the case with all divisions of the Black Divorce Courts (which were all circuit courts), the Southern Divorce Court was staffed with Presiding Officers graded as Regional Court magistrates.

At the same time, in February 1997 the Minister of Justice established a Family Court Task Team in the Department of Justice entrusted to 'take responsibility for the implementation of a pilot project in regard to the Courts referred to in section 2(k) of the *Magistrate's Court Amendment Act*'—that is, the Family Courts.[14] The minister's actions were in response to mounting political pressure to demonstrate a concern for women and the family. In his parliamentary address in June 1996, he had indicated a desire to establish a Family Court in terms of existing legislation 'as soon as possible.'[15]

The Task Team identified its vision as the establishment of a Family Court structure that would have a number of features. It would have its own identity, be accessible to the community, be sensitive to the community's needs, operate according to simple, appropriate procedures, offer counselling and mediation support services and provide quality service in a pleasant user-friendly environment.[16] It should ideally be created in terms of new legislation, but this ideal was subject to constraints: the enactment of such legislation would take time, and financial and skilled human resources were limited. The Task Team consequently recommended that the Pilot Project Family Courts be established within the framework of existing legislation as soon as possible. Regarding finances and human resources, in an attempt to streamline the process it was suggested that existing resources be utilised, and that staff be transferred from the Maintenance, Family Violence and Children's Courts of the Magistrate's Courts to the various Pilot Project Family Courts.[17]

[10] *The Family Advocate and Family Counselling Service Act.*

[11] Hoexter, 1997, n 8, para 8.11.4, p 126.

[12] Act 9 of 1929, s 10.

[13] *Divorce Courts Amendment Act*, No 65 of 1997.

[14] 'Pilot Project for "Family Court"', 23 Jan 1997.

[15] *Hansard: Nation Assembly Deb*ates, 13 June 1996, Col 2848.

[16] C Loots, Department of Justice, Family Court Pilot Project, 'Concept Document Outlining the Principles and Procedures which are Applied in Establishing a Pilot Project', 6 Nov 1997.

[17] *Ibid.*, p 2.

In terms of a Department of Justice document, the Task Team recommended that the Pilot Project Family Courts should be both an interim measure and a source of information for the creation of a permanent family court structure.[18] The Task Team decided that the newly deracialised divorce courts should form the basis of the divorce section of these Pilot Project Courts. Five sites were established as Pilot Project venues, four in major cities and one in Lebowakgoma, a poor rural area, as the Task Team felt that there was a need to include a rural pilot court. Local situations in each case have determined the timing of the start of these courts. Thus, for example, whilst the Cape Town Family Court enjoyed its official opening at the beginning of 1999 and has been in full operation for well over a year, its counterpart in Port Elizabeth was officially launched on 23 June 2000, although operating beforehand (as explained below).

The Centre for Socio-Legal Research at the University of Cape Town is currently monitoring the Divorce Court component of two pilot project courts in economically and demographically contrasting provinces, the Western and Eastern Cape, and it is these two Pilot Project Courts which provide the basis of the report below. The hypothesis for the comparison was that, by contrasting the pilot projects of the Western Cape—one of the richest provinces in South Africa—and of the considerably poorer Eastern Cape, the role played by provincial finances in the effectiveness of the courts would become evident.

THE PILOT PROJECTS' STATUS

The Cape Town Family Court Pilot Project was launched at the Magistrate's Court on 29 January 1999 by the Minister of Justice. Contrary to the Hoexter recommendations, the court was located at Regional Magistrate's Court level. At the launch, the Pilot Project was presented as a Family Court Centre, with the incorporation of a Divorce Court into an existing structure comprising the Maintenance Court, Children's Court, Family Violence Court and inquiries in terms of the *Mental Health Act*. These last four components were already physically grouped together within a Magistrate's Court building, but had never functioned as one composite unit. The Ministry of Justice claimed that the Family Court Centre would 'bring under one umbrella all matters relating to the Family to be dealt with by the judiciary'.[19] The Mayor of Cape Town promised at the launch that the Centre would offer the public free counselling in divorce matters.[20]

In contrast, the Family Court in Port Elizabeth was officially launched some 17 months later. The first summons for the Divorce Court was issued in Port Elizabeth in September 1999. Prior to this date, the Southern Divorce Court had

[18] C Loots, Department of Justice, Family Court Pilot Project, p 1.

[19] Ministry of Justice, 'The official launch of South Africa's first Family Court Centre in Cape Town', handout.

[20] Motshidisi Mokwena, 'Family Court a Unique Forum for Matters of Kin', *Cape Times*, 1 Feb 1999.

continued to sit in Port Elizabeth as part of its circuit sittings. Unlike in Cape Town, the Family Court is not located in one single venue and its various components are housed in two adjacent buildings. The Divorce Court and the Children's Court share one building, whilst the other physical components of the Family Court are alongside, separated from the first by a mechanics garage. This second building houses the court dealing with family violence interdicts and the Maintenance Court.

An indication of the ad hoc nature of the Pilot Projects is that there appears to be uncertainty as to the exact relationship between the old Southern Divorce Court and the Divorce Court of the Port Elizabeth Family Court Pilot Project. Interviews have indicated that the new Divorce Court is regarded by some attorneys and officials as a mere extension of the Southern Divorce Court, rather than as a component of an—albeit temporary—new creation, the Pilot Project Family Court. The lack of an official launch of the Pilot Project fuelled this confusion. It is further compounded by (or perhaps is a result of) the fact that the Presiding Officer of this new Divorce Court is also the president of the Southern Divorce Court and was known in that capacity by the legal fraternity prior to the Pilot Project's establishment. Moreover, the public perception in Port Elizabeth is reinforced by the Presiding Officer's understanding of his own role. He regards himself as fulfilling the role of a circuit officer of the Southern Divorce Court who has offered his services to the Pilot Project in that capacity in order to satisfy the requirement that divorces can be granted by a magistrate only at Regional Court level.[21] In contrast, although the Presiding Officers of both the Cape Town and Port Elizabeth Pilot Projects are appointed to the Southern Divorce Court, the Cape Town Presiding Officer had no prior association with that court and consequently there is no confusion regarding the role she is fulfilling.

THE PILOT PROJECTS' FACILITIES

In light of the fact that both Pilot Projects are intended to serve the same purpose—providing an affordable and family-friendly service to the public—it is difficult to ignore the glaring disparity that initially existed between the two in regard to their respective facilities.

Despite the components all being housed in one building, the Cape Town Family Court Centre does not correspond with the composite image projected at the launch, or any of the earlier recommendations. Central to both Commissions' vision had been the need to treat families in an unfragmented way.[22] The linkage of the various components of the Centre via a central reception area was regarded as vital. This has not occurred, and the various courts dealing with family-related matters continue to operate as isolated entities. More crucially, no infrastructure

[21] Interview with Port Elizabeth Presiding Officer, 28 Feb 2000.

[22] Hoexter, 1997, n 8, para 8.2, p 112; and Hoexter, 1983, n 3, para 7.1.2, p 487.

for the formal sharing of information between the components has been established, nor is there provision for the sharing of the services of social workers and other support structures, to enable families' problems to be understood holistically.

The Commission also emphasised the need for the court to be user-friendly. It was recommended that special attention be given to the layout of the court and that it should contain comfortable waiting rooms, enough conference rooms and ample child-care facilities.[23] This view had been further endorsed by the National Task Team, who promised in their vision statement that the family court structure would provide 'quality service in a pleasant user-friendly environment.'[24] This proposed user-friendliness has failed to materialise. Extremely cramped accommodation was initially allocated to the Cape Town Pilot Project, to the extent that babies crawled among those queuing in the passages and mothers were forced to change their children's nappies on the floor.

In contrast to the Cape Town Family Court, the Port Elizabeth Pilot Project was allocated spacious accommodation from its commencement, thereby enabling it to offer a service more akin to the proposed vision of the Hoexter Commission. There the Family Court contains adequate waiting facilities, conference rooms and a room to accommodate mothers and babies. Whilst there is no central reception area in the Family Court linking all four components, the Divorce Court and Children's Court enjoy shared reception facilities, as do the Family Violence and Maintenance Courts.

The initial obvious inconsistency between the physical attributes of the respective Family Courts, and in particular the Divorce Court components, has impacted on the quality of service that could be offered to the public by the respective centres. As discussed below, it is only recently that the Divorce Court of the Cape Town Pilot Project has managed to secure more appropriate accommodation.

THE PILOT PROJECT DIVORCE COURT FINANCES

Critical to the success of any new initiative is that it be sufficiently funded. Although both Eastern and Western Cape Pilot Projects were set up without budgets for the running of the Pilot Project Divorce Courts, as a result of other circumstances there has not been a uniform approach to the financing of the Pilot Projects. The contrast between the financial backing given to the Cape Town and Port Elizabeth Projects has resulted in very different outcomes to those hypothesised when this study began.

In Cape Town, as a result of the lack of budget, the Presiding Officer and Registrar were seconded temporarily from their posts elsewhere in the Department

[23] Hoexter, 1997, n 8, para 9.14, p 136; and Hoexter, 1983, n 3, para 9.11, p 529.
[24] Loots, n 16.

of Justice, and clerks were paid on a monthly basis from ad hoc funds. Equipment was sorely lacking. Initially there were no computers or even typewriters, and the Presiding Officer's administrative and secretarial work had to be done by the Chief Magistrate's secretary in a neighbouring building. Altogether, it provides an interesting example of how to set up a new state court with no budget whatsoever. At the outset, the court was not even authorised to type its own orders, but as from the beginning of 2000 this changed and one computer was allocated for this purpose. The faxing and photocopying of documents still had to be dealt with outside the Divorce Court section, and basic stationery necessities required by the officials (such as pens) were not supplied. Court files had to be begged from the Magistrate's Court and only one official rubber stamp—essential to validate most documents—was provided for use by all the staff, causing considerable delays. Budgets for the courts were finally allocated in June 2000, marking the end of the initial phase of the Pilot Project Divorce Courts' lives.

The situation in Port Elizabeth has been very different. Although a budget has now been allocated, the Family Divorce Court Pilot Project initially utilised the Southern Divorce Court budget and furniture, and office equipment—including computers—for the Divorce Court were inherited from the Industrial Court. The Divorce Court shares the use of a photocopier with the adjacent Children's Court component and enjoys access to a facsimile machine, albeit in the Department of Justice situated several city blocks away. This disparity between the two pilot projects in budgetary allocation has been a further factor influencing the quality of service that the respective courts have been able to provide to the public. It has also been a major factor in producing a service situation the exact reverse of what we expected to find when contrasting the courts in the two provinces.

PILOT PROJECT DIVORCE COURTS' ACCOMMODATION AND PROCEEDINGS

As our research focused on the Divorce Courts of the Family Courts, what follows is a description of the situation of these sections in the Cape Town and Port Elizabeth Pilot Projects respectively. In Cape Town, the Hoexter recommendations were totally ignored in the initial allocation of the Divorce Court premises. For more than a year, the divorce court component consisted merely of a small court, three cramped offices for the two Clerks and Registrar respectively, the Presiding Officer's office, and one other room which was used to house the Help Desk, comprising two tables staffed by volunteers to assist the public in filling in the form required to initiate a divorce action.[25] There were—and still are—no partitions in the room used by the volunteers staffing the Help Desk, with the result that there is a lack of privacy. No waiting rooms existed for the Divorce Court or its Help

[25] S Burman and L Swanepoel, 'Seeking the Friendly Face of Justice: Community Assistance in the Family Court', *Social Work/Maatskaplike Werk* (forthcoming, 2000).

Desk, resulting in the narrow corridors serving as makeshift waiting rooms, with consequent chaotic queues and arguments.[26]

From mid-1999 the Divorce Court staff were involved in negotiations to move to larger premises on the lower floor of the building. The process was hindered by logistical and political obstacles, resulting in the allocation of rooms occurring in piece-meal fashion. It was only in March of this year that the months of negotiation bore fruit. With telephone lines finally laid, the entire complement of staff have been able to join the Help Desk and relocate to more appropriate rooms in what were the quarters of the Master of the Court.

Quite the reverse situation existed in Port Elizabeth where, from the outset, the divorce court component enjoyed most generous accommodation. It consists of a vast courtroom, a second room which can be used as another courtroom, a large office for the Presiding Officer, two additional, smaller consulting offices, and an airy, open-plan office for the Clerk. This last area, which doubles as office space and a reception area, is furnished with comfortable armchairs—inherited from the Industrial Court, as is the rest of the furniture in the divorce component. There is currently no Help Desk operating, but should one be established in the future, there is ample space. A Help Desk is, however, unlikely to come into existence as the Presiding Officer is adamant that the rules of the court relating to indemnity for ill-given advice do not make provision for the court to employ non-legal persons in such a capacity.[27]

An adequate courtroom is important to any court structure. Not only should it be able to accommodate all those requiring it, but it should also be able to sustain an air of dignity. The allocation of courtrooms to the Cape Town and Port Elizabeth Divorce Courts respectively existed in sharp contrast to each other.

Since its inception there has been a growing public demand for the services of the Cape Town Divorce Court, with the courtroom subsequently proving to be totally inadequate. When a larger court downstairs was not available, the original small court had to be used. This court could accommodate a limited number of people and the remainder were forced to wait outside in the corridors; they could enter only when their matter was called. During the period of monitoring, this was the only court available for use and the Clerk's work in the court was constantly interrupted by the need to manage those outside the courtroom. The fact that the courtroom door was continually opened resulted in the corridor hubbub disturbing the case being heard. The incessant flow of people also impacted on the atmosphere in the court, disrupting the proceedings and detracting from the air of dignity befitting the importance of the matters being heard. Monitoring revealed that attorneys tended to add to the disruptions by, for example, consulting with their clients while court was in session, until the Presiding Officer publicly enforced the formality of the court.

[26] Initially the Help Desk was located on the same floor as the other Divorce component offices, but was later relocated downstairs. Despite the new venue, there is still no waiting room for the clients and corridors continue to be used for this purpose.

[27] Interview, n 21.

Noise was a constant problem in this courtroom, not only from the number of people inside and outside the court, but in addition from the persistent background roar of traffic in the street below. This was both irritating and impacted on the quality of the tape-recording of the proceedings. The only way to alleviate the disturbance from the traffic was to close the windows, which made the room unbearably stuffy and hot. In response to this, and after many months of investigation, an alternative courtroom was found on the ground floor of the building, which is large enough to accommodate everyone needing it. Initially, however, the availability of this courtroom was not guaranteed, and permission had to be sought in advance for its use. Since January 2000, this has been rectified.

None of these difficulties was encountered in Port Elizabeth. There is ample waiting space in the Divorce component and the courtroom is large enough in any event to accommodate everyone. There is no need to open the courtroom windows as the courtroom is effectively air-conditioned. It backs on to a fairly quiet road and there is minimal disturbance from traffic.

The Presiding Officers in both courts attempt to ensure that the proceedings run as smoothly and professionally as possible, taking care to create an atmosphere that is more relaxed than that in the High Court. They both strive to maintain a sense of order, while retaining an equilibrium between formality and informality in court procedures. Neither officer waives the fundamental rules of court procedure, but each is willing to allow a degree of flexibility so long as compliance with technical requirements is achieved. In Cape Town, the Presiding Officer is particularly sympathetic to unrepresented clients and, for example will stand cases down to allow a plaintiff to procure copies of the return of service should they be without the originals when called to give evidence. In addition, the Cape Town Presiding Officer assists witnesses by posing pivotal questions that circumvent lengthy explanations. When a translator is used, the Presiding Officer is more tolerant than the Presiding Officers in the earlier Southern Divorce Court research were found to be, and allows clients to elaborate on the grounds for divorce in a way that is appropriate to their culture.[28] She further takes the necessary time to explain difficult concepts and to satisfy herself that the parties have fully understood the nature of the court order, especially where parties are unrepresented. The Port Elizabeth Presiding Officer poses standard, similar questions to all clients, whether represented or not. He places particular emphasis on the binding nature of the oath and challenges parties on their endeavours at reconciliation.

SUPPORT SERVICES: COUNSELLING, MEDIATION AND FAMILY ADVOCATE SERVICES

Underpinning the Hoexter recommendations was an emphasis on counselling and mediation support services. The proposed Family Counselling Service would

[28] Burman, n 6.

discharge three main functions: first, a 'reception process' would be offered at the reception centre of the Family Court; second, there would be a conciliation process, the aim of which would be to facilitate communication between estranged spouses in order to ease the trauma of parting; and third, there would be a supporting service that would ensure that any further social welfare investigations would be undertaken speedily.[29]

The chairman of the Family Court Task Team further emphasised this sentiment at a workshop convened on 9 December 1998, where she expressed the Task Team's belief that backup services were vital if a family were to continue operating as a unit in their changed circumstances. Included in the team's vision statement is the recognition of the need for counselling and mediation support services.[30]

Despite this emphasis on the provision of conciliatory and support services, neither Pilot Project Divorce Court has attained this goal. The Cape Town Divorce Court was not allocated rooms to house the envisaged bodies and, although it is served by a Help Desk, the support and services offered here are very limited. Volunteers staffing the Desk are not required to hold any professional qualifications, and their function is purely to assist clients in completing the necessary court forms. The Port Elizabeth Family Court has elicited some involvement of non-governmental organisations, and whilst the Family Violence section has allocated a room for the Family and Marriage Society of South Africa (FAMSA) and the National Institute for Crime Prevention and Re-integration of Offenders (NICRO), there is no evidence of their presence in the Divorce section.

There is no formal mandate for the Presiding Officers of the Pilot Project Divorce Courts to liaise with the Family Advocate's Office. Unlike divorces in the High Court, the *Mediation in Certain Divorce Matters Act*[31] does not extend the Office's obligations to involvement in the Pilot Project Divorce Courts and, consequently, any involvement with the Family Advocate's Office has to be secured on an informal basis. The Presiding Officers of both the Cape Town and the Port Elizabeth Divorce Courts have done just this. The Presiding Officer in Cape Town encourages all clients with minor children to complete the necessary documents that will ensure that their matter passes through the Family Advocate's Office. In the majority of cases, full investigations are not required. Any concerns regarding access or custody which are communicated by the Office are clarified by the Presiding Officer in her questioning of the parties in court. In terms of a new arrangement with the Family Advocate's Office, as from March 2000 a Family Advocate attends court sittings once a week, in order to give any necessary input.

The Port Elizabeth Presiding Officer has adopted an alternative method. He does not encourage parties to complete the necessary documents to re-route their matter via the Family Advocate's Office. Instead, he chooses to postpone prob-

[29] Hoexter, 1997, n 8, para 9.11, p 132.
[30] Loots, n 16, p 1.
[31] Act 24 of 1987.

lematic matters involving minor children to a specific day of the week to enable the Family Advocate to liaise with the family on that day. On the basis of the Family Advocate's subsequent recommendation, the Presiding Officer will then determine whether the matter requires further investigation by the Family Advocate's Office.

THE PILOT PROJECT DIVORCE COURT'S JURISDICTION

The Pilot Projects Divorce Court's jurisdiction is governed by the enabling statute, which simply prescribes in general terms that jurisdiction pertains to law suits relating to divorce and the nullity of marriage.[32] The Rules of Court state that applications may be brought by way of notice of motion, but they do not elaborate on what applications will be entertained.[33] This is thus largely dependent on the individual Presiding Officer's interpretation of the rules. As the courts are so new, there is a lack of clarity as to whether applications to vary High Court orders fall within their ambit, and the final parameters may need to be tested in higher courts around the country. According to interview data, in the Western Cape there is additional confusion amongst the legal fraternity as to what set of rules is to apply to these Pilot Projects—which, by their very nature, are temporary.

Although the National Task Team did not address the question of the Pilot Projects going on circuit, both Hoexter Commissions originally recommended that rural areas be served by these courts in such a manner.[34] The Presiding Officers of both the Port Elizabeth and Cape Town Pilot Project Divorce Courts do take the court on circuit in their capacity as Officers of the Southern Divorce Court. The Port Elizabeth Presiding Officer covers the large area that includes Kroonstad, Welkom, Bethlehem, Bloemfontein, Kimberley, Queenstown, Umtata, East London and King William's Town. It was arranged that the Cape Town Presiding Officer would go on circuit to nearby Mitchell's Plain once a month, and also cover the far-flung towns of Vredendal, Worcester, Swellendam and George more infrequently. It has to date been on circuit twice to these venues. As the court originally had no budget of its own, transport, accommodation and subsistence expenses had to be obtained from the Regional Office of the Department of Justice. A further circuit is planned for later in the year.

As things stand, the Pilot Project Divorce Courts operate at magisterial Regional Court level. This is in sharp contrast to the 1997 Hoexter Commission's views, mirroring the earlier Commission's recommendations.[35] The 1997 Commission felt strongly that the Family Court should not be located at Magistrate's Court level but should be an entirely independent Superior Court. This view was premised on the fact that a court at a lower level would not enjoy a positive public

[32] S 1(a) *Administration Amendment Act* 9 of 1929 as amended.

[33] The short title of the rules is *Divorce Courts Rules, 1998.*

[33] Hoexter, 1997, n 8, para 9.3, p 130; and Hoexter, 1983, n 3, para 9.13, p 530.

[35] Hoexter, 1983, n 3, para 9.1, p 521.

image and would not 'gain the confidence of the ordinary man and woman in the street'[36]—a result of the Magistrates' Courts being commonly associated with criminal matters. The Cape Town Family Court Centre is in fact situated on the same floor as the Regional Magistrate's Courts in which criminal matters are heard and sometimes prisoners in leg-irons share the corridors with the Divorce Court's clients. This does not appear to have kept the public away, however, little as they like it. Our observations of the Cape Town Divorce Court revealed that it is much in demand and is being used extensively. This is evidenced by the length of its court rolls. The number of matters set down on any given week averages about 200.

In contrast, the Pilot Project Divorce Court in Port Elizabeth shares a building with only the Children's Court. The user-friendly atmosphere is thus not marred by the presence of prisoners. However, the demand for the Divorce Court's services is at present in its infancy due both to the fact that it only began operations at the very end of 1999 and that it currently sits approximately two weeks in every month. In addition, many do not know of its existence, as its services have not been actively advertised to the public at large. The court roll in the Port Elizabeth Divorce Court is therefore considerably shorter, tending towards an average of 20 to 25 matters per session. In light of the Cape Town Court's popularity, it seems possible that there may in the future be increased usage of the Port Elizabeth Court as more people become aware of its existence.

Represented and unrepresented clients alike frequent the Cape Town Court, with the former being represented by a variety of firms. Of the 1137 finalised cases monitored in Cape Town over a period of six months shortly after it was initiated, 45.3 per cent had legal representation, with the remainder unrepresented.[37] The court's clients hail from a range of socio-economic and cultural backgrounds. It is too early to be able to contrast this with the clientele in Port Elizabeth.

CONTRASTING THE PILOT PROJECTS WITH THE COURTS THEY REPLACED

The Family Court Pilot Project has been slotted into the framework of the Southern Divorce Court. In both Port Elizabeth and Cape Town, the Divorce Court component is still named the Southern Divorce Court and there continues to be confusion regarding the relationship between the two courts in Port Elizabeth, as discussed above. It must thus be asked in what ways these Divorce Courts differ from the earlier version of that court.

Established in the early 1900s, the Southern Divorce Court operated throughout the apartheid years. Certain difficulties associated with the operation of the court were peculiar to the prevailing political system, and were consequently

[36] Hoexter, 1997, n 8, para 8.7.5, p 119.
[37] From Mar to Aug 1999.

alleviated with the demise of apartheid.[38] Other problems which were identified at the time of research in the early 1980s were not directly related to the political system, however, and it is interesting to note the degree to which they have been alleviated, persist or possibly have even worsened.

Certain problems seem to have been alleviated to varying degrees in the new Divorce Courts. One such difficulty relates to the use of junior attorneys in the court. Earlier Southern Divorce Court research showed that firms tended to allocate the courtroom work to their junior members, who were often not well versed in the relevant regulations or law.[39] This trend is less prominent in the new Divorce Courts, where attorneys with a range of experience appear.

Second, the Presiding Officer of the earlier Southern Divorce Court bore the burden of ensuring that the best possible arrangements were made for the children of the marriage after the divorce.[40] The Presiding Officers of the Pilot Project Divorce Courts labour under a similar burden. They do, however—as shown above—have the safety net of the Family Advocate's Office to fall back on. In Cape Town, should the parties choose to complete the requisite documents, the Presiding Officer pays heed to any observations and comments that may emanate from the Family Advocate's Office.[41] She is guided in her questioning of the parties in court by such feedback. Should the Port Elizabeth Presiding Officer doubt whether the best interests of the child will be served by the requested arrangements, he may postpone the matter and subject the proposed arrangements to the Family Advocate's opinion.

The use of interpreters in the earlier Southern Divorce Court was problematic in many ways. As the court officials frequently spoke no South African indigenous languages, and the assistance of an interpreter was constantly required, the interpreters were in a position of considerable power.[42]

However, with the Divorce Court now open to all races, considerably less use is made of interpreters, as black clients are only a small minority.[43] In the Cape Town Court, of the matters monitored, only 5.3 per cent of the clients required that court proceedings be translated. The Presiding Officers of both Divorce Courts are fluent in English and Afrikaans but, as with the earlier Southern Divorce Court Presiding Officers, require the assistance of an interpreter for the other official languages. In Cape Town, the Xhosa-speaking Clerk of the Divorce Court provides this service, as earlier use of the Magistrate's Court interpreters proved problematic. This situation is not ideal, as the various clerks sit in court on a rotation basis. Should the need for an interpreter arise when the Xhosa-speaking Clerk is not in court, he has to leave whatever he is doing elsewhere and assist the court. In an attempt to minimise the possibility of misinterpretations

[38] For a detailed critique of these problems, see Burman, n 6.

[39] *Ibid.*

[40] *Ibid.*, p 181.

[41] Reg 2 of the Mediation in Certain Divorce Matters Regulations, 1990.

[42] Burman, n 6, at pp 175 and 182.

[43] 11.7% of the Cape Town Court clients were black people.

and place a check on the inherent control an interpreter has on proceedings, the Presiding Officer questions the interpreter should she feel that there is a disparity in length between the evidence of the witness and the translation.

In the Port Elizabeth Court, an interpreter has been assigned to the Divorce/Children's Court section of the Family Court. In the Divorce Court, the interpreter is present throughout the court sessions, both assisting with interpretation when required and performing the functions of clerk of the court. The Presiding Officer is able to evaluate the translation a little for accuracy from his limited knowledge of Xhosa. In both courts, the inherent problems associated with interpretation persist, such as the difficulty of translating nuances and the need at times to rephrase questions in order for the plaintiff to comprehend their meaning fully.

The earlier Southern Divorce Court would grant spousal or child maintenance orders only if the request was embodied in a consent paper.[44] This difficulty has been eradicated in the both the Cape Town and the Port Elizabeth Divorce Courts, where orders for spousal and/or child maintenance tend to be granted when requested in the summons.

Certain operational obstacles existed in the running of the earlier Southern Divorce Court, and many of these appear to have persisted in the new Divorce Courts. One such obstacle is that of time pressure. As a consequence of its circuit nature, the earlier Southern Divorce Court sat for only a limited number of days in each town. It thus worked under constant time pressure in an endeavour to get through all the matters that had been set down for that session. Both Pilot Project Divorce Courts sit permanently in Cape Town and Port Elizabeth respectively. The Cape Town Presiding Officer is still nonetheless under time pressure, but this is now due to great public demand, which has resulted in the court roll substantially increasing in length.[45]

The Presiding Officer of the Port Elizabeth Pilot Project Divorce Court sits two weeks every month in Port Elizabeth, undertaking a circuit for the Southern Divorce Court for the remaining two weeks. Although the demand for the services of the Pilot Project Divorce Court is as yet not great, should demand increase substantially, the Presiding Officer would be under pressure to accommodate Port Elizabeth clients in between his Southern Divorce Court circuit schedule.

A further problem of the earlier Southern Divorce Court was that of delays. Again as a result of its circuit nature, its clients experienced long delays in obtaining a court date, as they were able to set matters down for only the next visit of the court, sometimes several months off. Clients of the Pilot Project Divorce Courts may also be burdened by delays, but these result from other factors. With both the Cape Town and Port Elizabeth Pilot Projects, clients still have the option

[44] Burman, n 6, at p 176.

[45] From the period mid-1981 to mid-1982, 195 divorces were granted in the Cape Town Southern Divorce Court (see Burman. n 6, at p 172), compared with 640 cases finalised in the first six months of the Pilot Project Divorce Court in 1999 and 2680 matters finalised in the first six months of 2000.

of initiating their divorce via the Registrar in King William's Town (the seat of the Southern Divorce Court). Should this route be chosen, long delays may result due to the posting of the file between the respective town and King William's Town. A further delay of up to four months may occur in procuring the court order once the matter has been heard in court. Both Pilot Projects may thus have two court rolls for any particular session of court—one that they have drawn up from the summonses issued by themselves and one posted from King William's Town.

Should the summons be issued out of either Port Elizabeth or Cape Town, in the most favourable circumstances one can be pronounced divorced within a week of initiating the process. Both Pilot Project Divorce Courts are now empowered to type their own orders. In the case of Cape Town, this is a recent innovation. Prior to January of this year, the files of all matters—whether initiated locally or in King William's Town—had to be returned to King William's Town and the court order typed and sent from there. In the case of urgent orders, the Registrar could provide written confirmation that a divorce had in fact been granted. A strong demand for the Cape Town Court has recently placed considerable pressure on the staff of the court. Although a member of staff was hired specifically for the purpose of typing orders, her time is usurped largely by members of the public seeking assistance, and the court is thus behind in its typing of orders and has a five-month backlog of orders. In contrast, the Clerk of the Port Elizabeth Divorce Court (who serves also as the Registrar) is not under pressure to assist the public and is subsequently able to produce the orders within two days of the matter being finalised.

The application of customary law in divorce matters is a further continuing difficulty. Based on principles of family organisation that differ from those of the civil law, customary law can give rise to expectations incompatible with civil law principles. This came to the fore in research on the earlier Southern Divorce Court in custody and child maintenance issues, as the customary payment of *lobola* (bride wealth) transfers the child into the husband's family.[46] As with the Southern Divorce Court, the Pilot Project Divorce Courts apply civil divorce law, and so—theoretically—might encounter similar expectations generated by incompatible customary law. As monitoring of the Cape Town Court has illustrated, however, few black people have been making use of the court to date and it is not yet possible to assess the extent of this problem.[47] Similarly, in Port Elizabeth it is still too soon to ascertain the degree of use of the court by black people.

Research into the operation of the earlier Southern Divorce Court showed that Presiding Officers made only minimal enquiries into *actual* arrangements for the children post-divorce, such as the age of the person caring for them.[48] Although research has shown that the child's caregiver is often a child herself, or an elderly relative, this is frequently not brought to light in court in either the Cape Town

[46] Burman, n 6, at p 179.
[47] See n 40.
[48] Burman, n 6, at p 185.

or Port Elizabeth Pilot Project Divorce Courts, where only standard questions are posed in this regard.[49] The Cape Town Presiding Officer has made it clear that she elects, rather, to take judicial notice of the de facto socio-economic situation that exists in the country at present, which makes more desirable solutions impossible.

A final difficulty identified in the Southern Divorce Court that persists in the two Pilot Project Divorce Courts relates to the Clerk's responsibilities. In both the earlier court and the present two Pilot Project Courts, it is the Clerk who interacts most with the public, briefing the parties on court procedures. Clients are thus subject to the Clerk's time constraints and he/she carries the responsibility of ensuring that the public is adequately informed.[50] This is a heavy responsibility, especially in a court where it is expected that a high proportion of clients will be unrepresented and either semi-literate or from backgrounds that make the courts especially daunting.

However, research to date has revealed that only one of the problems encountered in the earlier research has definitely worsened in Cape Town. In the Southern Divorce Court in the 1980s, where a matter was defended, legal assistance for an indigenous plaintiff was hard to come by. Legal Aid regulations dictated that aid would not be granted if, inter alia, the applicant had committed adultery or was not considered to be a 'deserving case'.[51] Since then, far from improving in Cape Town, the Legal Aid Board's selection policy has deteriorated. A directive has been issued from the Legal Aid Board in Cape Town stating that, as from 1 October 1999, the Board is officially no longer offering financial assistance in any divorce matters whatsoever.[52] However, in contrast, the situation in Port Elizabeth has improved since the days of the earlier Southern Divorce Court. The local Legal Aid Board in Port Elizabeth is operating under a directive from the national board in terms of which funds *are* still available for divorces. These must, however, be channelled through the Southern Divorce Court. Consequently, the majority of the cases being heard in the Port Elizabeth Divorce Court are financed by Legal Aid.

CONCLUSION

The current version of the Southern Divorce Court is an improvement on its predecessor. However, merely improving on a highly deficient institution was not the

[49] S Burman, 'Intergenerational Family Care: Legacy of the Past, Implications for the Future' (1996) 22 *Journal of Southern African Studies* 585; S Burman, 'Law Versus Reality: The Interaction of Community Obligations to and by the Black Elderly in South Africa', in J Eekelaar and D Pearl (eds), *An Ageing World: Dilemmas and Challenges for Law and Social Policy* (1989), p 220; Sandra Burman, 'Child Care by the Elderly and the Duty of Support in Multigenerational Households' (1995) 4 *Southern African Journal of Gerontology* 13.

[50] Burman, n 6, at p 174.

[51] *Ibid.*

[52] Confirmed telephonically with Legal Aid Board officials on 7 Oct 1999 and 4 Nov 1999.

aim of any of the Family Court's progenitors. To evaluate the court at the end of this first stage of its existence, with budgets at last guaranteed, it is necessary to measure it against the blueprints that were formulated by the Hoexter Commission and the Ministry of Justice Task Team, and in those terms it is hardly recognisable.

The solution does not lie in simply remedying the inadequacies of the Divorce component, highlighted above, but in obtaining sufficient resources to upgrade and integrate all the components of the existing Family Court Centre in accord with the Hoexter recommendations. In the light of South Africa's current budgetary restrictions, this will be a major undertaking. At present, neither of the existing Family Court Centres we studied bears much resemblance to the blueprint, lacking most notably the essential common electronic database, integrated social work component and counselling services. What actually exists are the original components unchanged, except that the two new Pilot Project Divorce Courts are operating under a new name and in the institutional shell of a pre-existing circuit court. What is surprising is that the Cape Town court has taken on a life of its own and is proving more successful than could have been hoped, given the lack of funding, facilities and the public perception of the Southern Divorce Court prior to deracialisation as offering inferior justice. The Pilot Project Court has heard a far greater number of divorces than anticipated: it is clearly replacing the High Court as a forum for most divorces.[53] But, despite all obstacles, matters are handled efficiently and promptly and many of the Divorce Court's shortcomings, mentioned above, are countered by the notable commitment of the staff, who are prepared to put in many extra hours. Although the lower tariff may have contributed to its popularity, interview evidence in Cape Town indicates that it is not in fact necessarily proving cheaper for represented clients, as many attorneys are charging the same rates for their services in the Pilot Project Court as in the High Court. The success of the Cape Town Pilot Project Divorce Court is mainly attributable to the dedication of the staff, particularly that of the Presiding Officer. In Port Elizabeth, whilst the staff are both helpful and approachable, due to the superiority of the court's infrastructure the success of its operation is not as dependent upon the staff's input.

There is a danger, however, that the surprising success of the Divorce sections of the respective courts may result in the Family Court Centres being made permanent within their existing frameworks. The need to pass national legislation establishing Family Courts as envisaged by the Hoexter Commission may consequently be overlooked and the statute may never be passed. The vision of a family's matters being dealt with all together, under one roof by one social worker, will continue to go unrealised. The waste of time and duplication of work and human

[53] Prior to the Family Court, approximately 66% of the High Court's civil summonses were in respect of divorces but the figure has dropped to between 25 and 35%. A comparison of actual numbers of divorce summonses shows that the Pilot Project Divorce Court is now issuing approximately three times as many as the High Court: telephonic interview with the Registrar, Cape Town Pilot Project Divorce Court, 26 July 2000.

resources associated with the present structure will continue, exacerbating the emotional stress of families. A Family Court should exist both to minimise the trauma experienced by the family and to assist it to continue to function as effectively as possible in its altered form. In order to achieve this, family matters should be dealt with in a holistic manner, relevant information about the family should be electronically accessible to all components of the Family Court, and specific social workers should be allocated to families for the duration of their use of the court. This is the vision encapsulated by the Hoexter Commission as inspired by international examples. It is fervently to be hoped that the present inchoate South African Family Court will, against all the budgetary odds, emerge from its current misleading political window-dressing to achieve some approximation to its ideal.

7

Establishing Paternity in Judicial Proceedings in Spain: What Protection For Human Rights?

Encarna Roca and Isabel Miralles*

INTRODUCTION

Parental responsibility provides for the protection of under-age children in contemporary society. The law must establish a system which links adult and child in order to protect the child by giving the adult a number of legal obligations relating to the child. In our society, parenthood is a tool which provides this protection in the context of the family.

Marriage has been, and still is, the traditional and most common legal system for establishing paternity. According to this, the man married to the woman who has given birth is the legal father of the child. But, after the 1978 Constitution, Spain introduced a new possibility: biological parenthood can be established in order to protect children's human rights—among them the right to know their origin, and that due protection has been carried out by the real father. Conclusively, legal parenthood must legally coincide with biological parenthood; if it does not coincide, actions to sue for the determination of biological parenthood are foreseen by the law.

According to the 1978 Spanish Constitution, children have the right to sue the man they think could be their biological father, in order to establish legal parenthood by means of an action called *paternity research.* Consequently, Spanish law—both the Civil Code and the Catalan Family Code 1998—allows the use of blood tests in order to obtain definitive proof of a biological link. But an action like this will necessarily affect the human rights of the people involved. The right of children to be protected and the right of the parenthood coinciding with biological reality can be in opposition to the privacy of the sued adult. In many such cases dealt with by the Spanish Constitutional Court, the court has concluded that the

* Encarna Roca is Professor of Civil Law, Barcelona University. Isabel Miralles is a Reader of Civil Law, Barcelona University.

right of the child is paramount and must be protected, despite other rights being involved.

This chapter discusses the problems which can arise when several human rights are at stake in parenthood processes, and will discuss the solutions afforded by the Spanish courts and by the Spanish Constitutional Court.

THE FUNCTIONALITY OF THE FAMILY IN THE RULES ESTABLISHED IN THE 1978 SPANISH CONSTITUTION

After the coming into force of the Spanish Constitution in 1978, a number of civil laws changed. This occurred, firstly, through the application of the equality principle, contained in Article 14 of the Spanish Constitution and repeated—referring to filiation—in Article 39.2. Secondly, changes took place through the recognition of legislative powers to some autonomous communities in certain civil subjects. Here we will study only the Civil Code, even though there are the same or similar problems in the Catalan and Navarrese laws.[1]

The protection of the family is a constitutional demand. Article 39 of the Spanish Constitution establishes:

1. Public authorities guarantee the social and economic protection of the family.
2. Public authorities also guarantee a complete protection for children—these being equal before the law independent of their status—and for mothers whatever their marital status may be. The Law will facilitate research into paternity.
3. Parents must give all types of assistance to children born inside or outside marriage, during their minority and other appropriate cases in accordance with the law.

Reading this provision, it can be inferred that family law rules are a system of support for citizens' necessities. Effectively, Spanish constitutional law relating to the family develops what has been called a *mixed system*,[2] in which the way of protecting the family group members' interests is shared: private individuals must provide the group members with the constitutionally established assistance, according to Article 39.2 of the Spanish Constitution, and public authorities must give a double assistance: first, by primary assistance systems; and secondly, by acting in those cases in which private protecting systems are ineffective.

It is important to emphasise several basic premises:

- —According to Article 1 of the Spanish Constitution, Spain is set as a social and democratic state of law. This point is basic in order to interpret the so-called mixed system.

[1] There are two autonomous communities with a complete regulation of their own in the matter of parentage: Catalonia, where it is applied the Family Code (Act from the Catalan Parliament 9/1998, of 15 July, Arts 87–131) and Navarre, through the Special Civil Law Compilation, Arts 70–72.

[2] Encarna Roca, *Familia y cambio social (De la 'casa' a la persona)* (Editorial Civitas, 1999), p 68.

—As a consequence of what is said, public authorities must give full assistance to the family (Article 39 of the Spanish Constitution).
—The Spanish legal system is based on the protection of citizens' fundamental rights.

From this it follows that there is a need, on the one hand, to identify the purposes of family protection and, on the other, for distributing functions between public authorities and private individuals. The family is a private system which complements the public authorities regarding dispensation of services; it is not only about public authorities operating when private individuals do not act or when they act wrongly, but about both of them acting together in distributing each action field.[3] In this way:

—It is a concern of the public authorities to establish a system allowing citizens to have full possession of their fundamental rights and to have their social rights implemented. For this reason, the duty of the public authorities is organising systems of education, health, welfare, and so on.
—It is a concern of private individuals to give certain services of assistance within the limits of the family group, with the object of providing the group members with effective possession of their fundamental rights, according to the solidarity principle. This area concerns issues of parental responsibility, maintenance, alimony and maintenance for children under age in cases of separation and divorce.

Family law becomes an instrument to serve the individual. That is why family law rules cannot be considered as elements affecting private individuals' exclusive interests, as they have an important public nature.[4]

Public authorities assume that the protection of the family group lies in the fulfilment of social functions by the same group and they also assume that protection is due as far as it allows the respective individuals who make up the family group to achieve satisfaction of their rights. Legal rules on family are justified because they guarantee the fundamental rights of every individual making up the family. The basis for this line of argument arises from the state of law concept.

The Spanish Constitution does not place the family group in a powerful position before its individual members: the powers that it has legally recognised are structured to allow the efficiency of its members' rights. That is inferred from Article 32 of the Spanish Constitution, which bases marital relationships on the equality of rights and duties of the spouses, and from Article 14 of the Spanish Constitution, which establishes individuals' equality independent of their birth

[3] This thesis has long been accepted in the Italian doctrine. See Caferra, *Famiglia e assistenza. Il diritto della famiglia nel sistema della sicurezza sociale* (Zanichelli, 1984), pp 12ff and Bessone, Alpa, D'Angelo, Ferrando and Spallarossa, *La famiglia nel nuovo diritto* (Zanichelli, 1995), p 34; in the Spanish doctrine, the most interesting contribution is Igualada Ribot, *Alimentos entre parientes y subsidiariedad de la protección social* (Tirant lo Blanch, 1998), pp 69ff.

[4] CCJ 120/84 of 10 Dec states that, in the marriage process, 'some elements are not at one's disposal but of *ius cogens* precisely because of arising from and being an instrument at service of family'.

status. This means that, in those cases where a conflict exists between the family and individual interest, the latter prevails if it is based on the exercise of a fundamental right.

Because of that, a protection system exists for under-age children. Its purpose is to protect and defend against the infringement of the fundamental rights of minors. Therefore, the rights protected through the constitutional technique and identified as belonging to the group of fundamental rights prevail in all cases over a hypothetical family interest. But if the interests at stake do not have a constitutional rank, then priority is given to the family interest. This happens because, in the system based on constitutional rights, the family is an instrument whose essential aim is to supply its members with the exercise of their fundamental rights and the development of values enshrined in Article 10 of the Constitution.[5]

THE MEANING OF PARENTHOOD AND THE MEANING OF THE CONSTITUTIONAL RULES REGULATING PARENTHOOD

Starting from Article 39 of the Spanish Constitution, interaction between private and public sectors—that is, family and public administration—does not seem to present great difficulties. Article 39.3 of the Spanish Constitution, already described, imposes on parents certain duties that make up the characteristic content of so-called parental responsibility, which appears to be conceived as a function rather than a right. Unlike those legal systems which consider that parents have rights, the Spanish system treats parental authority as a function that the parents exercise for the benefit of their children, whether they are under age or legally of age but deprived of legal capacity. In this way, the minor's interest can be regarded not just as a public issue, because the private and public sectors meet at this point. Parents will act as agents to achieve the purposes sought by the law, so that together the private and public sectors will work for the best interests of the minor child.

Consequently, in the approach made by the mixed system we have referred to, those who primarily, and by a constitutional provision, are in charge of the best interests of minors—that is, the achievement of their fundamental rights—are their parents, and the public authorities act in two ways: firstly operating directly, by implementing welfare policies directed to achieve the full effectiveness of minors' rights—as, for example, compulsory schooling or the regulation of the parental responsibility function—and secondly, operating in a subsidiary way—that is, by controlling the correctness of the activities of the parents. Therefore, the family is functionally conceived.

Historically, the family law contained in the Civil Code 1889 seemed to be focused only on the solution of estate problems. However, the already ancient judgment of the Supreme Court of 24 June 1929 brought about a switch in the

[5] Art 10 of the Spanish Constitution says: 'The dignity of the individual, his/her inviolable rights, the free development of personality, the respect for the law and other people's rights are the foundation of public order and social peace.'

idea of parental responsibility.[6] Since then, parental responsibility has been legally conceived in a functional way, so that its purpose is to look after and care for the family interest, having as a feature 'an essential aspect of duty'.[7] This functional character is stressed by the system designed in the 1978 Constitution; in this way, the new Article 154 of the Civil Code[8] establishes that the object of parental responsibility lies in appropriate decision-making in order to aid the development of minors and the achievement of their fundamental rights. In fact, Article 154 provides that:

> Parental responsibility will be exercised always for the benefit of children, in accordance with their personality, and includes the following duties and authorities:
>
> 1st. To watch for over them, keep them company, to feed them, to educate them and to secure them a complete training.
>
> 2nd. To represent them and to administer their assets.

According to this, it can be asserted that the regular channel to assure the protection of a minor's interest is through the family,[9] and more specifically through the protection system legally laid down—in other words, parental responsibility.

THE NORMAL WAY TO ESTABLISH PARENTAL RESPONSIBILITY: PARENTAGE

Starting from this point, it is necessary to establish certain uniform foundations in order to determine who is compelled to exercise the functions of parental responsibility—that is, rules regarding parentage.

Rules to determine parentage are explained here as a legal technique whose essential aim is to provide infant children with a protection system during their minority. Thereby parental responsibility applies to those who are considered parents, according to the attribution of parentage.

Principles that rule the ascription of parentage can be inferred from the Constitution, although it only establishes a basis which was later developed by the Civil Code. There are two principles governing rules to ascribe parentage—and with them, usually, parental responsibility: coincidence between biological and legal truth; and application of the equality principle.

[6] See also the judgments of the Supreme Court of 24 May 1909, 14 Oct 1935, 3 Mar 1950, 26 Nov 1955 and 23 June 1965. The latter said that 'parental responsibility is made up of a whole of authorities and duties for the well-being of the children under age who are not emancipated'.

[7] LaCruz and Sancho Rebullida already regarded parental responsibility as a function, assigned to parents—not at their disposal—as organs for performing a child's care and capacitation: *Derecho de familia* (José M Bosch, 1966), p 439. In the same sense, see Vazquez Castan, *Comentarios al Código civil y Compilaciones forales* (Edersa, 1982), p 73.

[8] In the same way, Art 133 Catalonia Family Code establishes that 'parental responsibility is a necessary function' and that 'it is exercised personally and always for the benefit of children'.

[9] As Flaquer states: 'The slow and belated development of the welfare estate in Spain goes in parallel with the importance of the family as a material support agent and with the strength and persistence of family bonds throughout the life of individuals.'—*El destino de la familia* (Ariel, 1998), p 135.

Biological truth

The unanimous opinion of Spanish authors is that the Spanish Constitution requires biological parentage to coincide with that which is legally determined—therefore, those considered the legal parents are the biological parents.

Rivero,[10] a significant writer on the matter of parentage, considers that there are two legal methods to ascribe parenthood: one he refers to as the *realistic system*, ruled by 'the so-called "truthfulness principle" which, even recognising that legal parentage is not just a simple biological relationship, furnishes legal mechanisms allowing it to be reached'. He calls the second the *formalist system*, which:

> unconcerned about biological truth and reality and sometimes overvaluing other elements or values (family peace, legal certainty) or starting from the difficulty of proving paternity . . . establishes some initial outlines to determine parentage based on unilateral will and in some presumptions, obstructing then the establishment of parental relationship apart from legal schemes.

Certainly, the Spanish Constitution does not specifically support either of these two systems, but it can be inferred that the biological truth principle is the one considered the most preferable by the constitutional legislator. The reason for this derives from the constitutional admission of the paternity research technique that appears with this purpose in Article 39.2.

Effectively, the way in which Article 39.2 of the Spanish Constitution is expressed when it establishes that 'law will facilitate paternity research' implies that it does not amount to a right per se, but it is conceived as an instrument to allow the concerned person to obtain biological and other data in order to establish a parent–child relationship with the biological progenitor. This interpretation is deduced because it is included after imposing on the parents the duty of giving assistance to their children; therefore, to reach this object, paternity research is admitted.

This interpretation has been used in two judgments of the Constitutional Court. Judgment 7/1994 of 17 January considered the protection of duties derived from paternity to be preferable to the protection of the defendant's right to privacy in a case concerning paternity acknowledgment. The Constitutional Court argued that:

> the purpose of the rule that allows biological tests to be carried out is firstly the defence of the child's interests both material and moral; and it is obviously primary that the child has the right to have his/her biological filiation established.[11]

[10] Hernandez Rivero, '*Mater semper certa est?* Problemas de la determinación de la maternidad en el derecho español' (1997) *ADC* 5 at 10.

[11] This judgment has been studied by several authors. From the civil point of view, the most significant observations are Hernandez Rivero, 'Una nueva doctrina sobre la obligación de sometimiento a la prueba biológica en los procesos de filiación (Comentario a la STC 7/194, de 17 de enero)' (1994) 33 *Poder judicial* 349 and Quesada, 'De nuevo sobre las pruebas biológicas. A propósito de la sentencia del Tribunal Constitucional 7/1994, de 17 de enero' (1994) *RJC* 657.

Civil Code judgment 116/1999 of 17 June did not regard as unconstitutional the semen donor's anonymity in cases of artificial insemination, because the court understood that the aim of paternity research was the establishment of a legal link—that is, the parent–child relationship—whereas in the *Assisted Reproduction Techniques Act* (whose objection was that time treated by the Spanish Constitution), the use of this action would not be addressed to this purpose, but to the simple identification of the semen donor. The Constitutional Court said:

> It is as well to remember, as a starting point, that the paternity claim or research action is directed to constitute, between the involved individuals, a legal link including mutual rights and duties, making up the so-called parent–child relationship; therefore, the revelation of the progenitor's identity through the artificial procreation techniques is in no way addressed to the establishment of that legal link, but to a simple identification of the donor of the gametes which have been the origin of progeny. Therefore, the possible claim, with this specific and limited extent, takes a different ambit from that of the investigative action which derives from what Article 39.2, *in fine*, provides.[12]

The Court took a negative position and stated that paternity research was built in a functional way with the sole object of providing the establishment of a parent–child relationship which did not exist until the moment when parentage was ascribed by the judge; if the purpose was another, such as the knowledge of one's own origin, the action existed but it was different. We will discuss this subject again below.

Equality

The second principle that constitutionally governs the matter of parentage is the right to equality. In the Spanish constitutional system, the parentage technique amounts to a way to identify the holders of parental responsibility; it is not a system to identify marital status or a social class. Therefore, the application of any discriminatory rule in accordance with the filiation origin—in wedlock, out of wedlock, adoptive or through assisted reproduction techniques—cannot be inferred. In consequence, Articles 39.2 of the Spanish Constitution and 108 of the Civil Code state that all kinds of filiation produce the same effects.

Establishment of parentage is a right of children that will allow them to require from their parents the fulfilment of the duties that Article 39.3 of the Spanish Constitution impose on them, regardless of whether or not they are married. Therefore, according to these principles, we must examine the ways of ascribing parentage.

[12] This judgment has been studied by Aguila Camara, 'Sobre la constitucionalidad de la Ley de Técnicas de reproducción asistida (Comentario a la STC 116/1999, de 17 de junio)' (1999) 13 *Derecho Privado y Constitución* 117 and Roca 'Embriones, padres y donantes. La constitucionalidad de la ley 35/1988, de reproducción asistida humana, según la STC 116/1999' (2000) *RJC* 89.

Ascription of Motherhood

Until the assisted reproduction techniques started to be regularly used, the determination of motherhood followed a very clear rule: giving birth. Furthermore, this opens the door to ascribe fatherhood when the mother is married.[13] However, this technique is not the only one used by the legal system. The first case is the ignorance of motherhood, foreseen in Article 47.3 LRC.[14] However, the Supreme Court judgment of 21 September 1999 regarded as contrary to the Constitution the rule that allowed the mother to avoid her name being known in the recording of a child's birth, to avoid dishonour when she was not married. The Supreme Court stated the doctrine that had already considered it contrary to public concern in order to protect the minor's interests:

> At present and after the Spanish Constitution 1978 came into force we understand that this restriction, the concealing of clinical documentary proof of the mother's identity, has been repealed because of its obvious opposition to what [the Constitution] establishes . . . To be exact, the system provided by Articles 167, 182 and the concordant ones of Civil Registry Regulations . . . come into conflict with the principles of free research into paternity and of equality, and moreover they seriously erode Article 10 SC, because they affect the very dignity of mother and child, their attached inviolable rights and on the free development of their personalities . . . Coincidence between legal and biological parentage must be complete.

Hence the Supreme Court considers that motherhood must be registered in the recording of childbirth to avoid damage of the child's right to know his/her filiation and also to facilitate the pertinent claims.

The second problem appears when surrogacy motherhood techniques are used. Even though these techniques are forbidden according to Article 10 of Act 35 of 1988, a safe solution will be needed if they are carried out, given that possibilities of ascription of motherhood through identification of genetic material are very complex.

At this point, three legal techniques may be used: to ascribe motherhood to the genetic mother; to ascribe it to whom voluntarily has assumed this role by means of a surrogacy agreement; and to ascribe it through the traditional method of verifying the physical fact of childbirth.[15] The system chosen by the Spanish law is the one which best protects the child's interests. That is, the natural fact of child-

[13] Rivero, n 10, p 20.

[14] Rivero, n 10, pp 60ff. Art 47.3 of the *Civil Registry Act* (of 8 June 1957, still in force) says that 'it might be deleted this mention [of motherhood] . . . because of being unaware of who is the person that figures as mother'.

[15] This question has been studied in several European reports: limited to Spanish law, see *Informe de la comisión especial de estudio de la fecundación 'in vitro' y la inseminación artificial humanas* (Madrid, 1987), p 44.

birth, which is immediately verifiable, and also establishes the child's identity, provides a safe, fast and clear method to determine filiation and motherhood.

Ascription of Fatherhood

As there are no evident physical standards about who has to be considered a father, the legal system must turn to other techniques to ascribe fatherhood. These consist of presumptions, based on the supposed father living together with the biological mother for certain legally determined periods, without prejudice to the exercise of appropriate claims or objections when such presumed fatherhood does not coincide with biological fatherhood. According to this, fatherhood is legally established through the application of different standards, depending on whether the mother's relationship with the man to be declared father by the law is in or out of wedlock. This is because, although marriage does not legally require the spouses to have sexual relations only with each other, the law presumes fidelity within marriage (Article 68 of the Civil Code), so the husband will be presumed to be the father of any child to whom the wife gives birth. As mentioned previously, the presumption may of course be rebutted, and an action may be brought by the husband to establish that he is not the genetic father of the child.[16]

[16] What is said in the text may open the door to claims for damages, as has happened in judgments of 22 and 30 July 1999. The facts are quite similar in both cases. They concern husbands who had children from their marriages and who had separated with a following annulment or divorce; after the settlement of the matrimonial crisis, they discover that one of the children from marriage is not their child, since paternity objections have been brought successfully. The frustrated fathers had paid the maintenance assigned to their presumed children while they were living together and also after the separation. Both husbands in their respective actions had claimed the pertinent damages.

In a Supreme Court judgment of 22 July 1999, the right to obtain compensation was denied because the wife did not know either that the child was not from her husband until the claim was brought; as there was not a wilful misconduct, there was not a compensation duty: 'The assumptions involving application of Art 1902 of the substantive legal text originate, as a consequence, a compensation for the caused damage that may be extended to both economical and moral fields. But this is not relevant in the actual cases in which, as it was argued, it was not possible to apply that rule, because it no a wilful misconduct by Mrs C has been found.'

The second judgment, of 30 July 1999, is based on similar but different events: the wife impugned paternity of the two children from the marriage after the matrimonial crisis and it was determined that a third party was the children's father. The husband brought an action claiming economic and moral damages, and in the appeal to the Supreme Court he argued that the infringement of the fidelity duty carried with it a compensation, and given that this duty was a consequence of the matrimonial contract, Art 1101 CC should be applied. The Supreme Court's answer was conclusive: 'Undoubtedly, the breach of the conjugal duties specified in Arts 67 and 68 CC deserve an undeniable ethical and social reproach which maybe is stressed when infringing the mutual fidelity duty; in these cases there is no doubt that the only legal consequence that our substantive legislation establishes is to consider this breach as one of the matrimonial separation causes in Art 82, but without assigning, against the offender, economic effects, that in no case might be included inside alimony . . . nor might be demanded inside the generic rule of Art 1110, although those duties are considered to be contractual because of the very nature of marriage, since the contrary view would force to consider that any cause of irregularity of matrimonial life would compel it to compensation.'

ESTABLISHING PARENTAGE IN SPANISH LAW

Parentage in Wedlock

Article 108 of the Spanish Civil Code establishes that parentage, whatever its origin (in wedlock, out of wedlock or adoptive), will generate the same effects. Since the approval of the Constitution, Spanish law has removed any discrimination by reason of birth, opting for the legal equality of all children. The only difference—obvious and logical from any point of view—is the one maintained in order to settle the judicial actions that our rules provide to elucidate the 'biological truth'. Relating to actions, the fact of whether or not the parents are married to each other becomes of the utmost relevance; in other words, the action will be different depending on whether the children are born inside or outside marriage. That is why, ahead of any other reasoning, it is important to specify the systems of establishing parentage which establish whether children from that union were born in or out of wedlock.

The establishment of parentage is automatic when there is marriage. The rule states that children are born in wedlock when the father and the mother are married to each other. It does not matter whether the *conception* took place before or after the marriage. If there is marriage, the child becomes a child born in wedlock. In order to ascribe the child's fatherhood to the husband, all the legal systems have had to resort to a rule to establish the husband's paternity legally: in the case of the Spanish Civil Code, it can be found in Article 116, where there is the following presumption:

> The children born after the date of marriage and before the three hundred days following its dissolution or the spouses' separation *de facto* or *de jure* are presumed to be the husband's children.

Obviously this presumption is founded on the belief that the married woman's child has been procreated by her husband. If the contrary can be proved (through exercising the relevant legal action), this presumption will be rebutted.

Presumption of paternity is somewhat weakened in cases where the child is born within 180 days following the date of marriage, because the husband is allowed to rebut the presumption through a statement denying his paternity, unless he had admitted his fatherhood before the birth of the child (see Article 117 of the Civil Code).[17]

[17] Art 117 CC says: 'When the child is born within 180 days from the date of marriage, the husband will be able to destroy the presumption by means of an authentic statement formalised within six months after having knowledge of the childbirth. There are some exceptions: the cases in which he had expressly or tacitly acknowledged fatherhood or in which he had knowledge of the woman's pregnancy before the date of marriage, except—in the latter case—that the authentic statement had been formalised consenting both of them, before or after the marriage, within six months following the childbirth.'

There are two basic[18] systems or titles to establish parentage in wedlock according to Spanish law: recording of the birth together with the recording of the marriage of the parents; and a final judgment. This may be criminal (in cases in which there has been a rape by the husband after a de facto or de jure separation when, even in an existing marriage, there is no sexual cohabitation), or civil, when the judgment is the consequence of exercising a claim action (see Article 132 of the Civil Code).

Next to the establishment of parentage in wedlock, which could be called *original* parentage (the child is born inside a marriage valid at the time of conception or birth), the Spanish law admits the possibility of the child being born in wedlock in a *supervened* way, in the case of children born before the parents' marriage (although we repeat that there is no legal difference by reason of origin). In this case, *parentage will be in wedlock from the date of the parents' marriage*, provided that this parentage is legally established. This establishment implies acknowledgment of fatherhood or a court order to that effect. If any of these facts takes place, the child becomes a matrimonial child without other proceedings being necessary.

When the parentage established through any of these mechanisms is about to be attacked, the Spanish law gives the entitled individuals (father, mother, child and sometimes any other person who can prove a legitimate interest) the possibility to act judicially.[19] It provides two kinds of actions: a matrimonial parentage claim; and a matrimonial parentage objection.

Action to Claim Matrimonial Parentage

Action to claim matrimonial parentage[20] involves a judicial petition presented by someone who believes that parentage not appearing to be in wedlock—because of the lack of a presumption of matrimonial parentage or its wrongful destruction—must be recorded as matrimonial parentage. An example will clarify this statement. If the child is born 300 days after the spouses' separation, Article 118 of the Civil Code (already quoted) does not apply the presumption of the fatherhood of the husband of the mother (he is still a husband, since separation does not remove the marriage link). Nevertheless, if both spouses consent, the child may be recorded as being born inside marriage. In those cases where both spouses do not consent, the law gives the entitled individuals the right to exercise the claim

[18] I say they are basic since, moreover, the Spanish law indicates in Art 113 CC other establishment titles as the paternity presumption and the enjoyment of a legal status. But the two titles are not valid per se because they have to go together with other data.

[19] In the new *Civil Procedure Act*, in force from Jan 2001, the entitlement to take legal action is modified in cases in which the action concerns a child who is under age or legally incompetent; here it is assigned to the legal representative or to the public prosecutor (Arts 764–68).

[20] Leaving aside the specific problems about entitlement derived from the fact that the claimant enjoys or does not enjoy the professed legal status.

action contained in Articles 131 and 132 CC[21] to prove that the child is born from that couple's relationship.

Objection Action

An objection action, on the other hand, seeks to prove the ineffectiveness of a legal establishment. Denying matrimonial parentage any effect is only possible through a court decision. In Spain, there is the possibility of contesting both motherhood[22] and fatherhood, even though the first option is rarely used; case law—discussed later—can, however, be found on the objection of fatherhood. Firstly, the concept and the consequences when exercising the action must be examined. The action of matrimonial parentage objection seeks to prove that the legal presumption on which parentage establishment was based is false. The consequence sought is to leave without effect the parentage as legally established.

The husband and the child are both entitled to instigate such an action. The child may act by him or herself, or be represented by the mother (during the child's minority). In Spain, the mother does not have the right to contradict the fatherhood of the husband.[23] When the husband contests parentage and the mother acting for the child objects in order to maintain matrimonial parentage, it is necessary to nominate a minor's guardian *ad litem*.[24]

The main problem posed by the rule is the *time limit* in which to bring the action. Obviously, when an objection action is brought, the tension between two contradictory interests is clear: on the one hand is the interest of the man alleged to be the father to prove the falseness of his ascribed parenthood and to end the consequences involved by parental relationship; on the other is the child's need for certainty, as it does not seem proper that at any time the 'father' might contest the parentage relationship because of the emotional unsteadiness that it could mean for the minor. It is true that the time limit rules are not applied to the action brought by the child, but this is due to the fact that parentage objection by the child usually goes together with a claim for truthful parentage.

Assessing these data, the legislator has chosen to give the husband a maximum time limit for bringing his action to the court: one year from the recording of the birth in the Civil Registry, or since the husband had knowledge of the birth. This time limit does not lapse, so it does not admit any interruption: time runs on.

[21] Art 132: 'If there is not the corresponding enjoyment of a legal status, the matrimonial parentage claim action, that has no prescription, concerns the father, mother or child . . .'
Art 133: 'The non-matrimonial parentage claim action, when there is not the respective enjoyment of a legal status, concerns the child during his/her all life . . .'

[22] This action does not exist either in German or Swiss law, but it can be found both in French and Italian law.

[23] In Germany, the mother does not have an own entitlement either; however, she does in France and Italy.

[24] The Supreme Court judgment of 5 June 1997 made a pronouncement in the same sense since the court considered that parents' interests were opposite to those of child, having as a consequence the impossibility to 'bring to light the material or biological truth'.

This causes a series of problems which are difficult to solve. The aforementioned time limit could make sense at the time when divorce did not exist and, despite the fact that the spouses were actually separated, the mother's children were ascribed to her husband—even though they had not had any kind of relationship for years. In that hypothesis, it is understandable that time begins to count when the husband becomes aware of the birth. But the cases which lead to most judgments are not in this category. Most objections arise before or during the separation or divorce procedures, or at times when the mother's husband finds out—in the course of some medical treatment—that he is infertile. For this reason, sometimes our Supreme Court has admitted an objection by the father after the legal time, when for any reason he has been made aware of his 'false paternity'. The exercise of this possible objection is also limited to one year, but starting from the moment when the presumed father had knowledge of the fact that gives him the right to contest. The Supreme Court has justified this interpretation by saying that it is the one that best fits and interprets the constitutional rules. To discuss an actual case, we will refer to Supreme Court Judgment 353/1993 (of 30 January 1993) and Supreme Court Judgment 5104/1996 (of 20 June 1996). Briefly, the first case dealt with the following question: it was completely proved that the mother's husband could not be the minor's father (as he was absolutely infertile); the minor's mother clearly admitted that fact and she accepted the objection. We would point out that this acceptance was dismissed because our law expressly forbids any kind of agreement on the subject of parentage. However, the infertility was unquestionable and, as the action had been brought within one year since the detection of the proofs on which the objection was based, the court accepted the objection. Among other arguments, the court stated:

> The strict observance of the rule of Article 136 taking it apart from the rest . . . could lead to being in contradiction to the informant principles of the Act of 13 January 1981 in its evident tendency to the fact that in matter of marital status real truth must prevail over the presumption resulting from marriage.

The second judgment is a confirmation of that same legal argument, even though in that case the action was not upheld. The lack of success was due to the fact that it was proved that the objector husband had knowledge of his false paternity many years before bringing the objection action. In consequence, and faithful to the aforementioned line of thinking, the Supreme Court affirmed that the action must be considered:

> . . . lapsed because more than one year had passed since the plaintiff had knowledge of the fact that (according to what he says) made him to be aware of the mistake he had fallen into, because in both actions for separation (1984) and divorce (1988) he already alleges his infertility based on the medical reports adduced; thus in case it was an error it would have disappeared at a moment much earlier than 1990, the year when this action was brought.

The more recent Catalan legislation has adjusted its rules to what is undoubtedly the best solution. Article 106.1 of the Family Code (passed by Act 9 of 1998, on 15 July) admits the matrimonial parentage objection within two years to be counted *from the date when the birth became known or from the finding of the evidence on which the objection is based.*[25]

A last aspect to be discussed on the subject of parentage in wedlock is the possible objection to parentage which may be raised regarding children conceived and born before marriage. In these cases, the legal presumption of parentage is not relevant and that is why parentage is mainly established through acknowledgment of or consent to registration. The objection tends to be based on a person's own error or induced error (or another consent defect), which caused the acknowledgment. The proof of this defect is by a declaratory action; once the existence of the defect is proved, the erroneously established parentage must be modified.

Parentage Out of Wedlock

Parentage out of wedlock is parentage in which the parents are not married at the moment of conception or at the moment of birth, and they do not marry after the birth (Article 119 of the Civil Code).

Spanish law does not establish a presumption of parentage just because the parties concerned are living together; consequently, parentage ascription must be carried out in other ways, either voluntarily or imposed by the judgment that pronounces a parentage relationship. By contrast, other legal systems such as the German, Swiss, Austrian, Scandinavian and in some cases the French and Catalan (Article 94, Family Code)[26] apply presumptions of parentage out of wedlock.[27]

In this way, Spanish law draws a clear distinction between parentage in and out of wedlock. To focus on the subject, it is important to pay attention to the two

[25] The Catalan *Parentage Act* (Act 1/1991)—replaced by the Family Code (Act 9/1998)—shared the same viewpoint as the Civil Code. Against the article containing that rule, a Constitutional proceeding was submitted to the Constitutional Court (this proceeding implies that the judge who must resolve the case doubts whether a relevant article is contrary to the Constitution). The doubt precisely lay in whether it was constitutional to count the time limit for bringing the action after having notice of the birth, as it could imply discrimination, defencelessness and impossibility for the man who appears as father to inquire into paternity, against what is established in Art 39.2 of the Spanish Constitution. The Act change and the insertion of a transitional provision before the Act came into force have settled the question. Thus, because of lack of object, the constitutional process was considered finished by writ 57 of 9 March 1999.

[26] See Encarna Roca, *Familia y cambio social (De la 'casa' a la persona)* (Editorial Civitas, 1999) and Coll Badosa (coord.), *Compendi de Dret Civil Català* (Marcial Pons, 1999).

[27] The aforementioned Catalan article says:

1. It is presumed that the father of the son or daughter out of wedlock is:
   (a) the man the mother has lived with in the legal period of conception
   (b) the man the mother had sexual relations with in the period of conception
   (c) the man who has acknowledged paternity tacitly or in a different way from that of Art 93.
2. Presumptions referred to by para 1 may be destroyed by means of any kind of evidence at the pertinent suit.

usual mechanisms to establish parentage: acknowledgment; and judgment of the court.

Acknowledgment

Acknowledgment means that the progenitor declares the fact of biological fatherhood or motherhood by a statement that must be unilateral, personal, formal (such as a statement before the Civil Registry officer, a last will or public record) and irrevocable. As it is a voluntary act, its regulation requires no more than to establish the legal capacity of any person who may effectively acknowledge and—if necessary—when the acknowledged person's consent is necessary. In relation to the first issue, the Civil Code says in Article 121 that 'the acknowledgment conferred by incompetent individuals or by those who can not get married by reason of age will need the judge's approval after hearing the public prosecutor in order to be valid'. The second issue presents more difficulties because it is possible to acknowledge children who are under age as well as of age. If the child is under age, the acknowledgment will require the express consent of the minor's legal representative or the approval of the judge to be effective. If the acknowledgment is denied, the progenitor whose parentage has not been established will be able to bring a parentage claim action. If the children are of age, their express or tacit consent to acknowledgment will be required (according to Article 123 CC).

An acknowledgment will not be effective if other contradictory and therefore incompatible parentage has previously been determined.

Judgment

Judgment is usually the second mechanism to establish parentage out of wedlock; it is usually a civil judgment as a consequence of a parentage claim process. Our law does not exclude the criminal action to determine parentage when this is the consequence of an offence (rape, for instance). However, we will focus on the civil process.

The civil action to claim parentage out of wedlock requires the judge to establish a parentage which has not been officially determined. There are several reasons leading to this action. It may happen that, without an express acknowledgment by the progenitor, the child is being treated as a member of the family, similar to the treatment he or she would receive if parentage were legally established. When this situation exists and the child is known by the family name and accepted by the family and third parties as a member of the family, the law considers that there is the *enjoyment of a legal status* of filiation and it allows any person with a legitimate interest to bring an action to the court to establish that filiation.

If there is not the enjoyment of a legal status (such treatment by the progenitor), the child by him or herself may exercise the action when he or she comes of age or achieves emancipation, or it may come through the progenitor who had acknowledged the child. Being a question of legal status, the public prosecutor is also entitled to intervene in the action. It must be explained that the action concerns the child exclusively, so if the progenitor acts it is on behalf of the child and his or her interests. The progenitor who has acknowledged the child does not have the right of action on his own behalf.

JUDICIAL EVIDENCE

The purpose of this action is to prove real fatherhood or motherhood. The Spanish law does not allow such a process to be commenced without a minimum amount of evidence giving some credibility to the claim. Specifically, Article 127.2 CC says in part: 'the judge will not admit the action if it does not present some any evidence of the facts it is based on'. As affirmed by the Supreme Court judgment of 4 May 1999:

> The procedural requirement of the second paragraph is that there is some merit in the action and not to restrict or place an obstacle in the way of any right granted by the Constitution . . . and it is enough to show in the action documentation some concrete reference to means of proof to be examined, which will give credibility and probability to the facts of claim even though afterwards the action may not be upheld.

To facilitate the scope of the legal requirement, the Code itself in Article 135 establishes that:

> the parentage may be declared which is *resulting* from the express or tacit acknowledgment, from the enjoyment of a legal status, from the fact of living together with the mother at the time of conception, as well as from other facts of which parentage can be inferred in an analogous way.

The Supreme Court judgment of 17 November 1999 indicated:

> Article 135 of the Civil Code establishes two kinds of evidence to determine and specify parentage out of wedlock: direct evidence—biological proof and express acknowledgment—and indirect or presumptive evidence, being circumstantial proof of sexual cohabitation necessary and sufficient for procreation.

Since this rule, as any rule on this subject after the 1978 Constitution, is focused on the protection of the child's interests, doctrine and case law (with very few exceptions) have extended the reach of the aforementioned concepts allowing parentage research to take place on the basis of little supporting evidence. In this sense, the Supreme Court judgment of 15 March 1985 stated:

> The admission of the principle of parentage research in our legal system has meant a very strong change in the emphasis on the essential nature of the child's right to have his/her biological filiation declared.

In effect, the change which has taken place in Spain in recent years on the subject of parentage has implied a complete switch, as the aforementioned judgment stated. The present Civil Code rules, specifically Articles 127 and 135, have corrected the obstructionist strictness of biological parent–child truth research, which was the guideline before the law reform. As the Supreme Court judgment of 19 November 1985 stated:

> With this object they establish a wide range of proceedings in order to know that genetic truth which allows the courts to *use any system* foreseen by human reason corresponding to the social realities in which those rules have to be apply, taking into account their spirit and purpose, according to Article 3.1 CC—that is, the defence of the child's personal interests, as the child is in any case innocent of the progenitors' acts both in the moral and material fields.

The plurality of methods to establish the certainty of a claimed parentage is the consequence of the *child's interest being considered paramount.* The Constitutional Court remarked on this point when declaring:

> Precisely because of the possible conflict of interests, the child's welfare has to be considered the prevailing interest and, as doctrine has said repeatedly, in parentage cases there is no doubt about the underlying social and public interest in parentage statements, in which the children's rights to maintenance and inheritance, which are specially protected by Article 39.2 of the Spanish Constitution and go beyond the limits of a strictly individual right, are at stake. (Supreme Court writ of 31 May 1990)[28]

Following this same line of reasoning, after a slight hesitation, the Spanish courts proved to be very receptive when examining data from which parentage could be inferred. Pieces of evidence are diverse and it will accept any document proving possible intimacy at the time of conception, obviously without the requirement of the stability of the parties as parentage may of course be a consequence of sporadic acts. The courts have accepted: the fact of living together in a hotel on holidays (Supreme Court judgment of 8 October 1993); the statements of acquaintances of the couple, saying that 'they knew the relationship mentioned' (Supreme Court judgment of 10 June 1996); the existence of a certain 'correspondence proving feelings of an affectionate relationship' (Supreme Court judgment of 4 February 1993); the fact that the plaintiff was visited at her home by the defendant (Supreme Court judgment of 26 January 1993); the production of photographs from which a certain intimacy can be inferred (Supreme Court judgment of 29 April 1994); and 'hotel bills signed by the defendant and being in the possession of the plaintiff; payment of the christening expenses by the presumed father, as well as the payment of some other sporadic financial aid' (Supreme Court judgment of 27 January 1993). As indirect evidence, the courts have taken into account the treatment given to the minor, consisting of the paying of monthly amounts for the child's expenses, introducing the child to family and

[28] When an action of constitutional protection is brought to the Constitutional Court, the constitutional significance of the possible infringement must be previously decided. When the court understands that there is no infringement and therefore does not admit the claim, the decision is stated by means of a writ. When the claim is admitted, the decision is stated by means of a judgment.

friends, and caring about the child's studies (however, since she did not receive treatment as a child, she did not enjoy this legal status). Sometimes letters between the perceived parents 'with sentences like "I want you, I love you"' have been accepted; or a clear promise of marriage has been accepted as evidence (Supreme Court judgment of 28 February of 1997); or the evidence of 'engagement relationships between the litigants because of the fact of living together in the same apartment and occupying several times the same room' (Supreme Court judgment of 8 March 1996). These facts by themselves are not enough to be proof—they are merely pieces of evidence. Nevertheless, if they are joined with the refusal to take the biological tests from which parentage could be established without doubt, the Spanish courts have considered that, taken as a whole, the pieces of evidence and refusal to take the biological test allow the court to establish the claimed parentage (see below).

This does not mean that the Spanish courts give judgment in favour of all parentage claims. As has already been stated, the law requires evidence. When this does not exist, or it is not strong enough to base a claim on, the refusal of the biological tests by the defendant has been allowed without any kind of consequence. Thus, in the Supreme Court judgment of 1 October 1999, the only piece of evidence submitted with the claim was the statements of the claimant's witnesses, who had notice of intimacy between the claimant and the defendant through the claimant's own assertions. The court stated that:

> This refusal can only be significant for the purposes of proving the controversial progeny when it exists together with other pieces of evidence which lead the Court to the decision that the disputed parentage was proved.

The Constitutional Court, in its judgment of 17 January 1994, had already stated that 'nobody is compelled to undergo the tests without a justifiable basis, merely to please another person'. The requirement of this evidence is set, obviously, in order to deter baseless claims.

BIOLOGICAL PROOF AND PROTECTION OF FUNDAMENTAL RIGHTS

After this short look at the Spanish legislation on parentage actions, a question arises concerning the legal consequences that refusal to submit to the biological tests may imply, and the possible constitutional effects in case certain fundamental rights of the person compelled to submit to the tests might be considered harmed. By their nature, biological tests need the presumed father's cooperation, since the test requires certain actions on the part of the defendant; and his refusal is not only possible but also frequent.

In view of this fact, it is proper to ask whether this kind of test—as is often argued—may harm some personal fundamental right, and consequently whether the defendant's refusal would be lawful. As an interpretative rule, it is important to note that the admission of biological tests in parentage claims or objections is due to the rule of Article 39.2 of the Spanish Constitution: 'The law will facilitate paternity research.' From this fact, the possible constitutional tension will be between the protection of the minor's interest (essential according to Article 39 of the Spanish Constitution, as has already been stated) and the protection of fundamental rights belonging to the other party in the process.

Defendants have opposed taking the test on the basis that the tests would cause harm to their following fundamental rights: the right to not declare against oneself; the right to physical well-being; the right to privacy; and the right to personal freedom. Therefore, it must be asked whether the tests may be imposed forcibly. The evidential consequences flowing from the hypothetical progenitor's refusal to be put to those tests will be considered in the next section.

In relation to the first aspect—the right to not declare against oneself, contained in Article 24.2 of the Spanish Constitution—Rivero[29] mentions that Constitutional Court judgment 103/1985 (relating to the refusal to submit to a breathalyser test for the same reason), stated: 'the tested person is not compelled to admit his own guilt but to allow himself to be subject to *a special kind of expertise*, requiring cooperation which is not comparable to a declaration'. The same doctrine, not questioned nowadays, has been applied in parentage actions. The Supreme Court has stated that the party which must stand trial is, at the same time, the object of the process and in the last analysis the human body becomes the object of expertise to obtain biological and anthropological evidence. The refusal to submit to this kind of test would impede the effectiveness of what is ordered by Article 39.2 of the Spanish Constitution.[30] See also the Supreme Court judgments of 14 July 1988, 5 December 1988 and 28 May 1990.

The second reason for opposing biological tests—infringement of right to physical well-being contained in Article 15 of the Spanish Constitution—cannot be admitted either. Unlike in other countries,[31] in Spain it is not possible to impose biological tests against one's will. That is why, in order to legally support refusal to submit to the tests, the argument has been used that they infringe the right to physical well-being. Nevertheless, it seems clear that such a trivial test as a minimal blood extraction cannot qualify as 'an infringement of the personal right to physical well-being.' The European Commission for Human Rights, in its decision of 13 October 1979, stated:

> Such a banal act as a blood test is not an interference forbidden by Article 2.1 of the European Convention . . . a compulsory blood test [it adds] is a deprival of freedom, even when short-lasting; however, it is justified to guarantee the fulfilment of a legal duty.

[29] Hernandez Rivero, 'Las pruebas biológicas en los procesos de filiación y su relación con ciertos derechos fundamentales' (1992) 25 *Poder Judicial* 49.

[30] Art 39.2 of the Spanish Constitution *in fine* states: 'The law will facilitate paternity research.'

[31] For example, in Germany the parties must stand up to the tests. If they repeatedly refuse them without a fair consideration, the tests can be carried out by force. The same happens in Denmark, Austria and some states in the United States.

The Constitutional Court has stated that the defendant would only be able to legitimately refuse to submit to the biological tests 'when there is no real circumstantial evidence of the behaviour charged or when it could be a very serious risk for health.'[32]

The third reason is a presumed infringement of *the right to honour and personal privacy* contained in Article 18 of the Spanish Constitution. The right to honour lies in the individual's appraisal of himself and by others; privacy means the guarantee of a domain of information strictly reserved to family members. This has been the fundamental right more frequently invoked by those who raise objections to biological tests. The reason for this use/abuse can be found in the Supreme Court judgment of 13 March 1998 interpreting Organic Law 1/1982 (of protection of right to honour, privacy and image). The judgment dealt with a case in which the press published a story that the excellent sportive records obtained by an athlete could be due to the fact that (according to information obtained by the newspaper) the said athlete had a chromosomal structure more manly than womanly. The judgment states that privacy not only reaches data related to private or family life, but also is extended to biological or character aspects such as personal analytic data: clinical, bacteriological, morphological and other kinds of test.

But it is also evident that no right is absolute, and in the case of parentage there are some interests in conflict. Among them is the right of the child to know his/her origin, and this is a priority right according to the Spanish Constitution, as is clear from the right to investigate it:

> The preponderant interest given to parentage must be taken into account and with it to the legitimate and superior right of every society being at an advanced cultural stage where family and social interests prevail over those of the individuals, represented by the protection granted to privacy and well-being contained in Articles 15 and 18 of the Spanish Constitution (Supreme Court judgment of 30 November 1989; and, also in the same sense, Supreme Court judgment of 5 June 1997).

A good example of what has been said may be found in Civil Code Writ 103 of 3 March 1990 (the 'El Cordobés' affair) that stated:

> the constitutional right to privacy excludes other people's meddling in the sphere of a citizens' private and personal life. But *this cannot become a kind of impunity* leading to a breach of the strict fulfilment of obligations due to third parties.

The Supreme Court judgment of 28 April 1994 makes a pronouncement in the same sense, stating that biological tests could not attack the right to privacy or the right to honour, 'as honour is not attacked by the existence of a process; and

[32] The judgment also states: 'to safeguard every citizen's right to not be put to biological rests due to frivolous or unfair actions, the law establishes two steps: action admission and biological tests admission. But once the need for these tests is decided by the judge, seeing that it is not possible to prove parentage through other means of proof, the party concerned has the duty to make them feasible.'

nor does privacy suffer since legal biological tests, discretely carried out, could not infringe the privacy of the person subjected to them'.

To conclude this aspect, we will refer to an undoubtedly extreme case: after a person's death, and in order that the presumed child could be the deceased's heir, a statement of parentage out of wedlock was requested. The rest of the relatives objected, bringing forward as an argument the infringement of the right to the deceased person's honour and privacy. Civil Code writ 149/1999 (of 14 June 1999) stated that: 'this right is not infringed even when—as in this case—the corpse is exhumed to take DNA samples since it is a proportional expertise evidence appropriate for the sought purposes'.

The last opposition reason is the possible infringement of *the right to personal freedom* contained in Article 17 of the Spanish Constitution. The Supreme Court judgment of 14 May 1991 affirmed that:

> It is clear that the possibility to carry out the biological rests depends on the submission of the person involved, *because the higher principle of the individual freedom impedes the use of any kind of force or compulsion* to obtain the blood samples; from that denial the judge may deduce the appropriate legal consequences, *but it is legally impossible to forcibly compel a person to be put to those tests.*

LEGAL CONSEQUENCES OF THE REFUSAL TO BE PUT TO BIOLOGICAL TESTS

Because tests cannot be compelled, the courts have had to consider the consequences flowing from a refusal. The Supreme Court has held that, where the alleged progenitor refuses to submit to testing, this refusal cannot be construed as an admission of paternity but that is an important piece of evidence when the refusal is made without justification or is purely obstructive.

The case law doctrine may be summarised in the judgment of 13 June 1991:

> the refusal of the person involved—a procedural behaviour revealing a negative attitude because of the opposition to cooperate in such a significant fact for parentage—*does not imply any constitutional or legal infringement . . . and it can not mean a 'ficta confessio'*, nor determine either the claimed parentage statement when there are not other pieces of evidence.

Thereby, in Spain, the unjustified[33] refusal to be put to biological tests is not considered to be a confession of the controversial fact, even though it is undoubtedly a serious piece of evidence of the truthfulness of the fact that cannot be proved by other means. But the refusal itself is worthless. Only together with other evidence of the possible relationship between the theoretical progenitors would it

[33] The denial would be justified on the basis of the lack or impossibility of sexual relations from which the claimed parentage originated or, as one author indicates, if the test could imply a serious risk for the presumed father's health; it would also be justified if his religion impeded this kind of test.

permit the court to deduce the claimed parentage, and this has been the decision of countless judgments by the courts. This is the unanimous position (to such an extent that references need not be cited) adopted by our courts. And this has been the solution taken by the law. In effect, the reform of the *Civil Procedure Act* brought about by Act 1/2000 of 7 January (which was to be in force, according to the final provision, a year after being published in the *Boletín Oficial del Estado*)[34] has accepted this interpretation and has compiled it in Article 767.4, which says:

> The unjustified refusal to be put to biological tests will allow the court to declare the claimed parentage, provided that there are some other pieces of evidence and the proof of the said parentage has not been obtained by other means.

KEEPING FAR BIOLOGY: PARENTS AND CHILDREN IN ASSISTED REPRODUCTION

No legal system can have only one rule relevant to all cases. In Spain, the question of establishing parentage by formal, non-biological means is posed again in cases of assisted reproduction.[35] The mother's husband or partner will be the legal father of her children if he has consented to that operation. The consent to the medical treatment that leads to birth implies that the mother's husband or partner assumes, without the possibility to contest on this basis, the fatherhood of a child which is genetically not his (Article 8 of Act 35/1988,[36] the *Assisted Reproduction Techniques Act*).

The essential aim of the rules contained in Act 35 of 1988 is the protection of the rights of the children born as a consequence of these techniques. For this reason, Articles 5, 7 and 8 of the *Assisted Reproduction Techniques Act* deny the traditional claim and objection actions studied in the previous sections. The law takes this decision bearing in mind the valuation of the different interests present: the wish to have children of one's own; the need to not ascribe parentage to one who does not wish it, guaranteeing to oneself an absolute impunity through the anonymous donation of genetic material (Article 5, *Assisted Reproduction Techniques Act*); and the protection of the newborn child. All this leads to regarding as preferable the fact of formally ascribing parentage rather than initiating an investigation that, apart from infringing the right to the donor's privacy, would lack any legal sense provided that the newborn child has a safeguarded protection through *formal* criteria. In short, the law tries to give significance to a statement

[34] Hernandez Rivero, 'Incidencia de la publicación de la Ley de Enjuiciamiento Civil de 7 de enero 2000 en el ejercicio procesal de las acciones de filiación' (2000) *Revista Jurídica de Cataluña* (forthcoming).

[35] The same happens in the British legal system. See N Lowe and G Douglas, *Bromley's Family Law.* (9th edn, Butterworths, 1998), p 265.

[36] Act 35 of 1988, of 22 Nov, about Assisted Reproduction Techniques. This act was objected to by the *Partido Popular*, at that moment in the opposition, in 1989. The Constitutional Court decided that it was fully constitutional in Supreme Court judgment 116/1999, of 17 June. (*Boletín Oficial del Estado*, 6 July) p 67.

of will that occurs prior to birth and that causes the assumption of future parentage, even though it does not coincide with biological truthfulness.[37] Therefore, biological data are not longer useful in order to ascribe parentage since the donor will never be considered a biological parent, not even when this person's identity becomes known (Article 8.3, *Assisted Reproduction Techniques Act*). From this, it follows that biological truthfulness does not play an exclusive role in parentage, because in this case as well as in adoption the will of those who assume the parents' role is decisive.

Article 7 of the *Assisted Reproduction Techniques Act* establishes that 'the parentage of children born through assisted reproduction techniques will be regulated by rules in force, except for the specialities contained in this chapter.' Relating to motherhood, the rule is very simple: the fact of birth determines parentage, according to Article 10.2 of the *Assisted Reproduction Techniques Act.* Relating to fatherhood, rules become more complex. Article 7 of the *Assisted Reproduction Techniques Act* refers to rules in force,[38] already studied, although there are specialities by reason of the employed technique. The proceedings will be different depending on whether the couple is married or not.

Married Couple

When the assisted reproduction technique is carried out on a married woman and the genetic material used is from her husband, there is not any problem relating to ascribing fatherhood, because there is a coincidence between the biological element and the will declared in the certain document to which article 6.3 of the *Assisted Reproduction Techniques Act*[39] refers. Thereby the mother's husband is the father of her child.[40]

[37] In Spain, there is no unanimity about the acceptance of this system to ascribe parentage, excluding the later investigation. Hernandez Rivero, 'La investigación de la mera relación biológica en la filiación derivada de fecundación artificial' *La filiación a finales del siglo XX. Problemática planteada por los avances científicos en materia de reproducción humana* (Trivium, 1987), p 160; Echeverria Delgado, 'Los consentimientos relevantes en la fecundación asistida. En especial, el determinante de la asunción de una paternidad que biológicamente no corresponde', *La filiación a finales del siglo XX. Problemática planteada por los avances científicos en materia de reproducción humana* (Trivium, 1987), pp 201, 216; Almaraz Moro, *Aspectos civiles de la inseminación artificial y la fecundación in vitro* (Bosch, 1988), p 1; and Pantaleon, 'Contra la ley sobre técnicas de reproducción asistida' (1988) *Jueces para la democracia* 19 at 32ff are in favour of the admission of paternity research. Most authors who comment on Supreme Court judgment 116/1999 remain against it—for instance, Moran Gonzalez, 'Comentario a la sentencia del Tribunal Constitucional 212/1996 de 19 de diciembre de 1996 (II parte)' (1999) 10 *Revista de Derecho y Genoma Humano* 157 at 183; instead, Camara, n 12, p 143 and Roca, n 12, p 429 completely agree with the solution given by the court.

[38] These are Arts 115–26 of the Civil Code, Arts 89–97 of the Catalan Family Code and Art 70 of the Navarrese Compilation.

[39] Art 8.2 of the *Assisted Reproduction Techniques Act* establishes that: 'If [the woman] is married it will also be required the husband's consent', which must be 'a free, conscious and formal expression' (Art 6.4, *Assisted Reproduction Techniques Act*).

[40] The only problem would appear to be when the consent had been given as a result of error, violence or intimidation, but if the husband's genetic characteristics coincide with those of the child, I

When insemination has been carried out with the genetic material of a donor, the husband must give his written consent in order to have fatherhood ascribed to him, according to Article 8.2 of the *Assisted Reproduction Techniques Act.* This writing has to reflect clearly the consent for 'the fertilisation with the contribution of a donor,' and has to be prior to treatment starting. If there is no consent, or it is defective, it will be necessary to have recourse to the general rules of actions of fatherhood, and particularly to Article 136 CC.

Therefore the consent principle is applied before the ascribing of parentage by means of biological data, and for this reason Article 8.1 of the *Assisted Reproduction Techniques Act* establishes:

> Neither the husband nor the wife, when they have previously and expressly consented to the fertilisation, with the contribution of one or more donors, will be able to contest parentage inside marriage of the child born as a consequence of that fertilisation.

This means that lodging a parentage objection solely on the basis of genetic divergence is forbidden, for the benefit of the child.

Unmarried Couple

In case of insemination with a partner's semen, parentage may be ascribed to him for two reasons: because the child is biologically his; and because the will of the parties has intervened. Parentage ascription in the case of an unmarried couple is not automatic and requires the same proceedings as any kind of parentage out of wedlock—that is, those foreseen in Article 120 CC, even though to this end and also to claim parentage when the action is exercised, it will be regarded as 'certain writing' as referred to by the aforementioned Article 8.2 of the *Assisted Reproduction Techniques Act.*

When insemination is carried out with a donor's semen, fatherhood will be ascribed to the partner who has consented to the treatment within the terms required in Article 8.2 of the *Assisted Reproduction Techniques Act.* The objection action must be excluded if it is based only on using an assisted reproduction technique with a donor's genetic material when the consent to this technique had been given before starting it.

Exceptions to the general rules for ascribing parentage contained in *the Assisted Reproduction Techniques Act* are: refusing to let the child exercise a parentage research action; refusing to let the semen donor exercise a parentage claim action; and refusing to let the mother's husband exercise a parentage objection action. We will now go further into these questions.

think that there could only be claims for damages between husband and wife, and the will defect would not affect parentage.

Discovering Parentage as a Means

This refers to parentage research as an action intended to know one's origin. It is a common opinion among Spanish authors that personality protection under Article 10 of the Spanish Constitution allows the exercise of actions designed for knowing one's origin.[41] How, then, can the constitutionally protected right be brought into line with the semen donor's privacy? The *Assisted Reproduction Techniques Act* manages to do it in a very subtle way: by refusing to let the child born from these techniques have the right to know the donor's identity, even though permitting him or her to know his or her genetic origin.

The newborn child's interest is protected by so-called *relative anonymity*, which will allow the child to have access to some information, with the essential aim to protect the right to personality—one main aspect of which is health protection. Would the right to know one's origin be covered that way? The answer must be affirmative, although it will only extend to a part of that origin, provided that it does not extend to the donor's identity.

Furthermore, anonymity is rational since it permits the protection to the selfsame donor's privacy.[42]

Parentage Claim by the Donor

The system recognises rights, but it must also limit them. Thus the semen donor, who is the genetic father of the child born through *in vitro* fertilisation, cannot claim fatherhood on the sole basis of biology. The semen donor has had a biological role in procreation, but he does not have a social role, which is assigned by the law only to the mother's husband or partner who has consented to this technique.[43]

Parentage Objection

Is it possible for the mother's husband to contest fatherhood merely by adducing that the child born to his wife or partner does not have the same genetic features

[41] Rivero, n 37, pp 160ff and n 10, pp 22ff; Quesada, (1994b) 'El derecho (constitucional?) a conocer el propio origen biológico' (1994) *ADC* 243 at 253ff; and Gorina Garriga, *La Adopción Y El Derecho A Conocer La Filiación De Origen* (Aranzadi, 2000), pp 247ff.

[42] In those cases in which law opts for a formal system of ascribing parentage for the purpose of better protecting the minor's interests, two principles must be reconciled: biological truthfulness as a primary system to attribute parentage and therefore parental responsibility, and the free development of personality, on which a hypothetical right of the person concerned to know his/her origin would be based. Protection of a minor's interest impedes the transference of the consequences of parentage to the man who turns out to be the biological father in those cases in which paternity research is carried out in order to attain some of those purposes and not to ascribe parentage. See Quesada, n 41, pp 237ff; Garriga, n 41; pp 219–30, in relation to finding parents' identity in adoption.

[43] C Barton and G Douglas, *Law and Parenthood* (Butterworths, 1995), p 6.

as himself? This may happen on the occasion of an assisted fertilisation with donor's semen. The *Assisted Reproduction Techniques Act* radically excludes this possibility in Article 8.1, already quoted. Clearly this is a rule that protects the minor's interest and his or her fundamental rights.[44]

In short, the impossibility of bringing the objection action will cause the man who consented to the medical process to be held to be the father. The sole purpose of this is to protect the minor's interests.

CONCLUSIONS

Parentage is understood as a way to protect the newborn child. The basic reason is that the legal system assigns to the progenitors the parental responsibility for children under age, as a system to guarantee the effectiveness of the rights owned by the minor.

The preferable system to ascribe parentage (arising as an immediate consequence of the duty of protection) is the biological one. The Spanish legislation turns on this point: biological truthfulness must prevail over other circumstances. Nevertheless, this does not impede the legal viewpoint moving towards other positions in special cases (adoption and assisted fertilisation), precisely because of thinking that the minor's protection will only be achieved by applying the consent criterion.

The legal system establishes that tension between parentage and the protection of fundamental rights of other people involved in claim and objection actions must be decided in favour of protection of the minor. Therefore, the fact of carrying out biological tests to establish the disputed parentage does not imply for the compelled person any kind of fundamental rights infringement.

[44] Recently, the Italian Constitutional Court (*Corte Costituzionale*) has settled a similar case: it has declared the action of fatherhood ignorance inadmissible in those cases in which the husband had consented to the wife's insemination with semen of an anonymous donor: Judgment No 347, of 26 Sept 1998 (published in *Il Diritto di famiglia e delle persone*. XXVIII, 1999, p 505). As a consequence of this judgment, the *Corte di Cazzazione* in judgment 2315 of 16 March 1999, published in *Il Diritto di famiglia e delle persone*, 1999, p 622) has not admitted an objection action on this basis.

8

Suing Child Welfare Agencies: A Comparative View from New Zealand

Bill Atkin and Geoff McLay*

INTRODUCTION

Complaints about the handling and investigating of claims of child abuse have surfaced frequently in the past few years. Many involve notifications of physical abuse or neglect which have apparently not been followed through by the relevant social welfare agencies,[2] or allegations that an agency chose not to remove a child from a dangerous situation in order to maintain the child's family and in the hope that other less invasive measures would suffice.[3] Yet other complaints arise where claims of abuse have been too readily accepted when they should not have been, or the investigations have been wrongly conducted—a child removed from the family, where the allegations or suspicions that led to the removal ultimately prove to be untrue[4] or where someone else is later found to be responsible for the abuse.[5] In another variant, a child placed with a family by social welfare agencies harms that family. Behind each complaint is a very real human tragedy.

Accompanying this upsurge in complaints has been the attempt by dissatisfied families to bring civil proceedings against social welfare agencies they allege have failed them. In the United Kingdom, the House of Lords' *X v Bedfordshire* decision[6] appeared to have ended the chances of success for litigants in all but the 'dangerous child' cases. Then, remarkably, in *Barrett v Enfield London Borough Council*,[7] the House of Lords—perhaps prompted by the European Court of

* Bill Atkin is Reader in Law, Victoria University of Wellington and Geoff McLay is Senior Lecturer in Law, Victoria University of Wellington. This revised paper was first published by the *Child and Family Law Quarterly*, and is reproduced here with permission of that journal.

[2] Essentially the allegation in *Attorney-General v Prince* [1998] 1 NZLR 262.

[3] The allegation in *X (Minors) v Bedfordshire County Council; M (A Minor) and Another v Newham London Borough Council and Others; E (A Minor) v Dorset County Council; Christmas v Hampshire County Council; Keating v Bromley London Borough Council* [1995] 2 AC 633.

[4] These are the facts of *B v Attorney-General* [1999] 2 NZLR 296.

[5] The facts of the *Newham* case reported in *X (Minors) v Bedfordshire County Council*, n 3.

[6] *Ibid.*

[7] *Barrett v Enfield London Borough Council* [1999] 2 FLR 426.

Human Rights' judgment in *Osman v UK*[8]—reinterpreted *X v Bedfordshire* to allow many of the claims that we had thought barred by *X v Bedfordshire* to proceed at least to trial. *Osman, Barrett* and now the European Court of Human Rights in *Z and Others v United Kingdom*[9] and *TP and KM v United Kingdom*,[10] in which the court partially rejected *Bedfordshire*-style blanket immunities for welfare agencies, seem set to require the English courts to completely re-examine the issue and to develop law to replace those blanket immunities with a much more sophisticated approach.

Each case brought by children who might have avoided neglect or abuse by appropriate invention, or by children, parents or families whose lives have been tainted by inappropriate intervention, reflects very real human tragedy. The cases also inevitably bring into sharp focus the difficult and conflicting roles of social workers. There are stories of administrative good intentions gone awry—which is sometimes inevitable. But there are also stories of under-resourcing of social welfare agencies or of mistaken reliance on unproved or even disproven social work practices.[11]

The purpose of this article is to look at some of the factors that might go into the judicial mix in trying to sort out an appropriate liability regime for social welfare agencies. It does so by directly comparing English case law with that from New Zealand. After examining the conflicting case law from those jurisdictions, we suggest a number of starting points from which courts might successfully begin the complicated process of mediating the need to give just compensation to those adversely, but wrongly, affected by social workers' decisions and the equal need to prevent litigation from overwhelming the primacy of child protection. Whatever ought to be the proper basis for allowing or rejecting such claims, we regard the New Zealand position, as reached in the 1999 case of *B v Attorney-General*,[12] as untenable and as a warning to the English courts that, before deciding particular cases, much thought needs to be given to the interaction of tort law on the one hand and family law on the other.

TORT AND FAMILY LAW: AN INEVITABLE TENSION?

Tort cases in which courts have been prepared at least to consider the possibility of negligent actions against state welfare agencies provide a striking example of the tensions between the common law and modern family law. The somewhat conflicting New Zealand Court of Appeal decisions in *Attorney-General v Prince* and *B v Attorney-General*, and English decisions—among them *X v Bedfordshire* and *Barrett*—indicate the difficulty in articulating clear principles

[8] [1999] 1 FLR 193.
[9] [2001] 2 FLR 612.
[10] [2001] 2 FLR 549.
[11] This was, in essence, the allegation in *B v Attorney-General* [1999] 2 NZLR 296.
[12] *Ibid.*

that can reconcile two very different branches of what is traditionally seen as 'private law'.

At the heart of the traditional view of the common law is the desire to remedy a wrong.[13] Tort law looks backwards to assess what has gone wrong and ascribes responsibility to the party which has 'caused the loss'. The prime orientation of modern family law is to rebuild the family and protect children. Modern family law places great faith in welfare agencies achieving these joint, if sometimes conflicting, goals. This conflict in goals is reflected in the inconsistent ways in which courts have approached the question of welfare agencies' liability when the decisions that they have made to promote children's welfare turn out adversely for those children or their families.

While there is something very traditional about plaintiff children and families invoking the remedial function of the common law, there is something very untraditional about the kinds of the claims they make in the social welfare context. English (and Commonwealth) common law has come only very lately to a separate law of governmental or state liability, preferring instead the mantra that the state is under the same duties as private individuals.[14] Such a proposition might make sense when a social worker causes a car accident, but it is not so convincing when the social worker is exercising the uniquely governmental function of deciding whether to intervene in a family. An awareness that somehow governmental liability is different from ordinary tort law, especially when it involves the exercise of some form of discretion, has led to an extremely complex body of cases, of which *X v Bedfordshire* was, until *Barrett*, perhaps the leading authority.[15] That pre-*Barrett* case law sought (somewhat unwisely) to lay down general propositions about liability for government action, without sufficiently examining the particular context of the governmental role in question. One of the most important aspects of *Barrett* is that it requires judges to look at the context in which the discretion is given to government officials, and the context in which it is exercised. It is our view that, while family law and tort law clearly have different orientations, any perceived conflict between the two is not a reason for granting a blanket immunity in the style of *X v Bedfordshire*, or the drawing of artificial or arbitrary distinctions between different plaintiffs, as the New Zealand Court of Appeal did in *B v Attorney-General*.

[13] In the English Court of Appeal, Sir Thomas Bingham referred to the remedying of wrongs being the first 'loyalty of the law': *X (Minors) v Bedfordshire County Council*, n 3, p 663, reaffirmed by Lord Browne-Wilkinson at p 749.

[14] The leading Commonwealth exposition of this view is PW Hogg and PJ Monahan, *Liability of the Crown* (3rd edn, Carswell, 1989).

[15] For a critical view of both *Osman* and *Barrett* and the Commission decisions, see A Mullis, '*Barrett v Enfield London Borough Council*: A Compensation-seeker's Charter?' [2000] CFLQ 185. Mullis rightly raises the issue of the desirability of imposing legal liability, but to our eyes his critique of the cases—and especially of *Osman*—that the imposition of liability interferes in legitimate resource allocation decisions is simply not established on the facts of the cases; of course, it might have been had the exclusionary rule not prevented a proper trial of whether a resource allocation issue had been involved.

BREACH OF STATUTORY DUTY: MISSING IN ACTION OR CORRECTLY SIDELINED?

All the cases discussed in this article occurred in the context of various family or child protection statutes. Often those statutes impose mandatory duties to protect the child's best interests. Strikingly, the cases give scant consideration to the 'tort' of breach of statutory duty. The general demise of the tort of breach of statutory duty is beyond this paper. We suggest, however, that its demise in this particular context is not necessarily to be mourned, so long as the courts do not arbitrarily restrict negligence law.

Welfare Obligations Do Not Confer Private Benefits

The normal prerequisite for a successful breach of statutory duty claim is that the statute conferred a benefit on an identifiable section of the public, rather than merely providing a benefit to the general public. While the popular perception of social welfare legislation is that it does confer private benefits—albeit of a peculiar sort—on beneficiaries, English courts have been extremely reluctant to acknowledge that social welfare legislation is intended by parliament to create a private benefit enforceable by private right of action. In *X v Bedfordshire* itself, Lord Browne-Wilkinson observed:

> Although regulatory or welfare legislation affecting a particular area of activity does in fact provide protection to those individuals particularly affected by that activity, the legislation is not to be treated as being passed for the benefit of those individuals but for the benefit of society in general . . . The cases where a private right of action for breach of statutory duty has been held to arise are all cases in which the statutory duty has been very limited and specific as opposed to general administrative functions imposed on public bodies and involving the exercise of administrative discretions.[16]

The English courts have thus gone quite close to observing that what at first blush appeared to be privately enforceable rights are, in fact, simply laudatory goals for social welfare agencies to achieve. This, however, is in stark contrast to the acceptance by the House of Lords in *Barrett* that the obligations under the *Children Act* 1989 to provide for the welfare of a child in care are potentially enforceable in 'private' negligence law, as opposed to the 'public' breach of statutory duty tort.

The Advantage of Common Law Negligence over Breach of Statutory Duty

The failure of the courts to directly recognise social welfare-type duties as directly enforceable under the breach of statutory duty tort is not necessarily to be regret-

[16] See n 3, pp 731–32.

ted. On the one hand, cases dealing with breach of statutory duty and its requirement that parliament had intended a private right of action are notoriously incoherent and inconsistent. The search for parliamentary intention often proves elusive and becomes more a way of stating a conclusion than articulating a reason. On the other hand, breach of statutory duty might appear to be too absolute a weapon to employ against social welfare agencies. As Lord Browne-Wilkinson observed in *X v Bedfordshire*, liability under breach of statutory duty is often viewed as strict.[17] If the cases under consideration agree on anything, it is that some social welfare decisions will not give rise to liability, even if things turn out badly. Courts are concerned to preserve the element of discretion given by child welfare statutes to social workers to make appropriate decisions in particular cases, even when acting under a statutory duty. Courts are also concerned to preserve the ability to say that a particular decision involves a policy that a private law court should not review. This 'high policy' concern has caused significant problems in common law negligence cases and there is no reason to believe that it would not cause the same problems in breach of statutory duty cases.

Are Private Remedies Needed when Mechanisms Exist for Public Accountability?

Lord Browne-Wilkinson's conclusion in *X v Bedfordshire* that it was not just and reasonable to impose a duty of care on social workers in care and protection cases was, in his view, somewhat softened by the existence of so-called public remedies if the actions of the social workers had been inappropriate. Lord Browne-Wilkinson wrote:

> If there were no other remedy for maladministration of the statutory system for the protection of children, it would provide substantial argument for imposing a duty of care. But the statutory complaints procedures contained in section 76 of the 1980 Act and the much fuller procedures now available under the 1989 Act provide a means to have grievances investigated, though not to recover compensation. Further, it was submitted (and not controverted) that the local authorities' ombudsman would have power to investigate cases such as these.[18]

The New Zealand Court of Appeal, in contrast, implicitly rejected the significance of the public remedies in the care and protection cause of action.[19] The Crown had argued that complaints over the performance of Social Welfare could have been made through the ombudsman system or to the quasi-independent Commissioner for Children, an office expressly created to investigate issues of importance to child welfare.[20] However, dissenting from the imposition of a duty

[17] *Ibid.*, pp 731–35.
[18] *Ibid.*, p 751.
[19] *Attorney-General v Prince*, n 2, p 277.
[20] A recent prominent inquiry involved the failure of the Social Welfare to prevent the death of a

of care, Henry J directly refuted the effectiveness of the kinds of public accountability discussed by Lord Browne-Wilkinson:

> [T]hose [methods of accountability] suggested by the [Crown], namely recourse to judicial review or by way of complaint to the Ombudsman, appear to be a marginal value; the significance of the Office of Commissioner for Children under the [1989] Act must be doubtful.[21]

The role of public officers like the New Zealand Children's Commissioner is often advisory, and carries no powers to compensate. Vindication by the ombudsman, for example, is seemingly little comfort to those who have suffered real loss. Ombudsmen's reports are not perceived in the community as a real substitute for a court judgment.

In his speech in *Barrett*, Lord Slynn of Hadley indicated a similar scepticism of the sorts of administrative remedies that Lord Browne-Wilkinson had proposed.[22] There is more in this proposition that public remedies will sometimes 'oust' private remedies than the space given it by either the court deciding *Prince* or the House of Lords in either *X v Bedfordshire* or *Barrett*. We suggest that there is a fundamental clash of values in the common law's backward-looking compensatory approach and the forward-looking, preventive model of ombudsmen schemes or the Commissioner for Children's office. There appears to be a significant role for both to play in any system of public accountability.[23] Similarly, in *Z and Others v United Kingdom*, the European Court of Human Rights swept aside the United Kingdom's submissions that the availability of non-judicial remedies was, by itself, a sufficient answer to the United Kingdom's obligation to provide remedies for breaches of the European Convention for the Protection of Human Rights and Fundamental Freedoms 1950. The United Kingdom had argued that, as bodies such as the Criminal Injuries Compensation Board (CICB) or Local Government Ombudsmen had been available to review the failure of the council to protect children at risk, and in the case of the CICB had actually given some compensation, the United Kingdom's obligation to provide a remedy for breaches of the European Convention had been discharged. The court held that obligation of a member state was to give an effective remedy.[24]

The court indicated that administrative or quasi-judicial remedies, as opposed to judicial procedures, might in some circumstances be effective remedies, but not given the seriousness of the allegations in *Z and Others v United Kingdom* that the Bedfordshire County Council had systematically failed to protect children from

child at the hands of his mother's partner and which made a number of severe criticisms of the performance of social workers. See Commissioner for Children, *Final Report on the Investigation into the death of James Whakaruru* (Office of the Commissioner for Children, 2000).

[21] *Attorney-General v Prince*, n 2, p 289.

[22] See n 7.

[23] The concepts of accountability is usefully reviewed in S Braye and M Preston-Shoot 'Accountability, Administrative Law and Social Work Practice: Redressing or Reinforcing the Power Imbalance' (1999) 21 *Journal of Social Welfare and Family Law* 235.

[24] *Z and Others v United Kingdom*, n 9, para 108.

mistreatment. Indeed, it appears that the British government conceded to some extent that serious breaches of the Convention ought to be answerable in court.[25] However, the government accepted that, in the particular circumstances of this case, they were insufficient alone or cumulatively to satisfy the requirements of Article 13. It conceded that there had been a serious violation of one of the most important Convention rights; that the CICB could only award compensation for criminal acts, not for the consequences of neglect; and that any recommendation by the ombudsman would not have been legally enforceable. It had been under the obligation, in this case, to ensure that some form of compensation was made available for damage caused by the breach of Article 3, whether by a broader statutory compensation scheme, an enforceable ombudsman's award or through the courts.

THE IMPACT OF EUROPEAN HUMAN RIGHTS JURISPRUDENCE

Introduction

In England, the outcome of these social workers' cases now depends a great deal on European human rights jurisprudence. The European Convention for the Protection of Human Rights and Fundamental Freedoms 1950 has been applied with some vigour by the European Court of Human Rights in two recent decisions. Any common law rule that restricts the ability to sue social welfare agencies must be shaped by the Convention. The case of *Z and Others v United Kingdom* was, in fact, the proceeding brought by the children in the *X v Bedfordshire* case. The children alleged that Bedfordshire social workers had failed to remove them from a dysfunctional family home that was not just neglectful, but where conditions had been downright degrading. Its companion case, *TP and KM v United Kingdom* (reported in *Bedfordshire* as *M (A Minor) and Another v Newham London Borough Council*), involved the removal of a sexually abused child from her mother on the basis, subsequently shown to be incorrect, that the mother's partner was the abuser.

The Positive Obligation to Protect Children at Risk

In contrast to the Lord Browne-Wilkinson invocation of a blanket immunity that would completely prevent negligence suits, the court emphasised that the Convention required the British government to act to protect children at risk. Article 3 provides that 'no one shall be subjected to torture or to inhuman or degrading treatment or punishment'. The European Human Rights Commission had found

[25] See n 9.

that, given the special vulnerability of children, the United Kingdom was obligated to protect them from degrading treatment:

> The court has held that the obligation on High Contracting Parties under Article 1 of the Convention to secure to everyone within their jurisdiction the rights and freedoms defined in the Convention, taken together with Article 3, requires States to take measures designed to ensure that individuals within their jurisdiction are not subjected to torture or inhuman or degrading treatment, including such ill-treatment administered by private individuals . . . The Commission considers that the protection of children who by reason of their age and vulnerability are not capable of protecting themselves requires not merely that the criminal law provides protection against Article 3 treatment but that, additionally, this provision will in appropriate circumstances imply a positive obligation on the authorities to take preventive measures to protect a child who is at risk from another individual . . . The Commission notes in this regard the international recognition accorded to this principle in Article 19 of the United Nations Convention on the Rights of the Child, which enjoins States to take all appropriate measures 'to protect the child from all forms of physical and mental violence, injury or abuse.'[26]

Likewise, the court found that it was simply established Convention law that Article 3 gave rise to positive obligations on the state to prevent cruel or degrading treatment, and that the failure to do so could result in the state being liable for damages.[27] The court did acknowledge 'the difficult and sensitive decisions facing social services and the important countervailing principle of respecting and preserving family life.' The allegations against the Bedfordshire social services' repeated failure to intervene to protect the children were, however, beyond any such redemption as a genuine, but ill-fated, balancing of complex interests.

The Newham Case

In their respective companion reports and decisions on the *Newham* case, *TP and KM v United Kingdom*, both the European Commisson and the European Court were considerably more understanding of the House of Lords' decision not to allow a cause of action to proceed on the basis that the child had been wrongfully removed. While it was clear that a removal decision might breach either the child's or the mother's right to family life under Article 8(1), the Commission accepted the importance of the securing the safety of the child as a legitimate state role under Article 8(2).[28] Similarly, the court accepted that a wide margin of appreci-

[26] *Z v United Kingdom* [2000] 2 FCR 245 (Eur Com HR) at para 93 citing *A v United Kingdom* (1998) 5 BHRC 137 (ECt HR) at para 93, citing *A v United Kingdom (Human Rights: Punishment of Child)* [1998] 2 FLR 959.

[27] *Z and Others v United Kingdom*, n 9, para 73.

[28] *TP and KM v United Kingdom* (10 Sept 1999), Appl No 28945/98 (Eur Com HR) at para 71. Article 8(2) provides: 'There shall be no interference by a public authority with the exercise of this right [to respect for family life] except such as is in accordance with the law and is necessary in a democratic society in the interests of national security, public safety or the economic well-being of

ation ought to be granted to national authorities in protecting children's safety. That was not the end of the matter, however. A wide margin of appreciation was not necessarily appropriate in assessing subsequent decisions that affected parents' right of access to their children.[29] The court indicated that the degree of access that the mother might be permitted to a removed child might be reviewed by the court. Similarily, the court held that it could appropriately review the procedure adopted in reaching decisions to remove and the subsequently to return or not to return the child. The court accepted:

> Whilst Article 8 contains no explicit procedural requirements, the decision making process involved in measures of interference must be fair and such as to afford due respect to the interests safeguarded by Article 8.[30]

Osman and Blanket Immunities Preventing Suits against the Government

The Reaction against Osman

Without a doubt, the court's prior decision in *Osman* created significant difficulties for both the Commission and the court. In *Osman*, the European Court of Human Rights had held that granting a blanket immunity to the police that effectively immunised them from negligence actions based on their failure to protect citizens violated Article 6. The immunity, the court held, violated the right of potential plaintiffs to have civil actions determined by a court,[31] even if that court could find no other violation of the Convention. The decision was a source of dismay for English academics and judges, who largely rejected the court's analysis as a failure to understand that, in *Hill v Chief Constable of West Yorkshire*,[32] the House of Lords had not applied an immunity to prevent the plaintiff from recovering in what would otherwise have been a valid action, but rather had denied that there was a cause of action in the first place.[33] Despite this criticism, the

the country, for the prevention of disorder or crime, for the protection of health or morals, or for the protection of the rights and freedoms of others.'

[29] See n 10, paras 71–72.

[30] See n 11, para 72, quoting from *W v United Kingdom* (1998) 10 EHRR 29 at 28–29, paras 62 and 64.

[31] Art 6(1) provides: 'In the determination of his civil rights and obligations or of any criminal charge against him, everyone is entitled to a fair and public hearing within a reasonable time by an independent and impartial tribunal established by law.'

[32] [1989] AC 53.

[33] See, for example, Lord Buxton, 'The *Human Rights Act* and Private Law' (2000) 116 LQR 48; Lord Hoffmann, 'Human Rights and the House of Lords' (1999) 62 *Modern Law Review* 159; T Weir, 'Down the Hill—All the Way?' [1999] *Cambridge Law Journal* 4; P Craig and D Fairgrieve, '*Barrett*, Negligence and Discretionary Powers' [1999] *Public Law* 626; G Monti, '*Osman v UK*—Transforming English Negligence Law into French Administrative Law' (1999) 48 ICLQ 757; M Lunney, 'A Tort Lawyer's View of *Osman v United Kingdom*' (1999) 10 KCLJ 238; M Lunney, '*Osman* in Action—Article

European Court's scepticism in *Osman* of the appropriateness of striking out cases against public authorities appeared to have considerable influence in subsequent cases in England.

In *Barrett*, the House of Lords essentially distinguished the earlier *X v Bedfordshire* and thereby avoided the necessity of reconciling *X v Bedfordshire* with *Osman*.[34] None of the other Law Lords was prepared to join in Lord Browne-Wilkinson's criticism of *Osman*, preferring instead to simply reach the result that the European Court apparently mandated without directly considering it. The English Court of Appeal in the *Gloucestershire and Tower Hamlets London Borough Council* case dealt with *Osman* and used the Commission's report in *Z and Others v United Kingdom* to confirm that the courts should be reluctant to recognise blanket governmental immunities.[35]

The European Court Abandons Osman

The Commission had applied *Osman* to the facts of *Z and Others v United Kingdom*,[36] but had—perhaps not convincingly—distinguished the mother from the daughter plaintiff in *TP and KM v United Kingdom*, holding only that the daughter's Article 6 rights had been breached.[37] Perhaps as a result of the widespread English criticism, the court, by a twelve to five majority, simply confessed to having misunderstood English law in *Osman*.[38]

Under its analysis of common law negligence, the court held that the English Court of Appeal in *Osman*[39] had not immunised what would have otherwise been an actionable breach of a pre-existing obligations, but rather had found that there was no pre-existing obligation owed by the police at common law to the Osman family. Similarly, *X v Bedfordshire* was viewed by the court not as immunising the social services against otherwise valid claims, but—in denying that the various

6 and the Commission Reports in *Z v United Kingdom and TP and KM v United Kingdom*' (2000) 11 KCLJ 119; CA Gerty, 'Unravelling *Osman*' (2001) 64 *Modern Law Review* 159. The debate over *Osman* is inexorably bound up with the debate over the horizontal application of the *Human Rights Act* 1998 to the common law. The Buxton and Hoffmann articles show a strong correspondence between the force of opinion about *Osman* and the force of opinion about the appropriateness of horizontal application of the *Human Rights Act* 1998. That debate is outside the scope of this article. For the most vocal proponent of direct horizontality, see Sir William Wade, 'Horizons of Horizontality' (2000) 116 LQR 217; the best summary of the more moderate indirect effect doctrine is M Hunt, 'The Horizontal Effect of the *Human Rights Act*' [1998] *Public Law* 423. See also A Lester and D Pannick, 'The Impact of the *Human Rights Act* on Private Law: the Knight's Move' (2000) 116 LQR 380; N Bamforth, 'The True Horizontal Effect of the *Human Rights Act* 1998' (2001) 117 LQR 34.

[34] *Osman v UK* [1999] 1 FLR 193.

[35] *S v Gloucestershire County Council; L v Tower Hamlets London Borough Council* [2001] 2 WLR 909 at 934. Also citing the observations of Lord Woolf MR in *Kent v Griffiths and Others* [2000] 2 WLR 1158 at 1169, that *Osman* 'underlined the dangers of a blanket approach'.

[36] See n 26, para 109.

[37] The Commission argued that the mother's claim had been struck out in *Newham* because she lacked sufficient proximity to the local council and hence the council owed no pre-existing obligation to her, which was then subsequently immunised by the operation of public policy.

[38] *Z and Others v United Kingdom*, n 9, para 100.

[39] *Osman and Another v Ferguson and Another* [1993] 4 All ER 344.

councils owed a pre-existing duty in the first place—as presenting no possibly valid claim under existing UK law.

The Court Rediscovers Article 13

Whatever the correctness of the critique of *Osman*, the point remains that English common law appears, from a human rights perspective, to contain a significant gap in the legal mechanisms available to those children who alleged that the United Kingdom had failed to protect them from harm.[40] The court had no intention of letting the United Kingdom off for failing to provide an opportunity for the affected parties to vindicate the alleged breach of their Convention rights. Indeed, the British government had accepted before the court in *Z* that failing to provide such a remedy was itself a breach of the Convention. Rather than the contentious Article 6, the court following the lead of the United Kingdom's submissions preferred Article 13, which provides:

> Everyone whose rights and freedoms as set forth in the Convention are violated shall have an effective remedy before a national authority notwithstanding that the violation has been committed by persons acting in an official capacity.

Article 13 had been raised in *Osman*, but given its finding that the United Kingdom was liable under Article 6, the court had passed over any real consideration of Article 13. The court in *Z and Others v United Kingdom* now invoked Article 13 as the appropriate mechanism to require member states to provide adequate enforcement mechanisms for alleged human rights violations. The court now interpreted Article 13 as requiring member states to provide appropriate fora to inquire into the substance of complaints that member states had violated their obligations under the Convention.[41] Since the blanket immunity rule in effect denied the *X v Bedfordshire* plaintiffs any such court forum, the rule was, in effect, a breach of Article 13. In *TP and KM v United Kingdom*, the blanket immunity rule essentially prevented the mother from claiming a remedy for the Newham Council's failure to observe acceptable procedures:

> The exercise of the court's powers to return the child almost a year later was not an effective remedy. It did not provide redress for the psychological damage allegedly flowing from the separation over this period.

[40] The point was well made by Nuala Mole, adviser before the European Commission and the European Court of Human Rights, for both the plaintiffs in *Osman v UK* and in *Z and Others v United Kingdom* and *TP and KM v United Kingdom* in N Mole, 'International Law, the Individual' and AW Brian Simpson, 'Contribution to the Defence of Human Rights', in K O'Donovan and GR Rubin (eds), *Human Rights and Legal History: Essays in Honour of Brian Simpson* (Oxford University Press, 2000), p 26 (n 49). 'All of these eminent jurists (the critics of *Osman*) had difficulty with the court's findings that the decision of the Court of Appeal in *Osman* amounted to a procedural bar, rather than a definition of the content of the right. None has suggested what remedy should have been available in English law in order to satisfy Article 13.'

[41] *Z and Others v United Kingdom*, n 9, para 108; and *TP and KM v United Kingdom*, n 10, para 106.

> The court considers that the applicants should have had available to them a means of claiming that the local authority's handling of the procedures was responsible for the damage which they suffered and obtaining compensation for that damage.[42]

Effect of Human Rights Jurisprudence on New Zealand and English Law

The extent to which human rights concerns filter through to case law in New Zealand remains to be seen. On the one hand, while English cases are seen as influential, there is an increasing divergence in the common law of different jurisdictions, and certainly New Zealand courts will need to address the impact on the United Kingdom's European obligations on English developments (which New Zealand does not share) before adopting them into New Zealand law.[43] On the other hand, New Zealand judges may well view the English decisions as confirming that *X v Bedfordshire*-type immunities are simply inappropriate as a matter of common law, especially since New Zealand judges once clearly led their English counterparts in recognising duties owed by both central[44] and local government.[45]

One of the oddest features of the negative reaction to *Osman* in England was that it came at a time when the *Human Rights Act* 1998 was about to make the Article 6 point irrelevant. The *Human Rights Act* 1998 clearly contemplates actions directly against public authorities which fail to meet their obligations under the now incorporated Convention. The real importance of *Osman* was that, under the European Convention, the police might be liable for failing to protect citizens, and its corollary that other government agencies might also be liable for failing to protect citizens from harm. Indeed, the British government appeared to acknowledge that the children in *Z and Others v United Kingdom*, or the mother in *TP and KM v United Kingdom* would have had an action under the *Human Rights Act* 1998 had it been in force.[46] The court, after dealing with the British government's submission that a number of administrative remedies were available, recorded as telling the government's acceptance that there would be a remedy under the *Human Rights Act*:

[42] *TP and KM v United Kingdom*, n 10, paras 108–9.

[43] The debate over whether *Barrett* ought to be considered unpersuasive for New Zealand because of its 'European' character has already featured in judicial review proceedings of the refusal of the New Zealand government to grant legal aid to the appellants in *B v Attorney-General*: *HB v Attorney-General* (unreported, Wellington High Court, CP 92/00, 15 Dec 2000, McGechan J).

[44] The most famous example is *Takaro Properties v Rowling* [1986] 1 NZLR 22, reversed by the Privy Council in *Rowling v Takaro Properties* [1989] AC 473.

[45] *Brown v Heathcote County Council* [1986] 1 NZLR 76 and *Invercargill City Council v Hamlin* [1996] 1 NZLR 515.

[46] See N Mole, 'International Law, the Individual' and AWB Simpson, 'Contribution to the Defense of Legal Rights', in K O'Donovan and GR Rubin (eds), *Human Rights and Legal History: Essays in Honour of Brian Simpson* (Oxford University Press, 2000), p 27.

> [the UK Government] pointed out that from October 2000, when the *Human Rights Act* 1998 came into force, a victim would be able to bring proceedings in the courts against a public authority for a breach of a substantive right and the courts would be empowered to award damages.[47]

The application of human rights norms does not automatically make welfare agencies liable under tort law for social welfare decisions that turn out wrongly. What both decisions require is the careful identification of the reasons why a particular suit should not be allowed. For example, the Human Rights Commission, in *Z and Others v United Kingdom*, had accepted that the United Kingdom had pursued a legitimate aim in trying to preserve the social worker's role from undue interference, but was not persuaded that a blanket denial of liability was necessary. The Commission wrote, in relation to the Article 6 claim:

> The Commission accepts that this restriction pursued a legitimate aim, namely, to preserve the efficiency of a vital sector of public service . . . However, it is not satisfied that it was proportionate to that aim. It notes that the exclusionary rule gave no consideration to the seriousness, or otherwise, of the damage or the nature or degree of the negligence alleged or the fundamental rights of the applicants which were involved. As regards the multi-disciplinary aspects of child protection work, this may provide a factual complexity to cases but cannot by itself provide a justification for excluding liability from a body found to have acted negligently. The risk that liability would open a floodgate of litigation from discontented parents or relatives is a speculative factor which is only of limited weight. The conflictual nature of child care work equally reflects the fact that it frequently concerns matters of fundamental individual importance. The Commission notes that the tests of foreseeability of damage and proximity serve already as limitations of the categories of plaintiffs who can legitimately claim against allegedly negligent local authorities and is not impressed by the argument that liability would render the social services more cautious in the exercise of their powers.[48]

The court in *TP and KM v United Kingdom* similarly clearly believed that any responsibility to parents for disrupting their family life under Article 8 had to take into consideration the state parties' obligations to protect the children, under Article 3, from cruel and degrading treatment.[49] In the court's view, the removal and subsequent measures were clearly aimed at protecting the 'health or morals' and the 'rights and freedoms' of the child. Accordingly, they pursued legitimate aims within the meaning of paragraph 2 of Article 8.

In *Z and Others v United Kingdom*, the court was a little more reticent when expressing possible limitations on the liability of the state to prevent children suffering cruel and degrading treatment. At first blush, it is difficult to conceive of appropriate limiting factors to an obligation to prevent cruel treatment of chil-

[47] *Z and Others v United Kingdom*, n 9, para 107.
[48] *Z and Others v United Kingdom*, n 9, para 114.
[49] *TP and KM v United Kingdom*, n 10, para 69.

dren. But that is the wrong inquiry. The right inquiry is whether the system employed by the responsible authorities to detect and prevent abuse was appropriate, given both the seriousness of obligations under Article 3 to prevent the abuse and the importance of other obligations under the Convention, especially to respect family life. But in its analysis of whether the facts of *Z and Others v United Kingdom* showed a breach of Article 3, the court put to one side 'difficult and sensitive decisions facing social services and the important countervailing principle of respecting and preserving family life' because 'the present case . . . leaves no doubt as to the failure of the system to protect these children.'[50] The clear implication left is that, in appropriate cases, the countervailing duty would prevent the application of something akin to strict liability. Further, it was clear from *Osman* that the positive obligations of state officials to protect others' lives might be triggered by state officials' knowledge that the lives were under threat. The court acknowledged that there was a clear difference between traditional Article 13 cases, in which there was an allegation that a state official was directly responsible for cruel and degrading treatment, and those where the state had failed to protect others from cruel or degrading treatment. In state action cases, it was appropriate to require member states to carry out the investigations, while in failure to act cases the court considered that Article 13 may not always require that the authorities undertake the responsibility for investigating the allegations.[51] There should, however, be available to the victim's family a mechanism for establishing the liability of state officials or bodies for acts or omissions involving the breach of rights under the Convention.

THE ENGLISH AND NEW ZEALAND COMMON LAW APPROACHES COMPARED

The Need to Differentiate Cases

The nature of the particular decision which is alleged to have been negligently made is important to understanding the English and New Zealand court decisions in the area. New Zealand courts and the English courts, for instance, have identified a distinction between the decision to remove children from their parents (*Attorney-General v Prince*[52] and *X v Bedfordshire*),[53] and subsequent treatment of the child when in care (in *Barrett v Enfield London Borough Council*),[54] or the subsequent investigation of a complaint once child has been removed (*B v Attorney-General*).[55] While we will argue that distinctions have been applied

[50] *Z and Others v United Kingdom*, n 9, para 74.
[51] *Z and Others v United Kingdom*, n 9, para 109.
[52] See n 2.
[53] See n 3.
[54] See n 7.
[55] See n 4.

inappropriately, there can be no one approach to common law liability in the family law context. This should not be a surprise. Attempts to articulate one simple, easy principle have proved illusory in other areas of negligence.

It is necessary to draw distinctions between different case groups, but those distinctions ought to reflect the values implicit in modern family law statutes. In particular, common law liability ought not to be used to circumvent the priorities established by those statutes. The appropriate question for courts is not whether the negligent actions of the social workers occurred at a particular stage, but whether the imposition of a private tort duty would cut across the statutory scheme of modern family law. The key question for family lawyers under such an analysis is what exactly the priorities of modern family law are.

A Short Diversion into New Zealand Family Law

New Zealand family law statutes are notoriously confused in setting out priorities—the more recent family legislation in New Zealand often presents decision-makers with conflicting goals, which are supposed to be observed when exercising various powers. The New Zealand statute is not unique in this.

The *Children, Young Persons and their Families Act* 1989 instituted a dramatic new system for determining what outcomes should ensue for children in need of care and protection. Instead of relying on the apparent wisdom of professionals, social workers and other experts, primary decision-making was located in the so-called 'family group conference'. This gathering of members of the extended family—'whanau' in indigenous Maori terminology—is charged with formulating plans for the future of an abused or neglected child. While the responsible social worker has a residual right of veto over a plan where, for example, it is thought not to protect the interests of the child, the policy thrust is to avoid top-down solutions imposed on the family.[56] The state should intervene primarily to facilitate the family's decision-making, not to take over the child's life. Use of the court structure is designed to be a last resort, usually where the family group conference has failed.[57]

At the time of the passage of this legislation, a somewhat strange confluence of Maori values and New Right ideologies occurred. Maori wanted the ability to make decisions for their own children. New Rightists believed in the minimalist state and individual responsibility. When the state was seen much more as a protective agency performing public services, the thought of suing the state itself was relegated in favour of a wider public interest. But the model of the minimalist state reverses this. If the state is now merely a professional facilitator for individuals and groups, it lays itself open to greater accountability, including action through the courts. But when the genie is let out of the bottle, it is hard to restrict

[56] In 1999 there were 27,017 notifications of abuse, leading to 3,345 family group conferences.
[57] Despite this, the level of court orders under the Act is high: 1,551 in 1999.

the temporal scope of claims. Events that occurred prior to the passing of the 1989 Act have also come under scrutiny and have led to litigation. Some of these cases are reviewed below.

In the meantime, it is important to appreciate what tasks the state is given in child protection cases. For, while the family group is central to the process, much else must happen before a matter is placed before the family group, and much may happen afterwards. Some of the principal steps set out in the legislation are:

- —Under section 15, reports of abuse may be made to an official social worker or a member of the police. Such reports attract immunity from civil, criminal and professional proceedings.
- —The social worker or member of the police must 'as soon as practicable' investigate the report.
- —If the investigator 'reasonably believes' that the child is in need of care or protection, the case must be referred to a care and protection coordinator who, in turn, is obliged to convene a family group conference.[58]
- —After consultation with the family, the care and protection coordinator must fix the time and place for the conference and must determine who should be invited to attend. Under section 22, the child has a right to attend unless this would be 'undesirable'. The child's parents, guardians and care-givers, and members of the 'family, whanau, or family group',[59] also have a right to attend, unless the coordinator is of the opinion that such attendance would not be in the child's interests or would be undesirable for any other reason.
- —Where a plan agreed to by the conference is acceptable to the authorities, the department,[60] 'unless it is clearly impracticable or clearly inconsistent with the principles' of the Act, is required to give effect to the plan.[61] In some situations, this may involve placing the child in the custody or under the guardianship of the department.

The *Children and Young Persons Act* 1974, which applied in both *Prince* and *B v Attorney-General*, was repealed by the 1989 Act, and can be compared:

- —Where there was reason to suspect that a child was suffering or likely to suffer from ill-treatment or from inadequate care or control, or where the child's behaviour was causing serious concern, the department was required to arrange for 'prompt inquiry' for the provision of assistance to the parties involved.[62]
- —Where a member of the police or a social worker reasonably believed that a child was in need of care, protection or control, a complaint could be made

[58] *Children, Young Persons and their Families Act* 1989, ss 17 and 18. It appears that often statutory family group conferences are not convened, but instead 'family meetings' are held. The lawfulness of this approach may be questioned.

[59] 'Family' and 'whanau' are not defined in the Act, but 'family group' is defined to include an extended family, determined by biological and adoptive relationships as well as by significant psychological attachments not involving biological or adoptive links (s 2(1)).

[60] The Department of Child Youth and Family Services, formerly the Department of Social Welfare.

[61] *Children, Young Persons and their Families Act* 1989, s 35.

[62] *Children and Young Persons Act* 1974, s 5(2).

(but did not have to be made) to have the matter determined by the Children and Young Persons Court.[63]
— The court had a range of orders which it could make, including admonition and placing the child in state care.[64]

The 1989 Act is replete with statutory obligations. Many of them, however, involve an element of judgment. In determining the reasonableness of a report of abuse, a degree of assessment is required. Likewise, other decisions, such as the membership of a family group conference, are elastic. These are backed up by a range of 'principles', some of them conflicting.[65] For example, while the welfare and interests of the child are paramount and the child must be protected from harm, the child's relationship with the family, whanau or family group should be maintained and strengthened, consideration must be given to the stability of the family, and intervention into family life must be the minimum necessary for the child's safety and protection.

The statutory scheme is, therefore, a confused patchwork of duties, discretions and principles. The 1989 Act is not so different in this respect from the 1974 Act, except that the current law places much more weight on the importance of the family and 'family group.'[66] Getting the balance right between safety and over-intervention in family life is always hard in child abuse cases. It is even harder when the statutory framework is as described. To be looking over one's shoulder at the prospect of civil litigation, such claims for damages simply add to the pressures of a difficult situation. Failures can readily be understood and even excused. But does this mean that, in the absence of bad faith, there should be general immunity? Are there not standards which even government officers are expected to meet? What if decisions are made in the face of obvious evidence pointing in the opposite direction—for example, where a father accused of sexual abuse could not have been responsible because all access to the child had ceased?[67] In other words, when carrying out straightforward tasks which involve less of an element of assessment and judgment, should aggrieved parties be prevented from suing?

In *Attorney-General v Prince* (discussed below), the New Zealand Court of Appeal accepted that a duty of care could be imposed. One of the strongest reasons behind this decision was the lack of ambiguity in the statutory scheme—in the Court of Appeal's view, the *Children and Young Persons Act* 1974 unambiguously required prompt inquiry of reports of abuse. Subsequent legislation also emphasises the importance of the family group and of cultural values. While the 1989 Act ultimately places the interests of the child above those of the family group or wider culture, the ambiguous relationship between the welfare of the child, the welfare of the family group and the values of the culture in which both exist have left New Zealand judges uneasy about whether common law liability should exist.

[63] *Ibid.*, s 27.

[64] *Ibid.*, s 31.

[65] *Children, Young Persons and their Families Act* 1989, ss 5, 6 and 13.

[66] In fact, in 1983 amendments were made to the 1974 Act which represent the first signs of a legislative recognition of the importance of the family group: ss 4A–4C.

[67] As in *Parkinson v Attorney-General* [2000] NZFLR 552.

Courts Making Different Distinctions and Reaching Different Results

Distinctions, however, are never free from an appearance of arbitrariness. The paradox of the New Zealand and English case law in care and protection cases is that courts, while making essentially the same distinctions, have reached the reverse results. In New Zealand there appears to be liability for the failure to investigate a complaint, while in England there is no liability (the European Convention aside), if *Bedfordshire* is followed, for the decision to remove or not to remove the child from their family. The position is, however, reversed in the respective jurisdictions once that decision to remove has been made. In *B v Attorney-General* the New Zealand Court of Appeal held that social workers' common law duty did not exist after a decision was made to remove the child, and did not extend even to an earlier incompetent investigation into the child's allegation that she had been abused by her father. In *Barrett v Enfield London Borough Council* the House of Lords held that social workers might be held liable for decisions they had made in regard to the welfare of a child once that child had been placed in care.

Negligence Claims Brought by Parents, Families or Affected Third Parties

Claims in this group can be broken into two sub-groups. The first is where a family alleges that a social worker has failed in a duty to the family, independent of statute, which that social worker has breached by placing a 'dangerous' child with the family and that dangerous child has later caused harm to the family members. The second group involves cases where a parent alleges that a social worker's decision to remove a child from his normal family environment has compromised the parents' interests. The dangerous child cases are the clearest cases in which courts are prepared to hold that there will be common law liability. In these cases, the judges typically see little conflict between the statutory scheme of the statute under which the social worker has been acting and the imposition of a private law duty of care. The disadvantaged parent cases, on the other hand, represent the situation in which courts have been most reluctant to impose a private law duty of care. Courts in these disadvantaged parent cases believe that the imposition of such a duty of care would cut across the statutory scheme under which the welfare agency is acting, the primary goal of which is the protection of the child.

The 'Dangerous Child'

The two most prominent English dangerous child cases are the 1979 *Vicar of Writtle* case,[68] and the much more recent decisions of the English Court of Appeal and the House of Lords in the case of *W v Essex.*[69]

[68] *The Vicar of Writtle v Essex County Council* (1977) 77 LGR 656.
[69] *W and Others v Essex County Council and Another* [1998] 3 WLR 534.

The *Vicar of Writtle* case involved the failure of social services to alert a foster home that the child entrusted into its care was suspected of fire-raising at his school. Unfortunately the child, while in the plaintiff's care, set the foster home on fire, causing widespread damage. While Forbes J acknowledged that the welfare service had considerable discretion in the way in which it dealt with children under its care, he held that there had been no exercise of that discretion. Indeed, there was a policy at the head office that information about a child's propensity to light fires would be important information for a prospective foster parent to know. The judge's analysis was very similar to Lord Reid's approach in *Dorset Yacht Club*,[70] where the legitimate exercise of discretion to rehabilitate the Borstal boys might have meant that the Home Office ought not to be liable if the rehabilitation were to go wrong. Far more important was the close relationship that the judge perceived between the social worker who placed the child and the foster home that accepted him.

The English Court of Appeal decided in *W v Essex* not to strike out a statement of claim that alleged that the foster parents' children had been sexually abused by a child that the defendant's social workers had placed with the family. The Court of Appeal's decision was notable as the only one of three post-*X v Bedfordshire* decisions involving actions against social workers to be allowed to proceed to trial, before the House of Lords' decision in *Barrett*. The other two Court of Appeal decisions—*Barrett*[71] itself and *H v Norfolk County Council*[72]—had involved, respectively, allegations about the way a child had been treated by the social welfare agency once in care, and an allegation that a child had been sexually abused by a foster parent. In both *Barrett* and *H v Norfolk County Council*, the English Court of Appeal held that the cases were governed by *X v Bedfordshire* and, as imposing a duty of care would cut across the statutory scheme of child protection, the plaintiffs' claims ought to be struck out. In contrast, in *W v Essex*, the majority of the Court of Appeal focused on the relationship that existed between the social worker and the foster family, almost outside the statutory context. In the view of Judge and Mantell LJJ, the assurances of the social worker that the child did not have a record of sexual abuse and the social worker's knowledge that the child would only be accepted by the foster parents if there were no record of sexual abuse gave rise to a *Hedley Byrne* reliance type of relationship.[73] In contrast, Stuart-Smith LJ in dissent held that the recognition of liability based on negligent misstatement would cut across the statutory scheme in a way that was impermissible after *X v Bedfordshire*. The correctness of the majority's

70 *Home Office v Dorset Yacht Co Ltd* [1970] AC 1004.

71 *Barrett v Enfield London Borough Council* [1997] 2 FLR 167.

72 *H v Norfolk County Council* [1997] 1 FLR 384.

73 *Hedley Byrne & Co Ltd v Heller & Partners Ltd* [1964] AC 465. The Court of Appeal unanimously rejected the plaintiffs' contention that there had been a contract between the social worker and the plaintiffs which the social worker had breached. For a critique of the court's refusal to find a contract, see B Coote, 'Common Forms, Consideration, and Contract Doctrine' (1999) 14 *Journal of Contract Law* 116.

approach has been underlined by the House of Lords' decision on appeal that not only might the abused children be able to claim against the social welfare agency, but also that the parents might be able to, at least for the 'nervous shock' of discovering that their children had been abused. Lord Slynn of Hadley wrote of the question of whether a duty might be owed to the parents:

> It seems to me that it cannot be said here that the claim that there was a duty of care owed to the parents and a breach of that duty by the defendants is unarguable, that it is clear and obvious that it cannot succeed. On the contrary whether it is right or wrong on the facts found at the end of the day, it is on the facts alleged plainly a claim which is arguable. In their case the parents made it clear that they were anxious not to put their children at risk by having a known sex abuser in their home. The council and the social worker knew this and also knew that the boy placed had already committed an act or acts of sex abuse. The risk was obvious and the abuse happened. Whether the nature of the council's task is such that the court should not recognise an actionable duty of care, in other words that the claim is not justiciable, and whether there was a breach of the duty depend, in the first place, on an investigation of the full facts known to, and the factors influencing the decision of, the defendants.[74]

The House of Lords then left it open for trial whether the parents would be able to establish that they suffered harm under the requirements of nervous shock.

Judges in the 'dangerous child' cases tend to minimise the importance of the social worker's statutory discretion or role in 'rehabilitating' a troubled child and emphasise the reliance by the foster families. This can be contrasted with the care and protection cases where that same discretion forms the major barrier which any claim against social workers in this context must get over.

Claims by Disadvantaged Parents and Families

In contrast to the success of claims by foster parents for harm by a dangerous child, claims that the interest of parents (or the families) have been compromised by negligent decisions by social workers have been notably unsuccessful, with the limited exception of the European Court of Human Rights' holding in *TP and KM v United Kingdom.*

In the *Newham* case, which was heard together with *X v Bedfordshire* by the House of Lords, the plaintiff child alleged that she had been wrongfully removed from her mother by a social worker who suspected (wrongly, as it turned out) that the child was being abused by the mother's partner. In Lord Browne-Wilkinson's view, such a duty would cut across the statutory scheme. Lord Browne-Wilkinson wrote in *X v Bedfordshire* that:

> The relationship between the social worker and the child's parents is frequently one of conflict, the parent wishing to retain care of the child, the social worker having to consider whether to remove it. This is fertile ground in which to breed ill-feeling and litigation, often hopeless, the cost of which both in terms of money and human

[74] See n 69, p 605.

> resources will be diverted from the performance of the social service for which they were provided. The spectre of vexatious and costly litigation is often urged as a reason for not imposing a legal duty. But the circumstances surrounding cases of child abuse make the risk a very high one which cannot be ignored.[75]

Unsurprisingly, parents who had sought to make the similar claim that they had been deprived unnecessarily of their children by a social worker making the wrong determination that the parent was abusing the child have been unsuccessful. In the New Zealand case of *E v K*,[76] Morris J struck out such a claim by a father who had alleged that a social worker had wrongly determined that he had abused his child. Morris J accepted that there was a relationship of proximity between the social worker, in investigating sexual abuse allegations, and the subject of those allegations. But he held that policy would prevent the imposition of a duty of care. In particular, a duty to a child abuse suspect might cut across the paramountcy principle that is at the heart of modern family law. A duty of care might create a conflict of interest for a social worker, whose job under the *Children and Young Persons Act* 1974 was to guard the interests of the child.[77] An appropriate analogy was with private-sector professionals, including lawyers, who have an obligation to protect the interests of their clients. We partially agree with this 'conflict of interest' analysis—an important part of whether there can be a duty of care ought to be the degree to which the imposition of such a duty might place the prospective defendant in an impossible position.

Care needs to be taken with comparisons to private-sector professionals. They are perhaps a little misplaced in the case of social workers exercising statutory powers of removal, as there are really no comparable private professionals who can exercise the kinds of powers with which social workers are entrusted. Even with psychologists, who might be said to be acting as private professionals employed to assist the social workers—or, indeed, simply to treat the patient at hand—it is easy to be too absolute about the duty being owed only to the patient. As Morris J himself acknowledged, lawyers in a range of contexts can owe duties to non-clients.[78] Certainly in the education cases considered at the same time as *X v Bedfordshire*, Lord Browne-Wilkinson accepted that psychologists, employed by local school authorities to assess children as to whether they had special edu-

[75] See n 3, pp 750–51.

[76] [1995] 2 NZLR 239.

[77] *Ibid.*, p 249.

[78] Examples include the frustrated testamentary beneficiary cases, but also include, in some instances, the failure to ensure that a non-client gets advice. See also Master Venning in *N v D* [1999] NZFLR 560. Lawyers may owe a duty to a third party when giving a solicitor's certificate: *Allied Finance v Haddow* [1983] NZLR 22, and in the family law context it was held that a lawyer advising one party on a matrimonial property agreement (under s 21 of the *Matrimonial Property Act* 1976) owed a duty to the other spouse: *Connell v Odlum* [1993] 2 NZLR 257. It ought to be noted that, at least in commercial contexts, the New Zealand Court of Appeal has emphasised in cases such as *Brownie Wills v Shrimpton* [1998] 2 NZLR 320 that in the absence of special circumstances there will be no duty to advise a non-client.

cational needs, might owe duties to children they assess, even though they were not, strictly speaking, their patients.[79]

Morris J's decision was essentially followed by Gallen J in the first-instance decision in *B v Attorney-General*.[80] In this case, a daughter had made an allegation to a school friend that her father had abused her. Upon hearing the allegations, social workers removed both the daughter and her sister from their father's care. A subsequent, and prolonged, hearing established that the child had not meant her allegations. The father and the daughters sued the department and the psychologist employed to assist it, alleging that the conduct of the investigation had unnecessarily prolonged the length of the separation and greatly increased the family's legal costs in fighting the allegations. Gallen J acknowledged that the social worker's decision to remove the children from a parent accused of abuse, and the conduct of the subsequent investigation of that abuse, would foreseeably affect the father. However, it was inappropriate to allow a private law claim of negligence to be brought by the father because of the importance of safeguarding a child at risk.[81] His Honour also referred to the urgency with which social workers must work. We doubt that this factor was in fact a key one in *B v Attorney-General*, since the father accepted that there could be no liability for the initial, protective decision to remove the children, but rather sued in relation to the ongoing refusal to return the children. An appeal failed.[82] The Court of Appeal did not deal directly with the claim brought by the father. Both the joint judgment of Keith and Blanchard JJ and the concurring judgment of Tipping J dealt with the father's claim in the same manner as that of the children. If the children could not succeed, the father certainly could not. But, perhaps more importantly, running the father's and the daughters' claims together obscured the different considerations that ought to apply to what are, in fact, very different claims.

These decisions, however, have to be contrasted with that of Master Venning in *N v D*.[83] Master Venning accepted that not only was the relationship between a psychotherapist and her patient's father, who was accused of abusing the patient, sufficiently proximate but, in contrast to Morris J's decision,[84] the duty of care should not be defeated by public policy. Master Venning sought to distinguish this case on the basis that in *E v K* the social worker had been performing a statutory power to protect the child from future abuse. In *N v D* not only was the psychotherapist not acting in accordance with a statutory duty, but she had gone beyond simply treating the patient to alerting another psychologist who was

[79] See *Phelps v Hillingdon London Borough Council; Anderton v Clwyd County Council; G (A Minor) v Bromley London Borough Council* [2000] 3 WLR 776, where the House of Lords allowed the possibility of such a duty.

[80] [1997] NZFLR 550.

[81] *Ibid.*, p 565.

[82] See n 4.

[83] [1999] NZFLR 560.

[84] And, we might add, an extensive citation and analysis of *E v K* and *B v Attorney-General* in the High Court, on which we have ourselves drawn.

charged by the Family Court to prepare a quite separate report for a custody hearing. The Master concluded:

> In this case the plaintiff is the person that the defendant identified as having committed sexual abuse on the child. That allegation was passed on to third parties apart from the child's parents. The defendant intentionally passed the result of her findings on to the report writer in the Family Court proceedings. In those circumstances the defendant must have known, or should have known, that in passing on that accusation of sexual abuse it would impact upon the plaintiff as the person against whom the allegation was made. The relationship is direct and close.[85]

The Master emphasised that, unlike the other two cases, the child was not at risk at the time the psychotherapist made her views known more widely. The Master also focused on the need, echoing Lord Bingham MR in the *Newham* case, for the affected parent to have a real remedy.[86]

We wonder whether it is appropriate to make such a distinction. Can it really be said that it is only a statutory duty that requires professionals to contact relevant authorities? We wonder whether Morris J's concern that the professionals not be charged with common law duties that might prevent them from properly protecting their clients ought also, prima facie, apply in cases outside the statutory scheme of the child welfare statutes. Certainly Morris J's concern not to create conflicting duties on child welfare professionals was echoed more recently by a Canadian judge who refused to impose a common law duty on a counsellor whom a family alleged had failed to properly treat a patient, leading the patient to make allegations of sexual abuse against her father.[87] Beames J reviewed a number of US authorities, in which courts had imposed liability on therapists to third parties, but rejected for similar reasons a private law duty in Canada. The judge there wrote:

> Notwithstanding the societal interests in preventing false accusations of abuse, I conclude that the detection and reporting of abuse are more important societal goals, and further, because the healing of victims may be dependent upon the maintenance of confidence between a therapist and patient and upon the undiluted duty of a therapist to the patient, it is only in the most compelling circumstances that a court should extend a duty of care from a therapist to those third parties who may be identified in the course of therapy as alleged perpetrators. Those cases which have found such a duty . . . have done so on a very limited basis, based upon the particular facts in the case. Amongst other factors, those cases where a duty has been found have involved the therapist either personally undertaking, or encouraging their patient to make, public accusations against the perpetrators.[88]

However, we also wonder whether this prima facie reluctance to impose a duty might be countered in *N v D* by the other two factors the Master mentioned. After

[85] See n 83, p 564.
[86] See n 84, p 564.
[87] *Gardner v Rusch* (1999) 179 DLR (4th)336.
[88] *Ibid.*, p 349, para 36.

all, as the Master himself argued, in certain circumstances professionals have been held to owe duties to those other than their clients.[89] Firstly, this case was not an emergency one—the child was out of any immediate danger and the psychotherapist had treated the alleged victim for a long period of time before she made the allegations. Secondly, the psychotherapist chose to put herself outside the umbrella of the statutory scheme and its protection. We suggest that the conflict of interests analysis is perhaps the most important factor, but it cannot be the only factor in determining liability.

The Care and Protection Cases

Introduction: One Distinction, Different Results

It is possible to argue that the courts have adopted a consistent approach to suits brought by affected families, and have rightly focused on the fear that allowing parents to bring suit in the second sub-category might cut across the statutory scheme of child welfare legislation. No such consistency is evident in care and protection cases.

Both New Zealand and UK courts have essentially adopted the same prime requirement—that a private law duty does not 'cut across the statutory scheme'—but the inconsistent results reached by those courts indicate that this phrase is less of a test and more a way of justifying the result that the court has reached.

Elsewhere, one of us has compared in detail the reasoning of the New Zealand Court of Appeal in *Prince* with that of the House of Lords in *X v Bedfordshire.*[90] We do not intend to describe in the same detail those two cases. Nevertheless, it will be necessary to repeat some of the arguments in that paper before considering more recent cases, *Barrett* and *B*.

In *Prince*, the New Zealand Court of Appeal was prepared to allow a claim that social workers had failed to investigate an allegation that the teenager Prince was being neglected by his adoptive parents. The Court of Appeal was prepared to let such a claim go to trial on the basis that a duty of care to investigate such allegations would not cut across the statutory scheme of the *Children and Young Persons Act* 1974. But the majority argued further that such a duty would, in fact, reinforce the duties placed by the statute on the Department of Social Welfare to guard the interests of children at risk. In doing so, the Court of Appeal purported to adopt the same approach as Lord Browne-Wilkinson had in *X v Bedfordshire.* Given the existence of different statutes in two different jurisdictions, it was quite conceivable that there might be liability under one regime but not under the other. However, an analysis of the *Children Act* 1989, and its predecessor legislation, and

[89] See n 83, p 568.

[90] G McLay, '*Attorney-General v Prince*, 'Convicted Killer Can Sue Social Welfare'—*Prince*, the Strange Fate of *Bedfordshire* Down-Under' [1999] CFLQ 75.

the *Children and Young Persons Act* 1974 reveals almost identical statutory wording. The difference in results, therefore, cannot be explained simply by the observation that different statutes were involved. Rather, the decision in *Prince* seemed to reflect a different weighing of the policy factors that Lord Browne-Wilkinson had thought so important in denying a duty of care in *X v Bedfordshire.*

The difference in approach is perhaps best exposed by comparing the different weighing of two policy factors: firstly, the difficulty of a social worker's job and the potential that liability might somehow promote defensive social work; and secondly, the availability of administrative procedures through which the social worker's behaviour might be measured.

The Extraordinary Delicacy of the Social Worker's Task

Lord Browne-Wilkinson correctly termed the social worker's job as involving 'extraordinary delicacy' and expressed the not uncommon fear that the imposition of a duty of care might adversely affect the way that social workers discharged their statutory duty. But, rather than being focused on the performance of the statutory obligations to protect children, social workers would be focused instead on avoiding liability, to the detriment of the children they were supposed to protect:

> The question whether there is such a common law duty, and if so its ambit, must be profoundly influenced by the statutory framework within which the acts complained of were done . . . in my judgment a common law duty of care cannot be imposed on a statutory duty if the observance of such a common law duty of care would be inconsistent with, or have a tendency to discourage, the due performance by the local authority of its statutory duties.[91]

As discussed above, New Zealand courts have been alive to this fear when adversely affected parents have brought suit. The New Zealand Court of Appeal, however, rejected this is as a reason for not imposing liability in *Prince.* Indeed, the New Zealand Court of Appeal was somewhat sceptical of the validity, in the absence of hard data, of this adverse deterrence argument. Writing for the majority, Richardson J concluded:

> [the Crown] submitted that the imposition of a duty would or could cause the department and social workers to adopt a more cautious and defensive approach to their duties. He drew our attention to a considerable body of professional literature on that point and to the recognition of it in the *Bedfordshire* case . . . But like lawyers and doctors, social workers are professionals. At that triggering step [the court's characterisation of the initial decision to investigate a complaint] (and at other steps) they should be expected to have shouldered willingly a standard of reasonable skill and care that the private sector counterparts were expected to discharge. And in the

[91] See n 3, p 739.

> absence of any data as to potential claims based on the roles and responsibilities of department and social workers under the 1974 Act, which was replaced eight years ago by a very different legislative scheme, it would be unwise to give any particular weight to the resource implications of allowing for a common law duty of care.[92]

The force of the comparison between social workers' exercising powers to remove children, and normal professional responsibility of others, is that it dispels Lord Browne-Wilkinson's conclusion that the extraordinary delicacy of the social workers' task was any different from the delicacy which we associate with those professional groupings. As courts have been quite willing to impose duties on those professionals, the courts should not necessarily refuse to impose duties of care on social workers. There is some truth in this analogy. However, what the analogy cannot resolve is the source of the duty of care that is being imposed by the courts. Social workers involved in care and protection cases in fact exercise powers which are uniquely public—that is, the power to remove children from their families—and which have little or no private-sector comparison. On the other hand, social workers involved in the subsequent care of children might be said to be doing something much more analogous to private-sector nurses, or nannies or guardians.

Indeed, the Court of Appeal did not really identify the statute as being the source of the social worker's common law obligation, preferring merely to say that the common law duty simply reinforced the statutory obligations, rather than being derived from them. The majority expressed the point in the following way:

> Given the important features of the 1974 Act which we have been emphasising, it cannot be said that a common law duty of care in these terms would cut across the whole statutory scheme. At that early triggering step a specific positive duty rests on the Director-General. At that step it does not require participation with other agencies. The duty suggested does not conflict with any other duty by the department and its officers. On the contrary, it enhances it.[93]

B v Attorney-General: The Court of Appeal Restricts Prince

Because of the way that *Prince* had been pleaded, the Court of Appeal had considered an allegation that the Social Welfare Department had failed to make any investigation into allegations that Prince's adoptive parents were neglecting him. The Court of Appeal's decision in *Attorney-General v Prince* was largely focused on that complete failure to investigate (what it termed the 'triggering stage'), as opposed to the situation where investigation had gone wrong. The significance in *Prince* of an allegation that there had been no investigation was that it ruled out any argument that the social workers involved had exercised any discretion that would justify the court in saying that the social workers had legitimately exercised their professional discretion.

[92] See n 2, pp 284–85.
[93] *Ibid.*, p 284.

Before the Court of Appeal's decision in *B v Attorney-General*, it was possible to argue that *Prince* should not necessarily be restricted to situations where the social workers had failed to institute an investigation at all. The focus in Richardson P's judgment on the obligations of the Director-General to undertake an initial investigation might simply have been taken as a reflection of the procedural status of *Prince*. The court did not necessarily rule out the possibility of liability for inadequate investigations and, indeed, appeared to imply that there might be liability in some cases. However, because it was a striking-out application, the Court of Appeal needed to reach a definite conclusion only about the possibility of liability under the best possible scenario for the defendant.

B v Attorney-General, however, involved an allegation that the subsequent substantive investigation of a child's claim that her father had abused her had been negligently undertaken, leading to a child and her sister being kept from their perfectly innocent father for over eighteen months. It was the father's and his daughters' contention that, had the investigation been properly undertaken, the allegations would have been easily disproved. Rather than focusing on the obligations of the social workers to protect the interests of the child in any investigation, including an obligation not unnecessarily to deprive a child of her parents, the Court of Appeal restricted *Prince*. The court held that the duties the court had imposed in *Prince* did not apply once investigations had moved beyond the initial triggering stage. Keith J, writing for himself and Blanchard J, concluded:

> That temporal issue is critical in the circumstances of this case. By contrast to the facts alleged in *Prince*, the facts complained of here occurred after the immediate triggering step. That step was the response by the department to the information provided by the mother of the friend of [the daughter] including the decision to arrange for the prompt inquiry. By contrast, the criticised actions were various actions and failures occurring in the course of the investigation which followed and which continued beyond the initiation of the court process.[94]

This temporal distinction was key in the court's view because of the scope of the duties imposed on the Director-General by section 5 of the 1974 Act. Keith J wrote:

> We have no doubt that the breaches of duty alleged in this case fall outside that initial period of positive statute obligations during which, in accordance with *Prince*, a common law duty of care may also arise. In this case the process moved rapidly from the initial stage, involving a duty, to the operational stage of information-gathering and considering the exercise of statutory powers and then to the exercise of those powers. At this stage the department is exercising a discretion . . . the difficulties may be greater when a decision is made not to launch court proceedings. In some cases that decision may be so unreasonable as to amount to a failure of the department to do its duty. But we do not in this case have to give a precise definition to the line. The facts here lie clearly beyond it.[95]

[94] See n 4, pp 303–4.
[95] *Ibid.*, p 305.

The distinction was drawn between the duty to institute an inquiry as part of the initial triggering stage and the subsequent conduct of that investigation, during which no duty was possible. This distinction was possible because the Court of Appeal in *Prince* left unclear the underlying source of the social worker's duty. While the Court of Appeal in *Prince* had focused on the statutory duties imposed by section 5 of the 1974 Act, it is unclear whether the majority necessarily viewed the 1974 Act as the source of social workers' duty. Rather, the majority spoke of the common law duty, however it arose, as reinforcing the statutory obligations of the social workers. The Court of Appeal in *B v Attorney-General* appeared to interpret the duty in *Prince* as being defined by the obligations in the 1974 Act. If, of course, the duty at common law had arisen independently of the statute, as *Prince* appeared to indicate, then there is no reason why that duty should be restricted to the obligations imposed by the statute.

From a tort law perspective, a comparison of *Prince* and *B v Attorney-General* leads to the odd proposition that, while social workers might be liable if they do nothing, they are not liable so long as they do something (unless what they actually do is so unreasonable as to be, in effect, a failure to do anything at all). In essence, the New Zealand court had reached an odd position whereby social workers might be liable for non-feasance but not liable for misfeasance. This reflects a reversal of the normal common law rule that professionals, in the absence of a special relationship, owe no duty to act to protect others, but do owe a duty to take reasonable care once they have decided to act to protect others.

From a family law perspective, the distinction also appears to us unsustainable. The initial investigation of abuse cases must be done in great haste, and a preliminary determination made quickly so as to prevent any further abuse. Yet at this stage the Court of Appeal in *Prince* seemed prepared to impose a duty. Bad decisions at this stage can be remedied in the next steps of the process. The element of haste is, however, far less apparent once the social worker has gone beyond that initial triggering stage. At the later investigatory stage, one can expect a degree of reflection on what is going on that is as reviewable by a court as the exercise of professional obligations in other fields. It is illogical that, had the investigation in fact been conducted in *Prince*, rather than not at all, the social workers should not be liable simply because they were beyond the so-called triggering stage. The oddity of the distinction is perhaps best illustrated by the reasoning of Potter J in the subsequent *Parkinson* decision in the High Court.[96] Despite the facts of *Parkinson* being very similar to those in *B v Attorney-General*, the plaintiff father attempted to distinguish the case so that it could proceed. Potter J clearly viewed the investigation undertaken by the social workers of an allegation of abuse to be the same kind as in *B v Attorney-General*. Her Honour wrote of the investigation:

> In *B* the court considered that to impose a duty of care would prejudice the prompt and efficient exercise of the operational powers and discretions by the Department. In my view the conduct leading up to inquiry, the inquiry, and the views the officers

[96] *Parkinson v Attorney-General* [2000] NZFLR 552.

> formed in that inquiry, relate to the operational stage of information-gathering in which the court in *Prince* and *B* held no duty arose.[97]

The oddity of this conclusion, which is a fair reflection of the holding in *B v Attorney-General*, is that it represents a reversal of the normal understanding that operational decisions are the ones that are most appropriate for courts to assess, in comparison to high policy, which is not.

Similarly, it seems wrong to us that there should be any formula along the lines suggested by Keith J that makes liability depend on whether an investigation can be termed as 'so bad' as not to be an investigation at all. This adds an unnecessary complication to what ought simply to be considered an inquiry as to whether the social workers had behaved according to normal professional standards. Any difficulty as to the delicacy of the social workers' task should be dealt with by the courts in the same way as with other professionals, by asking not whether they got it completely right or completely wrong, but whether they followed a reputable professional methodology in their investigations.

Why the Court of Appeal seemingly accepted such an approach in *Prince*, but rejected it in *B v Attorney-General*, remains a mystery. It is true that the clash of interests involved in *B v Attorney-General* was potentially more complicated than that in *Prince*. The court needs to be much more subtle when reviewing a concluded investigation than a case of no investigation, but is such an inquiry really so much harder than other professional cases? One wonders whether the fact that the father was also bringing a claim meant that the court was concerned about recognising conflicting duties—on the one hand, the social worker's statutory duty to protect the children, while on the other a common law duty to the father. If it was, then these concerns unfortunately remained unexamined and undifferentiated from the children's case. Further, we do not believe that there is necessarily a conflict. The temporal distinction between beginning an investigation and conducting the investigation that the court drew to deny liability might have been better employed to militate against any conflict of interest preventing the social worker from fulfilling the prime role of protecting the child. A duty to the father at the preliminary stage might interfere with social worker's duty to act urgently to protect the child. A duty to the father to conduct the subsequent investigation professionally may not carry the same risks to the child.

The House of Lords and the Proper Place of Discretion: Barrett v Enfield London Borough Council

If New Zealand lawyers could have believed that, after *Prince*, social workers might owe duties of care to children affected by their decisions, after *X v Bedfordshire*, English lawyers would have made the reverse prediction about the liability of English social workers in care and protection cases. For New Zealand lawyers, perhaps a little depressed by the restrictive approach of the Court of Appeal in

97 *Ibid.*, p 570.

B v Attorney-General, the decision of the House of Lords in *Barrett*, released after *B v Attorney-General*, raised the prospect that the New Zealand courts were more conservative than their English counterparts. For English lawyers, who had become accustomed to *X v Bedfordshire* being used to strike out a range of cases brought against Social Services, the decision in *Barrett v Enfield London Borough Council* must have been a revelation.

The plaintiff Barrett alleged that the Social Services section of Enfield London Borough Council had been negligent in a number of important decisions relating to how he was cared for during a childhood largely spent under its protection. The House of Lords held that, in contrast to *X v Bedfordshire*, the claim should not be struck out.

Again, the decision in *Barrett* is worthy of an extended paper in its own right.[98] For the purposes of this paper, we want to compare the approach taken by the House of Lords to the crucial issue of whether a duty can be imposed when a social worker exercises a discretion in regard to a child in care. We believe that the approach of the House of Lords in *Barrett* is far closer to the New Zealand Court of Appeal's decision in *Prince* than it is to its own previous holding in *X v Bedfordshire*. Indeed, their Lordships' approach appears to be more consistent with the New Zealand Court of Appeal's approach in *Prince* than the Court of Appeal's own decision in *B v Attorney-General*.

Ever since *Dorset Yacht Club*, common law courts have struggled with the problem of imposing a common law duty on public officials who exercised a discretion.[99] As we have seen, the House of Lords' perception that the task of social workers was extraordinarily complex played a major role in the House of Lords' striking out of the care and protection causes of action in *X v Bedfordshire*. *X v Bedfordshire* is, however, only one of a series of cases in which the House of Lords and Privy Council have wound themselves into knots over how the courts ought to deal with discretion. The speeches of Lords Slynn of Hadley and Hutton in *Barrett* are important advances in this general debate, but we submit that their reasoning also significantly advances the approach adopted by the English courts in care and protection cases. After *Barrett*, the fact that a defendant was exercising a statutory discretion appears to play at least three roles in a negligence case.

Firstly, the fact that a discretion was exercised might rule out a claim under a justiciability rule that decisions involving matters of high policy are inappropriate to review at common law. Secondly, the fact the discretion has been exercised might be relevant when it comes to consider whether it is just and reasonable to impose a duty of care (as in *X v Bedfordshire* or seemingly in *B v Attorney-General*). Lastly, whether a discretion has been exercised remains an important consideration in whether the duty of care has been breached (seemingly, in *Prince*). In *X v Bedfordshire*, Lord Browne-Wilkinson had placed the social worker's exercise of

[98] See P Craig and D Fairgrieve, n 33.

[99] See T Geuther, 'The Search for Principle—the Government's Liability in Negligence for the Careless Exercise of its Statutory Powers' (2000) 31 VUWLR 629 and J McLean, 'The Ordinary Law of Tort and Contract and the New Public Management' *Common Law World Review* (forthcoming).

discretion clearly within the second role, and used the exercise of discretion as a reason to deny a duty of care. The significance of *Barrett* is to show how unlikely, but not impossible, it is that social workers would have exercised a discretion so as to make the claim non-justiciable. Certainly, it is now important to determine whether there are, in fact, issues of policy that a private law court should not review. There is seemingly no blanket exception of the type suggested by *X v Bedfordshire*. Lord Slynn of Hadley wrote:

> In the present case, the allegations . . . are largely directed to the way in which the powers of the local authority were *exercised*. It is arguable . . . that if some of the allegations are made out, a duty of care was owed and was broken. Others involve the exercise of a discretion which the court may consider to be not justiciable—eg whether it was right to arrange adoption at all, though the question of whether adoption was ever considered and if not, why not, may be a matter of investigation in a claim for negligence.[100]

The fact that liability arises from the exercise of discretion is something that may defeat liability either at the duty stage or, to our minds, preferably at the breach stage, but only after the courts have heard the facts of the case. That *Barrett* had restricted the kinds of cases where it will not be just and reasonable to impose a duty of care was made plain by the English Court of Appeal in *S v Gloucestershire County Council*, in interpreting Lord Slynn of Hadley's observations quoted above.[101] That case involved allegations that a council had been negligent in the placing of children with a foster-parent who subsequently abused the children. May LJ concluded that the negligence claims ought to go to trial, summarising the position after *Barrett* in the following way:

> (a) Depending on the particular facts of the case, a claim in common law negligence may be available to a person who claims to have been damaged by failings of a local authority who were responsible under statutory powers for his care and upbringing . . .
> (b) The claim will not succeed if the failings alleged comprise actions or decisions by the local authority of a kind which are not justiciable. These may include, but will not necessarily be limited to, policy decisions and decisions about allocating public funds.
> (c) The border line between what is justiciable and what is not may in a particular case be unclear. Its demarcation may require a more extensive investigation than is capable of being made from material in traditional pleadings alone.
> (d) There may be circumstances in which it will not be just and reasonable to impose a duty of care of the kind contended for. Here again, it may often be necessary to conduct a detailed investigation of the facts to determine this question.

[100] *Barrett v Enfield London Borough Council*, n 7, quoted in *S v Gloucestershire County Council; L v Tower Hamlets London Borough Council* [2001] 2 WLR 909 at 928.

[101] See n 35.

(e) In considering whether a discretionary decision was negligent, the court will not substitute its view for that of the local authority upon whom the statute has placed the power to exercise the discretion, unless the discretionary decision was plainly wrong. But decisions of, for example, social workers are capable of being held to have been negligent by analogy with decisions of other professional people. Here again, it may well be necessary to conduct a detailed factual enquiry.[102]

Barrett: A Disclaimer

Barrett and *Tower Hamlets* can be distinguished from *X v Bedfordshire, Prince* and *B v Attorney-General.* Indeed, the House of Lords itself clearly distinguished *Barrett* from *X v Bedfordshire.* While *X v Bedfordshire* and *Newham* involved the decision to remove or not to remove the child from the family, *Barrett* involved an allegation that social workers had failed to take care in the way a child was treated while in care. *Barrett* could be distinguished by New Zealand courts on the basis that decisions relating to the subsequent care of children are conceptually different from decisions to remove a child from the parents. However, we submit that the House of Lords' approach to the role of social workers' discretion is highly relevant to both situations.

CONCLUSIONS

Our conclusions can be summarised as follows:

— Three factors are necessarily involved in considering whether there ought to be a duty of care. The first is the statutory scheme under which the social workers and the psychologists are working. The second is the potential creation of a conflict of interest in recognising a duty of care to someone other than the child in care. The third is the time in the investigation that the alleged negligence has occurred.

— The fact that those involved in child welfare decisions have exercised professional discretion should not necessarily mean that a duty of care ought not to be recognised. Courts should be wary of arguments that seek particular immunities for social workers or associated professionals simply on the basis that they exercised professional judgment. There may, as indicated by Lord Slynn of Hadley, be some decisions that may not be justiciable, but we doubt that there are many of these.

— The conflict of interest line of argument seems to us to be the most important reason for holding that sometimes it will not be just and reasonable to impose a duty of care. Social workers and psychologists, especially at the

[102] See n 35, p 932.

initial stage of the investigation, must not be placed in an untenable position where the child's safety is balanced against liability to others.

—The New Zealand Court of Appeal in *B v Attorney-General* was right in seeking to distinguish between the initial stage of investigation and the associated decision to remove the child from the subsequent substantive investigation. However, the use it made of this distinction was inappropriate.

—In particular, we believe that, in the absence of malice (including perhaps premeditation) that might bring into issue possible defamation or misfeasance in a public office actions, plaintiffs other than affected children should not be able to sue during initial procedures (*Barrett* situations involving subsequent care are different). The potential danger to the child creates an urgency that might prevent the due professional weighing of the evidence.

—We believe that at this initial stage, in accordance with *Prince*, social workers ought to owe a duty to the child to investigate the claims.

—We believe that the Court of Appeal was wrong in *B v Attorney-General* to prevent the children from suing the social workers and the psychologist involved merely because their alleged negligence occurred after the preliminary decision to remove the children had been taken and the investigation commenced.

—The fathers' claims in *B v Attorney-General* and in *N v D* present the greatest difficulty for courts. On the one hand, the same conflict of interest is present at the later stage as it was in the initial stage. Once the immediate safety of the child has been secured (which may sometimes mean an urgent removal of the child to a place of safety), the child is not in danger and there is no overwhelming urgency that might prevent a due balancing of the evidence. It is this balance that the Court of Appeal in *B v Attorney-General* ought to have addressed, but did not.

9

Adoption—A Public or Private Legal Process? The Changing Social Functions of Adoption in Ireland and the Wider Implications for Coherence in Family Law

Kerry O'Halloran*

INTRODUCTION

Adoption, in Western societies, now serves a range of functions very different from the one it was initially designed to meet. Its traditional legal function[1] of 'providing homes for children who need them' with third-party applicants is dying out. As a consensual process for securing homes for indigenous healthy babies with unrelated applicants, it probably has no future.

Far from continuing as a fairly simple and essentially private family law process, adoption has in recent years become quite complex, with a growing public law dimension. It no longer sits comfortably in private law and its proceedings are now as likely as not to be contested. It is becoming functionally distorted by legislative and judicial demands that it respond to the pressures now affecting the family in modern society. As a consequence, adoption has become pivotal to the changes in family law. Understanding what is happening to adoption is key to understanding much of what is happening to its related body of family law.

This paper has three parts. The first deals with adoption as a social phenomenon by considering its culture specific nature. It begins with a brief historical survey of the different social roles adoption has played in a range of cultural contexts and then outlines some of its more typical roles in contemporary Western society. The second part focuses specifically on the experience of adoption in Ireland. It identifies and differentiates between the characteristics of adoption in the two jurisdictions on the island. Finally, the third section considers the strategic implications of current trends in adoption for the future coherence of family law.

* Assistant Director (Research), University of Ulster, Northern Ireland. This paper was first published in the [2001] 1–64 *International Family Law Journal* 43.

[1] See the Houghton Committee *Report of the Departmental Committee on the Adoption of Children* (1972), where the view is expressed that 'The child is the focal point in adoption; providing homes for children who need them is its primary purpose.'

ADOPTION AS A SOCIAL PHENOMENON

Adoption is a culture-specific legal entity. Different societies have found different uses for it. In Western society, it was typically represented by three parties: the natural parent/s; their lovingly relinquished healthy baby; and the unrelated married but childless heterosexual couple. It is instructive to note just how far adoption has in fact deviated from this model.

Historical Overview of Adoption Functions

The following brief historical overview of adoption as a social phenomenon reveals that its usefulness, at various times and places, has rested in particular on a capacity to meet the needs of adopters with a range of quite different motives.

Adoption and the Inheritance Motive

Adoption has its legal origins in the law relating to the ownership and inheritance of property.[2] The concern of those with land but without children to legally acquire heirs—and so consolidate and perpetuate their family's property rights for successive generations—is one which is common to all settled, organised and basically agricultural societies. In China, India and Africa, adoption has long served this purpose,[3] but it was the tradition established over the several hundreds of years and throughout the extent of the Roman Empire which laid the European foundations for this social role. A Roman could adopt only if he did not have an heir, was aged at least 60 and the adopted was no longer a minor.[4] This tradition was revived in France by the Civil Code of 1902 which required that the adopter be at least 50 and without legal heirs, while the adopted must have reached his majority.[5] Heir adoption therefore owed its origins to an 'inheritance' motive and, all other factors being favourable, found early acknowledgment in law.

Adoption and the Kinship Motive

Closely linked to this property-based social role is the practice of kinship adoption.[6] For some agricultural societies, such as those of India and China, these were synonymous as a relative was the preferred adoptee. All the ethnic groups

[2] See, for example, MK Benet, *The Character of Adoption* (Jonathan Cape, 1976).

[3] *Ibid.*, p 22. Also see E Goody, *Contexts of Kinship* (Cambridge University Press, 1973).

[4] *Ibid.* As Benet explains: 'Full adoption, *adrogatio*, was only possible for a person who was himself *sui iuris*—that is, a member of no family but his own. A minor could not be *adrogated* because a minor *sui iuris* had *tutores* or guardians . . . "The adopter" must be 60 or from some cause unlikely to have children.' (p 30)

[5] *Ibid.*, p 77.

[6] *Ibid.*, p 14.

peripheral to American society—Negroes, Indians, Eskimos and Polynesians—have long practised kinship fostering and adoption as a means of strengthening the extended family, and their society as a whole, by weakening the exclusive bond between parents and children[7]—though, curiously, the present form of kinship adoptions on the island of Ireland, the so-called 'step-adoption', has evolved for quite opposite reasons. Elsewhere this occurs as an open transaction between two sets of parents. To the Hindus of India, adoption outside the caste is prohibited.[8] For the Polynesians, the adoption of anyone other than a relative is an insult to the extended family.[9] Kinship adoptions seem to rest on an 'exchange' motive, whereby the donor nuclear family acquires a stronger affiliation with the wider social group, in exchange for relinquishing parental rights.

Adoption and the Allegiance Motive

The purpose of such adoptions is sometimes to secure social advancement for the adopted person.[10] This is not unlike the Roman practice of non-kinship adoption for the purpose of allying the fortunes of two families. A Roman patrician—or even an emperor—would adopt, for example, a successful general as his successor.[11] In Japan, also, the adoption of non-relatives was traditionally seen as a means of allying with the fortunes of the ruling family.[12] In Ireland, under the Brehon Laws, much the same ends were achieved by reciprocal placements of children between clans as a demonstration of mutual allegiance.[13] This bears a strong resemblance to the feudal practice of paying fealty and showing allegiance to a lord by placing a child for court service. Again, in sixteenth and seventeenth century England, it was quite common for the more wealthy households to take in the sons and daughters of poorer parents on service contracts—for example, as pages or servants.[14] Non-kinship adoption, in this form, would seem to be based on an 'allegiance' or 'service' motive.

Adoption and the Welfare Motive

Distinctly different from such historical forms of adoption is the relatively modern practice of non-kinship adoption of abandoned or neglected children for philanthropic motives. In societies where the functioning of the whole system was

[7] *Ibid.*, p 17.
[8] *Ibid.*, p 35.
[9] *Ibid.*, pp 35, 48–50.
[10] As Gibbons explains, at the time of the Roman Empire, a returning successful adventurer might seek to ingratiate himself 'by the custom of adopting the name of their patron' and thereby hope to secure his position in society. See *The Decline and Fall of the Roman Empire* (Harrap, 1949), p 131.
[11] *Ibid.*, p 30, Marcus Aurelius being a good example.
[12] *Ibid.*
[13] See R Gilligan, *Irish Child Care Services: Policy, Practice and Provision* (Institute of Public Administration, Dublin, 1991).
[14] See N Middleton, *When Family Failed*, (Victor Gollancz, 1971).

accepted as being of greater importance than that of each individual family unit, then the modern problem of unwanted children did not seem to arise. An extra pair of hands was always useful in societies tied to the land. But when the economy of a society changed from being land based to industrial, wage earning and mobile, then the nuclear family unit became more independent and children often simply represented more mouths to feed. On the island of Ireland, the gap left by the fading authority of social systems based on feudalism, the Brehon Laws and the extended agricultural family was filled by the state through the provision of basic containment and shelter as required by the Poor Laws.[15]

However, the fact that children with welfare needs were available did not, until recent years, provide any guarantee of their adoption. For example, during the first half of the twentieth century, many thousands—perhaps hundreds of thousands—of children were exported by philanthropic societies from these islands, where they were unwanted, to Australia and Canada.[16] In both jurisdictions of Ireland, the welfare of the child is now an explicit statutory criterion—not for determining a child's availability for adoption, but only of the grounds for making an adoption order.

Modern Adoption Functions

The modern role of adoption in contemporary Western society is quite different from any of its historical manifestations as outlined above. This reflects the nature of changes in the related cultural context. From its historical role in fairly closed societies with their well-defined boundaries and strong independent identities, adoption has now adapted its functions in relation to the needs of nuclear impermanent family units within a more fluid cosmopolitan society. As the following brief survey shows, the current types of adoption very much reflect the characteristic pressures on the family in a modern Western society.

Adoption of Children in Public Care

The flow of children from the public child care sector into the private law adoption process has been a relatively recent development. For many generations, when care in the family of origin has failed—whether due to criminal abuse perpetrated by a culpable parent or neglect by a well-meaning but inadequate parent—children have entered the public care system. The long-term residential care option in children's homes, then generally (if not universally) relied upon, too often proved damaging to the welfare interests of thousands of children placed in public care by court orders. Consequently, modern child care legislation introduced and has gradually broadened the grounds allowing such children to be available for

[15] See J Robbins, *The Lost Children: A Study of Charity Children in Ireland 1700–1900* (1991).
[16] See P Bean and J Melville, *Lost Children of the Empire* (Unwin Hyman, 1989).

adoption. This change of policy, introducing non-consensual adoption for older and often abused or impaired children—many with behavioural problems or special needs—might not have achieved its success if it had not coincided with both a dramatic decline in the availability of freely relinquished healthy babies and a continued increase in the number of childless couples wishing to adopt.

Inter-country Adoptions

For some decades, the number of babies available for adoption has been declining in all modern Western societies. At the same time, circumstances of war, natural disaster and endemic poverty have induced other countries to permit the adoption of orphaned or abandoned children by couples in Western societies. The welfare interests of such children can usually only be improved by this modern 'child rescue' approach. However, the availability of some children is conditioned by the social economy of their country of origin, and it may be that the dislocation to family and culture resulting from adoption may prove in the long term not to be conducive to the promotion of their welfare interests. Arguably, inter-country adoption will only satisfy the welfare test where, as with other adoptions, rehabilitation in the family of origin has become impossible.

Trans-racial Adoptions

Some of the rationale and many of the same tensions prevailing in inter-country adoptions exist also in the trans-racial context. Inter-country adoptions are also often trans-racial. Sometimes—as in Australia with Aboriginal children—trans-racial adoptions are promoted by a deliberate but pernicious government policy to favour one race at the expense of another. Usually, and most recently in the United Kingdom, the wisdom of having any formal policy on trans-racial adoptions—whether promoting or discouraging them—has been questioned.

The controversy surrounding trans-racial adoption has tended to centre on whether or not there was a racial match between child and adopters. The emerging consensus is that, where possible, placement arrangements should reflect a child's ethnic background and cultural identity insofar as such considerations are compatible with the welfare interests of that child, which must always have priority. In particular, the courts have upheld the value of preserving established relationships as a key component of welfare interests in trans-racial as in all other kinds of placements, the duration of current care arrangements and age of the child being of crucial importance.

Adoption of Children with Complex or Special Needs

Again, the reduction in all Western societies of indigenous healthy babies available for adoption has led to adopters broadening their outlook. This has been matched by a commensurate change in the factors governing the availability of children. Whereas previously children with complex health care or special needs, unwanted or inadequately cared for by their natural parents, would have been consigned to long-term institutional care, they are now quite often successfully placed for adoption.

Adoption of Children Born by Assisted Conception

The introduction of techniques of artificial insemination and the practice of surrogate motherhood have resulted in many children becoming available for adoption by private arrangement. This new form of 'adoption to order' is not without its problems, and many court cases have been generated by the withdrawal of consents freely given before birth of the children concerned. It also gives rise to concern for the child's long-term sense of identity and rights of access to information.

Welfare and Family Adoptions

Adoption of a child by the natural parents, grandparents, relatives, foster-parents or others with an established relationship with that child has grown to become the most prominent feature of modern adoption law. But, in particular, it is the increasing recourse to adoption by mothers of non-marital children applying jointly with their husbands to adopt those children, in order to legally seal the boundaries of their new marital family units, that has become contentious. The effect of an adoption order in such circumstances may be to marginalise not only the natural father but also his side of the family. In general, the use of adoption by family members has been viewed as unsatisfactory because it adds a veneer to an existing legal status in the relationship between child and adopter which may obscure that relationship. The possible obscuring of family relationships and potential loss of contact with significant relatives are among the reasons why family adoptions may not necessarily be conducive to promoting the welfare interests of the children concerned.

Same-sex Adopters

Adoption by a single homosexual male or lesbian, where the applicant is living with a partner of the same gender, has for some time been legally possible but until recently has not become professionally and socially acceptable. Judicial notice has been taken of research findings indicating that child rearing by same-sex couples has not had any deleterious effects on the children concerned. This has led to the current position where judgments emphasise that, providing such applicants can otherwise provide for the welfare interests of the child, their sexual orientation is of little relevance. Many such adoptions result from surrogacy arrangements.

The broad conclusion to be drawn from the material presented in the first part of this paper is that the functions of adoption are very much determined by its cultural context. To this can be added the observation that, in modern Western societies, the traditional form of adoption has largely been displaced by new variants, some of which are wholly driven by private interests (e.g. family adoptions) and others by the public interest (e.g. public care adoptions). Sustained adopter demand in the face of the shrinking consensual availability of healthy white babies has broadened the adoption market.

ADOPTION: JURISDICTIONAL CHARACTERISTICS ON THE ISLAND OF IRELAND

The island of Ireland was partitioned in 1922. Adoption law and practice, in its two jurisdictions—the Republic of Ireland (RoI) and Northern Ireland (NI)—now operate within separate and distinct legal systems but share many characteristics in common. It is with their contemporary distinctive differences that this part of the paper is concerned. These differences are identified and their significance assessed by taking comparable readings at the same operational stages of the adoption process in each jurisdiction.

Current Jurisdictional Differences in Adoption and the Public/Private Balance

The legal framework for adoption in each jurisdiction is now quite separate and distinct. In RoI, the law is to be found in a body of unconsolidated adoption legislation,[17] together with the *Guardianship of Infants Act* 1964 and the *Child Care Act* 1991. Adoption proceedings are heard in an administrative rather than a judicial setting, with hearings held by the Adoption Board and orders made by it. In NI, the law lies in the Adoption (NI) Order 1987 together with the Children (NI) Order 1995, supplemented to some extent by the discretionary powers of the judiciary as exercised in the wardship jurisdiction of the High Court. Adoption proceedings are heard in a judicial setting and adoption orders are made by the court.

Differences in Eligibility/Suitability Criteria

Access to the adoption process is clearly crucial. Queries regarding who may be a party to adoption proceedings, who may be prohibited from participation and the conditions under which this may happen constitute the acid test of how the public/private balance has been struck. The eligibility and suitability criteria as applied to natural parents, the child and the adopters gives effect to this balance.

[17] Notably, the *Adoption Acts* of 1952, 1964, 1976, 1988, 1991 and 1998.

Natural Parents

A natural parent will appear in adoption proceedings either as the donor parent or as the respondent.

In the southern jurisdiction, only an unmarried mother is entitled to voluntarily relinquish a child for the purposes of adoption. This she may do in favour of a relative and, until the introduction of the 1998 Act, she could have done so in favour of a complete stranger. She is not legally obliged to serve advance notice on any professional or government agency, nor is their approval for the placement required. The only legally operative criteria is that her decision to relinquish is accompanied by her full and informed consent. This decision—the consent to placement for adoption—is by far the most common reason for natural parents to subsequently appear in court as respondents. The unmarried father of the child in question may appear as a respondent to challenge the mother's decision, but only if he has first acquired guardianship rights.[18] The unmarried mother may also appear as a respondent if she retracts her consent. Finally, one or both married parents of a child subject to a care order may appear as respondents in adoption proceedings lodged by the child's foster parents. While the natural mother's donor role receives very strong recognition in the law of RoI, the role of parent respondents is comparatively weak and seldom succeeds.

In NI, whether married or not, any parent with full parental responsibility is entitled to voluntarily relinquish a child for adoption, though the consent of the other parent must be obtained or the need for it dispensed with. This right is only exercisable via an adoption agency, unless the placement is with a relative. Parents may have their rights removed by a care order and then further abrogated by a freeing order which authorises an adoption placement against parental wishes. The criteria for appearing as respondent in adoption proceedings is much the same as in the southern jurisdiction. However, in NI the respondent may well be a divorced father objecting to the adoption of his legitimate child and the court would be unable to make the adoption order unless statutory grounds existed for his consent to be dispensed with. Clearly, the jurisdictional differences centre around the strength of marital status in RoI.

The Child

In RoI, the twin criteria normally determining the availability of a child for adoption are non-marital parental status and parental consent. There is no evidence to show that child welfare (as represented by factors such as the child's wishes, the 'blood link', degree of bonding, complex health or other special needs) is itself a matter attracting a determinative weighting at point of entry to the adoption process. A marital child can only become available for adoption on a coercive

[18] The *Adoption Act* 1998 introduced a requirement that such a father be consulted prior to placement so that he may be advised of his right to apply for guardianship, access and/or custody of the child.

basis, as it is not possible for a marital parent to voluntarily relinquish a child of the marriage. The consensual adoption of children by relatives—most usually the child's natural mother and her spouse—is a particular feature of adoption in this jurisdiction. Evidence of criminal abuse or neglect of a child is in itself insufficient grounds for the compulsory placing of that child for adoption; any adoption initiative in respect of a child subject to a care order must come from foster parents—that is, it is a private rather than a public initiative. Suitability criteria are not determinative as evidenced by the very few children with special needs or subject to care orders being placed for adoption and the considerable numbers of healthy babies and young foreign children[19] being adopted.

In NI, the child's legal status and welfare interests—rather than the marital status of the parents—are the primary determinants of eligibility for adoption. Once a child's legal status has been compulsorily changed by the court to a ward or child in care, or as a consequence of a voluntary parental decision to allow care arrangements to be made, then the child may be made the subject of a freeing order and be placed for adoption. The freeing process can only be initiated by an adoption agency—in other words, it is a public rather than a private initiative. The issue of the appropriateness of freeing is determined by the objective application of the welfare test. The 'reasonableness' grounds have introduced a legal rule which measures eligibility by the effects rather than by the cause of parental fault or default. In this jurisdiction, the 'suitability' threshold is higher in respect of first party applicants and lower as regards third parties. In relation to the former, suitability criteria may prevent an adoption by prompting a discretionary judicial transfer to alternative family proceedings. This availability of adoption alternatives is an important and characteristic point of difference between the two jurisdictions. In relation to the latter, the availability of adoption orders subject to a contact condition in favour of a natural parent or sibling is again an important point of jurisdictional difference. It very much demonstrates the leverage available for judicial assertion of the public interest to compromise the private interests represented by an adoption order. The lower suitability threshold is also apparent in the active targeting of special needs children and those with complex behavioural or health needs for adoption, coupled with special post-adoption allowances and other forms of support. This results in a higher proportion of adoption orders in the northern than in the southern jurisdiction being made in respect of children who would otherwise be in public care and a lesser proportion in favour of foreign children.

The Adopters

There are jurisdictional differences in the law relating to both third party and to family adopters.

[19] In 1998, of the 400 orders made, only one adoption order was made in respect of a child with special needs, one in respect of a child subject to a care order, but 27 adoption orders were made in respect of children from overseas.

In RoI, eligibility criteria are framed to ensure that third party applicants closely conform to the constitutionally approved marital family unit. Only in statutorily specified instances will applications from anyone other than a married couple be accepted. All third party applicants must also satisfy a statutory requirement that they be of the same religion as the natural parents, or be of a different religion if this fact is known to the natural parents. The only third party applicants eligible to adopt a marital child are the foster parents of that child who have to satisfy carer tenure criteria. In contrast, family adopters in the southern jurisdiction do not have to satisfy rigorous eligibility and suitability criteria. There is an assumption that the welfare of a child can only be enhanced by family adoption. There is no requirement to serve notice of an intention to make a family placement, no opportunity for professional assessment prior to application and no possibility of a discretionary judicial decision to issue an alternative order on the grounds that such an order would be more compatible with the child's welfare than adoption.

In NI, unlike the southern jurisdiction, the legal standing of parents or other relatives does not attract preferential treatment in law. At point of application, the same professional scrutiny applies as it does to third party applicants, but parents or relatives must then also demonstrate that adoption rather than any other order available in family proceedings is a better means of promoting the welfare of the child concerned. Adoption orders issued to such applicants are quite likely to be made subject to conditions of contact. This highlights another distinctive characteristic of this jurisdiction, viz that the welfare principle has greater statutory weighting than in the southern jurisdiction. The public interest dimension is particularly evident in respect of third party adopters who, if foster parents, have statutory rights to apply to adopt after five years of carer tenure, whether or not the consent of their child care agency is available. They are also eligible for adoption allowances.

In short, several points of jurisdictional difference are evident in relation to eligibility/suitability criteria. Access to the adoption process is considerably more restricted in RoI for all prospective parties. A common restraining factor is marital status. Whether applicant, subject or relinquishing parent, access is much more dependent upon whether or not the individual is from a marital family unit than would be the case in NI. There are also differences affecting each class of participant. Applicants such as natural parents and relatives attract much less professional scrutiny in the southern than the northern jurisdiction, while foster parents comprise a much higher proportion of total annual applicants in the latter jurisdiction. Many more children subject to care orders and/or with special needs are eligible for adoption in the latter. Intimately related to all the foregoing is the fact that the proportion of natural parents who are unwilling participants in adoption proceedings is much higher in NI. These differences are, arguably, the consequence of a markedly more interventionist social policy towards all family units on child welfare grounds in the northern jurisdiction as opposed to a more protectionist policy towards marital family units in RoI.

Differences in Process

How the parties arrive at the point where an application is heard and determined depends upon the extent to which the adoption process serves primarily public or private interests. The balance between the two is apparent in the rules governing that process, and in the responsibilities of the different bodies and persons participating in it. On the island of Ireland, there are significant jurisdictional differences in process. Most obviously, the process is both longer and broader in the northern than in the southern jurisdiction. Also, the fact that adoption proceedings are judicial in the northern jurisdiction but administrative in the south is very evident, as is the less intrusive and less extensive nature of mediating bodies in the latter jurisdiction. Finally, the tight regulatory framework within which the adoption process in the northern jurisdiction operates is quite different from the official approach in the south.

Length and Breadth of Process

In NI, the process is lengthened at commencement by a statutory pre-placement counselling stage during which adoption agencies are required to provide a counselling service to all natural parents whose consent is available or will be sought for an adoption.[20] In the context of family adoptions, professional scrutiny is now mandatory some three months before application in relation to both 'self-placements', where the child remains with the adopting natural parent, and direct or indirect placements with relatives.[21] Such counselling will also occur in the context of the coercive use of freeing and/or wardship proceedings as a preliminary to an adoption placement, such coercive preliminaries being a distinctive and characteristic feature of the role of public child care agencies in the northern jurisdiction.[22] In this jurisdiction, the process is also extended at the closing stage by the statutory availability of disclosure procedures, use of contact registers, possible conditions attached to adoption orders and the opportunities for adoption allowances and other forms of ongoing support from government bodies.

In RoI, the fact that, in the context of family adoptions, the process does not start until an application is lodged in court is a distinctive point of jurisdictional difference.[23] The waiving of preliminary professional scrutiny and opportunity for public service support in this context emphasises the process's distinctively private characteristics. The reverse is true in the context of adoption in a public care context, where the process cannot begin for at least a year after placement with foster parents. At the end of the process, closure occurs abruptly with the making of an adoption order. The absence of any statutory post-adoption allowances or

[20] See Art 17(1) and Art 18(1), respectively, of the 1987 Order.

[21] See Art 22 of the 1987 Order.

[22] See Art 18(1) of the 1987 Order in relation to authority for a non-consensual freeing order.

[23] See s 10(1) of the 1991 Act. This may not occur until several years after placement, by which time the adoption is a virtual *fait accompli* as there can be no reasonable alternative.

support scheme, any statutory possibility of ongoing contact arrangements, or access to statutory information disclosure procedures effectively terminates the public dimension.[24]

In RoI, the adoption process does not encompass as wide a range or as uneven a mix of participants as in NI. The very small proportion of children entering the adoption process who are either legitimate or the subject of a care order continues to be a particularly distinctive characteristic of adoption in RoI.[25] Intimately related to that fact is the recent relatively large proportion of adopted children who originate from overseas.[26] Other distinctive characteristics distinguishing the southern jurisdiction are that the proportion of parental applications, which for decades had been much lower than in NI, is now much the same if not greater,[27] and the proportion of applications from grandparents is higher,[28] while the proportion from single third party applicants and from foster parents is much lower. By way of contrast, the process in the northern jurisdiction is characterised by the proportion of children whose eligibility has been determined by coercive intervention of the state; the number of those who are legitimate, and/or have special needs; the consistently high proportion of parental applications; and the growing proportion of foster parent applicants.

Fora and Mechanisms for Exercising Authority

Decisions regarding the placement of a child for adoption—where, with whom, with what sort of support—clearly indicate where the balance is being struck between public/private interests in adoption. In NI, there is a statutory duty upon all adoption societies to ensure that all placement decisions are taken by formally constituted adoption panels. In the southern jurisdiction, there is no statutory duty on either statutory or voluntary societies but its assumption by appropriate bodies is a notable characteristic of the adoption process in this jurisdiction. A similar situation exists in relation to the provision of an adoption service. In NI, specific and prescriptive duties are placed upon all child care agencies, whereas in the south there is a statement of broad principle that a service for the adoption of children should be provided, its implementation being left entirely to the discretion of the child care agencies.

[24] Some such opportunities may be available through private or agency-based practice, but not as a statutory service.

[25] The Adoption Board's report for 1989 shows orders having been granted in respect of: three children who were legitimated under the 1964 Act; three whose availability was determined under s 3 of the 1988 Act; and nine declarations made by the Board under the latter Act. In addition, three orders were made under s 3 of the 1974 Act. By way of comparison, the 1998 report gives the following statistics for the respective groupings: zero, one and sixteen; with none under s 3 of the 1974 Act.

[26] The Board's annual reports gives the following percentages: 1991, 7.49%; 1992, 36.98%; 1993, 6.51%; 1994, 5.41%; 1995, 6.39%; 1996, 8.85%; 1997, 10.32%; and 1998, 18.06%.

[27] For example, in 1987 the proportion of parental applications in RoI amounted to some 22.6% of the total, rising to 63.23% in 1998. In NI, they constituted 55.78% in 1987.

[28] In RoI, the proportion has remained stable at approximately 3.5% of the total; in NI, professional caution, judicial discretion and the statutory availability of alternatives would result in few successful applications.

Again, the public/private balance is evident in the extent to which the child's interests are protected during the period from placement to hearing. In RoI there is no specific statutory provision giving rise to any protective duties owed to a child placed for adoption.[29] Ultimately, all placements must be notified to the Adoption Board, but this does not trigger any specific protective duties. In NI, all placements are safeguarded and the duties to safeguard the child's welfare interests are statutory, specific, prescriptive and comprehensive. They rest most rigorously upon all placement agencies but apply also, though with less intrusiveness, to family adoptions from notification to hearing.[30] Further, in the northern jurisdiction, from the time of application all consensual placements and those made in respect of children subject to care order cannot be terminated without prior approval of the court.[31]

Regulating the Process

It is in the regulatory framework that the public/private balance is most important. In RoI, the Adoption Board is the only agency positioned to hold an overview of the workings of the adoption process. It, however, restricts its role to one of minimalist intervention: monitoring practice and registering and deregistering adoption agencies at their initiative. In NI, the DHSS and the High Court supervise the adoption process. The statutory powers available to the DHSS and employed by it to supervise the work of adoption agencies are very directive. An onus is placed on each agency to justify itself in terms of its contribution to the needs of the adoption process,[32] and the DHSS is required to inspect the quality of practice of every such agency.[33] The High Court also acts as a watchdog in relation to agency practice and will use its powers of judicial review to intervene when alerted to possible improper practice. This authoritative regulatory approach resting on a body of specific rules, with definite sanctions for non-observance, is a distinctive characteristic of the adoption process in NI.

Differences in Grounds for Dispensing with Consent

The statutory grounds for dispensing with parental consent are relevant at two stages in the adoption process: when authorising a non-consensual placement; and when making a non-consensual adoption order.

In RoI, the main adoption statute[34] provides for the possibility of non-consensual adoptions only in circumstances where it can be shown that the initial

[29] As regards 'family' placements, the care and maintenance provisions of ss 56 and 57 of the *Health Act* 1953 require advance notification of placement to be served on the local health board. As regards placements made by child care agencies, these are subject to the boarding out regulations. All adoption agency placements must be notified to the health board within seven days.

[30] See Art 23 of the 1987 Order and Reg 12 of the Adoption Agencies Regulations (NI) 1989.

[31] See Rules of the Supreme Court (NI) (Amendment No 6) 1989 and the County Court (Amendment No 3) Rules (NI) 1989; also Arts 28 and 29 of the 'protected' children procedures of the 1987 Order.

[32] See Reg 6 of the Adoption Agencies Regulations (NI) 1989.

[33] See Art 4 of the 1987 Order.

[34] *Adoption Act* 1974, s 3.

placement decision was authorised by an informed parental consent which was subsequently withdrawn—that is, the law is actually predicated on parental consent. No statutory grounds exist for dispensing with parental consent at time of placement.[35] Much—if not most—case law is focused on the contractual grounds for affirming or discounting the consent given by young unmarried mothers to the placement of a child for adoption. Even if given within six weeks of the birth of the child concerned, such consent will be upheld by the courts in RoI, though it is statutorily invalid in NI. It is a hallmark of the fundamentally consensual nature of adoption in the southern jurisdiction that responsibility for the placement decision is one which the legislators have left to the parent/s. Such grounds as exist under the 1974 Act to provide for the possibility of non-consensual adoption do so only in respect of the consent of an unmarried mother and become operative only if she has already given a valid consent to placement. The more recent *Adoption Act* 1988 introduced parental failure as grounds for dispensing with the necessity of parental consent to adoption with equal application to married and unmarried parents. However, these grounds are not synchronised with those that constitute criminal fault or default in child care legislation. Mere parental culpability, however grave, is insufficient; the conduct must be such as to amount to an 'abandonment' of parental responsibilities.[36] The grounds also require that the form of parental failure be due to 'physical or moral reasons', which places an emphasis on causes rather than effects of failure. Finally, it is not the fact of parental culpability which triggers a public agency initiative to place for adoption, but the fact of foster care tenure which may or may not give rise to a private initiative to apply to adopt the child in question. This formulation of the grounds for dispensing with parental consent has been worded so as to ensure compatibility with and subservience to constitutional principles with their emphasis on the 'inalienable and imprescriptible rights'[37] of parents. The result is that, in the southern jurisdiction, the grounds for non-consensual adoption are confined to a very narrow definition of culpability and to private rather than public responsibility for commencing relevant proceedings.

In NI, in the context of third party adoptions, the specific synchronisation of some grounds for dispensing with parental consent with those of child care legislation is a distinctive characteristic.[38] Parental culpability is not necessary, but will be wholly sufficient, and a single act[39] can justify commencement of a non-

[35] Except under s 14(2) of the *Adoption Act* 1952 which is restricted to circumstances where the parent/guardian either suffers from mental infirmity or their whereabouts are unknown.

[36] See s 3(1)(I)(C) of the 1988 Act: the degree of parental failure must be such as 'constitutes an abandonment on the part of the parents of all parental rights'.

[37] See Arts 41 and 42 of the Constitution.

[38] See, in particular, Art 16(2) of the Adoption (NI) Order 1987:
(e) has persistently ill-treated the child;
(f) has seriously ill-treated the child.

[39] See Art 16(2)(f) of the 1987 Order.

consensual adoption process. Other such characteristics include the fact that these grounds are available at time of placement as well as at the hearing for an adoption order; that non-consensual adoptions often result from consensual care admissions;[40] that a public agency initiative, using the freeing procedure, will most usually trigger a non-consensual placement; that judicial discretion may be employed in construing grounds of 'unreasonableness' to dispense with parental consent;[41] and that application may be made solely on the basis of length of carer tenure.[42] In the context of first party adoptions, the fact that they are classified as 'family proceedings', together with the requirement that the court be satisfied that the order being sought is in the child's best interests, provides the judiciary in this jurisdiction with the freedom to make a different order (eg a residence order or parental responsibility order) which is not available to their counterparts in the south. It should also be noted that the use of wardship, with its reliance on the principle that the welfare interests of the child are of paramount importance, has long played a key role in supplementing statutory powers and authorising non-consensual placements in NI, but not in RoI.

Differences in Applying the Welfare Test

Whether an adoption order can be made is determined in accordance with the statutory criteria relating to eligibility, suitability and consent. Whether it will be made is determined by the welfare test. The test has three functions: it identifies the 'substance' of welfare in relation to the child concerned; it indicates the professionals permitted to bring welfare related matters before the court; and it defines the weighting to be given to such matters in deciding whether or not to make an adoption order.

In both jurisdictions, the making of an adoption order is conditional upon a finding that to do so would be at least compatible with the welfare interests of the child concerned. In both, the wishes of an older child regarding his or her proposed adoption have to be ascertained and taken into account, but only in NI is there evidence that determining weight can be attached to those wishes.[43] In both jurisdictions, expert witnesses may be called to give evidence and in both that evidence may have a determining weight, but in NI such witnesses are more likely to be called upon to assist the court rather than, as in Ireland, to appear on behalf

[40] Art 18(2) of the 1987 Order simply requires that:

(a) the child is in the care of the adoption agency.

There is no requirement that this be on the basis of a care order.

[41] Art 16(2) of the 1987 Order permits considerable judicial discretion by simply requiring that a parent:

(b) is withholding his agreement unreasonably.

[42] See Art 13(2) and Art 29 of the 1987 Order.

[43] The influence of UK case law relating to children's rights exercises a direct influence. See, in particular, *Gillick v West Norfolk and Wisbeck Area Health Authority* [1986] AC 112 and *Re M v M (Child Access)* [1973] 2 All ER 21.

of one party. In NI, all family adoptions are subject to prior mandatory professional screening, the results of which are judicially taken into account in determining welfare. It is the case that in NI there has been a greater experience of contested adoptions, and for some decades the number of applications by step-parents and foster parents has brought many older children with established relationships into the adoption process than has been the case in RoI. This would have given the judiciary in the north more opportunities than have been available to their counterparts in the south to address the wishes of children.

Whether contested or not, more information on matters constituting the welfare factor as specified in approved report outlines is required to be brought before the court in NI than is the case in RoI. Jurisdictional differences exist in relation to matters held to constitute 'welfare', particularly regarding the child's established relationships and the period when welfare is considered relevant. In RoI, the 'blood-link' factor has gained considerable judicial endorsement and has the capacity to transform welfare into the determining factor in third-party non-consensual applications.[44] The welfare of the child is a factor which is relevant at the time of the hearing; there is no statutory requirement to take into account the likely effect of an adoption order on welfare throughout childhood. In NI it is the 'bonding' rather than the 'blood-link' factor which is often of determinative significance and is apparent—for example, in the availability of contact conditions to license the continuation of relationships which would otherwise be legally terminated by adoption. There is a statutory duty requiring the court to consider the capacity of an adoption order to promote welfare throughout childhood, but even if it could only do so in adulthood, this would be sufficient justification for making the order.[45] This more holistic long-term approach is also evident in the statutory disclosure procedures. In the northern jurisdiction, the making of an adoption order requires a predictive assessment of welfare and allows for legal compromises to be made to condition the future exclusiveness of the order.

The duty to bring welfare considerations before the court rests more heavily and on more professionals in the northern jurisdiction. In RoI, unlike NI, there is no explicit statutory requirement that a child's wishes be sought and taken into account, nor is any specific professional statutorily charged with the duty to represent such wishes before the court. In the northern jurisdiction, there is a statutory requirement that the wishes of the child be ascertained. Also, in all cases welfare interests will be represented by a guardian *ad litem*, in contested cases legal interests will be asserted by a solicitor and in complex cases the Official Solicitor may also be involved.

In NI, a legal difference exists in relation to the application of the welfare factor to different classes of applicant. So, although first party applicants are not subject to pre-placement scrutiny by an adoption panel, they still have to prove in court

[44] See, for example, *RC & PC v An Bord Uchtala & St Louise's Adoption Society* (8 Feb 1985), unreported, HC.

[45] See *Re D (A Minor) (Adoption)* 1991, unreported, *The Times*, 23 Jan CA.

that no other form of proceedings would provide a more appropriate means of meeting a child's welfare interests. Applicant relatives have to undergo professional assessment to ensure that their particular circumstances would not pose a future threat to the welfare of the child due to factors of age or distortion of family relationships. Non-consensual applicants may find their adoption order qualified by a contact condition imposed to safeguard an aspect of a child's welfare. Finally, in the northern jurisdiction, the welfare factor is always the first matter to be addressed in non-consensual applications. Moreover, as the grounds of 'unreasonableness' are most frequently relied upon, the welfare test therefore has to be met twice by such applicants. Welfare interests are statutorily required to govern all decisions taken during the course of each application. In short, the welfare factor has a more specific, comprehensive and significant impact upon adoption in NI than in RoI.

Differences in Outcome

In both jurisdictions, legislative intent began by being almost exclusively concerned with regulating the consensual third party applications of indigenous, white, healthy and in all respects 'normal' non-marital babies. From that common starting point, both jurisdictions have steadily adjusted their respective legislative provisions in response to emerging areas of common social need, but in accordance with a marked difference in the balance struck between public/private interests.[46] The extent to which each jurisdiction has moved away from the common baseline may be seen in the diversified outcome of their respective adoption processes.

Adoption Orders and Third Party Applicants

This, the type of order originally legislated for, has declined in the two jurisdictions, both in aggregate and as a proportion of total annual orders. Both jurisdictions share the same characteristic that placements are almost always religion specific (ie Catholic child with Catholic adopter, Protestant child with Protestant adopter).

In RoI, consensual applications have always been in respect of illegitimate children and this very largely continues to be the case—the majority of applications

[46] For example, in RoI legislation, adjustment has been made to allow for the adoption of some children born within marriage, who are the subject of care orders or have been born overseas, but such developments have remained subject to constitutional principles which firmly establish the importance of maintaining the privacy, autonomy and legal integrity of the marital family unit, not to be violated by coercive and permanent legal intervention unless complete parental failure can be proven. In NI, the use of adoption as an expedient form of custody order, its availability to carers with tenure and its application to children accommodated by statutory authorities with parental consent and to those with 'special needs' are all extensions of its original role, but it remains subject to proof that the public interest in safeguarding and promoting the welfare of the child can be best ensured throughout childhood.

concern children under the age of two years.[47] However, the adoption process in this jurisdiction is now including a small but increasing number of children born within marriage and a similar small number who, having been the subject of care orders, have subsequently been adopted by their foster parents.[48] There has also been a relatively recent and significant increase in the number of overseas children adopted.[49] The proportion of third party applications which are contested has always been very small and invariably arises in circumstances where a natural mother withdraws her consent to the adoption of her non-marital child. In this jurisdiction, there is no legislative provision for conditions to be attached to adoption orders.

In NI, unconditional third party consensual adoption orders now form a minority of the annual output.[50] In many instances, an adoption will have commenced on a non-consensual basis but the consent issue will have been resolved by the use of freeing procedures before placement. Orders in respect of children from overseas are not numerically significant, but those made in respect of children suffering from learning difficulties, physical disability or behavioural problems are not uncommon. Unconditional but contested adoption orders, where the opposition is from a culpable parent or parent, form a significant and growing proportion of annual orders made. The child concerned will often be the subject of a care order and may well be legitimate. In addition, an increasing proportion of orders are now made with attached conditions permitting contact with a member of the adopted child's family of origin. Qualified orders are now characteristic of the adoption process in NI in that they represent an increasing public service commitment to acknowledge and promote the independent interests of a child, over and above the interests of natural and adoptive parents, before and after the issue of an adoption order.

Adoption Orders and First Party Applicants

In RoI, the number of orders granted in favour of a natural mother and her spouse has grown rapidly in recent years and now constitutes the most significant char-

[47] For example, the board's annual report reveals that in 1989 the number of children aged 24 months or less at time of placement with third party adopters amounted to 358 out of a total of 366; in 1998 the comparable figures were 127 and thirteen.

[48] For example, in 1989 the same report shows four such children who were subject to declarations made by the Board in favour of their foster parents under the 1988 Act and three who were adopted as a consequence of High Court proceedings taken under that Act. The comparable figures in the 1998 report are sixteen and one respectively. Effectively, the only children born within marriage and available for adoption (as opposed to those who, having been legitimated, are then adopted) are those in the care of foster parents.

[49] The Board's annual reports provide the following data: 1991, 58 children were entered in the register of foreign adoptions; 1992, 297; 1993, 45; 1994, 39; 1995, 40; 1996, 54; 1997, 51; and 1998, 120.

[50] For example, in 1987, of the 285 adoption orders granted, 167 were in favour of a natural parent or relative. Of the remaining 104, it may be safely assumed that a large number were contested. This would leave less than a third to represent the traditional use of adoption.

acteristic of the adoption process.[51] Other types of first party applications—by a natural mother acting alone or by a natural father and his spouse—have remained consistently low.[52] The application is seldom contested or unsuccessful, the subject is almost invariably a non-marital child and the order granted will always be full and unconditional.

In NI, unconditional consensual orders have for some years constituted the main outcome of the adoption process.[53] The orders are more likely to concern children who are legitimate and older than their counterparts in the south and, because such applications are open to professional and judicial challenge on their merits, some children are likely to be diverted to other proceedings. Because first party applications in this jurisdiction may well concern marital children, some are contested by natural parents who may well succeed. Characteristic of adoption in this jurisdiction is the fact that some orders will also be made subject to a contact condition.

Adoption Orders and Relatives

A consistent characteristic of the RoI adoption process is that a significant minority of orders are made in favour of grandparents. This has never been the case in NI, where few such orders have ever been made and where applications would be open to professional or judicial challenge.

Other Orders

In RoI, a contested adoption application may, very occasionally, result in the issue of a guardianship order or possibly a wardship order. In NI, whether contested or not, an adoption application may at judicial discretion conclude in the issue of any order available in the family proceedings court—most probably a residence order under Article 8 of the Children (NI) Order 1995.

The Effect of an Adoption Order

In RoI, the outcome of the adoption process is as it always has been—either no order or a full order with its characteristic permanent, exclusive and absolute legal effects on all parties. In NI, the legal effects can be quite different. The statutory introduction of information rights, contact registers, schemes for payment and

[51] From 59 of the 1,115 orders granted in 1980 to 188 of the 615 granted in 1989, reaching 252 or 63% of the 400 orders made in 1998.

[52] For example, the board's report for 1989 shows that, out of a total of 226 family adoptions, only two orders were in favour of 'natural mother alone', none for 'natural father and wife' and two for 'natural father alone'. Comparable figures in the 1998 report are: none; none; and one respectively.

[53] For example, in 1987, first party applicants constituted 159 of the 285 orders granted. Given that these are seldom contested, it may be conjectured that half the total were first party consensual adoptions.

support and the possibility of conditions being attached to adoption orders or the issue of alternative orders have together resulted in a transformation of the traditional characteristics of adoption.

Jurisdictional Trends and New Legislation

In recent years, both jurisdictions have formally subscribed to international protocols and conventions such as the UN Convention on the Rights of the Child, the Convention for the Protection of Human Rights and Fundamental Freedoms and the Hague Convention on the Protection of Children and Cooperation in Respect of Intercountry Adoption. They have likewise become equally subject to decisions of the ECHR. For example, the following rulings apply to both: that the presumption favouring family life extends to include an unmarried father;[54] that the definition of 'family' is not restricted to one based on marriage but includes unmarried couples and non-marital children;[55] that the existence or otherwise of 'family life' can be determined as a matter of fact;[56] and that there is no legal right to adopt or to access artificial reproduction treatment.[57] These developments are naturally promoting a trend towards jurisdictional convergence. However, both are also anticipating the introduction of new indigenous legislation, some provisions of which can be expected to sharpen existing divergent trends.

Proposed New Legislation: RoI

In RoI, two adoption bills have been prepared and are expected to become law early in 2002. The first deals with adoption information, post-adoption contact and associated issues. This will regulate tracing and reunion services and will provide for information rights for adopted persons, birth parents and other parties to an adoption. It will also deal with access to records and with the care and management of records held by various agencies.

[54] See *Soderback v Sweden*, 28 Oct 1998 ECHR. Also see *Johansen v Norway* (1997) 23 EHRR 33 and *Rieme v Sweden* (1993) 16 EHRR 155.

[55] See *Keegan v Ireland* 18 EHRR 342 where the court held:

'the notion of "the family" . . . is not confined solely to marriage-based relationships and may encompass other de facto "family" where the parties are living together outside of marriage. A child born out of such a relationship is *ipso iure* part of that "family" unit from the moment of his birth and by the very fact of it.' (at para 44)

Also see *Marckx v Belgium* 2 EHRR 330, where the court held that Art 8 makes no distinction between the 'legitimate' and 'illegitimate' family and where it was also stated that:

'"family life" within the meaning of Art 8 includes at least the ties between near relatives, for instance, those between grandparents and grandchildren, since such relatives may play a considerable part in family life.'

[56] See *X, Y and Z v UK* [1997] 2 FLR 892, where it was held that, in determining whether a relationship can be defined as 'family life', the following factors are relevant:

'including whether the couple live together, the length of their relationship and whether they have demonstrated their commitment to each other by having children together or by other means . . .'

[57] See *X v Belgium and The Netherlands* Application No 6482/147, (1975) 7 DR 75, where it was held that unmarried persons cannot claim a right to adopt.

The second results from the RoI becoming a signatory to the Hague Convention and will provide for the Adoption Board to become the central authority for intercountry adoptions. In effect, the board will assume a more powerful management role in the adoption process. This will be a significant point of departure from practice in NI where there is no single body with equivalent powers and responsibilities. These legislative initiatives indicate that in some largely administrative and regulatory respects the law is converging with established practice in NI.

Proposed New Legislation: NI

In July 2001, Westminster published the Adoption and Children Bill for England and Wales and by so doing served notice that similar legislation would have to be prepared in NI. Just as the Children (NI) Order 1995 largely re-enacted the *Children Act* 1989, so it can be confidently predicted that any new adoption legislation initiated in England will, in due course, be almost identically replicated in NI. The Bill proposes to significantly amend the existing adoption legislation and the 1989 Act. In particular, it will make the welfare interests of a child, throughout the life of that child, the matter of paramount consideration for both court and adoption agencies. This will be probably the single most important change to adoption law for many decades. It and other provisions will make non-consensual adoptions considerably easier to obtain. The anticipated legislation will set adoption law on a fundamentally different and divergent track from that of its southern neighbour.

ADOPTION: STRATEGIC IMPLICATIONS OF CURRENT TRENDS IN ADOPTION FOR THE FUTURE COHERENCE OF FAMILY LAW

The third and final part of this paper focuses briefly and tentatively on the implications arising from the material presented above. It is suggested that the case study of adoption, as experienced in particular on the island of Ireland, offers a more general insight into the future of family law as a coherent discipline.

The Trends in Adoption on the Island of Ireland

The jurisdictional differences in adoption law clearly indicate a deference to their respective cultural contexts. In RoI, the importance and pervasiveness of traditional cultural hallmarks continue to determine legislative provisions and shape practice. The special position of the Roman Catholic Church, religion in general, the legal integrity of the marital family unit, an established non-interventionist child care policy and a strong tradition of reliance upon extended family networks to supplement or substitute for parental responsibilities can all be seen to colour the law and practice of adoption. In NI, these cultural characteristics are largely noticeable by their absence. In their place are the hallmarks of British legal pragmatism as extended to NI, where it shapes the law and practice of adoption and all other areas of family law. The legislative provisions and practice appropriate for the increasingly multicultural polyglot society which has developed in England are also in place in NI. Certain traditional legal presumptions favouring, for example, the marital nuclear family, Christianity and the maternal bond have been displaced by concepts such as 'unreasonableness', 'appropriateness' and, of course, 'the welfare of the child'. The traditional defence of the marital family as an inviolable legal entity has long been undermined by an interventionist child care policy (consensual as well as coercive) and the removal of fault as the only sufficient ground for judicial severing of spousal or parental bonds. In NI, the fact that the law now facilitates the decisions of adults to form, end and re-form family units, subject only to the proviso that in doing so they safeguard the welfare interests of any child involved, has become the most obvious jurisdictional hallmark of family law.

Having said that the characteristic jurisdictional differences in adoption owe a great deal to their respective cultural contexts, it must also be acknowledged that the tide of change impacting upon the family is forcing similar legal responses in both jurisdictions. The recent change of use in the legal functions of adoption is broadly similar in both jurisdictions and there is definite evidence of jurisdictional convergence in reasons for recourse to adoption. Moreover, these trends are representative of those occurring across many other modern Western societies.

However, this is now subject to an important caveat. The jurisdictional convergence in terms of the balance in public/private interests promises to be derailed by the eventual introduction of the paramountcy principle alongside the parental consent provisions in the adoption law of NI. This will significantly accelerate the flow of children from the public child care system into the private adoption law process. The possibility of an equivalent legislative provision being introduced into the adoption law of RoI is most unlikely.

Trend Towards Increased Privatisation

Jurisdictional convergence is most conspicuous in relation to the use of adoption by a natural parent and spouse to jointly acquire maximum rights and full parental status and thereby deny rights and status to others. This reversal in the traditional role of the natural parent from donor to applicant is a striking example of the extent of change in the social functions of adoption. The assertiveness with which private applicants now use adoption can also be seen in the increase in applications relating to children—usually healthy babies—from other countries. This choice is to some extent a forced one because of the sharp and continuing decline in numbers of children voluntarily relinquished in both jurisdictions. However, it is a choice quite often made despite the availability within the jurisdiction of children from the public child care sector and/or with special needs.

Trend Towards a Sustained Decrease in Consensual Adoption

The voluntary relinquishing of indigenous children for adoption is rapidly declining as a proportion of annual adoptions on the island of Ireland as elsewhere in modern Western societies. With it is declining the legal importance placed on parental consent as the cornerstone of adoption law.

Increasingly, both family and third party adoptions are being contested. As adoption becomes more adversarial, so also are governing principles being transferred from other areas of family law and applied to issues relating to parental consent. Concepts such as 'unreasonableness' and 'bonding' have become crucially important, as has the principle of the welfare of the child. Reliance on expert witnesses is also becoming a feature of adoption proceedings.

Trend Towards an Increase in Availability of Children from the Public Child Care Sector

The well-documented failure of public child care agencies to satisfactorily provide for the welfare of children who have been made the subjects of care orders, combined with sustained demand from prospective adopters and the rapid decline in numbers of voluntarily relinquished children, has led to a situation whereby an increasing proportion of adoption orders are being made in respect of children from public child care backgrounds. While both jurisdictions now provide for entry to the adoption process of children subject to care orders, the public interest in facilitating permanency planning for such children ensures that they constitute a far greater proportion of annual adoptions in NI than in RoI, where the constitutional and legislative constraints favour the private interests of marital parents.

Implications for Family Law as a Discipline

In modern Western societies, being a parent is now largely a matter of private individual choice. Serial parenting arrangements, together with the medical developments which allow adults to choose or reject the option of parenthood, have undone the centrifugal significance that the nuclear marital family once had within the body of private family law. In public family law, an increase in the incidence or detection of child abuse and neglect has led to the development of ever more pervasive interventionist strategies by public child care agencies in relation to families. On both the private and public fronts, there has been a retreat from the traditional presumption that the legal integrity of the family should be upheld and a falling back to the safer ground that, however families constitute or reconstitute themselves, they must ensure the welfare interests of any child involved.

Adoption in the Context of Public Law Proceedings

Traditionally, as 'guardian of last resort', the state has undertaken to provide for the public care of children in circumstances where private care was impossible—usually where parents were dead, missing or could not exercise proper control. More recently, in keeping with the ethos of 'partnership' between child care agencies and parents, such care may also be provided with parental consent, usually for reasons of parental respite, training or illness. In either case, the law has been at pains to ensure that the limited and specific duties of public child care agencies should not be convertible into a power to make a compulsory adoption placement. Parental consent was upheld as the essential legal passport for a child to pass from public care to private family via adoption. This is no longer the case. Equating the grounds for entry to public care with those of non-consensual third party adoption has been a most significant development for family law as a discipline. Extending to foster parents the right to apply to adopt, solely on the grounds of carer tenure, also marks a significant diminution of parental rights in favour of welfare interests.

Adoption in the Context of Private Law Proceedings

Traditionally, guardianship, wardship, matrimonial proceedings and adoption proceedings each occupied their own separate well-defined and discrete space within the body of private family law. The legal functions were tightly contained, exercised on a one-off basis to achieve permanency in the status awarded by their respective orders. Currently, each seems to have slipped its moorings, is drifting uncertainly and bumping into and shifting the position of the others. At the same time, *the locus standi* of parents—traditionally central to those proceedings—is being challenged by a new recognition accorded to those who bear direct and continuous care responsibility.

Wardship Proceedings

In the United Kingdom, including NI, wardship for a time became central to the realignment of other proceedings. It asserted the principle that the welfare interests of a child were to be treated as of paramount importance in any public or private issue concerning the upbringing of that child. By assuming responsibility for complex cases concerning children, wardship acted as a safety valve for private family law and bought time for a composite legislative reformulation in the construct 'family proceedings' as anchored on the *Children Act* 1989 and its NI counterpart, the Children (NI) Order 1995. The new arrangement radically diminished the traditional ambit of guardianship, restricted any future development of wardship, essentially removed the public interest threshold for orders in matrimonial proceedings and left open the possibility of acquiring further status-changing orders.

Guardianship Proceedings

One of the oldest of the private law jurisdictions has now virtually disappeared. The essentially protective order of guardianship would seem to have been largely consigned to history; the welfare of the child is now to be accorded a higher priority than that required of a guardian. The functions of this order are now absorbed into new family proceedings orders such as residence orders.

Matrimonial Proceedings

Of course, it is the changes in the law relating to marriage which have had the greatest impact upon family law as a discipline. Deference to individual choice has brought with it an abandoning of the importance previously attached to legal status and to the principles which governed changes in status. Also greatly undermined has been the importance previously attached to the principle of the welfare interests of the child in the context of uncontested matrimonial proceedings. The scaling down of the public interest in decision-making relating to the future care arrangements for children, following the breakdown of their parents' marriage, has been a watershed for family law in the United Kingdom. There is now a clear difference between the bearing of the welfare principle in contested and uncontested proceedings.

Other Care Arrangements

The incremental extension to carers of opportunities to acquire the rights and duties previously restricted to parents serves to illustrate the trend towards a general dilution of private parental interests in favour of establishing a public interest in protecting the position of those who voluntarily undertake child care responsibilities.

Adoption

Adoption, in recent years, has developed to become largely an expedient add-on to matrimonial proceedings, to tidy up private ownership rights in respect of children, deny inconveniently intrusive rights to others and seal the legal boundaries of a new marital family unit. This is a very strong indicator of how far family law has shifted—from embodying and giving effect to a body of coherent social principles representing a clearly understood definition of the public interest to becoming instead a vehicle for facilitating adult choice.

CONCLUSION

Adoption is a culture-specific set of legal functions. On the island of Ireland, as elsewhere in modern Western societies, it now straddles both private and public law. It has become intimately linked to private proceedings, particularly divorce, and to public proceedings, particularly where care orders are made in circumstances of serious child abuse. How adoption responds to these two feeder channels is of crucial importance not just for procedural efficiency, but mainly because of the need to rebuild a principled and integrated coherence for family law as a discipline. This paper has tried to show that there is now a dissonance in governing principles within adoption and between it and other public and private proceedings.

The problems arise partially from the fact that objectively defined parental rights and duties have now been displaced by the essentially subjective concept of 'welfare' as a basis for determining family proceedings. It can only be satisfactorily realised relative to the needs of each individual child and cannot therefore be applied with any consistency. Problems also follow from the fact that the role of the concept varies according to whether or not proceedings are contested. The weighting given to it—paramount or otherwise—often depends on whether parental consent is at issue. Nowhere is this more evident than in adoption, where paramountcy does not come into play until parental consent is first resolved. This points to an inbuilt contradiction threatening the coherence of modern family law—if the public interest in the welfare of the child is to be the new grundnorm for the discipline—the integrating principle across public and private proceedings—how can it be balanced in a consistent manner with private parental and carer interests in all proceedings, whether or not they are contested?

PART II
Practices

10
Children and the Transformation of Family Law

Carol Smart*

INTRODUCTION

Anyone who adopts an historical perspective on family law[1] will be struck by the extensive changes that have occurred in this field of law over the last decade. Of course, almost every decade throughout the twentieth century has brought changes—most particularly after World War II when the disadvantaged position of wives became more apparent and as divorce was made accessible to a much wider constituency. These changes, combined in a complex fashion with social, economic and cultural transformations, have not produced a state of stasis or of resolution, but rather have generated a field of legal policy which is in perpetual motion and reformulation. Family law cannot stay still while the family itself is being transformed and redefined, nor can it these days escape the consequences of operating beneath a close political scrutiny by media, pressure groups and government alike. Family law is a site of contested meanings and moralities as government seeks to reduce the cost of divorce to the Exchequer, as pro-family rights groups seek to reintroduce matrimonial fault, as gays and lesbians seek to extend the right to marry, as fathers seek to redefine their roles, and as mothers still seek to combine care work with paid work and avoid poverty after divorce.

These are not, however, the only matters of significance that we need to take into account in understanding recent policy changes. This is because, amongst the 'noise' associated with the transformations cited above, there has been a quieter set of developments which have centred on the place of children in the family, before and after divorce. I do not, of course, suggest that children were ignored throughout the twentieth century only to be 'discovered' in its final decade. This would give the wrong impression entirely because a commitment to the 'welfare

*Professor, Centre for Research on Family, Kinship and Childhood, University of Leeds. A version of this paper was first published in the *New Brunswick Law Journal*.

[1] I am speaking of England and Wales in this context, but I am certain that similar changes have been occurring in other common law jurisdictions as well and so I hope that this paper will carry a relevance beyond the shores of the United Kingdom.

of the child'[2] has been a major principle in family law since the end of the nineteenth century. But I do suggest that the 'place' that children occupy in the principles and practice of family law is beginning to change considerably as our ideas of childhood and about children change and as children themselves begin to become the speaking subjects of law, rather than the objects of law's benevolence.[3] It is on this quiet, incomplete revolution that I shall concentrate in this lecture. In the first section I shall take the English *Children Act* 1989 as my starting point for a discussion of how post-divorce family life has been changing over the last decade. I shall, however, move quickly on to how children themselves see post-divorce family life. I shall then focus on how children and childhood are being redefined and reconceptualised in family policy terms, especially in relation to the UN Convention on the Rights of the Child. Finally, I shall draw these issues together to give consideration to what these changes might mean for the practice of family law in the broadest sense.

Changing Post-divorce Family Life

The *Children Act* 1989[4] occupies an important cultural place in the history of family life in England and Wales because it symbolises the shift in policy emphasis away from the centrality of marriage and spousal relationships toward the centrality of parenthood and parent–child relationships.[5] Hale, who was the main author of the Act, has argued that there has been a clearly discernible trend in English family law away from a preoccupation with adjudicating on the conduct of adults towards one another and away from prioritising marriage over other forms of family life.[6] Family law has become more concerned with the extent to which arrangements between parents (married or not) meet the best interests of their children. The *Children Act* embraced this idea in particular through measures to abolish the legal concepts of 'custody' and 'access' to children on divorce. Basically, the Act severed the traditional relationship between marriage and parenthood (in which marriage provided legal rights in relation to legitimate children) by decreeing that the termination of a marriage no longer affected parents' legal relationship with their children.[7] This measure removed the need for courts to decide upon which parent should be granted custody and which should be

[2] Of course, the extent to which this principle was put into practice varied considerably, and the meaning of welfare changed constantly throughout the twentieth century: C Smart and S Sevenhuijsen (eds) *Child Custody and the Politics of Gender* (Routledge, 1989).

[3] J Roche, 'Children: Rights, Participation and Citizenship' (1999) 6(4) *Childhood* 475.

[4] I shall be referring only to the private law provisions of this Act.

[5] B Hale, 'Private Lives and Public Duties: What is Family Law For?' The 8th ESRC Annual Lecture 1997 (1998) 20 *Journal of Social Welfare and Family Law* 125.

[6] This trend may be in the process of being reversed by the current (UK) Labour government which has expressed a preference for marriage as a basis for family life over other forms of family formation: Home Office, *Supporting Families: A Consultation Document* (The Stationery Office, 1998).

[7] J Roche, 'Children: Rights, Participation and Citizenship' (1999) 6(4) *Childhood* 475.

given access because both parents retained the full set of 'rights and responsibilities' generated by legal marriage even after the termination of the marriage. Moreover, unmarried parents could be placed in exactly the same position as married parents by making, or by being awarded, a Parental Responsibility Agreement/Order. This measure, in effect, gave primacy to the biological status of parenthood over the legal institution of marriage. This was reinforced by the Act's presumption that there would be 'shared' parenting after divorce and that the first and paramount consideration of the courts should be the best interests of the child.

As I have argued, the Act did not start this trend towards the primacy of parenting, but it was a powerful lever in the shifting cultural significance of marriage versus parenthood. Moreover, this shift coincided with other important developments. For example, the rise of the Fathers' Rights Movement[8] was important to the extent that it identified men in family law as fathers/parents rather than solely as husbands or breadwinners. This gradual identification of (some) men with the 'new fatherhood'[9] was part of a process of shifting the terms of the debate towards a focus on the parent–child relationship. The claims that men made were increasingly made by them as fathers rather than as husbands, and they were increasingly made in terms of the welfare of children rather than in terms of the rights of adults. It has been argued that fatherhood has become more significant to men with the rise of divorce precisely because divorce has been associated in the recent past with a loss of both a partner and of children.[10] As one father we cited in *Family Fragments*[11] stated:

> *Leon:* I hadn't really thought about it. We were still living in the house together for about a year when we were going through really difficult times, moved into separate rooms. It was a case of I'd always worked really hard, I'd come home, gone up to the study and the children were there. My role as a father was to go out to work, to bring the money in, to try and look careerwise and the children were young and it was a case of just saying 'Hello, sit on my knee, then off to bed'. And I was just there and I probably didn't pay them much attention at all. *It was only when I realised that they might not be part of my life that gave me a real shock and it made me more aware and during that year I made more effort to spend time with the children.*

[8] I am not concerned here with the 'rights' or 'wrongs' of this movement, nor with the extent to which it could be argued that Fathers' Rights were a foil for 'men's rights' and an attempt to reduce women's rights.

[9] By the 'new fatherhood', I mean fatherhood defined more in terms of shared (practical and emotional) caring rather than traditional fatherhood defined in terms of being the breadwinner and head of household.

[10] 'Becoming a father is not difficult, but being a divorced father certainly is. At the moment when it is too late, the family personified by the child becomes the centre of all hope and concrete effort; the child is offered time and attention in a manner which during the marriage was allegedly out of the question, "although I really would like to spend more time with him/her". Divorce confronts the man with his own feelings as a father; he is the one to mourn for, having realised too late what liberation means, just as its objective slips away.' (U Beck and E Beck Gernsheim, *The Normal Chaos of Love* (Polity, 1995), p 154).

[11] C Smart and B Neale, *Family Fragments* (Polity, 1999).

POST-DIVORCE FAMILY LIFE: THE PERSPECTIVE OF CHILDREN

In the United Kingdom, there is a growing tendency to talk about 'parenting across households' rather than family breakdown.[12] This shift in terminology represents two elements. The first is an ideological shift away from framing family transitions in perpetually negative terms. The term 'breakdown' inevitably implies that disaster or a set of harms has befallen the family or its members. It fixes in the imagination the idea that something has gone wrong which should not have gone wrong—and which could never occur in 'intact' families. The shift away from the term 'breakdown' is therefore a sign of a shift away from an automatically value-laden frame of reference. The second element in this shift is in the positive—even optimistic—assumption that parenting can actually continue even if parents are not co-resident. This idea was virtually unthinkable prior to the *Children Act.* The family and parenthood were both usually imagined[13] to be located within a single household with a clear physical boundary between one family and another. Family members outside the household were assumed to be 'extended' kin and therefore less important or significant; whilst grown-up children living apart were described as having 'left' the family of origin. The recognition that important, emotional, caring relationships which are still called family can exist across households marks an important shift in policy thinking—and possibly in the national psyche.

Parenting across households is not only imaginable now, it is also the lived experience of a growing number of children who retain close bonds and/or contact with both parents after divorce or separation. The *Children Act* has meant that the old 'custodial' model of post-divorce parenting (in which one parent—usually the mother—has the children living with her exclusively, and where the other parent—usually the father—takes them out for trips and visits on alternate weekends) is no longer the only possibility. This kind of arrangement can be entirely satisfactory, of course, but now there are alternatives—especially the co-parenting model where children spend half (or approximately half) their time with each parent in different households. This shift towards parenting across households, or co-parenting, has the potential to change the nature of childhood in late modernity—and with it the potential to change children's experiences of both childhood and parenthood.

Our research with children[14] suggests that divorce can provide children with a new, reflexive position from which to understand and evaluate parenthood and

[12] M Maclean and J Eekelaar, *The Parental Obligation* (Hart, 1997).

[13] Of course, not all families lived like this. Oral histories show that children often lived with relatives, especially in working-class families; and of course in upper-class families, children were often sent away to boarding schools. The growth of a multicultural society in Britain has also meant that norms about family life have changed. However, the populist image of the family used by governments and the media alike has been based on the limited nuclear family, single-household model.

[14] We have recently completed two research projects on children's experience of post-divorce family life. The first was funded by the ESRC and concentrated on children who were being co-parented.

post-divorce family life. The quotation from Leon above suggests that divorce can shake or even destroy the taken-for-grantedness of parent–child relationships (just as it surely disrupts the taken-for-grantedness of spousal relationships). We found that this happened for children as well:

> *Q: Has you relationship with your dad changed at all?*
>
> *James H (12):* No, it's just the same . . . Sort of, like, appreciate him more. Sort of think about it more. Whereas before I just like took it for granted that he was there.
>
> *Selina (16):* I think I've probably got closer to mum and dad just because of the situation. Like, my friends will take their parents for granted [and say things] like 'Mum's always there when I get home' or 'Oh God, mum was moaning last night', kind of thing. But I don't 'cos when they're there I know it's only for a short time and I like appreciate them a lot more, I think.

Children could begin to see their parents as 'people' with their own needs, interests, habits and even flaws. They were able to reflect upon how good they were as parents or whether different parents provided different kinds of care and support:

> *Nina (11):* I don't think we'd like it living with dad . . . mum looks after us nearly all the time, she's better with us and she does things that I'm comfortable with and that are right for me and dad sometimes doesn't know what to do and gets panicked. I can't really talk to my dad about my feelings and stuff, sometimes there's like long silences . . . I'd end up feeling bored and sick of it [with him].

It is not unusual for adults to revisit their childhood and re-evaluate their parents' parenting abilities, but it is possibly a recent development for children to do this during their childhoods and it may be that being parented across households provides an emotional space for children to be more reflexive. It was the case that some children could compare[15] how they were being parented by their different parents and could make choices about which they preferred:

> *Q: What's it like when you're going off to dad's?*
>
> *Alistair (11):* Well it depends whether he's been nice to me the week before. Sometimes I want to go but not usually . . . I like mum the most . . . I didn't like it when I

That is to say, they were spending more or less equal amounts of time with both parents in different households. We interviewed 65 children in depth in this study, aged between four and seventeen years. The second study was funded by The Nuffield Foundation and was a follow-up study of the children of the parents we had interviewed in *Family Fragments?* Here we interviewed 52 children aged between five and twenty-two years, the majority of whom were between seven and fifteen. The Research Officers on the projects were Dr Bren Neale and Dr Amanda Wade.

[15] I should make clear that we did not ask children to compare their parents, nor did we ask them questions about whether they preferred to be at one house rather than another. Where comments of this sort emerged it was as part of a conversation about their experiences in a broad sense and children could volunteer as much or as little as they wished.

> was seeing dad more. I never saw my mum at weekends. So I asked for it to change. Now it's much better. Dad used to be much nastier than he is now, especially to mum. He shouts at me, he used to give me smacks a lot, but he's better than he was.

It also gives children potentially a wider range of childhood experiences which can focus on 'small' things:

> *Q: Is it difficult to remember what to do at each house?*
>
> *Lisa (8):* No, not really, 'cos they're different places and they look very different. As soon as you walk in you think, 'Ah, late night tonight, stories, cornetto', and at mum's house you think, 'Ah, nice early night tonight, nice little bowl of cereal and some lovely hot chocolate'.

Being parented in two households could increase children's range of experiences as well as the number of new challenges they might have to face, but it also provides the opportunity for them successfully to negotiate such challenges:

> *Karl (15):* When I'm here, I don't sort of think, 'Hang on, what am I doing? Why am I doing this, I don't normally do this'. You know, I just sort of, wherever I am, I just sort of do whatever it is. I'd get really confused if my mum and dad swapped places, that would just totally confuse me. I'd be doing all the wrong things at the wrong house! But, you know, you just sort of got to get used to it, I do what I do here, I just do that automatically.

The fact that parents lived in two separate households did not in itself necessarily constitute a problem for the children we interviewed—at least not once they had got used to the changes that inevitably accompany having parents in two places. As long as parents were supportive of their children in this new lifestyle, the children could thrive. However, if parents made the transitions difficult, if they restricted the toys or clothes that children could take with them, or if they required children to convey painful messages, then the situation could become extremely difficult for the children. We also found that certain practical things such as the physical distance between the households could be a problem, and for younger children there was always the problem of losing toys. One ten-year-old boy spoke of the Bermuda Triangle that existed between his mother's home, his school and his father's home, in which huge numbers of toys and school items were forever lost. Having parents in two places obviously made life more complicated, but this alone was not enough to make most children feel it was not worth the extra effort involved. Where being parented across households worked well, the children saw a continuity in their family life and they continued to feel cared for and part of their whole family. However, this does not mean that they did not feel an element of resentment or that the arrangement was better for the parents than for the children.

> *Q: What do you think of your family living in two houses?*
>
> *Ryan (7):* I think it's crap. I wish my dad was next door so I could see him whenever I wanted . . . or that he stayed here.
>
> *Q: Who do you think this arrangement works best for?*
>
> *Lisa (8):* Both of them [parents]. I don't like it. There are good advantages and bad advantages . . . but I don't like living away from the two of them.
>
> *Charmaine (11):* Yes, I think it's probably a lot easier for my parents because they're not swapping around all the time . . . But it's fine now because it's been about four years so I've got used to it.
>
> *Selina (16):* I mean, they've still got their house, haven't they? They're not moving. And I don't think they realise how hard it is. I don't think they understand how hard it is! But then no one would until they actually did it themselves.

These quotations make it clear that, even where the arrangement was working fairly well, there was a price to pay, and the children could feel that they were the ones paying it. But, as I suggest above, children were much more likely to feel that the price was too high if there were additional burdens placed on them beside the need to be regularly moving. Some children, for example, felt that they could not suggest changes to their arrangements because it would only provoke long arguments between their parents, or because one parent would feel betrayed. The boy we quote below only managed to change his 50:50 split with his parents because his mother agreed to support him and because she took legal advice first on whether her former husband could prevent an adjustment to the arrangements. Because Tom was twelve years old, she was advised that he was old enough to have his views taken into account.

> *Tom G (12):* I used to split my time really sort of evenly [between my parents] but I find my dad quite a prat to put it bluntly, so I've sort of been taking away days from him and coming to mum's instead because I don't like being depressed . . . My dad always seemed to criticise me about my homework and boss me around and tell me to do things over and over again and not let me do anything in my own time or anything.

Being co-parented could therefore feel quite oppressive to some children. One girl of thirteen was angry that whenever she tried to change the arrangements she would be reminded that the legal battle to achieve equality had cost thousands of pounds and so she felt completely stuck in the middle of her parents' battle. Other children felt it was not worth the effort of trying to change things.

One of the most poignant things that the children spoke of was the fact that, even though they saw both of their parents an equal amount of time, it did not mean that they did not miss the parent they were not with. This sense of perpetual loss might be chronic rather than acute most of the time, but it could become acute at the point of transition from one household to another. While children who might only see a non-residential parent occasionally also suffer these same emotions, for co-parented children it is built into their lives in a totally regular way and is combined with leaving 'home' as well. Thus not only do they leave one parent, but they leave their bedroom, their local friends and possibly their pets on a weekly or half-weekly basis.

> *Selina (16):* I find on Sunday evening I always *miss* where I've just come from. Either way. It's not like I miss mum more than dad or anything like that. When I get here and I've been at mum's all week I miss mum and I miss Paul [step-dad] and I miss *that*—'cos it's two different families and two different ways of doing things. You know, even things like clearing the table, whatever . . . I always come on Sunday night and I start unpacking all my stuff, whatever, if I've come from mum's, and I'll start just to miss mum a bit 'cos I've had her all week. And then by Monday I go to school and by Monday night it's just 'I'm at dad's now' and I'm in that mood . . . It's just Sunday evenings really that make me [sad]. If I *get* upset about it, it's always on a Sunday night. Like, I have a cry or whatever. Or write it down. I always write stuff down. Just like, a thought book. I just write things in it when I need to. And then . . . I'm all right again by Monday.

For very young children, a whole week away from one parent could seem far too long but for older ones the responsibility of having to see both parents for the same amount of time each meant that they felt they had far less freedom than their peers and that they had less time to spend with their friends. It could produce a situation of 'over-parenting' in which all of a child's spare time was accounted for and where some children gave up trying to sustain friendships because they were so busy being parented.

> *Harold (12):* I like my family . . . I think you should spend an equal amount of time at your mum and dad's . . . We sleep Mondays, Wednesdays, Fridays and Sundays at our mums and Tuesdays, Thursdays and Saturdays at our dad's . . . I see them both every day. I come back to mum's after school and then round to my dad's for an hour or so.
>
> *Q: If a friend invited you out for the day and you had arranged to be with dad, what would you do?*
>
> *Harold:* I haven't got [many friends] . . . I wouldn't go on the trip really, I wouldn't want to, I'd prefer to stay with mum or dad . . . I wouldn't like them to [have new partners] because I wouldn't like to spend time with the other person.

This last quotation introduces one final area of potentially significant change to post-divorce family life. Prior to the *Children Act*, there was a presumption—albeit one which was on the decline—that the best thing for children following divorce was for the parent with custody to re-marry and to create a reconstituted nuclear family so that the children would have a 'proper' family life. Research had shown that step-families could face a number of problems, but it is clear that the ethos of the 1970s and 1980s was geared towards 'starting again' as a 'proper' family.[16] New husbands were presumed to become the main father figure for the children and it was not uncommon for children to be adopted, or at least for them to take their step-father's name so that they would 'look like' a proper family to the outside world.

The *Children Act* undermined these presumptions by emphasising the ongoing relationship between non-residential parents (presumed to be fathers) and their children. By endorsing an omnipresent biological father, the Act left little room for the step-father to replace him. In reality, of course, children would often not accept a step-father or step-mother as a substitute parent anyway—especially if they had a good and ongoing relationship with their biological parent. But the *Children Act* has formally endorsed this shift away from the idea that a mother's (or father's) new partner also becomes a new parent. We found that, where children were being parented across households, they were not inclined to see a parent's new partner as a substitute parent, or even a parent at all:

> *Bob (13):* Michael [mum's live-in partner] has always been there to help with things like my bike and stuff but he's never, ever, like if I was upset, come into my room to say 'Are you OK?' or 'What's happened?' He's just like there to help you with easy things.
>
> *Q: He doesn't try to be a parent?*
>
> *Bob:* Well, if he did basically I'd tell mum that I wasn't happy living with him. Cos the way I see it you can only ever have one person that's not just your dad but like your dad, or your mum, doing dad or mum things.
>
> *David (16):* I don't think of [dad's live-in partner] as a part of the family, I just think of her as dad's friend.
>
> *Andrijka (10):* [Mum and dad's new partners] are a big part of my life. But I don't really think of them as family and people who I love. I think of them as—I don't know, friends I suppose.

It is likely, therefore, that not only are 'biological' families changing, but so are 'reconstituted' families, and some children are increasingly able to define the nature of their relationships with adults who share their lives. Mothers can be seen as having boyfriends—even live-in boyfriends—but these men need not impact particularly on the children co-residing with them. In fact, these new partners are seemingly forced into finding new ways of relating to these children because they cannot fall back into the old pattern of substitute parent with presumptions about authority and obedience.

If parenthood after divorce or separation is changing as a consequence of these developments, it follows that childhood too is likely to be changing. Of course, childhood is unlikely to change in only one direction or in only one dimension.

[16] J Burgoyne and D Clark, *Making a Go of It* (Routledge & Kegan Paul, 1984).

Nor is it likely to change solely as a reaction to changes in parenting.[17] However, it would be unrealistic to imagine that parenting across households puts childhood back together as it might have been had the divorce rate remained at pre-war levels. Divorce has changed modern childhood and the trend towards co-parenting (if it is actually realised) will change it again.

REDEFINING CHILDHOOD

Alongside actual changes in how childhood is organised, experienced and lived in post-traditional societies, there are (inevitably) changes in perceptions of and definitions of childhood. These latter changes are evidenced in changes to social policy and law, in pressure groups and new social movements, in marketing and media, and in academic disciplines where children are the focus of study. In this section I shall, for reasons of space, confine myself to family law rather than trying to discuss the broader fields of social policy, health and education. However, I shall start by referring to some important conceptual shifts which are creating a new climate in which new policy demands may become more feasible.

In 1975, John Holt published one of the first academic texts in the United Kingdom on the 'liberation' of children. It was called *Escape from Childhood: The Needs and Rights of Children*. It was seen as a very polemical book in the same sort of tradition as early feminist work which was demanding women's liberation.[18] The sorts of ideas that Holt was working with—namely giving political rights to children and democratising the two most important sites of oppression for children, which he saw as the family and the school—were controversial. Holt argued against the commonsense idea that the acquisition of rights should be linked to age because he saw such distinctions as purely arbitrary and as no proof of competence. But he also argued against basing rights on a notion of competence because tests of competence were not applied to adults. He suggested that adults could also be incompetent and that it was discriminatory to use this measure as a method of disqualifying children when it was not used for adults.

His arguments were not successful in the sense of persuading parents and governments to change how they conceptualised and hence treated children, but he did rekindle a debate about childhood and created a space for more critical thinking which challenged the naturalist assumption that children were inevitably incompetent and immature and that they should remain outside the modern concepts of citizenship and democracy. Holt's work was mirrored by the establishment of pressure groups such as The Children's Legal Centre in London, and radical lawyers and social workers began to operationalise some of these ideas,

[17] Influences from the media, the internet, the education system, high crime rates, high urban traffic density and so are going to be very influential as well, of course.

[18] D Archard, *Children: Rights and Childhood* (Routledge, 1993).

especially around the position of children in public care who had no voice at all in how they were treated and 'disposed' of. Some radical educationalists also sought to take forward these ideas, setting up schools where the children participated in the running of the institution and where they could choose which classes to attend.

The ideas generated by Holt and others in the 1970s, and more recently by academic lawyers in the 1990s,[19] have gradually begun to create a climate in which the idea that children are citizens too has become 'thinkable'. These developments have been assisted by the establishment of the UN Convention on the Rights of the Child to which the United Kingdom became a signatory in 1991. What is particularly important about the Convention is its focus on family life and not just on the idea of citizenship in the public arena. It shifts the emphasis away from the idea that parents have rights over children to focus on the way in which parents have responsibilities towards their children, including the responsibility to allow them to participate in family life.[20] Article 12 is of particular importance in this respect. It states:

1. Parties shall assure to the child who is capable of forming his or her own views the right to express those views freely in all matters affecting the child, the views of the child being given due weight in accordance with the age and maturity of the child.
2. For this purpose, the child shall in particular be provided the opportunity to be heard in any judicial and administrative proceedings affecting the child, either directly, or through a representative or an appropriate body, in a manner consistent with the procedural rules of national law.

The Convention bridges two dominant views on how children should be attended to in legislation. The first is the welfare principle, which is a major theme in the wording of the Convention. The second, which is more apparent in the sections quoted above, is the idea of the child as an actor who can intervene on their own behalf. The Convention does not, however, seek to resolve how to marry these two potential conflicting principles in practice.

In terms of family law in the United Kingdom, it has been the welfare principle which has dominated—at least until recently. The idea that the courts should put the welfare of children first in cases of divorce or disputes between parents, or between parents and the state, was a powerful counter-balance to the idea that children were 'owned' by their parents. It also allowed courts to settle disputes between adults in ways which did not ignore the needs of children who were not

[19] M Freeman, *The Moral Status of Children* (Martinus Nijhoff, 1997); J Eekelaar, 'The Emergence of Children's Rights' (1996) 6 *Oxford Journal of Legal Studies* 161; J Fortin, *Children's Rights and the Developing Law* (Butterworths, 1998) J Roche, 'Children: Rights, Participation and Citizenship' (1999) 6(4) *Childhood* 475.

[20] Children's Rights Office, *Building Small Democracies* (Children's Rights Office, 1995).

represented in these legal conflicts. However, the idea of the welfare of the child did not envisage a *participating child* who could speak for him or herself. The welfare principle was based on a presumption that professionals knew what was best for the generic child, and even for the specific child, and that their evidence should be sufficient to allow for children's interests to be represented. In turn, the professionals' understanding of the needs of the child was based on research which cast the child as the dependant within the family and with levels of competency which were likely to be related to age.

The way in which children became visible in family law—particularly in issues of divorce—was therefore a long way away from Holt's earlier vision of the child as a speaking citizen with rights comparable to an adult. The British philanthropic, paternalist tradition evinced concern for the child, but still preferred her to be seen and not heard. The welfare principle did not make the child into a legal subject.[21]

Inroads were made into the dominance of this principle by three major developments. The first was the *Gillick* decision.[22] This case concerned whether doctors could prescribe contraceptive pills to a girl under sixteen years of age without informing her parents or gaining their consent. It ruled that children under the legal age of consent could consent to medical treatment if they had 'sufficient understanding and intelligence' to comprehend what was proposed as well as the emotional capacity to make a mature decision. This decision allowed a child under sixteen to become a speaking subject as long as she was deemed to be sufficiently mature. It therefore freed children from an arbitrary and automatic assumption that before they reached sixteen they were incapable of making decisions and forming judgments. The second development was the Report of the Inquiry into the Cleveland Affair. This had focused on the question of whether doctors and social workers in Cleveland in Northern England, had been too zealous in the diagnosis of child sexual abuse to the extent that their interventions which were designed to 'save' children actually harmed them. The chair of the Inquiry was Mrs Justice Butler Sloss, who stated: 'The child is a person and not an object of concern.'[23] In this parsimonious sentence, she conveyed the idea that children should be allowed their personhood—a concept which arguably embraces dignity, respect and a voice, and that they should not be reduced to mere objects no matter how worthy the concern for their well-being. In this utterance, she sought to shift the balance between citizenship and welfare towards the former.

Finally, the third development was the *Children Act* 1989 itself. This Act placed the welfare of the child at its core, but also insisted that 'the wishes and feelings of the child should be ascertained'. It therefore pre-empted the UN Convention's Article 12 but, like the Convention, it did not address the competing tensions

[21] M Freeman, *The Moral Status of Children* (Martinus Nijhoff, 1997).
[22] *Gillick v West Norfolk and Wisbech Area Health Authority* [1986] AC 112.
[23] Report of the Inquiry into Child Abuse in Cleveland 1987 (HMSO, 1988), Cm 412.

which arise in practice from marrying together the idea of welfare which is defined by a professional corpus of knowledge and expertise, and the wishes and feelings of children which are unlikely to be framed in the same way. The tension between these two ways of attempting to represent children arises from the fact that they symbolise two very different theories of childhood. The welfare paradigm is based on the notion that the child is an adult in the making and that the concern of policy is to protect childhood so that a responsible, functioning adult can emerge. It is a future-oriented philosophy which is given scientific support by the dominance of medical and psychological research on outcome measurements.[24] The concern of the policy-makers, judges, welfare officers and others in the family law system is therefore not with the child's current views or experiences, but with what effect the present will have on their future. The opposing perspective is one which argues that, if we only see children as adults in the making, we ignore the extent to which children are able to be actors (persons) and to participate in decisions about their own lives in the present.[25] This approach also argues that children become competent actors if they are allowed to participate more fully and to have a wide range of experiences. It suggests that, rather than waiting for children to mature in accordance with a biological clock before giving them rights to participate, giving them rights to participate will allow them to mature as part of a cultural process.[26] The former perspective concentrates on children's biologically induced dependency, the latter on their socio-cultural agency.

This latter perspective has given rise to research[27] which is gradually making visible the extent of children's competence, rather than working from a presumption of childhood incompetence or a position of indifference to lived childhood based on a future-oriented focus on children's adulthood. As a consequence of being prepared to listen, it has been discovered that children have much to say. This in turn is generating much discussion about how children can participate, not simply in the legal process or in the divorce process, but in all aspects of family life.

THE IMPLICATIONS FOR FAMILY LAW/ FAMILY POLICY

> *Nina (11):* Well *she should be involved in sorting it out* but I don't think her parents should actually make her choose, or anything [Why?] Because she is going to feel awful if she says one parent and lets the other down, and they shouldn't make her do that.

> *Quentin (13): I think you should like have a debate* so you can say, like, why you'd choose your mum 'cos she's got more time for them and she can cook for them, and your dad

[24] S Rose, *Governing the Soul* (Routledge, 1989).

[25] A James and A Prout (eds), *Constructing and Reconstructing Childhood* (Falmer Press, 1990).

[26] T Cockburn, 'Children and Citizenship in Britain' (1998) 5 *Childhood* 99.

[27] An example of this is the body of empirical work funded by the Economic and Social Research Council in the United Kingdom on childhood.

could say 'Well, I've got a step-mum', but then the mum could say, 'Well, they really don't like it and they wouldn't be happy with her', say to the judge or someone . . .

Mark (15): I think he should have an opinion, I don't think he should necessarily decide, *he should get a say in it, he shouldn't just be left out,* I mean it's his life as well, he shouldn't be stuck with someone he didn't want to be with.

When we put to the children in our study a vignette which depicted parents requiring a child to decide who they wanted to live with after their divorce, we found that the majority felt that children should be able to participate in reaching such a decision, but that they should not have to be responsible for making the decision unless there were grounds for a serious dislike of one of the parents. Only the youngest children felt that they should not be involved at all and wanted to leave things to their parents.

This idea that children should be able to participate is gaining ground in family law in the United Kingdom, and there is a growing sense of enthusiasm to hear 'the voice of the child' at some stage in the divorce process. However, a number of authors have also pointed to the ease with which this demand can be made, compared with the difficulty there exists in operationalising it.[28] Parents may not allow their children to participate in even the most routine decisions in their families and so, when it comes to divorce, children may not have the skills or experience to play a part. The legal process may be reluctant to involve children because its procedures are not child-friendly or because of concerns that the child will become a pawn in the battle between parents. Children themselves may not want to participate, or one sibling might wish to while another does not. There is also the problem of balancing welfare with participation. By being invited to participate, a child might show a preference for an option that the court feels goes against their best interests.

There is also an equally important subset of issues which affect participation. For example, at what stage should a child be able to participate—at the point when parents first think about divorce or only after they have made the decision? Should children be invited to participate in decisions about how often they see each parent, or only on tactical issues such as where the transition should be? Should solicitors speak to the children and, if so, should the solicitors from both sides do so? Or should children only be invited to participate by court welfare officers or mediators? To what extent does participation in any of these forums amount simply to tokenism, with professionals informing children of what will happen and striving to achieve their consent rather than their participation in arriving at decisions?

[28] J Roche, 'Children: Rights, Participation and Citizenship' (1999) 6(4) *Childhood* 475; Adrian James and Allison James, 'Pump Up the Volume: Listening to Children in Separation and Divorce' (1999) 6(2) *Childhood* 189; L Ackers, *From 'Best Interests' to Participatory Rights: Children's Involvement in Family Migration Decisions* (University of Leeds: Centre for Research on Family, Kinship & Childhood, 2000), Working Paper 20; RA Hart, *Children's Participation: From Tokenism to Citizenship* (UNICEF, 1992), Innocenti Essays No 4.

Once we start to list these questions, it quickly becomes apparent that participation by children cannot simply be put forward as a solution to the discomfort we might feel about their exclusion. Moreover, inclusion in the legal process may be the last place to seek participation, not the first. As James and James argue:[29]

> Many parents believe, rightly or wrongly, that they *do* have rights over their children and that it *is* their right to make decisions about their children's future when they divorce. Such a view makes the assertion of children's agency and *their right* to be heard much more difficult to accommodate.

This suggests that a lot of work has to be carried out at the level of parent–child relationships before much headway can be made at the level of legal proceedings. The children we interviewed were not particularly interested in having a voice in legal proceedings; they wanted a voice in their family. But what is also interesting is that, in having a voice, they did not necessarily assume that this should mean that they determined the outcome of discussions. It seems that they wanted 'recognition', not control or rights. This brings us back to the concept of personhood which is hailed in Butler-Sloss's remark that 'children are persons and not objects of concern'. Of course, whilst we might accept that one route to personhood for children is to give them rights which are legally enforceable, the children we interviewed did not construct family relationships through this legal prism. We need, therefore, to consider whether solutions do lie in legal forums or whether we should start somewhere else when we try to attend to the specific situation of children.

In the field of law, it is always tempting to see legal rights as the solution to newly recognised problems, especially one which can be construed as a form of discrimination. The limits of rights have, of course, been much discussed,[30] and I will not rehearse all these issues again here. But the UN Convention necessarily takes us into a rights framework, and some researchers have argued strongly that children must have clearer rights as well as the right to separate representation in family matters.[31] It is therefore necessary to point to some problems with this approach. The first is that the rights approach takes and translates personal and private matters into legal language. In so doing, it reformulates them into issues relevant to law rather than to the lives of ordinary people. It also positions people in opposition to one another and this can be particularly problematic for children. But the rights-based approach also individualises issues in that it removes and isolates the individual who is claiming rights from their family or social

[29] Adrian James and Allison James, 'Pump Up the Volume: Listening to Children in Separation and Divorce' (1999) 6(2) *Childhood* 189 at 204.

[30] C Smart, *Feminism and the Power of Law* (Routledge, 1989).

[31] C Lyon, E Surrey and J Timms, *Effective Support Services for Children and Young People when Parental Relations Breakdown: A Child Centred Approach* (Centre for the Study of the Child, the Family and the Law, University of Liverpool, 1998).

context. This means that, for the duration of the conflict of rights, the individual cannot be part of their family or context and, after the conflict is over, has to find ways of re-entering into those relationships, assuming that they are not removed entirely. In some cases, of course, this might be appropriate, but in cases where there are problems over amount of contact, whether contact can be suspended for a period of time, whether one sibling can end contact while another continues and so on, the process of turning such claims into legally recognised rights could be extremely damaging for individual children.

The children in our studies seemed to be more interested in having a 'voice' and having their situation 'recognised' than in having enforceable rights. Williams[32] has argued in relation to welfare principles that what is more important than rights (for example, as consumers) is the ability for people to be able to voice their diverse needs and for these to become formulated into collective claims rather than individual demands.[33] These ideas are particularly important where children are concerned. Thus what needs to be heard is not so much the expression of the rights of individual children so much as the kinds of things that children in general have to say about post-divorce family life. Once such voices can be heard, the terms of the policy debate can begin to change. No longer would it be experts and judges who framed the policies or guidelines alone, and parents could hear what children in general think without it having to be distilled into a conflict with their own child. This is a slow process of cultural change in which legal rights play an important part in redefining the status of subjugated groups, but where the actual implementation of rights in individual cases may be counter-productive.

In family law there are, of course, procedures which fall short of adversarial battles over rights—or even fall short of the idea that each child in a divorce case should have their own lawyer to pursue their own separate interests. These could entail involving children in some way in mediation sessions, or it might mean that solicitors and court welfare officers take further their duty to 'ascertain the wishes and feelings of the child' by interviewing each and every child, whether there is a conflict between parents or not. These suggestions seem less than ideal also. It is not that solicitors and CWOs should never speak to children, but such interviews do not overcome the problem of the child's loyalty to both parents, nor the fact that the child is ask to reveal private matters which will then be 'used' in a legal forum. Being interviewed is not, in any case, equivalent to participation in family decisions—an ongoing process which may change with time. Involving children in mediation is also problematic. Should children be present while parents discuss them, especially if there is a great deal of hostility and even a history of violence? Or should children only be brought in when a compromise has been reached so that they can 'hear' what the arrangements will be?

[32] F Williams, 'Good-enough Principles for Welfare', (1999) 28(4) *Journal of Social Policy* 667.

[33] N Fraser, 'From Redistribution to Recognition? Dilemmas of Justice in a 'Post-socialist' Age' (1995) 212 *New Left Review* 68.

Ackers[34] would argue that it depends which level of participation you wish to achieve and that the level may not be one that is determined by the 'facts' of the case but by the quality of the relationships in the family, and by a recognition of existing power relationships in the family. It might therefore be entirely appropriate to involve a child in a mediation session where the father or mother is violent and where there is hostility if the child has witnessed this on many occasions already and has a stake in coming to an arrangement where they will feel safe.

The practicalities of the situation and the cost to the legal aid budget are such, however, that it is most unlikely that children will become more involved in the legal process except in cases where there is conflict. This brings us back to how children can be allowed to participate (should they wish to) where there is—in legal terms—no dispute. It is here that the idea of the voice of children in general becomes significant again. Through the mechanism of hearing what children have to say (even though they do not speak with a unitary voice of course), children can begin to assume the role of citizens of the family. We all know the extent to which children have been turned into vociferous consumers by being addressed as such by advertising campaigns. Such campaigns may be entirely problematic, but it is clear that children born in 2000 are quite different to children born in 1950 when it comes to their knowledge and desire for consumer goods. An equivalent change may be possible in relation to building the families into small democracies. This need not be carried forward on the basis of individual rights in which the child is construed as an autonomous individual consumer of oppositional rule-based entitlements, but more where the child is construed as part of a web of relationships in which outcomes need to be negotiated (not demanded) and where responsibilities are seen to be reciprocal. As eleven-year-old Jake said when we asked him what a boy should do when his parents asked him to decide who to live with after their divorce:

> I think there should be some kind of agreement between him and his parents as to what should happen, rather than him just deciding who he wants to live with. I think the people who are involved should get to decide, not by themselves, but by helping each other to reach some kind of agreement as to what would be best.

It would be hard to improve upon this recommendation.

ACKNOWLEDGMENTS

I am grateful to Bren Neale and Amanda Wade who worked with me on both of the projects on which these ideas are based. The ideas discussed here are part of

[34] L Ackers, *From 'Best Interests' to Participatory Rights: Children's Involvement in Family Migration Decisions* (Centre for Research on Family, Kinship and Childhood, University of Leeds, 2000), Working Paper 20.

our ongoing discussions and are owned by all of us alike. I am also grateful to the Nuffield Foundation and the ESRC in the United Kingdom for funding these research projects.

11

In Search of the 'Good Father': Law, Family Practices and the Normative Reconstruction of Parenthood

Richard Collier*

INTRODUCTION

The question of what constitutes 'good (enough) fathering' is one which has, throughout the 1990s, assumed a central importance within a range of conversations taking place around the legal regulation of family practices across Western societies. Indeed, it is difficult to under-estimate the present ubiquity of this 'fatherhood problematic' across a range of cultural artefacts. At the present moment in the United Kingdom, for example, questions such as whether 'families need fathers', what fathers are 'for' and what is happening to the status of fatherhood have come to pervade newspaper and magazine articles, talk shows, television dramas, popular novels and films. Within the legal jurisdiction from which I am writing—England and Wales—the specific relationship between fatherhood and law has been raised in a particularly clear way in relation to a series of concerns around the changing nature of 'family values' and family life—for example, around the issue of what is, and should be, the legal responsibilities, rights and status of men, whether married or unmarried,[1] within the 'new' or 'bi-nuclear' family;[2] in relation to the ways in which family and employment policies are presently conceptualising a need to change the behaviour of 'family men' during marriage and cohabiting relationships;[3] with regard to the promotion of

* Newcastle Law School, University of Newcastle Upon Tyne. A version of this paper was published in (2000) 22 *Studies in Law Politics and Society*, and this version is published with the permission of that journal. Earlier versions of this article were presented as papers at Amherst College and Cornell Law School, USA, at the University of Leeds, England and at the 10th World Conference of the International Society of Family Law, Brisbane, Australia. I would like to thank all who passed comments, in particular, Martha Fineman, Reg Graycar and Austin Sarat.

[1] Lord Chancellor's Department, *Court Procedures for the Determination of Paternity: The Law on Parental Responsibility for Unmarried Fathers—Consultation Paper* (Lord Chancellor's Department, 1998).

[2] E Silva and C Smart (eds), *The 'New' Family?* (Sage, 1999).

[3] R Collier, 'Feminising the Workplace? (Re)constructing the 'Good Parent' in Employment Law and Family Policy' in A Morris and T O'Donnell (eds), *Feminist Perspectives on Employment*

equality between women and men in both the workplace and the family; in relation to attempts to promote 'good enough' post-divorce parenting on the part of men,[4] whether in the context of securing the provision of child support[5] or in seeking to maintain post-divorce contact between father and child;[6] and, from a rather different area, in the context of debates about families, crime and citizenship, where ideas of parental responsibility have in a more general sense moved increasingly politically to centre stage.[7] Taking these developments together, a concern with fatherhood can be seen to be central to contemporary cultural representations *of* and political debates *about* the parameters of 'the family' and understandings of 'family life'.

This article seeks to ask a question *why* fatherhood should have emerged as a problem to be addressed by law at this historical moment and in the way that it has—broadly, that is, as something which is now widely seen as being in need of 'change' or reform. The specific aims of the article are twofold: the first is to investigate and unpack those forces which have come to produce a certain constellation of ideas around the meaning of what I shall term 'good fatherhood' during the late 1980s/1990s in England and Wales.[8] This is in essence, I shall argue, a 'progressive', optimistic model of fatherhood premised on the idea of there being a convergence of women's and men's lives, notable via a weakening of the sexual division of domestic labour. And secondly, the article seeks to map out how these ideas have fed into a more general fatherhood problematic—an idea which, I shall argue, is presently serving within the field of popular knowledge, the media and at the level of official government discourse to constitute the relationship between men and children in what are some frequently contradictory, misleading and at times oppressive ways.

CONTEXTS: LAW, THE NEW DEMOCRATIC FAMILY AND THE 'PROBLEMATISING' OF FATHERHOOD

How, at the outset, is the relationship between law and fatherhood to be approached? Uniting both doctrinal and socio-legal accounts of law and parent-

(Cavendish, 1999), pp 161–81; C Lewis, *A Man's Place in the Home: Fathers and Families in the UK* (Joseph Rowntree Foundation, 2000).

[4] C Smart and B Neale, '"I hadn't really thought about it": New Identities/New Fatherhoods', in J Seymour and P Bagguley (eds), *Relating Intimacies: Power and Resistance* (Macmillan, 1999).

[5] J Wallbank, 'The Campaign for Change of the *Child Support Act* 1991: Reconstituting the 'Absent' Father' (1997) 6 *Social and Legal Studies* 191.

[6] C Smart and B Neale, 'Good Enough Morality? Divorce and Postmodernity' (1997) 17 *Critical Social Policy* 3; C Smart and B Neale, 'Arguments against Virtue: Must Contact be Enforced?' (1997) 28 *Family Law* 332.

[7] L Gelsthorpe, 'Youth Crime and Parental Responsibility', in A Bainham, S Day Sclater and M Richards (eds), *What is a Parent? A Socio-Legal Analysis* (Hart, 1999), p 217.

[8] On differences within family law policy between Scotland and England and Wales, see further A Bissett-Johnson and C Barton, 'The Similarities and Differences in Scottish and English Family Law in Dealing with Changing Family Patterns' (1999) 21 *Journal for Social Welfare and Family Law* 1.

hood, as well as the intellectual and analytic methods of legal studies more generally, continues to be a presupposition about the centrality of law to strategies of intervention concerned with 'dealing with' particular social problems. It is, however, in contrast to the dominant epistemological frameworks of normative and socio-legal theory that Rose and Valverde[9] have recently sought to rephrase the question 'What does [family] law govern?' by beginning not with 'law' itself (whether in the form of statutes, cases or legal practices) but from a series of questions, or what they term 'problems or problematizations'. Far from seeking to *unify* law (whether jurisprudentially or genealogically), Rose and Valverde approach law in terms of the notion of problematisation—that is, the:

> way in which experience is offered to thought in the form of a problem requiring attention. The analysis of problematization is the analysis of the practices within which these problematizing experiences are formed . . . in order to analyse the ways in which problems form at the intersection of legal and extra-legal discourses, practices and institutions, it is necessary *to de-centre law* from the outset.[10]

In taking up and exploring this idea in the context of family law, I do not wish to argue that law is in any way unimportant in theorising fatherhood and family life. Far from it—and as we shall see, an appreciation of the power of law is essential to develop an understanding of the complex changes taking place in this area. Law is an important part of how 'our individual experiences are structured and reinforced by the discursive structures . . . that surround us, defining the contours of our everyday lives. These unexamined constructs reflect ideological concepts that act as *limitations on our imagination*.'[11] To focus the analytic gaze on how *ideas* of fatherhood become problematised at certain historical moments is to move away from pre-given notions, whether of fatherhood or law, and to draw attention to how fatherhood has been formed as a particular kind of experience and target for government at particular historical moments. Such an analysis seeks to explore 'the role of legal mechanisms, legal arenas, legal functionaries, legal forms of reasoning and so on in strategies of regulation'.[12] What interests me in what follows is, in short, the processes whereby a normative strategy around ideas of parenthood and family life has become authorised within family policy in England and Wales. First—drawing on developments in this area in recent years within

[9] N Rose and M Valverde, 'Governed by Law?' (1998) 7 *Social and Legal Studies* 541.

[10] *Ibid.*, at 545, my emphasis; cf C Smart, *Feminism and the Power of Law* (Routledge, 1989), Ch 1; see also N Rose, 'Expertise and the Government of Conduct' (1994) 14 *Studies in Law, Politics and Society* 359; M Valverde, 'Governing Out of Habit' (1998) 18 *Studies in Law, Politics and Society* 217.

[11] M Fineman, *The Neutered Mother, The Sexual Family and Other Twentieth Century Tragedies* (Routledge, 1995), p 7, my emphasis.

[12] N Rose and M Valverde, 'Governed by Law?' (1998) 7 *Social and Legal Studies* 541 at 546; cf M Foucault, 'Governmentality' in G Burchell, C Gordon and P Miller (eds) *The Foucault Effect: Studies in Governmental Rationality* (University of Chicago Press, 1995), pp 87–104. N Rose, 'Expertise and the government of Conduct' (1994) 14 *Studies in Law, Politics and Society* 359; N Rose, *Governing the Soul* (Routledge, 1989); N Rose, 'Transcending the Public/Private' (1987) 14 *Journal of Law and Society* 61.

this jurisdiction—it is necessary to make a number of points with a view to contextualising the discussion to follow about the relationship between law and the cultural construction of what I shall term the 'new fatherhood'.[13]

Law and the Politics of Fatherhood

It is important to remember, at the outset, that questions of law have long been central to concerns around fatherhood. At the end of the nineteenth century, for example, a debate raged about the emergence of the 'New Woman'—a figure who, with curious echoes for the present, was seen as questioning and undermining men's position as fathers in the family.[14] In England and Wales, and more recently, the various 'liberalising' family law reforms of the 1970s and 1980s have been widely interpreted as positioning women and men in different ways as, variously, the perceived beneficiaries or losers of legal reform.[15] The politically contested relationship between fatherhood and law over the past twenty years can, more generally, be seen most clearly in relation to such issues as:

—the perceived justice—or injustice—of the treatment of men by the courts and the legal profession, as propounded within specific jurisdictions, as well as internationally, by a range of fathers' rights and men's movement organisations.[16] Such groups have themselves been widely seen as increasingly 'setting the agenda' within a number of jurisdictions in the family law field;[17]

—in relation to political campaigns mobilised in direct opposition to attempts by the state to secure the provision of child support; or, more accurately, to

[13] A number of authors have similarly characterised these developments via reference to the idea of an emerging 'new fatherhood': see, for example, C Smart and B Neale, 'I hadn't really thought about it': New Identities/New Fatherhoods', in J Seymour and P Bagguley (eds), *Relating Intimacies: Power and Resistance* (Macmillan, 1999).

[14] E Showalter, *Sexual Anarchy* (Virago, 1992); EA Rotundo, *American Manhood* (Basic Books, 1993); MA Mason, *From Father's Property to Children's Rights* (Columbia University Press, 1994).

[15] On the 'zero-sum' conception of power implicit in such an approach, see further R Collier, 'From Women's Emancipation to Sex War? Men, Heterosexuality and the Politics of Divorce', in S Day Sclater and C Piper (eds), *Undercurrents of Divorce* (Ashgate, 1999); K O'Donovan, *Family Law Matters* (Pluto, 1993).

[16] J Arditti and K Allen, 'Distressed Fathers' Perceptions of Legal and Relational Inequities Post-divorce' (1993) 31 *Family and Conciliation Courts Review* 461; R Collier, 'From Women's Emancipation to Sex War? Men, Heterosexuality and the Politics of Divorce', in S Day Sclater and C Piper (eds), *Undercurrents of Divorce* (Ashgate, 1999); RF Doyle, *The Men's/Fathers Movement and Divorce Assistance Operation Manual: History, Philosophy, Operation* (Men's Defence Association/Poor Richard's Press, 1996); R Fay, 'The Disenfranchised Father' (1995) 9 *American Journal of Family Law* 7; P Foster, 'Are Men Now Suffering from Gender Injustice?' in A Sinfield (ed), *Poverty, Inequality and Justice: New Waverly Papers*, Social Policy Series No 6 (University of Edinburgh Press, 1993); SB Goldberg, 'Make Room for Daddy' (1997) 83 *ABAJ* 49.

[17] See, for example, R Graycar, 'Law Reform by Frozen Chook: Family Law Reform for the New Millenium', plenary address to the 10th World Conference of the Society of Family Law, Brisbane, Australia, July 2000 (copy of paper with author).

redress the historical lack of such provision on the part (largely) of men;[18] and

— in debates about the legal status of unmarried fathers[19] and around what was termed in England and Wales, prior to the *Children Act* 1989, the position of the non-custodial parent.[20]

Notwithstanding the long-established nature of each of these debates, it has been in relatively recent years that concerns about law, men and the family have moved increasingly centre stage within a context in which a broader political and cultural conversation has emerged about what is frequently referred to as the 'future of fatherhood' debate.[21] Central to this process within Britain has been the idea of the 'new democratic family', a notion which has, in a number of ways, served to *reposition* both motherhood and fatherhood as socially problematic objects of legal intervention.

Fatherhood and the 'New Democratic Family'

To clarify: ideas of what constitutes a family are, of course, fluid and subject to historical change. With such historicity in mind, it is possible to identify the emergence in recent years in Britain of what a number of commentators have referred to as a paradigm shift in how the state relates to the family.[22] Underpinning a range of initiatives undertaken by the New Labour government in Britain, subsequent to the election of May 1997, has been the presentation of a number of core values or assumptions. These values have been seen to be integral to 'third way' political thought more generally,[23] in relation to which the Labour government of Tony

[18] A Diduck, 'The unmodified family: The *Child Support Act* and the construction of legal subjects' (1995) 22 *Journal of Law and Society* 527; J Wallbank, 'The Campaign for Change of the *Child Support Act* 1991: Reconstituting the "Absent" Father' (1997) 6 *Social and Legal Studies* 191.

[19] A Bainham, 'When is a Parent not a Parent? Reflection on the Unmarried Father and his Child in English Law' (1987) 3 *International Journal of Law and the Family* 208; R Deech, 'The Unmarried Father and Human Rights' (1992) 4 *Journal of Child Law* 3; R Pickford, *Fathers, Marriage and the Law* (Family Policy Studies Centre/Joseph Rowntree Foundation, 1999); R Pickford, 'Unmarried Fathers and the Law', in A Bainham, S Day Sclater and M Richards (eds), *What is a Parent? A Socio-Legal Analysis* (Hart, 1999b).

[20] M Lund, 'The Non-custodial Father: Common Challenges in Parenting after Divorce', in C Lewis and M O'Brien (eds), *Reassessing Fatherhood* (Sage, 1987); J McCant, 'The Cultural Construction of Fathers as Nonparents' (1987) 21 *Family Law Quarterly* 127. Post-*Children's Act*, see B Simpson, P McArthy and J Walker, *Being There: Fathers After Divorce* (Relate Centre for Family Studies, University of Newcastle Upon Tyne, 1995).

[21] A Hochschild, 'Understanding the Future of Fatherhood', in M van Dongen, G Frinking and M Jacobs (eds) *Changing Fatherhood* (Thesis Publishers, 1995); J Mitchell and J Goody, 'Feminism, Fatherhood and the Family in Britain', in A Oakley and J Mitchell (eds), *Who's Afraid of Feminism? Seeing Through the Backlash* (Hamish Hamilton, 1997).

[22] G Pascall (1999) 'UK Family Policy in the 1990s: the Case of New Labour and Lone Parents' (1999) 13 *International Journal of Law, Policy and the Family* 258; see also A Barlow and S Duncan, *New Labour's Communitarismism, Supporting Families and the 'Rationalist' Mistake*, Working Paper No 10 (University of Leeds: Centre for Research on Family, Kinship and Childhood, 1999).

[23] A Giddens, *The Third Way* (Cambridge, 1998).

Blair (and the figure of the British prime minister personally) has been seen, within a Europe-wide context at least, to be a prime exponent.[24] Of particular prominence have been the values of social justice, emancipation, equality and social cohesion. From these values are seen to follow a number of policy objectives in relation to the family: the promotion of equality between women and men;[25] an attempt to find a new balance between individual and collective responsibilities; the protection of the vulnerable; the idea that there can be no rights without responsibility and, importantly, no authority without liberal democracy. Underlying, and central to, the promotion of each of these values has been a model of the family perhaps epitomised by the government's consultation document of 1998, *Supporting Families.*[26] What we have here is a family marked by the qualities of emotional and sexual equality, mutual rights and responsibilities in relationships, a negotiated authority over children, co-parenting and, of especial relevance to any discussion of fatherhood, a commitment on the part of both women *and* men to lifelong obligations to children.

The new democratic family ideal outlined above embodies a number of beliefs which can, in a number of respects, be seen to undercut—indeed, one might argue they are fundamentally incompatible with—those social values which have historically encircled the idea of the traditional patriarchal family (that is, the family form which has been the subject of wide-ranging feminist critique).[27] What we have here, for example, is something very different from a familial ideal premised on a rigid gendered division of domestic and child care labour. This 'symmetrical family' is premised on a notion of gender convergence between women and men in both the workplace and the family. This is not, moreover, a model of family life premised on unquestioning male authority and female submission.[28] Within

[24] See further, on broader constitutional aspects of the 'New Labour/New Britain' discourse, C Stychin, 'New Labor, New "Britain"? Constitutionalism, Sovereignty and Nation/state in Transition' (1999) 19 *Studies in Law, Politics and Society* 139; on communitarianism, SB Apel, 'Communitarianism and Feminism: The Case against the Preference for the two-parent Family' (1995) 10 *Wisconsin Women's Law Journal* 1; A Etzioni, *The Parenting Deficit* (Demos, 1993).

[25] Particularly clear in the recent attempts by the British government to promote 'family-friendly' policies—for example, by the enactment of the European Union Parental Leave Directive. The British Government has stated that it is seeking to 'make it easier for *both men and women* who work to avoid conflicts between their responsibilities' (M Beckett, *Hansard,* 21 May 1998, Col 1103, my emphasis). The Preamble to the Parental Leave Directive expressly states that the Directive is to act 'as an important means of promoting equal opportunities and treatment between men and women'.

[26] Home Office (1998) Green Paper *Supporting Families: A Consultation Document* (HMSO, Nov 1998).

[27] See, for example, M Barrett and M McIntosh, *The Anti-Social Family* (Verso, 1982); S Atkins and B Hoggett, *Women and the Law* (Blackwell, 1984); J Brophy and C Smart (eds), *Women in Law: Explorations in Family, Law and Sexuality* (Routledge, 1985); M Fineman, *The Neutered Mother, The Sexual Family and Other Twentieth Century Tragedies* (Routledge, 1995); K O'Donovan, *Family Law Matters* (Pluto, 1993); K O'Donovan, *Sexual Divisions in Law* (Weidenfeld & Nicolson, 1985); C Smart and S Sevenhuijsen (eds), *Child Custody and the Politics of Gender* (Routledge, 1989); C Smart, *The Ties That Bind* (Routledge & Kegan Paul, 1984).

[28] The issue of tackling domestic violence, for example, is a high-profile and politically contentious one. In Spring 1999 the Policing and Reducing Crime Unit of the Home Office commissioned a series of reviews designed to examine what 'worked' in tackling domestic violence, the definition of domestic violence being taken as 'any violence between current or former partners in an intimate relationship, wherever and whenever it occurs. This violence may include physical, sexual, emotional,

the language through which the new democratic family is being constructed, rather, legal obligation is fused with an explicit recognition of the social values of care and caring practices within contemporary British society. And it is a clearly expressed belief in the promotion of *equality* between women and men which has, in particular, been seen as fundamental to the new democratic family.

It is in relation to the above political context that the promotion of the new fatherhood has been presented as something which has positive consequences for the lives of both women and men as well as, importantly, for society as a whole. Yet some questions remain. How have the new democratic family and new fatherhood translated into specific policy initiatives? And what, in particular, does this mean for the 'everyday' lives of women and men?

Fatherhood, Law and Policy: Constructing 'Consensus'

In order to understand the way in which the new democratic family ideal has come to inform policy initiatives in England and Wales, it is instructive to consider further the broader context of policy development around the family within this particular jurisdiction. A plurality of different forms of expertise[29] have historically come together in the construction of family policy in England and Wales, with the *dramatis personae* of policy formulation and implementation encompassing (at the very least)[30] family welfare professionals, lawyers[31] and economists, as well as politicians and civil servants.[32] The authorities which have historically defined specific problems as objects of legal intervention (such as, let us say, the legal regulation of post-divorce fatherhood) have been established through, and worked within, a broader regulatory apparatus concerned with the scrutinising of familial well-being, welfare and what has been seen as—from one theoretical per-

psychological or financial abuse.' See further *Reducing Domestic Violence; What Works?* Policing and Reducing Crime Unit Crime Reduction Research Series (Home Office, (2000)). Notwithstanding such policy initiatives, however, it is important to remember in this regard that it was not until 1991 in England and Wales that the 'last bastion of husbands' legal sovereignty over their wives' (A Diduck and F Kaganas, *Family Law, Gender and the State: Text, Cases and Materials*, Hart, 1999, p 328), the notorious 'marital rape' exemption, was finally removed by the decision of the House of Lords (*R v R* Marital Rape Exemption: 4 All ER 481).

[29] N Rose, 'Expertise and the Government of Conduct' (1994) 14 *Studies in Law, Politics and Society* 359.

[30] R Dingwall and J Eekelaar, 'Judgements of Solomon: Psychology and Family Law', in M Richards and P Light (eds), *Children of Social Worlds: Development in a Social Context* (Harvard University Press, 1986).

[31] S Cretney, 'Lawyers Under the *Family Law Act*' (1997) June *Family Law* 405; C Piper, 'How Do You Define a Family Lawyer?' (1999) 19 *Legal Studies* 93; J Walker, 'Is there a Future for Lawyers in Divorce?' (1996) 10 *International Journal of Law Policy and the Family* 52.

[32] See generally, L Fox-Harding, *Family, State and Social Policy* (Macmillan, 1996); L Fox-Harding, 'Law, Policy and Practice: An Uneasy Synthesis', in J Eekelaar and M Maclean (eds), *Reader on Family Law* (Oxford University Press, 1994); R Dingwall, 'Dilemmas of Family Policy in Liberal States', in M Maclean and J Kurczewski (eds), *Family, Politics and the Law: Perspectives for East and West Europe* (Clarendon Press, 1994).

spective at least—the internalisation of controls within the liberal state.[33] The historical disciplining of social life via the regulation of family practices can itself be seen, of course, to have taken different forms across different populations, mediated notably by the contingencies of youth, class, race and ethnicity[34] and what has emerged from within the now-rich scholarship which exists in the field of law and the family is something of the way in which both women and men—but in particular, it has been argued, women as *mothers*—have been subjected to historical identification, explanation and disposition as 'familial individuals' in some particular and oppressive ways.[35] This is a process which has involved the production of a range of normative criteria around broader questions such as what constitutes a family, a 'good' marriage and 'good enough' parenting, as well as—my concern in this article, and I would suggest somewhat less explored—what is, or what is deemed *should be*, good fatherhood.

From such a perspective, it is possible to ask a number of questions about the way in which the new fatherhood ideal, as outlined above, has come to impact on policy debates. Those various academics, policy-makers, practitioners, counsellors and other experts of human relationships noted above have, during the latter part of the 1980s and throughout the 1990s, vigorously promoted what is now widely described within the relevant literature to be the *new consensus* or new orthodoxy which presently exists within the field of family policy in England and Wales.[36] This 'consensus' has been marked by a number of assumptions about the paramountcy of the welfare of the child, the importance of maintaining contact between men and children after divorce and separation and, more generally, about the desirability of getting 'men involved' in the family.[37] The 'search for the good

[33] R Collier, *Masculinity, Law and the Family* (Routledge, 1995); N Rose, 'Expertise and the Government of Conduct' (1994) 14 *Studies in Law, Politics and Society* 359; N Rose, *Governing the Soul* (Routledge, 1989); N Rose, 'Transcending the Public/Private' (1987) 14 *Journal of Law and Society* 61. Cf J Donzelot, *The Policing of Families* (Hutchinson, 1980).

[34] See further, N Rose, 'Expertise and the Government of Conduct' (1994) 14 *Studies in Law, Politics and Society* 359.

[35] S Boyd, 'Is There an Ideology of Motherhood in (Post)modern Child Custody Law?' (1996) 5 *Social and Legal Studies* 495; A Diduck, 'In Search of the Feminist Good Mother' (1998) 7 *Social and Legal Studies* 129; A Diduck, 'Legislating Ideologies of Motherhood' (1993) 2 *Social and Legal Studies* 461; M Fineman, *The Neutered Mother, The Sexual Family and Other Twentieth Century Tragedies* (Routledge, 1995); MA Fineman and I Karpin (eds), *Mothers in Law: Feminist Theory and the Legal Regulation of Motherhood* (Columbia University Press, 1995); A Phoenix, A Woollett and E Lloyd, *Motherhood: Meanings, Practices, Ideologies* (Sage, 1991); J Ribbens, *Mothers and Their Children: A Feminist Sociology of Childrearing* (Sage, 1994); D Riley, *War in the Nursery: Theories of the Child and the Mother* (Virago, 1993); E Silva (ed), *Good Enough Mothering? Feminist Perspectives on Lone Motherhood* (Routledge, 1996); C Smart, 'Deconstructing Motherhood' in E Silva (ed), *Good Enough Mothering: Feminist Perspectives on Lone Mothering* (Routledge, 1996).

[36] See further A James and M Richards, 'Sociological Perspectives, Family Policy and Children: Adult Thinking and Sociological Tinkering' (1999) 21 *Journal of Social Welfare and Family Law* 23.

[37] Research suggests that many mothers and fathers themselves perceive the reforms which have constituted the 'new consensus' as being, inasmuch as they focus on the welfare of the child and the maintenance of contact between biological parents, to be a 'good thing'. See further C Smart and B Neale, '"I hadn't really thought about it": New Identities/New Fatherhoods', in J Seymour and P Bagguley (eds), *Relating Intimacies: Power and Resistance* (Macmillan, 1999).

father' has thus been a key element within the constitution of this orthodoxy.[38] In this process, it is clear, a diverse range of professionals have claimed or acquired the power to identify and validate a particular normativity[39]—one which might appear, at least superficially, to be more technical than political.[40] Yet in this process, of course, what have also been generated are some particular notions of the 'good society' itself, a question which has a long, and inescapably political, history.

In the next section I wish to consider the way in which the new fatherhood has come to assume a particular significance within two areas—a comparison of which, I shall proceed to argue in the following section, can tell us much about the politically open-ended and conceptually problematic nature of the new fatherhood ideal per se—that is, firstly, in relation to recent attempts to promote via legal reform active parenting on the part of men during *subsisting* relationships; and, secondly, within the context of recent developments around the legal regulation of the *post-divorce* family.

RECONSTRUCTING FATHERHOOD: RESEARCH, POLICY AND THE REMAKING OF THE FAMILY MAN

Promoting 'Active Parenting' on the Part of Men in Subsisting Relationships

A recurring theme within the now-vast body of academic research on contemporary fathering and fatherhood has been that the promotion and encouragement of what has been termed 'active parenting' on the part of men should be a desirable objective on the part of government.[41] A number of empirical research studies have for some time highlighted, in particular, how men's interactions with children are frequently constrained, not simply by women's own desires and anxieties around motherhood, but also—and most powerfully, it has been argued—by the demands of men's paid employment.[42] Increasingly, as a result, there is widely seen

[38] C Smart and B Neale, *Family Fragments* (Polity, 1999).

[39] See further A James and M Richards, 'Sociological Perspectives, Family Policy and Children: Adult Thinking and Sociological Tinkering' (1999) 21 *Journal of Social Welfare and Family Law* 23.

[40] J Rodger, 'Family Policy or Moral Regulation?' (1995) 15 *Critical Social Policy* 5; on the United States, cf ML Fineman, 'Dominant Discourse, Professional Language, and Legal Change in Child Custody Decision Making' (1988) 101 *Harvard Law Review* 727.

[41] See, for example, the summary of research on fatherhood presented by C Lewis, *A Man's Place in the Home: Fathers and Families in the UK* (Joseph Rowntree Foundation, 2000); see also A Burgess and S Ruxton, *Men and Their Children: Proposals for Public Policy* (Institute for Public Policy Research, 1996); L Burghes, L Clarke, and N Cronin, *Fathers and Fatherhood in Britain* (Family Policy Studies Centre, 1997); G Dench, *Exploring Variations in Men's Family Roles: Joseph Rowntree Foundation Social Policy Research Findings No 99* (Joseph Rowntree Foundation, 1996); P Moss (ed), *Father Figures: Fathers in the Families of the 1990s* (HMSO, 1995).

[42] J Warin, Y Solomon, C Lewis and W Langford, *Fathers, Work and Family Life* (Joseph Rowntree Foundation/Family Policy Studies Centre, 1999); see also A Hochschild, *The Time Bind: When Work Becomes Home and Home Becomes Work* (Metropolitan Books, 1997); A Hochschild, 'Understanding the Future of Fatherhood', in M van Dongen, G Frinking and M Jacobs (eds), *Changing Fatherhood*

to exist a tension facing men within contemporary Western societies between, on the one hand, the still-dominant discourse around fatherhood (which continues to privilege the traditional idea of the 'father as provider', the traditional 'family breadwinner'[43] and, at the same time, what is generally positioned as the more progressive idea of the father as an emotionally involved 'hands-on' parent.[44] In seeking to negotiate the resulting tension, it is no wonder perhaps that, faced with such competing demands, it is now frequently seen to be, in the words of the author Fay Weldon,[45] a 'hard time to be a father'.

A number of policy interventions in England and Wales have recently sought to explicitly address this issue by attempting to shift the behaviour of men at what might be termed the *interface* of family and employment law. This promotion of active parenting on the part of men has become inseparable, notably, from what is the now broader cultural debate which is taking place in Britain, as elsewhere, around the perceived need to change working conditions in ways which are more 'family friendly' for both women *and* men.[46] Recent years have witnessed, for example, the implementation of the European Union Parental Leave (No 96/34), Working Time and Part-Time Work Directives; the implementation of a National Minimum Wage; the Out of School Childcare and 'Sure Start' Initiatives, along with a number of consultation papers on early education and day care; the establishment of the National Childcare Strategy; and, of particular importance to any discussion of fatherhood, the formation of a National Parenting Institute. Each has been seen as an intervention into a debate about men and women, work and family life which exemplifies how the new democratic family ideal has itself become enmeshed with—indeed, is inseparable from—the economic demands of advanced capitalist societies at the turn of the century—for example, the perceived 'demands' that both men and women should be engaged in paid employment; that lone parents (predominantly mothers) should be encouraged to get 'into work';[47] and, more generally, the belief that a flexible, efficient and appropriately credentialised workforce is now essential to the economically competitive future of essentially post-industrial, service-based economies such as Britain.[48]

(Thesis Publishers, 1995); A Hochschild with Anne Machung, *The Second Shift: Working Parents and the Revolution at Home* (Viking, 1989).

[43] J Bernard, 'The Good-provider Role: Its Rise and Fall' (1981) 36 *American Psychologist* 1.

[44] See, for example, D Lupton and L Barclay, *Constructing Fatherhood: Discourses and Experiences* (Sage, 1997), p 146.

[45] F Weldon, *A Hard Time to Be a Father* (Flamingo, 1998).

[46] R Collier, 'Feminising the Workplace? (Re)constructing the 'Good Parent' in Employment Law and Family Policy', in A Morris and T O'Donnell (eds), *Feminist Perspectives on Employment Law* (Cavendish, 1999), pp 161–81; New Ways to Work, *Balanced Lives: Changing Work Patterns for Men*, (New Ways to Work, 1999).

[47] A Bryson, R Ford and M White, *Making Work Pay: Lone Mothers, Employment and Well-being* (Joseph Rowntree, 1997); R Edwards and S Duncan, 'Rational Economic Man or Lone Mothers in Context? The Uptake of Paid Work', in E Silva (ed), *Good Enough Mothering? Feminist Perspectives on Lone Motherhood* (Routledge, 1996).

[48] See further H Bradley, 'Gender and Change in Employment: Feminization and its Effects', in RK Brown (ed), *The Changing Shape of Work* (Macmillan, 1997); J Brannen, G Meszaros, P Moss and

Allied to this work and family life agenda, and more generally, a range of measures have been undertaken which seek to encourage men to take on a more active parental role during subsisting relationships. We have witnessed broad-based initiatives, as well as numerous ministerial statements, aimed at attacking negative cultural stereotypes of fathers as somehow inherently abusive or uninterested in children (especially, it must be said, boys); seen a marked refocusing on the male parent across a range of health and welfare services; and experienced the publication of government literature directed to all expectant fathers. One recent government-funded initiative, the Fathers Direct program, perhaps exemplifies this more general approach to the encouragement of active fathering. Fathers Direct is the first nationwide service offering information, advice and support for British fathers.[49] In the words of the director of the scheme, it is 'setting out to change the whole culture which surrounds fathers, which undervalues the real passion that many have for their children. Fathers Direct will tackle the invisibility of all the good fathering which goes on.'[50] Interestingly (and, I shall argue below, revealingly), 'good' fatherhood in this context tends to be depicted here as something which is to be learnt, something requiring practice and hard work. It is both a status and a state of mind to be achieved in a 'struggle' against other demands. As such, it is a model of parenthood which curiously can itself be seen to involve a distinctly 'masculine' notion of unconnectedness and endeavour. 'Successful' fatherhood is portrayed as 'the product of acquired knowledge and mastery of action. Motherhood, in contrast, still tends to be represented as having an instinctive core.'[51] Or, as Smart and Neale put it,[52] what we have here is a model of fatherhood which continues to be understood largely within psychologistic, personal and individualised terms, devoid of any appreciation of the complex social and economic developments constituting broader changes in family practices.[53]

Noted above are examples of initiatives focused largely (though not exclusively) on changing the behaviour of men during subsisting relationships. In this context, the characterisation of the 'good father' as active parent would appear both socially desirable and, generally, politically legitimate (in that few voices now speak against such a depiction of progressive parenting). In the area of post-

G Poland, *Employment and Family Life: A Review of Research in the UK (1980–1994): Department of Employment Research Series No 4* (University of London, 1994); W Hutton, *The State We're In* (Jonathan Cape, 1995); R Pahl, *After Success* (Blackwell, 1995); R Pahl, *On Work* (Blackwell, 1988); J Rifkin, *The End of Work* (Tarcher Putnam, 1996); J Schor, *The Overworked American: The Unexpected Decline of Leisure* (Basic Books, 1991).

[49] This has involved, amongst other measures, the establishment of a Home Office helpline 'aiming to foster a nation of "involved" dads' (K Inman, 'Invisible Men', *The Guardian*, 17 Nov 1999) and financial support for Fathers' Groups and Clubs (T Lloyd, *Fathers Group Evaluation*, Working With Men, 1996; A Richardson, *Fathers Plus: An Audit of Work With Fathers Throughout the North East of England 1998*, Children North East, 1998).

[50] *The Observer*, 25 Apr 1998; see also A Burgess, *Fatherhood Reclaimed* (Vermillion, 1997).

[51] D Lupton and L Barclay, *Constructing Fatherhood: Discourses and Experiences* (Sage, 1997), p 147.

[52] C Smart and B Neale, '"I Hadn't Really Thought About It": New Identities/New Fatherhoods', in J Seymour and P Bagguley (eds), *Relating Intimacies: Power and Resistance* (Macmillan, 1999).

[53] See, for example, the discussion of E Silva and C Smart (eds), *The 'New' Family?* (Sage, 1999).

divorce parenthood, however, the new fatherhood ideal can be seen to have played out in some rather different and, I shall suggest, problematic ways.

Fatherhood and the Post-Divorce Family

An explicit ideological commitment to keeping biological fathers 'in touch' with 'their' children has been central to legislation such as the *Children Act* 1989 (henceforth CA), the *Child Support Act* 1991 (CSA) and the *Family Law Act* 1996 (FLA) in England and Wales.[54] This commitment has been, I have suggested, a key element of the broader and profound policy shift identified by academic commentators, family practitioners and welfare professionals alike as having taken place during the late 1980s and throughout the 1990s in this area.[55] It is a shift supported by a reworking of the welfare of the child or paramountcy principle,[56] which has seen a growing consensus on the part of both policy-makers and politicians that children, in particular, *suffer* through lack of contact with both parents.[57]

Ultimately, Smart and Neale[58] have suggested that what is at issue here has been no less than a clear and determined attempt to effect social engineering in the area of the family by, in Smart's words, 'changing the very nature of post-divorce family life'.[59] The core provisions of the above pieces of legislation have thus each—albeit in different ways—been seen as resulting in a reconceptualisation of post-divorce fatherhood in their foundational assumption about the desirability of ensuring this commitment to the maintenance of contact between biological fathers and children in the post-divorce and separation scenario.[60] At the risk of simplification, and without under-estimating just how much of this has been a result of subsequent judicial interpretation and case law rather than enshrined in the legislation itself,[61] in relation to both post-divorce and separation family eco-

[54] I Weyland, 'The Blood Tie: Raised to the Status of a Presumption' (1997) 19 *Journal of Social Welfare and Family Law* 173.

[55] A James and M Richards, 'Sociological Perspectives, Family Policy and Children: Adult Thinking and Sociological Tinkering' (1999) 21 *Journal of Social Welfare and Family Law* 23; C Smart, 'Wishful Thinking and Harmful Tinkering? Sociological Reflections on Family Policy' (1997) 26 *Journal of Social Policy* 1; C Smart and B Neale, *Family Fragments* (Polity, 1999).

[56] H Reece, 'The Paramountcy Principle: Consensus or Construct' (1996) 49 *Current Legal Problems* 267.

[57] F Kaganas, M King and C Piper (eds), *Legislating for Harmony: Partnership under the Children Act 1989* (Arena, 1995); C Piper, 'Ascertaining the Wishes and Feelings of the Child' (1997) 27 *Family Law* 796; C Piper, 'Divorce Reform and the Image of the Child' (1996) 23 *Journal of Law and Society* 364; B Rodgers and J Pryor, *Divorce and Separation: Outcomes for Children* (Joseph Rowntree Foundation, 1998).

[58] C Smart and B Neale, *Family Fragments* (Polity, 1999).

[59] C Smart, 'Wishful Thinking and Harmful Tinkering? Sociological Reflections on Family Policy' (1997) 26 *Journal of Social Policy* 1.

[60] I Weyland, 'The Blood Tie: Raised to the Status of a Presumption' (1997) 19 *Journal of Social Welfare and Family Law* 173.

[61] Mr Justice Hall, 'Domestic Violence and Contact' (1997) 27 *Family Law* 813; C Smart and B Neale, 'Arguments against Virtue: Must Contact be Enforced?' (1997) 28 *Family Law* 332; I Weyland,

nomics (the CSA) and understandings of parenthood as a largely gender neutral (ungendered) practice (the CA and FLA), a shift in family policy has taken place in which, alongside a refocusing on parental responsibility,[62] a reconstituted 'father figure' has emerged.[63] This, in essence, is a man who is 'once a parent, always a parent'.[64] The good (post-divorce) father is a man who is (a) to be economically responsible 'for life' for his first family—financially, he is not to move on financially unencumbered into future relationships (the provisions of the CSA); and (b) considered, as part of the good fatherhood ideal the law seeks to promote, to be active in joint parenting, both during marriage and partnership and after divorce or separation (CA and FLA).

I have sketched above a development in family policy which, of course, predates both the election of the New Labour government in 1997 and what I have suggested has been, within recent years, the heightening in Britain of questions of gender equality and convergence in debates about the way in which the state is seen to relate to both family and working life. I have argued that it has been implicit within the new democratic family ideal that social responsibility on the part of men traverses the fields of work and home; and, importantly, that it is via policies directed at *men*, and not women, that the greatest effect will be had in reducing existing divisions of domestic labour and promoting equality in the workplace and the family. Underlying these attempts at, to use Smart's term, 'socially engineering'[65] the new fatherhood has been a conceptualisation of fatherhood which, I now wish to argue, rests on a particular understanding of parenthood as a certain kind of social problem. However, this is an understanding of parenthood which involves a problematisation of family practices which is itself profoundly flawed in the assumptions that it is making about men, parenting and the materiality of family practices and 'family life'.

GENDER, PARENTING AND THE LIMITS OF THE NEW FATHERHOOD

Central to the new orthodoxy or consensus in family policy, we have seen, has been a model of the responsible parent as formally gender-neutral. At the risk of simplifying, within the new democratic family ideal it is assumed that men can

'Judicial Attitudes to Contact and Shared Residence since the *Children Act* 1989' (1995) *Journal of Social Welfare and Family Law* 445.

[62] J Eekelaar, 'Parental Responsibility: State of Nature or Nature of the State?' (1991) 1 *Journal of Social Welfare and Family Law* 37; S Edwards and A Halpern, 'Parental Responsibility: An Instrument of Social Policy' (1992) *Family Law* 113.

[63] A James and M Richards, 'Sociological Perspectives, Family Policy and Children: Adult Thinking and Sociological Tinkering' (1999) 21 *Journal of Social Welfare and Family Law* 23; C Smart and B Neale, '"I hadn't really thought about it": New Identities/New Fatherhoods', in J Seymour and P Bagguley (eds), *Relating Intimacies: Power and Resistance* (Macmillan, 1999).

[64] J Roche, 'The *Children Act*: Once a Parent, Always a Parent' (1991) 5 *Journal of Social Welfare Law* 345.

[65] C Smart, 'Wishful Thinking and Harmful Tinkering? Sociological Reflections on Family Policy' (1997) 26 *Journal of Social Policy* 1.

and do 'parent' just as well as women. Yet the concept of gender neutrality is itself, as a number of scholars have now argued, extremely questionable in this context in several respects.[66] Sociology's engagement with the complex ways in which structural and discursive practices both constitute and give meaning to sexual difference in specific instances has brought to the surface something of the nature of the sexed *as different* experiences of women's and men's 'gendered lives' in relation to contemporary family practices.[67] And, in so doing—whether it is in relation to the workplace or family—the integration of a 'politics of difference',[68] not least around questions of corporeality, reproduction and what has been termed the 'sexuatedness' of discourse,[69] has led to some fundamental and unsettling questions across jurisdictions, about attempts to promote social justice via the conceptualisation of the gender-neutral or ungendered citizen. Recent sociological work has suggested, in contrast, that family practices are *not* pre-given sites in or to which men and women 'come' as fixed and finished gender subjects. They are, rather, active forces in the social construction of ideas about 'family' men and women.[70] From this perspective, there are multifarious ways in which family practices play a key role in the constitution of such gendered subjects—via processes, for example, such as the encoding of cultural, social and economic capital, the construction of family work as a form of emotional labour and via normative notions of parental responsibility.[71] Each of the above is an idea which itself continues to be sexed (as different) in some far-reaching way.[72] Integrating lived

[66] See, for example, S Boyd, (1989) 'From Gender Specificity to Gender Neutrality? Ideologies in Canadian Child Custody Law' in J Brophy and C Smart (eds), *Women in Law: Explorations in Family, Law and Sexuality* (Routledge, 1985); M Fineman, *The Neutered Mother: The Sexual Family and Other Twentieth Century Tragedies* (Routledge, 1995); M Fineman, *The Illusion of Equality: The Rhetoric and Reality of Divorce Reform* (University of Chicago Press, 1991); M Fineman, 'Implementing Equality: The Rhetoric and Reality of Divorce Reform' (1983) *University of Wisconsin Law Review* 789.

[67] M Fineman, 'Feminist Legal Scholarship and Women's Gendered Lives', in M Cain and C Harrington (eds), *Lawyers in a Postmodern World* (Open University Press, 1994).

[68] IM Young, 'Together in Difference: Transforming the Logic of Group Political Conflict', in J Squires (ed), *Principled Positions: Postmodernism and the Rediscovery of Value* (Lawrence and Wishart, 1993); IM Young, *Justice and the Politics of Difference* (Princeton University Press, 1990); IM Young, 'The Ideal of Community and the Politics of Difference', in L Nicholson (ed), *Feminism/Postmodernism* (Routledge, 1990).

[69] KW Leng, 'New Australian Feminism: Towards a Discursive Politics of Australian Feminist Thought' (1995) 7 *Antithesis* 47.

[70] D Morgan, 'Risk and Family Practices: Accounting for Change and Fluidity in Family Life', in E Silva and C Smart (eds), *The 'New' Family?* (Sage, 1999).

[71] See J Eekelaar, 'Parental Responsibility: State of Nature or Nature of the State?' (1991) 1 *Journal of Social Welfare and Family Law* 37; C Piper, *The Responsible Parent* (Harvester Wheatsheaf, 1993); MG Wyness, 'Parental Responsibility, Social Policy and the Maintenance of Boundaries' (1997) *The Sociological Review* 304.

[72] Ideas of what it might mean to be a good father or mother, for example, play out in some very different ways in the context of social control over the children for whom they are deemed to be legally responsible: L Gelsthorpe, 'Youth Crime and Parental Responsibility', in A Bainham, S Day Sclater and M Richards (eds), *What is a Parent? A Socio-Legal Analysis* (Hart, 1999), p 217: C Piper, '*The Crime and Disorder Act* 1998: Child and Community Safety' (1999) 62 *Modern Law Review* 397; C Walsh, 'Imposing Order: Child Safety Orders and Local Child Curfew Schemes' (1999) 21 *Journal of Social Welfare and Family Law* 135). The culturally resonant figure of the anxious/over-attentive mother continues to be ascribed blame and responsibility for the youthful criminality of her sons—on

experience in such a manner, however, raises a number of questions about how the new fatherhood relates to what we might term the 'day-to-day' realities of family life—that is, to what numerous research studies indicate to be a continuing disjuncture between what we might term the *rhetoric surrounding* and the *realities of* contemporary parenting practices.[73] The assumption of gender neutrality runs counter, in particular, to what has been identified to be the pervasive dissociation of men from the domain of the familial—or, as Smart and Neale put it,[74] questioning the rhetoric of gender convergence, 'the pretence of fatherhood as an *active relationship* rather than a *passive status*'.

By 'dissociation', I mean to bring into focus what empirical studies of fatherhood and family life have highlighted to be the existence of some distinct and differential experiences for women and men.[75] Dissociation, in this sense, is *not* to imply simply that the demands of paid employment have historically functioned to physically 'separate out' men from a familial sphere in which they had already been, in many ways, constituted as an absent partner (be it physically, because of the demands of work and the cultural pull of the homosocial, or else absent in an emotional sense).[76] Nor, by itself, does it apply to the well-established idea of 'his' and 'hers' marriage.[77] It is not to overplay difference at the extent of similarity; nor is what is at issue here simply the argument that men are now somehow experiencing difficulties juggling work and family commitments which have in the past been more associated with women. Men can be seen to have been dissociated from the familial because of the way in which a gender construct of heterosexual masculinity has itself been historically institutionalised within dominant understandings of both family *and* working life.[78] Approaching parenthood as a

representations of motherhood in the context of the murder of James Bulger in Britain in 1993, see further A Young, *Imagining Crime* (Sage, 1996). The figure of the 'responsible' father remains, in this context and more usually, a much more shadowy and marginal presence: see R Collier, *Masculinities, Crime and Criminology: Men, Heterosexuality and the Criminal(ised) Other* (Sage, 1998), ch 3.

[73] This is not to say that the findings of such research studies necessarily filter through to the field of policy formulation. See further below.

[74] C Smart and B Neale, '"I hadn't really thought about it": New Identities/New Fatherhoods', in J Seymour and P Bagguley (eds), *Relating Intimacies: Power and Resistance* (Macmillan, 1999), p 118, my emphasis.

[75] See, for example, T Arendell, *Fathers and Divorce* (Sage, 1995); T Arendell, *Mothers and Divorce* (University of California Press, 1986); B Brandth and E Kvande, 'Masculinity, Child Care and the Reconstruction of Fathering' (1998) 46 *The Sociological Review* 293; M Eichler, 'The Limits of Family Law Reform, or the Privatization of Female and Child Poverty' (1990) 7 *Canadian Family Law Quarterly* 59; C Gray and S Merrick, 'Voice Alterations: Why Women have more Difficulty than Men with the Legal Process of Divorce' (1996) 34 *Family and Conciliation Courts Review* 240; C Grbich, 'Male Primary Caregivers and Domestic Labour: Involvement or Avoidance?' (1995) 1 *Journal of Family Studies* 114; C Smart and B Neale, *Family Fragments* (Polity, 1999); J Warin, Y Solomon, C Lewis and W Langford, *Fathers, Work and Family Life* (Joseph Rowntree Foundation/Family Policy Studies Centre, (1999)).

[76] See further D Morgan, 'The 'Family Man': A Contradiction in Terms?' (Fifth Jacqueline Burgoyne Memorial Lecture, 1 Feb, Sheffield Hallam University).

[77] J Bernard, *The Future of Marriage*, (Souvenir Press, 1973), 'New Man Fails to Survive into the Nineties', *The Independent*, 25 Jan 1996.

[78] R Collier, *Masculinity, Law and the Family* (Routledge, 1995).

material, embodied practice, however, particularly in terms of how ideas of sexual difference are themselves given meaning, involves surfacing precisely *how* such gendered experiences of parenting are produced and lived in the first place. 'Gender', as it were, does not float free from what women and men *do*. And at issue from such a perspective is the question of how diverse family practices are gendered during subsisting relationships and not, as it were, at the stage 'when things go wrong'. If we begin to integrate perspectives from that often neglected Other of French feminist thought, feminist materialist scholarship, a literature concerned with a materialist analysis of labour, what comes into view is men's direct *interest* in maintaining existing (and well-documented) sexual divisions of domestic labour. Far from revealing a pattern of gender convergence, empirical research points to the continuing existence of a pervasive sexual division of domestic labour.

Notwithstanding the attempts outlined above to promote active parenting on the part of men, the assumption underlying the new fatherhood remains that fathering is somehow revealed as problematic for law only at the point of divorce or separation. And yet:

> for the majority of heterosexual couples who follow traditional child-care arrangements, fatherhood still does not routinely provide an identity for a man nor necessarily an active, involved relationship with children . . . men's behaviour may well be changing [but] for the majority of fathers, fathering is something that they have to fit into a schedule dominated by paid employment, which tends to mean that their core identity is generated elsewhere.[79]

The context in which this core masculine identity is gendered is one which is marked by a constellation of parenting and employment practices which themselves continue, as a vast body of research across diverse fields suggests, to be profoundly gendered in some far-reaching material and, importantly, psychologically complex ways.[80]

The above argument addresses a conceptual limitation of the new fatherhood in terms of the 'gap' between rhetoric and reality of family life. It questions the way in which family practices have historically been, and continue to be, encoded in terms of sex(ual) difference, hierarchy and (normative) heterosexuality. It is in the light of such differences that it becomes revealing, and disturbing, to consider further the way in which the effects of the new fatherhood have played out in terms of family law practices—in, that is, the 'everyday' lives of those women and men who 'come before', or otherwise experience, the law.

[79] C Smart and B Neale, '"I hadn't really thought about it": New Identities/New Fatherhoods', in J Seymour and P Bagguley (eds), *Relating Intimacies: Power and Resistance* (Macmillan, 1999).

[80] S Day Sclater, *Divorce: A Psychosocial Study* (Ashgate, 1999); S Day Sclater, 'Divorce—Coping Strategies, Conflict and Dispute Resolution' (1998) *Family Law* 150; S Day Sclater, *The Psychology of Divorce: A Research Report to the ESRC* (University of East London, 1998).

Consequences: Contact, Conflict and Diversity—Contesting the New Fatherhood

It has become commonplace within sociological accounts of family life to see fatherhood as something which takes multiple forms, defined both by institutional structure and 'everyday' practice.[81] Smart and Neale,[82] for example, in taking up this notion of diversity, have argued that the new fatherhood is itself an ideal, undifferentiated social phenomenon. It is made up of what they suggest to be (at least) four distinct elements in the way in which it conceptualises men; as, variously, *providers of masculine identity* (seen by the authors as a potentially regressive stance); *enforcers of patriarchal power* (a highly reactionary, backward looking position); *carriers of rights* (involving a self-interested, individualised form of power); and, finally, *sharers of responsibilities* (presented as a collective and, for the authors, potentially progressive stance).[83] Such an analysis of the very heterogeneity of ideas of fatherhood is particularly interesting for the way in which it serves to highlight the open-ended and potentially contradictory nature of the new fatherhood.[84] For example, it is clear that the father figure continues, on the one hand, to be situated within a range of dominant discourses as a major guarantor of social and familial order. The practices associated with fathering remain, in particular, firmly within the context of conventional heterosexual masculine behaviour. It is taken as axiomatic that a 'family man's' primary commitment and identification will be, and should be, with his paid employment rather than with full-time child care. The experience of 'being a father' continue to involve, for most men (and all too clearly), a temporal and spatial trade-off between the domains of work and family.

At the same time, however, it is also clear that there is no 'one' model of fatherhood informing present debates. Within different contexts, for example, we find the idea of the 'feckless' irresponsible father[85] and the 'deadbeat' dad. These are negative images of 'bad' fathers which have become increasingly visible within both family law and 'law and order' debates in recent years in England and Wales, as well as elsewhere (albeit in ways, it must be said, which continue to fail to address some fundamental questions about what it might mean to speak of pater-

[81] On the concept of 'masculinities', cf RW Connell, *Masculinities* (Polity Press, 1995).

[82] C Smart and B Neale, '"I hadn't really thought about it": New Identities/New Fatherhoods', in J Seymour and P Bagguley (eds), *Relating Intimacies: Power and Resistance* (Macmillan, 1999).

[83] *Ibid.*, p 123.

[84] See also D Lupton and L Barclay, *Constructing Fatherhood: Discourses and Experiences* (Sage, 1997).

[85] R Collier, 'The Campaign Against the *Child Support Act* 1991: "Errant Fathers" and "Family Men"' (1994) *Family Law* 384–87; J Wallbank, 'The Campaign for Change of the *Child Support Act* 1991: Reconstituting the "Absent" Father' (1997) 6 *Social and Legal Studies* 191; S Westwood, '"Feckless Fathers": Masculinities and the British State', in M Mac an Ghaill (ed), *Understanding Masculinities* (Open University Press, 1996).

nal *presence* in the first place).[86] In a different context, we have seen the increasing visibility of the gay father within debates about the changing contours of family life.[87] In the context of debates about the legal recognition of gay and lesbian relationships, the mutual redrawing of parenthood as gender-neutral, and of the welfare of the child as paramount, itself can be seen to have led to what is at least the possibility of developing a wider legal recognition of relationships outside the parameters of heterosexuality. These are ideas which impact on understandings of fatherhood as *a priori* normatively heterosexual. In addition—although it is of an ambiguous status,[88] all too easily displaced by still-powerful notions of a 'natural father's love'—there exists the increasingly visible discourse of 'dangerous father'. This speaks to a rather different reality, one in which it is 'family men' themselves who constitute a dangerous presence in the lives of women and children, notably in the form of domestic violence and sexual abuse.[89] Each of the above developments suggests that any purported hegemony of the

[86] Note, for example, the ongoing high-profile debate in Britain, as elsewhere, around the impact of 'working parents' on the psychological and educational well-being of their children. The dominant research paradigm in which this debate has been framed has focused almost exclusively on 'working mothers' rather than 'working fathers'. It is taken as given that a man's primary commitment will be towards paid work. See R Collier, *Masculinity, Law and the Family* (Routledge, 1995); D Morgan, 'The 'Family Man': A Contradiction in Terms?' (Fifth Jacqueline Burgoyne Memorial Lecture, 1 Feb 1994, Sheffield Hallam University). On the arguments of the 'pro-family' of the New Right in this context, see D Morgan, *Family Connections: An Introduction to Family Studies* (Polity, 1996); R Whelan (ed), *Just a Piece of Paper? Divorce Reform and the Undermining of Marriage* (Institute of Economic Affairs, 1995). Cf V Randall 'Relax, You're a Good Mum', *The Observer,* 10 Oct 1999.

[87] S Fraser, 'Father dear father' *Scotland on Sunday,* 9 Jan 2000. J Weeks, C Donovan and B Heaphy, 'Everyday Experiments: Narratives of Non-heterosexual Relationships', in E Silva and C Smart (eds), *The New Family?* (Sage, (1998); R Verkaik, 'Lord Irvine intervenes to encourage gay judges', *The Independent,* 11 Nov 1999; see also, for example, 'Lesbians can make better parents', *Sunday Express,* 14 Feb 1999). To argue as much is not to underestimate the intransigence of a heterosexual centre in giving up its privileges: see D Herman and C Stychin (eds), *Legal Inversions: Lesbians, Gay Men and the Politics of Law* (Temple University Press, 1995); S Reinhold, 'Through the Parliamentary Looking Glass: 'Real' and 'Pretend' Families in Contemporary British Politics' (1994) 48 *Feminist Review* 61; C Stychin, *Law's Desire* (Routledge, 1996). Nor is it to deny the scale and depth of all-too-evident deep-seated resistance to any perceived move away from a position whereby heterosexuality is seen as socially normative: see D Cooper and D Herman, 'Getting 'the Family Right': Legislating Heterosexuality in Britain, 1986–1991' (1991) 10 *Canadian Journal of Family Law* 41; also S Beresford, 'Lesbians in Residence and Parental Responsibility Cases' (1994) *Family Law* 643; R Collier, 'Straight Families, Queer Lives', in D Herman and C Stychin (eds), *Sexuality in the Legal Arena* (Athlone Press, 2000). These are tensions which are not lost on (at least some) members of the British Cabinet themselves: 'Marriage Message Splits Cabinet', *The Observer* 13 Feb 2000. At the time of writing it has been announced that schools in Britain will be forced to teach children that marriage is the 'proper' relationship under legally binding plans being drawn up by the government.

[88] By this I mean that dominant constructions of fatherhood continue to make assumptions about what is presumed to be, in all instances, the 'natural' qualities of father love. This has been particularly evident in cases where men have killed members of their families, and then themselves, where media depictions are commonplace of such men 'who have loved too much'. For an insightful psychosocial account of masculinity and jealousy, see further C Yates, 'Masculinity and Good Enough Jealousy' (2000) 2 *Psychoanalytic Studies* 77.

[89] AM Liddle, 'Gender, Desire and Child Sexual Abuse: Accounting for the Male Majority' (1993) 10 *Theory, Culture and Society* 103; M Macleod and E Saraga, 'Challenging the Orthodoxy: Towards a Feminist Theory and Practice' (1988) 28 *Feminist Review* 16.

'good' (heterosexual) family man is itself far from secure and that, at present, cultural representations of fatherhood are diverse.[90]

My point is not simply that all these different images or representations of fatherhood presently co-exist, however—nor, by itself, that some may be more powerful than others. What we can witness in recent years has been the construction of a normative model of fatherhood which has had a number of effects in terms of how it has impacted on the courts, lawyers and family welfare professionals, as well as, importantly, on parents themselves. The consequences are particularly clear in relation to the way in which the new fatherhood has informed understandings of the issue of *contact*, something which is, as we have seen, central to both the new consensus in family law and the new democratic family ideal. What have emerged from reported cases on contact, for example, are a number of principles which themselves rest on certain assumptions—the presumption, for example, that contact is inherently desirable[91] and that it is in the interests of the welfare[92] of the child (as well as the integrity of the court),[93] that the court should enforce such orders and that contact is a right[94] of the child themself. Yet, without negating either the desirability of establishing contact in certain situations, or the complex problems which can revolve around maintaining contact,[95] a considerable body of research suggests that post-divorce co-parenting, far from being an unproblematic social good, can in fact serve in certain circumstances to fuel conflicts between divorcing parents.[96] Research suggests that, far from reducing conflict, there has in fact been an increase in the frequency of disputes over contact subsequent to the passing of the *Children Act* 1989; that disputes are now taking

[90] See also K Harrison, 'Fresh or Frozen: Lesbian Mothers, Sperm Donors and Limited Fathers', in MA Fineman and I Karpin (eds), *Mothers in Law: Feminist Theory and the Legal Regulation of Motherhood* (Columbia University Press, 1995); S Ruddick, 'The Idea of Fatherhood', in HL Nelson (ed), *Feminism and Families* (Routledge, 1997).

[91] *Re M (Contact: Welfare Test)* [1995] 1 FLR 274. *Re O (Contact: Imposition of Conditions)* [1995] 2 FLR 124.

[92] *Re W (A Minor: Contact)* [1994] 2 FLR 441. Also *Re S (Minors: Access)* [1990] 2 FLR 167.

[93] *A v N (Committal: Refusal of Contact* [1997] 1 FLR 533.

[94] Which can be traced back to the case of *M v M (Child Access)* [1973] 2 All ER 81 per Wrangham J.

[95] B Cantwell et al., 'Presumption of Contact in Private Law: an Interdisciplinary Issue' (1998) 28 *Family Law* 226; K Hewitt, 'Divorce and Parental Disagreement' (1996) *Family Law* 368; S Jolly, 'Implacable Hostility, Contact and the Limits of the Law' (1995) 7 *Child and Family Law Quarterly* 228; cf C Willbourne and J Geddes, 'Presumption of Contact: What Presumption?' (1995) 25 *Family Law* 87.

[96] This is notably the case in circumstances where it is the product not of a shared ideology, but of legal or financial coercion or other unresolved tensions: S Day Sclater and C Yates, 'The Psycho-Politics of Post Divorce Parenting', in A Bainham, S Day Sclater and M Richards (eds), *What is a Parent? A Socio-Legal Analysis* (Hart, 1999); C Hooper, 'Do Families Need Fathers? The Impact of Divorce upon Children' in A Mullender and R Morley (eds), *Children Living with Domestic Violence* (Whiting and Birch, 1994); F Kaganas, 'Contact, Conflict and Risk', in S Day Sclater and C Piper (eds), *Undercurrents of Divorce* (Ashgate, 1999); see also R Bailey-Harris, G David, J Barron and J Pearce, *Monitoring Private Law Applications under the Children Act: A Research Report to the Nuffield Foundation* (University of Bristol, 1998); C Smart and B Neale, *Family Fragments* (Polity, 1999); C Smart and B Neale, '"I hadn't really thought about it": New Identities/New Fatherhoods', in J Seymour and P Bagguley (eds), *Relating Intimacies: Power and Resistance* (Macmillan, 1999).

longer to resolve;[97] and—perhaps ironically for a measure in which the welfare of the wishes of the child are supposed to be paramount—that the irrebuttable presumption in *favour* of contact or shared parenting can itself run entirely counter to the views and feelings children would themselves express on many occasions, were they ever to be properly consulted.[98]

It is in relation to another context, however, that the issue of contact becomes particularly problematic. This is in what research suggests to be the considerable number of cases where violence exists—in the vast majority of cases, that is, violence on the part of men; violence which is not the 'rare exception', but which can be seen as a systematic feature of many family relations, especially during the processes of divorce and separation.[99] In the context of the ideological promotion of the harmonious divorce, recent research in England and Wales suggests that issues of violence are themselves being systematically 'marginalised' within divorce mediation practice.[100] Indeed, Smart and Neale[101] suggest, one consequence of the present ideological power of the new fatherhood has been that family law would itself now appear to have moved into a position where it is 'almost impossible to conceive of a father who is harmful to children unless he inflicts direct violence on them'.[102] Following a succession of judicial decisions focused on the case of the 'implacably hostile' mother, and the issue of whether the mother has unreasonably and 'without virtue' withheld or prevented contact between father and child,[103] there are signs that the case law in this area is now in a state of some

[97] R Bailey-Harris, G David, J Barron and J Pearce, *Monitoring Private Law Applications under the Children Act: A Research Report to the Nuffield Foundation* (University of Bristol, 1998); G Davis and J Pearce, 'On the Trail of the Welfare Principle' (1999) 29 *Family Law* 144; G Davis and J Pearce, 'The Welfare Principle in Action' (1999) 29 *Family Law* 237; G Davis and J Pearce, 'A View from the Trenches: Practice and Procedure in Section 8 Applications' (1999 29 *Family Law* 457; J Pearce, G Davis and J Barron, 'Love in a Cold Climate: Section 8 Applications under the *Children Act*' (1999) 29 *Family Law* 22.

[98] C Smart and B Neale, 'It's my life too'—Children's Perspectives on Post-divorce Parenting' (2000) *Family Law* 163 at 168.

[99] M Hester and L Radford, *Domestic Violence and Child Contact Arrangements in England and Denmark* (Policy Press, 1996); M Hester, C Pearson and J Radford, *Domestic Violence: A National Survey of Court Welfare and Voluntary Sector Mediation Practice* (Policy Press: 1997); C Humphreys, 'Judicial Alienation Syndrome: Failures to Respond to Post-separation Violence' (1999) 29 *Family Law* 313; compare K Inman, 'Invisible Men', *The Guardian*, 17 Nov 1999; on domestic violence and child abuse, see S Burton, L Regan and L Kelly, *Domestic Violence: Supporting Women and Challenging Men* (Policy Press, 1998); M Hester and C Pearson, *From Periphy to Centre: Domestic Violence in Work with Abused Children* (Policy Press, 1998); A Mullender and R Morley (eds), *Children Living with Domestic Violence* (Taylor and Francis, 1994); on developments around contact generally, see A Bainham, 'Contact as a Fundamental Right' (1995) 54 *Cambridge Law Journal* 255.

[100] R Bailey-Harris, J Barron and J Pearce, 'From Utility to Rights? The Presumption of Contact in Practice' (1999) 13 *International Journal of Law, Policy and the Family* 111; D Greatbatch and R Dingwall, 'The Marginalization of Domestic Violence in Divorce Mediation' (1999) *International Journal of Law, Policy and the Family* 174.

[101] C Smart and B Neale, '"I hadn't really thought about it": New Identities/New Fatherhoods', in J Seymour and P Bagguley (eds), *Relating Intimacies: Power and Resistance* (Macmillan, 1999b), p 134.

[102] *Ibid.*; see also F Kaganas and C Piper, 'Contact and Domestic Violence' in S Day Sclater and C Piper (eds), *Undercurrents of Divorce* (Ashgate, 1999).

[103] S Maidment, 'Parental Alienation Syndrome—a Judicial Response?' (1998) *Family Law* 264; J Rosenblatt and P Scragg, 'The Hostile Parent: A Clinical Analysis' (1995) 25 *Family Law* 152.

uncertainty.[104] Nonetheless, it is also clear that the new fatherhood ideal is continuing to play out in some all too powerful ways in this context.

The problematic nature of the effects or consequences of the new fatherhood does not stop here. If the new fatherhood has involved some questionable assumptions about the desirability of contact, it has also impacted on the related assumption that the promotion of consensus between the parties is itself an *a priori* social good (and, indeed, that it might be possible for the law to 'legislate for harmony' in this area in the first place.[105] Recent research suggests, in contrast, that the psychological ambivalences of loss accompanying the end of human relationships jar in a number of respects with the powerful rhetoric of the harmonious divorce as it is presently being promulgated.[106] Indeed, Brown and Day Sclater[107] argue that the dominant welfare discourse—of which I have argued the new fatherhood is part—itself functions in practice so as to negate the legitimacy of—to deny for both women *and* men—the space to articulate conflictual feelings of loss, guilt and anger which almost inevitably accompany the break-up of human relationships. Their argument has some important implications for the new fatherhood, for it is clear that the welfare discourse forming such a central strand in the vocabularies of professionals involved in family dispute resolution is itself being routinely invoked by mothers and fathers in giving accounts of *what* they have done and *why* they have done it.[108] In view of how parents are culturally and legally exhorted to put their own feelings and interests 'to one side' for the sake of the children, this in itself is unsurprising. Yet what is also clear is that divorcing parents are not unproblematically 'accepting', as it were, the premises of the welfare discourse and its various prescriptions for behaviour and feeling in terms of their everyday actions.[109] Research studies suggest, rather, that many divorcing and separating couples routinely *reinterpret* the neutral language of welfarism being conveyed to them in terms of the lived realities of their family lives as they are presently experienced[110]—that is, a social experience mediated by the context

[104] Advisory Board on Family Law, *Children Act* Sub-Committee, *A Consultation Paper on Contact Between Children and Violent Parents: The Question of Parental Contact in Cases Where There is Domestic Violence* (Lord Chancellor's Department, 1999); P Harris, 'Contact and Domestic Violence: A Response from Peter Harris, the Official Solicitor' (1999) 158 *Childright* 16.

[105] F Kaganas, M King and C Piper (eds), *Legislating for Harmony: Partnership under the Children Act 1989* (Arena, 1995).

[106] S Day Sclater, *Divorce: A Psychosocial Study* (Ashgate, 1999); see also S Day Sclater and C Yates, 'The Psycho-Politics of Post Divorce Parenting', in A Bainham, S Day Sclater and M Richards (eds), *What is a Parent? A Socio-Legal Analysis* (Hart, 1999).

[107] J Brown and S Day Sclater, 'Divorce: A Psychodynamic Perspective', in S Day Sclater and C Piper (eds), *Undercurrents of Divorce* (Ashgate, 1999).

[108] S Day Sclater, *Divorce: A Psychosocial Study* (Ashgate, 1999); also S Day Sclater and C Yates, 'The Psycho-politics of Post Divorce Parenting', in A Bainham, S Day Sclater and M Richards (eds), *What is a Parent? A Socio-Legal Analysis* (Hart, 1999); C Smart and B Neale, *Family Fragments* (Polity, 1999); C Smart and B Neale, '"I hadn't really thought about it": New Identities/New Fatherhoods', in J Seymour and P Bagguley (eds), *Relating Intimacies: Power and Resistance* (Macmillan, 1999).

[109] S Day Sclater, *Divorce: A Psychosocial Study* (Ashgate, 1999); also S Day Sclater and C Yates, 'The Psycho-politics of Post Divorce Parenting', in A Bainham, S Day Sclater and M Richards (eds), *What is a Parent? A Socio-Legal Analysis* (Hart, 1999).

[110] C Smart and B Neale, '"I hadn't really thought about it": New Identities/New Fatherhoods', in J Seymour and P Bagguley (eds), *Relating Intimacies: Power and Resistance* (Macmillan, 1999).

of a 'reality' of family practices which is marked by gender difference; a context in which it would appear that women and men are not interpreting the purportedly gender-neutral language of welfarism in the *same* ways, and in which their emotional investments accommodate a diversity of actions, each of which might equally be presented by the individual concerned as being 'in the best interests of the child'.[111] Research emerging from both the United Kingdom and internationally suggests that it is precisely the material and emotional dependencies surrounding child care (and, increasingly, elder care) which tend, in particular, to mediate women's and men's negotiations and experiences of the breakdown of heterosexual relationships,[112] as well as the issue of how they might seek to work around and negotiate specific tensions between individual employment and family commitments in particular circumstances. These are, I have argued, distinctly gendered processes. Yet any consideration of such gendered dimensions is an issue systematically effaced by the purportedly gender-neutral ideology which has framed the emergence of the new fatherhood. In contrast, a debate has been constructed around the idea of the new 'sharing' fatherhood, premised on the notion of gender convergence, in which any critique of marriage has itself been systematically marginalised:

> Men who love their children are assumed to be sharing equally in the work of the family . . . the social conversation about men and the sexual political issue of domestic work omits the most significant fact about male resistance to change—that it suits

[111] From such a perspective, a rather different light is shed on the well-documented ways in which men, in the unsettling processes of divorce, have been seen to pursue agendas based on rights and justice—B Neale and C Smart, 'In Whose Best Interests? Theorising Family Life Following Parental Separation or Divorce', in S Day Sclater and C Piper (eds), *Undercurrents of Divorce* (Ashgate, 1999)—rather than, as has been suggested is the case for divorcing women—S Day Sclater and C Yates, 'The Psycho-politics of Post Divorce Parenting', in A Bainham, S Day Sclater and M Richards (eds), *What is a Parent? A Socio-Legal Analysis* (Hart, 1999)—a discourse which expresses the emotional needs of the mother herself for independence and freedom from the constraints of ties to her former male partner. Empirical research points to many cases where men routinely (if unconsciously) misrepresent the actuality of the personal circumstances of their wife/partner in a post-divorce representation of empowered 'mythic' women who are somehow the 'winners' (with men being the 'losers') in divorce: C Smart and B Neale, '"I hadn't really thought about it": New Identities/New Fatherhoods', in J Seymour and P Bagguley (eds), *Relating Intimacies: Power and Resistance* (Macmillan, 1999), pp 130–31. Perhaps ironically, research suggests that many women with children are systematically 'losing a fortune out of divorce settlements because they are "too nice" . . . [and] not driving a hard enough bargain for fear of further damaging family relationships': The *Independent on Sunday*, 30 April 2000, reporting research published jointly by the Joseph Rowntree Foundation and the Family Policy Studies Centre which found that, in attempting to 'maintain family harmony', many women appeared reluctant to call on lawyers until the final stages of divorce proceedings. The report, A Perry, G Douglas, M Murch, K Bader and M Borkowski, *How Parents Cope Financially on Marriage Breakdown* (Family Policy Studies Centre, 2000), is backed by government figures which show that, after a divorce, it is becoming increasingly common for women to suffer a loss of income.

[112] In short, it cannot be assumed that fathers and mothers *respond* to these child welfare norms in the same way: C Piper, *The Responsible Parent* (Harvester Wheatsheaf, 1993), p 176. Of all the contingencies which inform the complex ways in which different individuals negotiate and/or actively resist positionings offered them by the welfare discourse, it would appear to be in relation to a differential relationship to/with *children* that the various sexed (as different) negotiations of heterosexual relationships are frequently experienced in an acute way.

> men. This seems to be too unpalatable to be made explicit—to say it about gender relations underlines the romantic ideology of modern sharing marriage. Meanwhile men's interests continue to be served by the same discourses which deny them, and which continue to invite us to wait until men are ready to change. (McMahon 1999: 7–8)

The analysis presented above of the relationship between fatherhood and law suggests that a range of cultural discourses would appear at present to be problematising fatherhood (the fatherhood problematic referred to above), yet they are doing so in such a way as to systematically, behind an ostensibly progressive rhetoric of equality and gender convergence, *depoliticise* issues of power and material interest within contemporary family practices.

CONCLUDING REMARKS

Appeals for the need for more 'authoritative' research continue to be invoked regularly within debates around family policy in Britain as if, it would at times seem, with the undertaking of one more study the Truth of family life will be known.[113] Yet the history of family policy is littered with examples of the contingency of such appeals to Truth in the context of the pragmatics and everyday experience of political and policy decision-making.[114] In his foreword to the book *Undercurrents of Divorce*,[115] Michael King has written of the need to challenge the prevailing wisdom in family law, that 'secular cannon concerning the relationship between children's welfare and the reduction of conflict between parents'. He refers to the need to go 'against the grain of official policy or the new orthodoxy on divorce and reconstituted families', whilst recognising that such an approach 'is likely to irritate, and provoke, those judges, politicians, and civil servants who tell themselves and one another that now, at last, we have just about "got it right"'. The well-documented 'bitter controversies'[116] which exist in the field of family law reform show 'how much confusion and ambivalence' remains 'about what we want the law to do'.[117] In England and Wales, at least, 'getting it right' in family policy would appear to be, notwithstanding years of socio-legal research in the field, as elusive as ever.[118]

[113] See further, on the uses of social science data in relation to the family, ML Fineman, and A Opie, 'The Uses of Social Science Data in Legal Policy Making: Custody Determinations at Divorce' (1987) 1 *Wisconsin Law Review* 107.

[114] Recent events concerning the delayed implementation of Part II of the Family Law 1996 can be seen as a case in point in this regard: R Collier, 'From Women's Emancipation to Sex War? Men, Heterosexuality and the Politics of Divorce', in S Day Sclater and C Piper, *Undercurrents of Divorce* (Ashgate, 1999).

[115] S Day Sclater and C Piper, *Undercurrents of Divorce* (Ashgate, 1999), p ix.

[116] The Honorable Mrs Justice B Hale, 'The 8th ESRC Annual Lecture: Private Lives and Public Duties: What is Family Law For? (1998) 20 *Journal of Social Welfare and Family Law* 125.

[117] *Ibid.*

[118] At the time of writing, there has been no conclusive statement from either the Lord Chancellor's Department or government about the fate of Part II of the *Family Law Act* 1996, the

I would make four concluding points in seeking to focus on the implications of this argument for developing a critical analysis of the relationship between fatherhood and law.

Beyond 'Fatherhood': Reconceptualising the Relationship Between Men and Children

First, it is necessary to go beyond the present fatherhood debate and consider what emerges when we reframe these issues in terms of the changing relationship between men and children more generally. That is, it is important to consider what the very terms in which the debate has been couched tell us about the nature of men's location, not just in relation to the private family, but within the social per se.[119] What has become increasingly visible and politicised is the frequently problematic nature of the presence of men *in* the lives of children, whether it is in the capacity as biological or social fathers, as caregivers or as welfare workers across a range of institutions and organisations.[120] This is not simply a matter of stating that the politics of the rhetoric of gender convergence are vastly overstated. What has surfaced from within sociological scholarship is a rich picture of what we might more accurately term men's everyday *invisibility* from the routine, day-to-day care of children in society—whether individually, collectively, whether of their (our) own of other people's children—and what this might tell us about the

provisions of which were widely heralded at the time of enactment as bringing about the introduction of 'no fault' divorce. As yet, Part II of the *Family Law Act* remains unimplemented.

[119] This development itself, as I have argued elsewhere R Collier, *Masculinities, Crime and Criminology: Men, Heterosexuality and the Criminal(ised) Other*, (Sage, 1998), relates to more complex changes in and around the concept of parenthood—and thus, implicitly, around ideas of *childhood*. In contrast to what have been termed previous 'adultist' approaches to law and the family—A James and M Richards, 'Sociological Perspectives, Family Policy and Children: Adult Thinking and Sociological Tinkering' (1999) 21 *Journal of Social Welfare and Family Law* 23—within a new paradigm in the sociology of childhood, it is the figure of the child which has emerged as an active, and contested, socially symbolic subject (see, for example, V Bell, 'Governing Childhood: Neo-Liberalism and the Law' (1993) 22 *Economy and Society* 390; A Diduck, 'Justice and Childhood: Reflections on Refashioned Boundaries', in M King (ed), *Moral Agendas for Children's Welfare* (Routledge, 1999); A James, *Childhood Identities, Self and Social Relations in the Experience of the Child* (Edinburgh University Press, 1993); A James and A Prout (eds), *Constructing and Reconstructing Childhood* (Falmer Press, 1990); C Jenks, *Childhood* (Routledge, 1996); J Qvortrup, 'Childhood and Modern Society: A Paradoxical Relationship?' in J Brannen and M O'Brien (eds), *Childhood and Parenthood* (Institute of Education, 1995); J Brannen and M O'Brien (eds), *Childhood and Parenthood: Proceedings of the International Sociological Association Committee for Family Research Conference* (London: Institute of Education, 1995); U Beck and E Beck Gernsheim, *The Normal Chaos of Love* (Polity, 1995); C Smart and B Neale, '"It's my life too"—Children's Perspectives on Post-divorce Parenting' (2000) *Family Law* 163. In this process, this 'childhood question' has served to challenge and disturb some taken-for-granted ideas about the relationship between men and children.

[120] K Pringle, *Men, Masculinities and Social Welfare* (UCL Press, 1995). Epitomised by current debates around the parameters of 'appropriate' physical contact between men and children: 'Is a Father Allowed to Miss his Children *Physically*? Should I Feel Guilty that I Do?': B Morrison, *As If* (Granta Books, 1997). See further R Collier, 'The Anxious Parent and the Vulnerable Child', in J Bridgeman and D Monk (eds), *Feminist Perspectives in Child Law* (Cavendish, 2000).

politics, value and ethics of care and caring within contemporary advanced capitalist societies. Far from being either anti-family or a marginal(ised) ideological concern, although they continue all too often to be depicted as such within much mainstream socio-legal study in Britain,[121] these are issues about men and children which are precisely the kinds of questions being asked within developing feminist scholarship concerned with the ethics of care.[122] At issue here are issues which cannot, in short, be confined simply to a debate about *fatherhood* and law. They are about how society understands and values the relationship between women, men and children in a more general sense. Yet these are questions which, it would seem, rarely filter through to a field of policy debate and formulation,[123] a domain which remains fixated on the private family, a debate about heterosexual family values and the importance of the biological link between family men and children.

Contesting the Language of Masculine/Familial Crisis

Secondly, and following on from the above, it is important to recognise and challenge the way in which contemporary discussions of fatherhood are now enmeshed with—indeed, they have become inseparable from—the dominant languages of masculine and familial crisis which have, together, marked the reconfiguration of heterosexual relations presently taking place across Western societies.[124] The material *effects* of the seemingly ubiqutious idea of the 'crisis of masculinity' are not to be under-estimated. Indeed, one reason why fathers' rights groups and organisations now appear increasingly influential, at least within some

[121] Note, for example, James and Richards' (1999) depiction of Smart's work as 'it must be said' deriving from a 'feminist perspective': A James and M Richards, 'Sociological Perspectives, Family Policy and Children: Adult Thinking and Sociological Tinkering' (1999) 21 *Journal of Social Welfare and Family* 23.

[122] S Sevenhuijsen, *Citizenship and the Ethics of Care: Feminist Considerations about Justice, Morality and Politics* (Routledge, 1998); C Smart and B Neale, *Family Fragments* (Polity, 1999); JC Tronto, *Moral Boundaries: A Political Argument for an Ethic of Care* (Routledge, 1993); JC Tronto, 'Women and Caring: What can Feminists Learn about Morality from Caring?' in A Jaggar and S Bordo (eds), *Gender, Body, Knowledge* (Rutgers University Press, 1989); see also S Benhabib, *Situating the Self: Gender, Community and Postmodernism in Contemporary Ethics* (Routledge, 1992); M Griffiths, *Feminisms and the Self: The Web of Identity* (Routledge, 1995).

[123] On what can happen when feminist views *are* seen as informing policy debate, see further: 'Legal Commissars Subverting Family Values' and 'Twice Married Feminist Behind Radical New Laws', *Daily Mail*, 1 Nov 1995.

[124] See, for example—and in different ways—the arguments of S Faludi, *Stiffed: The Betrayal of the Modern Man* (Chatto & Windus, 1999); M Midgley and J Hughes, 'Are Families Out of Date?' in HL Nelson (ed), *Feminism and Families* (Routledge, 1999); L Nicholson, 'The Myth of the Traditional Family' in HL Nelson (ed), *Feminism and Families*, (Routledge, 1999); cf D Blakenhorn, *Fatherless America: Confronting Our Most Urgent Social Problem* (Basic Books, 1995); N Dennis and G Erdos, *Families Without Fatherhood* (Institute of Economic Affairs, 1993); P Morgan, *Farewell to the Family? Public Policy and Family Breakdown in Britain and the USA* (Institute of Economic Affairs, Health and Welfare Unit, 1995); D Popenhoe, 'American Family Decline, 1960–1990: A Review and Appraisal' (1993) 55 *Journal of Marriage and the Family* 527.

jurisdictions, can be seen to relate to the way in which the new father has been constituted as a familial subject in ways rather different way to the past. The new father makes claims to rights, equality, rules and justice which resonate well with the more general direction, concepts and categories of family law reform;[125] his concerns about justice appear to be shared by many who have expressed a growing dissatisfaction with the perceived limits of what was a broad discretionary system in the family law field. Of particular importance in empowering the new father, however, has been—and remains—the way in which he has been constituted and understood through reference to the language of gender neutrality.

The dominant notion of gender-neutral parenting has certainly served to displace that combination of an ontology of sexual difference, hierarchy and normative heterosexuality which had been historically central to the discursive constitution of father-presence as socially desirable in the first place.[126] And it is no wonder that, in so doing, the hitherto cultural and legal importance of the traditional, authoritarian patriarchal father figure should have become far less socially significant and legitimate. However, it is important to recognise the ways in which gender neutrality has itself reconstituted the father figure in some particular ways. The analysis presented in this article of recent developments around fatherhood in England and Wales has leant weight to the arguments of those who have suggested that gender neutrality has in many ways led, in practice, to a devaluing and systematic negation of the social importance of mothers and mothering, a position which Fineman[127] describes as 'motherhood descending'.[128]

Beyond the 'Private' Family: Law, Society and the Gendered Dimensions of Care and Dependency

Thirdly, and underscoring each of the above points, what is so difficult to see in the present political climate[129] is any engagement with the conceptual basis of the

[125] Although it is also important to note, and in addition, the generally more sophisticated language and organisational structures utilised by such groups.

[126] R Collier, *Masculinity, Law and the Family* (Routledge, 1995).

[127] M Fineman, *The Neutered Mother: The Sexual Family and Other Twentieth Century Tragedies* (Routledge, 1995).

[128] See also the argument of N Dowd, *Redefining Fatherhood* (New York University Press, 2000).

[129] At the time of writing, it was clear that 'the family' would be a prominent issue in the forthcoming British election, expected to take place in 2001. Marriage continues to be routinely depicted within family debates in Britain as a 'best case' scenario. In the words of the Lord Chancellor: 'The institution of marriage is at the heart of society. But relationships people have chosen for themselves *short of marriage* also deserve society's support, not least in the interests of the children. *These relationships too are part of society* . . . when a marriage or a cohabiting relationship short of marriage comes asunder, then the state must step in . . . because children come first.' (Lord Chancellor, speech to the UK Family Law Conference, 25 June 1999, my emphasis) A broader agenda of 'saving marriages' has itself recently emerged as central to the formulation of contemporary family policy. Various ministerial pronouncements that 'other' relationships are not to be 'judged' and that 'these too are part of society' sit uneasily alongside a clearly stated beliefs in 'the strengthening of marriage as a basis for bringing up children', and that such a belief should itself be 'the cornerstone of Labour's modern family

idea of the private family itself; and, related to this, what the autonomy of men to 'opt out' of caring relations tells us about the gendered way society values intimacy. There remains, notwithstanding rhetorical nods towards diversity, little questioning of how we think about the private family and its relationship to society within dominant political debates in Britain. To even raise such questions is, I recognise, to be accused by some of engaging in 'utopian' thinking. Yet engaging with such question about the gendered dimensions of care and dependency is itself arguably an *inherent* part of—indeed, it is inescapable within—present debates about the relationship between law and family practices (what—or whose—'family values' does the law seek to uphold or promote?). Such issues do not, I have argued, suddenly 'appear' at the point of divorce; they exist during subsisting marriage, being pathologised at the stage of relationship breakdown where they tend, more usually, to be constituted as a sign of individual moral failure—and not, as they might be, as a sign of a growing diversity in the content and form of heterosexual attachments and caring situations.[130] Crucially, the vocabulary of gender neutrality, like the epistemic frame of sex/gender from which it derives, paradoxically appears disconnected to any appreciation of the gendered nature and material realities of care are caring—a recognition, for example, that the choice and commitment to care *about* is not necessarily the same thing as caring *for*.

Normative Pluralism? Family Practices and the Limits of Law

Fourthly and finally, it is not, I believe, ultimately surprising that there should exist tensions and contradictions surrounding the relationship between law and fatherhood. These tensions are, rather, indicative—indeed, they are emblematic—of a more general 'normative pluralism' and conceptual chaos within the family law field.[131] At stake in present debates around law and fatherhood is something more than simply a balancing exercise between questions of individual rights and social utility. Rather—whether it is in relation to the changing status of unmarried fathers, the post-divorce family or the 'work and family life' issues discussed above—what we are dealing with can be seen to be a number of different and incompatible ways of approaching decision-making in the family law field. As Dewar[132] argues, transferring such inescapably political issues about principles, philosophy and the meaning of 'family values'—for example, what constitutes a desirable or undesirable model of 'family life'—to the field of law and administration makes it unsurprising that the legal arena should then be marked by such

policy' (Jack Straw, Home Secretary, *The Guardian*, 24 July 1998; see further G Pascall, 'UK Family Policy in the 1990s: The Case of New Labour and Lone Parents' (1999) 13 *International Journal of Law, Policy and the Family* 258.

[130] E Silva and C Smart (eds), *The 'New' Family?* (Sage, 1999).

[131] J Dewar, 'The Normal Chaos of Family Law' (1998) 61 *Modern Law Review* 467.

[132] *Ibid.*

unresolved (or, perhaps, unresolvable) tensions. This article has argued, following Dewar's analysis, that some potentially unworkable contradictions run through contemporary dominant conceptualisations of fatherhood. Yet they do not simply pervade, and cannot be confined to, diverse legal constructions of fatherhood. They are all too clear in what men themselves are saying about their lives. Far from the positive 'push for change' inherent in the new fatherhood ideology, research into the materiality of family practices—that is, what women and men actually do—suggests, certainly, the existence of a great deal of confusion, anger, frustration and, frequently, psychological pain on the part of men. Yet research also attests to widespread resistance, stalling and reluctance to change on the part of men, as well as a continuing material, cultural and symbolic empowerment across a number of social fields (not least the supposedly increasingly egalitarian and equal workplace). What is so revealing at the present moment is how much of the rhetoric in these debates about fatherhood in fact constitutes an attempt to bolster and reaffirm heterosexual marriage *in the face of* the threat posed by the changes in women lives and the resulting dissatisfaction on the part of many women with existing sexual divisions of labour. What is consistently passed over is the way in which men, as a sex group, stall and resist change, whilst at the same time—and paradoxically—an entire debate about fatherhood has been constructed in terms of a demand for men *to* change.

This article has not sought to negate the role and importance of law in promoting social change. Nor has it presented a reductive, essentialist reading of gender difference. It has, rather, sought to question the ways in which apparently positive changes may themselves be in many ways superficial, 'merely altering form, while leaving aspiration and expectation undisturbed'.[133] Whilst the possibilities of shifting gendered parenting practices may not be limitless, constrained materially in all kinds of ways, the 'creative tensions within the discourses of gender, sexuality and familial power relations [do] provide women and men . . . with choices [which] should not be overlooked'.[134] What is required, I have argued, is a richer and more nuanced account of family practices than that contained within recurring representations of 'new fathers', 'feckless' fathers, 'deadbeat dads' or, indeed, 'feminist fathers'.[135] In order for law to contribute to developing a more inclusive society, as well as an improved sense of well-being amongst both women and men, it is essential that the conceptual framework which informs the implementation of policy questions is critically assessed.[136] There is, for example, much

[133] M Fineman, *The Neutered Mother, The Sexual Family and Other Twentieth Century Tragedies* (Routledge, 1995), p 6.

[134] S Oerton, *Beyond Hierarchy* (Taylor and Francis, 1996).

[135] ID Balbus, *Emotional Rescue: The Theory and Practice of a Feminist Father* (Routledge, 1998).

[136] On recent theoretical interventions in the field of family law in the United States and the United Kingdom more generally, see further (for example): S Boyd, '(Re)placing the State: Family, Law and Oppression' (1994) 9 *Canadian Journal of Law and Society* 39; S Boyd, 'Some Postmodernist Challenges to Feminist Analyses of Law, Family and State: Ideology and Discourse in Child Custody Law' (1991) 10 *Canadian Journal of Family Law*, 79; J Dewar, 'The Normal Chaos of Family Law' (1998) 61 *Modern Law* 467; J Dewar, 'Family, Law and Theory' (1996) 16 *Oxford Journal of Legal Studies* 725;

to gain—for both women and men—from the developing notions of care evolving within feminist scholarship of engaging with principles of actuality, which address the realities of caring situations; principles of care which locate the child within a set of social relations and, importantly for men, seek (among other things) to value different styles of parenting; and principles recognising the complex psychosocial dynamics around loss and selfhood—issues all too frequently effaced within the strict adherence to abstract principles of justice and welfare which marks dominant practice.

Leaving aside its continuing elusive nature, it is far from clear that the idea of the 'symmetrical family', based in the revolving door of working women and caring men, is in itself an obvious good. The entire framework in which such a family is conceptualised continues to assume that heterosexual marriage is the most desirable context for personal life. Yet, far from trading in an untheorised and ultimately obfuscatory discourse of 'saving marriages', research which is addressing how family practices are themselves (re)constituted and lived at the turn of the new century points to an appreciation of the more complex realities of contemporary 'family life'; and it is these realities—what women and men actually *do* in their everyday lives, as opposed to what they should be doing—which suggest that legal interventions such as those presently taking place around the 'search for the new father' in England and Wales will fail to significantly shift the cultural practices of women and men around family life. Whether such conceptual concerns have any place in contemporary *realpolitik* is, of course, another matter. They are, however, precisely the kinds of issues which critical law and society scholarship should be addressing in discussions of the past, present and future direction of family law.

M Fineman, *The Neutered Mother, The Sexual Family and Other Twentieth Century Tragedies* (Routledge, 1995); K O'Donovan, *Family Law Matters* (Pluto, 1993); see also A Bainham, 'Changing Families and Changing Concepts—Reforming the Language of Family Law' (1998) 10 *Child and Family Law Quarterly* 1; LD Houlgate, 'Must the Personal be Political? Family Law and the Concept of Family' (1998) 12 *International Journal of Law, Policy and the Family* 107; note also M Minow, '"Forming Underneath Everything that Grows": Toward a History of Family Law' (1985) *University of Wisconsin Law Review* 819.

12

Different Approaches to Post-Divorce Family Relationships: The Example of Contact Centres in France

Benoit Bastard*

In France, as in many other countries, contemporary families are being confronted with changes and difficulties.[1] This paper addresses issues relating to divorce and visiting rights. This is a complex area, because the aim is to achieve two different and potentially conflicting objectives:[2] respecting the will of the spouses when they do not want to stay in an unsatisfactory relationship; and maintaining—and, if necessary, restoring and reinforcing—the relationships between a child and the non-custodial parent. In France, we consider that children have the right to be cared for at all levels—economical, practical and psychological—by two parents.

Confronted with this tension between two goals which are difficult to achieve simultaneously, professionals have developed new responses which differ from traditional legal action. Whereas French civil judges have traditionally been passive and dependent on the will of the parties in all matters, including family affairs, over the past decade, there has been a shift towards judges taking a more active role. In order to maintain some form of relationship between children and their non-custodial parent, they have encouraged the development of new services and developed referrals to other professionals, particularly mediators and contact centres.

This paper focuses on the experience of French contact centres, offering some thoughts about the implications of these centres on changes to family structure. I stress two aspects of the French experience. First, I argue that these centres have developed a new framework in order to obtain more compliance with social expectations concerning visiting rights. I then overview the debate on family relationships and their future which has emerged from analysis of the operation of

* Sociologist and member of the Nationale de la Recherche Scientifique, France; member of the board of the French Association of Contact Centres.

[1] This paper is based on research conducted on children contact centres in France, with Laura Cardia-Vonèche (University of Geneva, Switzerland).

[2] Irène Théry, *Famille: une crise de l'institution*, Notes de la Fondation Saint-Simon, no 83, 1996.

these centres. Before presenting these arguments, I present some basic information about contact centres in France.

SOME DATA ABOUT CHILD CONTACT CENTRES IN FRANCE

Divorce and Family Law

France has a population of 58 million. In 1996, we had 279,000 marriages. As in many developed countries, one marriage out of three ends in divorce (125,000 divorce per year). More than two million children under eighteen do not live with their mother and father. Among them, 85 per cent live with their mothers most of the time. Great concern has been expressed during the last decade about the fact that a large number of these children have little contact with their fathers. Visiting rights are difficult to implement, and only one half of these minor children of divorced parents see their father on a regular basis (regular meaning more than once a month). One-third of the children who do not live with both parents never see their father.[3]

The French civil law was reformed in 1975 to introduce divorce by mutual consent. Joint custody (*autorité parentale conjointe*) was introduced in 1987 and became the usual decision in a divorce in 1993. In 1996, mediation was introduced in the French code of civil procedure and is now due to be introduced into the civil code regarding divorce and family matters more generally.

It has to be noted that the civil judge (*juge aux affaires familiales*) meets the parties at least once when they ask for a divorce. During this meeting, where the judge meets husband and wife separately without their lawyers, a strong emphasis is placed on reaching agreements on the decisions to be made concerning children and financial affairs.[4] The judge may also meet the children involved. The emphasis on agreement is also—to a certain extent—shared by lawyers (*avocats*).

Meeting places for exercising visiting rights

In the late 1980s, contact centres emerged in France as a responses to the difficulties encountered by children and parents in difficult divorce cases. They were created through local initiatives which were not connected to one another. In Bordeaux, the initiative came from a group of lawyers, social workers and psychologists. They shared their experiences about the trauma they observed in both children and parents when parents were in a state of high conflict. They

[3] Catherine Villeneuve-Gokalp, 'La Double Famille des Enfants de Parents Séparés', (1999) 1 *Population* 9.

[4] See Laura Cardia-Vonèche, Sylvie Liziard and Benoit Bastard, 'Juge Dominant, Juge Démuni? La Redéfinition du Rôle du Juge en Matière de Divorce', (1996) 33 *Droit et Société* 277.

considered that the difficulties, in the case of children, were linked to the interrupted relationship between the child and their non-custodial parent. In Grenoble, a social worker with the family court was very dissatisfied by the conditions under which she had to practise—for instance, arranging contact between a non-custodial parent and his child in her car.

From these many local reflections and initiatives emerged the same concept: the idea of creating a specific 'neutral' space where some appropriate support could be given by professionals. The new centres were called Point-Rencontre ('meeting place') in Bordeaux, La Passerelle ('The Bridge') in Grenoble, Le Couvige in Clermont-Ferrand, and so on.[5]

This new concept spread quite rapidly throughout the country. In 2000, there were between 100 and 120 of these centres.[6] A generic name has now been adopted with the creation of a network of centres: *lieux d'accueil pour l'exercice des droits de visite*—a name which is not easy to use in French, but still refers to the idea of a place where people can meet for the purpose of implementing visiting rights. The French network is called Fédération des lieux d'accueil pour l'exercice des droits de visite and it has 60 centres as members. Standards and guidelines for practice (*Code de déontologie*) were adopted by the Fédération in 1998.

French child contact centres are usually in the form of an *association*—which is usual for non-profit projects. Still, they are run by professionals: social workers, psychologists, family counsellors, therapists. Those professionals are usually employed by other institutions and devote some of their time—often on Saturdays—to the activity of the centres. The guidelines adopted by the Fédération insist that the services must be provided by paid professionals.

Nearly half of the centres ask for payment from 'clients'. However, the guidelines stipulate that money issues should never be a reason for not maintaining contact between children and their non-custodial parent. Payments requested are small, and most of the funding comes from state or public local agencies. These resources are scarce and often difficult to obtain.

Parents are referred to the centre by a judge in 80 per cent of cases. Little systematic data is available to date on the parents and children who use the centres, but we do know that the father is the visiting parent in 80 per cent of cases.[7]

Child contact centres are located in a flat or a house. In some cases, this is the sole use of these premises, but some centres are located in premises which have other uses during the week—a welfare centre, for instance.

At a given hour, the custodial parent comes with the children and leaves them; the other parent arrives and take the children to his/her home if such rights have been allowed by the judge or agreed between the parents. If this not the case, the

[5] On the creation of these services, and for an analysis of their activity, see Benoit Bastard, Laura Cardia-Vonèche, Nathalie Deschamps, Caroline Guillot and Isabelle Sayn, *Enfants, parents, séparations. Des lieux d'accueil pour l'exercice du droit de visite et d'hébergement* (Fondation de France, 1994).

[6] A list of French centres can be obtained from the Fédération des lieux d'acceuil pour l'exercice des droits de visite, 12 rue Gambetta, 64000 Pau, France.

[7] Bastard, Cardia-Vonèche, Deschamps, Guillot and Sayn, n 5.

visit takes place 'on site' at the centre. The usual duration of the visit is from two hours to half a day—this is the case in 75 per cent of situations.

One of the main characteristics of the French centres which should be emphasised is the lack of any close 'supervision'—meaning one professional being present during the whole visit. On the contrary, if one looks at a centre like Point-Rencontre in Bordeaux, up to 30–50 families may be present, with different schedules, during a five-hour period of opening. Some of these parents and children will not stay in the centre, though most do. Point-Rencontre is a large centre with many rooms where parents stay with their children without the permanent supervision of a particular member of the staff. Three professionals are present at the desk and intervene when they consider it necessary to do so.

In the French experience, the spirit in which the service is offered is not so much focused on 'supervising' visitation (as in the United States), but rather on supporting and maintaining the relationship between children and the visiting parent. Straus explains this very important difference:

> Compared with programs in France, the emphasis of US programs appears to be more on providing security and objective observations than on taking a unilateral stance in support of maintaining the relationships between non-custodial parents and their children. The difference appears to stem in part from the intense attention in the US that is being directed to the problems of domestic violence and to protecting battered women and their children.[8]

What is the role of professionals in the child contact centres? They help children to separate from their custodial parent and to meet the other parent—a father or a mother they might be reluctant to meet or be in a relationship with. They also try to reassure the custodial parent regarding their own and their child/children's safety. Finally, the professionals work with the visiting parent in order to facilitate his/her relationship with the children—for instance, they support these parents in caring for young children or in talking with adolescents. There is a strong insistence that parents be on time for all visits.

As stated in the guidelines of the French Fédération, most of the services claim to maintain confidentiality on the contacts they arrange. It means that they give no evaluation to the courts or welfare services about the state of the relationship between the children and their visiting parent. Still, the relations between centres and the courts vary from one place to another. Many judges have supported the development of the services, seeing them as a resource for intervening in conflicting families, but the relationship between the courts and contact centres has not yet stabilised. Many judges would prefer the centres to have a more active contribution concerning decisions regarding visiting rights.[9]

[8] Robert Straus, 'Surveillance des Rencontres Enfants-parents aux Etats-Unis. Un État des Pratiques' (1996) 33 *Droit et Société* 317. See also Robert B Straus and Eve Alda, 'Supervised Access: The Evolution of a social service' (1994) 32 *Family and Conciliation Courts Review*.

[9] On the relationships between child contact centres and courts, see Isabelle Sayn, 'Une Relation 'dans L'intérêt de l'Enfant'? Le Juge de la Famille et les Lieux d'Accueil du Droit de Visite' (1996) 33 *Droit et Société* 329.

A NEW FRAMEWORK FOR REGULATING FAMILY RELATIONSHIPS

Child contact centres appear to be a new institution in the civil law field. Whereas the civil judge was traditionally passive and depended on the parties themselves, these centres represent a shift towards a more active form of intervention.

This intervention does not aim to change people. Parents are taken 'as they are'—with their conflict and their problems (alcohol, drugs, violence)—provided they are able to be present for their children. In this respect, contact centres are part of a larger trend affecting the landscape of social intervention. They represent, in the family sphere—as in other sectors like addiction—the idea of a 'low-threshold' institution. The intervention is focused not on the individuals but on their relationships, and it aims at maintaining social links.

On the one hand, nothing is imposed on parents and their children in the centres. Parents are given an incentive by the judicial decree which refers them to the service (though the service is not mandated by the judge). The professionals have a limited role. They support the contact by acting and talking with parents and children, but they usually try to withdraw and make themselves unobtrusive whenever possible. In fact, these services wish to give parents opportunities: nothing could happen without their participation.

However, if nothing is imposed, everything is in fact suggested. The services represent a strong incentive to self-regulation. As mentioned earlier, mothers are encouraged to separate from their children—they are told they can do so because the centre is a secure. Fathers are strongly encouraged to create new relationships with their children—they are constantly reminded of the importance of being present, sober, and so on so that their children can benefit from the visits. Finally, children are allowed—indeed, encouraged—to meet their other parent.

The collective setting helps to normalise the situations presented at the centres, providing an invisible normative framework which constrain people and invites them to self-regulation.

DIFFERENT TYPES OF SERVICE AND THE CHANGE IN FAMILY STRUCTURE

French centres are diverse and do not share the same conception of their intervention. They have different ideas of what professionals have to do as well as about the types of parent–child relationship centres should promote. For this, they rely on at least two different backgrounds. One is mediation. Centres that are connected with the mediation movement—for instance, La Passerelle in Grenoble, when it was created—consider that visiting rights can be implemented only if the conflict between parents is reduced. This is why they use any occasion—at the beginning or the end of the visit—to engage in discussion with parents, to evaluate the state of their conflict, to prepare any decision that could improve the organisation of the contacts. Without organising any formal mediation session—both parents being present—they are able to undertake 'shuttle' negotiation between them. From their perspective, it is assumed that the child benefits from interactions between their separated parents and it may be possible for both parents to be simultaneously present in the centre on some occasions.

Other centres are strongly opposed to this first orientation. Like Point-Rencontre in Bordeaux, which figures as the leader of this latter trend, they exclude any idea of mediation and consider that is neither useful nor feasible to try to restore the relationship between parents when they are in high conflict. They consider it could give the children false expectations about the reconstitution of their parents' relationship. So they disregard mediation and their work is devoted to restoring separate links between the child and each of their parents after divorce.

This opposition in the way contact centres operate can be used to introduce a more general reflection on the different models of family relationships that underlie the intervention strategies of these centres.

Both types of centre—pro- and anti-mediation—share a very strong belief that a child should not lose contact with their non-custodial parent. From this perspective, they are opposed to family relationships which are too 'osmotic' and in which a child could become '*la chose d'un de ses parents*'. They share a model of family relations consisting of differentiated links between the individuals who are concerned. However, they disagree on the model that could be appropriate to achieve both objectives: having the couple separated and maintaining the relationships between children and the non-custodial parent.

In the first model—mediation oriented, as at La Passerelle—the underlying assumption is that the relationship between the child and the non-custodial parent is always mediated by the parental relationship. As mediators used to say, parents are parents forever and the parental couple should survive. Maintaining contact between them is in the interest of the child.

In the second model—the one that has been elaborated in Bordeaux—it is considered that the relation between a child and their non-custodial parent is independent from the representation of a couple. There should be an individualised relation between a child and each of their parents.

CONCLUSION

These observations are strongly linked to a debate about the future of family relationships which is part of the process of reform of the French civil code. A report to the government written by a Law Professor, Françoise Dekeuwer Desfossez, is strongly in favour of the model in which the parental couple is seen as the necessary basis of the relationship between parents and children. According to this report, coparenting (*coparentalité*) is the only way to organise parent–child relationships, either in marriage or divorce. The idea of a 'parental couple' is strongly emphasised:

> L'enfant ne procède pas seulement d'individus mais d'un couple, c'est-à-dire de deux personnes unies par une histoire. Les changements de la constellation familiale ne remettent pas en cause la référence fondatrice représente pour un enfant le couple de ses parents.[10]

According to the authors of this report, this is the only available solution. They refute the notion of a family in which the child would be the only link between his/her parents:

> L'enfant ne peut être considéré comme la source et l'origine d'une famille qui lui préexiste en fait. Le couple préexiste à l'enfant. L'enfant ne peut se prétendre le créateur d'une famille au sein de laquelle il est en droit d'attendre, auprès de ses père et mère, sont statut d'enfant.[11]

But can we consider that the couple is still reliable as the basis of the family? And what is the danger when we put the child at the centre of the family structure? Jean Gréchez, the former leader of Point-Rencontre in Bordeaux and the president of the French Fédération, expresses the view that we should admit that this idea of a couple surviving the break-up is unrealistic and corresponds to a wish to maintain the idea of the indissolubility of marriage:

> Parler d'un couple parental qui survivrait au couple conjugal, ce pourrait être une vague réminiscence de l'indissolubilité du lien du mariage dans la religion catholique, un transfert du religieux ou de l'imaginaire enfantin sur le discours social actuel.[12]

Finally, the creation and the development of these new centres signal a shift towards judges and social workers taking a more active stance when it comes to parents and children confronting separation and divorce. This more active way of dealing with divorce is not associated—at least at first glance—with an idea of imposing a specific model of family relationships, but with a strong incentive towards self-regulation.

Still the analysis of these new services raises questions about the models of family that our societies wish to encourage in divorce situations—or even more generally. Describing the French experience of children contact services raises the following question: do we think that 'coparenting' and the notion of a 'parental

[10] 'Children do not proceed only from individuals, but from a couple, that is to say two persons linked by an history. Changes in family paterns do not.' Françoise Dekeuwer-Défossez (ed), *Rénover le droit de la famille. Propositions pour un droit adapté aux réalités et aux aspirations de notre temps. Rapport au Garde des Sceaux, ministre de la Justice* (La Documentation française, 1999), p 18.

[11] 'Children cannot be considered the source and the origin of a family which, in fact, existed before their birth. The couple pre-exists the child.' *Ibid.*, p 17.

[12] Jean Gréchez, 'Apprentissage de la Loi et Processus d'Évolution Psychique au Point-Rencontre' (1996) 132 *Dialogue* 79.

couple' is able to offer a valid solution for having both a real separation (or divorce) and a continued link between children and their two parents? Which alternative organisation of the parent–child relationship could we imagine when parents want to have a clear break and have no idea about how to maintain any contact between them?

13

Legal and Educational Interventions for Families in Residence and Contact Disputes

Joan B Kelly*

Extensive family and divorce research of the past decade has provided us with a more complex and useful understanding of the sources of children's adjustment problems, both in marriage and after divorce. A parallel line of research has focused on educational and legal interventions designed to ameliorate the impact of separation and divorce on children and their parents. Taken together, this information has widespread implications for legal practice, agency and court-sponsored interventions, and for state and national policy formation.

This chapter briefly summarises relevant research in both of these areas, and describes a hierarchy of educational and legal interventions that can benefit children of separated and divorcing parents by minimising the effects of the separation and divorce process on children and their parents.

MARITAL CONFLICT AND CHILDREN'S ADJUSTMENT

To place the consequences of separation and divorce in the proper context, it is important to understand what aspects of marriage create negative outcomes for children *prior* to the separation. The type and extent of marital conflict is an important predictor of children's adjustment after divorce. Indeed, some studies find it a more powerful predictor than the divorce itself or post-divorce conflict.[1] Children in high-conflict marriages have symptoms similar to those of children of divorce: conduct disorders, anti-social behaviours, difficulty with peers and

* Joan B Kelly, PhD is a psychologist, researcher, mediator and lecturer, who was formerly Director of the Northern California Mediation Center, and President of the Academy of Family Mediators. She is currently President of the California Dispute Resolution Institute. A version of this article was published in (2001) 15 *AJFL* 92, and has been published with the permission of that journal.

[1] C Buehler, A Krishnakumar, G Stone et al., 'Interparental Conflict Styles and Youth Problem Behaviors: A Two-sample Replication Study' (1998) 60 *Journal of Marriage and Family* 119; M Kline, J Johnston and J Tschann, 'The Long Shadow of Marital Conflict: A Model of Children's Postdivorce Adjustment' (1991) 53 *Journal Marriage and Family* 297.

authority figures, depression, and academic and achievement problems. Staying together for the sake of the children in high-conflict marriages is not necessarily in the children's best interests. Children whose high-conflict parents divorced when they were in their pre-adolescence were significantly better adjusted ten years later, compared with those young adults whose high-conflict parents stayed married.[2] High levels of marital conflict experienced during childhood have also been linked in young adults to more depression and other psychological disorders, when compared with those reporting lower levels of family conflict during childhood.[3] Such research has demonstrated that the psychological damage often attributed in past decades to the children's divorce experience can in part be accounted for by the experiences of these children in marriages prior to separation.[4]

Assessing Dimensions of Conflict

Conflict between parents regarding child-rearing differences, household responsibilities, extended families and financial disputes is common in many marriages. The threshold at which risk occurs for children in each family as a result of marital conflict is complex in its determination and largely unknown. The presence of conflict and verbal disagreement is not by itself a reliable predictor of child adjustment, as such conflict may be mild, very severe, infrequent or constant. Since labelling parents as 'high-conflict' in some jurisdictions leads to limitations on legal and physical custody rights and options for at least one parent, more discrimination in assessing the extent and type of parental conflict, both during marriage and after separation, is warranted. These dimensions of conflict include the intensity or severity, the focus of the conflict, parental conflict styles, success at resolving conflict, and the presence of buffers protecting the child against parental conflict. An additional consideration is whether the high conflict was part of the marital dynamic and history, was stimulated by the separation itself and/or was generated during protracted, hostile adversarial processes. Such a differentiation of conflict dimensions assists us in understanding why some children appear to be well-adjusted in families with considerable parental conflict, whereas others do

[2] P Amato, L Loomis and A Booth, 'Parental Divorce, Parental Marital Conflict, and Offspring Well-being during Early Adulthood' (1995) 73 *Social Forces* 895.

[3] PR Amato, 'The Consequences of Divorce for Adults and Children' (2000) 62 *Journal of Marriage & Family* 1269; P Amato and B Keith, 'Parental Divorce and Adult Well-being: A Meta-analysis' (1991) 53 *Journal of Marriage & Family* 43; N Zill, D Morrison and M Coiro, 'Long-term Effects of Parental Divorce on Parent–child Relationships, Adjustment, and Achievement in Young Adulthood' (1993) 7 *Journal of Family Psychology* 91.

[4] Amato, *Ibid.*; PL Chase-Lansdale, AJ Cherlin and KE Kierman, 'The Long-term Effects of Parental Divorce on the Mental Health of Young Adults: A Developmental Perspective' (1995) 66 *Child Development,* 1614; A Cherlin, F Furstenberg, L Chase-Lansdale, K Kiernan, P Robins, D Morrison and J Teitler, 'Longitudinal Studies of Divorce on Children in Great Britain and the United States' (1991) 252 *Science* 1386.

not.[5] The consequences of parental violence on child adjustment, and research efforts to understand different types of intimate partner violence, will be considered separately.

Although frequency of conflict was the most common research measure in prior decades, the *intensity* of fighting in marriages now appears to be a more sensitive and effective measure in assessing children's adjustment. High-intensity conflict is more severe, is more often typified by shouting, threats, belligerent behaviours and demeaning language, and is linked to more symptoms in both boys and girls, compared with children experiencing less aggressive parental conflict.[6] Parental conflict that erupts over and focuses on the child, rather than on other marital, parenting or financial issues, is also associated with more symptoms in children, particularly fear, anxiety and self-blame.[7] The manner in which parents fight is also associated with different outcomes in children. Overtly hostile conflict styles (physical and verbal behaviours such as slapping, screaming, derision and contempt) were linked to more adjustment problems in children, compared with children whose parents used covert conflict styles (passive-aggressive behaviours, resentment, tension), or when compared with frequency of conflict.[8]

When parents demonstrate some ability to resolve their conflict through talks, compromise or negotiation, even if there is high conflict, there is less of an impact on their children's adjustment, compared with parents who make no such attempts or never resolve conflict.[9] Many high-conflict parents are capable of reaching agreements in custody mediation on a wide array of child-related issues, and should be encouraged—if not mandated—to use these services.[10]

Recent research focusing on buffers which help shield children in high-conflict marriages has identified the following protective factors: a good relationship with at least one parent or caregiver; parental warmth, especially for boys; and the positive support of siblings.[11] Child characteristics, such as intelligence and good

[5] For a more extensive review of conflict and child adjustment, see JB Kelly, 'Children's Adjustment in Conflicted Marriage and Divorce: A Decade Review of Research' (2000) 39 *Journal of the American Academy of Child and Adolescent Psychiatry* 963.

[6] E Cummings and P Davies, *Children and Marital Conflict* (Guilford Publications, 1994); MR Dadds, E Atkinson, C Turner, GJ Blums and B Lendich, 'Family Conflict and Child Adjustment: Evidence for a Cognitive-contextual Model of Intergenerational Transmission' (1999) 13 *Journal of Family Psychology,* 194; E Vandewater and J Lansford, 'Influences of Family Structure and Parental Conflict on Children's Well-being' (1998) 47 *Family Relations* 323.

[7] J Grych and F Fincham, 'Children's Appraisal of Marital Conflict: Initial Investigations of the Cognitive-contextual Framework' (1993) 64 *Child Development* 215.

[8] C Buehler, A Krishnakumar, G Stone. et al., 'Interparental Conflict Styles and Youth Problem Behaviors: A Two-sample Replication Study' (1998) 60 *Journal of Marriage and Family* 119.

[9] E Cummings and P Davies, *Children and Marital Conflict* (Guilford Publications, 1994).

[10] RE Emery, *Renegotiating Family Relationships: Divorce, Child Custody and Mediation* (Guilford Publications, 1994); JB Kelly, 'The Determination of Child Custody' (1994) 4 *The Future of Children: Children and Divorce* 121, The David and Lucile Packard Foundation, 300 Second Street, Los Altos, CA 94022. www.futureofchildren.org; JB Kelly, 'A Decade of Divorce Mediation Research: Some Answers and Questions' (1996) 34 *Family and Conciliation Courts Review* 373.

[11] ML Caya and JH Liem, 'The Role of Sibling Support in High-conflict Families' (1998) 68 *American Journal of Orthopsychiatry* 327; R Emery, *Marriage, Divorce, and Children's Adjustment,*

cognitive capacity, may also provide buffers against high conflict,[12] particularly in the context of some of the above protective factors. These buffers remain important after separation, and need to be considered in making decisions about residence and contact. If the child enjoyed a good relationship with both parents—for example, in families with intense or frequent conflict—then placing restrictions on contact or shared decision-making because of the conflict may deny the child the beneficial effects of the buffer.

Some high-conflict parents seen at separation have a marital history of mild to moderate conflict, and do not experience much conflict about their children. In such instances, the reasons for separation and the manner in which the separation occurred may have engendered intense anger and conflict, which—with appropriate interventions—is likely to diminish over time.[13] Other high-conflict parents have severe personality disorders and psychiatric illnesses, which make it less likely that rage, vindictiveness, and struggles for control and power will subside substantially without special interventions.[14] As a result of the stress of divorce, all separating parents are quite vulnerable to developing or increasing their anger, conflict and suspiciousness, particularly with exposure to certain adversarial processes and practices, including personally demeaning and attacking affidavits,[15] false allegations, and advice to not speak to the other parent. Such parents may require more intensive legal and educational interventions to diminish the conflict regarding their children after divorce.

How Does Marital Conflict Affect Children?

Severe conflict in marriage impacts on children's adjustment in both direct and indirect ways. Direct effects include children's modelling and replication of aggressive parental behaviours, symptoms of anxiety, fear, physiological arousal, illness and depression, and their failure to learn effective social interaction and dispute resolution skills from their parents.[16] Further, research indicates that intense conflict has negative physiological effects on young children's capacity to

2nd edn (Sage, 1999); V Neighbors, R Forehand and D McVicar, 'Resilient Adolescents and Interparental Conflict' (1993) 63 *American Journal of Orthopsychiatry* 462; E Vandewater and J Lansford, 'Influences of Family Structure and Parental Conflict on Children's Well-being' (1998) 47 *Family Relations* 323.

[12] J Grych and F Fincham, 'Children's Appraisal of Marital Conflict: Initial Investigations of the Cognitive-contextual Framework' (1993) 64 *Child Development* 215.

[13] RE Emery, *Renegotiating Family Relationships: Divorce, Child Custody and Mediation* (Guilford Publications, 1994); JB Kelly and JR Johnston, 'The Alienated Child: A Reformulation of Parental Alienation Syndrome' (2001) 39 *Family Court Review* 249; J Wallerstein and J Kelly, *Surviving the Breakup: How Parents and Children Cope with Divorce* (Basic Books, 1980).

[14] Kelly and Johnston, *Ibid.*; JR Johnston and V Roseby, *In the Name of the Child: A Developmental Approach to Understanding and Helping Children of Conflict and Violent Divorce* (Free Press, 1997); JR Johnston, MG Walters and S Friedlander, 'Therapeutic Work with Alienated Children and their Families' (2001) 39 *Family Court Review.*

[15] D Ellis and N Stuckless, *Mediating and Negotiating Marital Conflicts* (Sage, 1996).

[16] E Cummings and P Davies, *Children and Marital Conflict* (Guilford Publications, 1994).

self-regulate strong emotion.[17] Indirect effects of high marital conflict are the manner in which both father–child and mother–child relationships are negatively affected. With mothers, persistent, intense marital conflict undermines the quality of the mother–child relationship, through a spillover of negative emotion and more negative parenting practices and behaviours.[18] In particular, mothers are less warm and accepting of their children, and use more erratic and harsh discipline, compared with mothers in low-conflict marriages.[19] Children's reports of interparental conflict are related to their own assessments of parental acceptance and inconsistent discipline.[20] Interparental hostility is also linked to more troubled sibling and peer relationships in school-age children.[21]

Fathers in intensely conflicted marriages withdraw more from the parenting role, and from their children, than do fathers in low-conflict marriages, and are more negative and intrusive with their children.[22] This may be related in part to the repeated observation that mothers are often gatekeepers of paternal involvement, which may intensify in conditions of high conflict. Maternal attitudes toward the extent of fathers' parenting predict father involvement more strongly than do fathers' desires or ability to parent.[23] The negative consequences of intense conflict on the parenting of both fathers and mothers, and on parent–child

[17] M DeBellis, 'Post-traumatic Stress Disorder and Acute Stress Disorder', in R Ammerman and M Hersen (eds), *Handbook of Prevention and Treatment with Children and Adolescents: Intervention in the Real World Context* (Wiley, 1997); A Lieberman and P Van Horn, 'Attachment, Trauma, and Domestic Violence: Implications for Child Custody' (1998) 7 *Child and Adolescent Psychiatric Clinics of North America* 423; JD Osofsky, 'The Impact of Violence on Children', in (1999) 9 *The Future of Children: Domestic Violence and Children* 33, David and Lucile Packard Foundation, Los Altos, CA.

[18] SA Anderson and DR Cramer-Benjamin, 'The Impact of Couple Violence on Parenting and Children: An Overview and Clinical Implications' (1999) 27 *American Journal of Family Therapy;* IA Appel and G Holden, 'The Co-occurrence of Spouse and Physical Child Abuse: A Review and Appraisal' (1998) 12 *Journal of Family Psychology* 578; J Belsky, L Youngblade, M Rovine and B Volling, 'Patterns of Marital Change and Parent–child Interaction' (1991) 53 *Journal of Marriage and Family* 487; A Harrist and R Ainslie, 'Parental Discord and Child Behavior Problems' (1998) 19 *Journal of Family Issues* 140; PK Kerig, PA Cowan and CP Cowan, 'Marital Quality and Gender Differences in Parent–child Interaction' (1993) 29 *Developmental Psychology* 931.

[19] E Cummings and P Davies, *Children and Marital Conflict* (Guilford Publications, 1994); EM Hetherington, *Coping with Divorce, Single Parenting, and Remarriage* (Lawrence Erlbaum Associates, 1999); A Krishnakumar and C Buehler, 'Interparental Conflict and Parenting Behaviors: A Meta-Analytic Review' (2000) 49 *Family Relations* 25.

[20] NA Gonzales, SC Pitts, NE Hill and MW Roosa, 'A Mediational Model of the Impact of Interparental Conflict on Child Adjustment in a Multiethnic, Low-income Sample' (2000) 14 *Journal of Family Psychology* 365.

[21] CM Stocker and L Youngblade, 'Marital Conflict and Parental Hostility: Links with Children's Sibling and Peer Relationships' (1999) 13 *Journal of Family Psychology* 598.

[22] SA Anderson and DR Cramer-Benjamin, 'The Impact of Couple Violence on Parenting and Children: An Overview and Clinical Implications' (1999) 27 *American Journal of Family Therapy* 1; IA Appel and G Holden, 'The Co-occurrence of Spouse and Physical Child Abuse: A Review and Appraisal' (1998) 12 *Journal of Family Psychology* 578; J Belsky, L Youngblade, M Rovine and B Volling, 'Patterns of Marital Change and Parent–child Interaction' (1991) 53 *Journal of Marriage and Family* 487.

[23] See WJ Doherty, 'Responsible Fathering: An Overview and Conceptual Framework' (1998) 60 *Journal of Marriage and Family* 277; and JH Pleck, 'Paternal Involvement: Level, Sources, and Consequences', in M Lamb (ed), *The Role of the Father in Child Development*, 3rd edn (Wiley, 1997) for reviews.

relationships, indicate that effective divorce education programmes should focus on restoring good parenting patterns and attitudes in both parents.

VIOLENCE IN MARRIED AND SEPARATED FAMILIES

Marital Violence and Children's Adjustment

Violence occurs more frequently in marriages with intense or severe conflict, and is more strongly associated with adjustment problems in children than is marital conflict.[24] School-age children repeatedly exposed to violence are more aggressive, and have more depressive symptoms, anxiety, phobias, distractibility and intrusive thoughts compared with children in non-violent families.[25] More recent research into partner violence has also reported symptoms of psychic trauma and post-traumatic stress disorder in infants, young children and older youths, particularly when other risk factors—including child abuse, psychiatric illnesses in parents and poverty—are present.[26] The degree of trauma is related to the strength of children's emotional attachment to both the perpetrator and victim, with the strongest reactions linked to violence against caregivers with whom they are close.

Aside from the direct impact on children's adjustment of exposure to violence, as with intense marital conflict, children's adjustment is negatively affected by poor parenting practices in violent marriages. The parenting of violent fathers,

[24] JW Fantuzzo and WK Mohr, 'Prevalence and Effects of Child Exposure to Domestic Violence' (1999) 9 *The Future of Children: Domestic Violence and Children* 21; E Jouriles, W Norwood, R McDonald, J Vincent and A Mahoney, 'Physical Violence and Other Forms of Marital Aggression: Links with Children's Behavior Problems' (1996) 10 *Journal of Family Psychology* 223; C McNeal and P Amato, 'Parents' Marital Violence: Long-term Consequences for Children' (1998) 19 *Journal of Family Issues* 123.

[25] JR Kolbo, EH Blakely and D Engleman, 'Children who Witness Domestic Violence: A Review of Empirical Literature' (1996) 11 *Journal of Interpersonal Violence* 281; JD Osofsky, 'The Impact of Violence on Children' (1999) 9 *The Future of Children: Domestic Violence and Children* 33, David and Lucile Packard Foundation, Los Altos, CA, www.futureofchildren.org; D Pelcovitz, SJ Kaplan, RR DeRosa, FS Mandel and S Selzinger, 'Psychiatric Disorders in Adolescents Exposed to Domestic Violence and Physical Abuse' (2000) 70 *American Journal of Orthopsychiatry* 360.

[26] CC Ayoub, RM Deutsch and A Maragonorr, 'Emotional Distress in Children of High-conflict Divorce: The Impact of Marital Conflict and Violence' (1999) 37 *Family and Conciliation Courts Review* 297; M DeBellis, 'Posttraumatic Stress Disorder and Acute Stress Disorder', in R Ammerman and M Hersen (eds), *Handbook of Prevention and Treatment with Children and Adolescents: Intervention in the Real World Context* (Wiley, 1997); JW Fantuzzo and WK Mohr, 'Prevalence and Effects of Child Exposure to Domestic Violence' (1999) 9 *The Future of Children: Domestic Violence and Children* 21; KL Kilpatrick and LM Williams, 'Post-traumatic Stress Disorder in Child Witnesses to Domestic Violence' (1997) 67(4) *American Journal of Orthopsychiatry* 639; A Lieberman and P Van Horn, 'Attachment, Trauma, and Domestic Violence: Implications for Child Custody' (1998) 7(2) *Child and Adolescent Psychiatric Clinics of North America* 423; JD Osofsky, (1999). 'The Impact of Violence on Children', in (1999) 9 *The Future of Children: Domestic Violence and Children,* 33. David and Lucile Packard Foundation, Los Altos, CA; JD Osofsky, 'The Impact of Violence on Children' (1999) 9 *The Future of Children: Domestic Violence and Children* 33, David and Lucile Packard Foundation, Los Altos, CA, www.futureofchildren.org

including more coercive, irritable and emotionally aggressive interactions and physical punishment, appears to be more negative for children's outcomes than the more emotionally withdrawn, erratic and less effective parenting practices of non-violent, and violent, mothers. Violence in marriages is also associated with more physical abuse of children, compared with non-violent marriages. It is estimated that, in violent marriages, children are abused by one or both parents between 45 and 70 per cent of the time.[27] They are also at higher risk of sexual abuse,[28] and more likely to be the victims of sibling violence than children in non-violent households.[29] The cumulative and negative impact of exposure to parent violence is intensified by the child's own experience of physical abuse and poorer parent–child relationships, as noted above. Thus it is not surprising that children in violent, high-conflict marriages have more adjustment problems, of greater severity, than do children in non-violent high-conflict marriages, and both groups have significantly more negative outcomes than children in non-violent, low-conflict marriages.[30]

Types of Couple Violence

For the past two decades, much of the research and public policy debate on domestic violence has focused on men who batter women. As necessary and valuable as this has been, until recently the debate has failed to distinguish between different categories of violence in intimate relationships, and the sequella of such violence after separation. There has been limited but useful research which provides a more differentiated understanding of the use of violence in relationships during marriage, cohabitation and after separation. Most of the research demonstrates that most couple violence is bidirectional, is initiated in roughly equal frequency by both men and women, varies in frequency and levels of severity, and has different psychological and physical characteristics and outcomes.[31] In a study of extreme high-conflict parent couples after separation, five categories of marital

[27] Fantuzzo and Mohr, *Ibid.*; G Margolin, 'Effects of Domestic Violence on Children', in PK Trickett and CJ Shellenbach (eds), *Violence Against Children in the Family and the Community* (American Psychological Association, 1998).

[28] RF Wilson, 'Children at Risk: The Sexual Exploitation of Female Children after Divorce' (2001) 86(2) *Cornell Law Review* 251.

[29] G Margolin, 'Effects of Domestic Violence on Children', in PK Trickett and CJ Shellenbach (eds), *Violence Against Children in the Family and the Community,* (American Psychological Association, 1998).

[30] JR Johnston and L Campbell, 'A Clinical Typology of Interparental Violence in Disputed Custody Divorces' (1993) 63 *American Journal of Orthopyschiatry* 190; C McNeal and P Amato, 'Parents' Marital Violence: Long-term Consequences for Children' (1998) 19(2) *Journal of Family Issues* 123.

[31] JW Fantuzzo and WK Mohr, 'Prevalence and Effects of Child Exposure to Domestic Violence' (1999) 9 *The Future of Children: Domestic Violence and Children* 21; MP Johnson and KJ Ferraro, 'Research on Domestic Violence in the 1990s: Making Distinctions' (2000) 62 *Journal of Marriage and Family* 948; Johnston and Campbell, *Ibid.*; MJ Kwong, K Bartholomew and DG Dutton, 'Gender Differences in Patterns of Relationship Violence in Alberta' (1999) 31(3) *Canadian Journal of Behavioral Science* 150.

and separation violence were identified: ongoing/episodic male battering; female-initiated violence; male controlling interactive violence; separation-engendered and post-divorce violence; and psychotic and paranoid reactions.[32] In contrast to male battering, interactive violence was initiated by both men and women, was least severe in intensity of all categories, rarely involving injuries, typically ceased after separation, and did not involve fear of the partner. Separation-engendered violence involved only one or two episodes, and typically violence did not recur when a restraining order was obtained. Most importantly, these men and women had never been violent during the marriage. These two categories of violence occurred most frequently, and the violence caused by severe mental illness was least frequent, in this sample. Such research indicates that different orders, interventions and treatment should be considered and implemented for the perpetrators in each category, but research lags far behind in this regard, in part because of the near-exclusive focus on male battering in family law and legislation. Partners involved in interactive violence, for example, appear to be capable of participating meaningfully in divorce education programmes and custody mediation, whereas mediation is often inappropriate for women who have been battered. Restraining or protective orders are most effective in situations of mutual interactive and separation-engendered violence, but often are meaningless and flagrantly violated in situations of battering, or violence which is the result of paranoid and disordered, psychotic thinking.

Other studies have described four categories of violence in partnered relationships: common couple violence; intimate terrorism; violent resistance; and mutual violent control.[33] Common couple violence, the most prevalent form of couple violence, occurs least frequently, is mutual in instigation and participation, and involves the least serious injuries, if any. It is quite similar to Johnston and Campbell's interactive violence.[34] In contrast, intimate terrorism is perpetuated almost exclusively by males, escalates over time, often involves serious injury and threats to injure the children, and is more often reported in samples of women in shelters or services for battered women.[35] Two subtypes of intimate terrorism have been identified and studied: the violent-antisocial (cold, cruel, calculating), and the dysphoric-borderline (dependent, needy, impulsive).[36] Such research brings into question standard policies of ordering the same anger management programmes for all violent perpetrators, as opposed to more differentiated interventions of varying length, intensity and focus. Whereas both men and women involved in interactive or common couple violence, and separation-

[32] Johnston and Campbell, *Ibid.*

[33] See MP Johnson and KJ Ferraro, 'Research on Domestic Violence in the 1990s: Making Distinctions' (2000) 62 *Journal of Marriage and Family* 948.

[34] JR Johnston and L Campbell, 'A Clinical Typology of Interparental Violence in Disputed Custody Divorces' (1993) 63 *American Journal of Orthopyschiatry* 190.

[35] MP Johnson and KJ Ferraro, 'Research on Domestic Violence in the 1990s: Making Distinctions' (2000) 62 *Journal of Marriage and Family* 948.

[36] N Jacobson and J Gottman, *When Men Batter Women: New Insights into Ending Abusive Relationships* (Simon & Schuster, 1998); Johnson and Ferraro, *Ibid.*

engendered violence, may benefit from well crafted programs for managing anger, such programmes are likely to be ineffective for intimate terrorists with sociopathic personalities.

A number of studies report similar prevalence rates of violence perpetrated by men and women (12–13 per cent). These studies most often reflect the incidence of common couple violence in larger community samples.[37] However, these prevalence rates do not address the fact that male violence is likely to be more severe, cause more serious injuries, and result in more fear among female partners, compared with female violence. Considerable research is needed to further understand various categories of violence, in terms of how they differentially affect children's adjustment, whether some mothers and fathers with a history of violence can capably parent, and what orders and interventions will be effective in separation and divorce situations.

DIVORCE AND CHILD ADJUSTMENT

Children of divorce have significantly more adjustment and achievement problems than do children in never-divorced families.[38] More recent and large-scale studies in the United States, using sophisticated methodologies, report smaller differences and great overlap between divorced and never-divorced children than did earlier studies. The magnitude of the differences is quite small and the majority of children of divorce fall within the average range of adjustment on standardised measures.[39]

Aspects of the divorce experience do increase risk for many children, particularly loss of economic and psychological resources, diminished parental support, discipline and contact, continued high interparental hostility, disruptive life changes, and the remarriages and redivorce of residential parents. For those youngsters who are already at the higher-risk end of the bell curve as their parents separate and divorce, separation escalates the risk of more enduring, negative outcomes. On the other hand, certain protective factors are associated with more positive outcomes, including psychological stability of parents, good parent–child

[37] MJ Kwong, K Bartholomew and DG Dutton, 'Gender Differences in Patterns of Relationship Violence in Alberta' (1999) 31(3) *Canadian Journal of Behavioral Science* 150.

[38] For reviews, see PR Amato, 'The Consequences of Divorce for Adults and Children' (2000) 62(4) *Journal of Marriage & Family* 1269; R Emery, *Marriage, Divorce, and Children's Adjustment*, 2nd edn (Sage, 1999); EM Hetherington, *Coping with Divorce, Single Parenting, and Remarriage* (Lawrence Erlbaum Associates, 1999); JB Kelly, 'Children's Adjustment in Conflicted Marriage and Divorce: A Decade Review of Research' (2000) 39(8) *Journal of the American Academy of Child and Adolescent Psychiatry* 963; B Rodgers and J Pryor, *Divorce and Separation: The Outcomes for Children* (Joseph Rowntree Foundation, York, England YO30 6WP, 1998).

[39] PR Amato, 'Life-span Adjustment of Children to Their Parents' Divorce' (1994) 4(1) *The Future of Children: Children and Divorce* 143, The David and Lucille Packard Foundation, 300 Second St., Los Altos, CA 94022. www.futureofchildren.org; PR Amato, 'The Consequences of Divorce for Adults and Children' (2000) 62(4) *Journal of Marriage & Family* 1269; R Emery, *Marriage, Divorce, and Children's Adjustment*, 2nd edn (Sage, 1999); Hetherington, *Ibid.*

relationships, the continued involvement of both parents after divorce, pre-separation positive child adjustment, and existing positive external resources, including regular child support payments.[40]

Common Adjustment Problems in Divorced Children

The nature of the problems seen in divorced children include externalising behavioural problems (acting out, anti-social behaviours and problems with authority figures and parents), internalising problems (depression and anxiety), social and economic difficulties, and academic achievement problems. Although a number of older studies have reported that boys have more adjustment problems than girls,[41] other results are not consistent. The interactions between gender, age at separation, pre-separation adjustment, sex of residential parent, quality of relationships with both parents, and level of conflict confound efforts to resolve the gender issue. One large nationally representative sample of married and divorced–never remarried families assessed at two points in time found no gender differences that could be linked to divorce.[42] Boys had significantly more externalising behaviours than girls in the overall population, regardless of family structure, including being suspended or expelled from school, getting in trouble with police, and running away from home.

Academic Performance

Divorce has been associated with lowered academic performance and achievement test scores, but some of the differences are evident prior to separation.[43] The academic differences between children of divorced and married parents are modest and are reduced, but do not disappear, when the income and education of the parents are controlled for.[44] Compared with children in married families, children of divorced parents miss more school, do less homework, watch more TV and have less parental supervision of homework.[45] The school dropout rate of divorced

[40] See PR Amato, 'The Consequences of Divorce for Adults and Children' (2000) 62(4) *Journal of Marriage & Family* 1269; Emery, *Ibid.*; Hetherington, *Ibid.*; S McLanahan, 'Father Absence and Welfare of Children', in Hetherington, *Ibid.*; RL Simons, KH Lin, LC Gordon, RD Conger and FO Lorenz, 'Explaining the Higher Incidence of Adjustment Problems among Children of Divorce Compared with those in Two-parent Families' (1999) 61(4) *Journal of Marriage and Family* 1020.

[41] Hetheringon, *Ibid.*

[42] E Vandewater and J Lansfor, 'Influences of Family Structure and Parental Conflict on Children's Well-being' (1998) 47(4) *Family Relations* 323.

[43] S-L Pong and D-B Ju, 'The Effects of Change in Family Structure and Income on Dropping Out of Middle and High School' (2000) 21(2) *Journal of Family Issues* 147; Y Sun and Y Li, 'Marital Disruption, Parental Investment, and Children's Academic Achievement' (2001) 22 *Journal of Family Issues* 27.

[44] S McLanahan, 'Father Absence and Welfare of Children', in EM Hetherington, *Coping with Divorce, Single Parenting, and Remarriage* (Lawrence Erlbaum Associates, 1999).

[45] Hetherington, *Ibid.*; McLanahan, *Ibid.*

youngsters is more than two to three times as high as that of never-divorced children, but when economic discrepancies are included in analyses, the dropout rate is related more to poverty than to separation or family structure.[46] Divorced children are also less likely to earn a college degree, not just for economic reasons but because parental aspirations for educational attainment decrease for adolescents in divorced families but increase for adolescents in married households.[47]

When fathers are involved with children's school and schoolwork after separation, there is less decline in academic functioning. Youngsters with more involved fathers are less likely to be expelled or suspended, get better grades, and like school better, compared with children who have less involved fathers after divorce. In fact, children with more involved fathers do not differ in school performance and achievement from children in married families.[48] This would suggest a re-evaluation of the extent and pattern of distribution of child contact with fathers. When father contacts are limited to weekends only, the peripheral nature of their involvement may limit potential cognitive, psychological and monitoring contributions to children's academic work and achievements.

Standard of Living Before and After Separation

Many children experience a substantial decline in their standard of living in the custodial home after divorce, leading to greater economic instability and reduced access to resources that never-divorced children are more likely to have, including better schools and neighbourhoods.[49] Newer studies indicate that a substantial number of divorced families were poorer prior to separation, compared with still-married families, suggesting that the stresses and outcomes associated with limited resources were present for some time in these families.[50] After divorce, inadequate child support, unemployment and weak enforcement policies are largely responsible for economic decline, beyond the greater financial burden of supporting two households. It is estimated that the economic problems of divorced households account for as much as half of the adjustment problems seen in divorced children.[51]

[46] S-L Pong and D-B Ju, 'The Effects of Change in Family Structure and Income on Dropping Out of Middle and High School' (2000) 21(2) *Journal of Family Issues* 147.

[47] S McLanahan, 'Father Absence and Welfare of Children', in EM Hetherington, *Coping with Divorce, Single Parenting, and Remarriage* (Lawrence Erlbaum Associates, 1999).

[48] CW Nord, D Brimhall and J West, *Fathers' Involvement in Their Children's Schools* (National Center for Education Statistics, US Dept. of Education, Washington, DC 20208–5574, 1997).

[49] PR Amato, 'The Consequences of Divorce for Adults and Children' (2000) 62(4) *Journal of Marriage & Family* 1269; S McLanahan, 'Father Absence and Welfare of Children', in EM Hetherington, *Coping with Divorce, Single Parenting, and Remarriage* (Lawrence Erlbaum Associates, 1999).

[50] KA Clarke-Steward, DL Vandell, K McCartney, MT Owen and C Booth, 'Effects of Parental Separation and Divorce on Very Young Children' (2000) 14(2) *Journal of Family Psychology* 304; S-L Pong and D-B Ju, 'The Effects of Change in Family Structure and Income on Dropping Out of Middle and High School' (2000) 21(2) *Journal of Family Issues* 147.

[51] S McLanahan, 'Father Absence and Welfare of Children', in EM Hetherington, *Coping with Divorce, Single Parenting, and Remarriage* (Lawrence Erlbaum Associates, 1999).

Impact of Divorce on Young Adults

As young adults, divorced children have more relationship problems, and poorer socio-economic attainment than do young adults in never-divorced families.[52] Again, the magnitude of the differences is small, and the pathology of young adults has been exaggerated in small clinical studies.[53] By their mid-thirties, young adults from divorced families are not distinguishable from those whose parents did not divorce.[54] For young adults, painful childhood experiences and memories are the hallmark of divorce, rather than enduring pathology or adjustment problems.[55] The longer-term resiliency of the vast majority of children of divorce is clearly evident.

POST-DIVORCE FACTORS AND CHILDREN'S ADJUSTMENT

Adjustment and Parenting of the Residential Parent

Living in the custody of psychologically disturbed or character-disordered residential parents is associated with impaired emotional, social, and academic adjustment in children after divorce.[56] One longitudinal study indicated that the delinquent activities of mothers as adolescents were significantly linked to the antisocial behaviours of their children fourteen years later.[57] The type and quality of parenting after separation and divorce is also crucial. When residential and non-residential parents adequately monitor their children's activities, discipline authoritatively, maintain age-appropriate expectations, and provide appropriate emotional support, children and adolescents are better adjusted compared with divorced children whose parents provide less appropriate parenting.[58] These

[52] PR Amato, 'The Consequences of Divorce for Adults and Children' (2000) 62(4) *Journal of Marriage & Family* 1269; R Emery, *Marriage, Divorce, and Children's Adjustment*, 2nd edn (Sage, 1999); McLanahan, *Ibid.*

[53] J Wallerstein, J Lewis, and S Blakeslee, *The Unexpected Legacy of Divorce: A 25 Year Landmark Study* (Hyperion, 2000).

[54] PL Chase-Lansdale, AJ Cherlin and KE Kierman, 'The Long-term Effects of Parental Divorce on the Mental Health of Young Adults: A Developmental Perspective' (1995) 66 *Child Development* 1614; R Emery, *Marriage, Divorce, and Children's Adjustment*, 2nd edn (Sage, 1999); EM Hetherington (ed), *Coping with Divorce, Single Parenting, and Remarriage: A Risk and Resiliency Perspective* (Lawrence Erlbaum Associates, 1995).

[55] L Laumann-Billings, and RE Emery, 'Distress among Young Adults from Divorced Families' (2000) 14(4) *Journal of Family Psychology* 671.

[56] RE Emery, M Waldron, KM Kitzmann and J Aaron, 'Delinquent Behavior, Future Divorce or Non-marital Childrearing, and Externalizing Behavior among Offspring: A 14-year Prospective Study' (1999) 13(4) *Journal of Family Psychology* 568; JR Johnston, 'Research Update: Children's Adjustment in Sole Custody Compared to Joint Custody Families and Principles for Custody Decision Making' (1995) 33(4) *Family and Conciliation Courts Review* 415; N Kalter, A Kloner, S Schreiser, and K Okla, 'Predictors of Children's Post-divorce Adjustment' (1989) 59(4) *American Journal of Orthopsychiatry* 605.

[57] Emery et al., *Ibid.*

[58] PR Amato and JG Gilbreth, 'Nonresident Fathers and Children's Well-being: A Meta-analysis'

findings provide compelling reasons to offer divorce education programmes focusing on appropriate parental behaviours and disciplinary practices following separation.

Access to the Contact Parent

A number of large studies have reported no overall relationship between frequency of contact with the non-residential parent—usually the father—and children's adjustment.[59] Clearly, frequency of contact does not ensure positive meaning in the father–child relationship, as fathers range from very involved and caring to those who are self-absorbed, inconstant or emotionally abusive. Recent studies focusing on the quality of the father–child relationship, level of conflict, maternal acceptance of visits and type of paternal parenting provide strong evidence of father impact on child adjustment.[60] When parental conflict is low, high levels of father–child contact after separation and divorce are significantly related to positive outcomes in children.[61] However, several studies indicate that when conflict is very high, children—particularly boys—living with their mothers are more likely to be negatively affected by frequent contact or transitions.[62] Frequent contact in such circumstances may create even more strain between mothers and sons, adding to the greater acrimony between them following divorce compared with mothers and daughters.[63] No research has been conducted on high-conflict families that use neutral exchange points—such as schools or daycare, which eliminate face-to-face contacts between angry parents that children might otherwise experience—to implement contact.

Newer data indicate that maternal dissatisfaction with visits is more predictive of child well-being than is conflict.[64] Mothers dissatisfied with higher levels of paternal involvement had less well-adjusted children, *regardless* of levels of

(1999) 61 *Journal of Marriage and Family* 557; C Buchanan, E Maccoby and S Dornbusch, *Adolescents After Divorce* (Harvard University Press, 1996); EM Hetherington, *Coping with Divorce, Single Parenting, and Remarriage* (Lawrence Erlbaum Associates, 1999); E Maccoby and R Mnookin, *Dividing the Child* (Cambridge University Press, 1992); B Neighbors, R Forehand, R and D McVicar, 'Resilient Adolescents and Interparental Conflict' (1993) 63(3) *American Journal of Orthopsychiatry* 462.

[59] See PR Amato, 'The Consequences of Divorce for Adults and Children' (2000) 62(4) *Journal of Marriage & Family* 1269; R Emery, *Marriage, Divorce, and Children's Adjustment*, 2nd edn (Sage, 1999).

[60] Amato, *Ibid.*; PR Amato and JG Gilbreth, 'Nonresident Fathers and Children's Well-being: A Meta-analysis' (1999) 61 *Journal of Marriage and Family* 557; ME Lamb, 'Non-custodial Parents and Their Impact on the Children of Divorce', in RA Thompson and PR Amato (eds), *The Post-divorce Family: Research and Policy Issues* (Sage, 1999).

[61] PR Amato and S Rezac, 'Contact with Residential Parents, Interparental Conflict, and Children's Behaviour' (1994) 15 *Journal of Family Issues* 191.

[62] *Ibid.*; T Johnston, Summary of research on the decrease of court involvement after the appointment of a Special Master, unpublished manuscript (2000).

[63] EM Hetherington, *Coping with Divorce, Single Parenting, and Remarriage* (Lawrence Erlbaum Associates, 1999).

[64] P King and H Heard, 'Nonresident Father Visitation, Parental Conflict, and Mother's Satisfaction: What's Best for Child Well-being?' (1999) 61 *Journal of Marriage and Family* 385.

conflict. Overall, the majority of mothers in this large study were satisfied with high levels of paternal involvement, and tended to view some conflict as a normative part of coparenting after divorce.

When fathers feel close to their children and engage in active parenting, high levels of paternal involvement are also linked to better outcomes in their school-age children.[65] Active parenting includes help with homework and projects, providing emotional support, and using authoritative discipline. The ability to actively parent—which is more likely if there is meaningful midweek as well as weekend contact—is linked as well to better academic performance, compared with those children with less actively involved fathers. Further, joint legal custody is linked to higher rates of father contact,[66] and to more positive child adjustment, compared with children whose mothers have sole legal custody. There was no difference in conflict levels in the two groups. Although the joint legal custody families functioned better prior to final divorce on a number of variables, these findings remain significant after controlling for a large number of pre-separation variables, including income, education, anger, marital conflict, involvement in child rearing and child adjustment.[67]

Very young children, as well, need sufficient regular contact with their non-residential parents to develop and maintain strong attachments, assuming the parent has adequate caretaking abilities. When infants and toddlers are limited in their contacts to several hours a week or every other week, their attachments to their fathers may weaken and become more insecure. In such circumstances, young children often express more anxiety and resistance at the time of transition.[68]

Limited time with the non-residential parent has lingering consequences for older adolescents and young adults as well, in terms of feelings of loss, missing their fathers and economic assistance.[69] The majority of 820 college students, eight years after divorce, reported that they had too little time with their fathers, and wanted more contact with them over the years. They indicated that their fathers also wanted more time, but that their mothers were opposed to more contact. The living arrangement preferred by 70 per cent of these students was equal time with each parent. Among the 10 per cent of this sample who did live in shared physical time arrangements, 93 per cent said that this was the best living arrangement for them.[70] Young adults who lived in sole custody arrangements also expressed

[65] PR Amato and JG Gilbreth, 'Nonresident Fathers and Children's Well-being: A Meta-analysis' (1999) 61 *Journal of Marriage and Family* 557.

[66] J Selzer, 'Father by Law: Effects of Joint Legal Custody on Nonresident Fathers' Involvement with Children' (1998) 35(2) *Demography* 135.

[67] ML Gunnoe and SL Braver, 'The Effects of Joint Legal Custody on Mothers, Fathers, and Children Controlling for Factors that Predispose a Sole Maternal vs Joint Legal Award' (2001) 25(1) *Law and Human Behavior* 25.

[68] JB Kelly and ME Lamb, 'Using Child Development Research to Make Appropriate Custody and Access Decisions for Young Children' (2000) 38(3) *Family and Conciliation Courts Review* 297.

[69] WV Fabricius and JA Hall, 'Young Adults' Perspectives on Divorce: Living Arrangements' (2000) 38(4) *Family and Conciliation Courts Review* 446; L Laumann-Billings and RE Emery, 'Distress Among Young Adults from Divorced Families' (2000) 14(4) *Journal of Family Psychology* 671.

[70] Fabricius and Hall, *Ibid.*

more feelings of loss, and more often viewed their lives through the lens of divorce, compared with those young adults who grew up in more shared physical custody arrangements.[71]

After controlling for income, fathers with more contact with their children, and fathers with joint legal custody, made greater financial contributions to their children's college expenses, compared with fathers with less contact or no legal custody. For each increment in contact with children, fathers paid incrementally more.[72]

Parental Conflict During Separation and After Divorce

Most children exposed to intense and frequent marital conflict experience much less conflict on a day-to-day basis after separation, and over time hostility between parents diminishes significantly. And, while protracted, bitter litigation causes longer-term negative consequences for contact frequency and paternal involvement: three years after divorce, only 8–12 per cent of parents remain in very high conflict.[73] It is important to separate the extent of legal conflict parents engage in from the amount of *actual* conflict that children experience after separation, either during transitions or within each residence. Some parents, despite intense legal conflict, are able to encapsulate that conflict and protect their children.[74] When parents continue their bitter conflict after divorce, it is the extent to which they put their children in the middle of the conflict that determines children's outcomes. If parents have high conflict, but leave their children out of it, then their adjustment does not differ from children whose parents have low or no conflict.[75] Cooperation between parents is always preferable, but is not essential if children's other needs can be met. Many parents engage in parallel parenting in the years after divorce, each of them parenting adequately in their own domains, without apparent harm and even with seeming benefit to children.[76]

[71] L Laumann-Billings and RE Emery, 'Distress Among Young Adults from Divorced Families' (2000) 14(4) *Journal of Family Psychology* 671.

[72] WV Fabricius, SL Braver and K Mack, 'Divorced Parents' Financial Support of their Children's College Expenses', paper presented at the Association of Family and Conciliation Courts annual conference, New Orleans, June 2000 (manuscript under review).

[73] P King and H Heard, 'Nonresident Father Visitation, Parental Conflict, and Mother's Satisfaction: What's best for child well-being?' (1999) 61 *Journal of Marriage and Family* 385; E Maccoby and R Mnookin, *Dividing the Child* (Cambridge University Press, 1992).

[74] EM Hetherington, *Coping with Divorce, Single Parenting, and Remarriage* (Lawrence Erlbaum Associates, 1999).

[75] C Buchanan, E Maccoby and S Dornbusch, *Adolescents After Divorce* (Harvard University Press, 1996); C Buchanan, E Maccoby, E and S Dornbusch, 'Caught between Parents: Adolescents' Experience in Divorce Homes' (1991) 62 *Child Development* 1008.

[76] E Maccoby and R Mnookin, *Dividing the Child* (Cambridge University Press, 1992); MF Whiteside and BJ Becker, 'Parental Factors and the Young Child's Postdivorce Adjustment: A meta-analysis with implications for parenting arrangements' (2000) 14(1) *Journal of Family Psychology* 5.

LEGAL AND PSYCHOLOGICAL INTERVENTIONS

The accumulated body of divorce and child adjustment research has provided considerable clarity in terms of our understanding of the needs of children at separation or after divorce—particularly which factors will promote good outcomes and which will minimise risk for children. The adversarial process too often undermines attempts to meet those needs. The central failings of the adversarial process in divorce are the failure to protect children from escalating conflict, the destruction of the possibility of civility between parents, the win–lose atmosphere which encourages parental irresponsibility, and the diminution of important parent–child relationships. These failings emerge from the basic nature of the adversarial process itself, which pits parents against each other, promotes polarised and positional thinking about each other's deficiencies, and discourages communication, cooperation and more mature thinking about children's needs at a critical time of change and upheaval. The destruction of a productive parental relationships is thus often ensured.

Attorneys frequently remind us that fewer than 5 per cent of custody disputes go to trial, as if trial were the only destructive part of the process. The damage starts early in the adversarial process, and for many continues over a prolonged period of time. False allegations and hostile affidavits increase anger in at least one parent and have enduring, damaging effects. For example, hostile, personally attacking affidavits are associated with more post-divorce violence, compared with the use of factual declarations.[77]

Instead of relying primarily or exclusively on adversarial processes to reach settlements, it is crucial that all separating and divorcing parents be offered a hierarchy of interventions which provide multiple opportunities to settle custody and access disputes, both during and after divorce (see Figure 13.1). This multi-layering of services provides opportunities to exit the legal system at the earliest point possible. It promotes the concept of minimising legal conflict and inter-parental hostility. It also acknowledges the range of abilities of separated parents to settle their disputes, and the fact that some custody disputes and problems require more extensive legal or judicial intervention.

Interventions should start with the most benign and least expensive services, *available immediately after separation*, and step up to the most coercive and expensive forms of justice for those parents unable to reach any agreement in any other forum. Each step provides opportunities for settlement. The overall goal is to contain or reduce parental conflict, understand and respect children's psychological and developmental needs, model civility and communication about children, and promote responsible parenting.

In the past two decades, states and jurisdictions in several countries have developed and implemented divorce education programmes, custody and divorce mediation services and, for chronically disputing parents, a variety of

[77] D Ellis and N Stuckless, *Mediating and Negotiating Marital Conflicts* (Sage, 1996).

mediation/arbitration models. Some jurisdictions have also implemented judicial settlement conferences following unsuccessful mediations for reaching temporary orders. For the most part, empirical research has demonstrated that aspects and outcomes of these interventions are sufficiently effective to be implemented on a larger scale.

Divorce Education Programmes

Structured educational programmes for separating and divorcing parents have been developed and widely implemented in the United States and elsewhere.[78] These programmes are either mandated by state legislation (in Utah, for example), are required by local rule, or are ordered or recommended at the discretion of the judge. Because attendance is low at voluntary divorce education programmes, mandatory programmes have been adopted on a wider-scale basis. Most divorce education programs are designed only for parents, although several well-designed programmes offer assistance and education to the whole family by providing parallel child sessions.[79]

The broad goal of divorce education programmes is to help children to cope more effectively with separation or divorce by helping parents. In this respect, the programmes are seeking to mobilise parental strengths that have eroded during troubled marriages[80] and after separation.[81] A parallel goal is to mitigate the more negative impacts of divorce, in particular to educate parents about the potential effects of their behaviour and attitudes on their children.[82]

Most divorce education programmes seek to:

- —inform parents how children typically respond to separation and adjust after divorce;
- —alert parents to the negative impact of continued high conflict and other harmful behaviours on their children's adjustment;
- —discuss benefits of and skills for developing a civilised parenting relationship;

[78] MJ Geisler and KR Blaisure, 1998 'Nationwide Survey of Court-connected Divorce Education Programs' (1999) 37 *Family and Conciliation Courts Review* 36.

[79] *Ibid.*; JE Glenn, 'Divorce Education for Parents and Children in Jackson County, Missouri' (1998) 36(4) *Family and Conciliation Courts Review* 503; *Kids' Turn*, 1242 Market Street, 4th Fl, San Francisco, CA 94102 www.kidsturn.org (2000).

[80] E Cummings and P Davies, *Children and Marital Conflict* (Guilford Publications, 1994); A Krishnakumar and C Buehler, 'Interparental Conflict and Parenting Behaviors: A Meta-analytic Review' (2000) 49(1) *Family Relations* 25.

[81] EM Hetherington, *Coping with Divorce, Single Parenting, and Remarriage* (Lawrence Erlbaum Associates, 1999).

[82] SL Braver, P Salem, J Pearson, and SR Deluse, 'The Content of Divorce Education Programs: Results of a Survey' (1996) 34 *Family and Conciliation Courts Review* 41; MJ Geisler and KR Blaisure, 'A Review of Divorce Education Materials' (1998) 47 *Family Relations* 1167.

—focus parents on children's need for a continuing relationship with both parents, separate from their own feelings and attitudes;
—describe positive parenting behaviours and discipline practices;
—discuss adult adjustment to divorce and coping with change;
—focus on responsibilities of residential and contact parents; and
—describe courts processes, including mediation.

Empirical research indicates that client satisfaction is quite high, even among those mandated to attend.[83] In a statewide mandated divorce education programme for parents, 24 per cent were resentful of having to attend, but 93 per cent later rated the programme worthwhile and 81 per cent said it should be mandatory. Relitigation rates were significantly lower in one study among parents participating in the education groups, compared with those in control groups,[84] but others found no difference.[85] Participating in divorce education programmes *early* in the legal process is more effective than doing so later, and high-conflict parents appear to benefit the most. Several studies, including one random assignment study,[86] found that parents participating in divorce education programmes indicated greater willingness to have their children spend more time with the other parent, more intent to cooperate, and less likelihood of putting their child in the middle of their disputes, compared with control group parents not participating in a programme.[87] Reports from programme leaders and attorneys indicate that a certain (but unknown) percentage of parents exit the adversarial process with voluntary custody and contact agreements reached following the divorce education intervention.

With respect to content, programmes which incorporate current and reliable divorce research findings, and which focus on building parent skills for improved communication between parents and conflict reduction behaviours, are more effective in producing change in parents, compared with more didactic or feeling-oriented programmes. And programmes incorporating video, exercises and demonstrations, discussion, handouts and didactic presentations are more effec-

[83] J Arbuthnot and D Gordon, 'Does Mandatory Divorce Education for Parents Work? A Six Month Outcome Evaluation' (1996) 34 *Family and Conciliation Courts Review* 60; MJ Geisler and KR Blaisure, '1998 Nationwide Survey of Court-connected Divorce Education Programs:' (1999) 37 *Family and Conciliation Courts Review* 36; K Shifflett and EM Cummings, 'A Program for Educating Parents about the Effects of Divorce and Conflict on Children: An Initial Evaluation' (1999) 48 *Family Relation* 79; N Thoennes and J Pearson, 'Parent Education in the Domestic Relations Court: A Multi-site Assessment' (1999) 37 *Family and Conciliation Courts Review,* 195.

[84] J Arbuthnot, K Kramer and DA Gordon, 'Patterns of Relitigation Following Divorce Education' (1997) 35 *Family and Conciliation Courts Review* 269.

[85] L Kramer and A Kowal, 'Long-term Followup of a Court-based Intervention for Divorcing Parents' (1998) 36 *Family and Conciliation Courts Review* 452; Thoennes and Pearson, *Ibid.*

[86] K Shifflett and EM Cummings, 'A Program for Educating Parents about the Effects of Divorce and Conflict on Children: An Initial Evaluation' (1999) 48 *Family Relation* 79.

[87] K Kramer, J Arbuthnot, D Gordon and J Hosa, 'Effects of Skill-based Versus Information-based Divorce Education Programs on Domestic Violence and Parental Communication' (1998) 36 *Family and Conciliation Courts Review* 9.

tive than programmes relying on just one format.[88] More recently, programmes have begun to integrate materials and processes that address domestic violence.[89]

Divorce education programmes for children have developed more slowly. They are generally offered for different age groups, and are designed to help children develop a better understanding of, and skills for, coping with their parents' divorces.[90] Such programmes for children are not viewed as therapy, but do provide cognitive and emotional support in the group setting. Programmes often run over four to six sessions, and incorporate drawings, discussion, reading, role-playing, and advice books to parents and other children experiencing divorce.[91]

Parent feedback and empirical research strongly suggest that well-designed divorce education programmes should be a first, early and mandatory intervention for all parents separating or divorcing (see Figure 13.1). Well-designed divorce education programmes bring children's voices and their needs into sharp focus for parents in a completely non-adversarial manner. They help parents to understand that children's needs are distinct from those of adults, that marital and divorce anger need to be separated from decisions about children, and that their children's future social and emotional well-being will, in part, be determined by their behaviours.

Custody Mediation

Custody mediation has provided divorcing couples with a powerful and effective alternative to the adversarial process in the past two decades, and should be widely available for all parents disputing custody and access before proceeding to more adversarial processes. Because of its effectiveness in many dimensions, many professionals and policy-makers recommend that it be mandatory as a second-step settlement intervention (see Figure 13.1).[92] What is required with mandatory mediation is the *attempt* to mediate parental differences on custody and contact, not settlement. Mandatory mediation conveys an important public policy and social message to parents and lawyers that settlement efforts and civilised discussion focusing on children are preferred.

[88] *Ibid.*; MJ Geisler and KR Blaisure, '1998 Nationwide Survey of Court-connected Divorce Education Programs' (1999) 37 *Family and Conciliation Courts Review* 36.

[89] GW Fuhrmann, J McGill and ME O'Connell, 'Parent Education's Second Generation: Integrating Violence Sensitivity' (1999) 37(1) *Family and Conciliation Courts Review* 24.

[90] JE Glenn, 'Divorce Education for Parents and Children in Jackson County, Missouri' (1998) 36(4) *Family and Conciliation Courts Review* 503.

[91] See, for example, *Kids' Turn*, 1242 Market Street, 4th Fl, San Francisco, CA 94102, www.kidsturn.org (2000).

[92] D Ellis and N Stuckless, *Mediating and Negotiating Marital Conflicts* (Sage, 1996); RE Emery, *Renegotiating Family Relationships: Divorce, Child Custody and Mediation* (Guilford Publications, 1994); R Emery, *Marriage, Divorce, and Children's Adjustment*, 2nd edn (Sage, 1999); JB Kelly,

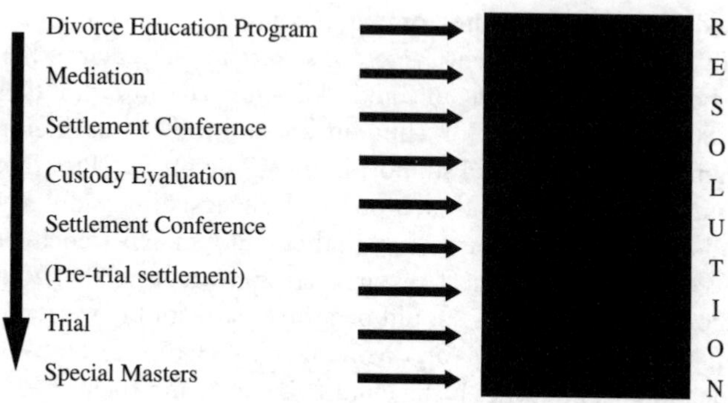

FIGURE 13.1

Empirical research in four countries demonstrates that custody mediation is viewed by a large majority of its participants as quite satisfactory, and that it often contains parental conflict during and after the process.[93]

Men and women are more satisfied with both mediation processes and outcomes, compared with control or comparison groups using adversarial processes to settle their divorce disputes. They feel heard and understood, and retain control over their outcomes.[94] Mediation is efficient in time and expense, works also with many high-conflict parents, and settlement rates are acceptably high (55–85 per cent), depending on the setting and prescreening processes. Relitigation rates are lower, and compliance with agreements occurs at higher rates among mediated samples.[95] Parents randomly assigned to custody mediation were more likely to reach agreement prior to a court hearing, compared with the adversarial group.[96] Mediation was associated with less conflict between parents during and after divorce, more cooperation, child-focused communication, and offers of parental

'The Determination of Child Custody' (1994) 4(1) *The Future of Children: Children and Divorce* 121, The David and Lucile Packard Foundation, 300 Second Street, Los Altos, CA 94022, www.futureofchildren.org; JB Kelly, 'A Decade of Divorce Mediation Research: Some Answers and Questions' (1996) 34(3) *Family and Conciliation Courts Review* 373.

[93] S Bordow and D Gibson, *Evaluation of Family Court Service* (Family Court of Australia Research and Evaluation Unit, 1994); Ellis and Stuckless, *Ibid.*; Emery, *Ibid.*; JB Kelly, 'A Decade of Divorce Mediation Research: Some Answers and Questions' (1996) 34(3) *Family and Conciliation Courts Review* 373; A Love, L Moloney and T Fisher, *Federally Funded Family Mediation in Melbourne: Outcomes, Costs and Client Satisfaction* (Office of Legal Aid and Family Services, Attorney-General's Dept, Barton, ACT 2600, Australia, 1995).

[94] RE Emery, *Renegotiating Family Relationships: Divorce, Child Custody and Mediation* (Guilford Publications, 1994); Love et al., *Ibid.*; Kelly, *Ibid.*

[95] Ellis and Stuckless, *Ibid.*; R Emery, *Marriage, Divorce, and Children's Adjustment,* 2nd edn (Sage, 1999); Kelly, *Ibid.*

[96] RE Emery, *Renegotiating Family Relationships: Divorce, Child Custody and Mediation* (Guilford Publications, 1994).

support to each other after divorce, compared with parents in an adversarial divorce process.[97] In the longest longitudinal study to date, non-residential parents (mostly fathers) using mediation were reported to be significantly more involved with their children twelve years later, compared with fathers in the random assignment litigation sample.[98]

Empirical research has not supported the early claims advanced by critics of mediation that women were disadvantaged in custody or child support outcomes.[99] Among unexpected findings were that women who were victims of domestic violence were satisfied with the mediation process and outcomes,[100] and preferred mediation when offered a choice of mediation or a more evaluative process.[101] Mandatory mediation in the public sector requires protective policies for those unable or afraid to negotiate on their own behalf, including the routine utilisation of screening, opt-out provisions for victims for domestic violence, use of separate sessions and support persons, and protective orders. It is essential that mediators have specialised training in mediation, divorce and custody matters, child development and domestic violence in order to offer effective services.[102]

Special Master and Arbitration Interventions

Newer mediation/arbitration interventions have been implemented for the approximately 8–12 per cent of parents who continue in chronic high-conflict post-divorce and relitigate frequently (see Figure 13.1). Whether legal actions are initiated by one or both parents, such parents use a disproportionate amount of the court's time and resources, deplete their own economic resources, continue to view each other as enemies, and more often place their children in the midst of this conflict.[103] Among this group are parents with serious psychological problems and character disorders. Many of the disputes are minor, intended to control,

[97] See Emery, *Ibid.*; JB Kelly, 'A Decade of Divorce Mediation Research: Some Answers and Questions' (1996) 34(3) *Family and Conciliation Courts Review* 373.

[98] RE Emery, L Laumann-Billings, M Waldron, DA Sbarra and P Dillon, 'Child Custody Mediation and Litigation: Custody, Contact, and Coparenting 12 years after Initial Dispute Resolution' (in press) *Journal of Consulting and Clinical Psychology*.

[99] JB Kelly, 'A Decade of Divorce Mediation Research: Some Answers and Questions' (1996) 34(3) *Family and Conciliation Courts Review* 373.

[100] B Davies, S Ralph, M Hawton and L Craig, 'A Study of Client Satisfaction with Family Court Counseling in Cases Involving Domestic Violence' (1995) 33 *Family and Conciliation Courts Review* 324; L Newmark, A Harrell and P Salem, 'Domestic Violence and Empowerment in Custody and Visitation Cases' (1995) 33 *Family and Conciliation Courts Review* 30.

[101] Newmark et al., *Ibid.*

[102] RE Emery, *Renegotiating Family Relationships: Divorce, Child Custody and Mediation* (Guilford Publications, 1994); JB Kelly, 'The Determination of Child Custody' (1994) 4(1) *The Future of Children: Children and Divorce* 121, The David and Lucile Packard Foundation, 300 Second Street, Los Altos, CA 94022, www.futureofchildren.org; JB Kelly, 'A Decade of Divorce Mediation Research: Some Answers and Questions' (1996) 34(3) *Family and Conciliation Courts Review* 373.

[103] JR Johnston and V Roseby, *In the Name of the Child: A Developmental Approach to Understanding and Helping Children of Conflict and Violent Divorce* (Free Press, 1997).

punish, or obstruct the other parent, and have little or no basis in law or psychology for decision-making. A number of US jurisdictions have implemented Special Master or Parent Coordinator programs, in which experienced custody evaluators, mediators and family law attorneys are given limited and court-ordered authority to settle parenting disputes.

This non-confidential intervention is designed to focus on children's developmental, social and psychological needs, and to reduce parental conflict by providing an immediate non-adversarial forum for resolving disputes. These disputes may include scheduling, access, school, vacation-planning and child-rearing disputes that the parents are unable to settle themselves. Some children view their Special Master as their champion and protector, and call to ask specifically for their own session so that their voice can be heard on issues of importance to them.

The majority of Special Masters and Parent Coordinators use a model combining mediation/arbitration/parent education. They meet with parents and children to gather information about disputed issues as they arise, assist parents to mediate differences, but make timely decisions if parents cannot agree. Although in most jurisdictions, parents jointly stipulate to use the Special Master or Parenting Coordinator in a detailed Order signed by the court, in other jurisdictions the court will order parent arbitrators over the objection of one parent. While Special Masters function outside of the adversarial system, in a non-adversarial manner, they are responsible to the court, write and file decisions, and adhere to rules and structures for appeal and judicial review.

The most effective process for developing and implementing such programs is through the collaborative work of an interdisciplinary committee of experienced family law attorneys, custody evaluators and mediators appointed by the family law judge. Such committees explore the statutory authority for Special Masters in their particular jurisdictions, draft Special Master Orders which describe Special Masters' authority, length of service, and protections for parents, children and the Special Master.

Empirical research on the use of the Special Master is quite limited, but indicates that relitigation is dramatically reduced, and the majority of parents report being satisfied and experiencing decreased conflict with the other parent.[104] In one California county, for example, in the year prior to getting a Special Master, 166 cases had 993 court appearances. These same 166 cases had thirty-seven appearances in the year following the appointment of the Special Master.

Group programs have been developed for high-conflict, chronically litigating parents.[105] These interventions, often taking twelve to sixteen hours, have as their

[104] T Johnston, Summary of research on the decrease of court involvement after the appointment of a Special Master. Unpublished manuscript (1994). MH Vick and R Backerman, 'Mediation/arbitration: Surveys of professionals and clients', paper presented at the Boulder Interdisciplinary Committee on Child Custody, Boulder, CO.

[105] JR Johnston, 'Developing and testing group interventions for families at impasse', unpublished report to the Statewide Office of Family Court Services, Judicial Council of California, San Francisco, CA; S Kibler et al., 'Pre-contempt/contemnors Group Diversion Counseling Program: A Program to Address Parental Frustration of Eustody and Visitation Orders' (1994) 32 *Family and Conciliation Courts Review* 62.

goal to focus parents on their children and protect them from parental conflict. Some programmes offer education and skill-building in a sequencing of large and small group sessions, followed by one-on-one exercises and negotiations between disputing parents, under leaders' observation.[106] Other programmes provide therapeutic group mediation with concurrent child group sessions, and focus on individual families, their children, and their impasses.[107] Both types of programme have demonstrated increases in cooperation, a decrease in physical violence for women and men, a decrease in disagreements, and improved abilities in parents to communicate and focus on their children's needs.[108]

Giving Children a Voice in Divorce

Divorce represents one of the most major, and perhaps the most traumatic, life changes that children will experience. Yet children are not consulted on any of the issues radically affecting their future residential situations and parental relationships. It is not just parents who have strong interests in custody and access decisions and their long-term consequences, but the children directly affected by these parental and court decisions. In believing that children should not be asked to choose who they want to live with, we have gone to the extreme of not consulting children about any of the parenting and living arrangements precipitated by the separation and divorce. Yet they have wisdom and insight which most adults dismiss or under-estimate.[109]

Consider John, aged thirteen, who angrily told the mediator/author about his mother's fight for sole physical custody: 'My mum doesn't understand that a kid needs both of his parents. I get different things from my mom and my dad.' Or Maria, aged nine, who asked the author to tell her mum that she really missed her dad since the divorce and wanted to spend more time with him at his house. She added: 'Tell her I hope she won't be angry.' And Seth, aged eleven, who had run away from his mother's house and expressed an urgent need to change custody to his father, two years after final divorce. 'Nobody in the courts will listen to me. My mum is angry all the time . . . being with her is like having needles stuck in my brain. I can't think, I can't study, I'm trying too hard all the time just to stay calm and not blow up.' Or Tom, a thirteen-year-old who stated he would kill himself before spending overnights with his father: 'He never earned the right to be a father, and now he thinks he can demand that I spend half my time with

[106] Kibler, *Ibid.*

[107] JR Johnston, 'Developing and testing group interventions for families at impasse', unpublished report to the Statewide Office of Family Court Services, Judicial Council of California, San Francisco, CA, 1999.

[108] *Ibid.*

[109] JB Kelly, 'Interviewing Children in Mediation: A Structured Model for Giving Children a Voice in Divorce', unpublished manuscript; C Smart, 'Children and the transformation of family law' (2000) 49 *University of New Brunswick Law Journal* 1; C Smart and B Neale, 'It's my life too'—Children's Perspectives on Post-divorce Parenting' (2000) 30 *Family Law* 163.

him!' In these cases, angry parents were arguing about how much time the children would spend with each of them. These youngsters had an array of valuable opinions, strong feelings and deeply felt wishes which they wanted the author to convey diplomatically to their parents.

Children need opportunities and safe forums to promote their participation and present their voice. They should be consulted for their ideas about post-separation living arrangements, *not* to be the decision-makers, but for providing input for parents and others to consider. Children report feeling isolated and angry at being excluded from such important life events.[110] While they prefer informal family forums,[111] over using professionals, they will talk extensively in brief, structured mediation interviews conducted by experienced mediators with prior child training, and in group programmes. Many low to moderate conflict parents can be assisted to obtain their children's viewpoints in safe, supportive ways. Even if children's cognitive skills in generating and expressing reasons for their preferences are not fully developed, a large body of research indicates that opportunities to participate with parents and others in issues that directly affect children is associated with more positive mental health and educational achievement.

In listening respectfully to children, being willing to seriously consider and integrate their ideas, and helping them feel more empowered at a time of great upheaval, anxiety and change, we may help children to cope more effectively with the divorce experience. When we give children a voice, and give their parents opportunities to settle disputes and improve their coparental relationship within a hierarchy of well-conceived educational and legal interventions, we may significantly diminish the negative short- and longer-term impact of separation and divorce on children.

[110] J Wallerstein and J Kelly, *Surviving the Breakup: How Parents and Children Cope with Divorce* (Basic Books, 1980).

[111] C Smart and B Neale, 'It's my life too'—Children's Perspectives on Post-divorce Parenting' (2000) 30 *Family Law* 163.

14

Agents or Dependants: Children and the Family Law System

Pauline Tapp, Nicola Taylor and Mark Henaghan*

INTRODUCTION

This paper outlines the findings of a comprehensive review of 829 New Zealand family law judgments for the years 1990, 1994 and 1998. Judgments were included from the Family Court (723), High Court (100) and Court of Appeal (six) with respect to decisions concerning adoption, custody, access, care and protection, abduction/wrongful removal, violence, child support, matrimonial property, paternity and other guardianship issues such as medical treatment, change of name, relocation, and appointment of another guardian. For comparative purposes, a selection of 91 Australian and 203 English judgments were also analysed, but have not been reported on in this paper.

Our primary access to the law in action is through published judgments. While caution must be exercised when assumptions are made about judicial beliefs, it is nevertheless critical that all professionals involved with family law are aware of the conceptions and values they bring to their work. Traditionally, the law has characterised children as dependent, immature, incompetent and in need of protection. However, this does not fit well with the conception of children as competent and articulate actors with social and moral agency as encompassed in the UN Convention on the Rights of the Child. The emphasis is now on regarding children as citizens in their own right, who are entitled to be treated with dignity and respect, and to be involved as partners in adult endeavours.[1] By examining

* Pauline Tapp is Associate Professor in the Faculty of Law, University of Auckland, New Zealand; Nicola Taylor is a Research Fellow, Children's Issues Centre, University of Otago, New Zealand; and Mark Henaghan is Professor, Faculty of Law, University of Otago. The authors gratefully acknowledge the financial support of the New Zealand Law Foundation which enabled the research on which this paper is based to be undertaken.

[1] B Mayall (ed), *Children's Childhoods: Observed and Experienced* (Falmer Press, 1994); P Moss and P Petrie, *Children's Services: Time for a New Approach* (Institute of Education, University of London, 1997); A Prout and A James, 'A new paradigm for the sociology of childhood?' in A James and A Prout (eds), *Constructing and Reconstructing Childhood: Contemporary Issues in the Sociological Study of Childhood* (Falmer Press, 1990), pp 7–34; J Qvortrup, 'Childhood Matters: An Introduction', in J Qvortrup, M Bardy, G Sgritta and H Wintersberger (eds), *Childhood Matters: Social Theory, Practice*

what New Zealand judges choose to report in their judgments, we have systematically documented, over a decade, the trends in thinking about children. Our paper thus outlines the methodology, findings and implications of this research which we undertook during 1999 and 2000.

Small numbers of family law cases have previously been analysed in terms of their respect for children's autonomy rights,[2] but a systematic analysis of a large sample of judicial decisions has never before been conducted in New Zealand—nor internationally, as far as we can ascertain. In view of the importance of family law proceedings to children and families, and in light of New Zealand's obligations under the UN Convention on the Rights of the Child, it is important that legal judgments are studied over time. They provide one means of determining whether and how the Convention principles are being implemented in New Zealand through the relevant domestic statutes underpinning judicial decision making in family law proceedings, and provide important information on the nature of legal decision making in New Zealand case law.

Thus one of the primary purposes of our research has been to examine how children's rights have been taken into account in judicial decisions concerning a range of family law matters during the 1990s. Our study also explored judicial conceptions of childhood as revealed in comments about children's rights, children's views and child development in each judgment. It is these judicial conceptions which form the basis of this paper. Clearly, different conceptions of childhood influence our legal system and the decisions reached in individual cases:

> Different adult conceptions of childhood will result in different opinions about the right of a child to express a view and the relevance of the child's voice. Those who see children as primarily immature, subject to pressure and requiring protection, will have a different view from those who place primary emphasis on family autonomy, and see the child's interests as subsumed within those of the child's family. Feminists may regard the child's interests as inseparable from those of the child's mother. A different view will be held by those who regard the child as a social actor and right holder who will benefit from having their autonomy recognised.[3]

We first describe the methodology used in our research project, and then draw examples from the analysed judgments to illustrate judicial conceptions of children as dependants or as social agents.

and Politics, (Avebury, 1994), pp 1–24; AB Smith and NJ Taylor, 'The Sociocultural Context of Childhood: Balancing Dependency and Agency', in AB Smith, NJ Taylor and M Gollop (eds), *Children's Voices: Research, Policy and Practice* (Pearson Education, 2000), pp 1–17.

[2] P Tapp, 'The Use of the United Nations Convention on the Rights of the Child in the Family Court', in *New Zealand Family Law Conference Proceedings* (New Zealand Law Society, 1998), pp 235–64; P Tapp and M Henaghan, 'Family Law: Conceptions of Childhood and Children's Voices—The Implications of Article 12 of the United Nations Convention on the Rights of the Child', in AB Smith, NJ Taylor and M Gollop (eds), *Children's Voices: Research, Policy and Practice* (Pearson Education, 2000), pp 91–109; M Henaghan and P Tapp, 'Judicial and Legislative Conceptions of Childhood and Children's Voices in Family Law', in AB Smith, M Gollop, K Marshall and K Nairn (eds), *Advocating for Children: International Perspectives on Children's Rights* (University of Otago Press, 2000), pp 65–83.

[3] Henaghan and Tapp, *Ibid.*, p 69.

GOALS OF THE STUDY

The purpose of this research was to undertake a comprehensive review of 829 New Zealand family law judgments.[4] The project examined trends in judicial decision making over time by analysing New Zealand Family Court, High Court and Court of Appeal judgments in the years 1990, 1994 and 1998. The following areas of family law were included: adoption, custody, access, care and protection, abduction/wrongful removal, violence, child support, matrimonial property, paternity and other guardianship issues (for example, medical treatment, change of child's name, parental relocation, appointment of a guardian), with a view to determining to the degree apparent from the judgments:

—demographic details—re families and court proceedings;
—purpose of the court proceedings;
—appointment and influence of counsel for the child, amicus curiae and specialist report writers;
—whether the child's views or wishes were ascertained and how;
—whether and how the child's views or wishes were presented to the court;
—the weight that children's wishes and views were given in the judgment;
—the extent to which 'age and maturity' criteria were taken into account in giving weight to the child's views and wishes;
—whether the United Nations Convention on the Rights of the Child was referred to in the judgment, and if so, which articles of the Convention;
—whether other international conventions were referred to in the judgment;
—the use made of social science literature and research in the judgment;
—any other factors which influenced whether the child's views and wishes were considered (eg disability or culture);
—judicial comments on child development, family relationships and children's rights;
—the decision reached and the factors which influenced this.

RESEARCH METHODOLOGY

The research was undertaken during 1999 and 2000 by an interdisciplinary team comprising:

—Associate Professor Pauline Tapp, Faculty of Law, University of Auckland—barrister and solicitor, family law specialist;
—Ms Nicola Taylor, Research Fellow, Children's Issues Centre—barrister and solicitor;

[4] The New Zealand judgments were also compared with a selection of 91 Australian and 203 English cases reported in 1990, 1994 and 1998, but the data are not included in this paper.

—Ms Megan Gollop, Project Officer, Children's Issues Centre—psychology and counselling background;
—Mr Michael Gaffney, Project Manager, Children's Issues Centre—education and research technology background;
—Professor Anne Smith, Director, Children's Issues Centre—developmental psychologist; and
—Professor Mark Henaghan, Dean, Faculty of Law, University of Otago—barrister and solicitor, family law specialist.

The study utilised a mixed methodology involving both quantitative and qualitative aspects, and was funded by the New Zealand Law Foundation.

The years 1990, 1994 and 1998 were selected for inclusion in the research because of their proximity to important dates relating to the UN Convention on the Rights of the Child. This Convention was adopted by the United Nations General Assembly on 20 November 1989 and so we selected 1990 as the first full year following its adoption. New Zealand became a signatory to the Convention in 1989, and took the formal step of ratification on 13 March 1993. We therefore included the 1994 judgments as being those in the first full year following New Zealand's ratification. Finally, 1998 was the most recent year for which we could obtain a complete set of judgments, given that the research commenced during 1999. The four-year spacing between each set of judgments thus enabled trends to be identified across the 1990s. The methodology also lends itself to an extension of the study in 2002 (and at four-yearly periods thereafter!) to continue the analysis of trends in family law and judicial decision making over time.

Collecting together the judgments proved to be the most complex part of the research. However, we were greatly assisted by Butterworths of New Zealand Ltd's offer to provide the research team with access to their library in Wellington for the purpose of identifying and copying the judgments we needed. The judgments selected for inclusion in the research had to involve children aged eighteen years and younger. Those judgments concerning procedural or technical matters only were also identified and coded via an abbreviated coding format. Examples of judgments classified as procedural were cases concerning the admissibility of evidence, or costs issues—that is, those matters requiring some preliminary or technical matter to be decided before the court could hear the full dispute.

A coding template containing 38 categories reflecting the goals of the study was developed by the research team. This enabled a combination of quantitative and qualitative data to be extracted from each judgment.

Quantitative Data

—**case administration**—type, locality and country of court, judge, date of hearing, date of judgment, type of case;
—**demographics**—applicant/appellant, respondent, child(ren)—date of birth, age, sex, ethnicity;

—**legal procedures**—counsel for the child appointed, *amicus curiae* appointed, type of specialist report(s) prepared plus statutory provision requested under, children's views mentioned by the judge, how the children's views were ascertained, age and maturity criteria mentioned;
—**conventions and research literature**—UNCROC mentioned plus which Articles, other international conventions cited, references to social science literature and research.

Qualitative Data

—**text summaries**—brief details of family background, purpose of application/proceedings, judge's decision;
—**direct quotes from the judgment**—concerning children's views, child development, family relationships, children's rights;
—**inferences and conclusions drawn from the judgment**—judge's views on the specialist report, influence of child's views on the case outcome, factors which judge identified as influencing his or her decision.

Some of these categories were not mutually exclusive. For example, sometimes the quotes relating to child development could also be factors which the judge identified as influencing his or her decision. They could thus be coded in both fields of the coding template. We also had a 'miscellaneous' category to record any particularly significant or unusual feature of the case which was not captured in the other coding fields.

Our approach to the coding was to read each judgment, extract the relevant information and enter this directly on to a word processing coding template. Some judgments were able to be coded fairly quickly, within about thirty minutes—these were mainly matrimonial property or child support cases which contained little information about the children and did not involve specialist reports. Other judgments took several hours to code—particularly those complex custody, access or care and protection cases which had a lengthy history of court involvement, several specialist reports, counsel for the child appointed, and which included the expression of children's views. The data extracted from each judgment were later copied and inserted into a Filemaker Pro database for analysis.

RESULTS

In total, there were 829 New Zealand judgments included in the research sample—723 (87.2 per cent) from the Family Court, 100 (12.1 per cent) from the High Court and six (0.7 per cent) from the Court of Appeal (see Table 14.1).

Of the 829 New Zealand judgments, 691 (83.4 per cent) were fully coded and 138 (16.6 per cent) were partially coded because they concerned procedural

TABLE 14.1: Full Set of New Zealand Judgments by Year, Court and Mode of Coding

Year	*Family Court*		*High Court*		*Court of Appeal*		*Total*
	Fully Coded	*Procedural*	*Fully Coded*	*Procedural*	*Fully Coded*	*Procedural*	
1990	225	24	10	10	0	1	270
1994	256	29	13	29	0	3	330
1998	178	11	9	29	0	2	229
Total	659	64	32	68	0	6	829

TABLE 14.2: Grouped Ages of Children and Young People by Mode of Coding

Age	*Fully Coded No. of Chn*	*Fully Coded % of Chn*	*Procedural No. of Chn*	*Procedural % of Chn*	*Total*
0–4 years	256	19.8	36	18.2	292
5–12 years	587	45.4	61	30.8	648
13–18 years	209	16.1	24	12.1	233
19+ years	14	1.1	0	0	14
Missing	228	17.6	77	38.9	305
Total	1,294	100%	198	100%	1,492

matters. The judgments concerned legal proceedings in 43 different court locations throughout New Zealand. The number of judgments written, or contributed to, by each judge ranged from one to 179.

A total of 1492 children were identified in the 829 judgments. The fully coded cases concerned 1294 children (86.7 per cent), and the procedural cases concerned 198 children (13.3 per cent)—see Table 14.2. Dates of birth or ages were not recorded in the judgments for 305 (20.4 per cent) of the children and young people, but were stipulated for 1187 (79.6 per cent) of them.

It should be noted that, while the research focused upon children and young people aged between birth and eighteen years inclusive, there are young people aged nineteen years and over included in the study because their cases involved younger siblings who fell within the age criteria. Any case involving young people who were *all* aged nineteen years and over was excluded from the study. The median age of the children aged from birth to eighteen years in both the fully coded and procedural judgments was eight years. Data on gender were missing for 402 (27 per cent) of the children and young people mentioned in the 829 New

TABLE 14.3: Type of Family Law Proceedings by Court and Mode of Coding

Type of case	*Fully coded*		*Procedural*	*Total*
	Family Court	*HC / CA*	*All NZ Courts*	
Abduction	24	4	9	37
Access	105	2	18	125
Adoption	18	1	3	22
Care and protection	69	5	16	90
Child support	159	2	19	180
Costs	1	0	20	21
Custody	155	14	37	206
Guardianship	61	6	7	74
Matrimonial property	107	1	26	134
Paternity	25	0	14	39
Sexual abuse	3	0	0	3
Spousal maintenance	1	0	2	3
Violence	55	0	4	59
Other	15	0	14	29
Total	798	35	189	1,022

Zealand judgments. A total of 573 (38.4 per cent) children and young people were male, and 517 (34.6 per cent) were female.

Table 14.3 depicts the type of family law proceedings with which the 829 New Zealand judgments were concerned. It should be noted that as a number of the judgments concerned more than one issue (for example, custody, access and violence) the totals in the table add to more than 829.

The largest category of judgments concerned custody matters (206 judgments in total, of which 169 were fully coded). This was followed by cases involving child support issues (180 judgments in total, of which 161 were fully coded); matrimonial property issues (134 judgments in total, of which 108 were fully coded); access issues (125 judgments in total, of which 107 were fully coded); care and protection issues (90 judgments in total, of which 74 were fully coded); guardianship issues (74 judgments in total, of which 67 were fully coded); violence issues (59 judgments in total, of which 55 were fully coded); paternity issues (39 judgments in total, of which 25 were fully coded); abduction/wrongful removal issues (37 judgments in total, of which 28 were fully coded); adoption issues (22 judgments in total, of which 19 were fully coded); costs issues (21 judgments in total, of which one was fully coded); sexual abuse issues (three judgments in total which were all fully coded); and spousal maintenance issues (three judgments in total, of which one was fully coded). Twenty-nine judgments concerned such other issues as the transfer of proceedings, wardship, separation orders, availability of reports, and fifteen of these were fully coded.

Counsel for the child was appointed in 329 of the 691 fully coded New Zealand judgments (47.6 per cent). Specialist reports were mentioned in 286 (41.4 per cent) of the 691 fully coded New Zealand judgments. Four hundred and five judgments (58.6 per cent) made no mention of a specialist report. A total of 318 specialist reports were referred to, making it clear that in a number of cases more than one report was cited. The most common specialist reports were those provided by psychologists (199 judgments), followed by social workers (72 judgments), medical professionals (24 judgments), and psychiatrists (23 judgments).

JUDICIAL CONCEPTIONS OF CHILDHOOD

The New Zealand Family Court was established so that the concerns of the family could be considered holistically.[5] In our view, this aim has not been achieved for two primary reasons. First, the perception of children as dependants has meant that they are not seen as active participants in family matters, but rather as immature beings or becoming persons, who adults must protect and make decisions for. Secondly, the lack of a coherent family policy framework has meant the law has continued to deal with child and family matters in an isolated and discrete fashion. The separation of child support matters from the issues relating to access to a child was, in fact, a deliberate policy. The Minister of Social Welfare responsible for much of the development of the *Child Support Act* 1991 commented:

> We need to pay attention to the manipulation that occurs in the area of family policy, particularly in relation to matters of access. Do not confuse rights of children to ongoing support after the day of separation and important matters that need to be dealt with by the Court or an alternative system in relation to access. At the moment one of the great drawbacks of the system is that children are traded on and, the only person who loses are the children and the person who is the caregiver.[6]

However, it is interesting to note the recognition given to the inter-relationship between family finances and child care in the Matrimonial Property Amendment Bill 1999. This proposed to empower the court to both compensate a parent for caring for a child after separation and to postpone vesting of property where this would cause undue hardship for the parent caring for a child.

It is the thesis of this paper that the UN Convention on the Rights of the Child (UNCROC) provides a guide to enable the legislature and the Family Court to perceive the child as a social agent entitled to respect and a rightful participant, with members of the child's family, in court processes. Discussion with and by the whole family is, it is submitted, more likely to achieve solutions which will be

[5] *The Royal Commission on the Courts 1978* (Government Printer).

[6] The Hon J Shipley, 'The Crown's Investment in New Zealand's Children for Today and Tomorrow', in G Maxwell, I Hassall and J Robertson (eds), *Toward a Child and Family Policy for New Zealand* (Office of the Commissioner for Children, 1991), pp 13–15.

understood and accepted by the family than under the present system of adult decision making.

These two impediments to a holistic family law framework are vividly illustrated by the laws and practices concerned with the implementation of Articles 12 and 13 of UN Convention. Although all New Zealand family law statutes (other than the *Adoption Act* 1955 and the *Status of Children Acts* 1969 and 1987) provide for the appointment of counsel for the child,[7] so that there is the capacity to give effect to Articles 12 and 13 of the Convention, the child's voice is excluded from the vital pre-trial processes. The legislature and the court have not heeded the substantial research evidence that children and the legal system benefit when children are given information about what is happening in their families and an opportunity to provide input into decisions.[8] It should be noted that only the *Domestic Violence Act* 1995, section 9, provides for an application by a child. In contrast, the *Child Support Act* 1991, which has as one of its objects 'the right of the child to be maintained by their parents' (section 4(a)), does not permit a child to bring an application for child support.[9]

Despite the provisions for appointment of counsel for the child our research has shown that all too often judges and the legal profession reflect the common social and child sciences' conception of children as dependants, rather than as social actors and partners in family endeavours. This finding is in line with that of Neale and Smart[10] in the United Kingdom, and is reflected in the mixed role expected of counsel for the child in the *Best Practice Guidelines for Counsel for the Child*, ratified by the New Zealand Law Society Board on 18 February 2000.

In analysing the 829 judgments included in our research sample, it was very evident that in the cases concerned with child support, spousal maintenance and matrimonial property—areas traditionally regarded as adult matters—children's views were rarely mentioned.[11] Also, the children were objectified—that is, their existence was mentioned, but the child was not given the dignity of a name or an age. This invisibility of children in financial matters is in stark contrast with the research that home and neighbourhood are of considerable importance to a child

[7] *Guardianship Act* 1968, s 30; *Domestic Violence Act* 1995, s 81; *Child Support Act* 1991, s 226; *Family Proceedings Act* 1980, s 162; *Matrimonial Property Act* 1976, 26(2*); Children, Young Persons, and Their Families Act* 1989, s 159.

[8] Australian Law Reform Commission and Human Rights and Equal Opportunities Commission, *Seen and Heard: Priority for Children in the Legal Process*, Report 84 (1997); P Beck and N Biank, 'Broadening the Scope for Divorce Mediation' (1997) 14(3) *Mediation Quarterly* 179; R Chisholm, 'Children's Participation in Family Court Litigation' (1999) 13 *Australian Journal of Family Law* 197; F Garwood, 'Conciliation: A Forum for Children's Views?' (1992) 6(4) *Children and Society* 353; M Richards, 'The *Family Law Act* 1996 of England and Wales—Pilot Research on Information Meetings' (1998) 3(2) *Butterworths Family Law Journal* 43.

[9] *Hyde v CIR* [2000] NZFLR 385.

[10] B Neale and C Smart, *Agents or Dependants? Struggling to Listen to Children in Family Law and Family Research—Working Paper 3* (Centre for Research on Family, Kinship and Childhood, University of Leeds, 1998).

[11] Only once in matrimonial property, and three times in child support, but in all instances with no noticeable effect on the outcome.

when parents separate.[12] Atkin and Black[13] have noted how the fiscal emphasis of the *Child Support Act* 1991 results in the law being separated from the reality of family life with the potential to harm children and families.

It is submitted that the Convention requires that children be regarded as partners in family endeavours who are entitled to information, an opportunity to express their view, and to have their views understood from their perspective and taken seriously. While judicial use of UNCROC is increasing,[14] too many judges, even in the traditional child law areas, still perceive of children as dependants—as arational, inarticulate, immature, becoming persons who must be subject to socialisation and control by adults before they can graduate to the world of adult responsibility.

PERCEPTIONS OF CHILDREN AS DEPENDANTS

Judges who are protective of a child, who regard the child as an immature person, may fail to realise that each child is an individual who, despite their chronological age, may have acquired competence and a unique understanding of their situation from experience. Such a judge may not understand the importance of learning to enter the child's world to understand their perspective and forms of communication if court orders are to be of real assistance to the child and the family. This failure is well illustrated by a child abduction case decided under the *Guardianship Amendment Act* 1991.[15] Although finding that the child objected to being returned, the judge made an order for return because:

> Clearly [the child] has taken his mother's approach to the issue of returning . . . [The child] after all is only 10.5 years of age and in my view has to have major decisions made for him in his life. I accept that he is perhaps mature beyond his years, but children of his age have simplistic answers to problems. Often such answers are immediate and superficial. The report writer noted that [the child] had devised a plan to disrupt his travel back to Australia. In my view formulation of such a plan indicates a degree of immaturity in [the child]. That he has so strongly been influenced by his mother again indicates a degree of immaturity only to be expected of a 10.5 year old.

This approach not only dismissed the expert report writer's opinion that the child had a history of independent decision-making and self-reliance, but also failed to take account of the evidence that the child, rather than being under the control of his mother, in fact had concerns for his mother's well-being. Such a failure to

[12] P Amato, 'Children's Adjustment to Divorce: Theories, Hypotheses and Empirical Support' (1993) 55 *Journal of Marriage and the Family* 23; P Amato and A Booth, *A Generation at Risk: Growing Up in an Era of Family Upheaval* (Harvard University Press, (1997).

[13] W Atkin and A Black, 'Child Support—Supporting Whom?' (1999) 30 *VUWLR* 221.

[14] In the study, UNCROC was referred to in 22 (3.2%) of the fully coded New Zealand judgments by ten different judges—six in 1994 and sixteen in 1998.

[15] Family Court, 1998, FP009/1378/98.

respect the child's reality may not bode well for the success of the child's (forced) return to Australia.

This approach can be contrasted with that of a judge who saw the child as a social agent and was able to understand the child's perspective.[16] The judge accepted the nine-year-old's objection to returning. His Honour commented, in relation to the child having threatened to make a scene at the airport:

> That indicates not only strength of feeling, but a degree of immaturity . . . [The child's] responses show a degree of wilfulness and recalcitrance . . . While this is in one sense not helpful or attractive, all humans of whatever age reinforce strong views by overstatement. I think that it would be unsound to infer from these expressions a lack of maturity. They are after all the only means available to him to try to enforce his strongly felt preference.

A failure to understand the perspective of the children, and the forms of communication they might use when caught between loyalty to parents and when talking with an authority figure, may have led one judge[17] to prefer his own view of the children's wishes, gained during his interview with them, to the view expressed consistently and over a long period by the children to their counsel and to the expert. Counsel for the children submitted that considerable weight should be given to the children's wishes. The children were living with their mother when their father applied for custody. In confirming the mother's custody, the judge commented:

> My ascertainment of the wishes of each child is that it is a wish in the nature of a preference to live with their father such that they would respond positively to a paternal custody arrangement, but not such that indications for maintaining the present custodial arrangement would be negated by the wishes of the children.

Judges who regard children as dependants may fail to understand that a child's welfare requires that they be given the opportunity to learn from experience:

> Children's interests are most likely to be promoted when they are given opportunities for *graduated* decision making.[18]

If the child is to develop into an autonomous individual, some greater 'risk' may need to be accepted as a child matures chronologically or through experience.[19] Possibly in an endeavour to protect a child from adult responsibility, or perhaps to retain adult control, a judge[20] went against the strongly expressed wish of a fifteen-year-old to be with her mother. This was due to the judge's belief that

[16] High Court, 1994, M12/94.

[17] High Court, 1994, AP16/93.

[18] GB Melton, 'Parents *and* Children: Legal Reform to Facilitate Children's Participation', in AB Smith, M Gollop, K Marshall and K Nairn (eds) (2000), *Advocating for Children* (University of Otago Press, 2000), pp 141–58.

[19] B Franklin, 'The Case for Children's Rights: A Progress Report', in B Franklin (ed), *The Handbook of Children's Rights: Comparative Policy and Practice* (Routledge, 1995).

[20] Family Court, 1990, FP691/89.

the child's father was better able to meet her needs and that she would benefit from contact with her half-siblings. Although counsel for the girl had asked that the child's concern be heard, His Honour took a paternal approach. He stated:

> I want it to be known to [eldest child] particularly that [she and her brother] have been through much and I am sensitive to that. This is essentially a Court where the adults must be required to make decisions and to be given decisions. I have never regarded it as proper that children be unduly brought into disputes. I have deliberately chosen not to bring [child] in because she must, I think, accept my judgment in this matter and accept from me that I am doing what I can to make things better.

Hopefully the child was able to accept the decision. However, the cases of *K v K*[21] *(No. 1)* and *K v K (No. 2)*[22] provide a lesson in the dangers of going against the strongly expressed wishes of a child of this age. In those cases, the later court had to accept that the initial decision to require the ten-year-old boy to live with his mother, against his strong wish, could not work for either the benefit of the child or his mother.

PERCEPTIONS OF CHILDREN AS AGENTS

Other judges whose judgments we analysed in the study perceived children as social agents. They understood that children are persons entitled to be treated with respect as active members of families whose views are relevant to the resolution of family matters. Judges spoke with the child or children concerned in 33 of the judgments included in the research sample. These judicial interviews were generally:

> not to question [the children] about items of disputed evidence, but simply to size each of them up and to listen to whatever any of them might wish to tell me about what they wanted to happen.[23]

These judges were able to understand the importance for some children of having input into decisions. In one case, where the judge[24] spoke with the child, His Honour noted that he:

> sensed in him great relief that he had been able to state his preferences and that they had been listened to.

This sense was confirmed by the adults involved subsequently telling the court that, since the child had spoken with the Judge:

> he has been a different boy. He is happy at home . . . he has a better outlook on his schooling.

[21] (1988) 5 NZFLR 257
[22] (1988) 5 NZFLR 283
[23] Family Court, 1994, FP043/278/91.
[24] Family Court, 1990, FP067/048/84.

A High Court judge who regularly speaks with the child involved appeared to have been surprised by the strength of the children's desire to be heard. His Honour commented:

> I should make clear that, despite strong endeavours by me to stop the children expressing a preference, they both, on more than one occasion, loudly and clearly told me they wished to continue to live in New Zealand. It was something which took me by surprise. I had no intention of asking them that question. I do not believe it was a schooled response. We were simply talking about places and people and things.[25]

His Honour also noted his belief that the children had a greater perception of what was going on around them than many might have anticipated. Judges understand and respect the great trust children are reposing in them as a result of their participation in a judicial interview. A High Court judge commented in an access case:

> There is a considerable element of trust in children expressing their views to the Court in this way. I am sure that the parties will realise that it is absolutely vital that the confidence and trust displayed by the children in this way is not abused.[26]

Regarding a child as a person in the 'here and now' enabled some judges to enter the child's world and understand their perspective—a vital skill if the decision is to have a real chance of being understood and accepted by the child. One Family Court judge[27] spent an hour talking with an eleven-year-old and, despite strong argument from counsel for the father who submitted that the girl 'was only a child and should not be able to control the situation', understood and accepted the child's wish not to have direct contact with her father. The girl, whose parents were separated, had been sexually abused when in the care of her mother by various of the mother's associates. The girl had now settled with a caregiver. She experienced her father's pressure for contact as aggressive and abusive. It had resulted in interference with her ability to concentrate at school and was causing her ill-health. Her Honour commented that the child needed to be reassured that her views were listened to if gains she had made in counselling were not to be lost.

In another access case, a judge emphasised the importance of listening to a nine-year-old child who did not wish to have access with his father:

> This child ought to be heard and listened to carefully. With a background of such high marital discord including violence, and given his personality traits, it is clear that this boy needs to believe that he is worth listening to . . . I consider that long-term gain is more likely to be made if [the child] is not forced against his wishes to see his father, but is allowed to take the initiative himself in future.[28]

Another judge accepted in an access dispute that whether or not the father had been psychologically violent to the mother was to some extent irrelevant because:

[25] High Court, 1990, M88/84.
[26] High Court, 1990, AP/72/89.
[27] Family Court, 1998, FP085/38/95.
[28] Family Court, 1990, FP203/88.

> it is clear that this is what [the six-year-old child] believes. It is clear that she has this perception. It is clear that she is saying 'I do not want contact with father.'[29]

Judges who were prepared to listen to children found that children could propose useful solutions to the dilemma facing their family. One of the issues being litigated by parents who were unable to communicate about their son's care was which soccer club the boy should play for.[30] The child, though his counsel, suggested that he should play for his father's club on the weekends he was with his father, and for his mother's club on other weekends. In his view, this was the best way to stop his parents arguing. He said if he played solely for his mother's club his father would not be able to be involved at all in his soccer, whereas if he played for his father's club his mother would have difficulty transporting him to practices and games. The boy's suggestion assisted the parents to reach an agreement. Another child's proposal in an intractable access matter was accepted by the judge, who commented:

> I considered that [the child's wishes as expressed to the Judge] are entitled to substantial weight. I am also satisfied that they are his own reasoned wishes. He has had to cope with finding himself in the centre of a family feud. I am quite satisfied that each side has tried to use him in an attempt to score points against the other. [The child] has found his own solution to that problem and it should be respected.[31]

Judicial understanding of the Convention and its direction to respect the dignity of the child has led to an increase in judicial (or judicial directed) explanation to the child of the order of the court and the reasons for it. Such explanation was given in six of the judgments included in our research, and appears to have been regarded as useful when children were under parental pressure or the order was contrary to the child's expressed wishes. One judge commented:

> So concerned have I been as to the outcome of this case, that I have already consulted the children, as to the orders I propose making. I deliver this decision having already conveyed to the children, with only the lawyers present, my views, the orders I propose making, and having elicited their responses to those orders.[32]

As the two older children were opposed to contact with their father, the judge made an 'open' access order which would permit the children to make contact with their father if and when they so desired.

Where a court order was contrary to the children's expressed wishes, and the judge believed that the father had influenced the children against the mother, the judge directed that counsel for the children and the expert reporter explain the result of the court proceedings to the children that night before either of the children's parents did so.[33]

[29] Family Court, 1990, FP004/734/87.
[30] Family Court, 1998, FP284/91.
[31] Family Court, 1990, FP067/048/84.
[32] Family Court, 1998, FP560/97.
[33] Family Court, 1990, FP054/213/89.

In line with the Convention, a ten-year-old child's desire, conveyed through his counsel, not to express a wish was respected in a relocation dispute. The judge commented:

> I admire [child's] good sense in refusing to give any indication of his preference in this case. I infer he wants to avoid choosing against either parent, despite some pressure having been asserted from his mother's household . . . It is an adult dilemma, and [the child] is entitled to remain at the periphery, free of responsibility, with the expectation that the adults will make the decision, having proper regard to his needs.[34]

The courts recognise that neither the Convention nor section 23 of the *Guardianship Act* 1968 (the paramountcy provision) impose responsibility for the decision on the child and that the child's views are one factor—albeit a central one—in the determination of the child's welfare. Thus a nine-year-old child's wish for shared care, impelled by his sense of justice and his need to make his father happy, was unable to be given effect to because:

> Given the intense level of conflict between the parties, their complete inability to communicate, and the almost paranoid distrust each has of the other, a joint custody order . . . is quite out of the question.[35]

When a court makes an order contrary to a child's wishes, it can still show respect for the child by ensuring the reasons for the decision are explained to them. This occurred in a custody case where the judge said:

> It is not a question of the rights of the parents, but of what is best for the child. This means that the wishes of the child and the parents may at times be frustrated at great personal hurt and seeming injustice if the child's interests sufficiently so demand . . . From what I gleaned from my discussion with [the child] I consider he will accept the decision and will hopefully understand that the decision has been made taking into account his wish, but having regard to his welfare as the first and paramount consideration.[36]

CONCLUSION

The Convention requires that the legal process respect the dignity of the child and recognise that the child is a partner in family matters who is entitled to information and to have an opportunity to be involved in conversations about matters affecting the family. While the Convention does not repose responsibility for decisions concerning children on children, it does not allow adults to take total responsibility for such decisions without regard to the views of the children concerned. The matter should not be seen as one of dominance or authority, but rather of partnership. It is submitted that this quote from a Family Court judge

[34] Family Court, 1998, FP048/850/94.
[35] Family Court, 1998, FP009/1744/95.
[36] Family Court, 1994, FP009/773/93.

in one of the study judgments demonstrates how easy it is to overlook the message of the Convention:

> When contemplating matters of custody, lawyers, family members and even Judges, can sometimes fall prone to 'welfare-of-the-child-is-paramount' disease. A myopia can suggest that the child is properly at the centre of the family. Any decision about custody involves the family. The child is raised within a matrix of family relationships. The Court is required to give paramountcy to the welfare of the child when considering custody, but this does not mean that a family should rotate around a child. To do so would be unhealthy for both the child and adults. Any sensible social unit comprising adults and children will be directed by the adults, although they ought to take account of the needs of the children.[37]

The United Nations Committee on the Rights of the Child has advised that the Convention is to be regarded as:

> holistic in spirit, avoiding any hierarchy of rights or explicit categorisation by type . . . The holistic vision of childhood also brings intellectual, moral, emotional and spiritual needs into analysis alongside the physical.[38]

Such an approach to children's rights requires that all legal matters arising from parental separation be considered together. This would then enable the family processes and the legal processes to truly consider the importance for *this* child in *this* situation of the various options so that the child has the maximum opportunity to develop into an individual who is able to fully participate in society. Different aspects will be of importance for different children. One child may place emphasis on remaining in their home, neighbourhood and school, while another may place most emphasis on remaining with their siblings or having the resources necessary to develop a particular talent. That children can be sensitive to 'adult' matters and need them to be discussed and taken into account in decisions about 'child' matters is illustrated by the child in the study who wished to change to a shared care arrangement. This was due to his concern about his father's child support obligation and because he was aware that his father wanted shared care. The judge did not order shared care, but gave effect to the wish of the child expressed a year earlier and granted the father care of the child one week in every three.[39]

We consider that a holistic approach to family matters is more likely to result in acceptable and sustainable solutions. Such an approach would allow for a consideration and balancing of matters regarded with importance by the child, matters of importance to the parents and significant others, and practical matters such as employment, accommodation, finances and new personal commitments. A holistic approach would provide for a true family plan to be prepared which could consider the interests of all involved.

[37] Family Court, 1998, FP048/8.

[38] M Black, *Monitoring the Rights of the Child. Innocenti Global Seminar Summary Report* (UNICEF International Child Development Centre, 1994), p 21.

[39] Family Court, 1994, FP014/6/89.

Judicial decisions can have a major effect on children's lives, and the lives of their families. We trust that our research has shown the rich resource which court judgments provide for exploring what judges have to draw upon and to say about children in the context of family law proceedings. We consider that amendments are required to both statutes and to professional practice to place greater emphasis on children as social actors, and their Article 12 and 13 rights to have their views heard and taken into account. Our analysis has revealed that children are frequently an invisible and voiceless group within those areas of family law concerning property and finances. Even in other types of cases where children's welfare and views are more explicitly evident, the conceptions held about children generally can be used to avoid asking the particular child in the case for their views, or where these are expressed, to devalue them in the decision-making context. Children are an important part of the courts' constituency—recognising this will enhance the likelihood of effective decisions being made for both the child and their family.

POSTSCRIPT

The authors acknowledge that extreme caution is required when using judgments to make assumptions about judicial beliefs. A judgment is the court's answer to the request by the parties to resolve a matter or dispute for them. Except to the extent that it addresses questions of law, the judgment will be addressed to the parties—that is, the adults—and will contain the information the judge believes they require to enable them to understand, accept and implement the court's order. In some judgments, for example, it is apparent that the judge is aware of the children's wishes, but does not expressly base the decision upon them, possibly in order either to preserve the child's confidentiality or to avoid putting the child in a position of conflict should the parent(s) become aware of the child's views. In these cases, it is evident that the judge in fact gave effect to the child's views as the judge perceived them. Judgments may also be influenced by unstated matters such as the judge's perceptions of the parties and their lifestyles, the judge's conceptions of childhood and the judge's values. The conclusions and recommendations drawn by specialist report writers may be another influence.

The limitations of a judgment as a source of full data about what occurred in a case can be illustrated by the fact that in numerous cases included in the study where counsel for the child was involved, there was no reference in the judgment to any information provided by counsel or any submissions made by them. Yet the judges frequently recorded their thanks to counsel for the child for their constructive assistance in the cases, implying that their role was a significant, albeit relatively unmentioned, one.

15
The Reconstituted Family in Italian Law and Society

Valeria Mazzotta*

INTRODUCTION

The profound social, cultural and economic changes that have affected West Europe over the last twenty years have brought about the achievement of a new demographic reality that has greatly influenced the concept of the family. Beginning from the early 1960s, the so-called 'postmodern family'—a discursive concept coined by demographers and sociologists to indicate the relationship types superseding the institution of marriage and the contextual achievement of new affective relationships—was born, in addition to the existing families based on marriage.

It is a phenomenon that, to different extents and at different times, has involved every industrialised country. In Italy, it became important only around the late 1960s and early 1970s, largely because of the introduction of divorce at that time (L 898/1970), and because in 1975 reforms to the family law, based on equality between spouses and the extension of legal protection for minors, were passed.

It needs to be borne in mind that, in Italy, a traditional concept of the family is deep rooted, so change has been slower to occur there than elsewhere—such changes include a decrease in marriage rates, an increase in cohabitation, higher rates of separation and divorce, the social relevance of single-parent families, a comprehensive decline in the number of births and an increased increment of births outside marriage. Even today, the Italian situation has peculiar features: though the important sociological and cultural changes typical of the most advanced countries have been assimilated, a marked preference for marriage still exists, while the number of separations and divorces is limited.

Even so, it is widely accepted that the traditional model of the family is in question, and that new models of the family are occurring more and more frequently. This gives rise to the question of what is to be defined as a family.

This is not an easy question to answer—there is no single explanation because it depends on many different factors rooted in social and cultural values. In the

* Doctor in Law, University of Bologna, Italy.

TABLE 15.1: Separations and Divorces in Italy, 1991–99[1]

Period	*Separations*	*Divorces*
1991	44,920	27,350
1992	45,754	25,997
1993	48,198	23,863
1994	51,445	27,510
1995	52,323	27,038
1996	57,538	32,717
1997	60,281	33,342
1998	62,737	33,510
1999	64,622	33,852

TABLE 15.2: Number of Divorces per 100 marriages[2]

Country	*1970*	*1975*	*1980*	*1985*	*1990*	*1994**
Austria	18	20	26	31	33	34
France	12	16	22	30	32	35
England	16	32	39	44	43	44
Netherlands	11	20	26	34	29	29
Sweden	23	50	42	46	44	44
Hungary	25	28	29	33	31	30
Italy (sep)	3	6	8	10	13	16
Italy (div)	5 (1971)	3	3	4	8	8

*last available periods

same way, the law—which comes from society and represents present values and conceptions transformed into legal formulae—has had to adapt more and more to the particular needs of the sociocultural context of reference, so that the institution of the family has taken on different forms and meanings in different periods.

Although a variety of family models existed in the past, this was usually the result of involuntary factors—such as the early death of one of the spouses or mass emigration—which did not in any way affect marriage as a legal institution. In modern times, the coming of divorce and the weakening of traditional values have led to different family models, in which the autonomy of each partner is very important and has achieved a new relevance which was unknown in the past,

[1] Istat 2001 (Central Bureau of Statistics), see www.istat.it/Anotizie/Acom/sepdiv.html

[2] Istat (1997), see www.istat.it/Anotizie/Acom/sepdiv.html

allowing for the superseding of traditional schemes and the consequent spread of affective realities that satisfy the individual's emotional needs.

A further significant element is the acquired economic independence of women. This evens out the disparities in the distribution of power between the couple, and contributes to the crisis of marriage as a legal institution because the fear of no longer having access to financial security is no longer an obstacle to separation, or to a single life.

Marriage has partly given up its hegemonic role in favour of other family models, and in this way it is to be asserted that the family—the fundamental cell of society—still maintains its essential role: if the old concept of family was once based on the indissolubility of marriage, today it rests on a different foundation. This is the case in Italy too, even if this is so is to a lesser extent than in other countries.

However, it is undeniable that even in Italy there is a slow but progressive spread of alternative family models, evidence of the process of the transformation which is now being debated by the mass media who, in addition to politicians and the economy, are not content to simply report the process but are keen to drive it one way or the other. As Bernardini[3] argues, 'the family is a battle field where opposing interests and ideologies meet.'

Table 15.3: Alternative Family Models[4]

	No. of families	*No. of People in family*	*% of inhabitants*
Non-widowed single	2,194	2,194	3.8
Cohabitants	342	895	1.6
Married reconstituted families	382	1,128	2.0
Non-widowed mothers	611	1,472	2.6
Non-widowed fathers	103	255	0.4
Total		5,944	10.4

Table 15.4: Types of Marriage, 1990–96[5]

	1990	*1996*
Civil marriages (% of marriages)	16.8	20.3
Second marriages (% of marriages)		
Males	5.0	6.0
Females	3.3	4.4

[3] I Bernardini, *Una famiglia come un'altra* (Rizzoli, 1997), p 24.
[4] Istat (Central Bureau of Statistics, 1998.
[5] Istat (Central Bureau of Statistics), 2000.

THE RECONSTITUTED FAMILY

The increase in the rates of separation and divorce has led to a diffusion of the reconstituted family: according to recent data, in Italy the number of families reconstituted after an earlier marriage breakdown comes to 555,000—equal to 3.8 per cent of the total number of couples. Of these, 363,000 couples are married and 192,000 live together outside marriage.[6]

Even if these figures are less than the numbers recorded in other countries—for example, in the United States reconstituted families now make up 50 per cent of the present family structures, and 75–80 per cent of all individuals who divorce subsequently marry again—it is still a relevant phenomenon, destined to increase in the near future.

Analysing the phenomenon, what strikes us most is the lack of a precise word to identify it: usually the term 'reconstituted family' is used, as a literal translation of the English term that refers to a family composed of the ex-spouses, granted custody of the children, together with the new spouse. However it is incorrect to refer only to the former married couple, with children from the previous or new marriage, because in reality very often the new partners choose to live together as husband and wife, simply postponing the marriage; moreover, an approach to reconstituted families which focuses on emotional relationships must lead us also to consider families without children in the definition. Therefore, the most suitable definition of a reconstituted family is the one suggested by sociologist Laura Zanatta[7]: 'a married or not married couple, with or without children, where at least one of the two partners comes from a previous marriage or de facto relationship'; this is significant because in Italy there are many cohabitants without children. The diversity is greater in the centre and north of Italy, and divorced men, in comparison with women, are more prepared to remarry.

As far as cohabitants are concerned, the choice may be determined by many factors, with the rejection of marriage as an institution being only one. More often, the decision is made conditional on economic resources and the fear of losing economic benefits, such as maintenance or custody.

While the reconstituted family has always existed, in the past it was the death of a partner which induced a second marriage—not so much for love as for economic and social reasons.[8] Nowadays, however, it is the breakdown of marriage which is the main reason for new relationships, in addition to the fact that divorce brings two people the option of a new marriage.

The degree of complexity of a reconstituted family depends also on the presence of children from the former or current marriage. An important fact is that, in Italy, the family structure is less complex as, in 40 per cent of cases, new couples often have no children other than those born to the present union.

[6] *Ibid.*

[7] L Zanatta, *Le Nuove Famiglie* (Il Mulino, 1997), p 70.

[8] *Ibid.*, p 71.

TABLE 15.5: Family Structure[9]

Type of structure	%
Only children from the present relationship	39
Only children from a previous relationship	10
Children from both the present and the previous relationship	9
Without children	42

THE SEPARATION SCENE, FAMILY MEDIATION AND NEGOTIATION

Italian family law regulates two kinds of separation: judicial separation and separation by agreement (an equivalent of the British separation of spouses, based on a separation agreement).

The 'fault' separation no longer exists, having been eliminated by the Family Law Reform in 1975; however, a fault judgment survives as *addebito*—the Italian term may be translated as 'charge' or 'allegation'—which permits those involved in a judicial separation to ask the judge to attribute the responsibility for the marriage breakdown to one or both of the spouses whenever the intolerability of living together has led to a violation of matrimonial duties—such as, for example, the duty of fidelity. As has been cleverly argued by an expert in the subject,[10] the opportunity to consider infidelity as the basis for a charge—considering that the charge has economic consequences, such as the loss of maintenance or inheritance rights from the former spouse—leads to the use of accusatory and hostile terms when describing the new relationships of the separated spouses, and it is upon these assumptions that the new family has its foundations.

Judicial separation is a war waged on a battlefield, where the ex-spouses, supported by their lawyer, fight bitterly to redeem their dignity—which has often, for people whose marriages have broke down, been significantly injured. In this context of hard conflicts, children are often the involuntary protagonists in a cruel fight. They become victims of the quarrels and at the same time objects of blackmail and subjects of tutelage. Involvement of children in the process of separation is certainly not an expression of parental responsibility—as outlined also by the Ministers Committee of Europe Council in 1985—which remains towards children even after separation or divorce. Nevertheless, it is the desire for social rehabilitation that often inspires the fight for custody, rather than the interests of the child.

This is of particular importance to the reconstituted family because the success of the new family largely depends on the way the parents behave during the mat-

[9] *Ibid.*, p 80, based on Istat 1994–1995 data processing.
[10] Bernardini, n 3, p 35.

rimonial crisis. If, during the process of separation and divorce, they are able to talk and agree in a friendly manner, the success of the new family of each spouse is more likely, and children may find in the new partner of his/her parent the peace of mind necessary for proper parenting.

The intervention of a judge as arbitrator and the related involvement of a decisive power in the conflict is avoidable, because parties can opt for a separation based on agreement—that is, a separation of spouses which presupposes an agreement between the spouses to submit to ratification by the court. The court's close examination of the content of the agreement is intended to ensure that the actions of the parents are firstly in accordance with the interest of the children, and secondly in accordance with the peremptory rules about proprietary relations between spouses.[11] The court may well refuse to ratify the agreement, but it is not able to integrate or modify the spouses' agreement, which remains the foundation of the separation; thus ratification is only a formal requirement.

A well-written and peaceful separation agreement, not too generic or rushed, contributes to assuring the autonomy of the ex-spouses in their new lives, and also affects the welfare of the children, benefiting the formation of the new family. In this way, we may say that the separation agreement is the spouses' greatest responsibility—a very useful way of trying a peaceful settlement of the spousal dispute, with positive effects on the post-crisis arrangement.

The separation agreement, together with the de facto separations and the divorce based on joint request, can be placed in the sphere of the so called 'dejuridicisation' of divorce,[12] or 'privatisation of the treatment of matrimonial crises'[13] The lack of legal regulations governing the reconstituted family in some way represents a positive factor contributing to this phenomenon.[14] the components of the new family are given freedom to create their own family roles and they frequently resort to negotiation in order to reach an agreement—sometimes in advance—regarding the matrimonial crisis. (A similar debate in relation to cohabitation contracts and to civil union agreement is going on with regard to this subject in France.)[15]

Among the various ways of dealing with matrimonial conflict, aimed at making the most of the spouses' self-regulation, some attention should be given to family mediation, which permits the involved parties to work on the emotional aspects of the conjugal crisis, and also helps them to reorganise their own lives with regards to the emotional, legal, economic and fiscal sides of separation and divorce.

[11] M Sesta, *Lezioni di diritto d famiglia* (Cedam, 1997), p 93.

[12] P Ronfani, 'Dalla separazione patologica alla separazione responsabile. Il dibattiti tra gli studiosi', in G Maggioni, V Pocar and P Ronfani, *La separazione senza giudice* (Angeli, 1975), pp 13–33.

[13] L Carraro, 'Il nuovo diritto di famiglia' (1975) I *Diritto della famiglia e delle persone* 105; G Maggioni, 'Il ciclo di vita dei separati dal conflitto coniugale al divorzio', in G Maggioni, V Pocaramd P Ronfani *La separazione senza giudice* (Angeli, 1975), p 230.

[14] G Oberto, 'Prenuptial agreement in contemplation of divorce e disponibilità in via preventiva dei diritti connessi alla crisi coniugale' (1999) II *Diritto della famiglia e delle persone* 175.

[15] P Nicoleau, *Droit de la famille* (Edition Marketing, 1997).

Family mediation is an alternative approach to settling matrimonial conflict, aimed at moving beyond the strictness of traditional legal procedures based on an accusatory system. It should help couples to reach an agreement based on their capacity to negotiate which would be satisfying for both parties; overall, it would help to maintain parental functions with equal shares of responsibility.

Supporters of mediation think that it is a suitable instrument for solving some of the questions related to the social spread of new family models like the reconstituted family, as it helps to overcome the feelings of failure that people involved in separation often experience, and also supplies an aid to soothing resentment, in this way permitting dignity and the recovery of self-respect. In particular, it has been said that mediation is ' consistent with the evolution process now in progress in the field of family relations'.[16]

In Italy, family mediation is not yet so widespread, even though the discussion is now happening and expectations are high. Nevertheless, it must be said that there has been very sharp criticism from countries where mediation has been in use for a long time, so much so that a return to institutional methods of dispute settlement is becoming more likely.

THE RECONSTITUTED FAMILY AND THE LAW

It is recognised that the main reason for conflicts inside the new family is the absence of legal and social recognition, resulting in weak role institutionalisation—so much so that, on the basis of divorce statistics, second unions are frailer and weaker than first marriages.[17]

Italian family law ignores reconstituted families: it sees such a union as a de facto situation of no importance. Considering that the phenomenon also relates to unmarried couples—by choice or while awaiting a divorce decree—living with the partner's children born inside a previous marriage, or the present one, reference must also be made to de facto family legal regulation. The de facto family is in fact almost completely ignored by Italian law, with recognition in law being granted only to filiation.

Natural Filiation

Under the Family Law Reform of 1975, children born in a de facto family are protected in the same way as legitimate children. That is to say, parents of children born inside marriage, who have acknowledged a child together or subsequently, have the same duties and rights as legitimate parents towards their children.

[16] V Pocar and P Ronfani, 'De l'institution à l'auto—regulation', in J Commaille and F de Singly, *La question familiale en Europ* (L'Harmattan, 1997), p 265.

[17] Zanatta, n 6, p 88.

Relations Between Cohabitants

Cohabitation is not regulated by law, although parliament is now considering some Bills concerning the de facto family. However, contemporary interest in the phenomenon has required jurists and judges to deal with the problems arising from cohabitation, so that nowadays we have a lot of studies and jurisprudential precedents about the de facto family, especially concerning personal and economic relationships, where the need for legal intervention is particularly strong.

However, as with the lack of a proper law it is not possible to automatically apply the rules concerning spouses, all the economic assignments effected by partners to each other are explained as the assumption of natural obligation. With regard to inheritance, jurisprudence does not consider the surviving partner to have automatic rights to intestate succession on death, except in the case of their appointment as heir or a legacy, not even with regard to the family home where the woman has lived with the children and her partner—even where the owner is legally separated, his former wife remains the only person to be entitled to the family house.[18]

A wider opening exists with regard to the cohabitant's right of succession to the tenancy of a quasi-matrimonial home on the death of the unmarried partner.[19] A right to recover economic and non-economic damages from the person who has caused a partner's death through negligence or other tort has also been recognised.[20]

From De Facto Family to Reconstituted Family

On the property side, the most frequent case of conflict between the reconstituted family members and the members of the ex-conjugal family is with regard to the alimony due to the former wife with a new partner.

The problem has been widely discussed by the Court of Cassation which, in a recent case regarding divorce maintenance,[21] stated that a new, stable and economically satisfying relationship may well give grounds for the cancellation of the payment of alimony to the ex-wife, because 'the income situation of the spouses entitled to maintenance is also formed by eventual economic donations, not occasional but permanently given by a third partner with whom the ex spouse lives'. In the case of a second marriage, the law provides for the ending of any alimony obligations.

[18] Constitutional Court 26/05/1989 n 310, (1989) I *Giustizia Civile* 1782.

[19] Constitutional Court 07/04/1988 n 404, (1988) I *Foro Italiano* 2515.

[20] Court of Cassation 28/03/1994 n 2988, (1994) I *Giustizia Civile* 1849.

[21] Court of Cassation 10149/1999 in www.repubblica.it/cittadino.lex/famiglia/famiglia990924_c_divorzio/famiglia990924_c_divorzio.html

The Matrimonial Home

The untouchability of the property right is overridden by the preference given to children's need for protection. Therefore, the matrimonial home will preferably be assigned to the spouse granted custody, leaving out of consideration the entitlement to a property right or a life estate.[22] Sometimes it happens that the tribunal acknowledges the right of the house owner to ask the cohabitant for a rent.

RIGHTS AND RESPONSIBILITIES

So far as the parent not granted custody and the social parent are concerned, it has been said that 'rights and responsibilities of the new families, the reconstituted families, are inconvenient and contradictory, as they refer to relationships partly ended, partly interrupted, partly uninterrupted and party new'.[23] There is a particular conflict between the natural parent and the social parent. The 'coresponsibility principle', which entails that the relationship between parents and children endures even after the breakdown of a marriage, means that the parent not granted custody will share with the ex-spouse the responsibilities regarding the upbringing of the children. However, on many occasions the natural parent often substitutes in daily life for the distant figure of the absent parent.

ADOPTION OF THE CHILD BY THE SPOUSE

At present, according to Italian family law (and as in another countries), the constitution of a second family does not have any legal effect on the attribution of parental responsibilities: no legal bond between the step-parent and the children is granted to the new partner.

Though the only family relationships regulated by law are the ones based on blood ties, social parenthood may be legally acknowledged through the adoption of the child born within a partner's previous marriage. Although the role of the parent not granted custody is not removed, considering the parent-like relationships often established, the possibility of establishing a legal relationship when a sentimental relationship with a social parent already exists seems to be very appropriate.[24]

[22] Court of Cassation SU 28/10/1995 n 11297, (1999) *Famiglia e diritto* 521, comment by V Carbone.

[23] LD Wardle, 'The Evolving Rights and Duties of Step-parents: Making Rules for New Families', in J Eekelar and P Sarcevic, *Parenthood in Modern Society* (Martinus Nijhoff, 1994), p 384.

[24] M Dogliotti, 'Affidamento e Adozione', in *Trattato diretto da Cicu e Messineo* (Milano, 1990), p 314.

TABLE 15.6: Minors Adopted, 1984–90

Period	*Minors adopted*
1984	324
1985	370
1986	441
1987	434
1988	477
1989	475
1990	519

This 'special' adoption is regulated by Article 44(b), L 184/1983. It acknowledges that the new spouse has the opportunity to adopt the child of the other spouse: the law meets the requirement to regulate the relations between the children born in the previous marriage and the new spouse of the biological parent, who would otherwise be a mere outsider.

As previously mentioned, the law does not regulate the share of responsibility within the reconstituted family: there are very few doctrinal and jurisprudential interventions on the subject. However, leaving adoption out of consideration, it must be believed that some legal relevance is given to the relationship with the children of the spouse: from Article 78 of the civil code, we can deduce a direct affinity bond between the step-parent and his or her partner's child, from which the unbreakable conjugal impediment (Article 87 1° c n. 4 civil code) and rent agreement succession (l 392/1978 Article 6 1° c.) follow.

Some welfarist tendencies may well be seen in Article 433 of the civil code, which indicates the subjects bound to provide support payments. Although the child of the partner and the spouse of the parent are not included, the family solidarity basis of the support obligation is illustrated by the fact that people related by direct affinity are within the scope of the obligation.[25]

The adoption of children of the spouse is included among the 'adoptions in particular cases' regulated by Article 44 of the adoption law: this article introduces some exceptions to the severe rules regulating adoption in general, in order to mitigate the system and also to extend regulation to situations that would otherwise remain without legal acknowledgment.

The peculiarity of special adoption is that it does not cancel the blood tie with the biological parent, nor presuppose a situation in which the minor is abandoned; it does not imply the entire substitution of the surname, but only an addition; and finally, the agreement of both the adoptee and of their representative is requested.

[25] P Ubaldi, comment to Constitutional Court 31/1/1990 n 44 in (1991) II *Nuove Leggi Civili Commentate* 1009.

If the natural parent withholds consent, according to Article 46 of the adoption law the judge can examine the reason for the refusal and can approve the adoption just as if it is in the minor's interest; however, if the dissent is for good reasons, the adoption is not possible.

In a recent case,[26] the Constitutional Court stated that the natural parents can always withhold their consent. The court stated that 'in the special adoption procedure, the natural parents of the adoptee are entitled to make use of any procedural flaw which may obstruct the definitive realisation of the proceedings being taken in the minor's interest'. The Constitutional Court not only confirms the opportunity to carefully evaluate the minor's interest in being adopted, but also shows itself as sensitive to the need to protect the role of the natural non-custodial parent, by keeping his/her parental authority.

Preconditions for special adoption are:

- —marriage between the adopter and the parent of the minor;
- —custody;
- —exclusive exercise of parental authority by the parent who is married to the adopter.

Adoption is not possible if the parents have joint custody. Even though joint custody is not easily practised, if the circumstances are favourable for a proper exercise of it, then the relationship between the minor and his parents is so strong that any other welfare purpose of the adoption must be excluded.

Even though special adoption is not legitimising, in order to make it easier for the step-parent to exercise his or her duty of education, the biological non-grantee parent is replaced by the social parent even with regard to parental authority, and that implies the performance of maintenance, instruction and education: as argued and confirmed by some recent studies,[27] this is useful if the natural parent has disappeared, but it is inadequate if he or she is present, because that parent will be completely deprived of a parental role. Not only that: the social parents, even with hesitancy and ambiguity, would tend to safeguard their own role of friendship and complicity with the minor, instead of assuming real parental authority.[28]

Adoption: A Proper Measure

The opportunity to proceed to adoption in the minor's interest has been well identified by the Constitutional Court which, asked to give a constitutional judgment

[26] Constitutional Court 29/10/1999 n 401 in (2000) *Famiglia e Diritto* 213, comment by L Laudisa.

[27] Zanatta, n 6, p 91.

[28] I Thery and MJ Dhavernas, *La parentè aux frontiere de l'amitiè: statut et role du beau-parent dans lesfamilles recomposee*, in MT Meulders-Klein, *Les recompositions familiales aujourd'hui* (LGDJ, 1995), pp 159–87.

on Article 44, sub-section 5° of the adoption law,[29] declared its unconstitutionality—though only insofar as it does not permit the judge to reduce the age gap of eighteen years between adoptee and adopter unless there are good reasons for the realisation of the family unit. The court correctly stated that the benefits of a secure family unit, useful to the development of the minor and his social comfort, prevails over the legal rule prescribing that the minimum age gap between adopter and adoptee cannot be less than eighteen years.

The decision mentioned above has high juridical, moral and social value which is displayed by the evident awareness of the court of the transformations involving the modern family. These changes could overwhelm the interests of minors as weak subjects, so that they need the protection of adoptive status, thus ensuring an adequate integration into the new family.

From this point of view, the Constitutional Court invites judges to carefully evaluate the circumstances of each particular case, and to restrict the force of the legal rules regarding the age gap if it is advisable.

When the Adoptee is of Age

The matter of the adoption of a person of age who is a child of the spouse, in cases where there are other minors born to the new family, has been the object of contradictory decisions, both of the Constitutional Court and the Court of Cassation, which have aroused the interest of many.

First, a general view of the legal regulation of the subject must be given. In addition to Article 44(b) of the adoption law, regarding the adoption of a minor by the spouse of the parent, Article 291 of the civil code regulates the adoption of a child of age ('civil adoption'). Article 291 has a property function: it aims at warranting the adopter's interest in perpetuating his or her own name, estate and family tradition, although the adopter has no legitimate nor legitimised descendants. At the same time, it gives the adoptee the privilege and benefits of adoptive status.

In order that the adoptive tie conforms to the natural filial tie, the age gap between adoptee and adopter cannot be less than eighteen years (but see above). Adoption is forbidden if there are legitimate children: from this point of view, the position of both an orphan and of a child of age is worse than the position of a minor, because a minor can be adopted by the new spouse of the parent even if there are children of the new couple, whereas for a child of age or an orphan it is not the same. That leads to the delicate problem of inequality of treatment because—as argued by an influential doctrine[30]—'the need for protection doesn't automatically stop when one comes of age'.

[29] Constitutional Court 31/1/1990 n 44.

[30] G Sbisà and G Ferrando, *Dell'adozione di persone maggiori di età e dei suoi effetti* in *Commentario al diritto italiano della famiglia, diretto da Cian* (Oppo, Trabucchi, Tomo IV, 1992) p 245.

An opening in this direction, and a consequent mitigation of the prohibition, was obtained by means of two judgments of the Constitutional Court that gave to the adoption of the child of age a further and different function more typically marked to solidarity and welfare needs. First, the court declared Article 291 of the civil code unconstitutional in the part where it forbids adoption to people with legitimate or legitimised descendants, who are of age and assenting[31]; subsequently,[32] the court declared that Article 297 sub-section 2° of the civil code—according to which the Tribunal can pronounce the adoption in the minor's interest even in the case of the disagreement of the spouse—was applicable also in the case of the inability of the children to give their consent as required.

However, an obstacle to the adoption of children of age remains for people with minor legitimate or legitimised children. The Constitutional Court confirmed its opinion in this sense, arguing that otherwise the minor would be deprived of the capability of giving his consent once he became of age, and also that the risk would be 'altering the aim of the adoption, which does not have the same needs and urgency as the special adoption regulated by Article 44 LA.'[33]

As far as the reconstituted family is concerned, the Constitutional Court pronounced a judgment on the matter of the adoption of an adult child of the spouse of the adopter.[34] In that case, however, it avoided any evaluation: the court asked for a constitutionality judgment with regard to Article 312 of the civil code which, referring to the adoption of the child of age, restricts the evaluation of the Tribunal to the advantage of the adoption for the adoptee whereas, in the case of minors, Article 55 of the adoption law asks of the Tribunal for Minors a more complex evaluation of the children's interests. The court declared that only the law can introduce an exception to the competence of the Tribunal for Minors.

As can be seen, the court's caution seems excessive, because in that case it was simply asked to extend its evaluation to the relevance to the family unit (Article 30, 1° and 2° sub-section, Constitution)[35]—even in the case of the adoption of an adult child of the spouse of the parent, because there is no difference with respect to the situation of the minor.

The Court of Cassation[36] has recently been called upon to pronounce judgment in a case similar to Constitutional Court 252/1996. Beginning with the deep differences between the adoption of a child of age and special adoption, the Supreme Court asserted that the adoption of the spouse's child has an independent configuration, as it is a very peculiar situation.

[31] Constitutional Court 19/5/1988 n 557, (1988) I *Foto Italiano* 2801.

[32] Constitutional Court 20/7/1992 n 345 in (1992) *Archivio Civile* 1151.

[33] Consitutional Court 23/2/1994 n 53 in (1994) *Diritto della famiglia e delle persone* 1169.

[34] Constitutional Court 16/7/1996 n 252 in (1996) *Famiglia e diritto* 506, comment by W Riedweg.

[35] According to Art 30 of the Constitution, 'the parents have the right to maintain, educate and intsruct their children, even if born outside of marriage'; according to 3° ss 'the law ensures to children born outside of marriage any legal and social protection compatible with the rights of the legitimate family'.

[36] Court of Cassation 14/1/1999 n 354 in (1999) *Famiglia e diritto* 113, comment by L Rossi Carleo.

In that specific case, the trial court had pronounced that the new wife, with children born within the new marriage, could not adopt her husband's adult child both because of the lack of a minimum age gap of eighteen years—according to Article 291 civil code—between her and the adoptee, and because of the existence of other minor children born to the new marriage who were unable—as minors—to give their consent to the adoption of the step-brother.

The court repealed the judgment, and stated that the specific case differed from both special adoption and the adoption of a child of age. It also highlighted the principle of the family unit: if there are both minors and 'of age' brothers, the adoption would help a 'more complete union of the couple and the children' as 'the relationships derived from the adoption are the same as the relationships inside the biological family, where importance is only given to personal and emotional ties'. In this way, the age gap limit cannot be considered a good reason to differentiate between similar situations, whereas the right to become part of a stable and suitable family must be given to orphans, either minor or of age, whether from the same family or having the same father.

The supreme constitutional principle of the family unit does not admit any derogation justified by the full age of the adoptee, which can be seen as an overriding of the original function of civil adoption, which is the inheritance function. The court is aware of the diffusion of the reconstituted family today as a consequence of the increase in divorce; therefore, the need to grant facilities to the new spouse, willing to adopt his partner's child, meets a concrete need in daily life.

In this way, there is a will to favour the formation of new families—in itself already characterised by 'a situation of strong living together'—and also to give the new spouse/step-parent legal recognition. Of course, legal recognition 'will develop a valid and useful relation also with the children born in the first marriage and not yet self-sufficient, without distinction between minors and those of full age'.

In light of the decision mentioned above, a conclusive consideration is inevitable: on the basis of Constitutional Court 44/1990, which cleverly enhanced the value of the family—and the unit of the family in particular—the Court of Cassation agrees with that part of the doctrine which identifies in the family unit 'the real expression of the equal social dignity of the members of the family.'[37] The consequence is that, as an independent interest of the single members of the family is absent but the interest of the whole group actually exists, the interest of the adoptee is realised by belonging to the family.

WHAT REGULATIONS GOVERNING PARENTAL RESPONSIBILITY EXIST WITHIN THE RECONSTITUTED FAMILY?

According to recent surveys, local authorities have a low but constant percentage of requests regarding the adoption of children born to one or other of the spouses

[37] P Perlingieri, *Riflessioni sull'unità della famiglia* in *Rapporti personali nella famiglia* (Napoli, 1982), p 7.

in a reconstituted family. It must also be observed that the spouse who is not a biological parent, but who has a parental function, usually thinks of themselves as being logically and naturally entitled to exercise parental responsibility together with, and in the same way as, his/her spouse, and that this is a demonstration that the reconstituted family aspires to be socially recognised as a 'normal' family with 'normal' children.

Nevertheless, in the majority of countries, no rights or duties are given to social parents with regard to the step-children—for example, no legal duty of maintenance exists with respect to the partner's child. Even in the United States, where the reconstituted family represents a widespread and accepted reality, the duty of maintenance corresponds more to a sort of natural obligation than to a legal duty, and is susceptible to termination at will, and at any time.

England is a partial exception: according to statutory law, when a second marriage has been dissolved, a maintenance order to support the step-child is possible, taking into account the extent to which the step-parent had assumed responsibility for the child and the liability of any other person to maintain the child.

However, except for a few countries—such as Holland, where the social parent has a duty to maintain his spouse's child until adulthood, or Switzerland, where the new spouse has a duty to help with the upbringing and the maintenance of his partner's children—the only way to give a legal basis to social parenthood is by adoption.[38]

One of the peculiarities of the reconstituted family lies in the existence of many parental figures—that is, in addition to the existing parents. The relationship between children born in the previous marriage and the new partner of the parent with custody is often very difficult, because of the relevance of social and legal issues. The reconstituted family represents 'a social aggregation with uncertain borders, that calls into question the criteria of parenthood and the concepts of social and biological parenthood with its duties and rights.'[39]

The lack, in the Italian language, of a suitable word for identifying the mother's second husband, not to mention other members of these new families, is significant: it is only possible to resort to unsatisfactory definitions which invoke dark and disliked figures and call to mind childhood novels where the step-mothers or step-sisters are always hostile characters.

From new familial bonds usually come new, very complicated relationships, together with the possibility of a mutual superimposition of biological and acquired parenthood requiring good relationships between the new family and the previous one, and favouring the maintenance of the child's bond with the parent not having the custody and with his/her relatives.

Although it is stated in advance that, while a marriage can easily be broken up, parenthood always lasts, and though non-judicial intervention such as family

[38] A Agell, 'Step-parenthood and Biological Parenthood: Competition or Co-operation' in J Eekelar and P Sarcevic, *Parenthood in Modern Society* (Martinus Nijhoff, 1994), p 414.

[39] V Pocar and P Ronfani, *La famiglia e il diritto* (Laterza, 1998), p 123.

mediation aims to help parenthood in the children's interest, nevertheless—considering the unavoidable relationship between step-parent and children—the relevance of the new figure's entrance into the minor's life cannot be denied.

Therefore, the social parent's role in bringing up their partner's child has to be established, while at the same time taking care not to eliminate or belittle the part of the natural parent. As has been argued,[40] the new spouse of the custodial parent is a step-parent, and in the same way as step-children are children, step-parents are parents, because they stand in the place of a parent with regard to their step-children: the step-parent lives with his/her step-children, plays the role of an adult to whom the children may refer, and usually contributes to the welfare and maintenance of the family. Nevertheless, the natural parent's role must be preserved so that, in the child's interest, the possibility of a regular 'pluriparenthood'—placing the social parent without threatening the genealogical parent's role—can be admitted.[41]

The problem is therefore how to make the rights and duties of the biological parent fit with the rights and duties of the social parent—to identify possible avenues for the legal relevance of parental responsibility within the reconstituted family. According to current law, there are no alternatives: either the social parent adopts the child, in this way eliminating any rights and duties of the non-custodial biological parent, or the role of the social parent has no legal relevance at all.

This does, however, seem quite an absolute and extreme conclusion. In fact, the step-parent–step-child relationship is different from the biological parent–child relationship, and it is in the child's interest to keep both relationships. A legal recognition of the parental responsibility of the step-parent does not necessarily require the legal termination of the parental rights of the non-custodial biological parent, nor the interruption of any contact, except if the biological parent voluntarily disappears with the precise intention of shunning his or her parental responsibilities.

Such a conclusion seems agreeable to those who claim that full legal recognition of the reconstituted family is necessary, with a consequent revision of the concept of the family inspired by a principle of equality between biological and social parents—that is, the attribution of parental responsibility to social parents—and that, at the same time considering the unavoidable difference between biological and 'step'-family, the law should also give individuals the option to break the rules.[42]

According to a second opinion,[43] the position of the non-grantee biological parent should be primarily safeguarded, except for the refusal of any educational

[40] Wardle, n 22, p 386.

[41] I Thery, *Droit, justice et demandes, reflexion sur un objet introvable* in MT Meulders-Klein *Famille et Justice* (LGDJ, 1997), pp 23–24.

[42] Wardle, n 22, pp 385–88.

[43] M Jaap and E Doek, 'Separazione e Secondo Matrimonio: l'Attribuzione delle Responsabilità Genitoriali', in (1993) 4–5 *Il bambino incompiuto* 47.

role, and attribution of parental responsibility to the social parent should be subject to the former's consent. Accordingly, the law should favour the self-regulation of relationships, and family mediation might also be useful within the reconstituted family.

Both opinions lend themselves to some observations: with regard to the first viewpoint, we may comment that the necessary joint parental responsibility of the social and the biological non-grantee parent would further devalue the role of the latter—which is often already very uncertain. As far as the second opinion is concerned, such a position runs the risk of increasing the number of cases of judicial intervention in conflicts between the different parents, albeit in the minor's interest.

Lastly, there is a further problem to solve. It has already been mentioned that the reconstituted family is often also a family composed of unmarried partners, so it is necessary to decide whether parental responsibility should also be extended to the unmarried social parent. Though a positive solution is desirable in the minor's interest, this brings up some difficulties with regard to coordination with the unsolved matter of the legal condition of the de facto family.[44]

WHAT INTERVENTION?

Although the reconstituted family is a new phenomenon, it is increasingly common. Considering the lack of applicable laws and the fact that new social policies are still based on the married family and on legitimate children, it is understandable that the legal regulation of relationships between parents and step-children under these circumstances represents a real challenge—one which, it is widely believed, the law cannot shirk any longer.

The attendant paradox is that, on the one hand, the legal systems of Western countries consider marriage to be a contract from which the parties may withdraw through divorce, but that, on the other hand, parenthood is still regulated on the basis of the nuclear family, the foundation of which is the exclusivity and perpetuity of biological parents even after separation, ignoring the social parent and the actual transformation of families.[45]

The reconstituted family puts forward the necessity of reconciling biological parenthood with social parenthood: this is a difficult task, all the more so in Italy where family policy has never been effectively started nor realised. Furthermore, in Italy more than anywhere else, the idea of family is connected to the indissolubility of marriage and legitimate filiation, so that the few legal interventions made are aimed at sustaining the family, rather than at meeting the needs of individual family members.

[44] Pocar and Ronfani, n 38, p 202.

[45] *Ibid.*, p 199.

In this way, prohibitions are very often imposed and the boldest initiatives are halted because they lack precedent. In such a scenario, the majority of regional legislation, and the performance of welfare responsibilities, tend to sustain the conjugal family.

However, Emilia Romagna represents an exception where, in some circumstances, a kind of 'institutionalisation' of new family models has been recognised. To this effect, a deliberation of the city council of Bologna is significant[46]: besides providing for supportive measures and housing policy in favour of the new social formations 'that bring to social attention new models of cohabitation', the council wished for legal recognition by means of adequate national legislation.

Even if the lack of suitable intervention could be justified on the basis that the number of new families in Italy is less than in other countries, the shortfalls in social policy cannot be overlooked. Future legislative interventions in the field of the family must necessarily be harmonised with European legislation, where the general trend is to see family policy as playing a supporting role to people.[47]

The intention is to give relevance to the individual who finds solidarity and reciprocity in the family. Generally speaking, these trends are the same in Italy. According to some surveys,[48] the family is one of the most important values while, as far as public intervention is concerned, Italians are prone both to a solidaristic and an individualistic concept of the family: on the one hand, Italians ask for public intervention welfare assistance; on the other hand, the state should leave the family out of consideration and consider the individual instead.

Even in Italy, there is an undeniable disjunction between the legal crystallisation of values and family practice, with reference to the reconstituted family for example, and even though 'atypical' unions are still few in number, the steady increase means they are not marginal.

Many bills concerning the family have already been tabled in parliament, but have been unsuccessful—many have not even been discussed, thus confirming the idea that public institutions are not yet ready to absorb social changes and transformations which require adjustments to family policy. Many ask for a complete project of intervention on the family, which would give relevance to the family as a social subject with functions of solidarity and reciprocity independent from the chosen model. Considering its peculiarities and the interconnections between the different relationships inside the new family, it seems quite wrong to regulate the reconstituted family too closely.

It may be that all the law is able to do is to create some legal instruments which can be adapted in a flexible way to any particular individual case.

[46] 1 March 1997, 'Deliberation of Bologna City Council concerning the protection of different family models'.

[47] W Dumon, 'Les Incertitudes des Politiques à l'Egard de la Famille', in J Commaille and F de Singly, *La question familiale en Europe* (L'Harmattan, 1997), p 89.

[48] Eurobarometro 1993.

16

Child-centred, Vertically Structured and Interdisciplinary: An Integrative Approach to Children's Policy, Practice and Research

Annie G Steinberg, Barbara Bennett Woodhouse and Alyssa Burrell Cowan*

INTRODUCTION

As we begin to recognise children as persons with rights and voices of their own, a modern discipline of the study of childhood is emerging. In response to the needs of children, childhood studies and formation of policy for children have become more integrative of the range of disciplines and professions concerned with children's welfare. Children's issues do not exist in a vacuum, nor are they the province of any single profession or discipline. Legal issues are intricately intertwined with issues of child development, history, economics and social science. Medical practice must be informed by statutory and constitutional law and knowledge about family sociology. Social work professionals in the field and the laboratory must apply judgments drawn from law and medicine as well as the social sciences. Moreover, advocates for children working at all vertical levels—from theory and policy formation to clinical and court practice—must remain in

* Annie Steinberg, MD is Assistant Professor, Departments of Psychiatry and Paediatrics, University of Pennsylvania School of Medicine, Co-Director of CCPPR and Director, Deafness and Family Communication Center, Children's Hospital of Philadelphia. Barbara Bennett Woodhouse, JD was Professor of Law at the University of Pennsylvania Law School and Co-Director of CCPPR until July 2001 when she became the David H Levin Chair in Family Law at the University of Florida's Levin College of Law, where she is founder and Director of a new Center for Children and the Law based on CCPPR's organising principles. Alyssa Burrell Cowan, MSW is Coordinator of the Center for Policy, Practice and Research at the University of Pennsylvania (CCPPR). This paper owes a great debt as well to our fellow CCPPR Co-Directors Richard Gelles, PhD, and Carol Wilson Spigner (aka Williams), DSW, both of the School of Social Work, whose ideas are reflected herein and whose collaboration and inspiration is central to this project. We are grateful as well to the deans of our respective schools, Dean Ira Schwartz (Social Work), Dean Arthur Asbury (Medicine) and Dean Michael Fitts (Law), as well as to University of Pennsylvania President Judith Rodin, for their continuing support and encouragement.

constant conversation, so that our theory and policy may never lose touch with the real lives of children and our practice may be reinvigorated by new theoretical perspectives.

This paper describes the genesis and philosophy of the Center for Children's Policy Practice and Research at the University of Pennsylvania (CCPPR) which can serve as a template for the creation of similar projects. The plan to create such a centre at the University of Pennsylvania was first conceived in 1998 by faculty from the Schools of Law, Medicine, Nursing and Social Work. In December of that year, a diverse group of colleagues from across the university began to meet to discuss how we might form a vehicle to integrate our common professional interests in children and their welfare. By Autumn of 1999, the idea had crystallised as 'CCPPR' with a physical home on campus, and was formally recognised as 'a joint project of the Schools of Law, Medicine and Social Work'.

The founders were convinced that the study of childhood, and the creation of child-centred social policies, can only be accomplished in an interdisciplinary setting. The mission of CCPPR was to mobilise the resources of all disciplines engaged in childhood issues across the campus to seek innovative solutions for the crises facing America's children. We chose the name because its acronym, CCPPR, matched our goals—to provide 'a double dose of CPR (cardiopulmonary resuscitation) for a child welfare system in need of resuscitation'. Rather than confining our involvement only to practice or policy or research, we sought to combine all three levels of activity in a vertical structure that would maintain linkages at all stages of scholarship, practice and reform. This paper will describe our methods and the projects we have undertaken, and will also discuss the pitfalls and challenges of this highly demanding integrative approach.

THE CRISIS IN CHILD WELFARE PRACTICE AND POLICY

Children must have a stable and nurturing environment in order to become self-sustaining adults capable of caring for their own families. However, the lives of far too many children in the United States are compromised by violence, poverty, inadequate health care and the failures of the systems designed to protect and treat dependent and delinquent children. In many respects, American children at the beginning of the millennium are facing a 'crisis of neglect'. Our accelerated age has resulted in community instability, fragmented families and a generation of pseudo-mature children forced to function in domains far beyond their developmental capabilities.

Children are increasingly both victims and perpetrators of sexual offences, hate crimes, homicide—even mass murder. The well-being of children and adolescents is often overlooked or ignored until the need for intervention reaches crisis proportion. Attempts by social service agencies, health care professionals, the justice system and government agencies to remedy the problems facing children and families are too often stop-gap, poorly implemented, fragmented and ultimately ill-fated.

By any measure, as the twentieth century closed, the United States continued to fail miserably in assuring the rights of all its children to be healthy, safe and secure in their own homes and communities. Consider the following data:

—As many as half of the children who are killed by parents or caretakers are killed after the children and their families have come to the attention of the child welfare system. Children are also killed in foster care, again while supposedly under the protection and supervision of the child welfare system.[1]

—The booming economy and apparent effective strategies to control crime and domestic violence have had no impact on child maltreatment. Child abuse and neglect reports have increased dramatically to about three million per year.[2] Child fatality numbers have remained at around 1,200 per year, with a rise of 8 per cent in deaths from child abuse between 1997 and 1998. Out-of-home placements remain at about 500–600,000 children on any given day.[3]

—The average length of stay for children in foster care is two years and nine months. More than half of the children in foster care on 30 September 1999 stayed in care longer than eighteen months. Approximately 118,000 children in foster care are waiting to be adopted.[4]

—Youths ageing out of foster care face many significant difficulties. A national study reported that within two to four years of leaving foster care only 54 per cent had completed high school, fewer than half were employed, 25 per cent had been homeless, 30 per cent had no access to needed health care, and 60 per cent of the young women had given birth to children of their own.[5]

—Children are often removed inappropriately, and children in foster care are also disproportionately African-American or minority children. Many critics of the child welfare system view the system as oppressive and destructive to minority families. In Philadelphia, a city with a large percentage of minority families, a stunning 7 per cent of all children are officially deemed abused and neglected.[6]

[1] Richard J Gelles, *The Book of David: How Preserving Families Can Cost Children's Lives* (Basic Books, 1996).

[2] Seth C Kalichman, *Mandated Reporting of Suspected Child Abuse: Ethics, Law, and Policy* (American Psychological Association, 1999).

[3] *Ibid.*; Ira M Schwartz and Gideon Fishman, *Kids Raised by the Government* (Praeger, 1999).

[4] Children's Bureau, *Administration for Children and Families*, US Department of Health and Human Services, The AFCARS Report, Current Estimates as of Oct 2000 (Children's Bureau, 2000).

[5] Children's Defense Fund, *Child Abuse and Neglect Fact Sheet* (2000), Retrieved 6 Nov 2000 from the World Wide Web: http://cdfweb.vwh.net/ss_child_abuse.html

[6] Martin Guggenheim, 'Somebody's Children: Sustaining the Family's Place in Child Welfare Policy (2000) 113 *Harv L Rev* 1716; Dorothy E Roberts, 'Is there Justice in Children's Rights? The Critique of Federal Family Preservation Policy' (1999) 2 *U Pa J Const L* 112.

—In 1998, four million children lived in households headed by their grandparents and 1.4 million of these children had neither parent present. The number of children living with grandparents with neither parent present in the home grew almost 52 per cent between 1990 and 1998, making it the fastest growing portion of children living with relatives.[7]

—Eight years ago, the National Commission on Children reported: 'If the nation had deliberately designed a system that would frustrate the professionals who staff it, anger the public who finance it, and abandon the children who depend on it, it could not have done a better job than the present child welfare system. Marginal changes will not turn this system around.' At least 25 state child welfare agencies are presently operating under a court order as a result of lawsuits arising out of the various failings of the agencies.[8]

—Health care, child welfare and legal systems designed to protect our children too often fail to respect children's rights to participation and voice.[9] Children who are subjects of child protective proceedings are unrepresented in a large percentage of cases. Case loads for children's attorneys are crushing. The average child protective hearing lasts ten minutes.[10]

Children are the least powerful of persons and as such are most in need of high quality advocacy, research and policy initiatives. Recent 'reforms' have exacerbated barriers to accessible health services and deprived families of economic support, potentially placing children at increased risk. In child welfare, the tried and true 'reforms'—pouring more staff, more funding, more training, more services into a flawed system—have failed to have even a small impact. Our knowledge of the underlying issues remains insufficient. Few individuals have the breadth of training and access to interdisciplinary perspectives necessary to make recommendations for substantive change.

BUILDING THE CENTER FOR CHILDREN'S POLICY PRACTICE AND RESEARCH

This section describes the components of the Child-centered, Vertically Structured, Interdisciplinary Project we use as a vehicle for confronting these problems, as well as some features of the academic, political and social community in which it is situated.

[7] Census Bureau, *Current Population Reports, Marital Status and Living Arrangements, March 1998 Update* (Census Bureau 1998).

[8] Schwartz and Fishman, n 3.

[9] Frank P Cervone and Linda M Mauro, 'Ethics, Cultures, and Professions' (1996) 64 *Fordham L Rev* 1975; Catherine J Ross, 'From Vulnerability to Voice' (1996) 64 *Fordham L Rev* 1571; Jean Koh Peters, 'The Roles and Content of Best Interest in Client-directed Lawyering for Children in Child-protective Proceedings', 64 *Fordham L Rev* 1505.

[10] American Bar Association, *America's Children at Risk: A National Agenda for Legal Action,* A Leon Higginbotham Jr and Catherine J Ross eds (ABA Press, 1993).

The Community Context

Often, the disjunction between policy and practice is exacerbated by physical and social barriers that separate field level and theoretical workers. The University of Pennsylvania has the advantage of being located in a large urban area which concentrates many of the most difficult problems of child welfare. Philadelphia, with a population of 1.5 million, currently has 24,557 children under the supervision of the Department of Human Services (DHS).

The university is well situated as a site for interdisciplinary work on behalf of children: the university community numbers 38,534 and includes the Schools of Medicine, Law, Social Work, Education, Nursing, Business, and Communications. These professional schools are in addition to the School of Arts and Sciences, which is organised into numerous departments including Sociology, History and many other fields of study, and trains students both at the undergraduate and graduate levels. The university is also home to many specialised research centres such as the Center for Bioethics, the Institute for Law and Economics and the Center for the Study of Youth Policy.

Finally, the city has a vibrant public interest community of non-governmental organisations (NGOs) concerned with children and youth. Involvement in juvenile and children's issues by the Juvenile Law Center, the Support Center for Child Advocates, the Education Law Center, the Public Interest Law Center of Philadelphia, the Women's Law Project, the Public Defender Association, Community Legal Services and Philadelphia Legal Assistance, to name a few, contributes to a lively debate about polices and practices affecting children. The City of Philadelphia's subdivisions that deal with children, including the District Attorney, Department of Human Services, Family Courts, Department of Health, and managed mental health care (Community Behavioral Health) are engaged in an ongoing dialogue with these NGOs as well as with the university community. In short, the community context of public, private and academic resources in close proximity to a population of children at risk presents a unique opportunity for innovative work on behalf of children.

The Structural Framework

CCPPR's founders realised that our goals and principles needed to be translated into a structured framework. Five structural factors emerged as integral to achieving our vision. We agreed that our project must be vertically integrated, interdisciplinary, team-based, child-centred and developmentally informed.

Vertical integration refers to a commitment to operate simultaneously at all levels of action. Traditionally, a project is focused on one among a variety of levels at which action and the production of knowledge about children take place. At the 'ground level' is the clinic, providing medical, legal and/or social services to individual children. At the second level is the research centre with a mission of identifying and carrying out research on issues of importance to children and youth. Operating at a third level is policy and political advocacy, engagement in providing consultation and inputs to policy-makers with the objective of achieving broad systemic reform. While some of the founders were firmly rooted in clinical practice and others primarily engaged in theoretical modelling, policy formation or research, all of us agreed on the importance of integrating these fields of activity. Too often, policy-makers become disengaged from the realities of practice. Theoreticians and researchers can waste time and energy on problems that are irrelevant to those in the field. We believed our collective capacities would be enhanced by adopting and maintaining a vertically integrated structure which ensures our continuing engagement at all levels.

Interdisciplinarity refers to a commitment to viewing the problems and study of childhood through a variety of critical and professional perspectives. Working in isolation, scholars and professionals from social work, medicine, law, political science, education and sociology are disabled from addressing problems that cut across a wide range of disciplines. Since children are our focus, we must pay attention to the child's whole experience and environment. One cannot isolate children's mental development and physical health from their access to justice and education, or their social well-being from the material and social conditions of family and community. A sense of historical perspective and sensitivity to race, class and gender must inform work at every vertical level. No one profession or discipline has 'the answer' and all must work together in order to identify and address the problems facing children and to effectively meet children's needs. Our structure was designed to ensure the maintenance of an interdisciplinary perspective.

Team-based structures assume that any endeavour, whether clinical or theoretical, is enhanced by collaboration. The very process of assembling a team forces us to identify and engage diverse perspectives and approaches. Team-based activities enrich the discussion and educate the participants. Team-based operations provide a learning environment for novices as well as for experienced professionals, and are an important tool for accomplishing the teaching mission of a university. Teamwork, however, is not necessarily 'efficient'. In fact, it is often more labour-intensive and time-consuming than individual effort. Despite this, we concluded that our structure must ensure a continuing commitment to collaborative, team-based activity.

Child-centred refers to a shared commitment to moving children and their experiences from the periphery, where they have traditionally been marginalised (barely seen and not heard), to the conceptual and practical centre. A child-centred perspective plays out differently in different contexts. In the realm of law, for example, a child-centred perspective asks that we reframe legal doctrines that have so often focused on 'parents' rights' so that they are refocused on to 'children's needs and experiences.'[11] It requires that we constantly ask: 'What does this policy or practice mean to children? Is children's welfare served or disadvantaged by this policy choice?' One of us, in her writings, has labelled this child-centred perspective as 'generism' and its practitioners as 'generists.'[12] A generist approach identifies the next generation as the primary focus of study and of action. Just as feminists focus on women, in studying or working with victims of domestic violence, economic dislocation, family dysfunction and access to medical services, a generist or child-centred perspective commits us to exploring the child's experiences. Domestic violence, family dissolution, economic, medical and mental health policies have specific implications for children—and they are sometimes quite different to their implications for adults. Our structure must explicitly and implicitly commit us to adopting and maintaining a child-centred perspective and resisting the pull of the adult-centric perspective.

Developmentally informed policy, practice and research must be cognisant of and consistent with what we know and are continuing to discover about child development. Child development is distinct from the idea of childhood. Childhood is, in many ways, a social construct. In some cultures, children 'work' side by side with adults almost as soon as they can walk, and in others they are segregated in 'play' and 'educational' settings well into young adulthood. Child development, however, is a very real physical and neurological process. While children and youths are entitled to equal dignity and equal justice with adults, they are also entitled to be treated differently from adults when doing so is necessary to meeting their needs, understanding their reality and protecting their developmental potential.

The Team-based Approach

The work of the CCPPR is carried out by interdisciplinary teams. The composition of a given team depends on the task at hand and draws upon the people most skilled in the particular fields relevant to the team's specific mission. Following is a listing of our teams and some of the matters they have handled.

Clinical Team

A clinical team will usually include a social worker, a legal professional and a medical or mental health professional, as well as students in each of these disciplines. Clinical teams carry out clinical evaluations and provide expert testimony in legal proceedings, such as those involving:

[11] Barbara Bennett Woodhouse, 'Hatching the Egg: A Child-centered Perspective on Parents' Rights' (1993) 14 *Cardozo L Rev* 1747.

[12] *Ibid.*

—ten and fourteen-year-old siblings facing future adoption and the formal termination of their mother's parental rights under the *Adoption and Safe Families Act* (ASFA);
—fourteen- and fifteen-year-old brothers charged with first degree murder in the shooting of their chronically abusive father;
—a twenty-month-old in need of a developmentally appropriate interstate custody/visitation plan;
—a nine-year-old boy denied counsel and sign language interpreter in child protective proceedings.

Research Team

A research team is composed of scholars engaged in preventive interventions related to child welfare and juvenile justice. CCPPR has been involved in research and design of a computerised risk assessment system, as well as an evaluation of a pilot program involving law enforcement in the investigation of child abuse cases. Grant proposals are currently underway for research into many child welfare issues.

Technical Assistance/Training Team

Agencies seeking to improve or evaluate their operations contract with CCPPR for consultation and training on a one-time or continuing basis:

—assessment of compliance by states and counties with consent decrees ensuring access by children to child protection, mental health and special education services;
—provision of a social worker, a lawyer and a psychiatrist to lead a discussion among district attorneys at the field level on the challenges of dealing with child sexual abuse cases.

Law and Policy Team

Team members are prepared to address law and policy issues at all levels, but especially the upper levels of the vertical structure. For example, law and policy teams have submitted 'friend of the court' or amicus briefs in important cases at the federal Appellate and Supreme Courts and have testified to Congress and state legislatures:

—amicus brief in *Brian B v Commonwealth*, filed on behalf of a coalition of corrections and education groups, with US Court of Appeals for the Third Circuit on the right to education of juveniles incarcerated as adults;
—amicus brief in *Troxel v Granville* submitted to US Supreme Court regarding the importance to children at risk of placement of ties to kin and extended family;

—testimony to Congress on the dangers to abused children of the *Religious Liberty Protection Act*;
—testimony to California Legislature on adverse effects on child abuse investigations of parental rights amendment.

INTERDISCIPLINARITY IN ACTION

The concept of interdisciplinarity is best understood with specific case examples. Below, we provide a detailed example of how our team worked together on behalf of an individual child, who we name Michael. This case description disguises the identity and alters the facts to protect the confidentiality of the family involved.

A Clinical Team Case Study: Michael Carter (a Seven-year-old Boy)

The Clinical Team Concept

One of the central components of CCPPR's approach is the interdisciplinary clinical evaluation team. The main role of CCPPR's interdisciplinary evaluation team is to provide evaluations to departments of child welfare, children's attorneys and family courts to assist them in determining the appropriate disposition for children and families involved in the child welfare system for reasons of child maltreatment.

The clinical team assembled for this case was headed by author Annie Steinberg, MD, a child psychiatrist/pediatrician. It also included Alyssa Burrell Cowan, MSW (then a second-year social work student) and a psychologist, Sacha Coupet, JD, PhD (who was then a third-year law student). Law Professor Barbara Bennett Woodhouse and Social Work Professors Carol Wilson Spigner and Richard Gelles were available to supervise the students and to participate in review of the team's case evaluations. In describing the team's activities, we will refer to the student members of the team by their disciplines (ie lawyer, social worker, etc).

Principles underlying the evaluations include assuring the child's safety, well-being and permanence, as well as assisting judges and child welfare agencies to affirm children's rights to continuity and stability in their attachments and familial relationships, and bodily and developmental integrity. The law-trained members of a CCPPR evaluation team do not form an attorney–client relationship with the child or any of the parties, but instead are utilised by the team as resources to educate the team on the relevant legal issues and assure that CCPPR's evaluation is responsive to these issues.

Procedural Context

Families are referred to CCPPR for these evaluations from a variety of agencies within Philadelphia, including children and youth services, family court, pro bono legal services, child advocacy organisations and individual attorneys and families. Regardless of who makes the initial referral, it is the policy of CCPPR to seek court appointment and/or agreement of all the parties so that CCPPR's recommendation can retain its child-centred focus rather than be allied with the parent or the state.

All children are entitled to lawyers in Philadelphia Dependency Court cases, and are usually represented by attorneys from the Child Abuse Unit of the Public Defenders Association (PD). Michael, however, was referred to CCPPR by the Support Center for Child Advocates (SCCA), a private, non-profit centre that represents and trains pro bono lawyers to represent children in especially difficult child abuse cases. SCCA attorneys often handle cases in which the PD's office is 'conflicted out' because a public defender is already representing a parent accused of criminal abuse or neglect. The court appointed an SCCA attorney to advocate on Michael's behalf because of concerns that his mother, due to her cocaine and alcohol addiction, was unable to care for him and his siblings.

Presenting Problem

Michael was a prime cause for concern because his mother had reported that he sat and rocked excessively, moving the furniture about the house with the fierceness of his rocking. In addition, Michael's school counsellor reported that Michael was having extreme problems at school, rocking back and forth in his seat and crying every afternoon, almost continuously. His teacher reported that, with one-to-one support, Michael was able to complete his school work and had no significant delays. However, without immediate supervision and support, he had difficulty maintaining attention and focus. In spite of his problems, the teachers reported that Michael was a likeable child who was kind and never aggressive towards others.

Prior DHS Involvement

Michael's family was not unknown to the child welfare system. Ten years before, a case was first opened as a result of a call to the child abuse hotline regarding Sheila Carter's (Michael's mother) crack use and lack of bonding to an older sibling, Trevor. Five years earlier, DHS initiated Services to Children in their Own Homes (SCOH), sending workers to the home to provide assistance to the child and caretaker. Because of concerns with the mother's stability and parental capacity, the maternal grandmother agreed to take temporary legal custody. As the children were now living with a capable adult caretaker, the case was closed the following month. The family again came to DHS's attention two years ago when Michael's sister, Becky, was molested by an adolescent relative who resided in the home. The molester was tried and incarcerated, and Becky went to live with her adult sister. It was unclear why DHS had not reopened the case following that incident, given the abundance of information regarding the ongoing use of cocaine and alcohol by Michael's mother.

A new crisis occurred when the maternal grandmother who had temporary legal custody died about a year and a half ago, and her two daughters (Sheila Carter and her sister, Pam Carter) moved into her home. Despite the change in the family structure and the loss of the caretaker, no reassessment was done of the children and their safety in the home, which was now headed by Sheila Carter and her sister, Pam—also a cocaine and alcohol abuser. Somehow, no new court order was issued regarding custody, despite the death of Michael's legal custodian. While Michael remained in legal limbo, he was also suffering renewed emotional distress. Because Michael's symptoms were emotional, and there had been no reports of physical abuse, DHS expressed doubts that sufficient evidence existed to support legal intervention. Because of the legal, social and medical complexity of the case, and the ongoing risk to the child, CCPPR accepted the referral from the child advocate to assess Michael and his family for an interdisciplinary clinical evaluation that might go beyond presumptions of adequate care and safety.

Evaluation Method

The philosophy behind a CCPPR evaluation is inclusive and integrative. It starts with inviting as many family members as possible to attend the session. This makes it possible for the evaluators to obtain a more holistic and balanced view of the family, as well as to construct a better assessment of the family's resources, strengths and weaknesses. The clinic's child-centred perspective conceptualises the child at the centre of a system of family and community resources. Every effort is made to avoid seeing the child as an isolated unit, out of context from the adults who know and care for him/her. An assessment of the quality of the child's attachment with siblings and with adults who have occupied a caretaker role in the past or present is an important part of the initial group evaluation. Prior to the evaluation session, the law-trained members of the team research the pivotal legal issues and brief the other team members on the standards that are pivotal to the case evaluation. In Michael's case, for example, the key legal issue initially appeared to be establishing a causal connection between a child's emotional distress and environmental or parenting deficits sufficient to deem the child 'dependent' or lacking 'proper parental care and control', the statutory standard for intervention.

Having many family members present for an evaluation when the family is chaotic and in crisis is less feasible if there is only one professional managing the session. With several team members participating, it is possible to discover much more information about the family and the child's life and to make a better assessment and recommendation to the judge. Moreover, having an interdisciplinary team provides a richer, more meaningful evaluation of the child and family. In this case, despite the chaos that prevailed when family communication style was manifested in the session, the pediatrician/child psychiatrist was able to observe and evaluate the child's mental status/health in order to make a neuropsychiatric diagnosis and generate recommendations for intervention; the psychologist was able to focus on the attachment relationships between child and family members; and the social worker interviewed several family members about their support system, and obtained the relevant family and social history. Meanwhile, the lawyer on the team was able to listen critically to all information, assessing its relevance to the legal principles and exploring ways in which the law, as applied to the emerging facts, might affect the options available to the other professionals. With this model, both before, during and after an evaluation session, the collaborating team members were challenged to integrate the approaches and perspectives of their colleagues into their own professional perspective and analysis of the problem and its solutions.

Drafting and Finalising CCPPR's Report

At the conclusion of this evaluation, the pediatrician/child psychiatrist, lawyer/psychologist and social worker combined all of their notes into an assessment and made recommendations to submit to the family court to assist the court in making a decision about Michael's disposition. Upon completion of the draft final report, the clinical team members reconvened with the supervising law and social work professors. They again reviewed the relevant legal rules and precedents that provided the backdrop for the family court's review of the report and its decision-making process. The lawyers made organisational suggestions for how to structure the written report in a manner that would be most accessible and most useful to the judge. It is CCPPR's policy to finalise its reports before sharing them with attorneys or agencies, to avoid pressure to alter the tone or conclusions.

Short-term Outcome

Because of CCPPR's clinical evaluation and final report, the Support Center for Child Advocates was able to persuade Michael's mother to enrol him in an inpatient psychiatric treatment program at the Children's Hospital of Philadelphia. Despite scarce mental health resources, aggressive advocacy by the team child psychiatrist was successful in securing Michael a bed in a children's psychiatric ward. Within the first few days of inpatient care, Michael's rocking stopped and he stabilised quickly. The team maintained contact with the inpatient treatment team as discharge possibilities were explored, and the CCPPR team social worker continued to work with the Support Center for Child Advocates and the Department of Human Services to examine disposition options, and ultimately to locate a stable foster home for Michael. As a follow-up for the court, we saw Michael and his foster mother six months later, when reunification was requested by the mother, despite her failure to adhere to a detoxification and rehabilitation program.

The Benefits of Child-centred Interdisciplinary Practice

As Michael's case shows, a purposefully interdisciplinary approach has many strengths. These benefits are present even outside the formal team structure, in more informal collaborations and consultations among scholars and practitioners from a variety of disciplines. Child-centred interdisciplinary work enhances clinical practice and improves case outcomes in a number of ways. It:

—yields potent advocacy for the child;
—integrates medical, legal and social domains with better results for children and their advocates;
—reduces burnout and sustains clinicians in challenging cases;
—offers the opportunity to shift paradigms;
—assures the integrity of vision and mission; and
—can mobilise resources effectively to promote more developmentally informed legal standards.

VERTICALITY IN ACTION

This section explores the benefits of operating in a vertically integrated structure. We describe in some detail a case in which CCPPR's goal was to influence law-making and public policy at the level of constitutional doctrine. We then explore some of the benefits of a vertical structure encountered in CCPPR practice.

Law and Policy Team Case Study: Amicus Brief to the US Supreme Court in *Troxel v Granville*[13]

The Law and Policy Team Concept

The goal of a CCPPR law and policy team is to make timely interventions in appellate court cases and legislative reform, in the hope of channelling the development of laws and policies that may have significant downstream effects—positive or negative—on the welfare of children. When a legislature is drafting or seeking public comment on a proposed legislation, members of CCPPR may be asked to participate in an advisory committee or to provide testimony and briefings to legislators. Another context in which law is formed is the appellate case in which higher level courts make pronouncements about the meaning of a specific law[14] or about constitutional law[15]; in cases raising constitutional or statutory issues of

[13] The text of the *Troxel* brief, as well as of *Brian B*, is on CCPPR's web page at www.ssw.upenn.edu/CCPPR.

[14] For example, *Suter v Artist M* (1992) 503 US 347.

[15] For example, *Smith v Organization of Foster Families* (1977) 431 US 816; *Moore v City of East Cleveland* (1977) 431 US 494; *Stanley v Illinois* (1972) 405 US 645.

importance to children, CCPPR will seek to submit an amicus brief on its own, or may join with others in authoring or signing a brief submitted on behalf of a coalition of child advocacy groups.

CCPPR has consciously chosen not to engage in direct representation of parties bringing impact litigation or class action law suits. While such suits are an important element in law reform and often serve to mobilise public institutions to better serve children and vindicate children's rights, direct participation comes at a price. Advocacy organisations engaging in such work must assume an adversarial role towards the agencies and government entities, limiting their ability to participate collaboratively in systems reform. When developing reforms in response to a successful lawsuit, the defendant cities and states will turn to resources that have been less directly involved in the prosecution of the case. CCPPR seeks to avoid such direct conflict in order to remain available as collaborator and consultant (ie through its Technical Assistance/Training Team).

Like the clinical teams, a law and policy team must be interdisciplinary and child-centred. Good laws and policies depend upon accurate social science and an understanding of developmental and medical issues, as well as on a clear understanding of constitutional principles and family law jurisprudence. The composition of a law and policy team depends upon the primary issues in a case. For example, our amicus brief in *Brian B* addressed the question of whether adolescents tried and convicted as adults have a constitutional right to education while incarcerated. The team included specialists in juvenile justice, corrections, economics, child development, neurology and education theory. The goal of our brief was to inform the judges on the unique developmental and neurological needs of the adolescent, and on the economic consequences to these children and society of depriving them of education. Additionally, we sought to provide social science data establishing that the policy of withholding education was irrational and arbitrary—and thus unconstitutional. The *Troxel* case described below posed the question: were the parents' constitutional rights violated when states intervened to protect children's relationships with family and kin outside the nuclear family circle?

Procedural Setting for the Troxel *Amicus Brief*

The State of Washington had passed a law that gave standing to anyone seeking court-ordered visitation—at any point in time. Visitation was to be granted if the court found that it would serve the best interests of the child. Mr and Mrs Troxel had sought and won expanded contact with the two young daughters of their deceased son. The girls' mother, Tommie Granville, protested that the court order violated her Fourteenth Amendment liberty to direct the upbringing of her children, as established in a line of cases from the United States Supreme Court beginning with *Meyer v Nebraska* (1923)[16] and *Pierce v Society of Sisters* (1925).[17]

[16] *Meyer v Nebraska* (1923) 262 US 390.

[17] *Pierce v Society of Sisters* (1925) 268 US 510.

The Washington Supreme Court agreed with Granville, and found that its own state's law violated the federal Constitution. The US Supreme Court granted certiorari to consider the case.

Supreme Court practice provides a vehicle for participation of interested entities other than the plaintiff and defendant in the specific litigation. The purpose of a 'friend of the court' or 'amicus' brief is to provide additional perspectives on the potential impact of the case. Many groups filed amicus briefs in the *Troxel* case, including parents' rights groups, grandparents' rights groups, Bar and professional groups, women's advocates and civil liberties groups. CCPPR's goal was to ensure that the justices considered the impact of their decision on children at risk of placement. While we at CCPPR agreed with the notion that parents are entitled to deference in raising their children, we were also highly sensitive to the important role played by extended family, partners and kin in creating a safety net for children at risk of placement in the foster care system. CCPPR sought permission to file an amicus brief drawing the court's attention to these other contexts in which children's relationships with non-parents must be protected from disruption.

Stanley v Illinois illustrates what can happen when the court decides a family law case without sufficient perspectives on the broader issues.[18] *Stanley* involved an unmarried biological father who had lived with and raised his children but was accorded no parental rights when their mother died. The court, in vindicating Stanley's claim, made unnecessarily sweeping statements about the rights of biological fathers. This dicta was interpreted by lower courts and legislatures as conferring rights on absent and unknown fathers, a principle that threw the law of adoption and child protection into chaos. The court was forced to backtrack, step by step, as it clarified in subsequent cases that, while a father has a unique opportunity to develop a protected relationship, he must seize this opportunity by acknowledging and supporting his child in order to claim constitutional protection of the relationship. Our goal was to prevent a similar unintended disruption of child welfare and family policy.

Assembling the Troxel *Team*

This team was led by Professor Barbara Bennett Woodhouse, who clerked at the US Supreme Court, has been admitted to practise in the Supreme Court, and has authored or co-authored a number of briefs to the court in cases involving children's rights. The team included two third-year law students, Sacha Coupet, a psychologist whose PhD thesis studied the role of African American grandmothers in providing care giving for grandchildren, and Keren Rabin, who researched the non-parent visitation statutes in the fifty states. In addition, the team included second-year MSW student Alyssa Burrell Cowan and sociologist Richard Gelles, a specialist in family violence and an author of the recently enacted federal *Adoption and Safe Families Act*, which stresses the need to involve

[18] Woodhouse, n 11.

children's extended family resources and kin in child protection and foster care. Social work professor Carol Wilson Spigner, who had served in the Children's Bureau in Washington, which is charged with child protection at the federal level, provided perspectives on systemic barriers and on issues of race and class, and pediatrician/child and adolescent psychiatrist Dr Annie Steinberg provided the psychiatric and developmental perspectives on the child's need for permanency and stability in attachment relationships and the effects of disruption of such relationships. Finally, Professor Elisabeth Slusser Kelly, law librarian at the University of Pennsylvania, provided research resources and consultation to the team.

Conceptualising the Brief

The first step was to provide team members with relevant legal materials, and answer questions about the legal principles. After discussion of the developmental and social issues, the team developed a strategy and a central policy theme. The strategy was to urge the court not to make sweeping statements about parents' rights in the course of deciding the *Troxel* case, but to decide it on the narrow facts presented. The grandparents in this case had never been the primary caretakers or co-resident with the children, and the mother was not seeking to terminate all contact. The mother was a fit and competent parent and no indications existed of risk to the children. The children were not parties to the case and had expressed no position with respect to visitation. Yet the danger existed that the court, which did not handle many family law cases, might approach the case as an opportunity to enunciate an abstract hierarchy of constitutional rights between adults, placing the autonomy of the biological parent first, regardless of specific facts, attachment relationships and the needs of children. The 'child-centred' theme we adopted was that sound policies in the custody and visitation would approach these cases on a case-by-case basis, and would 'avoid sharpening the battle of rights' among adult family members, focusing instead on maximising children's family resources.

Drafting and Finalising the Brief

Based on this discussion, the team leader (Barbara Bennett Woodhouse) drafted an outline, and each team member was assigned responsibility for writing or providing research for a specific section of the brief, according to their area of expertise. The team leader assembled all the texts, edited them and harmonised them into a first draft. This draft was then circulated to all members for comment and correction and was discussed at various meetings of the team. The argument was further refined, and additional scientific, sociological or legal sources were provided. In the past, the difficulty and expense of producing a printed brief conforming with the precise rules of the court on size, colour of cover, type and font have been a substantial financial and logistical barrier. Electronic publishing has greatly reduced these barriers. Thanks to a donation to support printing and filing costs, CCPPR is in a position to print and file such briefs despite its limited resources. An electronic text of the brief was sent to a professional printing service and it was printed and served on the various parties to the case and filed with the Clerk of the Supreme Court.

Outcomes

It is impossible to know what effect, if any, an amicus brief has on the court's deliberations. However, the court's decision in the *Troxel* case definitely avoids the dangers of oversimplification. Six members of the court agreed that Granville's rights to parental autonomy had been violated, but they were unable to reach consensus on the theory behind their ruling. The justices among them produced six separate opinions—a plurality opinion (written by O'Connor and joined by Rehnquist, Breyer and Ginsburg), two concurrences (by Thomas and Souter) and three dissents (by Scalia, Kennedy and Stevens). The plurality took a cautious approach, holding that the Washington statute was not necessarily void on its face, but *as applied to this mother and her family*, it infringed her protected rights. The judge had failed to give any deference to the mother's choices and, in ordering that the children visit twice a month, the judge had simply second-guessed her decision that the children's welfare would be adequately served by monthly visits. Justice O'Connor also stressed the need for deference to family court judges and the need for case-by-case adjudication in this area. Other justices, including Kennedy, in their opinions discussed the diversity of family forms and the importance of extended family and grandparents. Justice Stevens specifically addressed the difference between a family court case, balancing the rights and interests of many parties, and a case involving individual rights. He also stressed the child's interests in protection of attachment relationships as meriting independent weight. Whether coincidentally or not, many of the concepts stressed in the CCPPR brief were reflected in the writings of the justices. By starting cautiously, with a set of opinions that provides a full and nuanced discussion of the issues but avoids broad pronouncements, the court escaped the trap of oversimplification it fell into in *Stanley*.[19]

Practice, Policy and Research Implications

The court's difficulty reaching a consensus in the *Troxel* case indicates that the next decades will see much debate over the constitutional analysis of state laws and court practices that attempt to protect children's extended family and other caregiving relationships. The CCPPR must remain vigilant to insure that this debate remains child-centred and pluralistic. The voices of all children—not only children of divorce, but children in foster care; not only children from affluent

[19] Barbara Bennett Woodhouse, 'Protecting Children's Relationships with Extended Family: The Impact of *Troxel v Granville*', *ABA Child Law Reporter* (July 2000).

nuclear families but poor children from disabled, immigrant and minority populations—must be included in these debates. More research is needed that is sensitive to culture, class and race before we can fully understand the roles of extended family in preserving children's developmental potential or weigh the effects of disrupting attachment relationships in the name of parental autonomy. By the same token, more research is needed into the effects on family stability of coercive court interventions and more exploration is needed of alternatives that are less traumatic and disruptive to family functioning.

The Benefits of a Vertically Integrated Structure

The benefits of a vertically integrated structure are perhaps best understood when illustrated by concrete examples. Case evaluations that are part of a larger enterprise having a vertically integrated structure provide important linkages between clinical activities and policy, practice and research at other levels, and vice versa. And, as the *Troxel* case illustrates, constitutional law develops incrementally, in a case-by-case analysis that starts at the family court level. Issues presented at the trial court level develop—often years later—into the raw materials of constitutional doctrine at the Appellate Court and Supreme Court levels. The benefits of verticality include the following:

1. *A vertically integrated structure helps us to translate lessons learned in the trenches into systemic safeguards and policy reforms.* Michael's case, in which a child was reverted by default to the care of an unfit mother at his grandmother's death, brought home the importance of systemic safeguards that will avoid a child's slipping through the cracks when death of a custodian results in a change in the child's care taking resources. Through CCPPR, we are able to apply this learning not only horizontally (in other case evaluations) but also vertically (towards policy reform and systemic change), when we provide consultation through our Technical Assistance/Training Team, as well as when our Law and Policy Team engages in legislative drafting efforts.
2. *A vertically integrated structure makes plain the importance of interdisciplinarity at all levels, not just the clinical level.* Michael's case illustrated the importance of proper training of line workers, not only in social work practice but also in the legal standards that define and control actions in a wider range of problem-solving and decision-making. The DHS workers in this case mistakenly believed that physical symptoms caused by emotional abuse and neglect were insufficient as a matter of law to justify DHS intervention. CCPPR, because of its vertical structure, can translate lessons learned in the field into programmatic content for its Technical Assistance/Training Team. This is why our training and technical assistance teams working with agencies always includes a lawyer/law student, as well as other professionals whose roles are more obviously implicated.

The *Troxel* brief likewise illustrates the importance of interdisciplinary collaboration at the upper levels of law reform. Legal issues and drafting of good laws are inextricably intertwined with knowledge of sociology, systems administration and child development and decision-makers must have access to experts, not only at trial but at all levels where the law meets the facts. We are better advocates because we understand how the issues play out in medical and social as well as legal contexts.

3. *A vertically integrated structure provides team members engaged in law reform and appellate advocacy with persuasive narratives that can change the hearts as well as the minds of those with the power.* Michael's case shows the importance of continuity of contact with primary attachment figures, and the importance of extended family resources to children at risk of placement. For want of a grandmother, this child was nearly lost. This issue of the value of extended family, from the child's perspective, was addressed by CCPPR's Law and Policy Team in the *Troxel* amicus brief. A central section of our brief in *Troxel* was composed of narratives drawn from CCPPR's clinical evaluations. These stories were worth a thousand words of legal argumentation, bringing home the diversity of cases affected by the *Troxel* case and the importance to 'at risk' children of extended family relationships. The ability to use narratives in legal research and writing enhances scholarship as well as practice.[20]
4. *A vertical approach educates law-makers on the real world consequences of their decisions.* Law-makers are often isolated from the real-world consequences of their actions. They operate in a climate dominated by political strategists and powerful interest groups. Children are among the least powerful of citizens. Since they do not attend $1,000 a plate fundraising dinners, donate large sums of money or have the vote, their perspectives are most likely to be ignored in the political arena. In briefings to politicians and other decision makers, as well as in testimony, information about what would undoubtedly pose serious risks to children and the real-world costs of their proposed actions shifts the momentum away from an adult-centric and towards a child-centred perspective.[21] The ability to draw on personal experience with real-world cases lends credibility to predictions about real-world consequences.
5. *A vertical structure allows scholars to educate law makers on the extent and limitations of the existing knowledge base.* In general, the sociology and science in an amicus brief is acquired second-hand, through research in secondary sources. Because CCPPR is engaged in research as well as case work and policy work, we are more directly linked to the world of research. This makes us more cognisant of the limitations of the existing knowledge base. Our location in a research university gives us access to state of the art research in a wide range of fields. It also gives us access to 'associated faculty' who donate their time to

[20] Barbara Bennett Woodhouse, '"It all depends on what you mean by home": Toward a Communitarian Theory of the Nontraditional Family' (1996) *Utah L Rev* 569.

[21] Harry M Byrne Jr, 'Pennsylvania Bar Association, Family Law Section Paternity Task Force Report' (1999) 21 *Pennsylvania Family Lawyer* 79 (Oct).

explain and critique the methods behind published studies and experiments. In the *Brian B* case, CCPPR's amicus brief included current research on the education of at-risk juveniles. In the *Troxel* brief, we described the neurological effects on the brain of separation from attachment figures. In each case, the scientific or sociological data were presented directly, in the words of the researchers and scholars themselves. How different from the practice of pouring over books and articles, trying to extract a legal argument from materials written for an audience with a specific disciplinary background!

6. *A vertical structure encourages thinking about legal abstractions in concrete medical, educational and social context.* The *Troxel* case involves a seemingly abstract principle: the constitutional liberty interest of a parent in controlling the upbringing of their child. Neither the child nor the parent, however, exists in isolation. Maurice is another child for whom CCPPR did a clinical evaluation; Maurice longed to visit his paternal grandfather despite his mother's opposition. Experience at the individual case level with children such as Maurice allows legal advocates to see abstract issues in a developmentally grounded, child-centred larger context.

THE RISKS OF AN INTERDISCIPLINARY, VERTICALLY STRUCTURED APPROACH

If this approach is so wonderful, you may ask: why isn't everyone doing it? Certainly, many other groups around the globe are realising the benefits of interdisciplinary collaboration. But these benefits do not come free of costs. In this section we will reflect on some of the risks and down-sides of our project.

Communicating Across Cultural Divides

In our work, we have found it very easy to be awed, inspired and impressed by each other's professional competence. Each of us is boringly familiar with our own discipline, but the other collaborator's professional acumen never ceases to amaze. The stresses emerge when we try to deal with daily administrative chores. Medical, social work and legal cultures differ radically, from major issues such as client confidentiality and autonomy to minor issues such as the order in which authors are listed on a publication. Lawyers need crisp, clear answers and are trained to meet non-negotiable deadlines. Medical professionals evaluate and re-evaluate, always ready to change their diagnosis or run another test. Social workers are attuned to the social context, where others might focus on the individual. Institutional expectations, appointments and promotions, academic schedules, perspectives on professional autonomy and reporting structures, publication guidelines and economic constraints differ considerably for team members at the School of Law, Social Work and Medicine. Interdisciplinarity requires a constant commitment to communication. Tacit assumptions must be made explicit. Misunderstandings must be aired immediately. And protocols must be developed that respect the various professional cultures without making one or another dominant.

It is also more, not less, time consuming to work with partners from other disciplines. Time that would otherwise be used to write or work is given to consultation with others, to translating their perspectives into a work product in progress, to teaching and to listening and learning.

Trying to Be in Too Many Places at Once

The common expression for being over-committed is 'working 24/7'. We find ourselves working what often feels like 28/10, largely because we are trying to work in so many spaces. From the family court trenches to the Supreme Court covers a lot of territory. A major motivating force in specialisation is the difficulty of doing everything well or even of doing it at all. We recognise, as well, that a group can acquire a momentum that drives it, in spite of itself, into specialisation in one or another arena of action. It remains to be seen whether we can sustain the commitment to verticality.

In addition, we are literally 'in too many places' because we occupy different physical and institutional spaces. While email and electronic printing have reduced the physical distances between the Law School, the School of Medicine and the School of Social Work, we must still find time for the weekly face-to-face meetings that cement our partnership. Less tangible than the physical distances are the institutional distances. In many universities, turf wars would make a collaboration such as ours impossible. Even where the administrators encourage collaboration, it is difficult for each school to fully appreciate work taking place off-site and involving faculty from other schools. When the time comes to recognise faculty members' work, in promotions and tenure decisions, how well will this work translate into the idiom by which research and scholarship are judged within a particular school and discipline?

Money versus Time versus Independence

Finally, the enterprise needs money to survive. Consulting work can produce income to pay for the time of consulting doctors, and buy release time for faculty who need more time for research and practice, but it can also create dual loyalties, when our avowedly child-centred perspective conflicts with the needs of an agency living in the real world of politics. Grant money provides a way around this dilemma. But grant-writing is time consuming and increasingly difficult as more 'private' entities are drafted into providing public services, and must compete for shrinking charitable dollars. Alumni who give money to worthy causes are attracted to children's welfare, but we must compete with bricks and mortar and with endowment, as well as pressing institutional needs. In an era when much of the public sector is being urged to privatise, children find they have little purchasing power in the market.

CONCLUSION

CCPPR is confident that these barriers are surmountable. The benefits of the structure and mission we have chosen seem well worth the costs. As we continue to develop our model of child-centred, team-based, vertically integrated action, we look forward to sharing experiences with others, both in United States and elsewhere, who are seeking to improve the current systems serving children and youth.

17

Children's Rights and the Use of Force 'in Their Own Best Interests'

Jane Fortin*

INTRODUCTION

Does a commitment to children's rights force us to respect the wishes of immature and vulnerable children, and if not, to what extent are we justified in using physical force to make them comply with our views? Furthermore, if we are satisfied that physical force is justified, how much force can we use? These questions may be asked by parents—and indeed by many other adults—whose work involves caring for children. This paper explores the extent to which the law provides them with comprehensible answers.

THEORETICAL JUSTIFICATIONS

Parents and other caretakers who accede that children have rights of their own sometimes feel uneasy about disciplining their young charges. They appear to assume that those who have rights cannot be made to undergo discipline, far less physical compulsion. Indeed, we are all familiar with the media's habit of lampooning the notion of children's rights with cartoons showing children presenting outrageous demands to their parents. The American children's liberationists were certainly responsible for giving the children's rights movement a bad press in this respect. They implied that those wishing to promote children's rights were committed to the view that enjoying rights involves the rights-holders making autonomous choices, irrespective of the consequences. This led to something of a backlash, with critics pointing out just how detached from reality such views were, insofar as they ignored children's physical vulnerability and psychological immaturity and their need for parental devotion and care. Often, the views of the

* Reader in Law, King's College London.

* This paper was further developed in a later article which explored more fully the impact of the *Human Rights Act* 1998 on English law and policy governing the use of force on children. See J Fortin, 'Children's Rights and the Use of Physical Force' (2001) 13 *CFLQ* 243.

two sides seemed to polarise, with the critics rejecting the whole notion of children having any rights, by appeals to family privacy and parental autonomy. The 'kiddy libbers', on the other hand, portrayed their opponents as encouraging parents to treat their children abusively.[1]

Underlying these debates is a familiar theme: the idea that acknowledging that a person has rights inevitably rules out any paternalistic intervention to restrict his or her autonomy. This theme has been referred to by numerous writers commenting on developments in the principles of family and child law.[2] Their assessment is often couched in slightly different language, with the terms 'welfarism' or 'utilitarianism' or the 'welfare test' being utilised as an alternative to 'paternalism.'[3] The argument is that promoting children's rights—particularly their right to reach decisions for themselves—conflicts with attempts to promote their welfare. Thus Eekelaar argues that a welfarist relationship between A and B is inconsistent with the concept of B having rights against A, since:

> Although it might logically be held that B has the right that A should promote B's welfare in accordance with A's conception of that welfare, such a right is really no right at all. A person who surrenders to another the power to determine where his own welfare lies has in a real sense abdicated his own personal autonomy.[4]

The argument that there is a conflict between a rights-based system of principles and one incorporating 'a relationship-based welfare approach' has been revisited by Herring when considering the impact of the *Human Rights Act* 1998 on the principles of child law.[5] There have been a variety of responses. As MacCormick[6] and Campbell[7] have argued, such an assessment depends on the model of rights adopted. A concept of rights, particularly the right to autonomy, need not be incompatible with paternalism. MacCormick is emphatic that an interest theory

[1] For an assessment of the part played by the American school of children's liberationists and the subsequent widespread rejection of many of their ideas, see J Fortin, *Children's Rights and the Developing Law* (Butterworths 1998), pp 4–8.

[2] *Inter alia*: S Parker, 'Rights and Utility in Anglo-Australian Family Law' (1992) 55 *MLR* 311, especially at 319–25; J Dewar, 'The Normal Chaos of Family Law' (1998) 61 *MLR* 467, especially at 371–72; J Eekelaar, 'Families and Children: From Welfarism to Rights', in C McCrudden and G Chambers, *Individual Rights and Law in Britain* (Clarendon Press, 1994), especially pp 301–2 and 326–27; J Roche, 'Children and Divorce: A Private Affair?' in S Day Sclater and C Piper, *Undercurrents of Divorce* (Dartmouth, 1999), p 56.

[3] Parker employs the term 'utility' as a means of describing a 'welfare'-dominated approach to family law debates, which he argues is inconsistent with a 'rights-based' or 'justice' model. See S Parker, 'Rights and Utility in Anglo-Australian Family Law' (1992) 55 *MLR* 311 at 321. But, as Raz has explained, it is logically perfectly possible to combine utilitarianism with a conception of *prima facie* rights, despite some people finding such a conclusion unacceptable: J Raz, 'Hart on Moral Rights and Legal Duties' (1984) 4 *Oxford Journal of Legal Studies* 123, especially at 128.

[4] J Eekelaar, 'Families and Children: From Welfarism to Rights', in C McCrudden and G Chambers (eds), *Individual Rights and Law in Britain* (Clarendon Press, 1994), p 301.

[5] J Herring 'The *Human Rights Act* and the Welfare Principle in Family Law—Conflicting or Complementary?' (1999) 11 *CFLQ* 237, especially at 233.

[6] N MacCormick 'Children's Rights: A Test-case', in *Legal Rights and Social Democracy* (Clarendon Press, 1982), p 160.

[7] T Campbell, 'The Rights of the Minor' in P Alston, S Parker and J Seymour (eds), *Children, Rights and the Law* (Clarendon Press, 1992), p 15.

of rights allows him to acknowledge that children have rights despite their not always or even usually being:

> the best judge of what is good for them, so much so that even the rights that are the most important to their long-term well-being, such as the right to discipline or to a safe environment, they regularly perceive as being the reverse of rights or advantages . . .[8]

Similarly, Campbell argues that, since individuals of any age—even adults, but especially children—may make choices which will endanger their ability to fulfil their own future prospects for achieving a good life, their rights may be fulfilled by some form of compulsion, or restriction of their own choices.[9] Indeed, as Raz points out, independence is not all or nothing. In his view, various reasons may justify coercion: it may be necessary to protect someone else, or to protect the coerced person's own long-term autonomy, or some other interest.[10]

Paternalism need not, therefore, be seen as 'an odious tyranny.'[11] But Eekelaar and others have quite rightly expressed unease over the way that adults might attempt to justify restricting and coercing children in a tyrannical way, by claiming that they are fulfilling the rights of those children. Whilst one can argue that being made to go to school is necessary for maturation into a rational autonomous individual, and therefore that present compulsion is a precondition for subsequent choice, it is far less clear how much should be denied to children and the precise ends to be served by such denial.[12] A commitment to the concept of children's rights is certainly not inconsistent with paternalistic coercion and restriction, if without that coercion and without that restriction of the child's own choices, his or her life-chances would be gravely limited. Nevertheless, coercion which involves the use of force may not only injure but also humiliate a child, particularly if that child has now reached adolescence. The prospect of overpowering a physically well-developed teenager, in order to force him or her to carry out the wishes of adult society, is a distasteful one. Physical coercion which overrides a child's own strongly stated views should always be very carefully justified. Furthermore, parents and other adults acting as caretakers for their children should ensure that their paternalistic restrictions on a child's self-determination are limited to the prevention of childhood mistakes which seriously jeopardise their future well-being.[13]

Theoretical ideals of the type discussed above can provide parents and other adults acting as caretakers with a degree of confidence when dealing with difficult children. Nevertheless, these ideals could be of more practical assistance if

[8] *Ibid.*, p 166.

[9] *Ibid.*, p 15.

[10] J Raz, 'Liberty and Trust', in R George (ed), *Natural Law, Liberalism and Morality* (Oxford University Press, 1996), p 121.

[11] D Archard, *Children: Rights and Childhood*, (Routledge, 1993), p 11.

[12] *Ibid.*, pp 55–57.

[13] *Ibid.*, p 54.

they were translated into a set of legal principles which provides such caretakers with clear guidance about the extent to which physical coercion is permissible when it overrides a child's own strongly stated views. But do legal principles governing coercion exist at all? If so, do they accommodate the view that paternalistic coercion should be as restricted as possible, with the circumstances justifying its use being clearly comprehensible to all? Is there any coherence to them? Family lawyers know that, since the principles of law applying to children have accumulated—mainly through the development of case law—in an entirely ad hoc way, the answer to most of these questions is 'no.'

THE USE OF PHYSICAL PUNISHMENT

Many of these issues come to the fore when discussing the extent to which it is appropriate to use physical force to discipline children—a topic fraught with controversy. Adults in a variety of settings are obliged to exercise discipline over the children in their care and may be liable in tort if, through their failure to do so, a child suffers harm in an accident.[14] Nevertheless, there is an obvious difference between restraining a child from damaging him or herself, or another child or adult, or someone's property, and punishing that child afterwards for having misbehaved. A century ago, society considered it reasonable to beat children in both situations. But social attitudes to the use of physical force have changed radically since then. Developed countries no longer allow the physical punishment of adult criminals, nor do they condone domestic violence in a private setting. Alongside such attitudinal changes, many are now convinced that physical *punishment* of children, as opposed to their physical *restraint*, is unjustifiable. The arguments against physical punishment are well-worn. It not only involves an adult exploiting their power over the child, both physically and psychologically, in a way which would not be condoned if another adult was the victim, but the violence may also escalate into physical abuse. Physical punishment comes after the event so does not save the child from harm and in any case, there are other methods of discipline which do not invade a child's physical integrity in the same humiliating manner. It is probably damaging not only in the short term but also in the long term, insofar as it may teach the child violent habits.[15]

Concerns about the use of corporal punishment often focus on parents who beat their children. But in practice, school teachers who spend long periods with ill-disciplined children may sometimes feel tempted to resort to physical forms of discipline. Nevertheless, English law gradually responded to a small but steady stream of applications being taken by British parents and children to the

[14] For example, *Surtees v Kingston-upon-Thames Borough Council; Surtees v Hughes* [1991] 2 FLR 559; and *J v North Lincolnshire County Council* [2000] ELR 245.

[15] See the evidence against corporal punishment summarised in *Physical Punishment in the Home—Thinking About the Issues, Looking at the Evidence*, a consultation paper for Northern Ireland (Office of Law Reform, 2001), p 11.

European Court of Human Rights challenging the use of corporal punishment in schools.[16] The relative success of these applications led to the gradual curtailment of physical punishment by all professionals working in public agencies. Finally, in 1998, the use of corporal punishment in all schools was completely prohibited.[17] Teachers are now obliged to find other methods to discipline schoolchildren. Nevertheless, as discussed below, they may still use physical restraint in certain clearly defined circumstances.

The principles of English law currently governing the use of physical punishment by parents in the home remain unchanged and fail to accommodate any of the ideals governing the use of paternalistic coercion discussed at the beginning of this paper. The law neither clarifies the circumstances justifying its use, nor attempts to restrict the circumstances in which it is used, nor is it clearly comprehensible to all. Indeed, the Committee on the Rights of the Child was, in 1995, critical of the legal principles which currently allow parents to administer any form of physical punishment which could be described as 'reasonable chastisement.'[18] The committee pointed to the imprecise nature of this expression and the risk of it being interpreted in a 'subjective and arbitrary manner', contrary to the provisions of the UN Convention on the Rights of the Child.[19]

The British government failed to respond to the criticisms of the Committee on the Rights of the Child. Indeed, this is not surprising when one considers the sequence of events occurring in the mid-1990s. Soon after the committee's report was published, there was a new government in power with a firm resolve to deal with youth crime. It was aware of the research which shows that there is a clear reverse correlation between levels of parental supervision of teenagers and the extent to which they become involved in crime. Almost as strong is the correlation between levels of offending and having friends who are in trouble with the police.[20] The Home Office was keen to promote a relatively punitive approach towards parents who failed to supervise their children sufficiently to prevent their becoming involved in criminal and anti-social activities.[21] The parenting orders created by the *Crime and Disorder Act* 1998 were designed to ensure that inadequate parents attended parenting courses to ensure, amongst other things, that they learned to discipline their children more rigorously. These orders[22] can be made against parents whose children are the subject of child safety orders, anti-

[16] They were often successful in arguing that the use of corporal punishment in schools is contrary to children's rights under Art 3 of the European Convention on Human Rights and to their parents' rights under Art 2 of the First Protocol. See J Fortin, n 1, pp 228–38.

[17] See *Education Act* 1996, ss 548–49, as amended by the *School Standards and Framework Act* 1998, s 131.

[18] See *R v Hopley* (1860) 2 F and F 202 and *Children and Young Persons Act* 1933, s 1(7).

[19] See *Concluding Observations of the Committee on the Rights of the Child: United Kingdom of Great Britain and Northern Ireland*, CRC/C/15/Add 34 Centre for Human Rights, Geneva, 1995, para 16.

[20] J Graham and B Bowling, *Young People and Crime*, Home Office Research Study 145, (Home Office, 1995), especially pp 48–49.

[21] L Gelsthorpe and A Morris, 'Much ado about nothing—a critical comment on key provisions relating to children in the *Crime and Disorder Act* 1998' (1999) 11 *CFLQ* 209, esp at 218–19.

[22] *Crime and Disorder Act* 1998, s 8.

social behaviour orders or sex offender orders and will normally be made whenever a child aged under sixteen is convicted of an offence.[23] This historical background suggests that the new government was not particularly interested in liberalising parenting methods. Indeed, it might never have reassessed the law governing the use of physical punishment by parents had it not been compelled to do so by the European Court of Human Rights.

In Autumn 1998, a decision of the European Court of Human Rights showed that Article 3 of the European Convention on Human Rights could protect children from parental behaviour, even in the privacy of their own homes. Confirming the European Commission's unanimous decision, the European Court upheld the claims of an English boy that being beaten by his stepfather with a garden cane by way of discipline, off and on over the course of a week, when he was only nine, had infringed his rights under Article 3.[24] The court considered that, by authorising parents to use 'reasonable chastisement' on their children, English law does not adequately protect children from infringements of their rights under Article 3. Although, in the course of the case, the government expressly conceded that domestic law would have to be amended, the European Court gave no guidance over how this should be done.

The government's consultation process before reforming the law to conform with the requirements of the European Convention was a bizarre one. The consultation document made clear the government's reluctance to antagonise British parents.[25] Its dilemma was that the government's own research indicated that the majority of parents not only considered it acceptable to smack their children, but also that the law should tolerate their doing so.[26] Consequently, any radical change in the law risked the government courting considerable unpopularity with its electorate. Indeed, the public might see a law strengthening children's rights as being tantamount to restricting parents' rights, notably their rights to family autonomy and privacy, including their right to bring their children up as they think fit. One might counter such concerns by arguing that the law should educate public opinion. After all, some husbands might have attempted to use similar arguments against the introduction of laws protecting women against domestic violence.

It seems clear that, unlike many European governments, the British government is reluctant to attempt weaning parents off the use of physical punishment. Far from proposing or discussing the possibility of prohibiting all forms of physical punishment within the home, the consultation paper assumed that the law would continue to allow parents to use physical punishment as a form of discipline. It merely sought views on how to introduce guidance for parents and the courts over

[23] *Crime and Disorder Act* 1998, s 9.

[24] *A v United Kingdom (human rights: punishment of child)* [1998] 2 FLR 959.

[25] *Protecting Children, Supporting Parents: A Consultation Document on the Physical Punishment of Children* (Department of Health, 2000).

[26] In 1998, 88% of respondents to a National Statistics Survey agreed 'that it is sometimes necessary to smack a naughty child'; 8% disagreed and 85% of respondents agreed that parents should be allowed by law to do so. *Ibid.*, Annex A, para 2.

the type of punishment which would certainly amount to an infringement of the child's rights under Article 3 of the European Convention. So, in all likelihood, a formula will be introduced prohibiting physical punishment of a level and type deemed to amount to 'inhuman or degrading treatment.' It may, for example, rule out the use of implements and blows to the head.[27] Unfortunately, such a change will neither introduce real clarity into the law, nor protect children from unnecessary physical abuse—at least not in the way that the complete abolition of all physical punishment would do.

Government nervousness over antagonising its electorate, combined with ministerial ambivalence, may explain the official silence over any future changes in the law, despite the consultation process being long since completed.[28] Meanwhile, pending the required reform, the *Human Rights Act* 1998 requires the domestic courts to comply with the European Convention on Human Rights, as interpreted by the European Court of Human Rights. Consequently, parents and other adults charged with offences associated with physically chastising children cannot claim that the defence of reasonable chastisement will exempt them from criminal liability if their actions amount to 'torture or inhuman or degrading treatment' under Article 3 of the Convention.[29] Even more radical reform may emerge through case law when the courts respond to challenges brought on behalf of children arguing that the new law still fails to protect their rights under the European Convention.[30]

THE USE OF PHYSICAL RESTRAINT

Although the use of physical force as a form of punishment is unnecessary and should be prohibited, it is arguable that adults are justified in using physical restraint to prevent children damaging themselves or others, or property belonging to others. As already noted, there is good theoretical justification for such

[27] *Ibid.*, pp 14–15.

[28] It had been expected that the consultation process would be short. Indeed, the consultation paper—which was published in January 2000—sought responses by April 2000. Time elapsed, however, and the parliamentary elections took place in June 2001 without any proposals for changing the law having been announced. Meanwhile, the Scottish Executive completed its own consultation process, announcing in Sept 2001 its intention to reform Scottish law by banning all smacking of children under the age of three and a total ban on the use of implements, shaking and blows to the head. A consultation process has now also started in Northern Ireland. See *Physical Punishment in the Home—Thinking about the Issues, Looking at the Evidence*, a consultation paper for Northern Ireland (2001) Office of Law Reform.

[29] See Rose LJ in *R v H (Assault of Child: Reasonable Chastisement)* [2001] EWCA 1024 [2001] 2 FLR 431 at 439, in the context of a father's defence to a charge of assault occasioning actual bodily harm that he had used 'reasonable' chastisement when beating his son with a belt. Pending amending legislation, juries must be directed to consider the factors identified by the European Court of Human Rights in *A v UK (Human Rights: Punishment of Child)* [1998] 2 FLR as relevant to determining whether conduct is sufficiently severe to amount to a breach of Art 3, when deciding what is 'reasonable' chastisement.

[30] See J Fortin, 'Rights Brought Home for Children' (1999) 62 *MLR* 350, at 361.

intervention as a means of fulfilling the child's own long-term interests and the rights of others to live in a safe and peaceful environment. Nevertheless, there is a dangerous grey area between physical restraint which is justifiable on these grounds and abusive behaviour which cannot be justified under any circumstances. Furthermore, any adult who adopts aggressive forms of physical restraint on a child risks injuring him or her. For these reasons, there is an official awareness of the need for regulation, so that professionals working in public agencies are clear about the legality of such action.

The Use of Physical Restraint in Schools

The activities of school teachers have been increasingly regulated and some teachers would argue that these regulations pull them in conflicting directions. As already mentioned, they are now prohibited from using physical punishment as a way of maintaining discipline. Nevertheless, teachers may be confronted by situations which they consider will become dangerous unless they physically restrain a pupil, as opposed to physically punishing him or her. Indeed, it is increasingly common for children in British schools to be subjected by their peers to physical assaults, intimidation, theft, verbal abuse, racial and sexual harassment, or harassment on other grounds, such as gender and religion. Furthermore, schools are legally obliged to maintain discipline, insofar as they are under a duty of care to do so and failure may be actionable in tort by a pupil, particularly if it leads to his or her physical or psychological injury.[31] Bullying in schools is also being taken increasingly seriously, with both the civil and criminal law being utilised by way of sanctions.

The disruption and violence in some schools led, in 1977, to new legislation clarifying what measures could and could not be taken by teachers confronted by disruptive and aggressive pupils. A teacher can use 'such force as is reasonable in the circumstances' for the purpose of preventing a pupil committing any offence, injuring anyone or damaging their property, engaging in 'any behaviour prejudicial to the maintenance of good order and discipline' at the school or among the pupils, whether or not that behaviour occurs during a teaching session.[32] Whilst the objectives of the new legislation were clear, the 'reasonable force' formula was criticised for being far too broad. Hamilton argued that it might, for example, be used to prevent a pupil swearing in class or even on a school trip.[33] It was even suggested that the legislation might risk teachers being able to slip back into using corporal punishment under the guise of physical restraint. Although there will

[31] *J v North Lincolnshire County Council* [2000] ELR 245.

[32] *Education Act* 1996, s 550A, as inserted by the *Education Act* 1997, s 4.

[33] C Hamilton, 'Rights of the Child: A Right to Education and a Right in Education', in C Bridge (ed), *Family Law Towards the Millennium: Essays for PM Bromley* (Butterworths, 1997), pp 215–20.

always be room for argument over what is 'reasonable,'[34] this criticism seems over-harsh when the legislation is read with the official guidance accompanying it. This stresses that the use of physical force can only be used as a means of *control*, as opposed to punishment. It emphasises that it has to be very carefully justified and should not be used, for example, to prevent a pupil from committing a trivial misdemeanour or in a situation which could be resolved in another way. It stresses that force 'can be regarded as reasonable only if the circumstances of the particular incident warrant it' and any degree of force is unlawful if they do not.[35] Here the law and guidance combine to provide teachers with a clear set of workable principles which they must abide by. As long as the guidance is followed conscientiously, teachers should feel reasonably confident that when they use physical restraint to prevent dangerous situations becoming far worse, they will not risk infringing their pupils' rights under Articles 3 or 5 of the European Convention on Human Rights.[36]

The Use of Physical Restraint on Residential Homes

The staff of residential homes who look after children on behalf of local authorities are probably more likely than teachers to be confronted by highly disturbed and violent children intent on engaging in dangerous activities. The old days of large children's homes run by charities filled with clean well-scrubbed little orphans are a thing of the past. Today's residential homes are increasingly expected to provide a home for a volatile mix of children who are, for various reasons usually relating to age and temperament, quite unsuitable for fostering. If these older, more difficult children get 'out of control,' they can be a danger to themselves, each other, the staff and those living in the vicinity of the home. Residential care staff must have the authority to keep discipline in such situations. Governmental responses to this aspect of public agency work have changed direction, depending on the latest scandal disclosed by the media. It has swung from stressing the need to respect the rights of children in residential care to emphasising that the state is a proxy parent, with responsibilities to override the wishes of those same children when appropriate.

[34] See, for example, the case of Mrs Marjorie Evans, who was suspended for eighteen months from her post as head of a Welsh primary school, having been found guilty of slapping an unruly ten-year-old. She was eventually, in 2001, cleared of this charge. The court accepted that she had been restraining him from trying to punch and headbutt her.

[35] *Section 550A of the Education Act 1996: The Use of Force to Control or Restrain Pupils,* DFEE Circular 10/98, para 17.

[36] The extent to which the *Human Rights Act* 1998, and more particularly Art 5 of the European Convention on Human Rights, create difficulties for British teachers who physically restrain pupils is discussed in more detail by J Fortin in 'Children's Rights and the Use of Physical Force' (2001) 13 *CFLQ* 243 at 251–52.

The methods of control used in some Staffordshire residential homes in the early 1990s totally disregarded the rights of the children in their care, both under the European Convention on Human Rights and under the UN Convention on the Rights of the Child.[37] By then it had also become very clear that some residential care staff were able to exploit their position of trust and the vulnerability of their charges not merely by employing brutal and sadistic methods of control but by abusing them sexually.[38] Regulations and government guidance soon followed, ruling out the various types of degrading punishments devised by the staff in the Staffordshire homes, including depriving children of food and drink, isolating them and requiring them to wear special clothes. This guidance, though timely, stressed what residential staff could not do, rather than what they could.[39] It appeared to do little to help them deal with rebellious and disturbed children intent on damaging themselves and others. Attempts were later made to expand these regulations with more practical advice. The new guidance reminded staff that if they wished to deny a child his or her liberty though locking the child up, this should be done by obtaining a secure accommodation order under section 25 of the *Children Act* 1989.[40] It also emphasised that the regulations allowed physical restraint or coercion being resorted to in an emergency, if it was 'immediately necessary to prevent injury to any person, or serious damage to property.'[41]

Soon after this, standards of residential care again attracted adverse publicity. Some residential homes became notorious for housing children who were absenting themselves to take part in prostitution and crime, with the staff having such low expectations of being able to dissuade them from leaving that they made no attempt to do so. Further clarification of the guidance and regulations followed which emphasised that support for the rights of children need not come at the expense of the rights and responsibilities of parents and of the professionals supervising them. It stressed that carers should not feel constrained by an apparent need to abide by the child's wishes and that residential staff were entitled under section 3(5) of the *Children Act* 1989 to do what was reasonable in all the circumstances to safeguard and promote the child's welfare. Children themselves needed to understand that their carers 'would be expected to provide them with the safety, clear guidance and firm influence that characterises effective parenting

[37] A Levy and B Kahan, *The Pindown Experience and the Protection of Children*, The Report of the Staffordshire Child Care Inquiry (Staffordshire County Council 1990).

[38] See inter alia: *Report of the Committee of Inquiry into Children's Homes and Hostels* (1985) HMSO; *Ty Mawr Community Home Inquiry* (Gwent County Council 1992); A Kirkwood, *The Leicestershire Inquiry 1992* (Leicestershire County Council 1993); W Hughes, *Report of the Committee of Inquiry into Children's Homes and Hostels* (HMSO 1985). See subsequently Sir William Utting, *People Like Us: The Report of the Review of the Safeguards for Children Living Away from Home* (The Stationery Office 1997); and *Lost in Care*, Report of Inquiry into the Abuse of Children in Care in the Former County Council Areas of Gwynedd and Clwyd since 1974 (The Stationery Office 2000).

[39] Children and Young Persons, Children's Homes Regulations 1991 (SI 1991/1506), reg 8 and the *Children Act 1989 Guidance and Regulations* (1991) HMSO vol 4: Residential Care, at pp 15–19.

[40] For a detailed assessment of the use of secure accommodation orders, see M Parry, 'Secure Accommodation—the Cinderella of Family Law' [2000] 12 *CFLQ* 101. See also Fortin, n 36, at pp 257–60.

[41] *Guidance on Permissible Forms of Control for Children in Residential Care* (LAC(93)13), para 5.

for children.' They should prevent children leaving children's homes at inappropriate hours by using reasonable physical restraint or by bolting doors to restrict the child's exit when there were grounds for believing that they were putting themselves or others at risk or were likely to seriously damage property. Indeed, staff had a duty to anticipate the harm to children of their behaving in such a way.[42] These mixed messages not only created confusion amongst staff members but undermined confidence over their ability to deal adequately with dangerous behaviour requiring restraint.[43] The Department of Health's very obvious dilemma is clearly reflected in these various attempts to provide their staff with workable and appropriate guidance. It is obviously no easy matter finding a satisfactory balance between ensuring that some of the most difficult children in the country are dealt with firmly, in a way which protects their long-term interests, and ensuring that their carers respect those same children's rights to dignity and physical integrity.[44]

The Use of Physical Force by Parents and Doctors

Meanwhile, what of parents confronting difficult adolescents intent on absenting themselves from home, in order to consort with 'unsuitable' peers? The guidance for residential care workers described above argued that the provision of 'safety, clear guidance and firm influence' was the mark of effective parenting and stressed that carers should override a child's wishes if it 'was necessary to safeguard and promote their welfare and protect others.' But the law remains unclear about what force a parent can use to restrain a child intent on having his own way. The younger child presents few problems. The physically large male teenager determined to assist his friends to steal and drive away fast cars presents parents with a challenge of an entirely different order. As noted above, if he is made the subject of an anti-social behaviour order, the parents may themselves be the subject of a parenting order which is intended to teach them how to discipline him better. But what legal boundaries must they operate within?

The parents who conscientiously seek legal advice over how they can stop their son taking part in such dangerous and criminal activities will probably conclude that the law in this area is impenetrable. The *Gillick* decision,[45] combined with the Court of Appeal's later decisions in *Re R (a minor) (wardship: medical treatment)*[46] and *Re W (a minor) (medical treatment)*[47] certainly make it difficult for lawyers to give lay people comprehensible advice. The parents must understand that they are

[42] See letter of 20 Feb 1997 from Sir Herbert Laming to all Directors of Social Services, clarifying 'Guidance on Permissible Forms of Control for Children in Residential Care' (LAC(93)13) CI (97)6.

[43] D Berridge and I Brodie, *Children's Homes Revisited* (Jessica Kingsley 1998), pp 99 and 134.

[44] The extent to which this guidance, if followed conscientiously, would prevent residential care staff from infringing residents' rights under the European Convention on Human Rights, is discussed in more detail by Fortin, n 36, pp 56–257.

[45] *Gillick v West Norfolk and Wisbech Area Health Authority* [1986] AC 112.

[46] [1991] 4 All ER 177.

[47] [1992] 4 All ER 627.

not entitled to prevent their teenage son, however young, joining his friends if they consider that he has reached 'a sufficient understanding and intelligence to be capable of making up his own mind on the matter requiring decision.'[48] Such a formula presents no serious obstacle since few parents faced with such a situation would ever accede that their son had reached such maturity. A lawyer will also explain that legally, and according to the later Court of Appeal case law, they could insist on their son attending a course of treatment therapy designed to achieve behavioural changes, since they have parental responsibility and thus the right to consent to his course of treatment, his own reluctance to take part being therefore legally irrelevant. But what if he refuses to attend?

Again, the parents may feel frustrated at the law's lack of practical assistance. For it provides little guidance over the degree of force they may use to coerce a child into complying with their wishes. The infuriated parent who attempts to bundle his son into his car in order to take him to the therapist risks being charged with false imprisonment, it being outside the limits of 'reasonable parental discipline.'[49] Or does he? In *R v Rahman*,[50] the father wished to send his daughter back to Bangladesh, whilst the father in our present scenario merely wishes to ensure that his son receives what he considers to be essential treatment. He might seek to convince the court that the difference in his objectives are crucial. After all, the judiciary have themselves, in the medical cases referred to above, implicitly authorised the use of force by doctors in order to ensure that the adolescents received the treatment deemed to be essential to protect their future health and well-being. Arguing by analogy, if doctors can use force, so can parents.[51]

Such arguments, although superficially plausible, are unlikely to succeed. Hopes that the medical case law can provide parents with practical guidance over their legal rights will be dashed by a closer examination of these authorities. Despite the *implicit* authorisation of the use of physical force, the decisions are surprisingly reticent over the details. Indeed, the courts have barely mentioned the implications of authorising treatment against the wishes of a fully grown adolescent. There was no reference to the force the doctors were authorised to use when treating the anorexic girl in *Re W* nor the violent and self-harming psychotic in *Re R*. In *South Glamorgan County Council v W and B*,[52] the judge merely told the local authority that they had obtained authority 'to take all necessary steps' to remove a fifteen-year-old from home against her wishes, and take her to the doctors at a specialised unit where she could be assessed and treated.[53] In all these cases, the judiciary appeared to assume that the doctors would act in a professional manner,

48 *Gillick v West Norfolk and Wisbech Area Health Authority* [1986] AC 112, at 186 per Lord Scarman.

49 *R v Rahman* (1985) 81 Cr App Rep 349.

50 *Ibid.*

51 The extent to which parents can physically restrain their teenage offspring without infringing their rights under the European Convention on Human Rights is discussed in more detail by Fortin, n 36, pp 248–50.

52 [1993] 1 FLR 572.

53 Per Douglas Brown J, at 584.

only using as much force as was necessary in the circumstances. This may have been true, but it seems unsatisfactory for the courts to leave to speculation matters involving what, to these patients, appeared a gross violation of their rights. Defining and measuring the amounts of force justifiable in every set of circumstances will be difficult but this should not deter the courts from attempting to give credible guidance on such matters.

Amongst this unhelpful case law, *Re C (Detention: Medical Treatment)*[54] stands out, insofar as the judgment considers many of the issues relating to the ethics of forcing an adolescent to undergo treatment. There a specialised clinic treating a sixteen-year-old severely anorexic girl sought authorisation to use reasonable force to ensure that she took part in their force-feeding programme and to prevent her continually absconding, as she had in the past. Wall J agreed with her counsel that to detain her against her will was itself a Draconian remedy. He also agreed that using a secure accommodation order or the mental health legislation might safeguard her liberty more effectively than an order made under the inherent jurisdiction, since these involved built-in safeguards. But since he did not consider these alternative routes were legally available to him, he used the inherent jurisdiction but also inserted safeguards into the order, similar to those used in the secure accommodation regulations. He limited the duration of her stay in the unit to a maximum of four months and directed that treatment should be provided in accordance with the views of her doctors but 'to ensure that [she] suffers the least distress and retains the greatest dignity.'[55] Quite what effect that formula had in practice is questionable, but the decision is notable since it aired for the first time many of the concerns considered in this paper.

Whilst there are good theoretical reasons for arguing that a teenager like C should not be allowed to martyr herself by refusing life-saving medical treatment,[56] the methods adopted for ensuring the treatment given are questionable. As noted elsewhere,[57] had C been two years older, there would have been no alternative but to find a clinic able to provide her with treatment under the mental health legislation, with its many safeguards, or to leave her untreated. There seems to be a stark contrast between the anxiety shown by the courts to safeguard the rights of adult patients to autonomy, as recently illustrated by the case law restricting the circumstances wherein women can be forced to undergo caesarian sections,[58] and their readiness to use the inherent jurisdiction as a panacea to ensure that treatment units and local authorities easily obtain authority to treat adolescents against their will. The judiciary may not always appreciate that one of the dangers of allowing agencies to rely on the High Court in this way is that it does not encourage a more open discussion of the benefits of using the mental health

[54] [1997] 2 FLR 180.
[55] *Ibid.* at 200.
[56] See discussion above.
[57] J Fortin, *Children's Rights and the Developing Law* (Butterworths, 1998), p 121.
[58] For example, *St George's Healthcare NHS Trust v S, R v Collins and others, ex p S* [1998] 3 All ER 673.

legislation instead. As Gostin has said: 'Nothing degrades a human being more than to have intrusive treatment thrust upon him despite his full understanding of its nature and purpose and his clear will to say no.'[59] It seems clear that when adolescents start challenging the legality of enforced medical treatment under the *Human Rights Act* 1998, the judiciary will be forced to justify and delineate the use of force far more carefully.[60]

CONCLUSION

As discussed at the beginning of this paper, there are sound theoretical principles which justify coercive paternalism 'in a child's best interests.' Consequently, adults need not fear that by acknowledging that children are competent rights holders they become morally committed to respecting children's wishes in every situation. A measure of physical force may well be appropriate to ensure that a child does not seriously damage his or her long-term happiness and fulfilment by behaving in a dangerously ill-disciplined way at home, in school or in residential care. Equally, good theoretical justification exists for forcing a seriously ill child to undergo unwanted life-saving medical treatment. Nevertheless, the coercion used should be restrained and subject to as many checks and balances as possible. Physically punishing children for past misbehaviour, however, is an entirely different matter and difficult to defend on moral grounds. On this issue, it appears, society's attitudes are in a state of flux. With official encouragement, parents could learn to discipline their children without resorting to corporal punishment. But the government should be prepared to promote such attitudinal changes by legislating against its use by parents, just as they did for teachers.

As this review has shown, the law does not provide adults who care for children on a day-to-day basis with a clear body of guidance over the extent to which they can use physical force on their charges. By attempting to respond to conflicting public attitudes and policies, it is perhaps inevitable that the emerging legal principles lack coherence and clarity, even when applied to the areas for which they were designed. Thus, while official guidance for teachers is reasonably helpful, that produced for residential care workers is confused and contradictory. Doubtless, these ad hoc developments represent part of our slow progress from a society which condones the use of physical violence to one which shuns it, and considers its use degrading and humiliating for adults and children alike.

[59] L Gostin, 'Consent to Treatment: The Incapable Person', in C Dyer, *Doctors, Patients and the Law* (Blackwell Scientific Publications, 1992), p 76.

[60] The extent to which doctors can force unwanted medical treatment on seriously ill teenage patients without infringing their rights under the European Convention on Human Rights is discussed in more detail by Fortin, n 36, pp 262–63.

18

The Lawyer–Client Relationship in Family Law: Does Client Funding Status Make a Difference?

Rosemary Hunter*

INTRODUCTION

Most of the existing literature on lawyer–client relations in family law fails to deal with differences between clients—either observable, or as constructed by their lawyers. Studies have either not sought to differentiate between different groups of clients,[1] or have tended to focus exclusively on poor clients,[2] or relatively wealthy clients,[3] or clients involved in particular kinds of disputes.[4] These studies suggest that poorer clients are dominated and disempowered by their lawyers through the operation of legal professionalism.[5] Professionalism distances lawyers from clients, legal obligations are separated from moral obligations, and legal service is fragmented rather than integrated into a concern for the whole needs of clients. Better-off clients, on the other hand, appear to fare better in their lawyers' offices. On the basis of their observations of lawyer–client interactions, for example, Sarat and Felstiner insist that the fluidity of power is such that the lawyer does not always exercise power over the client, and that both lawyer and

* Professor of Law and Director, Socio-Legal Research Centre, Griffith University, Australia.

[1] For example, John Griffiths, 'What do Dutch Lawyers Actually do in Divorce Cases?' (1986) 20 *Law & Society Review* 135; Richard Ingleby, *Solicitors and Divorce* (Clarendon Press, 1992).

[2] For example, Jack Katz, 'Representing the Poor', in Richard L Abel (ed), *Lawyers: A Critical Reader* (New Press, 1997), pp 253–61; Christine Parker, 'The logic of Professionalism: Stages of Domination in Legal Service Delivery to the Disadvantaged' (1994) 22 *International Journal of the Sociology of Law* 145. See also Francis Regan, 'Rolls Royce or Rundown 1970s Kingswood?' (1997) 22 *Alternative Law Journal* 255; John Germov, 'Equality before the Law: The Limits of Legal Aid and the Cost of Social Justice' (1995) 33 *Australian Journal of Social Issues* 162.

[3] For example, Austin Sarat and William LF Felstiner, *Divorce Lawyers and Their Clients: Power and Meaning in the Legal Process* (Oxford University Press, 1995).

[4] For example, Gwynn Davis, Stephen Cretney and Jean Collins, *Simple Quarrels: Negotiating Money and Property Disputes on Divorce* (Clarendon Press, 1994), pp 79–83.

[5] Parker, n 3. See also Michelle S Jacobs, 'Legal Professionalism: Do Ethical Rules Require Zealous Representation for Poor People?' (1995) 8 *St Thomas Law Review* 97.

client can be considered more or less powerful at different times, or even at the same time.[6]

Unlike these previous studies, the research reported here set out specifically to compare the legal services received by legally aided and self-funding family law clients.[7] This research was conducted in the context of recent cuts to legal aid budgets, the capping of individual legal aid grants in family law, and generally low fees paid for legal aid work undertaken by private practitioners. From 1 July 1997, the former legal aid funding partnership between the federal and state governments in Australia was replaced by a new regime under which the federal government assumed exclusive responsibility for funding family law matters.[8] Federal legal aid spending was simultaneously reduced by 20 per cent. New family law funding priorities and guidelines were introduced to govern the disbursement of federal legal aid funds, which included an overall cap of $10,000 per party in cases involving children. Within this cap, solicitors are paid at hourly rates which vary from state to state, but in all cases are considerably lower than the Family Court's scale of fees. Moreover, Legal Aid Commissions impose separate caps on the amount payable for each stage of a family law matter, regardless of the number of hours actually worked by the solicitor. These very tight restrictions on legal aid funding have given rise to concerns that the quantity and/or quality of services provided to legally aided clients might be compromised.

It should be noted that Australia has a mixed system of legal aid delivery. Legal aid clients may either be represented by a salaried lawyer employed by a state or territory Legal Aid Commission, or they may be represented by a private practitioner, who will be paid a standardised fee for the service by the Legal Aid Commission, as outlined above. This paper relates only to the legal aid work undertaken by private practitioners. That is, it compares the way private practitioners think about and treat their clients according to funding status.

The only other study to have undertaken a similar inquiry was conducted in England and Wales by John Eekelaar, Mavis Maclean and Sarah Beinart.[9] In England and Wales, a much higher proportion of family law work is legally aided

[6] Sarat and Felstiner, n 4, p 19.

[7] The research was conducted by the Justice Research Centre, Sydney, and funded by the Commonwealth Attorney-General's Department and Department of Finance. For a full report of the research, see Rosemary Hunter, with Ann Genovese, Angela Melville and April Chrzanowski, *Legal Services in Family Law* (Justice Research Centre, Sydney, 2000). The opinions expressed in this chapter are those of the author, and do not necessarily reflect the views of the Attorney-General's Department or Department of Finance, the Board of Governors of the Law and Justice Foundation of New South Wales, the former Advisory Board of the Justice Research Centre, the project Steering Committee or the other authors of the report.

[8] 'Family law matters' in this context primarily consist of matters concerning the residence of and contact with children following the breakdown of their parents' relationship (whether married or de facto), and property division following the breakdown of a marriage. Proceedings relating to protection from domestic violence fall within state jurisdiction.

[9] John Eekelaar, Mavis Maclean and Sarah Beinart, *Family Lawyers: The Divorce Work of Solicitors* (Hart Publishing, 2000).

(65–75 per cent)[10] than is the case in Australia (around 25 per cent).[11] Eekelaar et al. found themselves observing a dual profession, involving 'two distinct professional sub-groups'—one doing predominantly legal aid work for low-income clients, and the other working with private clients.[12] In Australia, on the other hand, due to the lower proportion of legal aid work available, it is quite rare for private solicitors to work exclusively with legal aid clients. While salaried Legal Aid Commission solicitors in Australia do deal only with legal aid clients, private solicitors will either have a mix of legal aid and private clients, or will deal exclusively with self-funding clients. Thus, while Eekelaar et al. did consider differences in legal services provided to legally aided and private family law clients in England and Wales,[13] those services were not generally provided by the same solicitors, and there was considerably less scope for solicitors to express views on perceived differences between legally aided and self-funded clients.

Our research was conducted across four Australian states (New South Wales, Victoria, Queensland and South Australia), and was based on family law cases involving children[14] which had commenced proceedings in the Family Court, and were finalised in the six-month period September 1998–February 1999. Solicitors were recruited to the study by means of random sampling from lists of known family law firms,[15] clustered around the eight Registries of the Family Court in the four states. A total of 60 solicitors from 55 law firms ultimately agreed to participate. These solicitors were asked to identify cases they had handled falling within the above parameters, and to forward to the relevant clients information about the study and an invitation to participate. Our aim in relation to each of the cases in the sample was to interview the solicitor, examine the solicitor's file, and gain the client's views by means of a client satisfaction survey. In the end, 97 clients gave us permission to view their files, and 95 clients completed a survey. In the interviews, solicitors were asked questions specifically relating to each file that was analysed, plus a series of open-end questions concerning the time, cost, process and outcomes of family law cases, their general experiences with legally aided and self-funded clients, and views on quality of legal services.

In addition to the interviews with solicitors having cases in the study, we interviewed a further 20 private solicitors who had initially said they were not

[10] *Ibid.*, p 20.

[11] Hunter et al., above n 8, p 49.

[12] Eekelaar et al., n 10, p 57.

[13] They found that handling legal aid cases tends to be high-volume, low-reward work; cases are dealt with fairly quickly, much of the solicitor's activity involves reacting to short-term crises, and the solicitor takes on a significant social worker or general practitioner type role. On the other hand, solicitors give their private clients more scope to set the agenda in their cases, especially if they involve 'big money', but this is not necessarily most conducive to timely resolution: *ibid.*, p 58.

[14] It was necessary to focus the study on children's matters (primarily residence and/or contact applications), since legal aid is not generally available for property matters. However, the self-funding cases in the file sample often involved both children's and property issues.

[15] These were firms that either included an accredited family law specialist, took family law referrals from the local Law Society and/or undertook a substantial amount of legal aid work as advised by each state's Legal Aid Commission.

interested in taking part in the study, in order to determine whether there were any differences in responses between them and the solicitors who had agreed to participate. We were particularly concerned to determine whether the self-selecting group of participating solicitors professed higher standards of client service than their peers. The 20 non-participating solicitors answered the same open-ended questions as the participating solicitors, but their clients and files were not accessed. In fact, while the participating solicitors undertook a higher proportion of legal aid work on average than the non-participating group, the responses of the two groups in relation to quality of legal services did not differ in any significant respect. The interview responses of both groups were therefore analysed together, giving a total of 80 respondents to the solicitor interviews.

SOLICITORS' PERCEPTIONS

Turning first to what solicitors said in the interviews, a fairly consistent typology of clients emerged, which was strongly correlated with funding status.

Reasonable and Unreasonable Clients

A major type of family law client identified was the 'unreasonable client,' who was described as being demanding, less reliable, less grateful for the solicitor's efforts on their behalf, and less responsible. This unreasonable client is typically legally aided, with a majority of private solicitors (81 per cent) responding that legally aided clients are more demanding than self-funding clients. Solicitors complained that legally aided clients telephone excessively, and insist on immediate attention as if they are 'the only person in the world.' To a lesser extent, solicitors also asserted that the unreasonable (legal aid) client requires a greater amount of time, insists that the solicitor pay attention to trivial issues, has unrealistic expectations, dictates terms to the solicitor, expects a better service, is less cooperative, is more emotive, takes advantage of the service, has trouble understanding family law, requires more reassurance, and costs the firm more money.

The construction of the unreasonable legally aided client operates in opposition to the reasonable, self-funded client, who is more selective with their demands, more considerate of the solicitor, and suitably grateful for the service they receive. They are more willing to negotiate and compromise, and are more willing to listen to the advice of their lawyer. When the solicitors interviewed had the rare opportunity to act for a client with unlimited funds, the case was described as 'fun' or a 'breath of fresh air,' even if the client was demanding.

To some extent, solicitors acknowledged that legally aided clients might be more demanding because of their socio-economic position. Demanding clients came from situations of poverty or were social 'victims,' and thus needed more time and had 'special' needs. In addition, several solicitors commented that their legally aided clients may be illiterate, had suffered from severe domestic violence, had fewer support systems, or were more likely to be from a non-English speaking background. Their cases may involve other complicating factors, such as overlap with criminal law issues, health and social relationship problems, and involvement with other agencies such as the Department of Community Services.

By far the most popular explanation among private solicitors for why legally aided clients were so unreasonable, however, was that they were not paying for their representation, and therefore had no idea of the costs of their demands.[16] Some solicitors also relied on individualistic explanations for the legally aided client's apparent unreasonableness. For instance, they explained that their legally aided clients had more difficult personalities, were less intelligent, were unable to resolve issues or to take responsibility for their lives without help, could not make decisions, and were 'down the street with nothing to do', so could spend more time harassing their solicitor. These explanations developed into a form of victim blaming, with several solicitors complaining that legally aided clients suffered from a 'welfare mentality', where they expected 'something for nothing'.[17]

In contrast, solicitors explained that self-funding clients typically have a higher level of education and so have a greater ability to understand family law, and are reliable and responsible as they are more likely to be employed. They were described as being more focused, selective with their demands, having a greater awareness of costs, and more appreciative of the service.

This dichotomy put forward by solicitors between the reasonable (and grateful) self-funding client and the unreasonable legally aided client appears, however, to be more perceived than real. We attempted to gauge the level of demand imposed by clients on their solicitors by coding the files for behaviours such as frequent phone calls or letters from the client, frequent phone calls or letters from the other party, the client failing to attend interviews or court, the client being difficult to contact, serious illness of the client or a child, or major problems with the other party. Analysis of the files showed that, contrary to solicitors' expectations, legal aid clients were no more likely than self-funding clients to subject their solicitor to frequent telephone calls and correspondence.[18] Moreover, when the different types of demands were totalled, self-funding clients and legal aid clients had the same mean number of demands per case (0.95).

[16] The solicitors interviewed by Mather et al. made a similar point in relation to *pro bono* clients: Lynne Mather, Richard Maiman and Craig McEwen, ' "The Passenger Decides on the Destination and I Decide on the Route": Are Divorce Lawyers Expensive Cab Drivers"?' (1995) 9 *International Journal of Law and the Family* 286 at 290, 303. As discussed below, *pro bono* work in family law is extremely rare in the Australian context.

[17] The language of solicitors can often be quite derogatory. In one article, Sarat and Felstiner use the term 'law talk' to describe lawyers' 'cynical realist' diction: William LF Felstiner and Austin Sarat, 'Enactments of Power: Negotiating Reality and Responsibility in Lawyer–client Interactions' (1992) 77 *Cornell Law Review* 1463.

[18] Frequent phone calls/letters from clients were recorded in 28% of self-funding cases and 25% of legally aided cases handled by a private solicitor.

The perception that legal aid clients are more demanding seems to arise from the fact that solicitors are facing increasing difficulties in maintaining legal aid work, and tend to blame their legally aided clients for these difficulties. Legal aid work has become less and less economically viable for law firms, and the transaction costs of obtaining and keeping a grant of aid, and accounting to the Legal Aid Commission, are disproportionately high.[19] Instead of recognising that their source of dissatisfaction is with the Legal Aid Commission, or with the federal government which has ultimate control over the amount of funding available for legal aid in family law, and instead of feeling sympathy for their clients, many solicitors seem to be blaming their legal aid clients for the economic challenges they bring.

Capable Clients

Another of the types of client identified—the 'capable' client—was generally described as well-educated, intelligent, articulate, confident and literate. The capable client appears to be another opposition to the unreasonable client and, not surprisingly, the capable client is more likely to be self-funding.

Capable clients are offered a greater range of options in dealing with their cases—for example, they may be entrusted with some tasks, such as drafting, filing and serving documents, organising witnesses, or negotiating with the other party. In other circumstances, solicitors might use such 'unbundled' services[20] as a means of saving their client money or preserving a grant of aid, but solicitors also explained that capable clients are offered unbundled services in order to give the client a greater sense of ownership and control over the case. In addition, other options for client-controlled negotiation, such as community based mediation, were considered to be appropriate for the capable client.[21]

Less capable clients, who were invariably identified as legally aided, are offered less control over their case and provided with fewer options. This disempowerment is not just a result of the restriction of funds. These clients are perceived to be less able to deal with the responsibility of their own lives and, by extension, their own cases.[22]

[19] Correspondence with the Legal Aid Commission constituted around 30% of typical legal aid files—quite a high ratio of unpaid work on these files. See Hunter et al., n 8, p 241.

[20] See Forrest S Mosten, 'Unbundling of legal services in family law', Conference paper presented at Advanced Family Law Conference, Bond University, Queensland, 17 Sept 1993.

[21] Eekelaar et al. made a similar observation in relation to the group of clients 'for whom mediation should work well': 'they do not seek conflict, but wish to make things as easy as possible for their children, are able to work out the kind of outcome they seek and are articulate enough to be able to mediate if conflict arises': see n 10, p 69.

[22] See also Griffiths, above n 2, at 153, noting lawyers' tendency to adapt the legal information given to clients according to the client's (perceived) emotional and intellectual ability to absorb it. For example, one of the lawyers observed by Griffiths had a detailed printed sheet concerning divorce procedure, which was given only to 'intelligent, literate, and emotionally stable clients'. Another chose not to give too much information to 'simpler' clients because it would make them confused and upset.

From the client surveys, however, there was no difference between self-funded and legally aided clients in responses to the proposition 'My lawyer made me feel like I had some control over my case'. Rather, both self-funded and legally aided clients gave their lawyers lower than average scores on this point.[23] The lawyer interviews indicated a strong consensus view that lawyers need to manage all of their clients towards the achievement of consensual settlements within the scope of the *Family Law Act* and the norms laid down by the Family Court. It appears, then, that this management process, which limits clients' control over their cases, is only minimally mitigated by the return of some degree of control to clients deemed to be 'capable'.

Deserving Clients

In between the unreasonable legal aid client and the reasonable, capable self-funding client is the next type of family law client—the 'deserving' client, or 'worthy cause'. The deserving client is a person whose case has merit (as perceived by the solicitor), but who—for whatever reason—cannot receive a grant of aid from the Legal Aid Commission. The deserving client may also have an urgent case where the Legal Aid Commission may be willing to provide a grant of aid, but the client cannot afford to wait.

Deserving clients need to elicit empathy, and solicitors appeared to have particular criteria for assessing the validity of a client's claim to their compassion. The deserving client has to have trouble financing the case, the case has to have merit and involve an interesting legal problem, the client has to be unable to run the case themselves, be both completely at a loss and desperate and still sensible and reasonable, and be grateful for the service.

Deserving clients may occasionally be assisted *pro bono*, although more frequently solicitors said they would discount the bill, undercharge, give free advice, charge at a Legal Aid scale, or provide extra work free of charge.[24] Solicitors could only take on such deserving clients if it was unlikely that the case would cost the firm too much, if the other side was appalling, if the case had a good chance of success, if a child was at risk, if the client's account was already quite high, or they had run out of funds. This set of criteria suggests that the deserving client is quite a restricted category.

This point is borne out by the file analysis. There were no cases in the file sample in which the solicitor acted wholly *pro bono*, and only 10 per cent of the

[23] Clients were asked to respond according to a five-point scale, ranging from strongly disagree (= 1) to strongly agree (= 5). Mean scores on most other questions were in the range of 4.0 to 4.3, but the mean score for the control question was only 3.4.

[24] This appears to be consistent with a Senate Committee's observation that lawyers often argue that they do not need to provide further *pro bono* services, as they already contribute to legal services to the poor by doing legal aid referral work at reduced rates: Senate Standing Committee on Legal and Constitutional Affairs, *Legal Aid: For Richer and for Poorer—Cost of Legal Services and Litigation Discussion Paper* (Commonwealth of Australia, 1992), pp 94–101.

self-funded or mixed-funded cases in the file sample involved substantial discounting (that is, free work) by the solicitor. These discounts, where quantifiable, ranged from almost 20 per cent to over 50 per cent of the bill. The actual sums of money involved varied: in three of the cases, it was $400–500, although in two other cases it was larger—$1,800 and $4,500. In one case, the solicitor did not charge for nine months' work, while in another case the solicitor discounted the counsel fees and billed expert fees at half their actual cost.

Discounting, however, did not appear to be related to the client's income (where this information was available). For example, of the six cases in which the client's income was known to be under $10,000 per annum, two received a discount and four did not. In one of the discount cases, the client's income was around $16,000 per annum, in two others it was around $23,000 and in one it was over $34,000.[25] The size of the legal bill relative to the client's income also did not seem to be relevant. For example, seven clients in the file sample ran up bills greater than their annual income, but only one of these received a discount. Thus 'deservingness' is not simply a matter of relatively or absolutely limited resources, but includes the range of subjective factors referred to above, which are difficult to satisfy, and operate unpredictably in individual cases.

Ordinary People

The deserving client bears some resemblance to the last type of client referred to by solicitors: 'ordinary people'. The ordinary person is a particular form of 'worthy cause', who has limited means to run a case but is ineligible for a legal aid grant due to the means test. Solicitors felt that the ordinary person, who has 'no more left in his wallet' at the end of the week, was being disadvantaged by the legal aid eligibility guidelines. They considered there to be too great a gap between those who could get aid, who were usually social security recipients, and those who could afford to fund their own cases, so that those caught in between missed out.[26]

This perception is again undermined by data from the file analysis and client surveys, and from an earlier profiling study of family law cases undertaken by the Justice Research Centre, which suggest that the majority of family law clients have an average or below-average income[27] and would be spending a large proportion

[25] See also Phillip R Lochner Jr, 'The No-Fee and Low-Fee Legal Practice of Private Attorneys', in Abel, n 3, p 246, arguing that the beneficiaries of *pro bono* services are typically middle-class litigants, who may be experiencing a period of temporary disadvantage but whose long-range economic prospects are generally very good.

[26] This category of clients also appears in Eekelaar et al.'s analysis, as 'the population group about whom the Lord Chancellor expressed concern as being above the legal aid limits but not able to afford costly legal services': n 10, pp 68–69.

[27] In the profiling study, 43% of self-funding clients had incomes under $30,000: Rosemary Hunter, *Family Law Case Profiles* (Justice Research Centre, Sydney, 1999), p 74. In the current study, 66% of self-funding respondents to the client survey reported incomes of $30,000 or less, and self-funding clients' income was under $30,000 in 73% of cases in which income information was recorded in the client's file.

of their limited funds on family law proceedings. Once more, the difference between perception and reality suggests that there may be another explanation for solicitor constructions of clients, which relates more to the solicitor's view of who is deserving and who is not in the context of restricted legal aid funding.

A few solicitors suggested that one way to eradicate disadvantage for 'ordinary people' would be to tighten up legal aid guidelines even further. Since 'ordinary people' have everything to lose, whereas legal aid clients are 'only' risking their grant of aid, further limiting access to grants would apparently reduce both parties to the same level. This solution shows scant sympathy for clients who cannot afford to pay for their own lawyer. Fortunately, not all solicitors were quite so keen to reduce all clients to the lowest common denominator. A larger number of solicitors felt that the means test was set at too low a level, and should be raised to include the 'ordinary person'.[28] Nevertheless, legal aid clients and 'ordinary people' remained dichotomised. One may conclude that if the means test were to be raised, these 'ordinary people' would cease to be 'ordinary people' and become legal aid recipients, with a new group of 'ordinary people'—above the means test, but still earning relatively little in the solicitor's eyes—taking their place.

THE SERVICES PROVIDED

The attitudes expressed by private practitioners towards their legally aided and self-funding clients might be expected to translate into differences in the legal services provided to the two groups. For example, the notion that legal aid clients are more demanding suggests that their cases might involve more work, although solicitors also asserted in the interviews that they were only able to offer a minimal level of service to legal aid clients because they generated so little revenue. In fact, on the kinds of inputs we could measure from the files—such as the volume of correspondence produced by the solicitor, the volume of documents perused, the number of phone calls and personal attendances, the number of court attendances and documents filed—there was no significant difference at all between the amount of work undertaken on legally aided and self-funded cases. It is possible that legal aid clients fare worse on items we were unable to measure, such as time spent with the client, and in preparing affidavits (since legal aid files are not time-costed), but systematically more limited service for legally aided clients was not in evidence.

The client surveys also belied any expectations of different treatment. Clients were asked a series of questions concerning how well their lawyers performed on a range of client service items, including listening, understanding, returning

[28] Of course, as Abel warns, the potential problems of raising the means test to include the middle class are that middle-class clients may consume more than their fair share of resources, and lawyers may overlook the poor, finding it easier to identify and communicate with middle-class clients: Richard L Abel, 'Law Without Politics: Legal Aid Under Advanced Capitalism', in Abel, n 3, pp 282–90.

phone calls, providing explanations, explaining options and keeping clients informed. There was no statistical difference in the responses of legally aided clients and self-funded clients to these questions.

One possible conclusion from this finding is that there may well have been differences in the quality of services provided to the two groups of clients, but the survey instrument was incapable of discerning them. However, in other crucial respects the survey did prove sensitive to differences. In particular, as mentioned earlier, lawyers scored considerably lower on giving clients control over their cases than on other aspects of client service. This finding provides a clue to what seems to have been going on.

Although lawyers produced stereotypical classifications of their clients, they also stressed client management as an important element of their skill as practitioners. As mentioned earlier, solicitors in the family law jurisdiction see it as an important part of their role to manage the client's expectations and bring them to an understanding and acceptance of what the Act and the court require.[29] Only a small minority of solicitors (7 per cent), said they would allow a client to drive the case. The great majority preferred to manage the client's expectations in such a way as to meet the outcome the practitioner expected from the court, and this approach did not vary with funding status. The file analysis similarly indicated only a minority of cases (5 per cent) in which the solicitor acting for the other party was criticised for failing to manage their client more firmly.

The *Family Law Act*, its interpretation by the Family Court and the Family Court Rules provide the basic framework within which solicitors manage client expectations. Most solicitors indicated that the client's expectations need to be heard, but the next step is to test those expectations against the likely outcome, from the court's perspective, and to communicate this very clearly to the client at the earliest possible opportunity.[30] Solicitors overwhelmingly described using the law to manage clients as a way of ensuring that clients' expectations were realistic, or 'hosed down'. They felt that this was essential, as if the client was led to expect something beyond what was achievable or able to be delivered legally, they would be dissatisfied with their service, which would have negative repercussions for the lawyer and the client.[31]

Ultimately, then, this concern to guide clients towards an expected and accepted range of outcomes seems to be the dominant factor in client management, rather than the solicitor's attitude towards the client based on funding status.

[29] The same finding was made by Griffiths, n 2, pp 156–66; and by Mather et al., n 17, pp 298–301.

[30] See also Sarat and Felstiner, n 4, pp 57, 69. Sarat and Felstiner argue that 'defining the legally possible is one of the divorce lawyer's basic devices in efforts to exercise power in lawyer–client relations'. This may well be true, even if one does not accept that law is sufficiently open-textured to allow *any* outcome.

[31] See also Peter Carne, 'Management of Your Family Law Practice', Family Law Residential, Kooralbyn, Queensland, 1992: 'Right from the start the solicitor has to control the client. This control will hopefully ensure that the client will come through the matrimonial dispute less scathed emotionally and financially than he or she would have otherwise and, for the solicitor, avoids dealing with a client who at the end of the process is dissatisfied both with the result and the legal costs.'

EXIT FROM LEGAL AID

But while private solicitors' professional standards and shared norms of case management seem to have prevented an erosion of service quality to legal aid clients, the news is not all good. Lawyers doing legal aid work have maintained equivalent standards of service; however, there are now many fewer lawyers doing legal aid work. Over three-quarters of the private solicitors we interviewed (78 per cent, n = 62) reported that the amount of legal aid work that they were doing in family law had decreased. Of the solicitors who specified how much their legal aid work had decreased, nearly half (47 per cent) commented that this decline was from a 'substantial', 'huge' or 'considerable' amount to practically nothing. In some cases, solicitors had decreased their legal aid commitment from over 60 per cent of their caseload to none. The most popular explanation for this decline was that legal aid work did not pay sufficiently to justify continuing, or that inadequate funding provided by the federal government to the Legal Aid Commissions meant that there were simply no funds to provide grants to their clients. Some solicitors felt that when they accepted a legal aid case they were working effectively at a loss, whilst others claimed they would prefer to actually take cases on *pro bono* rather than accept a legal aid grant.[32] Some solicitors felt that the inadequate remuneration would mean that they would eventually have to compromise the quality of their service, and under these conditions they would prefer not to accept the work at all. In other words, rather than dropping service standards, solicitors have simply dropped out. Other researchers have also documented this 'flight' from legal aid work by family law practitioners in Australia.[33]

The legal aid system was given a new injection of funds from the beginning of the 2000–2001 financial year, partly with the objective of raising fees to attract private family law practitioners back into legal aid work. Solicitors' comments in the interviews suggest that, in order for the increased funding to have the desired effect, there will need to be both a substantial increase in fees, and an overall increase in the number of grants available. It is questionable whether the funding increase will be sufficient to achieve these aims.

To conclude, client funding status does not appear to make a difference to the service Australian family law clients receive, but it does make a difference prior to that. Although legal aid clients have not suffered a reduction in service quality as a result of cuts to legal aid, they do face greater problems of access—both to legal aid grants per se, and to lawyers prepared to run their cases.

[32] The discussion of *pro bono* services above suggests that this claim should be treated with a degree of scepticism.

[33] John Dewar, Jeff Giddings and Stephen Parker, *The Impact of Changes to Legal Aid on the Practice of Family Law and Criminal Law in Queensland* (report prepared for the Queensland Law Society and Family Law Practitioners Association of Queensland, 1998); 'National Legal Aid Survey of Legal Firms Doing Legal Aid Family Law Work', communication from National Legal Aid, 29 Nov 1999.

19

The Distribution of Stock Options on Divorce and Proposed Changes in American Divorce Law

David S Rosettenstein*

INTRODUCTION

The American Law Institute (ALI) is proposing[1] that states in the United States amend their laws to embody certain principles governing the financial remedies available on divorce. One of the interesting aspects of the proposed revision of the law is the way the proposals embody premises based on presumed assumed risks, and then embody solutions with their own risk characteristics. The paper looks at how these various elements of risk play out with respect to the treatment on divorce of stock option compensation packages provided by employers to a spouse-employee. Devices of this type are playing a rapidly increasing role in employee compensation in the United States,[2] and at least among certain classes of employees may be starting to overwhelm conventional compensation packages.[3] These compensatory devices carry with them substantial elements of risk.

* Professor of Law, Quinnipiac University School of Law, Connecticut, USA.

[1] *Principles of the Law of Family Dissolution: Analysis and Recommendations* (Proposed Final Draft Part I, 14 Feb 1997) [hereinafter PFD]. For a more comprehensive discussion of these proposals as they relate to many of the themes in this paper, see David S Rosettenstein, 'The ALI Proposals and the Distribution of Stock Options and Restricted Stock on Divorce: The Risks of Theory meet the Theory of Risk', (2002) 8 *Wm. & Mary J Women & L* forthcoming.

[2] A recent survey suggests that, in 1999, 19% of employees were eligible to participate in stock option plans, an increase from the 12% who were able to participate in 1998: *Wall Street Journal*, 18 Jan 2000, p A1. A survey of 350 large US companies in June 1999 found that 17% of them granted options to 50% or more of their employees, up from 6% in 1993. See Kelly Smith and Roberta Kirwan, 'America's best company benefits', *Money*, October 1999, p 125. The US Department of Labor's Bureau of Labour Statistics announced that during 2000 it would commence a test survey to determine the incidence of stock option plans and the impact on compensation costs across all industries and all occupations in the country. See Bureau of Labor Statistics, US Department of Labour, *Employment Cost Index—December 1999*, http://stats.bls.gov/oclt/ect/ecnr0022.txt, Notes (accessed 28 Jan 2000).

[3] A study by William M Mercer Inc in the middle of 1999 found that, among the chief executive officers of 350 major industrial and service concerns, compensation packages typically included options with a face value of more than three times the individual's salary. See Joan S Lublin, 'Net envy', *Wall Street Journal*, 6 Apr 2000, p R1 at R3.

Some of the carried risks may relate to the employment relationship, but some may relate to factors which are essentially external to that relationship.

THE AMERICAN LAW INSTITUTE'S PROPOSALS

Property Division

The analysis conducted by the ALI came to the conclusion that most jurisdictions in the United States in principle believed in the equitable distribution of assets on divorce.[4] However, beyond that there were significant differences between the states, in particular, as to what assets might be included in the distribution, whether a presumptive equal distribution ought to employed, whether this presumption should apply to all assets or only those acquired by a spouse's labour, and the extent to which, through property division, access should be available to a spouse's post-divorce earnings.[5]

On the issue of whether a spouse may lay claim to a particular item acknowledged as 'property', the ALI takes the view that property acquired during the marriage, otherwise than by gift or inheritance, is 'marital property'.[6] The ALI then goes on to adopt the position taken in the majority of states in the United States that if property is earned by labour performed by a spouse during a marriage, that alone is sufficient to support a spousal claim of shared ownership on divorce.[7]

As to the specifics of property division, the ALI is proposing that, when property comes to be divided on divorce, the spouses should receive net shares that are equal in value—though (and this is significant for our future concerns) not necessarily identical in kind.[8] The ALI view is that the equal division claim should be grounded on the premise of an equal contribution to the marriage, not necessarily to the accumulation of financial assets.[9]

The ALI's position is that property earned by labour performed during the marriage is distributable marital property, even if the property is received after the marriage.[10]

Compensatory and Restitutional Awards

The ALI analysis concludes that, while current awards of alimony reflect an unease with traditional rationales for such awards, no clear-cut justification for an

[4] PFD, n 1, Introduction, pp 1–2.
[5] *Ibid.*, Introduction, pp 2–3.
[6] *Ibid.*, § 4.03, p 87.
[7] *Ibid.*, § 4.03 cmt. a, p 88.
[8] *Ibid.*, n. § 4.15(1), p 194. See also § 4.03 cmt. a, p 88.
[9] *Ibid.*, § 4.15 cmt. c, pp 197–98.
[10] *Ibid.*, § 4.08, p 168.

alimony award has emerged, except to the extent that there is some recognition of the necessity to meet a claimant's 'need'. The ALI study concludes that it is necessary to develop a coherent justification for alimony, and to integrate this into the principles for allocating property. Accordingly, the ALI suggests that, as far as alimony is concerned, the law should cease to focus on a claimant's 'needs', and should instead focus on any 'loss' suffered by the claimant as a result of the termination of the marriage which might entitle the claimant to 'compensation'.[11]

The ALI analysis suggests that compensatory awards should fall into two groups. First, there would be those claims on behalf of a spouse who, after a marriage of significant duration, experiences a loss in living standard by virtue of having less wealth or earning capacity. This group also recognises claims by individuals who have suffered an earning capacity loss during marriage which endures beyond dissolution where the loss arises by virtue of having borne a disproportionate share of caring for children or by virtue of having cared for a sick or disabled spouse or third party in fulfilment of a moral obligation.[12]

Where the recovery is based on the duration of the marriage alone, the recovery recognises the claimant's expectation to continue to share in the other spouse's income. The extent of the claim will be premised on the marriage having exceeded a minimum duration and will be a function of the duration. The recovery is expressed as a percentage of the post-marriage income differential of the former spouses.[13] Under this approach, the spouses' post-divorce incomes are not automatically equalised, but rather the proposal envisages that the post-divorce gap will lessen the longer the marriage endured until ultimately a marriage of sufficient length will produce post-divorce equality of income.[14]

Essentially the same result follows where the award is premised on providing care. What these analyses do is establish the link to the wage earner's income together with the risks associated with the source of those earnings. Thus, for example, by caring for a couple's child, the care-giver loses risk autonomy in return for income replacement.

The second set of claims to be recognised comprises those which flow either from a claimant's inability to realise a fair return during the marriage on an investment in the other spouse's earning capacity, or where there is an unfair disparity between the former spouses' ability to recover their pre-marital living standard after a short marriage. These claims are restitutional in character.[15]

Where the recovery is premised on an investment in the other spouse's earning capacity, the recovery is linked and limited, in a formulaic way, to the extent of the claimant's contributions to the cost of educational and living expenses.[16]

[11] *Ibid.*, Introduction, pp 8–10; § 5.02 cmt. a, p 261.

[12] *Ibid.*, § 5.03(2), p 271.

[13] *Ibid.*, § 5.03 cmt. b, pp 274–75.

[14] *Ibid.*, § 5.05 cmt. g, pp 295–99.

[15] *Ibid.*, § 5.03, p 272; id, cmt. a, p 275.

[16] *Ibid.*, § 5.15(4), p 384.

Looked at in risk terms, the provider assumed the risk of the consequences of the failure of the relationship, beyond the value of the contributions. Accordingly, the obligation to repay becomes decoupled from the risks associated with the 'performance' of the recipient spouse's benefit.

The final significant basis on which the ALI is suggesting that a recovery can be made applies to short, childless marriages which otherwise do not permit a recovery under ALI principles. Recovery is allowed if, after the divorce, a disparity exists between the spouses' abilities to recover their premarital living standards where the disparity is inequitable because the claimant made expenditures or gave up educational or occupational opportunities in order to serve some purpose which the spouses considered was important to their marital life. When the marriage ends, the expended assets must be essentially unrecoverable, or the lost opportunities must leave the claimant with an earning capacity significantly less than it was before the marriage. Generally the recovery is quantified at half the amount necessary for the claimant to recover the premarital standard of living or the amount necessary to enable the claimant to have a reasonable chance to recover the opportunity lost.[17]

The remedy under the last two heads of recovery is for a specific amount, not a particular asset, and thus ordinarily should be freed from the risks associated with the obligor's assets or financial future.

Space considerations preclude a detailed analysis of the risk premises of the entitlement claims identified under the ALI proposals as well as the risks associated with specific remedial devices. However, the upshot of the ALI proposals is that one is called upon to identify:

— the value of the spouses' property for division purposes;
— the income differential and hence income of the respective spouses;
— the value of the spouses' resources for restitutionary purposes.

We now turn to consider how these analytical demands play out when applied in the context of stock option compensation schemes.

STOCK OPTION COMPENSATION SCHEMES

The Nature of the Scheme

A stock option gives the employee the right to purchase stock of the employer at a predetermined price.[18] The price is usually fixed at the then prevailing market price,[19] in circumstances where it is envisaged that the price will rise, so that the ultimate benefit to the employee will be the difference between the price at which

[17] PFD, n 1, Introduction, § 5.16, pp 394–95.

[18] Joseph W Bartlett, *Fundamentals of Venture Capital* (Madison, 1988), p 226.

[19] To avoid triggering a 'taxable event' when the option is granted, the exercise price must be the 'fair market value' of the stock at the time the option is granted. See Bartlett, n 18, pp 227–28. Stock options fall into two general classes based primarily on their conceptualisation for tax treatment

the option is to be exercised and the market price at which the employee is able to sell the stock after exercising the option. The employee is freed from risk to the extent that, if the stock price does not rise, the employee has not paid out anything, and does not have to do so. However, to the extent that the option represents compensation for labour performed or to be performed, the decline in the price of the stock will leave the holder of the option uncompensated. In this sense, the option is not risk-free.

Normally, the employee may not exercise the option before a specified period has elapsed and then only if the employee remains in the employment of the employer. The option is said to vest when both these conditions have been met.[20] Technically, it may be necessary to recognise four classes of option. The option may be vested (sometimes described as accrued) and matured—that is, the employee will have an absolute right to exercise the option immediately. Or the option may vested and unmatured—that is, the employee has an absolute right to exercise the option at some future date, but cannot currently do so. Thirdly, the option can be matured—that is, it can be exercised, but not vested, so conventionally the stock will only be received unconditionally if the option holder remains in employment at a date in the future.[21] Finally, if the option can only be exercised in the future and the privilege of exercising may be lost in the interim, the option is described as unvested.[22] Jurisdictions are not always careful in the use of the terminology,[23] and generally—and unless the context otherwise indicates—we will treat the option as unvested if it is subject to the risk of forfeiture. Ordinarily, the employee is only free to exercise the option for a specified period.[24]

A rudimentary analysis suggests that the option is intended to do two things. First, because the recipient must remain an employee for a minimum period in order to exercise the option, the option is a device aimed at ensuring that the employee remains in the service of the employer for at least a minimum period. Secondly, the device creates an incentive for the employee to do whatever he or she can to enhance the price of the stock, so as to increase the spread between the

purpose. If they receive 'preferred' tax treatment, they are Incentive Stock Options (ISO) under IRC § 422. Otherwise, they are Non-Qualified Stock Options (NSO). Of significance is that the holder of an ISO can avoid paying capital gains tax until the shares acquired through exercising the option are actually sold, if the stock acquired is held for a qualifying period before sale. The holder of an ISO pays tax on the difference between the exercise price and the value of the stock at the time the option is exercised. An NSO is taxed at ordinary income rates. See *Rehfeldt v Rehfeldt*, Appeal No. C–850056, 1986 Ohio App LEXIS 5603, at *6 (12 Feb 1986).

[20] The concept of 'vesting' may differ when used in the context of pensions and tax law. See *In re Marriage of Miller*, 915 P.2d 1314, 1317 n3 (Colo. 1996).

[21] This type of arrangement really involves a hybrid scheme, part-option, part-restricted stock.

[22] See *Davidson v Davidson*, 254 Neb. 656, 660 (1998). See generally, Laurence J Cutler and Samuel V Schoonmaker, IV, 'Division and valuation of speculative assets: Reasoned adjudication or courthouse confusion?' (1998) 15 *J Am. Acad. Matrimonial Law* 257 at 284–96; J Thomas Oldham, *Divorce, Separation and the Distribution of Property*, § 7.11[3][a] (Law Journal Seminars Press, 1999).

[23] *See Hall v Hall*, 88 NC App 297, 307 (NC App 1987). And even when the case is settled, confusion may result. See *Taylor v Taylor*, 57 Conn. App 528 (2000) (settlement agreement used vested, resulting in an assertion that the term only applied to exercisable options).

[24] In the case of an ISO, this period is no longer than 10 years: IRC § 422. The plan may impose a shorter period.

price at which the employee is free to exercise the option and the price that the employee is able to get for the stock on the open market. In concept, the device creates a unity of interest between employee and the employer's stock holders.[25] Notice, however, that despite these forward looking elements associated with options, the option itself may be awarded for prior services. This may be a significant feature when it comes to determining the portion of the option's value which is distributable as marital property, a topic to which we will return.

A stock option is usually subject to significant conditions. To start with, as was noted, the employee has to remain in the employer's employment. The option instrument may effectively leave the employer free to terminate the employment relationship, and thus deprive the employee of any potential benefits of the option, or the employer may have a limited right to do so. Not infrequently, the employer is also free to cancel the scheme at any time before the employee exercises the option. But, even if the employee is in a position to exercise the option, there may be constraints on the employee doing so. To start with, if the stock is publicly traded, the employee may be precluded from publicly disposing of the stock for a minimum period after acquisition under rules primarily targeted at regulating the behaviour of 'insiders'.[26] Tax laws may impose similar constraints.[27] Additionally, the grantor of the options may limit the ability to trade the stock for a period after acquisition for the purposes of controlling market liquidity and hence the price of the stock in general.[28] Finally, depending on whether or not the stock option scheme is one which meets standards established under the Internal Revenue Code, it may have various tax treatments available to it which, under the circumstances of an individual taxpayer and depending on market conditions, may be advantageous or treacherous.[29]

The Claimant's Access to the Incentive Scheme

As we saw earlier, a claimant has three routes which might lay the foundation for a claim to an incentive-based compensation scheme or its proceeds. First, the

[25] Thus, in one case, the stock plan provided that 'the purpose of the Plan is to give the Company a significant advantage in attracting, retaining, and motivating key employees and to provide the Company with the ability to provide incentives more directly linked to the profitability of the Company's businesses and increases in stockholder value': *Peterson v Peterson*, No. CA99–01–007, 1999 Ohio App 1999 LEXIS 5121, at *4.

[26] SEC Rule 144, 17 CFR § 230.144. Certain instruments offered to employees may be subject to shorter restriction periods than those required under Rule 144. See Bartlett, n 18, § 7.11, 1990 Cumulative Supplement, pp 28–30.

[27] In the case of an ISO, the option holder may not dispose of stock received under the option scheme earlier than two years from the date the option was granted and one year after the option was exercised. See IRC § 422(a)(1).

[28] See *Lomen v Lomen*, 433 N.W.2d 142 (Minn App 1988) (employee agreed that all shares purchased under the option agreement would be acquired for investment and not for resale).

[29] Bartlett, n 18, pp 230–32. For a general discussion of the tax treatment of stock options, including for income, estate, gift and charitable-giving tax purposes, see Richard J Petrucci Jr, 'Planning with employee stock options' (1999) 51 *CBA Estates and Probate Newsletter* 5.

assertion might be that the scheme represents marital property. Secondly, the claimant may assert that the option scheme constitutes portion or all of the other spouse's income and as such should be considered in calculating the parties' income differential for the purpose of a compensatory award. Thirdly, the argument would be that the scheme represents an item of value which could be used to satisfy claims based on contributions to the other spouse's education, or for the restoration of a premarital standard of living after a short marriage. A discussion of the first route will provide the opportunity to discuss the issues relevant to the second and third routes as well.

Property Distribution

Does the Incentive Based Scheme Constitute Property?

Where the claimants seeks a recovery on the basis that the item constitutes marital property, the first hurdle that needs to be overcome is to establish that the incentive-based scheme does constitute 'property'. This question arises in two senses.

Initially, there is the question of whether the contingencies associated with the scheme render it a mere 'expectancy' and thus not distributable as property.[30] This is well-spaded soil in the area of pension schemes where the concern is whether a 'non-vested' pension—that is, one where the employee will receive nothing if the employee fails to satisfy some initial conditions (usually involving remaining in employment for a minimum period of time)—is distributable. The vast majority of jurisdictions in the United States today take the position that non-vested pensions are distributable, on the theory that, unlike expected inheritances, the grantor of the employment benefit is not free to change his or her mind and eliminate the inchoate benefit.[31] Given the pension experience, the trend among jurisdictions in the United States is to treat unvested stock options as property on the basis that the employee has a contractual right which has value as intangible property.[32]

Does the Scheme Constitute Property or Income?

The second sense in which it is necessary to consider whether these incentive-based compensation schemes constitute property available for marital distribution relates to the issue of whether a better or more appropriate characterisation

[30] The fact that an item is apparently valueless does not in itself mean that it is not distributable property. See *Banning v Banning*, No. 95 CA 79, 1996 Ohio App LEXIS 2693 at *14, *20 (28 June 1996) (trial court erred in refusing to distribute stock option because the exercise price was above the market price of the underlying stock).

[31] See, for example, *Krafick v Krafick*, 234 Conn 795 at 797 (1995).

[32] See *Bornemann v Bornemann*, 245 Conn 508 at 519 (1998). This case lists a number of other jurisdictions coming to the same conclusion, as well as some states which have decided to the contrary.

of the benefit is as 'income' to be used in fixing and meeting the obligations reflected in compensatory awards.[33]

There are three possible scenarios to be considered. First, the grant may be made for services totally rendered during the marriage.[34] In this event, the benefit should be treated as marital property.[35] But care must be taken. Because the receipt of the value occurs after the marriage, the claimant should not be allowed to recover a share of the scheme as marital property while at the same time the receipt of the value by the employee is treated as income for the purposes of assessing a compensatory award.[36]

In the other scenarios, the grant is made during the marriage for services to be rendered partly within the period for which the marriage endures[37] or totally outside of it.[38] Some courts appear to take the position that the mere fact that the option is granted during the marriage makes the option in its entirety marital property.[39] But other courts reject this approach.[40] The ALI proposal seeks to exclude from consideration as marital property certain assets because their value is 'inextricably intertwined with . . . post-marital labour'.[41] The conceptual problem that we may face is that the employee spouse generally may not have an indefeasible entitlement to benefit from the option scheme except by virtue of satisfactorily exercising skills and labour for the full qualifying period that is required beyond the marriage.[42]

[33] The same analysis must be made when determining the employee's income for the purpose of calculating child support.

[34] The question of when, for our purposes, the marriage ended is not one to be taken lightly, but is beyond the scope of the present paper.

[35] Some states may preclude this where the options are not exercisable during the marriage. See, for example, *Hann v Hann*, 655 NE 2d 566 (Ind App 1995).

[36] In this regard, in the context of pensions, see *Majauskas v Majauskas* 61 NY2d 481 at 492–93 (1984). See also *Chen v Chen*, 142 Wis. 2d 7, *16 (Wisc App 1987) (value of stock options correctly not treated as income for the purposes of fixing maintenance).

[37] This may be true even if the grant itself is made after the point when the parties' interests are severed. See, for example, *Goodwyne v Goodwyne*, 639 So. 2d 1210 at 1213 (La App 1994).

[38] It may not be a simple matter to determine the period that the grant is intended to provide compensation for. Factors which may impact this determination may include whether the form of the compensation reflects an effort to secure optimal tax treatment; whether it was offered to induce the employee to accept employment, remain in employment, leave other employment; whether it is linked to the achievement of a particular goal; and whether the award is made on a regular or irregular basis. See *Davidson v Davidson*, 254 Neb. 656 at 665 (1998).

[39] See *Davidson v Davidson*, 254 Neb. 656 at 663 (1998) (discussing the analysis of the court in *Smith v Smith*, 682 S.W.2d 834 at 837 (Mo. App. 1984); *Bodin v Bodin*, 955 S.W.2d 380 at 381 (Tex App 1997). *But see Farish v Farish*, 982 S.W.2d 623 at 629 (Tex App 1998) (suggesting that it might be relevant to demonstrate that the options were conferred for services in a time frame other than the marriage).

[40] See *Demo v Demo*, 101 Ohio App. 3d 383 at 387 (1995) (option granted after the marriage based on job performance prior to marriage was not distributable).

[41] PFD, n 1, § 4.07 cmt. b, p 151.

[42] The converse situation also can be encountered. The qualifying labour primarily may have been contributed prior to the marriage, with the option vesting during the marriage. The employee asserts that the options are non-marital propery. The claimant asserts that the vesting during the marriage characterises the option in its entirety as marital property. See *In re Marriage of Fatora and Sullivan*, 1998 Del Fam Ct. LEXIS 195 at 16–17.

Is there a way to allocate some, but not all, of the resulting value to the marital portion of the claim? The slowly emerging trend in the United States is to allocate to each spouse a share of that portion of whatever value finally materialises, where the distributable portion is determined by the ratio of the time that the benefit was 'earned'[43] during the marriage relative to the overall time it took to 'earn' the benefit.[44] The relevant fraction is called the 'coverture fraction or factor', and its use is well established in the context of distributing defined-benefit pensions.[45] The underlying basis for determining the distributable portion of the option is commonly called the 'time rule'.[46] A few jurisdictions have opted for simplicity. If the option is granted during the marriage, it is distributable property regardless of when the services are to be performed.[47] Others take the view that, even if the option is granted during the marriage, it is not distributable property if it is not exercisable and may be forfeited in the future.[48] Finally, lest any court get too complacent, all the calculations may in reality turn out to be flawed, because option vesting dates may accelerate, in the course of corporate mergers, restructuring, or by virtue of performance benchmarks being exceeded.[49]

Notice, at this stage, that our concern is with the portion of the asset that is distributable, not with assigning a value to that portion. What that value should be is an issue to which we will now turn.

What Value Should Be Assigned to the Incentive Based Scheme?

The difficulty with valuing the benefits of schemes such as stock options is that they tend to have associated with them two sets of risk factors. One set of risks involves those associated with the marketplace generally. The other comprises risks associated with the employee beneficiary and his or her employment relationship as well as the relevant tax strictures.[50]

[43] Even this concept is not without problem. If the employee spouse was working for the employer before the incentive scheme was granted, the decision has to be made whether the appropriate time should commence from some point prior to the grant. In essence, the argument is that the compensation is, at least in part, retrospective in nature, not exclusively prospective. See, for example, *Nelson v Nelson*, (1986) 177 Cal App 3d. 150 at 154.

[44] While this concept may be simple, the application may not be. For example, what if, during the marriage, the spouse is granted an unconditional option (which is not exercised during the marriage) to buy restricted stock—that is, stock subject to risk of forfeiture? Essentially, the option would be vested, but the any stock purchased might not be vested until the restrictions were lifted. See *Harrison v Harrison*, (1986) 179 Cal App 3d 1216, 1224–25.

[45] PFD, n 1, § 4.08 cmt. f, p 179. See also *Macaleer v Macaleer*, No. 1900 Philadelphia 1998, 1999 Pa Super LEXIS 132 at 17 (19 Feb 1999). For a general discussion of the use of coverture fractions in the context of divorce cases, see 'Stock Options in Divorce—a National Trend, (1999) *Am J Fam L* 105–9.

[46] See, for example, *In re Marriage of Salstrom*, 404 NW2d 848 at 851–52 (Minn App 1987); *DeJesus v DeJesus*, 90 NY 2d 643, 652 (NY 1997). For an extensive discussion of this topic, see David S Rosettenstein, 'Exploring the use of the time rule in the distribution of stock options on divorce (2001) 35 *Fam LQ* 263 (2001).

[47] See the cases cited in *Bornemann v Bornemann*, (1998) 245 Conn 508 at 525.

[48] *Hall v Hall*, (1987) 88 NC App 297 at 307.

[49] See Oldham, n 22, § 7.11[3][a].

[50] A New Jersey court used an interesting technique in order to circumvent some of these problems. It impressed a constructive trust on the options in the hands of the employee, directed him to

Superficially, market risks would have a discounting effect on the value to an investor of a contingent asset which would vary with the risk preferences of the individual investor. If, however, we can come up with a valuation device which frees the value of an asset from the risk predispositions of the individual investor, then we have eliminated one whole set of concerns which would impact the valuation of the asset on divorce. This is the particular appeal of the Black-Scholes[51] type formula which is now widely mentioned in the cases,[52] even though they may be less widely relied upon.[53] Unfortunately, the basic formula embodies assumptions as to some elements which are of are of particular relevance to our concerns. For example, it is critically dependent on information regarding market volatility. That volatility is in turn a function of the information that is available to the market. However, the information that is available to the employee spouse may differ from that which is available to the market. Thus the volatility may be affected by a major development in a product line, or by an unannounced merger with another more or less volatile corporation.[54] The fact that the employee is privy to information which is not available to the market represents a transition point from market risk factors to personal risks.[55] In short, there may be a real problem in translating a particular employee benefit scheme into an item of 'universal' value. Finally, Black-Scholes modelling is premised on the existence of a market for the underlying instruments.[56] Such a market may not truly exist in the case of closely held corporations, although it might be possible in some circumstances to identify an appropriate 'surrogate' instrument—technically often described as a 'synthetic'.

exercise the options when instructed to do so by the claimant on condition that she provide him with the necessary funds, and ordered the employee to hold in trust any stock resulting from the exercise of the option, or to sell the stock as directed by the claimant, turning over the proceeds to her. However, the court forbade a sale which would violate the Securities and Exchange Commission's 'insider trading' rules. Moreover, the claimant had to indemnify the employee for any tax liability that attached to him. See *Callahan v Callahan*, (1976) 142 NJ Super 325, 330–31.

[51] For a collection of material relating to the formula and its applications see Robert W Kolb, *The Financial Derivatives Reader* (Kolb, 1992). Basically, the Black-Scholes formula requires one to know the price of the underlying stock, the time before the option matures, the price to exercise the option, the market interest rate and the volatility of the stock. See Fischer Black, *Fact and Fantasy in the Use of Options, in* Kolb, above p 180.

[52] See, for example, *Davidson v Davidson*, (1998) 254 Neb. 656 at 669.

[53] See *Wendt v Wendt*, No. FA 960149562S, 1997 LEXIS 3104 (Conn Super. 3 Dec 1997), at 27 (Black-Scholes' valuation formula rejected in favor of intrinsic valuation); *Chammah v Chammah*, FA 95145944S,1997 Conn Super. LEXIS 1896, at 14–15 (Black-Scholes and intrinsic valuation techniques rejected, the former as inaccurate for valuing 'employment issued stock options in a marital context'; the latter as inaccurate 'under the facts of this case').

[54] See Black, n 51, pp 184–85.

[55] For a nice example of this situation, see *Jordan v Duff and Phelps Inc.*, 815 F2d 429, 434–5 (7th Cir. 1987) (duty to disclose to employee of a close corporation who held restricted stock that the corporation was in merger talks with a public corporation, even though a publicly traded corporation would not ordinarily owe the same duty to its employees).

[56] The model may be able to handle the contingencies inherent in the option scheme, even if this restricts the option's marketability. See *Chammah v Chammah*, FA 95145944S, 1997 Conn Super. LEXIS 1896, at 14.

The relationship between the employee spouse and the employer is also something that is worth evaluating in attempting to assign a 'universal' value to a scheme. Unlike a freely traded option, an incentive based scheme may be subject to defeasance by the employer.[57] Given that the scheme is designed to operate as an incentive for the employee, in the employer's eyes that incentive is weakened to the extent that the beneficial interest is assigned to a non-employee spouse.[58] Accordingly, the employer might see it as in its self-interest to cancel the relevant scheme and replace it with another in which the former spouse will not participate. The employer's motivation to act would exist even in the absence of a collusive[59] enterprise between employer and employee,[60] and if the employee is important enough to the employer, the motive for collusion on both sides will be substantial. In one sense, this represents a manifestation of the risk atmosphere in which the employee alone operates.[61]

Where a compensation order is predicated on the establishment of the 'value' of an incentive-based compensation scheme, as where the realisation of a series of options is viewed a part of a process of generating income after the divorce, issues become more problematic. Fundamentally, the Black-Scholes technique does not normally address the risks associated with the employee spouse's actual realisation of the value—that is to say, it does not take into account those risk factors which do not apply to the market in general but do apply to the employee. These range from risks of the scheme's termination, as just mentioned, to an employee failing to satisfy qualifying conditions,[62] to being held accountable for a value which the model suggests is intrinsic to the scheme but which cannot in fact be realised given the particular tax treatment of the scheme.[63]

The fact that an option may only be exercised by an employee,[64] and then only after the divorce, means that the tax treatment resolves into his or hers alone, so that the distributable value should be the after-tax benefit of that individual, not

[57] See, for example, *In re Marriage of Hoak*, 364 NW2d 185 at 193 (Iowa 1985).

[58] The same result might follow if the distribution scheme adopted by the court required an employee to exercise an option and liquidate the benefit.

[59] An employer's interest in an option grant may extend beyond ensuring that the employee has an incentive to perform. The grant may turn the employee, or at least a group of employees, into a 'relational' investor with the power to entrench management. Management, in turn, would be in a position to enhance the employee's post-divorce interests. See generally, Edward B Rock, 'Controlling the dark side of relational investing' (1994) *15 Cardozo L Rev* 987.

[60] A conspiracy was alleged by the non-employee spouse in *Mendenco, Inc. v Myklebust*, 615 SW2d 187 (Tex Sup 1981).

[61] The claimant may have a risk atmosphere of his own. There is a report that a major accounting firm directed a senior audit manager to give up a claim in divorce proceedings to a share of his wife's multi-million dollar option package granted by the firm's client, or leave the firm, on the basis that a conflict of interest might result if he did not do so. See Elizabeth MacDonald, *Wall Street Journal*, 28 Feb 2000, p A3.

[62] See *Bornemann v Bornemann*, (1998) 245 Conn 508 at 529.

[63] For some examples of the impact of tax consequences on the value of options, see Black, n 51, pp 187–89.

[64] See, for example, *In re Marriage of Frederick*, (1991) 218 Ill. App 3d 533 at 540 (options could not be transferred except by will or laws of descent and distribution, and only the employee could exercise the options).

the aggregate of two separate values after tax treatments.[65] However, the courts may not be convinced that this is a universal truth.[66]

Not surprisingly, then—given the potential complexities of using a valuation technique like Black-Scholes—a number of courts have reached for a 'down and dirty' solution to the valuation question.

Where an option is exercisable, a court may be comfortable with the idea that the value of the option is the difference between the exercise or 'striking' or 'strike' price and the current market value of the relevant stock itself.[67] This is tends to be called the 'intrinsic value' method of valuation.[68] The use of this approach starts to become remarkable where the court adopts it with respect to options which are not immediately exercisable.[69] Even if the relationship between the option value and the underlying stock value is fixed, it is not simply the difference between the striking price and the market value of the stock. Nevertheless, one tends to get the impression that, given the choice in choosing a method of valuation which involves a process analogous to a graduate seminar in finance, and adopting a first-cut approach based on the simple difference between striking price and the stock's market value, the courts go for the latter,[70] and let the risks be damned.

As we saw, under the ALI proposals it may become necessary after the divorce to make compensatory payments which are designed to narrow the post-divorce income gap of the former spouses. The amount payable under any such award will be a function of the anticipated income disparity. Where the potential obligor receives compensation in the form of stock options, say, the question arises whether the Black-Scholes or intrinsic valuation techniques should be used to

[65] See *Harrison v Harrison*, (1986) 179 Cal App 3d 1216 at 1223, 1228.

[66] See *Nelson v Nelson*, (1986) 177 Cal App 3d 150 at 156. Here the court took the position that it was only if the employee was able to demonstrate what the tax situation would be when the options were exercised that the court would be required to take the tax ramifications into account. Nevertheless, the appellate court went along with a trial court scheme to attempt to allocate some of the possible tax burden to the non-employee spouse. The appellate court took the view that the 'more equitable distribution' scheme would have been to divide the options in kind and leave each party to the mercy of his or her own tax circumstance: at 156. Such an approach, while expedient, is hardly equitable. Some states are totally indifferent to the tax consequences. Thus, in Indiana, the court may not consider the tax consequences of exercising the option unless the tax consequences necessarily arise from the plan of distribution itself—presumably, for example, if one of the spouses was forced by the divorce decree to exercise and an option and then liquidate the cash value: see *Hiser v Hiser*, 692 NE2d 925 at 927 (Ind App 1998). In contrast, some courts have recognised the need to take into account the tax treatment that will result not only from possible gains, but also from possible losses. See *Chen v Chen*, 142 Wis 2d 7, *15–16 (Wisc App 1987).

[67] See, for example, *Richardson v Richardson*, 659 SW2d 510 (Ark. 1983); *Knotts v Knotts*, 693 NE2d 962 at 968 (Ind App 1998). One author views this as a 'less than optimal approach'—but it is not clear from whose perspective. See Oldham, n 22, § 7.11[3][b].

[68] See *Davidson v Davidson*, (1998) 254 Neb 656 at 669.

[69] See *Green v Green*, (1985) 64 Md App 122 at 137–38.

[70] Even where the underlying stock lost about 10% of its value during the trial—which the trial referee acknowledged—and over 20% more between the trial and the date the decree was entered—which the appellate court on pragmatic grounds considered did not require recognition. See *Rehfeldt v Rehfeldt*, Appeal No C–850056, 1986 Ohio App LEXIS 5603, at 8, 13–5 (12 Feb 1986).

determine at least an element of the individual's income. Some aspects of this problem have already been alluded to.[71] Courts have some experience regarding the relationship between the exercise of options and the generation of income in the context of determining child support. Thus, the Ohio Court of Appeals took the view that the Black-Scholes model was 'designed to reflect market forces under certain conditions and may not be reliable for purposes of litigation'.[72] Instead, it valued the option for income determination purposes by taking the increase in value of the underlying stock during a year referenced to the date of granting of the option, *but only with respect to options that were exercisable*.[73] The court rejected the valuation technique of the lower court which had taken the difference between the stock price on a date 'deemed reasonable under the facts and circumstances of the case', and subtracted from the stock price the exercise price. This amount was then divided by the number of months the option had been in existence, and this amount was then annualised to produce an 'average annual deferred income'. The appellate court rejected this approach taking the position that for the purposes of determining income it was only the appreciation in value of the stock during a given year that was relevant.[74] In terms of risk allocation, the appellate court, by limiting its analysis only to exercisable options, placed the risk of selecting between investment choices on the obligor, and freed the obligee from all risks associated with the option scheme itself.

A court in Tennessee adopted a technique of simply averaging the yields from two prior years of exercising stock options as part of its process of making a child support order.[75] Indeed, another Tennessee court suggested that it might be permissible to determine the obligor's annual income for child support purposes by averaging the benefits of a one-time exercise of stock options over the time the obligor had taken to acquire the options.[76]

The Ohio appellate court's technique just described works well in the context of that case because the employee obligor consistently received options on an annual basis, and the obligee was only entitled to participate in whatever income stream actually materialised. The Ohio *trial* court's approach has a certain aesthetic appeal, particularly where the options are awarded on an irregular basis. However, the appellate court's approach is practical—at least when applied to exercisable options. Unlike child support orders, the ALI compensatory awards are only modifiable in a limited set of circumstances, and therefore basing an award simply on historical average returns from exercising options is potentially highly problematic, given that a critical element in determining the returns—the market price of the underlying stock—ordinarily will be beyond the control of the employee spouse.

[71] See n 54 *et seq.*

[72] *Murray v Murray*, 128 Ohio App 3d 662 at 674–75 (1999).

[73] *Ibid.*, at 675–76.

[74] *Ibid.*, at 672–74.

[75] *Stacey v Stacey*, No. 02a01–9802–CV–00050, 1999 Tenn App LEXIS 668, at 12 (6 Oct 1999).

[76] *Smith v Smith*, Appeal No. 01–A–01–9705–CH–00216, 1997 Tenn App LEXIS 733, at 8 (29 Oct 1997).

CONCLUSION

In summary, when it comes to the division of property on divorce, to achieve an equal division we ordinarily will have to be certain that the benefit will materialise and that we know what its value will be.

However, incentive-based compensation schemes are subject to two sets of risk factors which make obtaining the necessary information problematic. First, there are market-related factors. These generally impinge on the value of the benefit. Ordinarily, unless a market acceptable value can be identified, it is difficult to imagine how any division other than on a basis of equal participation in the specific asset can be consistent with the ALI proposal of equal property division. Any other scheme of division would appear to allocate the risks of a sub-nominal return disproportionately on one party or the other. This is particularly true because of the other set of risks associated with these schemes—that is, those risks which are personal to the grant recipient. Under this set of risks, both the existence of the benefit and its value may be threatened. While the spouses were engaged in a common endeavour, facing these risks was acceptable. Although both the ALI proposals and the case law favour disengaging the couple as cleanly and quickly as possible, this does not appear to be readily achievable when it comes to these option schemes—at least if one hopes to be relatively fair as well. Fairness would seem to require that the couple continue to be exposed to the risk environment together.

When it comes to the compensatory awards proposed by the ALI, the benchmark is the anticipated income divergence of the parties following the divorce. Where the option scheme is viewed as a source of income to the employee spouse, it becomes critical to be able to assign a value to the expected benefit. And, as we saw, in this regard courts are in some trouble. The prevailing favourite approach for valuing options seems to be to rely on the 'intrinsic value' of the option, a method which is as inaccurate as it is simple. Even here, however, the technique, as well as the Black-Scholes approach, does not appear to have been used directly as a device for forecasting income. The limited experience which the courts have at this point, which arises in the context of child support cases, seems to involve a case-by-case approach. The accuracy and coherence of the result are doubtful, and none of the techniques adopted seems fit for universal application. On the plus side, contemporary awards of spousal maintenance are ordinarily modifiable and should certainly remain so if the income in issue is a function of the performance of an incentive-based compensation package.

Finally, to the extent that the ALI proposal envisages restitutionary awards, the amount recoverable is not a function of the value of any benefits receivable under an incentive-based compensation scheme. The claim exists in its own right. With a bit of luck, the employee will be able to exercise an option and meet his or her obligations. But, if this is not the case, the obligation persists and in the ALI's view this is not an unfair or inequitable result.

In the final analysis, the enhanced role that option packages are performing in the American workplace is providing new challenges to the country's divorce law regimes. To some extent, the ALI proposals may help simplify the situation, but in other contexts the combination of the ALI proposals and incentive-based compensation packages is going to make the divorce courts' role more complicated. Clearly, at this stage of the law's evolution, the courts are still in considerable difficulty. At the moment, they have no 'option' but to struggle to find techniques which reconcile risks assumed with risks encountered.

20
Registered Partnership in the Netherlands

Gregor Van Der Burght*

INTRODUCTION[1]

During the last forty years, an entire new field of personal relations law has developed in the sense that legal practitioners, case law and the legislation have become increasingly involved in the legal and financial problems people have to cope with when they live together. Some live together as a couple; others live in a commune. The complexity of the latter is greater than the former; however, the former is by far the most common arrangement, and the social interest and impact of it is far-reaching. This chapter is solely devoted to two-party relationships.

In this respect, the following applies to 'cohabitations' between a father and mother who are living together, or between two friends—male, female or mixed. Their sexual preferences and/or behaviour are not the lawyer's business. However, the patrimonial and financial consequences of the way they want to live are. Sometimes I will mention homosexual couples and heterosexual couples separately, but

* Professor of Private and Notarial (Tax) Law, Chairperson Notarial Law Department and Dean of International Affairs, Faculty of Law, Vrije Universiteit Amsterdam, The Netherlands.

[1] G Van der Burght in: Pitlo-Van der Burght/Rood-deBoer, Personen en Familierecht, Gouda Quint, Arnhem 1998; Cohen Henriquez and Moltmaker, Koninklijke Notari'le Beroepsorganisatie 1977, Cohen Henriquez, Weekblad voor Privaatrecht, Notariaat en Registratie (WPNR) 5511 e.v. (1980), 5667 (1984), 5845 (1987), Van der Burght, Nederlandse Gezinsraad, Deventer 1982 (discussieverslag 1983), Van Mourik, WPNR 5523 (1980), and again Rondom de personenvennootschap, 2e druk, Zwolle 1986, p 158 e.v., Tijdschrift voor Familie en jeugdrecht (FJR) 1986, p 160 e.v., with Robert, WPNR 5571 (1981), Polak, Van Opstall-bundel, p 129 e.v., Handleiding voor het concubinaat, Projectgroep Leiden, Deventer 1981. Robert and Waaijer, Introduction and discussion in 'Relatievrijheid en recht,' congres Leiden 1982, Deventer 1983, Samen-Leven, Ars Aqui (AA)1977, Henriquez-bundel, Schoordijk, WPNR 5356 (1976), Twee mensen en het recht, Boekenreeks NJB, Zwolle 1972. Van de Wiel, Nederlandse Vereniging voor Rechtsvergelijking, Deventer 1974. Straver a.o.., Tweerelaties, anders dan het huwelijk, Nisso-raports 1979–1981, Saal e.a., Samenleven in meervoud, Alphen a.d. Rijn/Brussel 1981. Wortman, Samenlevingsvormen buiten huwelijk, Ministry of Justice 1986, Wetenschappelijk Onderzoek en Documentatie Centrum 1986. Jansweijer, Private leefvormen, publieke gevolgen, Staatsuitgeverij 1987, Doets e.a., Alternatieve samenlevingsvormen in de sociale zekerheid, Deventer 1988. Vandenberghe, De juridische betekenis van het concubinaat, dissertation., Leuven 1970, Koppen and Lekkerkerker, WPNR 6067/8 (1992); Rapport Leefvormen, About registration: Van der Burght in, Relatievrijheid en recht 1982; Van Hoeken, Ars Aequi 1993, p 78 e.v. See further Van Mourik, p 231, FJR 1993; Nuytinck, inaugural address EUR, Ars Notariatus LXX, Deventer 1996; Jessurun d'Oliveira NJB 1996, p 755/6; Senaeve and Coene, Geregistreerd partnerschap, Antwerp 1998.

this is primarily to point out that the law still discriminates between these categories. Since the 1970s, discussions regarding the question of whether living together out of wedlock is contrary to good morals have virtually disappeared. However I might point out that in some European countries (such as Belgium), scholars still attach some importance to this issue.[2]

LIVING TOGETHER: THE CAST OF CHARACTERS

A growing number of couples do not live in 'holy matrimony'. Sometimes it is not even a point of discussion—particularly in the case of students or other youngsters. Older adults live together in a 'common-partnership' of their own free choice, but often the law forces them to live together in what is called an extramarital cohabitation, simply because the law does not allow them to marry and, beyond that, neglects to provide those couples with a legal framework for the financial consequences of their relationship.

The homosexual couples who have appeared on the scene over the past few decades started looking for alternative legal solutions for the patrimonial and financial problems involved in any long-term cohabitation. For them, it was impossible to marry so the law did not leave them a choice. This was also true for those couples who were not allowed to marry due to close blood relationships: brothers and sisters, fathers or mothers and sons or daughters—in other words, the prohibited degrees of kinship.

And finally, we meet couples who are able, but are not inclined, to marry for various reasons: principled objections to the bourgeois institution of matrimony; fear of the same disappointments they have experienced in previous partnerships; or the avoidance of the consequences of marriage in the fields of taxation and/or social security.[3]

All these couples have one thing in common: the lack of any statutory legal provision destined to rule their specific situation, particularly the patrimonial and financial consequences of living together. Some such couples have therefore created their own rules by entering a cohabitation contract.

No Contract

Most of those couples have had no contract, however—for instance, young people who start a relationship, expecting it to last only a short time. To their mutual surprise, the duration becomes much longer and when they eventually do break up they face serious difficulties. But even during their relationship, certain

[2] Senaeve and Coene, *Geregistreerd partnerschap*, (Antwerp, 1998).

[3] A phenomenon that is frequently seen among elderly couples who would lose their old-age pension or among those who benefit from a social security allowance.

questions can arise which need to be solved. For those couples who have not entered into a contract, the courts and legal scholars have developed valuable theories to protect them from disasters.

As there is no written contract, one has to assess by the facts what the legal content of the relation is. One may 'borrow' from the rules of matrimonial property law. A warning applies here, however, in those cases in which a couple has deliberately refused to enter marriage. A distinction also has to be made between couples who can and those who cannot marry. The facts will often prove that, although an agreement in writing does not exist, at least a tacit contractual relationship does, based on reasonable expectations and general behaviour.

Generally speaking, a total community of property will not exist, but the fact that the couple have financed several items together, or that the ownership of some items is not clear, will lead to the finding that there exists a limited community between them.[4] When the acting partner has also acted on behalf of the other one, he or she may be seen as a tacit representative.[5] On the other hand, lack of evidence of separate ownership could be used as ground for the opinion that the asset involved is common property—inspiration can be drawn from Article 1: 131 Dutch Civil Code (DCC).[6]

A partner who reduces his or her work time and consequently income, or altogether leaves the workforce in agreement with a partner to devote time to the common household—and perhaps the upbringing of the couple's children—may count on the right to care and sustenance by the other.[7] One may speak here of an obligation based on a contract.[8] At the very least, a moral (and thus not an enforceable) obligation exists,[9] in which case the fact that one partner has supported the other can serve as a recognition, and thus as a reinforcement, of the moral obligation to a fully fledged civil (enforceable) one.[10]

Another important matter to be solved is, as always, how to arrange the 'divorce'—splitting up is often difficult in these cases. The division of the common property will be ruled by the general principles of law. The existence of a post-cohabitation right to alimony is questionable, although one might imagine its

[4] Hof's-Gravenhage 5 Jan 1977, NJ 569.

[5] Rb. Utrecht, 15 Mar 1988, KG 262.

[6] Asser-De Boer 1, Personen en familierecht 1998, (Kluwer, Deventer,) no 572; compare Supreme Court: 11 Oct 1991, NJ 1992, 600 and earlier: High Court The Hague, NJ 1980, 556 and many other rulings by District Courts.

[7] An analogy can be drawn with Art 1: 81 Van der Burght, Nederlandse Gezinsraad, p 49 e.v., Henriquez, KNB 1977, p 20, Schoordijk, Algemeen gedeelte van het verbintenissenrecht naar het NBW, (Kluwer, Deventer 1979), p 76, and in Het huwelijk, Zwolle 1984, p 100 e.f. District Court 29 June 1973, en 28 June 1974, NJ 1977, 35. High Court Amsterdam 7 May 1992, NJ 1993, 723. No obligation: Asser-De Boer 1, no 568.

[8] Compare Supreme Court 9 Jan 1987, NJ 927.

[9] Compare Supreme Court 27 Feb 1980, BNB 113; 21 juni 1995 BNB 1995/269, HR 17 oktober 1997 NJ 1998, 692, District Court Amsterdam 22 Mar 1983, FJR 1984, p 216; compare Supreme Court Jan 1987, NJ 927 and 10 Apr 1998, NJ 711; Asser-De Boer 1, no 568.

[10] Henriquez, KNB 1977, p 20, Campagne, Alimentatie . . . een evolutie, diss., Utrecht, Deventer 1978, p 184. See Asser-De Boer 1, no 568.

existence in cases where it can be shown that one partner has sacrificed his or her personal career for the benefit of the other (and other members of the family). In these cases, alimony would be justified to compensate the first partner.

Contract

The content of the contract is designed by a civil-law-notary in most cases in The Netherlands.[11] Such content is in most cases limited to the patrimonial and financial consequences of the cohabitation. Generally speaking, the contract copies for the greater part the statutory provisions of the matrimonial property law—for example, a stipulation on the expenses of housekeeping which includes expenses for raising and educating children; a definition of 'income'; the creation of some kind of community of property; the right to support during the relationship; and (sometimes) post-cohabitation alimony.[12]

The acceptance of those contracts as proof of existence of a 'real' relationship or partnership is and was general. In business life, employees with notarial living together contracts are in some respect treated as married couples—for instance, in the fields of pensions and public transportation discount schemes.

LEGISLATIVE ACTIVITY

Introduction

From the early 1980s, the legislation paid attention to the position of those unmarried 'de facto couples' by creating special provisions in the field of inheritance tax law. Couples living together in a common household for more than five years after the age of twenty-two were considered married partners and treated as such, with a tax-free exemption of 600,000 Dutch Guilders and a tax rate of between 5 and 26 per cent from 1,700,000 Dutch Guilders upwards. The law was so 'liberal' that it even provided special rules for 'communes' of three or more persons, with each member receiving half the exemption sum of a partner and the same tax rates. Later on—still in the 1980s—the content of much tax and

[11] In The Netherlands as in continental Europe, South America, Russia, China, Indonesia, etc. (the countries of the Latin Notariaat), the official who draws up contract and designs regulations in the field of family law, for instance, is the civil law notary. This officially appointed civil servant should not be compared with the public notary known in the Anglo-American legal system, since the civil law notary is a specialised laywer with an academic education followed by at least six years of practice experience, during the first three years of which the young notarial lawyer has to follow, next to his day-to-day practice, a post-academic professional training and teaching course, all concluded by an examination. This notarial lawyer is, among other things (real estate, corporate law), an expert in the field of the matrimonial property and inheritance (tax) law.

[12] I do not see any objection to the legitimity of these contracts, irrespective whether one of the partners is still married to a third party. Cf Senaeve and Coene, o.c. p 65ff.

social security legislation was adjusted to actual situations in which parties lived rather than to their formal legal positions.

Registered Partnership

In private law, it took much longer before the legislation was willing or able to make special provisions for unmarried couples. On 1 January 1998, new legislation was implemented, introducing a new phenomenon called 'registered partnership'.[13] This legislation created a separate civil status alongside to the single and the married one. The registered partnership provides those couples who are 'registered' with a complete system of rules for their relationship—virtually the same rules as for married couples—in the fields of private, social and tax law.

The registered partnership was originally (1998) only open to Dutch nationals and those who had a legal permit to stay in The Netherlands. This restriction was removed by the Acts of December 2000: everyone who is eighteen years of age and older may now enter a registered partnership. All kinds of couples are entitled to register—same- and different-sex couples—with only two restrictions. Monogamy is the rule! Moreover, since marriage and registered partnership are mutually exclusive, no one who is already married or registered, no matter to or with whom, can register.

In the original legislative proposal,[14] the registered partnership was also open to parties within the prohibited degrees of kinship. In the final proposal, these couples were excluded: parties who are related by blood or adoption, legitimately or illegitimately, in the ascending and in the descending line, or as brother and sister, cannot register. The exclusion of the prohibited degrees of kinship from the registered partnership can be explained by traditional reasons, since—as will be described below—the registered partnership has no effect as to affiliation. So to this day for couples living together who are related within prohibited degrees, no legal institution exists that provides them with a legal framework for their way of life.

It is difficult to defend that a couple consisting of a father who is being looked after by his daughter for what sometimes is a lifelong period must be denied the facilities offered to all kinds of other couples. One reason for this decision of the Undersecretary of Justice was the fear that a parent would favour the child he was living with to the disadvantage of his other children. This would constitute a

[13] Changed by the Acts of 13 and 21 Dec 2000, Staatsblad 2001, nr 11 and 9. Caroline Forder, *The International Survey of Family Law* 1995 and 1997, Hoevenaars, WPNR 6264 (1997); Notarisklerk 1997, p 177 e.v.; Verstappen, TFJ 1997–12. Kraan, EchtscheidingBulletin (EB), 1997, no 10; Soons, Juridische berichten voor het notariaat (JBN) 1997, no 73; Kalkman, JBN 1997, no 84; Fernhout, EB 1998, no 1. In 1982 a proposal by the author to have a registration of partners who desired so was rejected; Van der Burght, Relatievrijheid en Recht, Deventer 1983.

[14] Second Chamber, Kamerstuk. 23 761, no 2; Art 80a, para 7 since the Acyts of Dec 2000: para 5; nr 3, at 5.

breach of the rules of forced heirship or compulsory portion still present in the Dutch inheritance law.[15]

Statistics[16]

The first year of the registered partnership's implementation (1 January 1998) shows the following figures:

Relationship	*Reg. Partnerships*
1. Between two males:	1686
2. Between two females:	1324
3. Between a male and a female:	1616
Total	4626

The majority of the couples of different sex still seem to prefer the 'traditional' marriage; during the same period, 86,956 marriages were concluded.

In the second year, 1999 the figures were:

Relationship	*Reg. Partnerships*
1. Between two males:	897
2. Between two females:	864
3. Between a male and a female:	1495
Total	3256

Whereas the number of marriages was 89,428.

And in 2000:

Relationship	*Reg. Partnerships*
1. Between two males:	815
2. Between two females:	785
3. Between a male and a female:	1322
In total	2922

And 88,034 marriages. The higher numbers during the first year may be a result of a 'catching-up' effect after the implementation.

Heterosexual Couples

Another feature of the Dutch registered partnership is the fact that heterosexual couples can also register, so there is an extra possibility besides marriage. The need

[15] It is, however, interesting to see that, according the new proposed inheritance law, the forced heirship only consists in a claim in money, whereas when a surviving partner is involved the child will be happy to receive anything at all at the death of that partner—all without any security.

[16] Central Bureau for Statistics, Voorburg/Heerlen, The Netherlands, 10/3/99, p 16.

for it is questionable[17] because, as shown below, effectively the difference between marriage and registered partnership is almost negligible. The choice to create this extra opportunity for heterosexual couples was endorsed by the Undersecretary of Justice because it was felt that some couples would prefer to enter into a registered partnership rather than into a marriage. As a comparison, in the Nordic countries only same-sex couples may enter a registered partnership.

Private International Law

In the field of private international law, problems are likely to occur. First, no other state recognises this new phenomenon (not even the Scandinavian countries who also have a kind of registered partnership).[18] In addition, registered partnerships and marriages are treated in the same way in the Dutch system, so a registered partner is a bigamist when he marries someone else.[19]

As an example, a Dutch woman and Dutch man register their partnership in the Netherlands. Later on they move to Italy, where they split up. Afterwards, the man wants to marry an Italian woman; however, according to Dutch law, he and his registered partner should enter an agreement to terminate their registered partnership (see below) or he should apply for a 'divorce' in court. When his registered partner is not willing, or cannot be found, to enter a mutual agreement to end their registered partnership, only the judicial court procedure remains. That is impossible in Italy, however, for the simple reason that this country does not recognise the Dutch registered partnership. The man has to return to the Netherlands and stay there for at least twelve months, after which period the Dutch court has jurisdiction over the man and his case, and only then can the man apply for a 'divorce'. In practice, the man will just marry the Italian woman anyway and there will be no objections because the declaration of competence to marry (Article 1: 49a DCC) is not required because it is not applicable to partnership. The Dutch law is bound to recognise the Italian marriage and the registered partnership, so when the man (and his wife)[20] visit The Netherlands, the man can be prosecuted for violating Article 1: 33 DCC and punished for committing bigamy.

Some are of the opinion that Article 1: 80a DCC paragraph 2 is an indication that it is a requirement of Dutch public policy not to recognise the Italian mar-

[17] Scandinavian countries having a registered partnership restricted it to same-sex couples. Nielsen, 'Family Rights and the Registered Partnership', in (1990) *International Journal of Law and the Family*; Nielsen in B Dahl (ed), *Danish Law in a European Perspective* (1996); Senaeve and Coene, *Geregistreerd Partnerschap* (1998).

[18] Second Chamber, Kamerstuk. 23 761 nr 7, p 2; only partnership of Dutch citizens registered in the Nordic countries will be recognised.

[19] Even marrying his partner will raise difficulties; see below.

[20] We should not speak of 'new' wife, for the reason that registration of partners does not entail the creation of 'husband and wife' but of 'registered partners'.

riage, for according to Dutch law partnership and marriage are of equal value and must be alike, so are mutually exclusive.[21]

Marriage Open to All

Originally, the intention was that, after the introduction of the registered partnership, the legislation would take a few years' break and evaluate the practice of the registered partnership and later on probably introduce the 'marriage open to all'. That would terminate the existence of the registered partnership. Therefore this partnership was sometimes characterised as a 'gay marriage' open to heteros—one which would be abolished as soon as the hetero-marriage was open to gays. However, politics has dictated otherwise.

At the end of 1999, a legislative proposal was submitted to parliament creating the possibility of both sexes entering into marriage.[22] This was the result of pressure by groups and organisations of homosexuals and lesbians, and it was ultimately supported by a small majority of the Commissie Leefvormen (State Committee on Ways of Living Together).

The Undersecretary of Justice was of the opinion that, when this new 'open marriage' came into effect, there would be still room for the registered partnership. His motivation was the number of different-sex couples[23] who have shown a preference for the registered partnership over marriage; however, an evaluation will take place five years after the open marriage came into effect.[24]

Objections on principle against the institution of this kind of marriage[25] no longer seem to count in politics. The ties with a long-lasting tradition, culture and language concerning one of the most important legal and social institutions are under threat, due to an increasingly stretched concept of non-discrimination.

The Undersecretary of Justice seems to be very relaxed about the practical legal problems law that the same-sex couples will have to cope with, especially in the field of international law. He admits that most countries will not recognise this open marriage, that legal relations will be 'limping' (as is the case with the registered partnership) and stresses that couples should be informed about these facts.

Finally, the Second and the First Chamber of Parliament accepted the draft bill that made it possible for same-sex couples to enter marriage, and on 1 April 2001 the Bill was enacted and came into force. Among the first same-sex couples to enter marriage on that date was a female civil law notary.

[21] Verstappen, *Tijdschrift voor Familie en Jeugd Recht* p 281.

[22] Kamerstuk 26, 672, 1998–1999, no 1–3.

[23] One may doubt the seriousness of this motivation: not more than 3,500 couples to 250,000 married couples!

[24] Kamerstuk II, 26 672 no 3 p 6 and Art III.

[25] Kenneth McK Norrie, 'Marriage is for heterosexuals: May the rest of us be saved from it', paper presented at 10th World Conference, International Society of Family Law, 9–13 July 2000, Brisbane, Australia.

THE REGISTERED PARTNERSHIP

To Enter into a Registered Partnership

Both parties must be at least eighteen years of age. The legal exception (Article 1: 31 paragraph 2 DCC) for n marriage at an earlier age when the woman is pregnant does not apply since, at its inception, partnership has no effect on affiliation; however, since the Acts of December 2000 Article 1: 31 DCC is fully applicable to registered partnerships.

Parties who wish to enter into a registered partnership have to give notice of their intended registration to the Registrar at the place of domicile of one of the parties. After at least fourteen days, the registration of the partnership takes place by signing a deed in the presence of the Registrar. As opposed to a marriage procedure, a 'Yes, I do' is not an official part of the ceremony; the Undersecretary of Justice judged that in this way there would be more room for a personal touch in which the partners could tailor the ceremony. In practice, 'Yes, I do' has, however, proved to be rather popular with partners coming to register.

Unlike with a marriage, the partners registering their partnership are allowed to engage in church ceremonies before going to City Hall.

Legal Effects of a Registered Partnership

The most striking feature of the registered partnership is that no affiliation will exist between a partner and the child(ren) of the other, not even when that child is conceived and born during the partnership. The registered partner who fathered the child has to recognise it as his own child, and can, together with the mother, apply for joint custody in the same way as couples who live together with or without a contract. In fact, this absence of affiliation is the main difference between marriage and registered partnership.

Another striking difference is the way in which the partners can terminate their relationship by mutual consent out of court, as an alternative to a divorce by a judge on unilateral request.

For the rest—that is, patrimonial and financial aspects—the legislation has not bothered to create a special regime for registered partners. By virtue of Article 1: 80a DCC, all provisions given for marriage are applicable to registered partnerships. This principle not only applies to private law, but to all fields of law: social security law, taxation law, administrative law, penal law, and so on. This paper is limited in scope to the private law consequences of the registered partnership.

Transplantation of Matrimonial (Property) Law

With the registered partnership, a legal relationship is created from which both parties derive rights and duties, such as the duty to provide each other with what is necessary, the duty to supply maintenance, inheritance rights, and so on. Also, a registered partnership has significant legal consequences with regard to the property of partners. This matrimonial property law is codified in chapters 6, 7 and 8 of Book 1, DCC, which deals with Family Law in general.

The decision of the legislator to transplant almost wholesale all provisions developed for marriage to the registered partnership can be questioned. Would it be the choice of the majority of couples who want to enter into a registered partnership to be treated as a married couple? That question is particularly important since the whole matrimonial concept was already disputed at the time of the implementation of the registered partnership. Since the 1970s, a discussion has been ongoing about creating a 'lighter' marriage, with less elaborate legal provisions than to date. A certain laziness on the part of the legislator cannot be denied.

The transplantation of the traditional marriage concepts to the modern registered partnership leads to the following.

Primary System

Chapter 6 of Book 1 of the DCC contains a general compulsory law applicable to all registered partnerships. Deviation by partnership covenant is only possible where the specific clause stipulates this. An example would be how to share the burden of the household expenses.

Questions arise in relation to the first article of chapter 6. According to the first sentence of Article 1: 81 DCC, partners owe each other loyalty, help and assistance. This is primarily a moral stipulation. For marriage, loyalty means the abstention from adulterous behaviour. But what does it tell us about the concept of loyalty for registered partners?

Article 1: 81 DCC next contains an open standard concerning the duties between partners to provide for and to take care of each other during their partnership. It is the legal rendering of what is dictated by reasonableness and fairness in a relationship of marriage, but is it reasonable to transplant that without any consideration to registered partners?

With regard to maintenance after divorce, the legal translation of reasonableness and fairness between spouses as embodied in the standard of Article 1: 81 DCC no longer applies. The rule of Article 157, paragraph 1 and 2 DCC provides—if applicable—that the ex-registered partners can claim maintenance; this, however, is only the case when the partnership is dissolved by court order.

Article 1: 82 DCC obliges registered partners to provide for, and to raise, their children. In matrimonial property law, it is understood that 'their' children means the children of both spouses living in the family, and is not necessarily restricted to whether there is an affiliation between all parties. I consider this interpretation applicable to the partnership, notwithstanding the fact that remarks in parliament were made to the effect that, after termination of the registered partnership, such a liability would not exist.[26] The legislation should have been clear about this subject, especially since affiliation is one of the most prominent subjects in this act.

Since 22 June 2001, partners are no longer obliged to live together (2001 Article 1: 83 (old) DCC). The legislation could not be denied a somewhat regulative streak. The same remarks as to the a somewhat regulative streak can be made about the content of Article 1: 84 ff. DCC. They contain very detailed[27] (and never, except perhaps by accident, practised) rules concerning how to cope with the financing the household expenses, including the expenses of raising and educating children.

Article 1: 85 DCC affects the position of registered partners towards third parties—that is, certain creditors. Registered partners are both liable for debts entered into in the course of the customary household. The law attributes actions of one registered partner also to the other partner, to such an extent that the other partner becomes co-debtor. It does not go further than this position; as co-debtor, the other registered partner is not a party to the contract. In essence, Article 1: 85 DCC protects the creditor from exonerations by the non-contracting registered partner where, for instance, the contracting partner has exceeded the authority given by the other registered partner. The contracts concerned are of relatively low value—that is, up to the amount for new curtains or at most a washing machine.

Financially more important are those provisions which may directly interfere to the detriment of a third party. Registered partners cannot unconditionally enter into certain contracts. These contracts may only be entered into with permission from the other partner. If there is no permission they are *violable*. This stipulation concerns *all* registered partners and is not limited to registered partners who share a household. There are no legal requirements for giving permission. The registered partner who gives permission does not become a party to the legal transaction. If a partner performs a legal act covered by Article 1: 88 DCC without permission, the other partner may rescind this act (Article 3: 55 DCC). There are four categories covered:

1. contracts pertaining to the sale of, to the mortgaging of, or to the giving of free use of, and acts pertaining to ending the use of a house in which the registered partners live together or where the non-contracting registered partner lives alone, as well as of goods that form part of such a house or form part of the goods and chattels present in the house;

[26] First Chamber, 1996/7, Kamerstuk 23 761, nr 157b, at 3.

[27] The law indicates from which income(s) and to which estate(s) these expenses should be paid. The order is as follows: first the incomes of partners must be charged; if the expenses are not fully covered, the property of the partners have to be charged. Furthermore, within both categories the following applies: property held in community must be charged first, private estates come second. In other words, expenses are charged to the incomes in community; if these incomes are exhausted, the property held in community has to be charged; if there are still further expenses to be met, the private property owned by the partners has to be charged.

2. donations, except those that are customary, or those that are non-excessive and those for which nothing shall be taken out of his assets, during the life of the partner concerned—that is, life-interest contracts in favour of third parties;
3. contracts whereby the acting registered partner, other than in the conduct of his *own personal* business or profession, commits himself as bond or as a co-debtor, or gives security for the debt of a third party. Permission shall not be required in case the legal act is performed by an administrator of a public company, or a private company with limited liability, who is the sole shareholder or, who is together with his co-administrators, the owner of the majority of the shares. It is important to know that, when holding a common portfolio with some friends with a contract with the bank, that all participants are being held personally liable in case the investment goes wrong; this situation is covered by this provision;
4. partners may only enter a contract of purchase by instalments with the permission of the other partner.

Is it correct and wise to burden the registered partners with these typical matrimonial rules?

Partnership Property Law

The central feature of Dutch matrimonial property law which is applicable to the registered partnership is the statutory or full community of property.[28] All the rules of the full community described hereunder are also applicable to any limited community of goods the registered partners might conclude.

Full Community of Property

From the first moment of the partnership, a full community of property arises, *ipso jure.* Registered partners can only prevent this by a partnership covenant—by notarial deed—in which they make provisions with regard to the legal consequences of their partnership—see below.

Each partner is fully entitled to every good of the community, while having to respect the right of the other, which is regarded as equally strong. Neither partner can alienate their share in the entire (community), nor do they have disposal over their rights in the individual goods that belong to the community. The commu-

[28] See: G Van der Burght, 'Family and succession law, The Netherlands', *International Encyclopeadia of Laws*, (Kluwer, London), no 194ff; Pitlo/Van der Burght, Rood-de Boer (1998), p 198ff; Asser-De Boer 1, no 289f, Huussen, Bronnen van de Nederlandse Codificatie sinds 1798 II, Bussum 1975. Van den Hoek-Kok, CN 1922, Comité voor een gemeenschappelijke actie tot hervorming onzer Huwelijkswetgeving: schets van een Toekomstig Huwelijksvermogensrecht, 1917, Bakker-Nort, Schets van de rechtspositie der getrouwde vrouw, diss. Groningen 1915, compare Meijers, WPNR 3298/9,(1933); Van der Burght, Het wettelijk deelgenootschap thesis University of Amsterdam, Deventer 1973, p 15f.

nity of property comes about by the joining of both estates. Both registered partners are fully entitled, under universal title, to all property which was owned by each partner separately before the partnership, and to what has been or will be acquired during the community of property.

By virtue of Article 1: 94 paragraph 2 DCC, both partners may bind the community by incurring debts. Article 1: 97 DCC stipulates who administers which property of the community. Administration of community property includes performing acts of alienation and performing factual acts with regard to the asset in question. The registered partner from whose side the property passed into the community is exclusively competent as to the administration of the property, though both partners own the property and both may make use of it.

The joining of estates will continue for as long as the full community of property is in existence between partners. If this ends under any of the circumstances described in Article 1: 99 DCC, no new goods are added to the community. From that moment on, the community of property is referred to as a 'dead' community waiting to be divided among its owners (registered partners; one registered partner and the heirs of the other; heirs of both registered partners; former registered partners).

The community contains all assets and debts that both registered partners had at the start of the registered partnership, as well as the debts and assets accumulated during the registered partnership, either as capital or as interest. This simple principle can, however, easily give rise to conflicts—for instance, over the moment in which an asset arises—for example, a life insurance policy is paid out—but also about the moment when a liability arises.[29]

The community commences from the moment of the registration of the partnership. In general, all assets and debts belong to the community. However, there are two exceptions to this general rule (apart from deviating terms in a partnership covenant): the exclusion stipulation of gifts and legacies; and the attachment of a good to a partner (Article 1: 94 DCC).

Liability for Debts

Between them, partners are responsible for half the debts of the community (Article 1: 102 DCC). Matters are more complex with regard to liability to cred-

[29] See also Supreme Court ruling of 17 Mar 1944, NJ 306, with regard to the arising of a liability due to a verdict to render accounts of administration (Art 772 Civil Procedure); does this liability arise at the moment of the verdict (ie during the partnership) or does it arise at the moment that the defendant in the action of account does not meet the duties which he was obliged to meet (ie after the partnership)? A similar problem occurred when a rehabilitation benefit was granted to (Dutch) Indonesian victims of the war. Does a benefit which is granted after dissolution of the community, but granted for damages suffered before the dissolution of the community, belong to the 'dead' community of property which is to be distributed? Or Supreme Court: 22 maart 1996, NJ 640: a 'Golden handshake' received after divorce but legally originating from the period before and 24 Oct 1997, NJ 1998, 692: compensation for a 'whiplash' received after divorce and destined to support the victim personally.

itors. Prior to the dissolution of the registered partnership, the community offers recourse to three sorts of debts: debts of the community incurred by each of the registered partners and the private debts (those not belonging to the community) of each. Prior to dissolution, a creditor will have recourse against the separate assets of each registered partner for debts incurred by the registered partner concerned (either separate debts or debts of the community). There would be no recourse against the separate assets of a registered partner for a debt of the community incurred by the other, or for separate debts of the other, for obvious reasons.

Even after the dissolution of the registered partnership, all creditors have recourse against the undivided community (Article 1: 100 paragraph 2 jo. 3: 192 DCC). Furthermore, creditors may oppose the division of the estate (Article 3: 193 DCC). A specific consequence of the dissolution of the registered partnership for a creditor is that he now has recourse against the ex-registered partner of his contracting party for half of his claim; for that half, the partner is jointly bound with the contracting partner (Article 1: 102, end DCC).

As a matter of course, the internal ratio where each registered partner (as well as their joint heirs) bears half of the debts of the community remains in force, even after the division.

Division of Community

When the community property is divided, it does not matter from whose side a good came into the community. There are some exceptions to this rule relating to the attachment of some goods. See also Article 1: 101 DCC, which grants partners a priority with regard to personal goods. Both participants are entitled to half of the assets of the community; on the other hand, they are liable for half of the debts of the community. The law does not refer to this, but it is obvious that, at the time of the distribution, parties arrange for the manner in which this 'financial responsibility in equal shares' shall be effected.[30] Should the balance of the community show a negative result, partners have to pay the remainder in equal shares, from their private assets.

Act on Pension Compensation

Pension claims are not part of the community property. Irrespective of the partnership property regime under which the couple has lived, the right to compensation exists, unless registered partners explicitly agreed to the contrary by a partnership covenant or by termination agreement (Article 2 paragraph 1 and Article 11 Act on Pension Compensation). Therefore, compensation shall also take place if the partners had a completely separate property regime.[31]

[30] See Supreme Court, 10 Apr 1992, NJ 447.

[31] Bod, inaugural address University of Nijmegen, p 34 and WFR 6156 (1995); Stevens, *Pensioen en andere toekomstvoorzieningen* VA, Deventer. Pitlo/Van der Burght, Rood-de Boer (1998), p 262ff.

Registered Partnership Covenants

In general, the law allows parties to draw up their partnership covenant according to their own wishes (Article 121). They may deviate from the full community of property; they may also deviate from some stipulations in chapter 6. It is contrary to public order to agree upon a partnership covenant (which has external consequences) under a suspensive or a resolutive condition. It is prohibited to stipulate that the share in the liabilities accruing to a partner shall differ from his share in the assets.

Both marriage covenants as well as partnership covenants must be entered into by a notarial deed, on penalty of being declared void. If this stipulation is not observed, the partnership covenant has not come into effect (Article 1: 115 DCC). Non-fulfilment of this stipulation of form leads to the absolute nullity of the partnership covenant; the contract has no effect whatsoever between parties, nor does it have any effect towards third parties. Conversion is not possible. The same applies to covenants entered into postnuptially without the required prior consent of the district court (Article 1: 119 DCC); these covenants are void.[32]

Systems

Three main systems of contractual partnership property law can be distinguished: the regime of separate estates, of a (limited) community and of separate estates—possibly with a (limited) community—and/or combined with a settlement stipulation. The DCC presents as an example three schemes:

1. *community of accruals*: only (the results of) incomes and profits accrued during registered partnership are common. In case of a deficit, that partner who caused it bears the loss (Article 1: 124 ff. DCC);
2. *community of accruals and losses*: as in the first scheme, but the parties bear the eventual losses equally (Article 1: 127 DCC);
3. *statutory joint participation.*

At the beginning of the regime, each partner draws up a list of the estate that that partner owns at the beginning of the partnership. This list has to contain a description of each separate good and it has to state its value as well as every debt. During the course of the regime, all acquisitions pursuant to the law of succession and gifts at the value at the time of acquisition, reduced with the charges that may be attached to those acquisitions, are added to the list of the initial estates of the partnership. This total is called 'initial capital'. After the ending of the regime, the private estates present are valued: the 'final capital'. A balancing of the initial capital against the final capital will show whether an increase in capital took place.

[32] When a partnership has existed for one year, partners may change their covenant or they may decide to enter into their first covenant.

If this is so, a settlement shall take place so that the estate of each partner shall be increased by the same amount (Article 1: 129 and 132–145 DCC).

Much more popular in matrimonial property law than the legislator's choice of regimes is the so-called 'Amsterdam settlement stipulation', which is—as is to be expected—equally sought-after among registered partners. The registered partners conclude a covenant containing separation of property while it is stipulated that, each year, the surplus of the incomes of both parties will be cleared on a fifty–fifty basis, after the costs of the joint households have been deducted.

TERMINATION

The partnership is dissolved upon the death of one of the registered partners, by a new marriage or registered partnership after obtaining court permission, or after the other party is missing for at least five years. The dissolution of the partnership can also be reached by agreement between the parties or at the request of one of them to the court. Separation from bed and board, which is possible for married couples, does not apply here.

Termination by Agreement

Termination by agreement is possible if certain requirements are met. Parties have to enter an agreement on the fact that there is an irreparable breakdown of their partnership. The position of the children is no part of the agreement for the obvious reason that partnership does not entail affiliation. However, when the couple has made special arrangements—recognition or joint custody—these matters must be dealt with. Next to that—though it is not compulsory—the legislator laid down in the DCC a recommendation that the parties should also make arrangements as to several important subjects:

- —*maintenance (alimony) for one of the parties*. It must be underlined that, where parties entered a termination agreement after termination by mutual consent, the needy partner *cannot* apply to the court and claim support from other party (Article 1: 80d, paragraph 2, jo. Article 1: 159);
- —*division of the common estate*, if applicable. And, I would add: settling the *statutory joint participation* (Article 1: 129 and Article 1: 132 through 145 DCC) or a periodical settlement stipulation;
- —*compensation of the pension rights/claims* (Article 1: 94 jo. 155 DCC);
- —solving the matter of *housing*.

Registrar

Within three months after entering this agreement, a written declaration has to be delivered to the Registrar. In that declaration, the parties declare that they have entered a termination agreement. This declaration has to be co-signed by a civil law notary, or by an 'advocate' (attorney/lawyer). The reason for the co-signing is not clear. The law does not give any hint that those officials have any further task. As to the date of the agreement and the three-month period, the signature of the advocate is irrelevant since that person has no authority in this field; for that purpose, only the signature of the notary could have any significance, but it is questionable whether the notary is acting in his notarial capacity and delivering an official statement as a notary as to the date. In other words, the couple may draw up the declaration, show it to an advocate of notary and ask them to sign it. The legislation would have acted more careful towards the interests of the partners by giving the officials mentioned a better and more meaningful description of their legal task.

Marriage as a Follow-up of Partnership

It is not possible to marry when registered (Article 1: 33 DCC, see above). This rule applies also to the partners marrying each other. They have to terminate their partnership. Until 22 June 2001, the only way to do so (apart from via the court) was to enter a contract in which they concluded that their partnership had irretrievably broken down. The next step was to draw up a declaration stating that they had entered an agreement to the effect that their relationship had broken down irretrievably; a notary or an advocate then had to co-sign this false declaration. The couple had to present this declaration in due time to the Registrar; the Registrar would then hear that the couple was planning to marry and therefore wanted to give notice of their intended marriage. In other words, their contract and their declaration was false and they had committed forgery, but they were forced to do so by the law.

After giving notice, the marriage could take place after two weeks. During that fortnight, several threats existed to the position of the parties involved. When one of them died, the other would not inherit, unless there was a testament specially for that fourteen-day period, which would rarely be the case. Bankruptcy was also a threat.[33]

Although the Undersecretary had been informed about this effect of his proposal, it was not until 22 June 2001 that a new Act removed these effects. Since that date, couples may simply request the Registrar to change their civil status from registered partnership to marriage and vice versa.

However, this new legislation has created another unwanted effect. Hitherto, in the case of divorce, the marriage could only be dissolved by the judge. However one may now request the Registrar to switch from marriage to registered partnership and subsequently present a declaration (co-signed by a notary or an attorney) in which parties declare that they have entered a termination agreement because of the irreparable breakdown of their partnership. Although

[33] The Undersecretary of Justice was not inclined to make provisions to 'smooth' the change from partnership into marriage: First Chamber, Kamerstuk 23, 761, nr 157d at nr 2.

there was always an awareness of this effect, it was not until 16 August 2001 that Members of Parliament discovered it and were able to put questions forward to the Minister of Justice.[34]

Divorce by Court Procedure

In case partners do not agree on splitting up, one of them can file for divorce at the District Court. The judge will act similarly as in case of a marriage and divorce.

WAYS TO USE REGISTERED PARTNERSHIP

The following are ways in which the registered partnership is very useful.

1. A businessperson wants to transfer a business and avoid taxes such as transfer tax or gift taxes. The businessperson enters into a registered partnership with a limited community as to the business goods with the successor. At the termination of the partnership, they are entitled to divide the community in such a way that the successor gets all the business property and owes the other an equivalent of half the value of that property. There are no taxes for the acquisition by the successor.
2. Alternatively, they could have entered a limited community of business goods and a sum of money from the successor. The end of the story is the same but now no debts are left There are taxes for the acquisition by the successor.
3. Or a much older businessperson entered a partnership with that younger successor. After a few months, they terminate their relation but do not dissolve their community, instead agreeing that in case of death the whole community will remain with the survivor. When the businessperson dies, the successor will get the business property in principle for free: again, there are no taxes. In the meantime, both ex-partners may marry or be registered with another person.

EVALUATION

My general feeling is that the Dutch legislator acted too hurriedly when designing the registered partnership. The restriction to only non-prohibited degrees of kinship was done without solid arguments and is a mistake. All criticisms[35] against the current matrimonial property system have not prevented the legislation from

[34] One may wonder why to protest against this 'secret route', because the proposals for divorce procedures out of court are almost ready.

[35] All the critisism is well known to the legislator: see the interim report of the Ministry of Justice dated Dec 1997.

making it applicable in its full form. All current problems have been transplanted into the 'new' civil status of registered partnership. Creating a new way of living together should offer more variety and a more adequate and flexible legal framework. Instead, the registered partnership contains outdated concepts. The long-lasting and often negative experience with matrimonial property law should have been a warning to the legislator.

CONCLUSION

The Dutch legislature has missed an opportunity to create a considered and up-to-date system of partnership. The opening of the registered partnership to different-sex couples was a predictable political move—the final step to opening marriage to all forms of relationship. The registered partnership looks like a playground to experiment with the termination of the relationship out of court in the future to be implemented in marriage. Even if one would not reject these objectives, it would have been wise that before that step to the 'marriage for all sexes' was made, the legal system of matrimonial law would have been revised fundamentally.[36] And finally, since there is a 'marriage for all sexes', the registered partnership only serves very few people who have a very personal aversion to a name: 'marriage'. And what's in a name?

[36] The draft-proposals concerning matrimonial property law—and the first Act dated 31 May 2001, in force on 22 June 2001—do not give the impression that a fundamental study was made: it contains some technicalities (the Dutch legislation changes technical details of that legislation every ten years; in practice normal people do not notice anything of that and it is primarily useful to tease students and to keep the post-academic education circus on the move) and seem to embrace the view that the man in the street is a lawyer! See G Van der Burght, Weekblad voor privaatrecht, notariaat en registratie, nr 6409 (2000) and nr 6437 and 6438 (2001).

21

A Comparative Study of the Transfer of Family Wealth: From Privilege to Equality

Maria Donata Panforti*

TIED AND PLANNED TRANSFER

Both past and present experience shows us that Westerners often want to plan how their wealth will be bequeathed when they die. In this paper, the ways in which they have been able to do so in the past and can do so now will be discussed in the light of three legal systems: the Italian, the English and the North American.

From around Roman times to the nineteenth century in Italy and from the twelfth to the eighteenth centuries in England, any planning of the transfer of family wealth usually took the form of a simple decision to create an indissoluble bond between the family and a certain property or set of properties—usually land. The aim of this was to ensure an adequate level of prestige and economic well-being for descendants through the compulsory maintenance of possession of those properties, usually fairly substantial in economic terms. The fideicommissum and similar practices—such as the English entail and strict settlement, which developed precisely to avoid the alienation *extra familiam* of these goods—can be found in Roman law and in the documents of the early Middle Ages. Subsequently they began to be more frequently exploited in the work of the Glossators and Commentators and the English conveyancers, and they were then used regularly from the sixteenth to the beginning of the eighteenth centuries.

After this, however, the provisions inserting simple ties into the transfer document became increasingly rare in English law and were actually forbidden (after various vicissitudes) by the Italian legal order. At the same time, new trends began to emerge—although they were different in all three legal systems. The wishes of heads of families with regard to inheritance slowly began to change and perspectives widened towards an overall planning of the transfer of family goods, taking into account all the goods amassed (and not only the land) and all the family members. Concern over keeping the most important possessions in the family—possibly by favouring the first male child—lost ground during the eighteenth

* Universita di Modena e Reggio Emilia, Italy.

century to the wish to 'look after' all the estate. This took the form of satisfying the expectations of the family members who had been ignored until then—other children, the wife, collateral relatives, and so on—as well as giving descendants the power to manage these effects on an increasingly discretionary basis. This made it possible to unfreeze the estate or the single elements that made it up, and to invest the gains in new forms of wealth.

Even though ideological and operational differences between different contemporary legal systems appear to be wide, a generally observable tendency towards the planning and orienting of the passing to others of one's own goods can be seen. This should come as no surprise, however. Of all legal fields, family law is the most closely connected to the history of society and traditions, and therefore also clearly to the values and drives of a particular sector of society. The family is above all—like most other influential legal institutions—a mind-set and a way of understanding relationships between couples, and it goes beyond the confines of single legal orders and political boundaries between states. Consequently, it is axiomatic that in the countries with a Western legal tradition the notion of 'family' is substantially shared, even if it has some mismatches and differences.

The transfer of wealth within families in the sense that interests us here—that is, individual forms of planning for the transfer of wealth—needs to be investigated through the specific characteristics of the relationship linking the provider to the beneficiaries at different historical moments, and also through checking to what extent and with which instruments (apart from wills) the legal order allows the individual to place binding rules on the current family group and whoever might form part of it in the future. Moreover, given that the notion of family has changed over the centuries examined in this paper, a prevailing family model and the nature of the ties that link together the individual members need to be described, as do the affective and economic expectations of the individual with respect to other family members.

Fideicommissary Substitution and Entail

The need to forbid the transfer of property to strangers, which has been recognised in Europe through the centuries, was once able to rely on special institutions, fideicommissary substitutions and individual fideicommissum in Italy, and the practices of entail and strict settlement in England. Although these were very different with respect to their technical details, they were functionally extremely similar. The fideicommissum—initially abolished in France after the Revolution (1792), but then subsequently reintroduced—survived in Italy (albeit with various degrees of success) until the introduction of the Civil Code in 1865.

In the past, then, the head of family who wanted to bequeath a certain property to his descendants could do so only by means of specific legal mechanisms. Today, given that these transactions have been abrogated or have fallen into disuse, property owners use transfer strategies with a variety of aims, such as the trust of land in England, estate planning in the United States or a combination of provisions created on a case-by-case basis by a trusted notary in Italy. One important feature differentiates the entail and strict settlement from fideicommissary substitutions and individual fideicommissa: the first two use instruments forming part of the law of property to which, following common law, they belong; while the latter came into succession law, above all via the will.[1]

The reasons for these different approaches are historical. In England in the fifteenth and sixteenth centuries, when heads of families increasingly felt it to be important to avoid the alienation of a property and to ensure that their legatees would inherit it, the legal discipline of real property was already in place and offered a rich variety of ways for doing precisely this—for example, there were many different types of limited length 'ownerships' which were binding and highly complex in terms of content. In contrast, the field of succession law was very underdeveloped (the use of wills was legalised only in 1540) and the contractual area was developed only (and with great difficulty) in the seventeenth century. It was thus absolutely necessary to use the techniques of the law of property: strict settlement was a mixture of forms of interests in land, each one expressed in such a way as to ensure certain profits for the beneficiaries *pro tempore* and to obstruct the cession of the property to strangers. Thanks to strict settlement, the English concept of estate exploited its prerogatives of flexibility and temporality.

On the Continent, instead, heads of families began to use the instruments from the field of the law of succession and in particular of wills, attracted by the testamentary model inherited from Roman law, which took on a new dimension, and the development of an understanding of ownership which increasingly emphasised the uniqueness of property. The result of this was fideicommissary substitution which, on account of its theoretical grounding, was mainly used in the field of *mortis causa* transactions—even if, as we shall see, its development allowed for the agreements to be drawn up *inter vivos*. The contrast with the strict settlement is clear: its different legal nature, being constituted by various sequential forms of interests in land, allowed it to be used also and above all as an agreement between living people, specifically by means of the deed of settlement.

Strict settlement and family fideicommissum both evolved from older institutions—the entail in the first case and fideicommissary substitutions in the other. In the period running from 1285 to the middle of the eighteenth century, the entail gave rise to a very strong tie through which the father gave the first male offspring (usually when he got married) a special form of 'ownership' over the land (this was the entail), establishing that it would pass on his death to the heirs or the first male child heir, and then to his heirs, *ad infinitum*.[2] The power to set up entails was introduced by statute with the De Donis Conditionalibus Statute in 1285, and for the two centuries following the bond set up by the head of family

[1] Strictly speaking, however, even fideicommissa set up between living people were valid. They only took on legal value after the death of the bequeather.

[2] The limits on this were fixed by the rule against perpetuities.

was absolute and unavoidable. After this, forms of 'barring the entail' were developed, enabling the obstruction to be skirted.

Analogously, the fideicommissary substitutions identified an heir who would inherit the property on the death of the testator and was obliged to pass it on, at his death, to the substitute indicated. This latter was subject to the tie of the first and was himself also tied. The affixing of the bond was thus achieved in 'the predetermination of the succession line of the appointed heir.'[3]

Entails and fideicommissary substitutions have some—though not all—features in common. Both provide for the compulsory destination of one or more properties, usually to the eldest son, for their inalienability to strangers and for their successive passing to a member of the family indicated by the father. Both avoid providing for younger male children, daughters and the widow, who are left sums of money, lesser rights and dowries, or else are provided for through agreements not forming part of the original document. Both, finally, refer to real property, the most important from both an economic and a dynastic point of view.

However, entail is a form of property which is constituted by an agreement *inter vivos* (using a special deed), which takes effect at a specific time, usually on the marriage of the beneficiary. In contrast, fideicommissary substitution is a testamentary clause which becomes effective only on the death of the testator.

Beyond these differences, both the entail and fideicommissary substitution treat the role of the head of family, traditionally described as 'patriarchal', and the role of family wealth in similar ways. The father, who is the owner of properties which he in his turn has inherited or has accumulated through work or business affairs, is the person who holds economic power and therefore exercises this over areas which are fundamental for his children's lives—for example, their choice of profession, marriage and choice of partner. By distributing his property with an entail or by providing for its future division through substitution, the head of family promoted an identical family model for the next generation. The new owner of the property, who inherited all the income-producing properties, was required to distribute discretionary sums of money to his brothers and other children; this meant that, while he exercised a considerable amount of control over them, he was also subject to continual demands for money.

The preservation of real property—the true objective of the practices at issue—was thus representative of a certain type of family in which the dynastic and economic ties between its members prevailed absolutely over considerations of any other kind, particularly over emotional issues. This helps to explain their success and continued growth during the seventeenth and eighteenth centuries in both the legal systems discussed here. In Italy, moreover, the increased use of fideicommissum can also be explained by the influence exercised by Spanish practices, since they were widely used there. Historians have shown that these

[3] C Zorzoli, 'Della famiglia e del suo patrimonio: riflessioni sull'uso del fedecommesso in Lombardia tra cinque e seicento', in L Bonfield (ed), *Marriage, Property and Succession* (Duncker & Humblot, 1992), p 167.

influences spread over the north of the country as well as the south. This is surprising because the Spanish had dominion only over the south.

The link between the bound transfer of wealth and the dominating family model is not perhaps sufficient to explain these complex agreements, which dealt exclusively with land and buildings. In the period discussed here, the effective economic importance of real property should in fact not be over-estimated, particularly when this is viewed in relation to personal wealth based on money, credits and business affairs.

It is likely that there were in reality other reasons than investment for profit underpinning the wish to tie property to the family. There was, for example, certainly the tendency, justified by the political instability at certain times, to identify in land the most secure form of profit, particularly when one considers that these obligations were very long term. Moreover, it is likely that one of the aims of the settlor in drawing up these agreements was to avoid wasting any money through the sale of property, since it had been acquired with great effort. Another important aspect of this is very possibly the feeling of attachment for these properties that came about independently of the economic system and the historical moment, on account of their singularity: one building cannot replace another in individual life histories.

Strict Settlement and Affective Individualism

At around the beginning of the 1700s, changes in the family model which had prevailed until then began to make themselves felt. In the long run very influential, these developments corresponded to a change which was taking place across Western civilisation and which concerned the way in which the individual was perceived in relation to society as a whole. This affected the individual's behaviour towards both spouse and children, as well as towards parents and relatives. Historians and sociologists talk about this as 'affective individualism'.[4]

It is well known that individualism emerged as a way of thinking during the seventeenth and eighteenth centuries, after a long gestation period in medieval times, and that it was so important as to be considered a dominant feature of Western culture,[5] with the effect of recasting entirely the foundations of the legal systems of the countries concerned. This individualistic conception started from the idea that every human being is unique. Society is not composed of groups (as it was in medieval society), but of single persons who are independent and self-reliant, each one of them upholding legitimate desires for freedom, property and happiness. On the legal plane, this conception led to the Declaration of the Rights of Man, to constitutions, to a re-evaluation of private property[6] and to a new hierarchy of values in family relations which placed the individual and the personal

[4] Cf L Stone, *The Family, Sex and Marriage in England 1500–1800* (Weidenfeld and Nicolson, 1977).

[5] A Laurent, *Histoire de l'individualisme* (Paris, 1983); L Dumont, *Essais sur l'individualisme* (Paris, 1983).

[6] Cf N Bobbio, *L'età dei diritti* (Torino, 1990).

search for happiness and wealth in opposition to the values of lineage and degrees of kinship.

While in medieval times people were important because they belonged to a group, and everyone was interchangeable because—as Stone wrote—the 'aim of life was to guarantee the continuity of the family, the clan, the village or the state', in the individualist conception everyone believed themselves to be unique and considered it legitimate to give weight to their aims and to search for happiness. These ideas had a profound influence on the whole network of family relationships—although clearly old models and conceptions continued to exist—and led to, for example, the idea of marriage satisfying individual expectations for internal happiness and sexual gratification rather than being based on the economic, dynastic and procreative concerns of the past centuries. It was during the nineteenth century that this new form of family became more widespread, also as the result of the new concept of 'romantic love'.[7] This presupposed the feasibility of establishing a bond between two people based on qualities intrinsic to the couple rather than on external factors such as lineage and property.

At the beginning of the eighteenth century, these developments were still some way off and difficult to predict. However, there was a new sensitivity towards individual rights and therefore a general willingness to offer children other than the first the opportunity to live with greater self-sufficiency. This began to be felt in the devices for transfer of property and stimulated the increasing substitution of the entail with the strict settlement.

In the light of these new ideas, the entail now seemed to place an inappropriate amount of emphasis on the right to succession of the first son, leaving—as has been described above—other members of the family with little control over their own lives, given that they were financially dependent on the heir, and the new head of family. The new conditions introduced by the strict settlement tied the land only for one generation, although people were encouraged to set up a new tie for the following generation. Moreover, in the deed settling the property on the first male descendant, provisions were also made for other sons, daughters and widows, and these could not be changed. In this way, the arbitrariness of the powers of the owner *pro tempore* was weakened and the traditional patriarchal power reduced.[8] Moreover, this way of arranging things meant that there had to be a certain degree of collaboration between father and son (who in this way ensured that his contractual power increased) in the new resettlement, and this led to a new climate of equality within the family.

The passage from the entail to the strict settlement was an important crossroads in the passage from tied transfer to modern planned transfer. The strict settlement still performed its old function of obstructing the alienation *extra familiam* of property while also introducing a new duty—that of allowing for the planning of the transfer of wealth from one generation to the next. Thus not only

[7] A Giddens, *The Transformation of Intimacy* (Cambridge, 1992).

[8] L Bonfield, *Marriage Settlements 1601–1740. The Adoption of the Strict Settlement* (Cambridge, 1983); Stone, n 4, p 269.

was the exit of certain property from the family patrimony voluntarily blocked, but the division—strategically planned—of the property between all the desired subjects was also legitimised.[9] The regulating powers of the head of family were therefore more restricted in this new arrangement in terms of time (since they lasted for one generation only), but they were extended in terms of the subjects and properties involved.

The strict settlement used many of the figures and institutions in the law of property (future interests), but it also—from the eighteenth century on—used the trust. The appointment of a trustee allowed for there to be some control over the effective respect for the will of the testator. The trustee's range of action was, however, restricted by the provisions laid out in the deed constitutive of the strict settlement, which established that the trustee's role was to carry out and guarantee performance of the settlor's wishes, even if the powers conferred were to some extent discretionary. The planning outlined in the wishes of the settlor was highly binding on the trustee, whose range of action in carrying out the terms of the trust was thus circumscribed.

This arrangement, in my opinion, was consistent with the top-down conception of family relationships typical of the times, even if these had already been influenced by affective individualism and ongoing change to some extent. It went hand in hand with a conception of property as the almost exclusive source of social prestige and political power, as well as long-standing economic affluence. In a society like that of England in the seventeenth and eighteenth centuries—rather static and not very dynamic—the strict settlement was congenial to the interests of the privileged class of landowners who formed part of the aristocracy.

In the meantime, the market was opening up: affluence and social status were no longer assured simply by the possession of property. For this reason, it became apparent to some that a new technique for the transfer of property was necessary. This should maintain intact the value of the family estate, reducing any depreciation in the interests of the beneficiaries while allowing some of the estate to be mobilised within the framework of a planned transfer of the family estate—perhaps even by selling some of the property—and more generally by allowing for rapid reactions to the variations of the market. It was necessary to go beyond the confines of the strict settlement, which had been set up in the light of the needs of the head of family, giving wider discretionary powers capable of determining specific and appropriated responses to contingent needs. This power was attributed to the trustee in a new form, which was used alongside the strict settlement; it was called the trust for sale and first came into being at the end of the eighteenth century and the beginning of the nineteenth.[10]

[9] The strict settlement gave rise to a development which led in England to the trust for sale and in the United States to estate planning. It is very important to understand the role that strict settlement played with its intermediate position between the entail (which kept the property within the family) and its modern opposite, the trust for sale, the aim of which is to give the trustee the duty of selling the property.

[10] On the historical recourse made to the trust for sale, cf WR Cornish and GN Clark, *Law and Society in England 1750–1950* (Sweet and Maxwell, 1989), pp 146ff.

Unlike the strict settlement, this new institution was able to deal with property of any type (eg enterprises, shareholdings) by conferring power on the trustee, rather than on the beneficiary *pro tempore*; the former became the beneficiary of the legal title and, above all—and this is why it is called as it is—it allowed the trustee to sell the property, substituting this with the proceeds of the sale. A trustee is given a nominal title to the property, which is held for the benefit of one or more others. The trustee is bound to oversee the sale of the property, subject to a discretion regarding its timing. As well as determining certain aspects of the administration of real estate of the family, the flexibility of the trust for sale, now regulated by the *Trusts of Land and Appointment of Trustees Act* 1996,[11] allows it to apply to a wide range of purposes, even those which are extraneous to the original ones. Amongst these are the co-ownership of buildings and the protection of the co-purchaser who is not the owner of the family home.

The Decline of Fideicommissum

As in England, the oldest institution in Italy—fideicommissary substitution—was also transformed into a new version: the family fideicommissum. However, while the procedure transforming the entail into the strict settlement had involved a substantial amount of innovation, specifically aimed at maintaining the links between the new ideas circulating in society and legal norms, in Italy the change seems to have gone in the other direction.

The family fideicommissum first began to appear in the sixteenth and seventeenth centuries. It was aimed at protecting the heirs of the testator only and at the same time at excluding the collaterals through the creation of a series of obstacles to provisions in their favour. It was absolute and perpetual and its aim was to favour the family unit and to protect its economic prosperity over time.

This device was used widely, particularly after the seventeenth century.[12] The doctrine specified various circumstantial situations from which the presumption of the testator's intention to constitute a family fideicommissum could be deduced. This was characterised as follows: as many heirs as possible were named in relation to the property; substitution was tied to the death of the heir; and the order of succession—that is, the sequence of future beneficiaries of the property—was determined. Moreover, the preservation of the estate and a declaration of the intention to preserve the estate within the family were required.

The deed took the form of 'a series of provisions which, taking as their centre the fideicommissum [were] linked by the common "cause" of the constitution of

[11] The law has modified the discipline and the name of the institution (it is no longer the 'trust for sale' but 'trust of land'), bringing it into line with its aims. Cf LM Clements, 'The Changing Face of Trusts: The *Trusts of Land and Appointment of Trustees Act* 1996', *Modern Law Review* (1998) pp 56ff.

[12] 'Ma specialmente dopo il 1600 cominciò a montar la piena dei fideicommissi'. Thus ran the famous statement by A Muratori, *Dei difetti della giurisprudenza* , Ch XVII. For example, towards the end of the century, more than three-quarters of the Grand Duchy of Tuscany was burdened by deeds of trust.

an inalienable family estate.'[13] The members of the family—descendants of the testator—enjoyed the property collectively but sometimes also individually, through the temporary subdivision of the hereditament. Often, the additional clauses of a will obliged the beneficiaries to live together in the family home.[14]

The individual fideicommissum was first used in the first few decades of the eighteenth century. Its most typical forms were the fideicommissum of primogeniture or *maggiorasco*[15]; the explicit aim of both was to halt any excessive breakdown in the hereditament which might have been stimulated by the family fideicommissum. By excluding women, automatically prohibiting alienation and prohibiting any legitime quote, all the estate was brought under the binding force of the tie and the administration of the property was therefore concentrated in only one member of the family, usually the eldest son. In this way, the estate could be transferred in a unitary manner, making it indivisible.

Fathers who left all their possessions to their eldest son had also to provide for their younger children. An income was usually left to other male children and they were sent into church or army careers. Daughters were usually given a dowry, whether they married, became nuns or stayed at home to look after their relatives.

The doctrine recognised the right of the heir to hold the inherited property in usufruct. He had the twin duties of restitution and inventory, as well as being forbidden to transfer the inherited property to others. Inalienability was so strong that the property that was named in the fideicommissum could not be expropriated even for debts owed to the state by the heir. All the same, it sometimes happened that the heir managed to sell one or more of the properties that were left to him.

In the actual fideicommissum, the relation between the current holder and the property always seems temporary because it was subject to the conditions fixed by the testator and restitution took place when these were seen to be fulfilled. This did not favour the kind of management that would maintain improvements in the real estate value in the long term, or the assumption of commitments that would be fruitful over time. Instead, it encouraged an exploitation of property that was intense and concentrated in time, also considering that the following heir (known as the *onorato*) did not have any real power of control over the actions of the possessor *pro tempore*. At most, always assuming that the testator had not excluded this, he could at his own cost ask the legatee to make up an inventory of the property or to give a description of it, or else he could ask for a fidejussory or mortgage guarantee (when the legatee possessed other personal property).

[13] Zorzoli n 3, p 177.

[14] This clause was often specified for daughters, for whom it was a condition in order for them to be allowed access to the bound property.

[15] Trifone, 'Maiorasco e minorasco', in *Nuovo Digesto italiano*, 1938, p 52. Strictly speaking, while with primogeniture only the eldest son was specified, with *maggiorasco* the oldest among the living descendants (irrespective of whether it was a daughter or a grandchild) could be singled out. Cf also Mainoni, 'Fedecommesso e sostituzione fedecommissaria', *Enciclopedia giuridica italiana* (1900), p 913.

It was the duty of the prince to concede exceptions to the prohibition to alienate, allowing the sale of the property on the fideicommissum, and in the case of the Milanese Senate these exceptions were conceded fairly easily. In sum, however, the individual fideicommissum—precisely because it passed all the family wealth to the eldest son—forced all the other members to be dependent on him, given his duty to make economic provision for his brothers and collaterals.

Before this, fideicommissary substitutions had not required the indivisibility of the property and its concentration in one person only. The family fideicommissum, from this point of view, was a retrogression because, as we have seen, the substitutions could now be limited to one or more properties. It also had a detrimental effect because it accentuated the restrictions on the circulation of the property, and partly because it allowed 'all the emotional life of families supported by a tyrant-victim, who was frequently overwhelmed by heavy responsibilities and debts and by continual requests for money from his brothers, aunts and sisters.'[16]

From a comparative point of view, in contrast to the strict settlement, the eighteenth century fideicommissum was the result of a sociocultural environment and an understanding of a conception of family relationships that was too hierarchical to last very long given the ongoing march towards equality that was taking place in the same period.

The progressive limitations of the fideicommissum and the emphasis it placed on technicalities led to the formation of a strong movement of opinion demanding a radical reform of the law, and in fact even demanding its abolition during the eighteenth century. In reality, even during the Middle Ages it had been responsible for causing endless disputes, frequently extending down the generations. Moreover, fideicommissa began to be perceived during the Enlightenment as an obstacle to free circulation. In certain geographical areas, 'two-thirds and sometimes even three-quarters of pieces of land were subject to feudal and deed of trust obligations, and were not subject to free bargaining.'[17] Clearly, family relationships were affected too, in the sense that the concentration of the property in one person meant that the ambitions, expectations and hopes of the other children were curtailed, and they were often obliged to embark on personal and professional careers that they did not want. In the general climate of criticism, many voices made themselves heard—for example, Filangieri, Muratori, Genovesi, Beccaria—and many progressive rulers restricted the effect of the clause in question.

In France, a law of 1792 abolished substitutions of any kind and prohibited the creation of any new ones. The Napoleonic Code—which initially adhered to the abolitionist argument—was, however, modified through law No 3 of September 1807 and the possibility for private citizens to draw up fideicommissa was reintroduced.

In Italy, the French Civil Code came into force when the country was conquered by the French army. Once the French dominion had ended, during the

[16] Romano, *Famiglia, successioni e patrimonio familiare nell'Italia medievale e moderna* (Torino 1994), p 81.

[17] Mainoni, n 17, p 923, who cites Pecchio, *Storia dell'economia pubblica*, vol 2, ch 3.

Restoration, the rules preceding the conquest were made legal again. As a result, the fideicommissum was reinstated in many local norms. On Italy's political unification, the new Civil Code of 1865 abolished the fideicommissum definitively: while fideicommissary substitution was abolished, the appointment of an heir remained valid. The fideicommissa that were still standing when the new Civil Code was enforced were dissolved. A new bilateral and divisible succession system was introduced in which all the children were included in the division of the paternal legal assets, independent of their sex or order of birth.

The development which in England gave rise to the strict settlement, and therefore to its transformation from an instrument restricting the alienability to one for the distribution of family wealth, had no counterpart in Italy, where the fideicommissum maintained its unique and original function of stopping the alienability *extra familiam* of the estate. The free circulation of property theorised in the economic thinking of the eighteenth century—necessary for the budding industrialisation and supported by progressive rulers as well as some intellectuals—came to a complete standstill and this explains to some extent why the decline of the institution was inevitable.

Thus in Italy during the nineteenth century the use of the fideicommissum came to an end, while in the same period in England and the United States the search for a more efficient means than the strict settlement gave rise to a new institution: the trust for sale.

Modern Instruments in Western Legal Systems

The regulation of the transfer of family wealth varies in contemporary legal orders and, although the various systems deal with some areas of regulation in similar ways, the differences between them are striking.

In English law, the scope and contents of a will can be very wide, given that there is no provision for a reserved share for family members. However, it is not used very widely because of the expenses involved and because its effectiveness depends upon the executors obtaining a grant of probate from the court. This need for official recognition of authenticity clearly leads to expenses and bureaucratic formalities. To avoid such costs, but to ensure that a certain property goes to the beneficiary named, two main instruments are used. The first is the trust, which can take the form of a discretionary trust (including the trust of land), or protective trust; the second is joint ownership, where the property is left to more than one person, usually to the husband and the wife. In the case of the death of one of the two, their share goes automatically to the survivor without requiring any additional procedure of succession. In most families, where the value of the property possessed is not very high, joint ownership is the most widely used form, while the trust seems to be the most suitable and frequently used form for properties which are more substantial.

In the North American system, despite the differences between the states, which allow for different choices in relation to the patrimonial regime of a married couple, the main institution is estate planning. This is based on a trust *inter vivos* and it allows the requirements of probate to be avoided, offering the possibility to the settlor to keep control over the property all through his or her life, and then to pass it on to successive generations. These trusts can be structured in a variety of ways—for example, so as to allow the trust, made operative by the death of the settlor, to treat the surviving partner as the beneficiary and again, after that person's death, to benefit other descendants, thus avoiding inheritance taxes.[18] These are always revocable and their use is always recommended where funds or shares, or more generally intangible property, are at stake.

Together with trusts, there are forms of co-ownership with survivorship provisions, life insurances, joint bank accounts, reversible pensions paid to the survivors,[19] and Totten trusts.[20] Again it should be remembered that American law allows antenuptial agreements to be drawn up, in which the legal consequences of the death of one of the couple, or their separation or divorce, can be regulated. These agreements are banned in Italian law because of a theoretical argument leading back to the principle of the impossibility of waiving the rights of the spouses.

In Italian law, there is in fact a general ban on regulating family interests *mortis causa* by contract. Moreover, the fact that inheritance agreements are forbidden by Article 458, together with the inadequacy of wills—the only provision *mortis causa* which is foreseen by the system—means that the transfer of wealth between family members is highly unsatisfactory both for the private individuals concerned and the doctrine.

Many alternatives to the will are used: third-party beneficiary contracts, particularly in the form of insurance policies; life annuities; fiduciary transactions; clauses of consolidation in corporation contracts; gifts with effects *post mortem*; and gifts *si premoriar* as well as other practices. The Italian order, in relation to other civil law systems, shows itself to be particularly determined to prohibit 'patti successori'—that is, all agreements through which the testator agrees to leave property to someone or through which the beneficiary of a future inheritance agrees to renounce it.

French law, despite adopting the same principle, which is expressed in the articles of the Civil Code, has weakened this prohibition in different cases. Some of these are provided for by the Code, some have been introduced more recently by additional laws. Among the agreements allowed is the new paragraph which has been added to Article 930. According to this paragraph, adopted in 1971, when

[18] By-pass trusts, which can extend over many generations, must not infringe the rule against perpetuities.

[19] A seminal contribution to the discussion is provided by JH Langbein, 'The Contractarian Basis of the Law of Trusts', (1995) 105 *Yale LJ* 625.

[20] Here, the settlor opens a bank account in his name in trust for another person. The holder of the account—the settlor—has full powers over the funds deposited in it until his death, when the beneficiary takes his place.

the testator has alienated a property with the agreement of all the born and all the living legitimate heirs and legatees, actions cannot be brought against third parties who have come into possession of the property.

In the German system, on the contrary, inheritance agreements are valid, with the sole exception of dispositive agreements. However, in this legal order the machinery of succession can count, together with the will, on another important institution: the hereditary contract (*Erbvertrag*), in which the married couple—or future married couple—agree to regulate their plans for inheritance, often nominating themselves as mutual heirs and then seeing to providing for the children, who may well be from different marriages.

PATRIMONY IN THE MEDIEVAL AND EARLY MODERN FAMILY

The argument put forward by legal historians that the family in the Middle Ages used its property to centralise its members seems to be sound, at least in relation to the legal orders and legal institutions being considered here.

Entails and fideicommissary substitutions reflected a similar economic concern: the head of family who was moderately wealthy feared that his descendants would not be able to increase this wealth and he doubted that, when left to themselves, they would even be capable of managing it in such a way as to maintain its full value. He therefore forced them to do with minimal disposable assets, by tying the property—in the form that it had at the moment of the drawing up of the fideicommissum—and withdrawing from them any decisional power in respect to this. It is this pessimistic view of the capability of family members that determined the use of entails and fideicommissa, and led to the denial of any discretion.

The idea of the precariousness of individual existence was probably also part of this attitude. Life expectancy, in a period of epidemics, war conflicts, shortages of food and where medicines were primitive, was very short. In particular, children's lives were very much at risk because of the high perinatal and infant mortality rate,[21] as were the lives of women since childbirth was so dangerous.

The precariousness of individual existence contrasted with the permanence in time of the household, which persisted through generations of families with the same surname, and was tied to the same territories, to the same lifelong-held houses, the same furnishings and lifestyles. The lineage, and the material goods connoting it and making it recognisable to strangers, is what persists in time when individuals seem so transitory.

The fideicommissum and entail were aimed at guaranteeing the continuity of landholding through the years. The original testator imagines (by projecting himself into the future) that he is taking care of later generations rather than just the single beneficiary *pro tempore*. This lack of interest for the single person—and

[21] In some regions of Italy, children were named only when they turned two.

the emphasis on the material and property aspects that the laws for planned succession allow for—were realised in concrete forms made necessary by the uncertain living conditions of the times, to which everyone was exposed.

It should not be forgotten that there was no social security for the old or the ill, apart from church charity. By making sure that property stayed as one unit by keeping it in the family, the settlor also ensured that he and the weaker members of the household would be looked after in their old age, since this—given that there were no public institutions available—was the main place where caretaking activities took place.

Historical research shows that in general not much investment was made in the cultural development of children in economic terms: the costs of education and professional training were very low, substituted—except in some exceptional cases—by apprenticeship to other families. Not much money was invested in the children during their childhood and youth, and this allowed the value of the inherited property to increase—or at any rate not to decrease.[22]

Linked by land and material goods, the family model that is described above based its private relations on a common dependence on the beneficiary *pro tempore* of the patrimony. Personal relations, cooperation as the result of affection, human solidarity and shared feelings were not crucial to this. Aggregation instead rested on economic subjection that presupposed in its turn a deliberate inequality among the family members.

The idea of equality[23] was not accepted within the family—the most inflexible of institutions with respect to changes in hierarchy—although it made its way slowly into the political thinking of the time, and revealed itself as one of the main and most innovative themes underlying the Declaration of the Rights of Man. There was an enormous disparity of situations and rights in the family which corresponded to positions of both privilege and economic disadvantage, and was discernible between husbands and wives on account of their different sexes, as well as between adults and children or adolescents, between sons and daughters, between legitimate and illegitimate offspring, and between elder and younger children. These inequalities reflected the social stratifications of a world in which the idea of organising the public and private spheres along different lines, or even of separating them, was accepted only very slowly. In a society which did not allow for an equality of rights between men, it is clear that the interrelating of the social and private lives of people could not allow for an equality of treatment within the family structure.

Thus within the family in the late medieval and modern times, the biological characteristics (ie being a man or a woman) and the order of generation (eldest son, other son) determined the rights and status of the individual. Thus the organisational structure of the family was based on elements of fact which were

[22] Cf P Aries, *L'enfant et la vie familiale sous l'ancien régime* (1960).

[23] Cf FH Lawson, 'Family, Property and Individual Property', in *The Comparison. Selected Essays*, vol. 2 (North Holland 1977), pp 302ff.

unchangeable by individual will, and they led to advantages for some and disadvantages for others.

With respect to the outside world, in the same way, membership of a given family group guaranteed the individual a corresponding social position and adequate chances for quality of life. The importance and prestige of the family as a whole determined individual status. Each member reflected the characteristics of the group of which they formed a part; this was normal in medieval times, the epoch of human groups *par excellence*, where these intermediate societies provided an important structure for continuity.[24]

The nuclear family therefore represented either a source of frustrations or privileges for the individual according to one's position in the internal hierarchy. Analogously, at the level of the relations of social life, being recognised as part of a particular household could either be lucky or could lead to social exclusion. At all events, the qualification and position of the person was not dependent on individual personality, character, merits, contacts or culture as much as it was on the group he or she belonged to.

In relation to entails and fideicommissa, the idea of belonging to a family group takes on particular importance. Here it is not understood as a group of people tied by biological links, living in the same house and times but as a sequence of descendants who, together with others, form a single extended family over time.

There is a recognisable temporal quality characterising the medieval and early modern family, particularly in relation to the contemporary family. The most typical model tended to extend beyond the length of life of its current members, to include its descendants. The family therefore extended into the future, composed of people whose lives were important because they represented the household through the decades and the centuries; they prolonged its existence in a dimension which was as fascinating and important as the measuring of time was then difficult and costly. In this way, the precariousness of human life was projected towards what was long-lasting—lineage and descent, both elements which went beyond the single lives which made them up.

Forward-looking and wealthy heads of families who belonged to a particular dynasty usually felt a sense of responsibility towards their descendants,[25] and this was reflected in the property and dynastic institutions for the obligatory transfer of property. However, substitutions and entails do not indicate only an attachment to the family in the fifth dimension, but also a firm belief in the lack of change in any of the assumptions underlying the economic system. I have argued that these institutions show a sense of diffidence by heads of families towards their descendants and the latter's ability to administrate effectively. As well, they reveal (and this is not less easy to understand) the unwavering belief of those heads of families in the unchanging nature of the hierarchy of property values. In other words, they believed that not only the economic framework, but also the network of conventions and social values, would remain the same.

24 N Elias, *The Society of Individual* (Oxford, 1991).

25 For an interesting comparison, cf C Lasch, *The Culture of Narcissism* (WW Norton, 1979).

Rather than mere legal and technical institutions, then, fideicommissa and entails appear in this light to be the vehicles of a particular view of things (a way of thinking and feeling that was in fact coming to its end). According to this view, the transitory nature of individual experience was rooted in a social framework and economic system whose parameters seemed permanent and untouchable.[26]

INDIVIDUALS, FAMILIES AND PROPERTY IN A CONTEMPORARY PERSPECTIVE

In the contemporary legal systems considered here, what are apparent are the many different legal approaches and points of continuing debate. It is clear, however, that while the technical solutions diverge, there is substantial agreement on the meta-legal problems.

One of the first things to note from the discussion above is that today's transfer of wealth in families is no longer determined by the head of the family. In many cases, the transfer of property no longer moves from the father to the descendants but from partner to partner in a married couple, and then to the children.

In contrast to the past, moreover, the changes in levels of fertility all over the Western world have reduced the number of children and, while this simplifies the division of property, it places emphasis on the need to provide descendants with an obviously equal treatment. Average life expectancy is now considerably longer than before and so there is more overlap between the generations (sometimes even stretching across grandparents and great-grandparents), making the temporal span longer. In addition, while the number of family members decreases, the different types of family structure increase: single-parent families, de facto families, reconstituted families, same-sex cohabitation or living together on the basis of mutual assistance, polygamous families, families where there is no biological link between the children and the parents—because procreation has been assisted, or more traditionally there has been an adoption—and foster families where the link with the children is atypical and short-term. And if, historically, some of these formulas have always existed—primarily families with one parent only—those which are formed today are marked by a freedom of choice on all sides, rather than by the death of the partner.[27] Thus the transfer of property has become more complex. This explains the difficulties in which the Italian system finds itself where only one family model is envisaged and regulated by the Civil Code, and where the only means of transfer of property on death is via the will.

[26] Bourdieu has underlined that belonging to a certain social class implies the sharing of tastes, values, and schemes for living which are as important as they are unconscious and beyond individual control. The social order does not penetrate with much force individual awareness and is felt to be part of the order of things, through the non-rational acquisition of values, virtues and competences. See P Bourdieu, *Distinction* (Harvard University Press, 1979).

[27] This point was made by N Rouland, *Anthropologie juridique* (1989).

As a result of the increase in average life expectancy, the transfer of wealth between parents and children now often takes place when everyone is alive. Moreover, in most families it no longer consists (or not only) in the transfer of tangible property but in the protracted commitment of capital for the scholastic or other training of the children. Nowadays, then, the care taken of descendants is no longer provided through the investment of accumulated sums left in inheritance, but is used to finance training as well as the acquisition of competencies and experience. While in the past money was spent on precious objects, goods, financial assets and real estate investment, now money is spent—at least by the middle classes—on language courses, sports activities, music lessons, study holidays and short periods of work or learning.

As a result, the passing of property from one generation to another in the same family can nowadays be described as 'planned' because—compared with the tied model—it no longer aims to keep property in the family but to organise its distribution to deal with the needs of life. In addition, it is now unthinkable that what is given to the eldest son should not be given in an equal amount to the other children too, and this means that the distribution must be handled carefully.

It is now more common to see oneself and one's family in the present, or at most in an 'extended present' rather than as part of a family extending through time.[28] Once viewed as so far off as to meet all desires, hopes and fears, the future is now contracted into a dimension close enough to be uncertain, but also directly consequential with respect to the choices made in the here and now. The future seems to be so close in time that planning for a far off period loses any sense.

Property transfer from parents to children is changing: the idea that a settlor should leave tangible property to descendants on death is moving to one of the slow use of current resources to enable the new generations to acquire the competencies that they feel are necessary for their style of life, in line with their expectations about what society might be like in times to come. Their parents tend to invest in what they believe will lead to a higher level of quality of existence; as a result, this kind of intergeneration transfer is much less class-ridden than the previous model for it is much less elitist and can be adopted by everyone.

Underpinning this way of thinking is the conviction that family property should allow family members to realise their ambitions—the gaining of wealth and success. Thus, rather than having their own autonomous importance, the accumulated goods are perceived in a functional perspective in relation to abstract objectives; seen in this light, the patrimonial principle loses the centrality which it had in the family model of medieval and early modern times.

The role played by patrimonial assets in the family today is highly ambiguous. On the one hand, it is now subordinated to a hierarchy of values which place the individual's happiness and the satisfaction of his or her sentimental and spiritual needs at the top; on the other, it is absolutely vital given that it allows the indi-

[28] H Nowotny, *Eigenzeit. Enstehung und Strukturierung eines Zeitgefuehls* (1989).

vidual to realise these needs—particularly when they presuppose the acquisition of specific competencies or experiences and high added costs (often the case when children are being catered for).

The current notion of the family—at least in its ideal version—is based on the affective tie between its members, and the *raison d'etre* of the family is seen as the fulfilment of their emotional and spiritual needs rather than the pursuit of patrimonial principles. Nevertheless, the family property still has importance in a concrete, everyday sense. Property no longer centralises families into groups, nor do families function as groups which protect their individual members. The patrimony instead is taking on a new role: that of the necessary condition whereby the family can realise its essential objective of satisfying the aims of personal promotion and the well-being of all its members.

Even the traditional succession *mortis causa*—either through its recourse to succession laws or through its 'planning' measures by agreements between living people—now conforms to choices made in the present. This is no longer viewed as a way of tracking the future of the family through the hierarchical selection of the beneficiaries, but as the specific giving of property to beneficiaries who will make use of it in ways and objectives which mirror their own personal choices.

The intergeneration transfer of wealth thus confirms the lines of development of the Western family. From a conception of the individual as a functioning member of the family group to which he or she belonged, we have moved to a vision of things in which the family is the instrument for the fulfilment of desires and satisfaction of the individual's needs.

22

The Constitutional Dimension of Customary Family Law in Papua New Guinea

Owen Jessep*

INTRODUCTION

In this chapter I would like to discuss some recent developments in relation to customary family law in Papua New Guinea. In particular, I will refer to the 1997 case of *Re Willingal*,[1] in which a constitutional challenge was mounted against a customary arrangement whereby an unwilling 18-year-old woman, Miriam Willingal, was to be given in marriage as part of a complicated compensation settlement between two kin groups. This case has potentially far-reaching implications for the future recognition in Papua New Guinea of various aspects of customary family law, including that of polygamy. Similar issues are currently provoking interest and debate in other parts of the Pacific[2] and in various African jurisdictions.[3]

Papua New Guinea is a Pacific nation lying directly to the north of Australia, with a Melanesian population of over four million people. It was formerly an Australian colony, becoming independent in 1975. A distinguishing characteristic of Papua New Guinean family law is the contrast and conflicts which are evident between family law legislation on the one hand, and customary family law on the other.[4] The statute law is mostly old Australian colonial legislation, which has con-

* Associate Professor of Law, University of New South Wales, Sydney, Australia.

[1] (1997) N 1506.

[2] See, for example, J Zorn, 'Women, custom and international law in the Pacific', *USP School of Law Occasional Paper No 5* (University of the South Pacific, School of Law, Port Vila 1999).

[3] In relation to current debates in Southern Africa, for example, see F Kaganas and C Murray, 'The Contest between Culture and Gender Equality under South Africa's Interim Constitution' (1994) 21 *Journal of Law and Society* 409; T Nhlapo, 'Indigenous Law and Gender in South Africa: Taking Human Rights and Cultural Diversity Seriously' (1994–95) *Third World Legal Studies* 49; P Letuka and A Armstrong '"Which Law? Which Family? Which Women?"—Problems of Enforcing CEDAW in Southern Africa', in N Lowe and G Douglas (eds), *Families Across Frontiers* (Nijhoff 1996), pp 207–27; V Bronstein, 'Reconceptualizing the Customary Law Debate in South Africa' (1998) 14 *South African Journal of Human Rights* 388; and L Fishbayn, 'Litigating the Right to Culture: Family Law in the New South Africa' (1999) 13 *International Journal of Law, Policy and the Family* 147.

[4] See generally O Jessep and J Luluaki, *Principles of Family Law in Papua New Guinea*, 2nd edn (UPNG Press 1994).

tinued in force notwithstanding almost a quarter of a century of independence.[5] At the same time, customary family law is also recognised (subject to certain qualifications) under the Constitution and several other statutes.[6] As a result, in some areas of family law a 'dual' system operates, in which persons can choose whether to follow statute or custom. In relation to marriage, for example, a person may either make a monogamous statutory marriage by satisfying the formalities of the *Marriage Act* (Ch 280 of the Revised Laws), or instead make a customary marriage formed in accordance with the relevant custom.[7]

One noticeable feature of judicial activity in recent years has been the readiness of National Court judges to challenge aspects of customary family law. In some instances, this has led to denial of recognition and enforcement of familial custom, on the basis that certain constitutional or legislative safeguards relating to human rights have been infringed. In order to appreciate the basis of this developing human rights jurisprudence, culminating in the decision in *Re Willingal* (1997), it is necessary to provide a brief account of the most relevant constitutional and statutory provisions.

CONSTITUTIONAL AND LEGISLATIVE BACKGROUND

By section 9 of the Constitution of Papua New Guinea, the laws of the country include the Constitution itself, various categories of legislation, and the 'underlying law'. According to section 20, until such time as an Act of Parliament provides otherwise, the underlying law is to be understood as set out in schedule 2 of the Constitution. By that schedule, the two principal sources of the underlying law are custom[8] and the common law. In relation to custom, schedule 2.1(1), so far as relevant, states that 'custom is adopted, and shall be applied and enforced, as part of the underlying law'. This is, however, made subject to sub-section 2, which provides as follows:

> (2) Subsection (1) does not apply in respect of any custom that is, and to the extent that it is, inconsistent with a Constitutional Law or a statute, or repugnant to the general principles of humanity.

[5] These pre-Independence statutes are continued in force by virtue of the Constitution of Papua New Guinea, sch 2.6.

[6] Customary family law claims can be instituted at all levels of the legal system, from the Village Courts to the Local and District Courts, and even (depending on the amount and issues involved) in the National Court. See Jessep and Luluaki, n 4, chs 4 and 5.

[7] For discussion, see Jessep and Luluaki, n 4, ch 2.

[8] In sch 1.2 of the *Constitution*, the term 'custom' is defined to mean: 'the customs and usages of indigenous inhabitants of the country existing in relation to the matter in question at the time when and the place in relation to which the matter rises, regardless of whether or not the custom or usage has existed from time immemorial.'

One further important statutory provision dealing with the recognition of custom should also be mentioned. Section 3(1) of the *Customs Recognition Act* (chapter 19 of the Revised Laws) is in the following terms:[9]

(1) Subject to this Act, custom shall be recognized and enforced by, and may be pleaded in, all courts except so far as in a particular case or in a particular context—
  (a) its recognition or enforcement would result, in the opinion of the court, in injustice or would not be in the public interest; or
  (b) in a case affecting the welfare of a child under the age of 16 years, its recognition or enforcement would not, in the opinion of the court, be in the best interests of the child.

It follows from the constitutional and statutory provisions outlined above that, in relation to any aspect of familial custom that appears to be relevant in a legal context, there are potentially six grounds for refusing to adopt that custom as part of the underlying law. That is to say, recognition of custom is not automatic, but is made subject to a screening process. These six grounds (three from the wording of schedule 2.1 of the *Constitution*, and three from section 3 of the *Customs Recognition Act*) are as follows:

(i) inconsistency with the *Constitution*;
(ii) inconsistency with a statute;
(iii) repugnancy to the general principles of humanity;
(iv) resulting in injustice;
(v) contrary to the public interest; and
(vi) contrary to the best interests of a child under 16 years of age.

Of these possible reasons for impugning familial custom (reasons which in practice may often be expected to overlap to some extent), several decisions of the National Court in the early 1990s had resorted to grounds (i) and (iii)—that is to say by referring to custom in relation to the Constitution, and also in regard to the 'general principles of humanity'. Brief examples of each approach will now be given.

In the 1991 case of *Re Wagi Non and the Constitution Section 42(5)*,[10] the husband had left his wife and their four children in the care of his relatives in his village when he travelled to another province for employment. After he had been away for five or six years without making contact with his family or relatives, the wife eventually became tired of waiting for him and formed a relationship with another man. The husband's relatives then complained in the Village Court that the wife had committed adultery, in breach of customary expectations, and

[9] Some further limitations concerning the applicability of custom in criminal and civil cases are found in ss 4 and 5 of the same statute (ch 19). Those sections are not relevant for purposes of this paper.

[10] [1991] PNGLR 84. For an interesting discussion of this case, see J Zorn, 'Women, Custom and State Law in Papua New Guinea' (1994–95) *Third World Legal Studies* 169.

obtained an order for compensation against her. When she failed to pay the amount required, the Village Court ordered her imprisonment. In the National Court, Woods J ordered her release, stating (among other reasons) that the custom relied on by the relatives of the husband should not be recognised, as it infringed section 55 of the Constitution. In substance, this section provides that: 'all citizens have the same rights, privileges, obligations and duties irrespective of race, tribe, place of origin, political opinion, colour, creed, religion or sex'.

Thus gender discrimination is made one of the criteria according to which laws may be challenged. In the opinion of the court:

> I cannot help feeling that the going off and leaving the wife and children without his support and protection yet expecting her to remain bound by custom is a custom that must be denigrating to her status as a woman. It is denying her the equality provided in the *Constitution*, s 55 . . . I am not saying that a man cannot have several wives and cannot travel but if he chooses to have wives and travel elsewhere he must accord them equality in care and participation and she must have the same freedoms that he has . . . The facts of this case suggest that this woman is bonded, almost in slavery, to the husband even when the husband neglects her. This must clearly be a denigration of the woman's humanness.[11]

Again, in *Re Kepo Raramu and the Yowe Village Court* (1994),[12] a Village Court had sentenced a woman to a term of six months' imprisonment for commencing a new relationship after her husband had died. On appeal, the National Court ordered her immediate release. One of the grounds relied on for this decision by Doherty J was the following:

> I am well aware of the custom in many areas that says women whose husbands have died are not to go around with another man . . . I do not know of any equivalent custom that says a man whose wife has died is not allowed to go around with other women, and, as such, I consider this custom strikes against the basis of equality provided in s 55 of the Constitution.[13]

Despite the lack of any clear judicial definition in Papua New Guinea of what might be meant by 'the general principles of humanity' (a legislative expression that first appeared during colonial times), the notion of 'repugnancy' to these principles has featured in several National Court family law cases. The first such instance occurred in 1991 in *Re Kaka Ruk and the Constitution Section 42(5)*,[14] on facts notably similar to those in *Re Wagi Non* (see above). In *Kaka Ruk*, a husband had complained to the Village Court that his wife had committed adultery with the husband's brother. After being unable to pay the compensation ordered by the court, she was gaoled. When the matter came to the attention of the National Court, Woods J found that the husband had neglected her during the time when he had been absent at work on a plantation, and this had led to her associating with his brother, to whom she was now pregnant. After referring to para 2(12) of

[11] [1991] PNGLR 84, Woods J at 86–87.
[12] [1994] PNGLR 486.
[13] [1994] PNGLR 486, Doherty J at 486.
[14] [1991] PNGLR 105.

the National Goals and Directive Principles in the Preamble to the *Constitution* (equality of spouses' rights and duties in marriage), and the 'repugnancy' test in schedule 2.1 of the *Constitution*, Woods J stated:

> This custom that the husband is seeking to apply which leads to her gaoling when he is in the dominating position and where the situation has been partly caused by his behaviour must be a custom that denigrates women and is thus repugnant to the general principles of humanity and should be denied a place in the underlying law . . . In this situation before me now the wife [was] caught between bride price problems and an unhappy marriage which has produced no children. She almost [had] no way out . . . People in Papua New Guinea must come to terms with the law that women are not chattels that can be bought and thus bonded forever. They are equal participants in the marriage and in society . . .[15]

Marital problems of this sort should be resolved by discussion and mediation, the court added, rather than by the precipitate application of criminal sanctions.[16]

A final illustration, also with reference to the 'repugnancy' doctrine, is found in the 1994 case of *Ubuk v Darius.*[17] This was a dispute over custody of a child aged twenty months, whose parents had lived together in a de facto relationship for about two years. When the relationship broke up, the man (who had been previously married by custom) returned to live with his customary wife and their children. He sought custody of the ex-nuptial daughter, and emphasised his wife's apparent willingness to look after her. He relied on evidence of local custom to the effect that if an informal relationship did not progress to the status of a customary marriage, the father was entitled to automatic custody of any child born in the meantime, subject to a payment of compensation to the woman for having borne the child. The court was not impressed. In the words of Sevua J:

> Whether one views it subjectively or objectively, the woman is a sex object. So where is the morality and value of humanity in this woman? . . . How does a woman in such a situation free herself from this seemingly sexual domination? I consider [these] customs repugnant to the general principles of humanity and, therefore, inapplicable to the present case. The applicant can gain no assistance from that customary law.[18]

In the event, custody of the child was given to the mother, with access to the father.[19]

The Case of *re Willingal* (1997)

In cases like those so far mentioned, the court typically relied on one or another of the filtering mechanisms set out in schedule 2.1 of the Constitution or in

[15] *Ibid.*, Woods J at 107.
[16] *Ibid.*
[17] [1994] PNGLR 279.
[18] [1994] PNGLR 279, Sevua J at 283–84.
[19] *Ibid.*, Sevua J at 284.

section 3 of the *Customs Recognition Act* to deny recognition to some aspects of familial custom. Several of these cases arose from competing expectations about the respective behaviour and duties of the parties to a customary marriage, a setting in which the National Court felt obliged repeatedly to intervene to protect women from excessive punishment at the hands of Village Courts.[20] The 1997 case of *Re Willingal*,[21] in contrast, reached the National Court after publicity in one of Papua New Guinea's national newspapers, which in turn led to the institution of proceedings by a non-governmental human rights organisation. These proceedings featured a whole battery of challenges against a custom requiring a woman's forced marriage.

As mentioned in the judgment of Injia J in this case, the *PNG Post Courier* of 3 May 1996 ran an article beginning with the chilling headline of 'Girl Sold in Death Compensation'.[22] The story dealt with the unfortunate situation of Ms Miriam Willingal, an eighteen-year-old high school student from the Western Highlands area of Papua New Guinea.[23] It is not necessary here to set out the full facts of the case, which began with the death of Miriam's father who appeared to have been the innocent victim of a police raid on a Highlands village. For various reasons, this then led to extended negotiations between the members of his kin group (to which Miriam also belonged) and the kin group of his mother, two clans which had for generations enjoyed a close relationship. This relationship was expressed, for example, through ties of intermarriage, and in provision of refuge and protection in times of tribal fighting. At issue after Miriam's father's death was the question of how to restore the balance between the two groups, in order to ensure their continued coexistence and alliance for the future.

Unlike the common practice in other types of compensation claims, where recompense is made merely by the handing over of pigs, money, and various personal items of value,[24] in this case the compensation being discussed between the two clans also included the transfer of two young women, who might then be expected to marry men from the deceased's clan. Since Miriam Willingal was, for various reasons, one of the most likely candidates to be pressured into taking part in this arrangement, she began to object. It is not entirely clear how the information reached the newspaper, although Miriam's affidavit, quoted in the judgment,

[20] For discussion, see O Jessep, 'Village Courts in Papua New Guinea: Constitutional and Gender Issues' (1992) 6 *International Journal of Law and the Family* 401.

[21] *Re Willingal* (1997) N 1506.

[22] At p 7.

[23] The case also achieved international publicity, being featured in an article in the *New York Times*: S Mydans, 'When the bartered bride opts out of the bargain', 6 May 1997, p A4. For discussion of some aspects of the case, see D Gewertz and F Errington, *Emerging Class in Papua New Guinea: The Telling of Difference* (Cambridge University Press, 1999), ch 6. The authors describe the unfolding drama revealed in the court case, further represented in public discussion and speculation, as a 'Papua New Guinean morality play' reflecting the themes of 'tradition, modernity, choice, and social distinction' (p 122).

[24] At pp 34–35.

ends with the statement: 'For the reasons stated . . . I went public hoping that somebody might help me.'[25]

In response to the publicity, the Individual and Community Rights Advocacy Forum Inc (ICRAF) instituted proceedings in the National Court under section 57 of the Constitution, claiming that Miriam's constitutional rights were being infringed by the proposed compensation arrangements between the two clans. Section 57 grants standing to any person with an interest in the protection and enforcement of constitutional rights to seek appropriate National Court orders. As a preliminary step, the court found that ICRAF, a community interest group in Papua New Guinea with a history of human rights advocacy, was entitled to make the application on behalf of Miriam.[26] Interim injunctions and protective orders were made by the court, pending a proper hearing of the matter which took place during the following month.[27]

At the trial, there was some disagreement among the witnesses (including expert witnesses) over the details, meaning and implications of the customary compensation claim. The broad outlines of the claim referred to 25 pigs, 20,000 kina and two women.[28] Some witnesses said that no particular women were identified in the negotiations, that no woman would be pressured to comply with the arrangement, and that the marriages might not take place until some years in the future. Other witnesses, including Miriam, gave a contrary impression, to the effect that pressure could be or had been brought to bear on individual women by the clan leaders, and that a delay in arranging the marriages would cause aggravation and ill-feeling between the two groups. On this crucial point, Injia J found that Miriam had already been subjected to pressure, that she did not like the idea of being used as a form of payment, and that she was afraid that the men of both clans might become impatient and try to force her to accept the planned marriage.[29]

Turning to the relevant law, Injia J had no doubt that Miriam's constitutional rights had been infringed, and gave multiple reasons for this conclusion. His general approach to the issue of recognition of custom appears in the following passage:

> The traditional customs of the people of [this area], like the rest of PNG, have existed from time immemorial and they serve complex value systems which only they themselves best know. It is not easy for any outsider to fully understand the customs and the underlying values and purposes they serve. Any outsider including the modern courts must not be quick to extract those customs and their values and pass judgments on their soundness or otherwise . . . But it is clear to me that the framers of our Constitution and modern day legislators were thinking about a modern PNG based on ethnic societies whose welfare and advancement was based on the mainte-

[25] At 34.
[26] At 6.
[27] At 7–8.
[28] At 24. At this time, the value of the kina was approximately equal to A$0.92.
[29] At 42.

nance and promotion of good traditional customs and the discouragement and elimination of bad customs as seen from the eyes of an ordinary modern Papua New Guinean. No matter how painful it may be to the small ethnic society concerned, such bad custom must give way to the dictates of our modern national laws.[30]

The court accordingly held that a number of provisions of the Constitution and of other statutes would be infringed were the custom to be enforced. To begin with, section 32 of the Constitution, which guarantees basic freedoms in accordance with the law, would be infringed if Miriam was not free to choose whom to marry.[31] Further, a forced marriage in these circumstances would amount to a breach of section 55 (here, discrimination on the basis of gender) 'because there is no evidence that the same custom which targets young women from the deceased's tribe also targets eligible men from the deceased's mother's tribe.'[32]

Turning to other legislation, the court found that the proposed marriage would also breach section 5 of the *Marriage Act* (Ch 280 of the Revised Laws), which was designed to protect women from being pressured into customary marriages.[33] As to the criteria and requirements of section 3 of the *Customs Recognition Act* (Ch 19), the court found that the custom in question was not only repugnant to the general principles of humanity, but would also—if carried out—produce injustice and be contrary to the public interest. The custom was repugnant to the general principles of humanity because 'living men or women should not be allowed to be dealt with as part of compensation payments under any circumstances.'[34] Further, it would be unjust for any woman from this area to live under the compulsion and fear of a forced marriage, while 'men from [the same area] and other men and women in other parts of Papua New Guinea live, associate and marry freely.'[35] Finally, and for similar reasons, to recognise the custom would not be in the public interest, because it would 'subject Miriam or any other woman from the [same] area to unnecessary life-time obligations, pressure and [they would] live under threat and fear in their young and single life.'[36]

For all of these half-dozen reasons, the court then proceeded to issue permanent injunctions and restraining orders against the various groups and their members.[37] With such an array of provisions all leading to the same result, the court stated that it was therefore unnecessary to consider additional arguments presented on behalf of the plaintiff. These further points raised at least four other constitutional grounds, such as whether the relevant custom also infringed section

[30] At 51–52, 54–55.

[31] At 45–46.

[32] At 48–49.

[33] At 47, 49. Section 5 empowers a Local Court Magistrate, on complaint by a woman, to forbid a prospective customary marriage, or annul a customary marriage which has already occurred, where the court finds that the woman has been subjected to 'excessive pressure', or that it would otherwise be a hardship on the woman to compel her to comply with the relevant custom.

[34] At 50–51.

[35] At 50.

[36] At 50.

[37] At 56–57.

36 of the Constitution (freedom from inhuman treatment), section 42 (liberty of the person), section 49 (right to privacy) and section 52(1) (freedom of movement).[38] In short, Miriam's challenge was upheld by the court, which comprehensively rejected the proposed customary arrangement.

DISCUSSION

There is little doubt that *Re Willingal* will be a leading authority for years to come whenever aspects of customary family law are in issue. The judgment contains a bundle of potential weapons for future litigants seeking to prevent the enforcement and recognition of particular elements of custom. The reasoning in *Re Willingal* drew on earlier decisions of the National Court, but at the same time extended the range and scope of the arguments available to challenge familial custom, especially where the custom appears to be one-sided, oppressive or especially patriarchal in its application. The possibility of additional forms of argument is also suggested in those points upon which the court in *Re Willingal* found it unnecessary to rule.

What will be the implications of Miriam's case for other aspects of customary family law? In recent years in Papua New Guinea, the most controversial family law topic has been that of polygamous marriage. Even more than the perennial controversy over elements of customary bride price, the practice of polygamy (which in practice means polygyny—that is, the right of a man to have more than one customary wife) has produced a constant flow of public debate.[39] While polygamy is virtually unknown in many parts of the country today, it remains a relatively common practice among leaders from the Highlands provinces. In legal terms, a polygamous customary marriage has generally been regarded as valid since colonial times, by virtue of section 3(1) of the *Marriage Act* (Ch 280) which allows customary marriages to take place 'in accordance with the custom prevailing in the tribe or group to which the parties or either of them belong or belongs'. Thus, in the passage previously quoted from *Re Wagi Non and the Constitution Section 42(5)*,[40] Woods J stated plainly: 'I am not saying that a man cannot have several wives', but went on to insist that all the wives must be treated fairly and equally.

Against advocates of the practice, who rely on the Constitution's support for traditional customs, objections have come from women's groups, and other community and church groups, as well as from magistrates and judges dealing with

[38] At 49.

[39] For discussion, see for example O Jessep, 'The Governor-General's Wives—Polygamy and the Recognition of Customary Marriage in Papua New Guinea' (1993) 7 *Australian Journal of Family Law* 29. Analogous contemporary discussions in various African jurisdictions are referred to in several papers in J Eekelaar and T Nhlapo (eds), *The Changing Family—Family Forms and Family Law* (Hart, 1998).

[40] [1991] PNGLR 84, Woods J at 86–87.

the frequent financial and custody disputes, not to mention criminal assaults and murders (whether between spouses, or between co-wives) arising from polygamous arrangements.[41] Since 1996, private members' Bills designed to abolish or ban polygamy have been circulated on several occasions in parliament. The latest of these was prepared in 1998 on behalf of the current Speaker of the Parliament, Mr Bernard Narokobi. This draft Bill was publicly declared to be aiming to 'outlaw polygamy,'[42] and purported to extend the law of bigamy by making it equally applicable to parties to multiple customary marriages.[43] As with previous efforts, however, the 1998 Bill failed to attract much parliamentary support. Indeed, a parliamentary response on this issue is quite unlikely in the foreseeable future. This is due not only to the lack of unanimity on the question, and the fact that a number of current members of parliament have polygamous marriages, but also because a government trying to deal with mounting problems of social, economic and political instability (such as those currently facing Papua New Guinea) is unlikely to see family law reform as very high on its list of priorities.

In this context, it is interesting to note the recently published views of the South African Law Commission on the same issue.[44] The Commission declined to recommend the banning or outright prohibition of polygamy for a number of reasons. These included the alleged obsolescence of the practice of polygamous marriages, the impossibility of enforcing a direct ban against polygamy, the risk of encouraging a proliferation of informal unions as an alternative (with minimal legal protection for the women and children involved), and the undesirability of pre-empting possible constitutional challenges to such customary practices.[45] A final ground referred to was the danger of appearing to take sides against some particularly African family forms, while other emerging family forms such as cohabitation outside marriage and same-sex relationships were the focus of current public debate and controversy in South Africa.[46]

All of these points of view, among others, can also be found in the Papua New Guinean situation. For present purposes, however, I would like to focus on the

[41] Among the frequent references in the press, the Catholic Church of Papua New Guinea has recently called for 'a total ban on polygamy' (*PNG Post Courier*, 21 Apr 1999), and a National Court judge has called for legislation to punish husbands when co-wives are led to injure or kill one another (*PNG Post Courier*, 7 May 1999).

[42] See *The National*, 7 Sept 1998.

[43] See Marriage (Amendment) Bill 1998, amending s 57 of the *Marriage Act* (ch 280). Although the Bill was not proceeded with, it may be noted that the drafting of the Bill was quite ambiguous. In particular, the main prohibition against entering additional marriages, contained in a new sub-s (1A), was made subject to the existing sub-s (8). This latter subsection, however, purports to protect parties to multiple customary marriages from the operation of the section, where the marriages are in accordance with the relevant custom applicable to each marriage. Consequently, the overall effect of the proposed amendment was far from clear.

[44] South African Law Commission, *Report on Customary Marriages* (Project 90, Pretoria, Aug 1998). See also *Recognition of Customary Marriages Act 120 of 1998* (South Africa), yet to be proclaimed; and T Nhlapo, 'African family law under an undecided constitution: The challenge for law reform in South Africa', in J Eekelaar and T Nhlapo (eds), *The Changing Family—Family Forms and Family Law* (Hart Publishing, 1998), pp 617–34.

[45] South African Law Commission, n 44, paras 6.1.13–6.1.23.

[46] *Ibid.*, para 6.1.24.

reference by the South African Law Commission to the possibility of a constitutional challenge to the customary practice of polygamy.[47] It is interesting to speculate on whether (assuming the absence of any parliamentary legislative initiative), a court in Papua New Guinea might be faced with a constitutional or other statutory objection to some aspect of customary polygamous marriage, based upon one or more of the arguments considered in *Re Willingal* (Miriam's case) and earlier cases. Such a claim might conceivably be ventilated in any legal context in which a party's rights or responsibilities will vary according to whether the marriage is legally valid or not (such as spousal maintenance, adoption, property claims, inheritance, fatal accidents, and so on). The contending party, then, could be a husband, a wife, a relative, an insurance company, or anyone else with an interest in the result of the litigation. Some years ago, it may be noted, a Task Force of the PNG Law Reform Commission expressed the view that the custom of polygamy was 'unconstitutional', because in practice the freedom to have more than one spouse was only extended to males. Rather than argue for a similar liberty to be extended to females, however, the Task Force concluded that parliament should insist on monogamy for everyone.[48]

In its claim that polygamy was unconstitutional, the Task Force presumably had in mind the prohibition on gender discrimination contained in section 55 of the Constitution, which was also one of the grounds for the decision in *Re Willingal*. While it is not necessary to go into the point here, there are in fact some complex problems of interpretation involved in applying section 55 to a customary practice which appears to be justified by a statute of pre-Independence origin (such as the *Marriage Act*, originally enacted in 1963).[49] Leaving aside these complications, it is nevertheless obvious that arguments based on some of the alternative grounds canvassed above might just as easily come to the fore—for instance, that customary expectations and practices relating to polygamy in a particular Papua New Guinean community might be inconsistent with other rights guaranteed to women by the Constitution, or might produce injustice or be contrary to the public interest (thereby infringing the terms of section 3 of the *Customs Recognition Act*).

A court's decision to invalidate, on any of the grounds mentioned, a particular polygamous marriage (that is, by denying recognition and enforcement to the relevant custom) might well be dependent upon the precise legal context in which

[47] *Ibid.*, paras 6.1.7–6.1.10, 6.1.21–6.1.23; and Nhlapo, n 44.

[48] PNG Law Reform Commission, Task Force on Family Law Reform, Press Release, 20 June 1990.

[49] For example, sub-s (3) of s 55 states that the prohibition on discrimination contained in sub-s (1) 'does not affect the operation of a pre-Independence law'. See Jessep, n 39, pp 38–39. As to the issue of polygamy and discrimination, see South African Law Commission, n 44, paras 6.1.5–6.1.12, 6.1.21–6.1.23. See also F Kaganas and C Murray, 'Law, Women and the Family: The Question of Polygyny in a New South Africa' (1991) *Acta Juridica* 116–34; K Becker and M Hinz, *Marriage and Customary Law in Namibia* (Namibia Papers Working Documents No 30, Centre for Applied Social Sciences, 1995), pp 117–19; and T Bennett, *Human Rights and African Customary Law under the South African Constitution* (Juta, 1995), pp 120–21.

the issue arose, as well as the nature of the evidence adduced in the instant case.[50] That is to say, the decision would not automatically or inevitably spell invalidity for polygamous marriages in general. Such a general consequence would most likely require legislative intervention.[51] On the other hand, the presence of a single National Court decision concerning a polygamous marriage, in which arguments of this sort were successful, might well provide an impetus for further developments by encouraging other litigants to mount similar actions (or present similar defences).

According to reports,[52] judges in South Africa, dealing with cases in which aspects of custom were being challenged on the basis of gender discrimination, have so far appeared reluctant to use their new Constitution as a blunt instrument with which to attack custom. By contrast, in Papua New Guinea the Constitution has now been in force for twenty-five years, and at least in the last decade some National Court judges have begun to make use of the Constitution as a weapon to invalidate some elements of customary family law. As in South Africa, it is likely that the real challenges in Papua New Guinea are yet to come, and in this respect *Re Willingal* (Miriam's case) may stand as a signpost for the future.

[50] For a relevant South African discussion of questions of evidence of customary law, see C Himonga and C Bosch, 'The Application of African Customary Law under the Constitution of South Africa: Problem Solved or Just Beginning?' (2000) 117 *South African Law Journal* 306.

[51] On the difficulties inherent in any legislative attempt to ban or discourage polygamy, see Jessep, n 39, pp 40–41.

[52] See Nhlapo, n 44; see also Fishbayn, n 3.

PART III

Pressures

23

Law Reform by Frozen Chook: Family Law Reform for the New Millennium?

Reg Graycar*

INTRODUCTION

The purpose of this discussion is to show just how limited our sense of the contours of what we loosely call 'family law' is, and how that limited framework affects (and impedes) how we talk about family law, what we teach about family law, what the community understands it to be and what happens when we set about undertaking law 'reform' in this field.

I will briefly address some of the structural and legislative limits of our family law discourses (most particularly, in Australia, the Australian Constitution), then look at examples of laws which, while they significantly impact on family relationships, have traditionally not been considered to fall within the field of 'family law'. I will refer to recent law reforms in New South Wales that extend a number of legal rights to lesbians, gay men and others in close interpersonal relationships as examples of ways in which the scope of family law is being changed. But my main concern is with the prevalence of ill-informed myths and distorted 'data' about family law and the role this plays in impeding effective debate, discussion and, ultimately, law reform in this country. I will draw on some recurring stories (perhaps they should better be described as 'fairytales' or 'myths and legends') and relate these to several 'law reforms' or proposals that I have been involved with over the past few years. My purpose in telling these stories, which are regularly seen and heard in national media, is to ponder why they have so much more resonance with politicians than does research information or official government statistical data (which very frequently contradicts these stories). I suggest that this is at least in part attributable to the gendered nature of the discourses that characterise federal or heterosexual family law.

I shall start by asking 'What is family law?' then explain how I will be using that term in this discussion.

* Commissioner, New South Wales Law Reform Commission, Australia. This article was first published in (2001) 21 *Oxford Journal of Legal Studies* 219, and has been reprinted here with the permission of Oxford University Press.

WHAT IS FAMILY LAW?

When we put the words 'family' and 'law' together, we tend to think of that area of law we call 'family law'. But, of course, family law is a very small part of the legal framework that structures important aspects of our lives: family law might more accurately be described as the law that governs the breakdown of marital and (only in very limited cases) marriage-like relationships.

The Constitution plays a key role in this. Drawn up over a century ago by the 'founding fathers',[1] the Constitution reflects their view that most issues that affect families are not matters of national importance. For the purpose of delineating the federal parliament's power to legislate, 'family law' was limited to marriage, divorce and related children's issues,[2] and this continued to be the scope of federal family law-making power in the year 2000.[3] The Constitution's vision of the family is not only limited by subject matter: its conception of family was (and remains) Anglocentric, nuclear, male-focused and heteronormative. To keep this clear, in the remainder of my discussion I shall refer to federal family law as 'marriage and divorce law'.

Aside from excluding large proportions of the Australian community, there is another fairly obvious gap: generally speaking, family law is not concerned with the regulation of subsisting domestic arrangements.[4] Rather, it is concerned much more with the breakdown of those arrangements and the consequences of that.

[1] For a discussion of how the place of family law in the Constitution was perceived by the 'founding fathers' (who, as their name indicates, were all (Anglo) men), see Michael Coper, *Encounters with the Australian Constitution* (CCH, 1987), pp 198–99. Helen Irving has argued that if women had been involved in drafting the Constitution, they may have had different priorities in relation to what were matters of national importance: see Helen Irving, 'A Gendered Constitution? Women, Federation and Heads of Power' (1994) 24 *University of Western Australia Law Review* 186 at 192–94.

[2] See Constitution, ss 51(xxi) and (xxii). S 51(xxi) provides the Commonwealth with power to legislate with respect to marriage, while s 51(xxii) refers to 'divorce and matrimonial causes; and in relation thereto, parental rights, and the custody and guardianship of infants'.

[3] Chief Justice Alastair Nicholson, 'Family Law in Australia: Bargaining in the Shadow of the Constitution' (2000) 55 *Family Matters* 22; Chief Justice Alastair Nicholson and Margaret Harrison, 'Experiences of the Family Court of Australia: The First 25 Years' (2000) 24 *Melbourne University Law Review* 756. The only real change is that the power to make laws with respect to ex-nuptial children was referred by the states (all except Western Australia) to the Commonwealth, between 1986 and 1990, under s 51(xxxvii) of the Constitution, so Pt VII of the *Family Law Act* 1975 (Cth) (the part dealing with children) now applies to all children (other than in Western Australia) irrespective of the marital status of their parents: *Commonwealth Powers (Family Law—Children) Act* 1986 (NSW); *Commonwealth Powers (Family Law—Children) Act* 1990 (Qld); *Commonwealth Powers (Family Law) Act* 1986 (SA); *Commonwealth Powers (Family Law) Act* 1987 (Tas); *Commonwealth Powers (Family Law—Children) Act* 1986 (Vic).

[4] There are some rare exceptions: see, for example, the decision in *Eliades v Eliades* (1981) FLC ¶91–022, where the Family Court made an order for spouse maintenance during the course of a marriage. But compare the comment of Mason CJ, Deane and Toohey JJ in *R v L* (the 'rape in marriage' case): 'Whatever the scope of the power of the Parliament to make laws with respect to marriage, it is apparent that the Commonwealth Act [the *Family Law Act* 1975 (Cth)] does not attempt comprehensively to regulate the rights and obligations of the parties to a marriage and in particular says nothing to express or imply an obligation to consent to sexual intercourse by a party to a marriage.' (1991) 174 CLR 379 at 386 (citations omitted).

So, in speaking of 'family law', we are often talking only about marriage, divorce and its consequences. There are two obvious problems with this: first, it fails to take into account the myriad of laws that regulate many aspects of our family lives and relationships and, secondly, not everyone is married (or a child of a marriage).

Professor Carol Smart has illustrated the second point very effectively by noting that in the United Kingdom (and the same is true in Australia and, I imagine, numerous other countries), on most official forms, we are asked to nominate single, married, divorced or separated, or widowed.[5]

> All of these categories, save single, automatically presume heterosexuality. All assume that domestic arrangements gravitate around a sexual relationship rather than, for example, care or companionship . . . [T]he central organising principle of these categories is marriage and only marriage. Thus people are assumed inevitably to be in a state of pre-marriage, marriage, or post-marriage.[6]

One need only look briefly at a few examples to see how complex and widespread is the legal regulation of family relationships.[7] Our tax system, while notionally based on the individual as the unit of taxation, has many aspects that are based on family relationships,[8] while the social security system is premised on ideas about who should support whom.[9] Our family relationships are also deeply implicated in our industrial or labour laws, for example, through the determination of the extent to which childbirth, child rearing and caring for family members are recognised and supported as more than private responsibilities.[10]

In a recent discussion paper, the Law Commission of Canada noted that a survey undertaken for the Commission revealed that, leaving aside tax laws, terms

[5] Carol Smart, 'Stories of Family Life: Cohabitation, Marriage and Social Change' (2000) 17 *Canadian Journal of Family Law* 20 at 23.

[6] *Ibid.*

[7] There has also been considerable attention to the broader question of what constitutes a 'family' in law: see, for example, Martha Minow, 'Redefining Families: Who's In and Who's Out?' (1991) 62 *University of Colorado Law Review* 269 and 'All in the Family & in all Families: Membership, Loving, and Owing' (1993) 95 *West Virginia Law Review* 275. In 1999 the House of Lords had to decide whether a same-sex partner was a member of the other partner's family for the purpose of the *Rent Act* 1977 (UK) c 42: *Fitzpatrick v Sterling Housing Association Ltd* [1999] 4 All ER 705; see further below n 29.

[8] See Miranda Stewart, 'Domesticating Tax Reform: The Family in Australian Tax and Transfer Law' (1999) 21 *Sydney Law Review* 453; Patricia Apps, 'Tax Reform, Ideology and Gender' (1999) 21 *Sydney Law Review* 437; Claire Young, 'Taxing Times for Women: Feminism Confronts Tax Policy' (1999) 21 *Sydney Law Review* 487.

[9] See Bettina Cass, 'Gender in Australia's Restructuring Labour Market and Welfare State', in Anne Edwards and Susan Magarey (eds), *Women in a Restructuring Australia: Work and Welfare* (Allen & Unwin, 1995), p 38 and Lois Bryson, 'Two Welfare States: One for Women, One for Men', in Anne Edwards and Susan Magarey (eds), *Women in a Restructuring Australia: Work and Welfare* (Allen & Unwin, 1995), p 60.

[10] Therese Macdermott, 'Who's Rocking the Cradle?' (1996) 21 *Alternative Law Journal* 207. In an analogous discussion of women's caring responsibilities in the context of changes to parenting laws brought about by the *Children Act* 1989 (UK) c 41, Carol Smart has described how, while women care for their children, men often care about their children. She points out the consequences this has for the rhetoric that often accompanies disputes about responsibility for children after divorce and separation: see Carol Smart, 'Losing the Struggle for Another Voice: The Case of Family Law' (1995) 18 *Dalhousie Law Journal* 173.

dealing with close personal relationships featured in one way or another in some 1800 statutory sections of federal Canadian law.[11] The Commission commented that:

> [I]n every case, the law identifies a close personal relationship by using concepts that are associated with the idea of family, and more particularly with the idea of marriage. Second, the policy objective behind the use of words relating to family and marriage is different in each case.[12]

As the Commission noted, recent trends toward recognising the relationships have added them to marriage by describing them as 'marriage-like' without reconsidering the underlying policies—that is, by treating marriage[13] as the unquestioned benchmark.[14] But the analogy approach has reached its use-by date. My argument is that it is now time to rethink why certain legal consequences attach to certain forms of relationships, but not to others.

This attention to the ways in which family relationships are mediated and constructed through such diverse areas of law as evidence, tax and (in New South Wales) judges' pensions,[15] to give a few disparate examples, is not unprecedented. In their 1972 Australian family law text, Henry Finlay and Alastair Bissett-Johnson included a chapter on the legal consequences of marriage, dealing with such issues as interspousal immunity, contractual capacity, competence and compellability in evidence law.[16] Given the effect marriage had on women's legal capacity (as Blackstone told us, 'on marriage husband and wife are one person in law' and the husband is that one),[17] it is not surprising that these aspects of the legal consequences of marriage were seen as a key element of family law. An analogous development has been the way that the removal of many of the restrictions has been used in helping to obscure what the Law Commission of Canada has described as the 'heritage of inequality' that underpins family law:

> [C]lose personal relationships between men and women have been marked by an unequal distribution of power . . . In modernizing policies and programmes, this heritage of inequality cannot be ignored.[18]

[11] Law Commission of Canada, *Recognizing and Supporting Close Personal Relationships between Adults*, Discussion Paper (LCC, 2000), p 8.

[12] *Ibid.*, pp 8–9.

[13] A clear analogy is the way in which formal equality discourses treat men as the benchmark—women are either the same as men or different from men, but the standard or measure remains unquestioned: see Catharine MacKinnon, *Feminism Unmodified: Discourses on Life and Law* (Harvard University Press, 1987) especially ch 2, 'Difference and dominance: On sex discrimination'.

[14] The *Judges' Pensions Act* 1953 (NSW) was one of those Acts amended by the *Property (Relationships) Legislation Amendment Act* 1999 (NSW) discussed below at nn 24–25 and accompanying text.

[15] HA Finlay and A Bissett-Johnson, *Family Law in Australia* (Butterworths, 1972), ch 5.

[16] Sir William Blackstone, *Commentaries on the Laws of England* (first published 1765–69, 21st edn, 1844), vol 1, 442. As Blackstone put it, 'the very being of legal existence of the woman is suspended during the marriage': *ibid.* For a discussion of the common law and married women, see Lee Holcombe, *Wives and Property: Reform of the Married Women's Property Law Act in Nineteenth-Century England* (University of Toronto Press, 1983), p 18.

[17] Law Commission of Canada, n 11, p 14.

[18] I am indebted to Professor Roderick MacDonald for this insight.

Yet one of the paradoxes of marriage and divorce law is that this inequality is rarely, if ever, expressly mentioned. This absence helps to maintain the myth of formal equality that underpins family law discourses and debates.

Critical and feminist family law scholars such as Katherine O'Donovan,[19] Michael Freeman,[20] Carol Smart,[21] Frances Olsen[22] and Martha Fineman[23] have raised some of these concerns, and in particular have highlighted how law regulates and constructs family relationships and how 'privacy discourses' have masked abuses of power and, literally, physical abuse within the family for years. Yet marriage and divorce law has generally remained a closed system: while the better books (and law school courses) now raise issues of violence in family relationships as part of 'family law', it is still uncommon to see a family law course that deals broadly with legal modes of regulating subsisting familial relationships rather than merely with the law of marriage, divorce and what are often called 'ancillary' matters (that is, property and children).

A NEW 'FAMILY LAW'?

But something very dramatic has been happening to family law. Lesbian and gay legal scholars have challenged their exclusion. The slogan 'we are family' has been heard not only on the streets and in the marches, but also in law journals and in the courts. The lesbian and gay law reform programme has highlighted the need to address the multiple forms of regulation that constitute family law—that is, the constellation of laws and practices that construct, privilege or devalue, impact upon, recognise or ignore the variety of relationships in which people live their lives. In 1999, the New South Wales parliament passed a law that amended some twenty pieces of legislation so that they apply to lesbians and gay men in cohabiting relationships, and a small number of Acts were changed so that they now apply to people living in 'domestic relationships'—that is, interdependent, non-couple caring relationships.[24] The laws in the first category include those dealing with property, death or injury, decision-making during incapacity and after death, and a number of miscellaneous statutes, such as the *Bail Act* 1978 (NSW) (which looks at who is affected by bail decisions) and the *Legal Aid Commission Act* 1979

[19] Katherine O'Donovan, *Sexual Divisions in Law* (Weidenfeld and Nicolson, 1985).

[20] M.D.A. Freeman, 'Towards a Critical Theory of Family Law' (1985) 38 *Current Legal Problems* 153.

[21] For an early example, see Carol Smart, 'Marriage, Divorce, and Women's Economic Dependency: A Discussion of the Politics of Private Maintenance', in Michael Freeman (ed), *The State, the Law, and the Family: Critical Perspectives* (Tavistock, 1984), p 9.

[22] Frances Olsen, 'The Family and the Market: A Study of Ideology and Legal Reform' (1983) 96 *Harvard Law Review* 1497; Frances Olsen, 'The Myth of State Intervention in the Family' (1985) 18 *University of Michigan Journal of Law Reform* 835.

[23] Martha Fineman, 'What Place for Family Privacy?' (1999) 67 *George Washington Law Review* 1207.

[24] *Property (Relationships) Legislation Amendment Act* 1999 (NSW). Six laws were amended to apply to 'domestic relationships': *Bail Act* 1978 (NSW); *Coroners Act* 1980 (NSW); *De Facto Relationships Act* 1984 (NSW); *District Court Act* 1973 (NSW); *Duties Act* 1997 (NSW); *Family Provision Act* 1982 (NSW).

(NSW) (which determines whose income and assets are taken into account under the means test for legal aid).[25] Similarly, laws passed in other jurisdictions traverse a wide range of areas of law. For example, in Ontario the law implementing the 1999 decision (grudgingly, if its title is anything to go by) of the Supreme Court of Canada in *M v H*[26] amended some 67 laws,[27] and the federal Canadian legislation which followed in 2000 amended 68 laws.[28] The statute that gave citizens of the US state of Vermont the right to enter into 'civil unions', passed in April 2000, extended every state law that currently applies to married couples to those in civil unions.[29]

THE BRIDE WORE PINK . . . TWICE

The major initiative for the 1999 New South Wales law reforms came from the community-based Gay and Lesbian Rights lobby. In 1993 that group published a draft discussion paper called 'The Bride Wore Pink', which formed the basis of consultation in the gay and lesbian communities.[30]

'The Bride Wore Pink' was a pioneering Australian law reform document. It raised questions about broad issues such as why certain rights and obligations attach to or flow from marriage (and, in some cases, other relationships). The overarching principle guiding 'The Bride Wore Pink' was that the basis for relationship recognition should be purposive.[31] Simply put, the kinds of relationships that laws should regulate ought to depend upon the purpose of the law in question. As these purposes vary, so should the type of recognition and obligation. For example, some laws that recognise relationships do so because of financial dependence or interdependence between the partners, while others are more con-

[25] A full list of those acts amended can be found in *Property (Relationships) Legislation Amendment Act* 1999 (NSW) sch 1, 2. See also the appendix to Reg Graycar and Jenni Millbank, 'The Bride Wore Pink . . . To the *Property (Relationships) Legislation Amendment Act* 1999: Relationships Law Reform in New South Wales' (2000) 17 *Canadian Journal of Family Law* 227.

[26] [1999] 2 SCR 3; 171 DLR (4th) 577. In that case the Supreme Court of Canada (Lamer CJ, L'Heureux-Dubé, Cory, McLachlin, Iacobucci, Major, Bastarache and Binnie JJ, Gonthier dissenting) held that s 29 of Ontario's *Family Law Act*, RSO 1990, c F.3 violated s 15(1) of the Canadian Charter of Rights and Freedoms, pt I of the *Constitution Act* 1982, being sch B to the *Canada Act* 1982 (UK) c 11, because the definition of spouse included unmarried opposite sex couples living in 'conjugal relationships' but not same-sex couples in such relationships. Significantly, the court directed the province of Ontario to ensure that its legislation complied with the Charter, and gave the province six months to do so, setting a deadline of 20 Nov 1999.

[27] *Amendments Because of the Supreme Court of Canada Decision in M. v H. Act*, 1999, SC 1999, c 6, (Family Law Act amendments in force 20 Nov 1999; fully in force 1 Mar 2000).

[28] *Modernization of Benefits and Obligations Act*, SC 2000, c 12.

[29] *An Act Relating to Civil Unions*, Pub L No 91, 2000 Vt Laws (2000) (in force 1 July 2000). While there has been no comparable legislative change in England, the House of Lords decided in late 1999 that a same-sex partner was a member of the other partner's family for the purpose of the *Rent Act* 1977 (UK) c 42: *Fitzpatrick v Sterling Housing Association Ltd* [1999] 4 All ER 705 (Lords Slynn, Nicholls and Clyde, Lords Hutton and Hobhouse dissenting).

[30] The paper is reproduced in (1993) 3 *Australian Gay and Lesbian Law Journal* 67.

[31] This is discussed in more detail in Graycar and Millbank, 'The Bride Wore Pink', n 25, pp 254–61.

cerned with emotional connection.[32] Live-in sexual relationships are not the only ones to give rise to financial or emotional ties, but they are the relationships most likely to do so. It was therefore proposed that live-in partner relationship recognition should be broad-based and presumptive—that is, it should apply unless excluded, rather than require people to opt in.[33] Other forms of close relationships may give rise to emotional or financial ties, but those situations may not be so predictable, nor as widespread, and therefore statutory coverage might be more limited.

After a series of consultations, the Gay and Lesbian Rights Lobby recommended in 1994, in a revised edition, that legal recognition in New South Wales should simultaneously and distinctly be accorded to same-sex couple relationships, as well as to other forms of interdependent relationships, and that the New South Wales Law Reform Commission (NSWLRC) should be asked to consider the broader questions over a longer time frame.[34] This, then, is basically what has happened and this was the position in 2000.[35]

The outcome, then, is that New South Wales law now recognises same-sex couples in the same way as married or heterosexual non-married couples for a number of legal purposes. Additionally, others who are not couples but are in defined 'domestic relationships' have been granted a more limited range of rights and obligations under some (but not as many) New South Wales state laws.[36] To this extent, New South Wales joins only with the Australian Capital Territory

[32] For example, the *Anatomy Act* 1977 (NSW), *Human Tissue Act* 1983 (NSW) and *Coroners Act* 1980 (NSW) are about respecting a partner's wishes regarding a deceased person. The *Guardianship Act* 1987 (NSW), s 33A assumes that a partner in a 'close and continuing' relationship is the one best placed to know the incapacitated person's wishes.

[33] For a more detailed discussion of this, see Graycar and Millbank, 'The Bride Wore Pink', n 25, pp 254–61.

[34] Lesbian and Gay Legal Rights Service, *The Bride Wore Pink—Legal Recognition of Our Relationships: A Discussion Paper*, 2nd edn (Lesbian and Gay Legal Rights Service, 1994) <www.rainbow.net.au/~glrl/The_Bride_Wore_Pink.htm> at 31 Dec 2000 (copy on file with author). All websites cited in this article are correct as at 31 Dec 2000. Copies of all internet sources are on file with the author.

[35] The NSWLRC was asked by the Attorney-General to undertake a review of the *Property Relationships Act* 1984 (NSW) on 6 Sept 1999. The terms of reference, a preliminary consultation paper and papers from a seminar held by the Commission in July 1999 are all available from the Commission's web page: NSWLRC, Digest of Law Reform Commission References: Reference 101—Relationships and the Law (2000) <www.lawlink.nsw.gov.au/lrc.nsf/pages/digest.101>; NSWLRC, Relationships and the Law: Review of the Property (Relationships) Act 1984, Preliminary Paper (2000) <www.lawlink.nsw.gov.au/nswlrc.nsf/pages/paperproperty>; Jeff Shaw QC, 'Opening Address' (Address presented at the Discussion Forum on Relationships and the Law, Sydney, 7 July 2000) <www.lawlink.nsw.gov.au/lrc.nsf/pages/seminar01.03>; Justice Claire L'Heureux-Dubé, 'Relationship Recognition: The Search for Equality' (Paper presented at the Discussion Forum on Relationships and the Law, Sydney, 7 July 2000) <http://www.lawlink.nsw.gov.au/lrc.nsf/pages/seminar01.01>; Hayley Katzen, Seminar Paper (Paper presented at the Discussion Forum on Relationships and the Law, Sydney, 7 July 2000) <http://www.lawlink.nsw.gov.au/lrc.nsf/pages/seminar01.02>; Owen Jessep, 'Financial Adjustment in Domestic Relationships in NSW: Some Problems of Interpretation' (Paper presented at the Discussion Forum on Relationships and the Law, Sydney, 7 July 2000) <http://www.lawlink.nsw.gov.au/lrc.nsf/pages/seminar01.04>.

[36] Details of all the amending legislation are available in an appendix to Graycar and Millbank, 'The Bride Wore Pink', n 25, pp 279–82.

(ACT) in moving beyond the couple in a sexual relationship as the unit upon which state laws and policies operate.[37] While this recognition of close personal relationships is very limited (more so than in the ACT, where the domestic partners need not live together), it is an extremely significant step in moving away from the sexual relationship as the key determinant of 'family'. Some academic commentators have recommended various forms of moving beyond the 'who's sleeping with whom' approach to family[38] but the New South Wales law, while limited, is still one of the first to be implemented. It is therefore an important step in the process of rethinking some of the underlying questions about the law's response to the variety of relationships in a way that is very timely, not only for the work of the New South Wales Law Reform Commission, but for the broader project of rethinking the contours of 'family law'.

We might think, then, that family law (not just as the law of marriage and divorce) is now the site of a much richer, more nuanced discourse but, as will become apparent, this is not the case in the federal, heterosexual marriage and divorce law arena. Some stories will illustrate this.

THE STORIES

In August 1999, *The Australian* published in its weekend magazine a cover story about the Family Court in which Lone Fathers' Association spokesperson Barry Williams gave us some insight into that organisation's sources of data on family law and social policy issues. He was described as believing that:

> official statistics on family violence . . . used by the Family Court, academia, law societies and other professional bodies, are incorrect. He maintains, for example, that men and women are equally violent. 'My ex-wife, for example, once chucked a frozen chook at me,' he says by way of illustration.[39]

On national television in May 2000, the same spokesperson claimed that 83 per cent of men were 'denied access to their children'.[40] In the same month, in a Sunday newspaper, the beliefs of the organisation were summarised:

> The group Lone Fathers believes such killings [domestic homicides] are symptomatic of the despair many divorced fathers feel at the loss of contact with their children,

[37] *Domestic Relationships Act* 1994 (ACT).

[38] For example, Professor Martha Fineman some years ago advocated a redefinition of 'family unit' away from what she called the 'sexual family' to the mother–child dyad: Martha Fineman, *The Neutered Mother, the Sexual Family and Other Twentieth Century Tragedies* (Routledge, 1995), ch 9. And Michael Freeman has also drawn on her notion (and critique) of the sexual family to argue that we omit elders from our sense of family, despite resort to notions of 'community care' (which is another expression for looking after elders within families): Michael Freeman, 'Family Values and Family Justice' (1997) 50 *Current Legal Problems* 315 at 325.

[39] Miriam Cosic, 'Uncivil War', *The Australian Magazine* (Sydney), 21–22 Aug 1999, pp 15, 20.

[40] Mike Munro (Interviewer) and Warwick Adderley (Producer), 'Child support', *A Current Affair*, Channel 9, 11 May 2000.

and accuses the Family Court of discriminating against men, with custody awarded to mothers in 83 per cent of contested cases.[41]

Also in May 2000 (the month of the federal Budget, which included an announcement of proposed changes to the Child Support Scheme),[42] media commentator and member of the recently established Family Law Pathways Advisory Council, Bettina Arndt, said: 'There's also powerful evidence of the appalling legacy of the green light given by the Family Court to lone mothers who decide to move children away from their fathers.'[43]

THE LAW REFORM DEBATES

The Family Law Reform Act 1995 (Cth)

In the past few years, I have been either directly involved with or have observed a number of different sets of 'family law reform' initiatives or proposals, and I will refer briefly to each of these. The first—and the one with which I have had most involvement—is the passage of the *Family Law Reform Act* 1995 (Cth), which made significant changes to Part VII of the *Family Law Act* 1975 (Cth), the part that deals with children's issues.[44]

A major stated aim of the reforms was to create a new normative standard of shared parenting for separated couples.[45] Apparently, it was believed that this might change the long-standing practice of one parent assuming day-to-day

[41] Sue Williams, 'A casualty of parents at war: A mother speaks out about the tragedy of ex-partner who took her little boy's life', *Sun Herald* (Sydney), 28 May 2000, pp 104, 105.

[42] Commonwealth Department of Family and Community Services, Budget 2000–2001 'What's new what's different' (2000), www.facs.gov.au/Internet/FaCSInternet.nsf/aboutfacs/budget/budget2000-wnwd_e.htm.

[43] Bettina Arndt, 'The child exchange rate', *Sydney Morning Herald* (Sydney), 18 May 2000, p 19. (This article was also published in *The Age* on the same day: Bettina Arndt, 'Bring home benefits for distant dads', *The Age* (Melbourne), 18 May 2000, p 15.) The inference is that the Family Court allows mothers to move without reason to do so; the reality, of course, is quite different. About half of all custodial parents who seek to relocate with their children are prevented by the court from doing so: see Helen Rhoades, Reg Graycar and Margaret Harrison, *The Family Law Reform Act 1995: The First Three Years* (University of Sydney/Family Court of Australia, 2000), ch 5.

[44] For an interim report of an Australian Research Council-funded research study of the impact of these changes, see Helen Rhoades, Reg Graycar and Margaret Harrison, *The Family Law Reform Act 1995: Can Changing Legislation Change Legal Culture, Legal Practice and Community Expectations?, Interim Report* (1999).

[45] This is not to suggest that there was a clear set of aims, but rather that a set of normative ideas underpinned the exercise. For a good example of the contemporaneous discourses, see the discussion in the House of Representatives: Commonwealth Parliamentary Debates, House of Representatives, 8 Nov 1994, 2842 (Daryl Williams); Commonwealth, Parliamentary Debates, House of Representatives, 21 Nov 1995, 3303–4 (Peter Duncan). See also Richard Chisholm, 'Assessing the impact of the *Family Law Reform Act* 1995' (1996) 10 *Australian Journal of Family Law* 177; Margaret Harrison and Regina Graycar, 'The *Family Law Reform Act*: Metamorphosis or more of the same?' (1997) 11 *Australian Journal of Family Law* 327; Helen Rhoades, 'Child law reforms in Australia—a shifting landscape' (2000) 12 *Child and Family Law Quarterly* 117.

responsibility for the children after parents separate.[46] While shared parental responsibility is a laudable aim, what is most significant about the Act, self-consciously labelled a 'Reform' Act, is that, unlike most exercises in law reform, it did not address any particular problem or respond to some identified 'mischief' that apparently flowed from the practice of children being raised predominantly by one parent.[47]

So, if the Part VII reforms were not a legislative response to an identified problem or to research data about what is in the best interests of children,[48] where did they come from? I suggest that they were a response to the anecdotes constantly recounted to politicians: the stories of aggrieved non-custodial fathers who told (and continue to tell) bitter tales of gender bias against them by the legal system, and particularly by the Family Court. The fathers' rights groups have been remarkably successful in capturing the attention of the politicians. This motivation for the reforms is obvious from the government's Second Reading speech,[49] and from the contemporaneous parliamentary debates where there are numerous references to the hope that a shared parenting law would alleviate the distress of non-custodial parents, the majority of whom are fathers.[50] The fathers' groups persistently claim that the court is 'biased' against them.[51] But their claims had (and have) no empirical support: the literature and the available studies show that the Family Court makes orders (in contested cases) in favour of fathers at twice the rate of those made by consent.[52] The fathers' anecdotes that so captured the attention of the politicians (and I should emphasise that this is a non-party political issue: the legislation was introduced by the previous Labor government) invoked the discourses of 'victimhood' and 'formal equality'[53] in much the same

[46] The law prior to the *'Reform' Act* had provided that, in the absence of a contrary order, both parties had joint custody and each had guardianship: *Family Law Act* 1975 (Cth) s 61. Nevertheless, the more common practice was (and remains) for the children to live with their mothers, but have contact with their (non-resident) fathers.

[47] This is discussed in more detail in Helen Rhoades, 'Posing as Reform: The Case of the *Family Law Reform Act*' (2000) 14 *Australian Journal of Family Law* 142.

[48] For a review of the research data on the outcomes for children after divorce and separation, see Bryan Rodgers and Jan Pryor, *Divorce and Separation: The Outcomes for Children* (Joseph Rowntree, 1998). See generally *ibid.*, pp 150–53.

[49] Commonwealth Parliamentary Debates, House of Representatives, 8 Nov 1994, 2757 (Peter Duncan).

[50] See, for example, Commonwealth Parliamentary Debates, House of Representatives, 21 Nov 1995, 3303–6 (Peter Duncan, Philip Ruddock).

[51] See Miranda Kaye and Julia Tolmie, 'Fathers' Rights Groups in Australia and their Engagement with Issues in Family Law' (1998) 12 *Australian Journal of Family Law* 19, 35; Miranda Kaye and Julia Tolmie, 'Discoursing Dads: The Rhetorical Devices of Fathers' Rights Groups' (1998) 22 *Melbourne University Law Review* 162; Regina Graycar, 'Equal Rights versus Fathers' Rights: The Child Custody Debate in Australia', in Carol Smart and Selma Sevenhuijsen (eds), *Child Custody and the Politics of Gender* (Routledge, 1989), p 158.

[52] Sophy Bordow, 'Defended Custody Cases in the Family Court of Australia: Factors Influencing the Outcome' (1994) 8 *Australian Journal of Family Law* 252; Frank Horwill and Sophy Bordow, *The Outcome of Defended Custody Cases in the Family Court of Australia*, Research Report No 4 (Family Court of Australia, 1983); see also Janet Fife-Yeomans, 'Court to investigate custody "bias"', *The Australian*, 1 Oct 1998, p 3.

[53] Kaye and Tolmie, n 51.

way as happened in the lead-up to the *Children Act* 1989 reforms in the United Kingdom.[54]

This is not the place to outline the findings of the research on the implementation of the *Family Law Reform Act* 1995 (Cth) in any detail,[55] but it is fair to say that when measured against some of the stated aims, these reforms have been unsuccessful in bringing about a change in parenting practices. Moreover, there have been some very serious outcomes that endanger children and their carers.[56] Not least, contrary to the stated aim of having parents agree about parenting issues, there has been a considerable increase in litigation[57] and, in particular, in the area of contravention applications, an area to which I will return shortly.

'Equal' Shares: The Matrimonial Property 'Debate'

A second example of a 'family law reform' initiative is the reform of matrimonial property laws.[58] In 1999 the federal Attorney-General's Department released a discussion paper that relied extensively upon discourses of formal equality to make recommendations for reform that were (judging from the submissions received in response) almost universally considered to be disadvantageous to women and the children in their care.[59] My interest for these purposes is not with the detail of the proposals,[60] but with how the underlying rhetoric in the paper drew upon

[54] Jeremy Roche, 'The *Children Act* 1989: Once a Parent always a Parent?' [1991] *Journal of Social Welfare and Family Law* 345 at 346, 355; Richard Collier, *Masculinity, Law and the Family* (Routledge, 1995), p 177; Arthur Baker and Peter Townsend, 'Post-divorce Parenting—Rethinking Shared Residence' (1996) 8 *Child and Family Law Quarterly* 217; Carol Smart and Bren Neale, *Family Fragments?* (Polity Press, 1999), pp 31–3f2.

[55] Preliminary findings can be found in Rhoades, Graycar and Harrison, *Interim Report*, n 44; and see the final report: Rhoades, Graycar and Harrison, *The First Three Years*, n 43.

[56] The clearest example is the reduction in the number of cases in which contact is denied at interim hearings in the context of allegations of violence, when compared with the constant (and much higher) rate of no-contact orders made at final hearings. This suggests that children are living in situations later held to be unsafe: see Rhoades, Graycar and Harrison, *Interim Report*, n 44, pp 59–61; Rhoades, Graycar and Harrison, *The First Three Years*, n 43, pp 78–81.

[57] Rhoades, Graycar and Harrison, *The First Three Years*, n 43, pp 100–01.

[58] For an extended discussion of some of the broad issues involved, see Regina Graycar, 'Matrimonial Property Law Reform and Equality for Women: Discourses in Discord?' (1995) 25 *Victoria University of Wellington Law Review* 9.

[59] Attorney-General's Department, Commonwealth, *Property and Family Law: Options for Change—A Discussion Paper* (AGPS, 1999).

[60] For some commentaries on the discussion paper, see Stephen Bourke, 'Matrimonial property law: A discussion of the reform options' (Address presented at the NSW Bar Association Public Forum: Property and Family Law, Options for Change, Sydney, 20 May 1999) www.familycourt.gov.au/papers/html/bourke.html; Chief Justice Alastair Nicholson, 'Proposed changes to property matters under the *Family Law Act*' (Address presented at the NSW Bar Association Public Forum: Property and Family Law, Options for Change, Sydney, 20 May 1999) www.familycourt.gov.au/papers/html/nicholson7.html; Family Court of Australia, *Response of the Family Court of Australia to the Discussion Paper 'Property and Family Law: Options for Change'* (1999) www.familycourt.gov.au/papers/html/propertysub.html; Reg Graycar, 'If it ain't broke, don't fix it: Matrimonial Property Law Reform and the Forgotten Majority', *Australian Family Law & Practice—Family Law News*, Report No 402 (17 Sept 1999), p 4.

some of the myths and stereotypes with which I am concerned. The paper asserted, for example, that the current system was subject to claims of 'bias' and that there had been considerable social change in the past twenty years (such as the increased proportion of women in paid work).[61] But let's not let the facts get in the way of a good story—what was not mentioned was the ever-increasing wage gap between women and men,[62] and the casual and part-time nature of much of the paid work that women do.[63]

The results of the Australian Divorce Transitions Project published in 2000, which revisited the mid-1980s work of the Australian Institute of Family Studies on the economic consequences of marriage breakdown,[64] show that women and the children in their care are still carrying the economic burden of marriage breakdown.[65]

The Family Law Amendment Bill 1999 (Cth)

In October 1999, at the same time as the government was conceding defeat in the face of enormous opposition to the matrimonial property proposals,[66] the Family

[61] Attorney-General's Department, Commonwealth, n 59. See especially ch 4, where it is stated in the concluding paragraph that the 'evidence supports the claim that, due to increased workforce participation, women are making an economic as well as nurturing contribution to marriage': p 32.

[62] Statistics from the Australian Bureau of Statistics (ABS) reveal that the difference in earnings between low- and high-income earners in full-time jobs has been increasing and that women's hourly earnings fell as a proportion of men's hourly earnings between 1994 and 1998: ABS, *Australian Social Trends 2000*, ABS Catalogue No 4102.0 (ABS, 2000), p 150.

[63] See ABS, *Casual Employment* [1999] (July) Labour Force Australia, ABS Catalogue No 6203.0, pp 3, 4–5.

[64] Peter McDonald (ed), *Settling Up: Property and Income Distribution on Divorce in Australia* (Prentice-Hall, 1986); Kathleen Funder, Margaret Harrison and Ruth Weston, *Settling Down: Pathways of Parents after Divorce* (Australian Institute of Family Studies, 1993).

[65] See Ruth Weston and Bruce Smyth, 'Financial living standards after divorce' (2000) 55 *Family Matters* 10. Their research, based on data from the Australian Divorce Transitions Project (ADTP), found that, of post-divorce households (including the categories of alone, sole parent, repartnered and partner with child), the most advantaged group comprised those living with a partner and no children. In the study, this group was almost solely constituted of men (presumably because it was women who were the primary caregivers of the children after separation). For a discussion of the ADTP, see Grania Sheehan, 'About the Institute's Australian Divorce Transitions Project' (2000) 55 *Family Matters* 6 at 6–7. The Australian Institute of Family Studies' findings are echoed in research recently published in England: see Alison Perry et al., *How Parents Cope Financially on Marriage Breakdown* (Family Policy Studies Centre, 2000). A summary of the findings is available at www.jrf.org.uk/knowledge/findings/socialpolicy/480.htm. For an insight into the outcomes for the clients of community legal centres, whose lives are very different from those who appear in the published law reports, see Nicola Seaman, *Fair Shares? Barriers to Equitable Property Settlements for Women* (National Association of Community Legal Centres, 1999). The reported cases often involve people with significant assets. For some high-profile examples, see *Ferraro v Ferraro* (1993) FLC ¶92–335 and *Whiteley v Whiteley* (1992) FLC ¶92–304.

[66] In a speech to the National Press Club on 27 Oct 1999, federal Attorney-General Daryl Williams said: '[T]he government released a discussion paper earlier this year seeking views on matrimonial property reform. We received a number of submissions and I thank all those who took the time to participate. Neither option in the discussion paper gained significant support.' He therefore announced the government's intention not to proceed, but to gather more comprehensive research and statistical information: Daryl Williams, 'Shaping family law for the future' (Speech presented at the National Press Club, Canberra, 27 Oct 1999) www.law.gov.au/ministers/attorney-general/articles/PressClub.html.

Law Amendment Bill 1999 (Cth) was introduced. As enacted, this legislation[67] makes several changes to the *Family Law Act* 1975 (Cth), two of which are particularly relevant for these purposes. First, the legislation establishes a punitive regime for dealing with breaches of contact orders/agreements.[68] Secondly, it provides a statutory basis for the recognition of private financial agreements.[69] In relation to contact enforcement, the dominant story underpinning the claimed need for tighter enforcement is the implacably hostile mother-caregiver,[70] who for no reason chooses to deny the father his rightful contact with his child (she's the one who also fabricates allegations of domestic violence or abuse for strategic purposes). Yet this woman has been clearly shown by the research to be a mythical creature.[71] In research which I conducted with Helen Rhoades and Margaret Harrison, one of our most striking findings when we interviewed parents was that most women who had experienced violence in their relationships still wanted their children to have some contact with their other parent, but what they sought (and often did not get) was an arrangement that ensured the safety of the children and themselves.[72] Our findings were that in the current climate of declining legal aid, women are being forced to make ill-advised agreements that prove unworkable and, not surprisingly, many of these break down. Instead of trying to make a more realistic arrangement, the contact parent is frequently bringing enforcement proceedings, well over half of which are considered by the court to be unfounded.[73] And, as for the private agreements, there is no evidence of any widespread community support for the enforceability of prenuptial agreements.[74]

67 *Family Law Amendment Act* 2000 (Cth). The Act came into effect on 27 Dec 2000.

68 *Family Law Amendment Act* 2000 (Cth) sch 1, though note the insertion, immediately prior to enactment, of s 70NG(1A).

69 The *Family Law Act* 1975 (Cth) also makes provision for binding arbitrations: ss 19D, 19E.

70 The term is used by Carol Smart and Bren Neale in 'Arguments against Virtue—must Contact be Enforced?' [1997] *Family Law* 332. In its report, *Child Contact Orders: Enforcement and Penalties* (1998), the Family Law Council, while identifying that the problems went wider than those experienced by contact parents, gave particular emphasis to many of these claims. For a commentary on the report, see Julia Tolmie, 'Child contact orders: Enforcement and penalties—the final report of the Family Law Council' (1998) 12 *Australian Journal of Family Law* 305.

71 See Marie Hume, 'Study of child sexual abuse allegations within the Family Court of Australia' in Family Court of Australia, *Enhancing Access to Justice—Family Court of Australia Second National Conference Papers* (1996); Thea Brown et al., 'Child abuse and the Family Court' (1998) *Trends and Issues in Crime and Criminal Justice*, Paper No 91, 2–3. See also Miranda Kaye and Julia Tolmie, '"Lollies at a children's party" and other Myths: Violence, Protection Orders and Fathers' Rights Groups' (1998) 10 *Current Issues in Criminal Justice* 52 at 55–56.

72 Rhoades, Graycar and Harrison, *The First Three Years*, n 43. Another issue rarely aired is the failure on the part of non-residence parents to exercise contact: this is discussed (briefly) by the Senate Legal and Constitutional Legislation Committee, Provisions of the Family Law Amendment Bill 1999 (1999) [2.18]–[2.19].

73 Rhoades, Graycar and Harrison, *The First Three Years*, n 43. A review of contravention judgments collected in 1999 for this research showed that 95% of the 110 applications received in that period were brought by non-resident parents alleging a failure by the resident parent to make the children available for contact. Sixty-two per cent of these applications were considered to be without merit, 45% were dismissed, and 17% were considered 'trivial' or of a 'minor nature' resulting in no penalty.

74 Senate Legal and Constitutional Legislation Committee, n 72. Only one of the submissions to the Committee gave unqualified support to binding pre-nuptial agreements: see [1.78]. For a detailed discussion of the proposed financial agreements, see Belinda Fehlberg and Bruce Smyth, 'Pre-nuptial agreements for Australia: Why not?' (2000) 14 *Australian Journal of Family Law* 80.

The Child Support Scheme[75]

In May 2000 the government announced plans in the Budget to change the Child Support Scheme again,[76] in particular to assist those men with second families.[77] It might be thought that this group is particularly financially disadvantaged. In fact, the Divorce Transitions data shows that the least disadvantaged of all groups post-divorce are men who have repartnered, including those living with children.[78] So, in an attempt to help these men, the disposable income of women and the children in their care will be reduced for the second time in two years.

Summary

To sum up, in a number of different contexts changes have either been made or proposed to 'marriage and divorce law' that respond to what are either purely anecdotal stories of problems with the law or rhetorical resort to notions like formal equality to suggest that previously recognised gendered disparities in outcomes for women and men have simply disappeared through resort to the rhetoric of 'social change'. In the remainder of this discussion, I question why this pattern of what I call 'law reform by frozen chook' persists at the federal level when in New South Wales it could be suggested that the seeds are being sown for a much more complex and realistic understanding of 'family law'.

SOME REFLECTIONS

While the examples of federal heterosexual marriage and divorce law reform have largely been based on loud rhetorical victim campaigns by aggrieved men, the New South Wales changes happened quickly and relatively quietly: there was almost no publicity and the parliamentary debates, while containing a few gems,[79]

[75] For some background discussions of this scheme, see Margaret Harrison, Patricia Harper and Meredith Edwards, 'Child Support—Public or Private?' in *Family Law in 84*: Hobart, 16–17 November 1984 (1984) vol 2; Cabinet Sub-committee on Maintenance, *Child Support: A Discussion Paper on Child Maintenance*, Discussion Paper (1986); Regina Graycar, 'Family Law and Social Security in Australia: The Child Support Connection' (1989) 3 *Australian Journal of Family Law* 70.

[76] For discussion of the changes that were made only one year before, which took effect from July 1999, see Margaret Harrison, 'Recent Issues and Initiatives' (1999) 52 *Family Matters* 61 and Linda Hancock, 'Reforming the Child Support Agenda: Who Benefits?' [1998] (March) *Just Policy* 20.

[77] Commonwealth, Department of Family and Community Services, n 42, p E5.

[78] Ruth Weston and Bruce Smyth, 'Financial Living Standards after Divorce' (2000) 55 *Family Matters* 10 at 15.

[79] One particular gem is the comment by an opposition member of parliament, responding to the Bill's focus on 'property': 'If this bill were about sexuality I would not be able to support it. However, as no-one is arguing that this bill is about sexuality, I will not oppose it.': NSW Parliamentary Debates, Legislative Assembly, 1 June 1999, p 739 (Stephen O'Doherty).

were relatively low key.[80] Only three members of the New South Wales Legislative Council voted against them and the opposition (Liberal Party) chose not to oppose the changes.[81]

However, this does not mean that there is no opposition to lesbian and gay law reform, nor that we have overcome homophobia in Australia. In the federal sphere, consider the recent Senate report on superannuation,[82] where some of the government senators[83] chose to rely extensively on the (small number of) submissions from groups such as the Festival of Light to reject a proposal to extend partner benefits to those in same-sex relationships.[84] Another particularly disturbing example is the response to the July 2000 Federal Court decision involving discrimination in the availability of fertility services.[85] That court decided, in response to a challenge brought by a single heterosexual woman, that Victorian legislation limiting access to fertility services to married women and those in de facto heterosexual relationships was inconsistent with the *Sex Discrimination Act* 1984 (Cth) and was consequently invalid by virtue of section 109 of the Constitution.[86] Within days, Prime Minister John Howard announced the government's intention to amend the *Sex Discrimination Act* 1984 (Cth) with a view to protecting the 'rights' of state governments to discriminate on the basis of marital status or sexual preference when determining who might have access to fertility services.[87] His stated concern that all children have a right to a mother and a father was widely perceived as an attack on lesbians and single heterosexual women who choose to have children and use fertility services as a safe method of doing so.[88]

[80] The speed with which these amendments happened and aspects of the parliamentary process are discussed by Jenni Millbank and Wayne Morgan, 'Let Them Eat Cake, and Ice Cream: Wanting Something "More" from the Relationship Recognition Menu', in Robert Wintemute and Mads Andenæs (eds), *Legal Recognition of Same-Sex Partnerships: A Study of National, European, and International Law* (Hart Publishing, 2001); Jenni Millbank and Kathy Sant, 'A Bride in her Every-day Clothes: Same Sex Relationship Recognition in NSW' (2000) 22 *Sydney Law Review* 181. See also Graycar and Millbank, 'The bride wore pink', n 25, pp 248–54.

[81] New South Wales, Minutes of the Proceedings of the Legislative Council, No 5 (26 May 1999), p 96.

[82] Senate Select Committee on Superannuation and Financial Services, Report on the Provisions of the Superannuation (Entitlements of Same Sex Couples) Bill 2000 (2000) www.aph.gov.au/senate/committee/superfinan_ctte/samesex/Contents.htm.

[83] A minority of three out of seven members.

[84] Senate Select Committee on Superannuation and Financial Services, n 82. Of the forty-one submissions received, only five opposed the Bill. The Committee received many more letters and emails in support of the legislation, but these were not treated as submissions: see ch 1 www.aph.gov.au/senate/committee/superfinan_ctte/samesex/Chapter%201.pdf.

[85] *McBain v Victoria* (2000) 99 FCR 116.

[86] *Ibid.*

[87] For extensive debate and discussion in relation to this proposed amendment, see for example the many articles published in *The Australian*, 2–5 Aug 2000; the *Sydney Morning Herald*, 2–5 Aug 2000 and *The Age* (Melbourne), 2–5 Aug 2000. Without the support of the Australian Labor Party and the Australian Democrats, such legislation seems unlikely to be passed unless individual members cross the floor.

[88] And note that the United Nations Convention on the Rights of the Child, to which Australia is a signatory, contains no definition of 'family' that would support this view, but rather refers to a child's family environment: Convention on the Rights of the Child, opened for signature 20 Nov 1989, 1588 UNTS 530, 28 ILM 1448, preamble (entered into force 16 Jan 1991).

After weeks of public 'debate' (much of it as ill-informed as the 'debates' about the 'federal marriage and divorce law' issues discussed above), the federal government introduced a bill that would leave it open to states to discriminate not only against lesbians and single heterosexual women, but also against women living with male partners to whom they were not married.[89]

And, returning to New South Wales, the amendments made by the *Property (Relationships) Legislation Amendment Act* 1999 did not apply to adoption, despite a 1997 recommendation by the New South Wales Law Reform Commission that the barriers on adoption based solely on sexuality should be lifted.[90]

While these examples reveal some clear fissures in the project of recasting aspects of relationships law, there is some room for cautious optimism. That is, the practical, purposive nature of the 1999 New South Wales changes, the reference to the Law Reform Commission to look further at the issue, and the lack of any substantive secular voice of opposition to them can be seen as positive developments.

So my question is: what is it about Australian marriage and divorce law debate that lowers the level of discourse so dramatically, that reduces it to stories of frozen chooks? If we hear these stories with amazement, and wonder how they can have so much impact, the converse is surely: what impact, if any, does research (including empirical research) have? Is this a problem peculiar to family law, or does it affect public policy-making more broadly? We see some aspects of it in the criminal justice context, where the analogy might be the constant law and order rhetoric such as the ill-informed calls for higher sentences and the death penalty as crime deterrents when evidence shows that not to be the case.[91]

[89] This is the effect of proposed cl. 22(1A) of the Sex Discrimination Amendment Bill (No 1) 2000 (Cth), introduced 17 Aug 2000, which would provide that '[n]othing in this section makes it unlawful to refuse a person access to, or to restrict a person's access to, assisted reproductive technology services if that refusal or restriction is on the ground of the person's marital status and is imposed, required or permitted by or under a law of a State or Territory'. A report in the *Sydney Morning Herald* suggests that this is designed to assist those states which wish to place further restrictions on those who can access the services, such as a five-year living together requirement for women in de facto relationships: Margo Kingston, 'De Factos Face 5-Year IVF Wait', *Sydney Morning Herald*, 22 Aug 2000, p 2.

[90] NSWLRC, *Review of the Adoption of Children Act 1965 (NSW)*, Report No 81 (1997) xli, recommendation 58. See *Adoption Act* 2000 (NSW), which implements many of the recommendations, but not the one in question. The adoption issue is an emotive one, but is often presented in a quite misleading way since there are very few children available for adoption in Australia. In fact, the rates of adoption have declined dramatically from a high of 9,798 adoptions in 1971–72 to 543 adoptions in 1998–99. Of those 543, only 127 were local (cf inter-country) adoptions by non-relatives. The other main category is 'known' child adoptions, mostly step-parent adoptions: Australian Institute of Health and Welfare, *Adoptions in Australia, 1998–99* (1999), pp 3–6. The relevant analogy in lesbian or gay families would be second parent adoptions.

[91] There is an accumulating body of research demonstrating that increased penalties do not have a demonstrable deterrent effect: Franklin Zimring and Gordon Hawkins, *Deterrence: The Legal Threat in Crime Control* (University of Chicago Press, 1973); Alfred Blumstein, Jacqueline Cohen and Daniel Nagin (eds), *Deterrence and Incapacitation: Estimating the Effects of Criminal Sanctions on Crime Rates* (National Academy Press, 1978); Roderic Broadhurst and Nini Loh, 'Selective Incapacitation and the Phantom of Deterrence', in Richard Harding (ed), *Repeat Juvenile Offenders: The Failure of Selective Incapacitation in Western Australia*, 2nd edn (Crime Research Centre, University of WA, 1995), p 55;

Perhaps family law is particularly susceptible to this kind of ill informed policy-making, since most people have a family of one kind or another. Therefore, it is presumed that we are all our own experts and the data and research material are of no more consequence (indeed, are of less consequence) than the stories of aggrieved participants.

I suggest that we will only be able to have a coherent debate about family law-related issues when we move beyond the paradigm of the 'gender wars' that characterise marriage and divorce law in this country.[92] Unfortunately, the field of family law has become less a terrain of debate and more a battlefield, with landmines (such as the recent child support proposals) going off in every direction. For every anecdote or story that has swayed a politician, family law and policy researchers could provide not only alternative anecdotes but also research data that contradict that story.[93] Yet, just like the stories of lesbians and single heterosexual women scandalously having children with impunity (as opposed to with men), the stories of frozen chooks influence the politicians. Stories about the women who actually use fertility services, data about the real-life poverty of children and the women who care for them, and about the violence that characterises many of the relationships from which they are trying to escape, all remain unheard.[94] How many times do we have to hear the hoary old chestnut, 'women may once have been disadvantaged, but now the pendulum has swung too far and it is men who are the victims'[95] or, as the federal Attorney-General is quoted as saying: 'For a couple of decades we had a focus on women's issues, and then

Neil Morgan, 'Capturing Crims or Capturing Votes? The Aims and Effects of Mandatories' (1999) 22 *University of New South Wales Law Journal* 267. For a discussion of the related phenomenon of law reform or policy-making by talkback radio see Russell Hogg and David Brown, *Rethinking Law and Order* (Pluto Press, 1998).

92 This is not a solely Australian phenomenon. Compare the language used in some recent family law publications from (respectively) the United States, Canada and the United Kingdom: Mary Ann Mason, *The Custody Wars: Why Children are Losing the Legal Battle and What We Can Do about It* (Basic Books, 1999); Nicholas Bala, 'A report from Canada's "Gender War Zone": Reforming the Child-related Provisions of the *Divorce Act*' (1999) 16 *Canadian Journal of Family Law* 163; see also Richard Collier, 'From Women's Emancipation to Sex War? Men, Heterosexuality and the Politics of Divorce' in Shelley Day Sclater and Christine Piper (eds), *Undercurrents of Divorce* (Oxford University Press, 1999).

93 In introducing a series of articles about family law reform that came out of a Family Law Teachers' Workshop held in Byron Bay in Sept 1999, and which formed vol 14(2) of the *Australian Journal of Family Law*, Professor John Dewar commented: 'The consistent message of all the research described here is that, in its day-to-day operation, family law fails to protect women and children from financial and physical harm. Yet this message seems to go unheeded by family law policy-makers. Family law policy often seems to be made in the teeth of, rather than on the basis of, the research and other empirical evidence available.' ('Introduction' (2000) *14 Australian Journal of Family Law* 79).

94 For discussion, see Regina Graycar, 'The Relevance of Violence in Family Law Decision Making' (1995) 9 *Australian Journal of Family Law* 58; Juliet Behrens, 'Ending the Silence, but . . . Family Violence under *the Family Law Reform Act* 1995' (1996) 10 *Australian Journal of Family Law* 35. More recently, research is starting to look at the link between violence and post-separation poverty: see Grania Sheehan and Bruce Smyth, 'Spousal Violence and Post-separation Financial Outcomes' (2000) 14 *Australian Journal of Family Law* 102.

95 There are examples of this theme in the parliamentary debates on the Family Law Reform Bill 1995: see, for example, Commonwealth Parliamentary Debates, House of Representatives, 9 Nov 1994, p 2963 (Robert Katter).

suddenly the table seemed to be turned and men seemed to be often the victim of . . . a family dispute.'[96]

The journalist who described family law disputes as gender wars has, in my view, identified a large part of the problem. It resonates with what the Law Commission of Canada described as the 'heritage of inequality'[97]—the underlying gendered power imbalance that is so rarely talked about explicitly yet is so central to the way in which laws dealing with relationships between women and men are constructed. There is considerable theoretical research on how the voices of the powerful drown out the voices of the powerless: in the context of divorce law reform, men have the ears of the politicians; the women and children simply do not.[98] And there are all sorts of pragmatic reasons for this. Since it is overwhelmingly women who are raising children after separation and divorce (not because of 'biased' courts, but because of a history of gendered patterns of caregiving), they are not as free as men are to spend time lobbying politicians and otherwise engaging in public activities.[99]

The amendments to the *Property (Relationships) Act* in New South Wales provoked nothing of this kind. It may be that people didn't know about the amendments; it may be that the changes to New South Wales laws were much more purposive and less symbolic, and therefore much less likely to 'excite' the passions. But it may also be simply that most members of the heterosexual community do not feel that giving rights to lesbians and gay men takes away rights or (economic) power from them.[100] By contrast, if federal 'family' laws were changed to respond to documented phenomena such as the high incidence of violence against women amongst the separating population,[101] and the poverty of women and children after divorce,[102] there would be a perception that power (and money) were being taken away from men.

[96] Cosic, n 39, p 20.

[97] Law Commission of Canada, n 11, p 14.

[98] One of the best discussions of this phenomenon is by Kim Lane Scheppele in her 'Manners of Imagining the Real' (1994) 19 *Law and Social Inquiry* 995. See also, for a discussion of the 'stock story', Richard Delgado, 'Storytelling for Oppositionists and Others: A Plea for Narrative' (1989) 87 *Michigan Law Review* 2411 at 2418–22.

[99] See Hancock, n 76, pp 28–30 for an analysis of how the majority of views put to parliamentary committees such as the 1992 Joint Select Committee come from non-resident parents. This issue of the differential access of women and men to political discourses was expressly put to the Joint Select Committee: see Reg Graycar, *Submission to the Joint Select Committee on Certain Aspects of the Operation and Interpretation of the Family Law Act, Part 2* (1991) pp 71–72; see also Martha Fineman, 'Illusive Equality: On Weitzman's Divorce Revolution' [1986] *American Bar Foundation Research Journal* 781 at 787–88; Ruth Lister, 'Women, Economic Dependency and Citizenship' (1990) 18 *Journal of Social Policy* 445.

[100] I am indebted to Jenni Millbank for this insight. Of course, as she rightly points out, this goes only so far—when it comes to children, there is another discourse entirely.

[101] Which, of course, has a negative impact on children: see Patrick Parkinson, 'Custody, Access and Domestic Violence' (1995) 9 *Australian Journal of Family Law* 41; Chief Justice Alastair Nicholson, 'Foreword' (1995) 9 *Australian Journal of Family Law* 1.

[102] See McDonald, n 64; Funder, Harrison and Weston, n 64; more recently, Weston and Smyth, n 65.

CONCLUSION

This is an ideal time to reconsider a whole range of legal rights and obligations that attach to relationships. We have not, until recently, questioned the centrality of the concept of marriage, yet have added on categories such as 'marriage-like relationships'. The lesbian and gay law reform process (and its limited success in New South Wales) really heralds the end of a period of adding by analogy without questioning marriage as the benchmark. We have reached a point where it is necessary to rethink the purposes of attaching rights and responsibilities to particular relationships. While it seems to be accepted that we need to do this to be able to include lesbians, gay men and their families more effectively in our communities, let's not let this opportunity to rethink families and family law pass us by. Only with a more informed debate about the purposes of aspects of legal regulation might we escape the constraints that the gender wars, with their heritage of inequality, have until recently imposed upon our family law discourses.

24

Can International Conventions Drive Domestic Law Reform? The Case of Physical Punishment of Children

Elaine E Sutherland*

What brings about law reform? In a democratic society, so the theory goes, it is the will of the people, expressed either directly or, more often, through elected representatives. In the United Kingdom, direct input from the electorate on specific issues is something of a rarity,[1] although the opportunity for particularly vocal, well-financed, highly organised groups to have a disproportionate impact remains a danger, particularly for minorities in any community.[2] Clearly, political and economic factors play a large part in law reform.[3] In the context of child

* Reader, School of Law, University of Glasgow; Professor, Lewis and Clark School of Law, Portland, Oregon, USA. This chapter was first published in (2001) 6 *Scottish Law and Practice Quarterly* 22–34 and is reproduced with kind permission of Butterworths, a Division of Reed Elsevier (UK) Ltd. A number of minor amendments, taking account of subsequent developments, have been inserted in the original text. I would like to express my thanks to the British Academy and the University of Glasgow for providing funding to assist me in attending the 10th World Conference of the International Society of Family Law in Brisbane, Australia, 9–13 July 2000, where an abbreviated version of this paper was delivered.

[1] Occasionally, a referendum will be held on a specific issue. For example, on 11 Sept 1997, the Scottish electorate was given the opportunity to vote on two issues: whether a parliament with devolved powers should be established for Scotland and whether such an assembly should have tax-raising powers. The strong 'Yes' vote on both issues (74.3% in favour of establishing a parliament, 63.5% in favour of it having tax-raising powers) was significant in leading to the *Scotland Act* 1998 which established the Scottish Parliament. The Welsh Assembly was created by the *Wales Act* 1998, which was preceded by a single-issue referendum in Wales, since it was never anticipated that the Welsh Assembly would have tax-raising powers.

[2] In 1999, the Scottish Executive made clear its intention to repeal s 2A of the *Local Government Act* 1986, which prohibited the local authority from 'intentionally promoting homosexuality' or the 'acceptability of homosexuality as a pretended family relationship'. While there was widespread support for abolition, a campaign to retain it was funded by a wealthy Scottish businessman using the (somewhat perplexing) banner of 'Keep the Clause'. 'Clauses' are parts of a Bill (ie the draft of legislation while it is being proposed), while the parts of an Act of Parliament are 'sections'. One part of the strategy was to organise and fund a postal public opinion poll which the organisers sought to give credence by calling a 'referendum'. The opinion poll was preceded by an expensive advertising campaign. Despite the vast expenditure, the section was repealed: see the *Standards in Public Life (Scotland) Act* 2000, s 34.

[3] The *Child Support Act* 1991 is a clear example of both political and economic factors driving a particular course of action. The Conservative government of the day was concerned about the cost of

and family law, moral and religious considerations undoubtedly have particular relevance and, consequently, a degree of influence.[4] The impetus for law reform may come from government itself, supported by internal research departments, and independent or quasi-independent research bodies also contribute. In Scotland, like many other countries, there is a law reform commission and an enormous amount of child and family law reform has been a product of the Scottish Law Commission.[5] Interest groups and professional lobbyists play their part. Academics like to believe that our outpourings have some impact. All of these elements can be described as the 'domestic' forces driving law reform. What of 'international' forces?

Undoubtedly, international pressure can contribute to the law reform process, often over what might be described as extreme issues.[6] However, examples abound of international condemnation having little or no impact on domestic law when there is sufficient domestic impetus driving a particular course of action.[7] Of course, part of the problem may be one of mixed messages. The politicians of country X may be prepared to join in criticising what is happening in country Y on a particular issue, but when economic interests—like trade—are at stake, country X will often find it very convenient to respect country Y's autonomy and confine its criticism to occasional statements backed up by no action at all. 'Inter-

providing state benefits to lone parents, particularly lone, never-married mothers. It also promoted a policy of 'family values', although it never defined the term. It produced a White Paper, *Children Come First* (Cm 2745, 1994), dubbed by critics 'The Taxpayer Comes First', heralding the introduction of the child support system which created a complex formula-driven system for the collection of money from non-resident parents, backed up by draconian enforcement powers. The early days of the system were dogged by errors and defects, prompting further reform. When the Labour government was elected, it undertook further reform of the system in order to simplify it and tackle some of the injustices of the original, while keeping the child support system in place; see *Children First: A New Approach to Child Support* (Cm 3992, 1998) and *Child Support and Pensions Act* 2000.

[4] The abortion debate is an obvious example here, but religion and morality often enter the picture over such issues as divorce and what, if any, recognition should be accorded to non-marital cohabitation and same-sex relationships.

[5] The Scottish Law Commission was established by the *Law Commissions Act* 1965 and its recommendations have resulted in such legislation as the *Family Law (Scotland) Act* 1985 (financial and property obligations within the family and on divorce); the *Matrimonial Homes (Family Protection) (Scotland) Act* 1981 (the right to live in the family home and protection from domestic violence); the *Age of Legal Capacity (Scotland) Act* 1991 (powers of people under the age of eighteen); Part I of the *Children (Scotland) Act* 1995 (children in the family setting) and the *Adults with Incapacity (Scotland) Act* 2000 (decision-making on behalf of adults whose own capacity to do so is impaired or absent).

[6] An example here is female genital mutilation (FGM). The UN Convention on the Elimination of All Forms of Discrimination Against Women, 18 Dec 1979 (19 ILM 33) requires states to eliminate discrimination against women, including abolishing discriminatory laws, customs or practices. The Declaration on the Elimination of Violence Against Women (UN Doc A/48/629), passed by the General Assembly in December 1993 (GA Res 48/104), includes FGM as one of the examples of violence against women. The UN Fourth Conference on Women, held in Beijing in Sept 1995, discussed the issue and the ad hoc committee on 'Women 2000: Fender Equality, Development and Peace for the Twenty-first Century' reported on 8 June 2000 that 'many governments have introduced educational and outreach programmes, as well as legislative measures criminalizing these practices'.

[7] The 'one child per family' policy, enforced in China, continues despite international condemnation of it. For a discussion, see, Xiaorong Li, 'License to Coerce: Violence against Women, State Responsibility, and Legal Failures in China's Family-planning Program' (1996) 8 *Yale LR & Feminism* 145.

national' pressure is given rather more substance when it is encapsulated in an international convention. There, at least, the views of the parties will be set out clearly, although the effect of conventions will vary depending on states becoming parties to a particular convention and the convention's own enforcement mechanisms.[8] The United Kingdom is a party to both the European Convention on Human Rights and Fundamental Freedoms[9] (the 'European Convention') and the United Nations Convention on the Rights of the Child[10] (the 'UN Convention'). Consequently, and to put it as simply as possible, the law operating in the various parts of the United Kingdom, including Scotland,[11] ought to comply with the provisions of these conventions.

The European Convention, concluded in the aftermath of the atrocities which ravaged Europe in the 1930s and 1940s, sets out a code on human rights designed to ensure that the horrors of that time should never be repeated. The United Kingdom was a party from the outset and, from 1966,[12] its citizens could take a case to the European Court[13] where they alleged that their rights under the Convention had been infringed. While it is a matter of some shame to admit it, the United Kingdom has appeared as defender in a considerable number of cases before the European Court, with a substantial number of findings against the state. Sadly, Scotland has contributed its share of these cases.[14] Thus, there was

[8] Philip Alston, 'Appraising the United Nations Human Rights Regime', in Philip Alston (ed), *The United Nations and Human Rights: A Critical Appraisal* (Clarendon Press Oxford, 1992), p 4; Geraldine van Bueren, *The International Law on the Rights of the Child* (Martinus Nijhoff, 1995), p 378; John P Grant, 'Monitoring and Enforcing Children's International Human Rights', in Alison Cleland and Elaine E Sutherland (eds), *Children's Rights in Scotland*, 2nd edn (W Green, 2001).

[9] Cm 8969 (1950).

[10] Cm 1976 (1992).

[11] While Scotland has always had its own, distinct, legal system and court structure, the Parliament of Scotland was dissolved on 25 Mar 1707 when the Parliaments of Scotland and England united. It was not until 1 July 1999, as a result of the *Scotland Act* 1998, that Scotland again had a separate legislature. While the UK parliament will continue to sit at Westminster, complete with representatives of Scottish constituencies, its jurisdiction to legislate for Scotland will be confined to 'reserved matters'. All other matters will be the province of the Scottish parliament and most legislation on child and family matters will fall into this category.

[12] The United Kingdom did not recognise the jurisdiction of the court until Jan 1966.

[13] The procedure for taking a case to the court was altered by Protocol 11 to the Convention. In the past, a case went first to the Commission, which would declare on admissibility and, if it found the case to be admissible, consider the merits and attempt to reach a friendly settlement. If no such settlement was reached, the Commission would send a report to the Committee of Ministers of the Council of Europe. If no proceedings were initiated within three months, the Committee of Ministers would rule on the matter. If proceedings were raised, the court would decide the issue. Protocol 11, which came into force on 1 Nov 1998, recognised that the old structure was not the most efficient way to deal timeously with the caseload generated by the Convention. It amended the procedure and abolished the Commission. Now a case goes first to a Committee of three judges which makes the initial ruling on admissibility de plano. Thereafter, a case goes to a Chamber of seven judges which fulfils much the same function as did the Commission, attempting to reach a friendly settlement, where appropriate, and, if no friendly settlement is reached, issuing a judgment. The case can be referred to a Grand Chamber of seventeen judges thereafter, within three months of the Committee's decision, where important issues are at stake.

[14] See, for example, *Campbell and Cosans v UK* (1982) 4 EHRR 293 (parental rights and corporal punishment in schools) and *McMichael v UK* (1995) 20 EHRR 205 (child protection procedures and parental rights).

always a degree of pressure on government to try to avoid the embarrassment of being found wanting by the European Court. In addition, it is a fundamental tenet of interpretation that, where any provision of domestic law is ambiguous, it will be interpreted by the courts in a manner which will ensure compliance with the United Kingdom's international obligations.[15] Thus, in cases of ambiguity, the interpretation favouring the Convention would often prevail. That is no help, of course, where the domestic provision is unambiguously inconsistent with the Convention—or, indeed, any other international instrument.

The status of the European Convention was altered dramatically by the passing of the *Human Rights Act* 1998, which incorporates its substantive provisions into the law of the various parts of the United Kingdom. The effect will operate on three levels. First, proposed legislation will be subject to pre-scrutiny. Where it is being introduced at Westminster, any incompatibility with the Convention must be declared.[16] In Scotland, the parliament will be unable to legislate in a manner inconsistent with the Convention.[17] Secondly, the courts will be able to issue a 'declaration of incompatibility'[18] in respect of Westminster legislation, while Acts of the Scottish parliament will be declared unlawful if they are inconsistent with the provisions of the Convention.[19] Thirdly, acts of public authorities may be challenged and declared unlawful where they violate the Convention.[20] Effectively, citizens of the United Kingdom will no longer have to make the long trek to Europe to mount a challenge: they will be able to benefit from European Convention rights in the courts at home.

The UN Convention, adopted unanimously by the General Assembly of the United Nations on 20 November 1989 and ratified by the United Kingdom on 16 November 1991, sets out the first truly coherent statement of children's rights intended to be of worldwide application. In terms of its scope, the fact that it came into force more quickly than any other human rights convention and the fact that only two countries[21] have failed to ratify it, it is an unprecedented document. If it lacks anything, it is a powerful enforcement mechanism.[22] There is no International Court of the Rights of the Child. Instead, enforcement is through the softer method of self-reporting by states. Two years after ratification, and every five years thereafter, states are required to submit a report of their own progress in complying with the Convention to the United Nations Committee on the Rights

[15] See, for example, *Kaur v Lord Advocate* [1980] SC 319; *Salomon v Commissioners of Customs and Excise* [1967] 2 QB 116; *IRC v Collco Dealings Ltd* [1962] AC 1; and *T Petitioner* [1997] SLT 724. For a particularly encouraging statement, supporting the importance of the UN Convention in the context of Scots law, see *White v White* 2001 SLT 485, per Lord McCluskey at 494.

[16] *Human Rights Act* 1998, s 19.

[17] *Scotland Act* 1998, s 35.

[18] *Human Rights Act* 1998, s 4.

[19] *Scotland Act* 1998, s 29.

[20] *Human Rights Act* 1998, s 6.

[21] The countries are the United States, which signed the Convention on 16 Feb 1995, and Senegal.

[22] This shortcoming is a common feature of human rights conventions. The International Covenant on Economic, Social and Cultural Rights (ICESCR) and the Convention on the Elimination of All Forms of Discrimination Against Women (CEDAW) have similar enforcement mechanisms.

of the Child.[23] The Committee scrutinises these reports and issues Concluding Observations on the particular country's progress. In the very tactful language of the United Nations, the Concluding Observations make references to 'positive aspects', 'principal subjects of concern' and 'suggestions and recommendations'. The hope is that, by the time of the country's next report, it will have addressed some—if not all—of the principal subjects of concern and implemented some of the suggestions and recommendations.

These, then, are two examples of 'international' pressure which might drive law reform. This article examines the issue of physical punishment of children and what has driven—and continues to drive—law reform in this context in Scotland.

PHYSICAL PUNISHMENT OF CHILDREN

Background

As a general rule, the legal system makes strenuous efforts to protect children in Scotland from violence. The criminal law uses the concept of assault to protect all members of the community, including children, from physical attack. In addition, a sophisticated mesh of legislation, regulations and guidance draws together social work, law enforcement, education and legal resources to protect children from abuse and neglect in the domestic setting.[24] However, the legal system demonstrates lamentable inadequacy in allowing a certain amount of violence against children under the euphemistic and vague umbrella of 'reasonable chastisement'. It should be noted that children are the only category of persons against whom such violence is permitted.[25]

The right to chastise a child stems from the notion of parental power[26] and, as such, can be delegated to others entrusted by parents with the care of the child.

[23] Art 44. The reports are known as the 'Initial Report' (two years after ratification) and 'Periodic Reports' (at five-year intervals thereafter). The Committee uses the term 'Second Periodic Report' to describe the first of the five-yearly reports. Timely compliance with the requirement to report has not been a feature of the Convention's operation. As of 21 Mar 2000, of the 191 initial reports due, only three had been submitted on time, with 52 states reporting under one year late, 86 states reporting over one year late, and no reports having been received from 50 states: CRC/C/96.

[24] The *Children (Scotland) Act* 1995, Pt II sets out, in detail, the responsibilities of local authorities to support children and their families, when intervention may be appropriate, the legal mechanisms for intervention, and the obligations of the local authority to children it is looking after. These statutory provisions are supported by further regulations and guidance, governing their operation. Three volumes *of Scotland's Children: The Children (Scotland) Act 1995 Regulations and Guidance* were published by the Scottish Office, governing *Support and Protection for Children and their Families*; *Children Looked After by the Local Authority*; and *Adoption and Parental Responsibilities Orders*. See also *Protecting Children—A Shared Responsibility: Guidance on Inter-Agency Co-operation* (Scottish Office, 1998). In addition, an extensive training program has been undertaken in respect of the personnel involved.

[25] While robust physical contact is an inherent part of many sports, the criminal law remains applicable. See *Ferguson v Procurator Fiscal Glasgow*, unreported, 11 Oct 1995, where a football player who was convicted of assaulting another player on the pitch was sentenced to three months' imprisonment.

[26] Erskine, Institutes, I, *v* 53.

As we shall see, at one time delegation to school teachers was permitted.[27] What amounts to 'reasonable chastisement' is somewhat unclear, and depends on the circumstances of the individual case and, in particular, on the age of the child and the extent of the violence. Thus, for example, it has been held to be reasonable for a mother to hit her nine-year-old daughter with a belt,[28] but unreasonable for a mother to slap a two-year-old on the face with such force as to knock him over.[29] In 1999, a father—himself a school teacher—was convicted of assaulting his eight-year-old daughter, having slapped her buttocks when she became hysterical in a dentist's waiting room.[30] Where the 'reasonableness' test is satisfied, it provides a defence to a charge of assault.[31]

Let us be quite clear about the issue under consideration. What we are talking about here is the deliberate infliction of violence by one human being on another. In any other setting, such conduct would constitute assault. The violence is meted out by someone who is usually bigger and stronger and inflicted upon a person who is usually smaller, weaker and more vulnerable. Usually, such behaviour would not only be regarded as criminal; it would—quite correctly—be viewed as morally reprehensible. For some reason, sections of Scottish society find the hitting of children by parents to be acceptable and may draw comfort from the use of such euphemisms as 'smacking'.[32] If we are to address this issue squarely, we must see physical punishment for what it is—violence against children inflicted by the very people they should be able to trust.

Nor should we allow ourselves to be sidetracked by believing that the assaulting parent should be excused because he or she may have had a 'good motive'—

[27] *Stewart v Thain* 1981 JC 13. The issue of physical punishment within the context of education is discussed below, but it should be noted that there has been incremental statutory intervention: *Education (No 2) Act* 1986, s 48; *Education Act* 1993, s 295; *Standards in Scotland's Schools, etc. (Scotland) Act* 2000, s 13.

[28] *B v Harris* 1990 SLT 208.

[29] *Peebles v McPhail* 1990 SLT 245. which has allocated £3 million to develop multi-agency programs, rising to £4 million in 2001; Scottish Executive Response to the Advisory Group Report on Youth Crime Review (same site).

[30] The father was struck off the teaching register by the General Teaching Council for Scotland. This meant he could no longer teach in any public sector school, although he could be employed in a non-teaching capacity. He could also be employed in the private sector. In Nov 2001, the Court of Appeal upheld his appeal against the decision, largely due to the procedures adopted by the GTC, and he has been reinstated. Clearly, harm may have resulted for the family—including the daughter—if this father had lost his job, and there was considerable public outcry over the suspension. However, it seems perfectly reasonable to conclude that a person convicted of assaulting a child is unsuited to teaching children generally.

[31] Conversely, where the reasonableness test is not satisfied, the parent may face conviction. See the unreported case, cited in the *Report on Family Law* (Scot Law Com No 135, 1992), at para 2.67, n 3, where a father who had whipped and caned his children from the age of seven was sentenced to four years' imprisonment. See also *C v HM Advocate* 1998 GWD 17–849, where a sentence of twelve months' imprisonment was not found to be excessive in respect of a mother's conviction for assaulting her eleven-year-old son to his severe injury by punching him, stamping on his head and biting him—all because she believed he had returned home late while she was out.

[32] One need only look at the—albeit falling—number of parents who hit their children in public to realise that these parents are clearly not embarrassed by their actions.

that is, the education or longer-term protection of the child. Motive may be relevant in sentencing but, as far as the criminal law is concerned, it is distinct from intention in determining guilt or innocence. Of course, it must also be remembered that, frequently, parents who assault children are driven by their own anger and frustration, albeit the 'good motive' can be presented later as some kind of rationalisation. If the legal system were to ban all physical punishment of children, parents would be given a clear message that they must find some other way to raise their children. A further danger exists. If the legal system takes the approach that some degree of violence towards children is acceptable, then it sends out a clear message to parents and creates a climate of tolerance of such violence. However hard it might then try to set limits on the acceptable level of violence, there will be parents who grasp the general message and fail to understand the subtleties of the limits. Some of these parents will overstep the limits—with potentially disastrous consequences.

We live in a world where, at least in the post-industrial societies, there is something of a sense of fear of youth. The tabloid press fuels public perception that young people are out of control and present a real danger to the rest of society.[33] This, in turn, leads to a conclusion that 'something must be done' and, for some, parents hitting their children may seem to be the answer. When examined more closely, however, it is not difficult to see that the use of violence by parents is of little value as an educational tool. In *B v Harris*,[34] a mother who slapped her nine-year-old and hit her with a belt was ultimately regarded as having exercised her right of reasonable chastisement. Briefly, it appears that the child had herself slapped a younger child who lived in the neighbourhood. When this was drawn to the mother's attention, she slapped her daughter. Her daughter swore at her (apparently in front of neighbours) and it was after this that the mother then hit her daughter with a belt. It is not clear which part of the girl's conduct led Lord President Emslie, delivering the opinion of the court, to conclude that she 'richly deserved punishment'.[35] But what messages were being sent to the girl in this case? Did she believe, originally, that it was acceptable for bigger, older people to hit smaller, younger people? In the attempt to make clear to her that such conduct was not acceptable, it is difficult to see how her mother's action could have done other than reinforce that notion. One is left with the impression of a nine-year-old who must have wondered why the highest court sitting in Scotland thought that her mother's conduct was not worthy of punishment[36] when her own, very

[33] Much of this perception is fuelled by events outside Scotland, including the numerous school shootings in the United States, and the Bulger case in England. In this respect, the *Report of the Advisory Group on Youth Crime* (www.scotland.gov.uk/youth/crimereview), published in June 2000, is an encouragingly positive document and the recommendations contained therein have been accepted by the Scottish Executive.

[34] 1990 SLT 208 (IH).

[35] *Ibid.*, at 209K.

[36] It should be noted that the case arose in the context of establishing grounds for referral to a children's hearing rather than the prosecution of the mother. Thus the court was not addressing the issue of punishing the mother.

similar, conduct was. If she thought about it at all she might, quite reasonably, have come to the conclusion that justice is indeed capricious.

The International Position

What of the international position? Certainly, many other countries have long since afforded children protection from violence meted out in the name of 'reasonable chastisement'. As long ago as 1979, Sweden banned all physical punishment of children and offending parents are liable to criminal sanctions. Seven other European countries have followed suit[37] and many others around the world are considering doing so.[38] Where all physical violence against children has been banned, the societies involved are not showing signs of imminent disintegration as a result.

What of the European Convention on Human Rights? Article 3 of that Convention prohibits 'inhuman or degrading treatment or punishment'. The issue of physical punishment of children provides a particularly clear example of the way thinking on a particular issue can develop and evolve in the context of the European Court of Human Rights. Having concluded, initially, that corporal punishment of children did not necessarily qualify as a breach, the court gradually edged its way towards countenancing the possibility that it might be so classified in particular circumstances.

In *Campbell and Cosans v United Kingdom*,[39] two Scottish mothers who were opposed to the use of physical punishment in schools sought undertakings from the schools that their children would not be subjected to this form of violence. When their requests were refused, they took their cases to the European Court. The court rejected the argument that corporal punishment in schools was inhuman or degrading treatment or punishment. However, it did find that, where the parents opposed such an approach to discipline, it breached Article 2 of the First Protocol to the Convention, which requires respect for the parents' religious and philosophical convictions in the course of a child's education. It is unsurprising, perhaps, that the focus in the early 1980s should be on the parents', rather than children's, rights.

That is not to suggest that the European Convention was inapplicable to children's rights. In the light of the decision in *Tyrer v United Kingdom*,[40] where 'judi-

[37] Austria, Croatia, Cyprus, Denmark, Finland, Latvia and Norway.

[38] Belgium, Bulgaria, Germany, Ireland and Switzerland are considering such a ban. In *State of Israel v Plonit*, 25 Jan 2000, Cr App 456/98, the Israeli Supreme Court banned all physical punishment of children. See R Schuz, 'Child protection in the Israeli Supreme Court: Tortious parenting, physical punishment and criminal child abuse' in A Bainham (ed), *The International Survey of Family Law: 2001 Edition* (Jordans, 2001). The Commissioner for Children in New Zealand has begun a campaign to end all physical violence against children and is seeking government support: 'Smacking should be illegal: Commissioner', *Otago Daily Times*, 15 Dec 1999.

[39] (1982) 4 EHRR 293.

[40] (1978) 2 EHRR 1.

cial birching' of a fifteen-year-old boy on the Isle of Man was found to breach Article 3, it became clear that the institutional setting for physical punishment would, ultimately, offer the state no absolute protection. A number of 'friendly settlements' were reached over the issue of physical punishment in schools, thus denying the court the opportunity to address the issue squarely for some time.[41] In *Warwick v United Kingdom*,[42] the Commission found the caning of a sixteen-year-old young woman at school was degrading punishment. The court had the opportunity to pronounce on the matter in *Costello-Roberts v United Kingdom*,[43] where it concluded, by a five to four majority, that the child's rights under Article 3 had not been breached in that case, because the minimum level of severity had not been reached. However, it made clear that corporal punishment could involve a breach of Article 3. Clearly, physical punishment in schools was being looked upon less and less favourably by the Commission and the court.

Finally, in 1998, in *A v United Kingdom*,[44] the court had the opportunity to consider physical punishment in the family. There, a nine-year-old boy had been caned by his step-father with considerable force on a number of occasions. In 1994, while not denying the factual allegations, the step-father argued that his actions amounted to 'reasonable chastisement' and was acquitted of the charge of occasioning actual bodily harm (broadly equivalent to assault in Scotland). In a unanimous judgment, the European Court found that there had been a breach of the child's rights under Article 3 and awarded him £10,000 in damages. That sum was payable by the UK government, rather than the step-father, since it is the state's responsibility to protect the child's human rights. While the Commission had indicated that the decision 'did not mean that Article 3 is to be interpreted as imposing an obligation on States to protect, through their criminal law, against any form of physical rebuke, however mild, by a parent of a child', its message was becoming clear. Physical punishment of children is growing less acceptable and will be subject to more rigorous scrutiny.

That the European Court's thinking should develop in this way is hardly surprising when we turn to the provisions of the UN Convention. Article 19(1) is quite explicit in requiring states parties to 'protect the child from all forms of physical or mental violence'. Other rights accorded to the child under the Convention are sometimes subject to qualification. So, for example, the right to freedom of thought, conscience and religion is subject to the rights and duties of parents to provide the child with direction in the exercise of this right.[45] No such

[41] See, for example, *Mrs X v United Kingdom* (No 7907/79), decided 2 July 1978, DR 14. It appears that the United Kingdom generated some 30 cases on this issue in 1985: Khan, 'Corporal Punishment in Schools' (1995) 7 *Education and the Law* 1.

[42] No 9471/81, decided 18 July 1986, DR 60.

[43] (1994) 19 EHRR 112.

[44] (1999) 27 EHRR 611. In *X and others v United Kingdom*, 10 Mar 2001, the European Court effectively overturned the decision of the House of Lords in *X (Minors) v Bedfordshire County Council* [1995] AC 633, and found that a local authority could be liable to children for its failure to protect them from violence in the home.

[45] Art 14.

qualification is placed on the child's right to protection from violence. Thus the usual justifications for parental physical punishment of children—like the suggestion that it is somehow in the child's interests or serves some educational purpose—are no response to the Convention's very clear prohibition. In addition, Article 37(a) requires states parties to ensure that 'no child shall be subjected to torture, or other cruel, inhuman or degrading treatment or punishment'. As we have seen, that phrase is found in the European Convention and, while the court has not yet found that it prohibits all physical violence against children, it does afford some protection. In the context of the UN Convention, in a sense, this is less important given the very clear prohibition on violence found in Article 19. Certainly, the Committee on the Rights of the Child was critical of the continued acceptance of corporal punishment of children in the United Kingdom. In its 1995 Concluding Observation on the United Kingdom, it commented:

> The Committee is worried about the national legal provisions dealing with reasonable chastisement within the family. The imprecise nature of the expression of reasonable chastisement as contained in these legal provisions may pave the way for it to be interpreted in a subjective and arbitrary manner. Thus, the Committee is concerned that legislative and other measures relating to the physical integrity of children do not appear to be compatible with the provisions and principles of the Convention, including those of its Articles 3, 19 and 37.[46]

The committee would rightly have expected this issue to be addressed squarely when the United Kingdom next reported. If that was the case, it must have been disappointed by the Second Report to the UN Committee on the Rights of the Child by the United Kingdom.[47] The report improves upon its predecessor in some respects, with separate sections being devoted to particular developments in different parts of the United Kingdom,[48] attempts to involve children in the course of drafting,[49] and input from NGOs.[50] However, on the issue of physical punishment of children, the report—having noted the committee's concern—simply indicates that consultation on the matter is underway, records that physical punishment is no longer permitted in respect of a child in state care and notes the

[46] Committee on the Rights of the Child, Concluding Observation on the United Kingdom, CRC/C/15/Add 34 (15 Feb 1995), para 16.

[47] HMSO, Aug 1999, due on 14 Jan, 1999 and recorded by the Committee as having been received on 14 Sept 1999: CRC/C/83/Add/3. An Executive Summary of the Report can be found at www.doh.gov.uk/unchild.htm.

[48] Sections are devoted to developments in Scotland, Northern Ireland and Wales, before the report moves on to particular aspects of the Convention when narrates progress and notes regional differences.

[49] Consultation with children was conducted through NGOs and, in Scotland, Save the Children was commissioned to undertake the 'Our Lives' project which sought the views of children and young people on the main themes of the Convention: see Second Report, paras 1.6.1–1.6.7.

[50] Government departments in the various parts of the United Kingdom were encouraged to involve local NGOs. The *Report to the Government on Progress Towards Implementing the Convention on the Rights of the Child* (Feb 1998) was produced by a group of non-governmental organisations which work with and for children, including the Scottish Child Law Centre and the Scottish Children's Rights Alliance. It pointed out a number of deficiencies in the UK's compliance with the Convention.

opposition of some NGOs to all physical punishment of children.[51] Reports, by their very nature, can be expected to be somewhat narrative, but the lack of any discussion of the current position of children in the family setting is, to say the least, disappointing. That, then, is the current international position. What of the domestic forces which have driven law reform on the issue of physical punishment and what difference has each made?

Physical Punishment in Schools

As we have seen, at one time, the concept of 'reasonable chastisement' applied to permit physical punishment of children in schools.[52] Of course, there were always parents opposed to this approach to education. In addition, the Society of Teachers Opposed to Physical Punishment (STOPP) lobbied hard to bring about changes in the law. However, these efforts made little progress until the landmark decision of the European Court in *Campbell and Cosans v United Kingdom*.[53] It will be remembered that the decision there was about parental rights, not children's rights, but that case and the others discussed above began to get government attention. As a result, the *Education (No 2) Act* 1986 was passed, prohibiting the use of physical punishment in state and publicly funded schools.[54] This did nothing to protect children in private schools. The *Education Act* 1993 went some way towards addressing this issue by requiring that, in all schools, physical punishment should not be 'inhuman or degrading'.[55] The process was completed by the *Standards in Scotland's Schools, etc. (Scotland) Act* 2000 which extends the same protection given to children in state schools to those in independent schools.[56]

Physical Punishment in the Family Setting

It is fair to say that public opinion on the issue is divided, as the Scottish Law Commission discovered in 1990 when it sought views on the possible abolition or modification of the parental right of 'reasonable chastisement'.[57] It received an unprecedented number of responses and, predictably enough, these spanned the

[51] Second Report, paras 7.12.1–7.13.3.
[52] *Stewart v Thain* 1981 JC 13.
[53] (1982) 4 EHRR 293.
[54] S 48.
[55] S 295.
[56] S 13. It should be noted that the Act also prohibits physical punishment of children in state-funded pre-schools. Private pre-schools remain outside this legislation, although child-minders are often required to register with the local authority and it may seek to refuse registration to an individual who refuses to forswear the use of physical punishment. See *Sutton London Borough Council v Davis* [1995] All ER 53.
[57] *Parental Responsibilities and Rights, Guardianship and the Administration of Children's Property* (Scot Law Com Disc. Paper No 88, 1990), question 11.

spectrum of opinion. The public opinion survey it commissioned in 1991 favoured continued legality of 'smacking', particularly in respect of younger children, but the outlawing of hitting any child with an implement.[58] Certainly, academic respondents were strongly opposed to all violence against children.[59] Organised opposition to physical punishment of children was mounted by a campaign group, End Physical Punishment of Children (EPOCH). In its report, the Commission recommended reform of the law to clarify and restrict, but not to abolish, the parental right in this respect. It proposed that, in both civil and criminal proceedings, it should not be a defence that a person struck a child in the exercise of a purported parental right if he or she struck the child (i) with a stick, belt or other object; (ii) in such a way as to cause, or risk causing, injury; or (iii) in such a way as to cause, or risk causing, pain or discomfort lasting more than a very short time.[60] However, even this modest reform proved too much for the legislature and the *Children (Scotland) Act* 1995 contains nothing on chastisement of children. Thus the law remains in its present, somewhat ambiguous, state.

In February 2000, the Scottish Executive re-examined the whole issue of physical punishment of children and published a Consultation Paper, *The Physical Punishment of Children in Scotland.* Clearly, the ruling in *A v United Kingdom* was responsible, at least in part, for that decision and the Consultation Paper makes explicit reference to it.[61] It also noted the provisions of both the European and UN Conventions, although it was somewhat dismissive of the latter on the basis that it gives no rights capable of enforcement in domestic courts.[62] Some of us like to believe that constant academic pressure[63] contributed to the decision and a well-organised lobbying campaign by the Children are Unbeatable! Alliance played its part.[64] Comments on the Consultation Paper were invited by 21 April 2000 and it was expected that, like the Scottish Law Commission before it, the

[58] *Report on Family Law*, paras 2.100–2.101. The survey was carried out in Sept 1991 by System Three Scotland. Similar views were expressed in a survey carried out by the Office for National Statistics Omnibus Survey in April 1998 in England.

[59] *Report on Family Law* (Scot Law Com No 135, 1992), paras 2.73–2.79.

[60] *Report on Family Law*, paras 2.67–2.105, Rec 11 and draft Bill, cl 4.

[61] At paras 4.3–4.8.

[62] At paras 3.24–3.25. As we shall see later, this attitude to the UN Convention is misplaced since domestic courts are paying increasing attention to it.

[63] Alison Cleland and Elaine E Sutherland (eds), *Children's Rights in Scotland* (W Green, 1996) para 5.39 (see also 2nd edn, 2001, ch 6); Rhona KM Smith, 'Spare the Rod and Spoil the Child?' 1999 SLT (News) 139; Elaine E Sutherland, *Child and Family Law* (T&T Clark, 1999), at para 6.19. A similar view has been expressed by commentators in respect of similar provision for 'reasonable chastisement' in other parts of the United Kingdom. See, for example, Jane Fortin, *Children's Rights and the Developing Law* (Butterworths, 1998), p 234; Michael Freeman, 'The Convention: An English perspective', in Michael Freeman (ed), *Children's Rights: A Comparative Perspective* (Dartmouth, 1996), p 99. For a US perspective on the international position, see SH Bitensky, 'Spare the Rod, Embrace Our Humanity: Toward a New Legal Regime Prohibiting Corporal Punishment of Children' (1998) 31 *U Mich JL Rev* 353. For a different view, see Barry Phillips, 'The Case for Corporal Punishment in the United Kingdom. Beaten into Submission in Europe?' (1994) 43 *ICLQ* 153.

[64] The Alliance is a UK body comprising over 260 organisations and individuals. There is a separate Scottish Alliance within the movement which coordinates its efforts in Scotland and, for example, has submitted a response to the Scottish Executive's consultation paper.

Executive would receive a large number of responses ranging across the spectrum of possible opinion. Even so, this hardly explains the inordinate delay that followed, although political expediency might.[65] Eventually, on 6 September 2001, the Deputy First Minister indicated that the Scottish Parliament would soon have the opportunity to consider draft legislation dealing with physical punishment of children.[66] Disappointingly, the proposed legislation will not ban all physical punishment of children and thus will fall short of the UN Convention standards. However, it will be an improvement on the current law. Essentially, it will prohibit physical punishment of children under the age of three years. As far as older children are concerned, blows on the head, shaking and the use of implements will all be prohibited, and the courts will be provided with a checklist of factors to take into account in assessing the 'reasonableness' of the violence used. In addition, the use of physical punishment will be banned in childcare centres, by childminders and in private pre-schools. Public and media reaction to the proposed legislation has been mixed and it remains to be seen what actually emerges from the legislative process.[67]

CONCLUSION: WHAT IS DRIVING LAW REFORM?

So, to return to the original question, what drives law reform? As the example of physical punishment demonstrates, there is the 'will of the people'—or, at least, those people who wish to organise and vocalise. Undoubtedly, the campaigning efforts of STOPP, EPOCH and the Children are Unbeatable! Alliance have had an impact in raising the profile of the debate on physical punishment of children. Certainly, scholarly writings can assist such groups, although academics must be prepared to write for a more populist audience if we are to have a wider impact.

What becomes clear from the example of physical punishment of children is that the European Convention and the European Court have had significant impact in driving law reform, with the latter (for want of a better expression) packing the real punch. The Convention was there for years before physical punishment of children was questioned seriously. It was only after the decision in

[65] A General Election to the Westminster parliament was held in the intervening period. While legislating on physical punishment of children in Scotland is the province of the Scottish parliament, pending legislation would undoubtedly have attracted the attention of the media throughout the United Kingdom—as, indeed, it did subsequently: see n 67 below.

[66] 'No smacking rule for children under three', Scottish Executive Press Release, SE3050/2001. The text of this, giving details of the proposed legislation, can be found at www.scotland.gov.uk/pages/news/2001/09/SE3050.aspx

[67] The Deputy First Minister's announcement was reported widely in the press, accompanied by the whole spectrum of possible opinion, the recounting of improbable scenarios and predictions of Scottish parents driving toddlers over the border to England in order to hit them (similar predictions of cross-border trips were made in Sweden when all physical punishment was banned there). British newspapers have raised the issue of the same level of protection being afforded to children in other parts of the United Kingdom: A Macleod and A Frean, 'Smacking of toddlers to be a crime', *The Times*, 7 Sept 2001.

Campbell and Cosans v United Kingdom that legislation removed and restricted the right to hit children at school. Granted, the Scottish Law Commission cited the European Convention when it recommended its reform of the law on parental physical punishment of children,[68] but that recommendation came to nothing. It was not until the decision in *A v United Kingdom* that the matter was reopened and government began to show serious commitment to law reform. No state which thinks of itself as 'civilised' likes to be criticised by the European Court. Despite its poor showing before the court, the United Kingdom still has such a self-image. The award of damages to victims adds further incentive for the government to respond. The incorporation of the European Convention into the legal systems operating throughout the United Kingdom will, of course, give further reason for compliance.

What of the UN Convention? As we have seen, it goes a great deal further in protecting children from violence than does the European Convention—at least as the latter has been interpreted to date. The lack of a hard enforcement mechanism has meant that, while it is cited in debate,[69] the force of clear and verifiable decisions is absent from the UN Convention. This may explain the rather cavalier dismissal of it by the Scottish Executive in its most recent consultation paper on the matter. However, it is far from irrelevant. Scottish courts are making increasing reference to the UN Convention.[70] Politicians are becoming more aware of its provisions.[71] However, the strongest hope for the UN Convention lies in the use being made of it by the European Court.

The court's jurisprudence in respect of physical chastisement of children has evolved over the years. It may be that it will continue to do so and that, ultimately, all physical punishment of children will be outlawed. This possibility is given greater support when one considers the European Court's recent willingness to use the UN Convention as an aid to construction of the European Convention's provisions.[72] Most recently, in *T v United Kingdom* and *V v United Kingdom*,[73] the case brought by the two boys convicted of killing Jamie Bulger in 1993, the court made reference to the provisions of the UN Convention when considering the rights of children being tried for a criminal offence. Granted, the articles of the

[68] *Report on Family Law* (Scot Law Com No 135, 1992), para 2.89.

[69] The Scottish Law Commission cited the UN Convention: Report on Family Law (Scot Law Com No 135, 1992), para 2.71.

[70] See, for example, *Sanderson v McManus* (1997) SC (HL) 55 per Lord Clyde at 65 (parental right to contact with children and the legitimate limits thereon); *Dosoo v Dosoo* 1999 SLT (Sh Ct) 86, per Sheriff Robertson at 87 (child's right to express views on contact with a parent and the right to confidentiality); *White v White* 1999 SLT 106, per Sheriff Principal Nicholson at 110 (different position of marital and non-marital father).

[71] In a debate in the Scottish parliament on 24 Feb 2000, on the physical punishment of children, a number of MSPs made reference to the UN Convention. In its final stages, the *Standards in Scotland's Schools etc (Scotland) Act* 2000 was amended to give children a greater voice in the context of education, largely as a result of Art 12 of the UN Convention.

[72] See, for example, *Costello-Roberts v United Kingdom* (1994) 19 EHRR 112 and *Keegan v Ireland* (1994) 18 EHRR 342.

[73] The cases are reported on the European Court website: www.echr.coe.int

UN Convention addressing this issue were given additional weight by the fact that the Committee of Ministers of the Council of Europe had specifically endorsed them by Recommendation.[74] However, it is clear that the court was willing to use the UN Convention as an indication of internationally accepted standards and, as such, something which could flesh out the European Convention when it did not address a particular issue explicitly. When one remembers that the European Convention was drafted with the atrocities of the Holocaust and the needs of postwar Europe in mind, it is not surprising that it did not focus on the rights of children. It can be anticipated that it will need refinement when children's rights are being examined. In this respect, the UN Convention has much to offer and, if it is used by the court increasingly in the future, the indirect impact of the UN Convention will increase.

In an ever-shrinking world where so many forces are driving towards globalisation, it is hardly surprising that international influences can have at least as much impact on law reform as can domestic movements. The interrelationship of the two should not be underestimated. International conventions are a product of domestic input, and it is the variety of local contributions that gives the opportunity for international instruments to reflect world opinion. In turn, international conventions have an impact at domestic level by informing debate and discussion. Clearly, the impact is strongest when the convention in question is supported by a hard enforcement mechanism, like the European Court. Nonetheless, even conventions with softer enforcement mechanisms, like the UN Convention, play their part.

[74] Recommendation No R (87) 20.

25

Emancipation of the African Woman: Fact or Fallacy?

Elmarie Knoetze*

INTRODUCTION

It is said that in South Africa the status of African women is dictated by a deeply entrenched tradition of patriarchy. Although this well-worn term has no precise definition, it is generally understood to mean the control exercised by senior men over the lives and property of women and juniors. In terms of this notion, the empowerment of men entails a corresponding disempowerment of women, who are deprived of the powers essential to realise their autonomy, such as contractual and proprietary capacity, *locus standi*, as well as the concomitant right of inheritance. Generally control of and access to property is regarded as a key to empowerment, a key which is often denied women through patriarchal social structures, allegedly institutionalised by the law.

RIGHT TO INHERIT

General Principles

In customary law, succession is intestate, patrilineal and based on the principle of primogeniture.[1] Upon the death of a family head his oldest son succeeds to the status of his father, denying his mother a right to inheritance, but providing her with support:

> Male primogeniture is consistent with the structure and functions of the joint family. The general heir, who succeeds to the office as well as to the estate, must be a male,

* Senior Lecturer in Law, University of Port Elizabeth, South Africa.

[1] For an exposition of the customary rules of succession, see JC Bekker *Seymour's Customary Law in Southern Africa*, 5th edn (Juta and Company, 1989), pp 273–310; NJJ Olivier et al, *Indigenous Law* (Butterworths, 1995), paras 142–53; TW Bennett, *A Sourcebook of African Customary Law for Southern Africa* (Juta and Company, 1991), pp 379–425.

> because only a man can be a head of a household in the traditional society. Intestate succession through the male line forestalls the partitioning of an estate, and keeps it in tact for the support of the widow, unmarried daughters and younger sons.[2]

According to the official sources of customary law, women could not succeed to the status of a man because they did not have the legal powers to play male roles. However, the death of a family head did not terminate his marriage, as ideally his widow would enter into a levirate union with one of the deceased's male relatives or an approved consort in order to perpetuate the family name through the procreation of children. In addition, the heir became responsible for the continued maintenance and support of the widow and any other surviving dependants. Thus, provided that a widow was prepared to remain at her late husband's family home, she was entitled to be maintained for the rest of her life.[3]

Rules of succession are inevitably shaped by the type of society in which they are supposed to operate. The various tribal systems of succession in South Africa thus bear the imprint of family and social structures prevalent in pre-colonial Africa. Customary rules of succession assumed, for example, that families were typically 'extended'—both through polygamous marriages and through connections with ascending and descending generations in the male line. Economic factors are another significant influence on the law of succession. In the predominantly subsistence economies of pre-colonial Africa, each family was more or less self-sufficient. Because all members of a family had an immediate concern with the husbandry of these assets, no one person could claim full rights and power over them. Thus, although the head of a family was overall manager of the family estate, his powers were in practice less important than his responsibilities to care for dependants.[4] From this, it is apparent that in customary law individual ownership was limited. All members of a family had an interest in the major productive assets, but control over these was vested in the family head:

> Although the property of the house is commonly spoken of as belonging to the family head, because this is a brief and convenient way of describing the matter, it belongs in law to the family as a unit, under his supervision and control; it has also been described as belonging in communal ownership to the family, which, of course, includes the family head.[5]

The socio-economic order which produced the customary law described above has, of course, not remained the same. The nature of family assets has, for example, changed in that a great deal comes from cash earnings by the husband and wife who, apart from buying household necessities and a family home, spend

[2] HJ Simons, *African Women: Their Legal Status in South Africa* (C Hurst Co, 1968), p 239.

[3] South African Law Commission Discussion Paper 93 Project 90, *Customary Law: Succession* (Aug 2000), p 23.

[4] South African Law Commission Issue Paper 12 Project 90, *The Harmonisation of the Common Law and the Indigenous Law: Succession in Customary Law* (Apr 1998), p 1; South African Law Commission, *Customary Law: Succession*, n 3, p 1.

[5] JC Bekker, *Seymour's Customary Law in Southern Africa*, 5th edn (Juta and Company, 1989), p 74.

the money on the education of their children, entertainment and so forth.[6] Diverse forces associated with colonialism, apartheid, Westernisation, the cash economy and ultimately constitutionalism have had a profound effect on both the economy and on African family structures. Thus the economic and social basis on which the system of male primogeniture rested has changed.[7] The cattle economy has been converted into a cash economy and the family is less 'extended' as members are scattered all over the country. This, it is alleged, has profoundly changed the position of the first-born.[8] Therefore, a major question to be posed is whether the customary rules of succession are appropriate to modern social conditions, and whether, in fact, they are even constitutional.

Constitutionality of the Male Primogeniture Rule

The customary law of succession must take account not only of changed social conditions, but also of South Africa's new constitutional dispensation. Constitutional norms of equal treatment and non-discrimination in terms of section 9 of the Constitution of the *Republic of South Africa Act* 108 of 1996 pose a major challenge to this order: the customary rule that the deceased's heir be male constitutes potential prima facie discrimination against females. In *Du Plessis v De Klerk* (1996 3 SA 850 (CC)), Sachs J warned that the direct enforceability of chapter 3 of the interim Constitution (containing the Bill of Rights) could require the court to indulge in a wholesale striking down of customary law because of the potential violation of the equality clause. Similarly, the South African Law Commission[9] expressed the view that:

> [t]he customary order of succession, which prefers the deceased's oldest male descendant as heir, clearly constitutes discrimination against females (daughters, granddaughters, sisters and mothers). Widows, on the other hand, are not members of their husbands' families, and hence could be said to experience no discrimination.

This viewpoint can be challenged by the application of the customary rule that payment of *lobolo* gives the husband control over the reproductive capacities of the wife, incorporating her into the husband's family.[10] In the Xhosa culture, for example, the woman becomes a member of the husband's clan by marriage, rendering sexual contact with one of his clan members incestuous.[11] On the other hand, not all ties with the wife's family are severed by marriage. Her father retains the role of her protector for the remainder of her life; he re-obtains control over his daughter in the event of dissolution of the customary marriage by divorce,

[6] Bekker and De Kock 'Adaptation of the Customary Law of Succession to Changing Needs' [1992] *CILSA* 367.

[7] South African Law Commission, *Customary Law Succession*, n 3, p 1.

[8] Bekker and De Kock, n 6, p 368.

[9] South African Law Commission, *The Harmonisation of the Common Law*, n 4, p 10.

[10] Bekker, n 5, p 150.

[11] *Ibid.*, p 123.

and during the marriage he plays a role in securing the stability of the marriage through the custom of *ukutheleka*. In terms of the latter, a father may 'impound' his daughter in the case of ill-treatment by the husband, requiring from him the payment of a penalty for the release of his wife.[12] Thus whether the wife fully becomes a member of her husband's family is debatable. Arguably the South African Law Commission could be correct in holding that the wife in a customary marriage is not by virtue of her exclusion from inheritance, directly unfairly discriminated against on the basis of sex. However, it is noteworthy that the South African Law Commission[13] does not draw a similar distinction between the rights of inheritance of widows *vis-à-vis* those of female blood relatives and in fact makes recommendations for the recognition of such succession rights.[14]

Although in earlier times succession to women was obviously not a serious social issue, it is one today. All women, to a greater or lesser extent, participate actively in the market economy. They are expected to run households and bring up children; sometimes they have the assistance of males and sometimes they have to operate alone: they do not necessarily enjoy the benefit of the heir's duty of support as this is conditional upon her residing at her late husband's homestead.

As far as gender discrimination is concerned, the prohibition in section 9 of the Constitution is reinforced by South Africa's obligation under the international Convention on the Elimination of All Forms of Discrimination against Women, which *inter alia* provides that states take all appropriate measures to ensure the same rights for both spouses in respect of the ownership, acquisition, management, administration, enjoyment and disposition of property (Article 16(1)(h).[15] The duty to ensure equal treatment was further reinforced in the *Promotion of Equality and Prevention of Unfair Discrimination Act* (No 4 of 2000), which requires the abolition of the 'system preventing women from inheriting family property' (section 8(c)), and the abolition of 'any practice, including traditional, customary or religious practice, which undermines equality between women and men' (section 8(d).[16]

The first issue to be addressed in the determination of the constitutionality of the customary rules of succession is obviously whether the Bill of Rights contained in the Constitution in fact applies to customary law. This issue forms part of the broader question of the direct/indirect, vertical/horizontal application of the Bill of Rights, and much has been written about it.[17] A critical discussion of

[12] Bekker, n 5, p 191.
[13] South African Law Commission, *Customary Law Succession*, n 3.
[14] See paras 4.5.1–4.5.3 of the Report, pp xviii–xix.
[15] See South African Law Commission, *Customary Law Succession*, n 3, p 6.
[16] *Ibid.*, pp 6–7.
[17] See, for example, D Lourens, 'Inheemse reg: Aard en inhoud in terme van die grondwet' [1994] *De Rebus* 856; JC Bekker 'How compatible is the African customary law with human rights? Some preliminary observations' [1994] *THRHR* 441; AJ Kerr, 'Customary law, fundamental rights, and the Constitution' [1994] *SALJ* 720; AJ Kerr, 'The Bill of Rights in the new Constitution and customary law' [1997] *SALJ* 346; AJ Kerr, 'Inheritance in customary law under the Interim Constitution and under the present Constitution' [1998] *SALJ* 262; G Rautenbach 'A commentary on the application of the Bill of Rights to customary law' [1999] *Obiter* 113; C Himonga and C Bosch, 'The application of

the applicability of the Bill of Rights to customary law falls outside the scope of this note, and certain assumptions regarding the applicability of the Bill of Rights will be made. However, the discussion necessitates certain preliminary remarks.

First, sections 211 of the Constitution of the Republic of South Africa and 1(1) of the *Law of Evidence Amendment Act* 45 of 1988 give recognition to South African customary law. In terms of section 211(1), the institution, status and role of traditional leadership, according to *customary law*, are recognised, and subsection 3 provides for the application of customary law by the courts, 'when that law is applicable' (emphasis supplied). Such recognition and application are, however, subject to the Constitution. Moreover, chapter 2 of the Constitution, containing the Bill of Rights, in terms of section 8(1) applies to 'all law'. The phrase 'all law' has been interpreted to include both South African common law and customary law.[18] The provisions of section 8 are seemingly confirmed by the *Promotion of Equality and Prevention of Unfair Discrimination Act* (No 4 of 2000), which in section 6 declares that neither the state nor any person may unfairly discriminate against any other person.[19] From this it follows that customary law is subject to the provisions of the 1996 Constitution.[20]

Secondly, the extent of the application of the Bill of Rights to customary law is far from clear. For example, in terms of section 173 of the Constitution, the courts have the inherent power to develop the common law, but no reference is made to the development of customary law. On the other hand, in terms of section 39(2), the courts must take the spirit, purport and objects of the Bill of Rights (which are freedom, equality and human dignity) into consideration when they interpret customary law. Furthermore: 'Customary law might still escape the full rigour of the Bill of Rights if it could be argued that the right to equal treatment should be limited by the customary rules of succession.'[21] Section 36(1) of the Constitution prescribes that a rule that potentially infringes one of the fundamental rights has to be reasonable and justifiable in an open and democratic society based on freedom and equality, that it should not negate the essential content of the right, and that the limitation should be necessary:

> In essence, a case of limitation requires a balancing of interests. In order to determine whether the limiting law is acceptable in an open and democratic society, one right (equal treatment) is weighed against another right (culture) and the limiting law (the customary system of succession).[22]

The weighing off of rights in the Constitution is indicative of the third uncertainty: the potential conflict that exists between various provisions in the Bill. For example, the 1996 Constitution recognises cultural diversity in sections 30 and 31 in that, in terms of section 30, everyone has the right to participate in the cultural

African customary law under the Constitution of South Africa: Problems solved or just beginning?' [2000] *SALJ* 306; TW Bennett, *Human Rights and African Customary Law* (Juta and Company, 1995).

[18] Rautenbach, 'A commentary', n 17, pp 123, 126.
[19] South African Law Commission, *Customary Law Succession*, n 3, p 9.
[20] Rautenbach, 'A commentary', n 17, pp 125–26.
[21] South African Law Commission, *Customary Law Succession*, n 3, p 9.
[22] *Ibid.*, pp 9–10.

life of his or her choice (eg customary law), but on the other hand it purports to impose constitutional rights premised on individual liberty and equality (eg section 9). The relationship between the right to culture and the right to equality and the significance attached to each is an important issue, which will be discussed later.

In the leading cases dealing with the customary law of succession under the new dispensation,[23] women apparently lost the war for equality in the battle of the sexes. In the first case, the court decided that the primogeniture rule does not *unfairly* discriminate against women in terms of the then section 8 of the interim *Constitution Act* (no 200 of 1993). The court's reasoning heavily relied upon the right of support a female is entitled to after the death of the family head:

> It is [a] common cause that in rural areas where this customary rule [of male primogeniture] most frequently finds its application, the devolution of the deceased's property unto the male heir involves a concomitant duty of support and protection of the woman or women to whom he was married by customary law and of the children procreated under that system and belonging to a particular house . . . [A] widow in particular may remain at the deceased's homestead and continue to use the estate property and the heir may not eject her at whim. If one accepts the duty to provide sustenance, maintenance and shelter is a necessary corollary of the system of primogeniture . . . [it is] difficult to equate this form of differentiation between men and women with the concept of 'unfair discrimination' as used in s. 8 of the Constitution.[24]

The court furthermore referred to the freedom granted to persons in the Constitution to choose this system as governing their relationships (section 31 of the interim Constitution and section 30 of the final Constitution) and hence came to the decision that the succession rule is not in conflict with the equality clause.

Although the court questioned the constitutionality of the principle in the second *Mthembu* case, it still refused the application as the applicant's daughter was denied a right to inheritance based on her illegitimacy (the existence of a customary marriage between applicant and the deceased could not be established: a discussion of this issue falls outside the scope of this note). In this case, the court considered that the development of customary law (to modify the primogeniture rule) in terms of section 35(3) of the interim Constitution as an endeavour rather to be undertaken by parliament, as it would have affected not only the customary law of succession, but also the family law rules. The court recognised that the rules of succession could not be looked at in isolation. Seen in perspective, customary rules of succession would fit in with the family customary law rules. Thus, due to their complexity, matters of law reform in the field of customary succession are best left to the legislature.

In the Supreme Court of Appeal judgment, the court firstly held that the applicant's minor daughter's illegitimate status, and not her gender, was determinative

[23] *Mthembu v Letsela* 1997 2 SA 936 (T), 1998 2 SA 675 (T), and 2000 3 SA 867 (SCA).

[24] 945E–I.

of her exclusion from inheritance. The court pointed out that a similar fate would apply to illegitimate sons. The court secondly stressed that the regulation in issue (Regulation 2(e) of Regulation R200 of 1987) was not ultra vires the common law as it *did not introduce something foreign to Black persons* (emphasis supplied). It merely gave legislative recognition to a principle or system which had been in existence and followed, at least, for decades. It is thus not inconceivable that many Blacks, even to this day, would wish their estates to devolve in terms of Black law and custom. It is therefore within the power of Blacks to choose how they wish their estates to devolve. This viewpoint of the court is very much reminiscent of the constitutional recognition of the right to cultural diversity in terms of sections 30 and 31 of the Constitution. Insofar as Blacks thus have a *choice* as to the devolution of their estates, it cannot be said that the law institutionalises the subordinate position of females by excluding them from inheritance.

On the argument that the court should develop the customary rule of male primogeniture to one of equal treatment of the sexes, in terms of section 35(3) of the interim Constitution, the court firstly pointed out that the deceased died before the interim Constitution took effect, and that in intestate succession the inheritance vests immediately upon the death of the deceased. The court was thus not bound by section 35(3) as both the interim and final Constitution do not operate retroactively. Secondly, only where the enforcement of previously acquired rights would, in the light of our present constitutional values, be so grossly unjust and abhorrent that it could not be countenanced, could it be declared contrary to public policy.[25] The court found that the case in question was not a case where the recognition and respecting of previously acquired rights would be so grossly unjust and abhorrent that they could not be countenanced. Therefore, on the facts, the invitation to develop the rule in the spirit, purport and objects of the Bill of Rights could not be entertained. An illegitimate child in customary law is said to 'belong' to the maternal grandfather or his successor, who is obliged to provide for him or her. There could thus be no question of the young girl being 'thrown out of her home' simply on the basis of her illegitimacy. A brief evaluation of these decisions raises the following points.

In the first *Mthembu* case, the court explicitly found it unnecessary to decide on the horizontal application of the Bill of Rights to customary law, and merely assumed that the Bill of Rights would apply to customary law. The Law Commission, in its Discussion Paper 93 of August 2000 (p 10), comes to the conclusion that, as courts are obliged to construe customary law so as to promote the spirit, purport and objects of the Bill of Rights, it amounts to 'indirect' application of the Bill of Rights to family relationships. With reference to customary law, it gives the court a ground for applying the so-called 'living law' (as socially practised) to laws set down in the official version of the system.[26]

[25] *Du Plessis v De Klerk* 1996 3 SA 850 (CC) para 20.
[26] South African Law Commission, *Customary Law Succession*, n 3, p 11.

From the first decision, it is clear that the court contemplated that the application of male primogeniture may not be appropriate in certain circumstances, these being in urban areas where the rule of support of the widow and children is often neglected. Thus, in such a case, the rules of succession do not serve the modern social conditions in an environment removed from the pre-colonial concept of the extended family. According to Himonga and Bosch,[27] the court missed out on the opportunity to draw a distinction between the 'living' and 'official' versions of customary law by not attaching significance to studies reflecting inheritance practices and patterns different from the official version:

> [T]his...should have motivated the court to investigate the possibility of the existence of a difference between the official customary rule it relied upon [that is, the rule of male primogeniture] and the law actually practised by the people (the living customary law). The fact that the judge missed the implication of this . . . may reflect a methodological orientation of the courts in their application of customary law. In this connection...the courts employ the rule-centred paradigm. This paradigm led them to search for rules in 'rule-centred literature studies, based on restatements of indigenous law'. As a result, the courts are not motivated to look outside these resources to other sources, such as the 'stories of women and children who have been marginalised in indigenous law [as well as] the stories of all people who live by indigenous law', to discover the content of the rules they seek to apply.[28]

The court indicated that the constitutionality of the rules of succession should be considered against the background of the right to participate in the cultural life of one's choice. This invokes not only the question of the weight attached to the right to gender equality vis-à-vis the right to culture, but also whether the interpretation of the right to equality should be done in isolation.

It has been argued that the right to culture cannot be used to protect the interests of a group at the expense of the rights to equality, non-discrimination and inherent human dignity.[29] Robinson acknowledges that:

> Culture and customs are valuable and important parts of people's lives and women experience some aspects of customary law as affirming. The positive aspects of customary law can be measured by the extent to which they affirm women's personhood or are not experienced as oppressive. When women make free and valid choices to participate in the cultural life of their communities those choices must be respected. When the law mandates the adherence to so-called cultural norms that are discriminatory that is subordination and thus impermissible.[30]

One might argue that the protection of the right to culture requires that the male primogeniture rules remain good law. Allowing women to opt in or opt out of cultural practices means that the customary law system is no longer a system, but simply a series of voluntary norms which members of a community may

[27] *SALJ* 332–333

[28] Himonga and Bosch, 'The Application of African Customary Law', n 17, p 333.

[29] Robinson, 'The Minority and Subordinate Status of African Women under Customary Law' [1995] *SAJHR* 469; Van der Meide, 'Gender Equality v Right to Culture' [1999] *SALJ* 105.

[30] Robinson, *ibid.*

follow or ignore. Consequently, the individual's rights are prioritised over the group's interest in cultural unity and cohesion.[31] Robinson opines that, for three reasons, this argument is not persuasive.[32] First, the right to culture should only be protected as long as the participation is by *choice*. It should not be a shield to defend aspects of customary law that deny the equality and dignity of women. Therefore, in a balancing of these competing interests, the right of the individual to equality should prevail because that outcome results in the lesser harm. Secondly, this argument falsely presumes that culture is static and absolute and thus rigid rules can accurately reflect and regulate actual social practices of a community. This viewpoint does not recognise the dynamic and diverse nature of customary law. For example, whereas females are in most tribes not appointed as chiefs, this practice is allowed by the Modjadjis, where succession to the position of chief and headman follows the female line.[33] Thirdly, Robinson considers the argument flawed because:

> in holding up culture as a sacred cow, there is no questioning of who defines culture and how it is defined. Cultures are hierarchical and replete with power imbalances that often disadvantage women. To the degree that laws regulating cultural practices reflect the unchecked authority of certain elements within a community and not the values of all groups within the community, they are not sacrosanct and should be examined to prevent the violation of individual autonomy and human rights as well as the domination of weaker elements within the community.[34]

To the argument that the right to culture should be subordinate to the right to equality, Van der Meide[35] adds that, although culture is practised within and defined by reference to a group, in the Bill of Rights it is an individual, not a collective, right. Generally, therefore, the right to culture cannot be used to protect the interests of a group at the expense of the rights to equality, non-discrimination and inherent dignity of individuals. A more fundamental question to the right to culture is what is meant with 'culture'. He argues that the 'official' version of customary law, institutionalised by the legislature, is 'at best of dubious authority and at worst "invented tradition"'.[36] Thus the corpus of rules used by the legal profession should be treated with circumspection, for it may have no genuine social basis. Consequently, in deciding which aspects of customary law are to be deemed unconstitutional, obvious targets would be rules of the official version that owe little to an authentic African tradition or to contemporary social practice.

The viewpoint of the South African Law Commission on the issue seems clear. According to it, the particular wording of the right to culture suggests that it may

[31] *Ibid.*

[32] *Ibid.*, p 469.

[33] Department of Provincial and Local Government 'A draft discussion document towards a White Paper on traditional leadership and institutions', Apr 2000, pp 25–27.

[34] Robinson, 'The Minority and Subordinate Status of African Women', n 29.

[35] Van der Meide, 'Gender equality', n 29.

[36] *Ibid.*

not limit the right to equality: 'An individual may claim the freedom to pursue a culturally defined legal regime, but only to the extent that that regime does not interfere with someone else's right to equal treatment.'[37]

In essence, Prinsloo[38] and Koyana[39] seem to be favouring a more socio-contextual approach. They welcome the decisions of *Mthembu* as an example worth following. Although Prinsloo does not explicitly weigh the competing interests of equality and culture against each other, he stresses the importance of the *context* within which a consideration of the constitutionality of a customary rule should be made:

> Wanneer 'n regsreël aan die vereistes van die oorgangsgrondwet, ook in die toekoms aan die grondwet van 1996, getoets word, is dit noodsaaklik dat die inheemse reg as 'n erkende regsreël naas die gemene reg oorweeg word en dat 'n mens waak teen 'n etnosentriese beoordeling van die inheemse reg. Dit vereis 'n goeie kennis en insig van die inheemse reg en beoordeling van die gewraakte reël teen die agtergrond van die betrokke regstelsel en die besondere kultuur. So 'n beoordeling word in hierdie saak [Mthembu] gevolg . . . Volgens regter Le Roux moet verder in gedagte gehou word dat elke persoon ingevolge artikel 31 van die [interim] grondwet geregtig is om deel te neem aan die kulturele leefwyse van sy keuse en dat persone wat hulle aan die inheemse reg wil laat bedien hierdie keuse vryelik uitoefen . . . Die woorde 'regverdigbaar wees in 'n oop en demokratiese samelewing gebaseer op vryheid en gelykheid' [in die beperkingsklousule] is in hierdie verband van besondere belang.

Koyana shows his satisfaction with the *Mthembu* judgment as follows:

> the recent judgement of Le Roux J . . . will go down in history as one of the first and greatest judicial pronouncements which vindicate customary law as the appropriate legal system to be applied by millions of Black South Africans whose lives are governed by it. More importantly, it has corrected the error of many who thought that the equality clause and the clause against discrimination in the new South African Constitution should result in the rules of customary law that at first glance discriminate against women on the ground of gender being abolished as being contrary to the Constitution.[40]

He warns against various absurdities that would follow the granting of relief that was sought and considers these as so far-reaching in all branches of customary law that 'the millions of Africans whose lives are governed by customary law, constituting the vast majority of people of South Africa, would regret that the new Constitution ever came into being.'[41] Koyana continues by giving the following examples of such far-reaching absurdities:

[37] South African Law Commission, *Customary Law Succession*, n 3, p 10.

[38] Prinsloo, 'Die inheemse opvolgingsreg getoets aan die grondwet—*Mthembu v Letsela* 1997 2 SA 936 (T)' [1998] *TSAR* 574.

[39] Koyana, 'Customary Law and the Role of the Courts Today' [1997] *Consultus* 126.

[40] *Ibid.*, p 126.

[41] *Ibid.*, p 127.

> In the field of the law of succession it would mean that where a man with 30 head of cattle, 80 sheep and 60 goats dies leaving say four daughters and one son younger than them all the eldest daughter would inherit the livestock. If she got married the following year she would be entitled to go with all the stock to her married home, leaving her widowed mother and brother and sisters with no cows to milk and no oxen wherewith to plough the lands, no goats to sell from time to time and get R400 for each and have cash for groceries and clothing, and no sheep to slaughter from time to time and have meat.[42]

Maithufi[43] also welcomes the decision, but cautions that it should not be read as express authority for the view that the male primogeniture rule does not unfairly discriminate between persons on the ground of sex. Maithufi's discussion is interesting in that he also refers to the *context* within which the male primogeniture rule finds its application. He draws a distinction between the succession to status and to the inheritance of the property of the deceased, and points out that the eldest male child will, by virtue of the male primogeniture rule, succeed to his deceased father's status, but not necessarily to his property. In fact, the homestead is usually allocated to the youngest son of the deceased who carries the duty to care for his mother. Other children of the deceased are also allotted a portion of the estate.[44]

That equality is the focal point of the Constitution is evident from the *dictum* in *Fraser v Children's Court, Pretoria North* 1997 2 SA 261 (CC) 272A that: 'There can be no doubt that the guarantee of equality lies at the very heart of the Constitution. It permeates and defines the very ethos upon which the Constitution is premised.' However, that equality has to be interpreted on the bases of sameness and similar treatment has been rejected. Instead, the court has adopted what De Vos[45] calls a 'contextual approach' in terms of which the actual impact of an alleged violation of the right to equality on the individual within and outside different socially relevant groups must be examined in relation to the prevailing social, economic and political circumstances in the country. Thus, depending on the context in which the complainant finds him or herself, a classification which is unfair in one context may not necessarily be unfair in a different context:

> Any consideration of whether a legally relevant differentiation actually constitutes a breach of section 9 will therefore first have to take into account the history of the impugned provision as well as the history of the group or groups to which the complainant belongs. Where such provisions contribute to the creation or perpetuation of patterns of group disadvantage for groups disfavoured in the past or groups that continue to be disfavoured in society, it will be very difficult for the court to find the measures constitutional. However, where the legally relevant differentiation is aimed

[42] *Ibid.*

[43] Maithufi, 'The Constitutionality of the Rule of Primogeniture in Customary Law of Intestate Succession—*Mthembu v Letsela*' (1997) 2 SA 936 (T)' [1998] *THRHR* 146.

[44] *Ibid.*, p 147.

[45] De Vos, 'Equality for All? A Critical Analysis of the Equality Jurisprudence of the Constitutional Court' [2000] *THRHR* 66.

> not at the creation or perpetuation of patterns of group disadvantage, but instead is aimed at breaking down those structural inequalities and thus at reaching for 'true' or 'substantive' equality, the court will be reluctant to declare the measures unconstitutional.[46]

Balatseng[47] calls for the interpretation of customary law in the context of its indigenousness, thus in its *cultural context* (emphasis supplied), and not according to Western norms and perceptions.[48] To interpret customary law literally in terms of the constitutional norms of individual liberty and equality and in isolation from its philosophical cultural background would be to force customary law into a preconceived human rights mould. According to Bekker,[49] the challenge to law reformers lies 'in understanding customary law against its own particular philosophical background, which is "communitarian", and to reconcile that with the tenets of individual human rights'.

It is submittedly this cultural contextual approach that was advocated by Prinsloo[50] where he says that in *Mthembu*'s case:

> regter Le Roux se benadering om die gewraakte inheemse regsreël teen die agtergrond van die volledige inheemse opvolgingsreg te beoordeel, is wys en navolgenswaardig. Indien 'n mens die gewraakte reël in isolasie beoordeel, kan 'n mens maklik tot 'n ander gevolgtrekking kom, soos die regter ook aangedui het. Kerr ['The Bill of Rights in the New Constitution and Customary Law' 1997 *SALJ* 350–52] wys ook op die vervlegtheid van die inheemse opvolgingsregsreëls en die belaglikheid wat kan ontstaan indien die inheemse regsreël dat slegs mans deur die manlike lyn mag opvolg onkonstitusioneel verklaar sou word; dit sou daartoe lei dat 'n dogter die voogdy oor haar ma sou uitoefen.

This was also the approach followed in the *Mthembu* Supreme Court of Appeal case, where the court pointed out that the male primogeniture rule is one not imposed by legislation, but exercised by choice by millions of Blacks. I am in respectful agreement that the right to equality thus cannot be interpreted in isolation—the cultural background of the system within which it operates, as well as the fact that legally speaking Blacks have a choice as to the system for devolution of the estate, necessitate a broader evaluation. The weakness of the *Mthembu* decisions perhaps lies in the lack of investigation into the socio-cultural context of the male primogeniture rule. As mentioned earlier, a system of succession ideally should reflect the way of life and natural wants of the people affected thereby, and arguably in modern society there has been a modification of succession practices. This is reflected by the fact that many African people lead partly modern, partly traditional lives:

46 De Vos, p 68.
47 Balatseng, 'Equality and Women under Customary Law' [1996] *Word and Action* 9.
48 See Rautenbach 'A commentary', n 17, p 116.
49 Bekker, 'The Equality Clause and Customary Law' [1994] *SAJHR* 122.
50 Prinsloo, n 38.

> Some are, to state the obvious, townspeople while others are tribespeople. Townspeople would obviously experience a mixture of customary and common law, whereas tribespeople will experience a predominance of customary law. Both groups would therefore to a greater or lesser degree experience the communal or socialist aspects of African law as well as the individualistic or capitalist nature of the common law.[51]

For purposes of law reform, an investigation into communalism *vis-à-vis* individualism would therefore be necessary. This would entail an enquiry into the extent to which African people prefer communalism to individualism: 'It is just possible that the law reformer ascribes to Africans an adherence to communalism that no longer exists or assumes that urbanised Africans are predominantly individualistic.'[52] The question of whether the court is best equipped to act as law reformer will be discussed later.

The applicability of the limitation clause (section 33 of the interim Constitution and section 36 of the 1996 Constitution) in determining whether the rule of male primogeniture was a reasonable and justifiable limitation of the rights entrenched in the Constitution was not considered at length in any of the judgments. In the first case, this was unnecessary since the right to equality limited itself with respect to the qualification of *unfair* discrimination and not mere differentiation between the sexes. Prinsloo[53] is of the opinion that the male primogeniture rule is not in conflict with section 9 of the Constitution because it constitutes a reasonable and justifiable limitation on the equality principle. Thus, based on the aforementioned, the discrimination in *Mthembu* was either not unfair, or could possibly constitute a reasonable, justifiable limitation in terms of the limitation clause. In terms of the former, discrimination is deemed unfair if it is gratuitous and where the person discriminated against stands to derive no benefit from it, but on the contrary his or her dignity is impaired or demeaned without any objective and justifiable reason for meting out disparity of treatment.[54] De Vos[55] points out that essentially the equality guarantee protects individuals' 'human dignity'. Human dignity will be impaired if a legally relevant differentiation treats people as 'second-class citizens' or 'demeans them' or 'treats them as less capable for no good reason', or otherwise offends 'fundamental human dignity' or where it violates an individual's self-esteem and personal integrity.[56]

In the second *Mthembu* case, the court held that, although public opinion might sometimes be relevant to an inquiry before the court, it is not a prerequisite for, or a decisive factor in, the discharge of a court's function to apply and

[51] Bekker and De Koc, n 6.

[52] *Ibid.*, p 372.

[53] Prinsloo, n 38.

[54] *President of the Republic of South Africa v Hugo* 1997 4 SA 1 (CC); *Prinsloo v Van der Linde* 1997 3 SA 1012 (CC); and *Harksen v Lane NO* 1998 1 SA 300 (CC).

[55] De Vos, 'Equality for all?', n 45, pp 65–66.

[56] *Ibid.*, p 65.

interpret the Constitution. It is respectfully submitted that to significantly modify the rules of a customary system of law, extensive public participation and comment are required, as such a system should reflect the way people live and to impose unwanted rules would lead to the creation of mere 'paper law'. By dismissing the submission of the importance of public opinion, the court arguably missed an opportunity to engage the people whose right to culture is protected by the Constitution.[57]

When interpreting customary law, not only the dynamic nature of the system should be kept in mind, but also the fact that the rules of succession, family law and even property law are interrelated. By allowing women to inherit, the rules of property law need modification; by allowing women proprietary capacity, the rules of delictual liability also need consideration. Koyana,[58] for example, illustrates that in the field of the law of delict the African girl could make out a case for the five head of cattle presently payable to her father as damages for her seduction and pregnancy to be paid to her directly. This complexity of customary law may impede or hamper the judiciary in pronouncements upon the constitutionality of a particular customary rule or custom.

Consequently, it is submitted that, because the court probably felt itself not equipped with evidence of public opinion on the issue and because of the complexity of the nature of the question involved, it declined the invitation to develop the customary rule of male primogeniture. This is not to say that the court is always reluctant to fulfil the duty of the development of customary law. In *Mabena v Letsoalo* (1998 2 SA 1068 (TPD)), the court held that a girl's mother is entitled to negotiate for and receive *lobolo* in respect of her daughter. She was also considered entitled to act as the girl's guardian and to consent to her marriage. Although it was impossible for the mother of the bride to be her daughter's guardian according to traditional law, the court recognised that there existed instances in practice where mothers negotiated for and received *lobolo* and consented to the marriage of their daughters. The court held that such a principle of living actually observed law had to be recognised by the court as it would constitute a development in accordance with the spirit, purport and objects of the Bill of Rights. Thus the court went beyond official customary law to look for the applicable customary rule in the practices of the people.[59]

The courts' decline in *Mthembu* to develop customary law along the lines of the Constitution suggests that the determination of the constitutionality of customary law rules is not a trivial, but rather a daunting task:

> At the heart of the prohibition of unfair discrimination lies the recognition that the purpose of our new constitutional and democratic order is the establishment of a society in which all human beings will be accorded equal dignity and respect regardless of their membership of particular groups. The achievement of such a society in

[57] Himonga and Bosch, 'The Application of African Customary Law', n 17, p 334.
[58] Koyana, 'Customary Law and the Role of the Courts', n 39, p 127.
[59] Himonga and Bosch, 'The Application of African Customary Law', n 17, p 336.

the context of our deeply inegalitarian past will be not be easy, but that that is the goal of the Constitution should not be forgotten or overlooked.[60]

Role of the Legislature

Undoubtedly the courts are placed in a difficult position. If they declare the particular rule of customary law unconstitutional without replacing it with some alternative, a lacuna will be created.[61] On the other hand, if they develop customary law without consultation, it might lead to communities not accepting the law. Thus not only was the court in the second *Mthembu* case of the opinion that the modification of the rule of male primogeniture falls within the functional duties of the legislature, but several authors hold a similar viewpoint.[62] Arguably, the proper medium for reform would be legislation, which permits full investigation of the social context and consultation with interested groups:

> Change is needed; but especially in a democracy, those affected by customary law need to have an opportunity to state their views with the assurance that 85 per cent of their system of law will not need to come from other sources. This is not to say that the values of the Bill of Rights are to be disregarded. If those affected by customary law are persuaded to adopt new values, such of those values as the legislature(s) adopt and enact are incorporated into customary law. The normal method of change in customary law . . . in circumstances such as present the best way of approaching extensive reforms is to appoint a commission or commissions in different provinces.[63]

If the development or adaptation of customary law is left to the legislature, one of two possible courses of action could be utilised: either legislation could be enacted to introduce new provisions consistent with the Constitution, or the Constitution could be amended by exempting African customary law and personal laws from the ambit of the non-discrimination clause, as is the case under the Zimbabwean Constitution (s 23(3)). With respect to the first-mentioned option, the question as to the extent of customary law revision arises as it has been suggested that 85 per cent of the present rules of customary law are inconsistent with the Bill of Rights.[64] If the Bill of Rights applies to all branches of customary law, the whole of the present customary law of intestate succession is inconsistent with the Constitution and therefore invalid, and so is much of the traditional law of marriage and parts of the law of property. It is argued that the traditional leaders who participated in the negotiation process for democratic transformation would never have consented to so much of customary law being invalid, and in terms of

[60] Per Goldstone J in *President of the Republic of South Africa v Hugo* (1997) 4 SA 1 (CC) para 41.
[61] Kerr, 'The Bill of Rights', n 17, p 355; Rautenbach 'A commentary', n 17, p 132.
[62] Bennett, *A Sourcebook of African Customary Law*, p 129; Kerr, 'Inheritance in Customary Law', n 17, p 269.
[63] Kerr (1998) *SALJ* 269.
[64] *Ibid.*, p 266.

section 211 of the Constitution, traditional leadership and the system of customary law are constitutionally recognised.[65] In terms of this argument, the constitutional recognition given to customary law must have meant the system of law in existence at the time subject to the normal processes of change, without requiring 85 per cent of the whole system to be substituted by rules deducible from the Bill of Rights.[66] One should perhaps also remember that:

> the process of judicial review under a [B]ill of [R]ights must always balance two constitutional goals: human dignity and democracy. Changing customary law on the basis of section [9] of the Constitution would realize the goal of human dignity, but it might do so at the cost of the wider community's democratic right to express its views on reform.[67]

With respect to the second option mentioned above, the Supreme Court of Zimbabwe in *Magaya v Magaya*[68] upheld the customary rule that a woman could not be appointed as heir.[69] The case concerned the application of African customary law of succession. The deceased had married two wives in terms of customary law; one female child was born of the first marriage and three male children of the second. The eldest female child claimed heirship to the deceased's estate, in conflict with the customary male primogeniture rule.

In this case, the court acknowledged that the exclusion of women as heirs under customary law could amount to prima facie discrimination on the basis of sex. Although the Zimbabwean Constitution does not include sex as a prohibited ground of discrimination, the court recognised Zimbabwe's international human rights law obligations concerning gender discrimination. However, section 23(3), exempting customary law from the ambit of the non-discrimination clause, saved the discriminatory aspects of the applicable succession laws. This decision was reached despite the existence of the *Legal Age of Majority Act* (No 15 of 1982), which bestows a person with majority on reaching eighteen years of age. The court in *Magaya* found that the Act was merely concerned with bestowing procedural competencies and was not intended to grant women additional substantive rights, which would include the right to inherit. Finally, the court reasoned that to allow women to inherit in a broadly patrilineal society would severely disrupt the African customary laws of that society.[70] In this regard, the court favoured the approach that 'pragmatic' and 'gradual' change should be effected. The court, quoting Bennett,[71] was of the opinion that, due to their complexity, matters of law reform in the field of customary law are best left to the legislature:

> In the case of succession a court could not simply rule customary norms void; it would have to stipulate how much widows could inherit and in what circumstances.

[65] Kerr (1998) *SALJ*, p 268.
[66] *Ibid.*
[67] Bennett, *Human Rights and African Customary Law*, p 95.
[68] (ZS) 16–2–1999 Case SC210/98 unreported
[69] Robb and Cassette, 'Customary Law of Primogeniture upheld in Zimbabwe' [1999] *De Rebus* 44 (Oct).
[70] *Ibid.*, p 45.
[71] Bennett, *Human Rights and African Customary Law*, p 95.

> Details of this cannot be determined in judicial proceedings. The proper medium for reform would be legislation, which permits full investigation of the social context and consultation with interested groups.[72]

The position in Zimbabwean law is, however, not as clear as suggested by the decision in *Magaya* above. Bennett[73] refers to the case of *Chihowa v Mangwende*,[74] where the court came to the opposite conclusion. In *Chihowa*, the deceased died intestate, leaving no male descendant, but a widow, two major daughters, a father and four brothers. One of the daughters applied for an order that she was entitled to succeed to her father's estate and the court granted the order on the basis that lack of capacity as the only barrier to females succeeding to the estates of their male relatives had been removed by the *Legal Age of Majority Act* (No 15 of 1982). Thus women were regarded as eligible heirs.[75] Of significance was the fact that this ruling applied to a female descendant of the deceased, and not to the deceased's widow. Thus, according to *Muriso v Muriso*,[76] *Chihowa* could not be read to allow a widow to be appointed the intestate heir of her husband's estate.[77]

In South Africa in 1998, the legislature did in fact respond to the call to undertake the duty of alteration of the customary law of succession in the drafting of the Customary Law of Succession Bill (No 109 of 1998). The main objective of the Bill was to extend the South African law of testate and intestate succession to all persons and to repeal section 23 of the *Black Administration Act* (No 38 of 1927), which regulates succession in respect of Black persons, as well as to enact new provisions of succession which will be consistent with the Constitution of the Republic of South Africa, and which reflect the rules of the common law of succession. While on the one hand introducing statutorily recognised rights of inheritance (testate and intestate succession) to both spouses in a marriage, the Bill, on the other hand, recognises the potential polygamous nature of a customary marriage by allowing spouses, where there is more than one, to inherit in equal shares. The Bill was not received favourably by all:

> The Bill met a hostile reaction from traditional leaders, notably those of the Eastern Cape House, who were scathing in their criticism of the terms of the Bill and the lack of consultation preceding it. Arguing that laws of succession are inextricably linked with the African concept of family an kinship, the House in a written submission declared itself 'fundamentally opposed to the Eurocentric approach which is prevalent in [our] country' and decried the extension of Roman-Dutch law principles to customary law.[78]

Subsequent to the publication of the Bill, a decision was taken not to proceed it, after a meeting was held by the Chairperson of the Portfolio Committee on

72 *Ibid.*, p 95.

73 *Ibid.*, p 127.

74 (1987) 1 ZLR 228 (S).

75 See also Nkala, 'Any Chance of Emancipation for the African Woman?' [1999] *De Rebus* 40 (Oct).

76 (1992) 1 ZLR 167 (S).

77 See Bennett, *Human Rights and African Customary Law*, p 127.

78 South African Law Commission 'Customary Law: Succession', pp x–xi.

Justice, the Chairperson of the Ad Hoc Sub Committee on the Quality of Life and Status of Women and representatives from the Law Commission.[79] Subsequently, the South African Law Commission expressed its view that, in the case of the conflicts of law, a common code of succession should provide for customary law to regulate the devolution of a deceased estate if all relevant factors, including the deceased's ways of life and, for purposes of deciding interests in land, the place where that land is situated, indicate that the deceased had his or her closest connection to that system of law. If, on the facts, it seems more appropriate to apply common law, or if the application of customary law would result in unjust or unfair consequences, common law should be applied.[80] In September 1999, instruction was given by the Ministry of Justice to the South African Law Commission to, as a matter of urgency, continue with the investigation into the customary law of succession. The result of such investigation was Discussion Paper 93 Project 90 'Customary Law: Succession' of August 2000. The main recommendations of the Discussion Paper with respect to the right of women to inherit can briefly be summarised as follows:

—The law of succession seeks to secure the material needs of those who were most closely related to the deceased and, given the profound changes that have occurred in the society and economy of South Africa, the current system of succession should be amended to cater more effectively for modern family forms (para 1(xv)).

—While the Constitution requires respect for the African legal heritage, it also stipulates that the right to culture, and hence customary law, is subordinate to the right to equal treatment. Moreover, because the right to equal treatment is applicable to the private relationships of individuals, any rules of the customary law of succession that discriminate unfairly on the grounds of sex, gender, age or birth must be changed (para 2(xv)).

—The recommendations contained in the Law Commission Report on the 'Harmonisation of the Common Law and Indigenous Law: Conflicts of Law' with respect to choice of law rules are endorsed (para 3.2(xvi)).

—The time has come to amend customary rules that discriminate on grounds of gender, age or birth in order to give the deceased's immediate family more secure rights, as the law is no longer effective to achieve its major social purpose—that is, to provide a material basis of support for the deceased's surviving spouse and immediate descendants (para 4.1(xvi)).

—The *Intestate Succession Act* (No 81 of 1987) must be applied to all intestate estates, even if a deceased was subject to customary law (para 4.2(xvi–xvii)). However, if application of the Act is to be extended, special provision must be made to exclude succession to offices of traditional leadership from the Act (para 4.3(xvii)).

[79] South African Law Commission 'Customary Law: Succession', p xi.

[80] South African Law Commission Report Project 90, 'The Harmonisation of the Common Law and the Indigenous Law: Conflicts of Law' (Sept 1999).

—Once the *Intestate Succession Act* is made generally applicable, the customary heir's duty to continue supporting a deceased's dependants should be repealed (para 4.4.1 (xvii)).
—The concept of 'surviving spouse' in terms of the *Intestate Succession Act* should be defined so as to include partners from informal unions (para 4.5.1(xviii)).
—Because the *Recognition of Customary Marriages Act* (No 120 of 1998) specifically recognises polygamous marriages, provision must be made in the *Intestate Succession Act* for inheritance by two or more wives of a deceased. Each wife should be allowed to share equally in the estate (para 4.5.2(xviii)).
—To avoid splitting up the assets of the matrimonial home and its contents, a spouse should in terms of the *Intestate Succession Act* have a guaranteed right of inheritance to the house and its contents, even if these items exceed the minimum amount to be inherited by the spouse, stipulated by the Minister of Justice (the amount is currently fixed at R125 000) (para 4.5.3(xix)).

CONCLUSION

There are tremendous challenges facing law reformers and courts in the modification and application of customary law in accordance with the constitutional imperatives within which this law has been recognised.[81] Comparison of the non-recognition of a woman's rights in succession as opposed to the equality status conferred by the *Recognition of Customary Marriages Act* (No 120 of 1998) on some African women gives a clear indication of the uncertainty in the scope of judicial review of customary law under the Constitution. As indicated, reform has already begun in the sphere of marriage law, but to abolish the principle of male primogeniture in succession seems to be an even more complex matter. Customary rules of succession seem to be firmly established—hence the hesitant attempts of the legislature and the judiciary to change them. This is complicated by the alleged difference between the official version as opposed to the living version of customary law. This leads to the conclusion that methodological and analytical tools of other social sciences will arguably have to be employed in combination with traditional legal methodological and analytical tools to assist the law maker/reformer to capture the customary law to be recognised and applied within the constitutional framework.[82] Law reform would need to proceed in a sensible and sensitive manner and would have to take into account the somewhat conflicting needs of a speedy resolution on the one hand, and broad consultation on the other.[83]

[81] Himonga and Bosch 'The Application of African Customary Law', p 340.
[82] *Ibid.*
[83] South African Law Commission 'Customary Law: Succession', p x.

26

The State, Race, Religion and the Family in England Today

Michael Freeman*

INTRODUCTION: SOME MODELS

Race and religion play different roles in different countries. As far as religion is concerned, there are many different ways in which the relationship between state and church can be expressed.[1] There may be an official religion (as is often the case in Islamic states). There may be an established church (as in England), together with a recognition of freedom of religion for those who do not espouse its tenets. There are secular states, states which are neutral as regards religion, states which have no official religion and states which do not tolerate or give any recognition to religion or religious groups. There are countries where church and state are kept separate (the United States is a model of this). A number of states have concordats with the Roman Catholic church (Italy, Spain and Portugal); others protect legally recognised groups. There is also the so-called 'Millett' model, wherein the state recognises different religious communities and allows each to follow its own personal religious law in particular matters, especially those which relate to the family (as in Israel).

There may not be as many models when it comes to conceptualising issues of race, but a number of different attitudes can be detected, ranging from supposed equality or equality of opportunities, to policies of separate but equal, to systems (thankfully now rare) where the interests of one race are dominant.

This chapter examines race and religion within English family law. It is intended as the first step in a project on which these issues will be explored in the context of different models in different parts of the world.

* University College, London.

[1] Partsch, 'Freedom of Conscience and Expression and Political Freedom' in L Henkin (ed), *The International Bill of Rights: The Covenant on Civil and Political Rights* (Columbia University Press, 1981).

THE HISTORICAL CONTEXT

In England, in the past, religion assumed what today would look to be a disproportionate and disruptive influence. This was particularly so in matters relating to a child's custody. Nineteenth century decisions are replete with references to the need to have sacred regard to the religion of the father.[2] Until recently, questions of race (and, concomitantly, of culture and colour) were not issues of any significance. But Britain is now a multicultural society: nearly 6 per cent of the population belong to non-white ethnic minorities. There is also considerable cultural diversity. The established Church of England may be in decline—church attendances have plummeted. But religion remains vibrant amongst minority religions: the per capita attendance at mosques and synagogues is considerably higher than that for the Christian churches.

One result is that religion and race issues have thrown up some of the most difficult—and certainly some of the most controversial—questions, particularly in relation to children. Legislation—the *Children Act* 1989—specifically recognises the importance of race[3]—the first English family law legislation to do so.

THE CHOICE OF RELIGION

> As a court [it has] no evidence, no knowledge, no view as to the respective merits of the religious views of various denominations.[4]

Re Carroll is an interesting case with insight into an earlier era. A Roman Catholic mother had placed her child for adoption with a Protestant adoption agency. She subsequently changed her mind and wanted her child back so as to place the child with a Catholic adoption society. The Court of Appeal held that the mother had the right to determine the child's future religious upbringing, to which end the child was returned to her. Scrutton LJ commented:

> In my opinion [the court] has this duty, where the character of the parent is not attacked, to give effect as to the religious education of the parent of a child too young to have intelligent views of its own. The responsibility for religious views is that of the parents, not of the Court. The Court should not sanction any proposal excellent in itself which does not give effect to the parent's views on education religious and secular.[5]

The courts once showed antipathy to atheism: the poet Shelley lost his right to custody, the Lord Chancellor of the day finding his views immoral and vicious.[6]

[2] *Re Agar-Ellis* (1883) 24 Ch D 317.
[3] *Children Act* 1989, s 1(3)(d) (the reference is to 'background') and s 22(5)(c).
[4] [1931] 1 KB 317.
[5] *Ibid.*, p 3.
[6] *Shelley v Westbrooke* (1817) Jac 266.

In modern times, they have occasionally taken the view that a particular form of religious upbringing is intrinsically harmful to the child, because it isolates them socially and educationally. Children have been removed from parents who are Exclusive Brethren for this reason—even where, as in *Hewison v Hewison*,[7] this breaks well-established attachment bonds. Even stronger opposition was taken in one case to the cult of Scientology, and it was held that its harmful effects (the judge described it as immoral, socially obnoxious, corrupt, sinister and dangerous) necessitated transferring the care of the children from the father to the mother (a Scientology 'court' apparently having given the father custody), even though they had lived with him for five and a half years in a stable relationship.[8] But in general the view which prevails is that it is not for the court to pass any judgment on the beliefs of a parent where they are socially acceptable and consistent with a decent and respectable life.

Where the residential parent has a religious practice which could potentially harm a child (for example, a Jehovah's Witness who will not countenance blood transfusions), courts have sensibly imposed undertakings rather than allowing the placement of the child to be determined on the religious issue alone.[9]

RELIGIOUS CONFLICTS

Courts have also sometimes required persons looking after a child to bring that child up in his or her religion, even where it is not theirs. This happened in the landmark decision of *J v C* in 1969: English foster parents, who were Anglicans, were ordered to continue to bring up the son of Roman Catholic Spanish parents as a Roman Catholic, and were not allowed as a result to send him to an Anglican choir school.[10] But the courts have now said that only in unusual circumstances should a court require that a child be brought up in a religion which is not that of the parent with whom the child is residing.[11]

This was said in *Re J*,[12] which is the most graphic illustration in recent times of religious conflict about a child's upbringing to challenge an English court. A Turkish Muslim father sought specific issue orders from the court in relation to his five-year-old son, one requiring the nominally Christian mother to raise the child as a Muslim and another requiring her to have the boy circumcised. The mother and the guardian *ad litem* opposed both applications. The father was not a devout Muslim and the court refused to make either order. As far as upbringing was concerned, it was not practical to make an order that a child whose home was with a mother who was a non-practising Christian should be brought up as

[7] [1977] Fam Law 207.
[8] *Re B and G* [1985] FLR 493.
[9] As in *Re C* [1993] 2 FLR 260.
[10] [1970] AC 668.
[11] [1999] 2 FLR 678.
[12] See n 11.

a Muslim. The judge saw this as an application of the principle in the Act that a court should not make an order unless making the order was better for the child than not making an order. He held that male circumcision was lawful—incidentally, the first authority to this effect in England—but that to circumcise a son was not a decision that could be taken by a parent alone, despite the fact that the Act provides that each person with parental responsibility (and both parents in this case had it) 'may act alone and without the other (or others) in meeting that responsibility'. This judicial inroad on a clear legislative provision was justified by the judge because circumcision is 'an irrevocable step'.[13] The only other issue relating to parental responsibility which divided the parents concerned the eating of pork—a matter, thought the judge, for compromise and agreement. But it was not 'in J's welfare interests . . . to make a specific order in relation to it'[14]—that is, presumably, it was not better for J that an order be made. If the circumstances had been such that an order was appropriate, the court would have had to decide whether the eating of pork was in this child's best interests. The boundaries of justiciability are fast being approached!

The Court of Appeal,[15] in upholding this decision, paid especial attention to the meaning of religion in the context of child care. The correct focus, said Thorpe LJ, was religious upbringing rather than religion, because no matter what religion the child belonged to by birth, the child's own perception of his religion would derive from involvement in worship and teaching within the family. A newborn 'does not share the perception of his parents or of the religious community to which the parents belong'.[16] This ruling is of greater significance to the Muslim community (where five to seven would be common circumcision ages) than the Jewish community, where it is invariably performed on the eighth day of a boy's life. And this is conceded by Thorpe LJ who felt 'confident' that, where it is the practice to carry out circumcision within days of birth, 'there is much less likelihood of forensic dispute'.[17] The Court of Appeal agreed with the first instance judge that, despite the clear language of the *Children Act*, there was a small group of important decisions (Dame Elizabeth Butler-Sloss P mentioned sterilisation as well as circumcision) which ought not to be carried out or arranged by a one-parent carer with parental responsibility. The issue of sterilisation is outside the scope of this paper, but I cannot let this reference to it pass without comment. The judge drew no distinction between therapeutic and non-therapeutic sterilisation: the view that parents in agreement could consent to a non-therapeutic sterilisation is quite unacceptable.[18]

The imperatives of religion were tested also in another recent English case, the heart-rending conflict known as *Re P*.[19] The case has many earlier echoes when

[13] See n 11, p 702.
[14] *Ibid.*, p 687.
[15] [2000] 1 FLR 571.
[16] *Ibid.*, p 575.
[17] *Ibid.*, p 576.
[18] Of course, in *Re B* [1988] AC 199, the House of Lords refused to accept the distinction existed. That it does is clear in Canada: *Re Eve* (1987) 31 DLR (4h.) 1.
[19] [1999] 2 FLR 573.

unimpeachable parents (so-called) have demanded the return of children long placed happily with foster parents or relatives.[20] *Re P* has the added complications that the child had Down Syndrome and an intensely orthodox Jewish heritage and background. The case records the end of a battle[21] by orthodox Jewish parents (a rabbi and his wife) to recover their eight-year-old daughter from Roman Catholic foster parents with whom the child had lived for seven years and with whom she had clearly bonded, though contact had not been lost with her family of origin. The girl had been placed with the particular foster parents when the biological parents could not cope, and attempts to find a suitable Jewish family had failed. The court accepted that the final loss of their daughter was tragic, but the conclusion was inevitable. This must be right. There could not be a clearer case of foster parents having become psychological parents. The evidence was clear that a move back now would bewilder and distress the child who might see it as a form of 'punishment' for something she had done wrong. Butler-Sloss LJ thought the residential status quo argument was 'sometimes over-emphasised', but had no doubt that it had 'real validity' in this case. Religion was a 'relevant' consideration: here it was an 'important factor', since 'no one would wish to deprive a Jewish child of her right to her Jewish heritage'.[22] What this meant to her was a bone of contention with conflicting expert testimony. But important though it was, said the court, 'the right to practise one's religion is subservient to the need in a democratic society to put welfare first'.[23] There can be absolutely no doubt that the court came to the right conclusion, but the juxtaposition of religion and welfare in the sentence just quoted raises as many questions as it answers. The implications of the statement are potentially far-reaching: to cite just one example, what are its implications for the religious practice of male circumcision?

RELIGION AND EDUCATION DECISIONS

The other main area which brings into conjunction state, family and religion is education. England has an established church and there are Church of England schools. There are also schools run by other Christian denominations—these raise no educational concerns or interest[24]—and by Jews, Muslims and others—and these sometimes do. The question whether parents from religious minority groups should have the right to educate their children as they wish did not provoke a great deal of interest in England until recently—the schools did not exist until at earliest a couple of generations ago—but now they fuel conflict and controversy. At issue is the conflict between parents' rights to educate their children as they see fit—a right increasingly embedded within English law in the last 20 years[25]—

[20] Most famously, *Re Thain* [1926] Ch 676 (where religion was not an issue).
[21] An earlier skirmish is recorded as *C v Salford City Council and others* [1994] 2 FLR 926.
[22] See n 19, pp 585–86.
[23] *Ibid.*, p 598 *per* Ward LJ, following *Hoffmann v Austria* (1994) 17 EHRR 293.
[24] Where concerns have been raised the focus has been on abuse, particularly sexual abuse.
[25] From the *Education Act* 1980 onwards.

against children's rights to a broad education which will prepare them for the outside world and the state's interest in a skilled and tolerant population. There are a number of international instruments emphasising freedom of thought, conscience and religion, but they tend to see these rights from an adult's viewpoint.[26] Even the UN Convention on the Rights of the Child which mandates states to respect the child's right to freedom of thought, conscience and religion, also directs them to respect the rights and duties of parents to 'provide direction to the child'.[27] The Convention does not give children the right to choose their religion—the Islamic states would not stand for this.[28] The Convention protects the liberty of individuals and groups to establish educational institutions, but these institutions are to comply both with Article 29(1) (which stresses the need for education to develop the child's personality, talents and abilities to their fullest potential) and also conform with 'such minimum standards as may be laid down by the State'. And Article 30 stresses the importance of minority groups by directing states to respect the right of a child belonging to an ethnic, religious or linguistic minority 'in the community with other members of his group, to enjoy his or her own culture, to profess and practise his or her own religion, or to use his or her own language'.

Problems occur where parents wish to have their children educated in a language other than English (Hasidic Jews, for example, believing the medium of instruction should be Yiddish), or who want a reduced (or virtually non-existent) secular curriculum (Hasidic Jews being an example of this too), or who want an education for their girls which will deny them equal opportunities now and in the future (Muslims often are accused of this).

American courts were grappling with these problems as early as the 1920s. In *Prince v Massachusetts*, the Supreme Court observed:

> It is in the interest of youth itself, and of the whole community, that children be both safeguarded from abuses and given opportunities for growth into free and independent well-developed men and citizens . . . neither rights of religion nor rights of parenthood are beyond limitation.[29]

Even so, in the celebrated case of *Wisconsin v Yoder*,[30] the Amish community succeeded in establishing their right to exempt their children from education after the eighth grade, contrary to the laws of Wisconsin which made schooling compulsory up to the age of sixteen. But Justice Douglas recognised that it was:

> the future of the student, not the future of the parents, that is imperilled by today's decision. If a parent keeps his child out of school . . . then the child will be forever barred from entry into the new and amazing world of diversity that we have today

[26] For example, the International Covenant on Economic, Social and Cultural Rights, Art 13(3).
[27] Art 14(2).
[28] See G van Bueren, *The International Law on the Rights of the Child* (Martinus Nijhoff, 1995), pp 156–59.
[29] 321 US 158 (1944). See also *Meyer v Nebraska* 262 US 390 (1923).
[30] 406 US 205 (1972).

> ... If he is harnessed to the Amish way of life by those in authority over him and if his education is truncated, his entire life may be stunted and deformed.[31]

The Supreme Court surely came to the wrong decision in *Wisconsin v Yoder*. It may have been over-impressed by the stability and prosperity of the Amish community, but with this precedent might find it difficult to be less tolerant of other closed communities.

Such a community could not succeed in England. Children could not be removed from school two years early on the grounds that they belonged to a minority community for whom such education was redundant. And that is right. In England, the test-bed for the problem has occurred when schools run by minority religious communities have been inspected by the state. The leading case, unfortunately not properly reported, is *R v Secretary of State for Education and Science, ex p. Talmud Torah Machzikei Haddass School Trust.*[32] The school (though it regarded itself as a 'talmud torah') was a boys' school run by the Belz section of the Hasidic Jewish community in Hackney in East London. The Secretary of State for Education started a procedure to de-register and close the school.[33] This was appealed (to the Independent Schools Tribunal) and an application for judicial review was also made. It was the school's case in the judicial review that the inspectors lacked competence to judge the school. Only one of the inspectors understood Yiddish, and he did not really understand the cultural traditions of the community and so the full significance of the lessons. The Department of Education conceded that the school would be suitable if it equipped a child for life within the community of which he is a member, rather than for the way of life in the wider society—but only so long as it did not foreclose the child's option when he was older to adopt another form of life (this is reminiscent of Justice Douglas's comment in the *Yoder* case). The judicial review application failed. The decision is nevertheless important—and, I would argue, regrettable. In this I note I am supported by Carolyn Hamilton[34] and Jane Fortin.[35] Whilst it is probably right that schools such as this one cannot be judged exactly like state schools, there are dangers in exposing children to an unduly narrow and uncritical curriculum. Should children be denied equality of opportunities because their parents want to live in closed communities? Hamilton makes the following point:

> Allowing a child to be educated within such an ideological, social and educational enclosure cannot amount to equality of opportunity, although it undoubtedly upholds the principle of plurality. However, the concession towards pluralism and parents' religious values and beliefs is too great.[36]

[31] *Ibid.*, pp 244–45.
[32] *The Times*, 12 Apr 1985.
[33] Under *Education Act* 1944, s 71 (this is now *Education Act* 1996, s 469).
[34] C Hamilton, *Family, Law and Religion* (Sweet & Maxwell, 1995), pp 259–63.
[35] J Fortin, *Children's Rights and the Developing Law* (Butterworths, 1998), p 290.
[36] See n 34, p 262. See also Holly Cullen, 'Education Rights or Minority Rights?' (1993) 7 IJLF 143, and James G Dwyer, *Religious Schools v Children's Rights* (Cornell University Press, 1998).

Ultimately, what the law needs to do is balance minority community rights and a child's right to achieve through education equality of opportunity. The balance in the *Talmud Torah* decision is tilted too far in favour of community and identity rights, and too far away from the child's education and developmental rights.

ISSUES OF RACE TODAY

Whilst religion has long been an issue, it was only in the final decades of the millennium that issues of race assumed importance—indeed, greater importance than religion.

The *Children Act* 1989 was the first children's legislation to be alert to race questions. Local authorities are expected to give 'due consideration' to, inter alia, 'the child's religious persuasion, racial origin and cultural and linguistic background.'[37] And, in making arrangements for the provision of daycare the legislation is designed to encourage persons to act as local authority foster parents to have regard to the 'different racial groups to which children within their area who are in need belong.'[38] In *Principles* laid down at the same time it was advised: 'since discrimination of all kinds is an everyday reality in many children's lives, every effort must be made to ensure that agency services and practices do not reflect or reinforce it'.[39] Giving 'due consideration' to racial origin means both understanding the connection between race and decision-making and applying that understanding to the individual child. Government *Guidance* regards ethnic origin, cultural background and religion as 'important factors for consideration'.[40] It stresses that, where reuniting the child with his or her family is the goal, there is a greater chance of success if the foster parents are of similar ethnic origin. But it acknowledges that 'there may be circumstances in which placement with a family of different ethnic origin is the best choice for a particular child.'[41] Legislation does not define race—even the *Race Relations Acts* do not do this[42]—and, as with religion, there are contentious questions on what is included, and what falls outside.

Only two years before the *Children Act*, the courts were saying—rather as they have now done with religion—that they would not prioritise it over other aspects of a child's welfare. In *Re A*,[43] the child—a Nigerian girl of nine who had been with white foster parents for five and a half years—was 'adamant' that she wished to remain with her foster parents. But this was not what tilted the balance: 'one must, of course, approach the statements of young children with a degree of

[37] S 22(5)(c). See also S MacDonald, *All Equal Under the Act*? (National Institute of Social Work, 1991).

[38] Sch 2, para 11.

[39] Principle 21 of *Principles and Practice in Regulations and Guidance* (Department of Health, 1989).

[40] Vol 4 (Department of Health, 1991), para 2.41.

[41] *Ibid.*

[42] The courts have given some assistance. See *Mandla v Dowell Lee* [1983] 2 AC 548 (Sikhs as a race).

[43] [1987] 2 FLR 429.

caution'[44] said Swinton Thomas J. The decision that the child should remain with her foster parents was dictated by paramountcy considerations. And, significantly, it was in striking contrast to the somewhat over-ideologised expert evidence to the effect that 'any child of West African background, regardless of the length of time that a child has been in an alternative family, must be placed back with a West African family'.[45] This expert had 'not met or spoken' to either the foster parents or the child.[46]

Another illustration of the conflict is *Re N*,[47] a case which contains a trenchant condemnation of the domination of social services departments by political correctness. The case related to a Nigerian girl of four and a half ('a person in her own right and not just an appendage of her parents')[48] who had lived with white foster parents since she was three weeks old. They wished to adopt. The father (a Nigerian by birth but now a naturalised American living in the United States) wanted care and control (the child was a ward of court). Bush J, after commenting that he had been 'bombarded by a host of theories and opinions by experts who derive their being from the political approach to race relations in America in the 1960s and 1970s,'[49] concluded that to separate the child from her foster parents would cause serious psychological damage both at present and in the future. The compromise, which seems to have given greater weight to the father's interests than the child's, was to reject adoption. This is not an institution known in Nigerian culture, and to the father it was a restoration of 'slavery'.[50] The foster parents were given care and control. This left the court—in whom were vested major decisions—and the mother—who played no part in the child's life—as the only persons with parental rights (and responsibility). Today it is probable that parental responsibility would have been vested in the foster parents by conferring on them a residence order, but this concept[51] was only operationalised in October 1991 with the implementation of the *Children Act*.

A third example is *Re JK*.[52] The illegitimate child of a Sikh mother, the child had been placed with white foster parents when six days old. She was now three, had bonded and regarded the foster parents as her parents. They wished to adopt but the local authority intended to match her with a family of a similar background to her natural parents. But Sikhs do not adopt (at least outside the family) and they attach stigma to illegitimacy. The local authority was clearly going to fail in its avowed aim: they were becoming so desperate that they were considering a Roman Catholic family (presumably of Asian origin). The evidence from a distinguished child psychiatrist was clear:

44 *Ibid.*, p 436.
45 *Ibid.*, p 435.
46 *Ibid.*, p 435.
47 [1990] 1 FLR 58.
48 *Ibid.*, p 60.
49 *Ibid.*, pp 61–62.
50 *Ibid.*, p 68.
51 *Children Act* 1989 s 8.
52 [1991] 2 FLR 340.

> to move the child at this stage from the only home that she has known . . . would be likely to cause irreparable psychological damage. She would probably never trust anybody again . . . She would almost inevitably reject any substitute parents with whom she was placed.[53]

The President of the Family Division agreed: 'It would be a terrible thing for this little girl to be moved from this home at this stage in her life.'[54] He saw the local authority as a 'prisoner'[55] of its own policy. He concluded the child welfare demanded that the foster parents be allowed to adopt.

These three cases are evidence of a judicial commitment to welfare over race. The judges in none of these cases were oblivious to the race issues (in *Re JK*, for example, there was reference to the need to take the child to the local Sikh temple and the foster parents were praised for so doing). But there are cases which seem to prioritise race (and colour) questions over welfare considerations. One,[56] which was particularly controversial at the time, had the Court of Appeal refusing to interfere with a trial judge's decision to remove a child of mixed race aged sixteen months from a white foster mother with whom he had been since he was five days old. The Court of Appeal held that the judge had been entitled to conclude that the advantages of bringing up a child of mixed race in a black family—one of Jamaican origin had been found—outweighed the importance of maintaining the status quo for the child, who was thriving in a stable home.

The most recent case suggests that this emphasis on race (or culture)—the two are not clearly distinguished and Bush J in *Re N* ridiculed this failure—has assumed new importance since the *Children Act* 1989.

In *Re M*,[57] a Zulu boy of ten was being brought up by an Afrikaans foster mother in London. He had been in London for four years. She wished to adopt, or at least keep him in England by obtaining a residence order. The Court of Appeal was impressed by the trial judge's view that the boy's development 'must be, in the last resort and profoundly, Zulu development and not Afrikaans or English development.'[58] There was expert evidence—the same child psychiatrist as in *Re JK*—that a swift return to South Africa would cause the child severe trauma. Astonishingly, the views of the boy were not sought. The court, following a passage in Waite LJ's judgment in *Re K*,[59] saw the immediate return of the boy as one of his rights as part of his welfare 'to have the ties of nature maintained whenever possible with the parents who gave [him] life.'[60] The boy himself certainly did not see it this way. The first attempt to remove him to South Africa failed when he resisted. He had to be removed forcibly and the 'experiment' of reintegrating him into South

[53] [1991] 2 FLR 340, p 344–45.
[54] *Ibid.*, p 347.
[55] *Ibid.*, p 347.
[56] *Re P* [1990] 1 FLR 96.
[57] [1996] 2 FLR 441.
[58] *Ibid.*, p 449.
[59] [1990] 2 FLR 64, 70.
[60] See n 57, p 452.

African culture and society failed abysmally. His parents subsequently agreed to his return to England. It is an interesting reflection on our times that, where once the courts would have justified their decision in terms of the sacred rights of parents, a generation later in terms of the pseudo-scientific 'blood tie',[61] now they invoke—disingenuously I would claim—the rights of the child.

[61] *Re C (MA)* [1966] 1 All ER is the most dramatic example.

27

Men and Women Behaving Badly: Is Fault Dead in English Family Law?

Andrew Bainham*

INTRODUCTION

The English divorce reports of the 1950s and 1960s are replete with bizarre and colourful examples of men and women behaving badly. There was Mr Williams, the Welsh miner whose voices told him that there were men in the loft waiting to commit adultery with his wife;[1] there was the infuriating and submissive Mr Le Brocq who drove his domineering wife to distraction by his steadfast refusal to have a good argument with her.[2] Wives too, it seems, were behaving badly. There was Mrs Horton, who was guilty of cruelty in spitefully damaging her husband's masonic regalia and Panama hat. 'These are serious charges,' said Bucknill J, 'they show a malevolence which is likely to bear fruit in acts of cruelty—an evil and unwifely spirit—far more serious to my mind than mere nagging.'[3] Most bizarre of all was surely the famous 'tickling' case of *Lines v Lines*,[4] where Mr Lines required Mrs Lines to tickle him all over every night. When the tickling stopped, the husband sulked. This, said the High Court, was cruelty because it caused the wife's health to suffer—the medical evidence being that she was suffering from acute anxiety and could not keep her fingers still.

* Christ's College Cambridge. This article is an expanded version of a paper presented to the International Society of Family Law's tenth world conference on Family Law: Processes, Practices and Pressures in Brisbane, Australia in July, 2000. It was first published in (2001) 21(2) *Oxford Journal of Legal Studies* 219, and has been reprinted here with the permission of Oxford University Press. I would like to thank my colleague Stuart Bridge of Queens' College, Cambridge for his helpful suggestions as to sources. I am also grateful to John Eekelaar for his comments on an earlier draft. The views expressed here and any errors which remain are mine alone.

[1] *Williams v Williams* [1963] 2 All ER 994 in which the House of Lords held that insanity was not necessarily a defence to a charge of cruelty.

[2] *Le Brocq v Le Brocq* [1964] 3 All ER 464 where the Court of Appeal allowed the husband's appeal against the finding of the lower court that this kind of silent, submissive and morose behaviour could of itself amount to cruelty.

[3] *Horton v Horton* [1940] p 187, an earlier petition presented around the outbreak of World War II. Here it was held that, in order to establish cruelty, it was necessary for the husband to prove wilful and unjustifiable acts inflicting pain and misery upon him.

[4] *The Times*, 16 July 1963.

There was, of course, a two-sided aspect to divorce petitions at that time. The petitioner might find that he or she could not rely on a matrimonial offence which he or she had connived at, colluded in or condoned. So, in the well-known 'wife-swapping' case of *Richmond v Richmond*,[5] Mrs Richmond could not rely on the adultery of her husband with Mrs Burfitt while she herself had agreed to commit adultery with Mr Burfitt on the same caravan holiday. The case illustrates a persistent feature of the relevance of fault in family law to which we must return later in this paper—that there is frequently a balancing exercise which must be performed. In family law, it is not merely a question of the misconduct of one partner. This must often be set aside and measured against the conduct of the other.[6]

When compared with the excitement of the 1950s and 1960s, the modern view of divorce as a 'process over time', with a 'statement of breakdown' and a 'period for reflection and consideration', seems very dull and uninteresting. A cardinal feature of the unimplemented *Family Law Act* 1996 would have been the abolition of fault, although the failure to implement the legislation means that, for the moment at least, adultery and behaviour remain as important bases for divorce and the little-used desertion remains at least in theory an option. The many different professions involved in divorce work, if not the present government, seem almost universally committed to the removal of fault from divorce law.[7] This prompts an examination of the role which fault may have to play in modern family law.

In the United States, there has been a substantial movement in favour of a revival of fault in the context of divorce which has triggered significant academic debate.[8] This attempt to rehabilitate fault has been accompanied by other trends which indicate a more interventionist approach to divorce and which see divorce as a matter of legitimate public concern rather than purely private agreement.[9] The focus in the United States has been on the relevance of fault to the basis of divorce, the redistribution of marital property and the level of alimony awards.

The spotlight in England has been very much on divorce, but if we look to wider issues of family law it quickly becomes apparent that fault continues to play a significant, albeit declining, part in legal outcomes across the whole spectrum of family disputes. In the next section of this chapter, I review the extent to which fault can be said to be relevant across a range of important issues which are the

[5] [1952] 1 All ER 838. In fact, although the wife here could not rely on her husband's adultery (because she had connived at it), she was able to secure an order for maintenance on the basis of desertion and wilful neglect to maintain.

[6] See the discussion of fault in relation to financial matters below.

[7] See in particular, M Thorpe and E Clarke (eds), *No Fault or Flaw:* The *Future of the Family Law Act* 1996 (Gordans, 2000), being the published proceedings of the President of the Family Division's Third Interdisciplinary Family Law Conference 1999.

[8] Contrast particularly Barbara Bennett Woodhouse (with comments by Katherine T Bartlett), 'Sex, Lies and Dissipation: The Discourse of Fault in a No-fault Era' (1994) 82 *Georgetown Law Journal* 2525 with Ira Mark Ellmann 'The Misguided Movement to Revive Fault Divorce, and Why Reformers Should Look Instead to the American Law Institute' (1997) 11 *International Journal of Law, Policy and the Family* 216.

[9] For a recent discussion, see Ira Mark Ellmann, 'Divorce' in S Katz, I Eekelaar and M Maclean (eds), *Cross Currents* (Oxford University Press, 2000), p 444, especially 449–50.

concern of family law. In the following section, I attempt to analyse the modern function of fault in family law and to evaluate its role for the future. Although my concern is with family law generally, the obvious place to start is divorce.

FAULT IN FAMILY LAW TODAY

Divorce

As noted above, English law retains, for the foreseeable future, fault-based 'facts'—effectively grounds—for divorce alongside the no-fault separation grounds.[10] We therefore have under the *Matrimonial Causes Act* 1973 a so-called 'mixed system'. After extensive review, the Law Commission, the government and parliament (the last after a struggle with right-wing extremists) accepted the principle of no-fault divorce.[11] It is impossible in one short section to do justice to all the arguments for the abolition of fault in divorce but, at the risk of over-simplification, they seem to come down to the following. First, the necessity to make unpleasant allegations in order to obtain a divorce does nothing to assist—and indeed frustrates—the law's objective of saving saveable marriages and disposing of those which cannot be saved with a minimum of distress and humiliation.[12] Secondly, the one-sided nature of petitions (with a petitioner making the allegations and a respondent on the receiving end) presents a dishonest and distorted picture of the real reasons for marital breakdown which are more complex.[13] Thirdly, and perhaps most importantly, the fault facts have been massively relied on to obtain the so-called 'quickie' divorce—it being the case that three-quarters of all divorces are obtained on this basis to avoid the inconvenience of having to wait out a separation period.[14] Hence the overwhelming majority of divorces, ostensibly based on fault, are really divorces by *consent* since they are undefended. This, it was thought, was dishonest (especially in the light of procedural considerations which had reduced divorce to an essentially administrative process in which allegations were never properly tested)[15] and resulted in a process which discredited the legal system.

[10] The three fault facts under the *Matrimonial Causes Act* 1973, s I are essentially adultery, behaviour and desertion for two years. Although conceptualised as facts which are merely evidence of irretrievable breakdown, these so-called facts are more appropriately viewed as grounds since a divorce may not be granted on the basis of irretrievable breakdown alone, but only on proof of at least one of the facts. See *Richards v Richards* [1972] 3 All ER 695.

[11] The principal sources being the Law Commission, *The Ground for Divorce*, Law Com No 192 (1990); Government Consultation Paper, *Looking* to *the Future: Mediation and the Ground for Divorce*, Cm 2424 (1993) and White Paper, Cm 2799 (1995) of the same name.

[12] These have been official objectives of divorce law since the *Divorce Reform Act* 1969 and are now stated as general principles in the *Family Law Act* 1996, s 1.

[13] Criticisms which can be traced back at least as far as the *Report of the Matrimonial Causes Procedure Committee* (1985) (The Booth Report).

[14] The median time for obtaining a fault-based divorce being approximately six months.

[15] The so-called 'special procedure'—special when it was introduced in the mid-1970s—has now become almost the universal procedure. Under this procedure, there is no requirement that either

Hence there is a groundswell of opinion which favours no-fault divorce, though the present government has recently announced its intention not to implement Part 2 of the *Family Law Act* 1996 which would, inter alia, have given effect to the no-fault principle.[16] It should not be thought, however, that the abandonment of fault as a basis for divorce was ever without its critics. Most obviously, there are conservatives who feel that to abandon fault is to remove the moral basis of marital obligations. The removal of adultery in particular might be thought to undermine the marital obligation of fidelity.

One of the more interesting theories in support of a return to fault is that of the economist Robert Rowthorn.[17] Rowthorn seeks to draw an analogy between the characteristics of marriage and those of modern business partnerships. It is Rowthorn's primary contention that marriage, like the business partnership, is an institution of trust which enables two people to have the confidence to make long-term investments in their relationship. Thus:

> the idea of fault is central to the notion of marriage as a commitment. By restricting unilateral exit from marriage without just cause, or by making the terms of dissolution depend on marital conduct, fault-based divorce penalizes those who break their marital vows and helps to protect those who fulfil their obligations.[18]

Ira Ellmann has identified and criticised four principal arguments of the proponents of fault-based divorce as follows.[19] First, it is frequently argued that no-fault divorce causes an increase in the divorce rate, though Ellmann can find no empirical evidence to support this. Secondly, it is argued that fault-based divorce has a deterrent effect on marital misconduct. Thirdly, and closely allied to the second argument, is the argument that no-fault divorce leads to unjust outcomes in property allocations and alimony awards.[20] Finally, Ellmann draws attention to a more subtle argument that no-fault divorce is but an aspect of wider cultural changes which reflect amoral thinking about marriage and the family:

> changes that discourage moral discourse about family relations, that focus on individual fulfilment more than mutual commitment, that emphasize marriage's

party appear in person and no effective opportunity for judicial investigation of allegations made in divorce petitions.

[16] The Lord Chancellor announced in June 1999 that the government did not intend to go ahead with the expected implementation of the *Family Law Act* in 2000. The reason given was that the interim results of pilot schemes relating to the statutory 'information meetings' were disappointing. On 16 Jan 2001, the government announced it would repeal Part 2 of the Act: Lord Chancellor's Department, Press Release, 16 Jan 2001. The effect of non-implementation for present purposes is that the mixed system of divorce will continue to operate in practice.

[17] Robert Rowthorn, 'Marriage and Trust: Some Lessons from Economics' (1999) 23 *Cambridge Journal of Economics* 661.

[18] *Ibid.*, at 686.

[19] See n 8, pp 219 *et seq.*

[20] As to which see below.

> potential for happiness and de-emphasize its obligations, and that value individual independence and disparage mutual interdependence.[21]

Ellmann concludes that none of these arguments is well-founded.

Academic commentators have also questioned whether or not there is a psychological need to apportion blame for marriage breakdown and whether society in general is wholeheartedly behind the direction of the reforms. As Shelley Day Sclater and Christine Piper have put it:

> For many, the notion of fault, of attributing blame to one party and exonerating the other, is what the legal system should be about, it is what ensures that justice is not only done but seen to be done.[22]

And Christopher Clulow[23] has warned against the introduction of a divorce law in which reconciliation is seen as the 'Gold Star' aim of the process and in which the process is so sanitised that 'good' divorces are those in which it is possible to achieve this aim and 'bad' divorces are those in which 'messy' emotions are to the fore and which actually result in divorce.

It is now clear that we will not see no-fault divorce in England in the foreseeable future. But the debate about fault in this context is in part a debate about what 'family justice' really is and, as we shall see, this is an issue which is by no means confined to divorce.

Domestic Violence and Occupation of the Family Home

It ought to be self-evident that domestic violence is about fault and the legal consequences which can attend culpable behaviour in the domestic context. To a large extent, this is true. Violence or harassment in the family context can give rise to criminal prosecution or to a civil non-molestation order which can be enforced by a power of arrest and breach of which can result in imprisonment.[24] So this is a context in which one might be forgiven for thinking that legal remedies hinge unmistakably on proof of fault. But when we turn to the remedy of the 'occupation order', formerly known as the 'ouster order', we can see that this is a highly problematic proposition.[25] It should be said at the outset that for many victims of

[21] See n 8, pp 228–29. For discussion of the problem of reconciling support for individual and communal identity in marriage, see Milton C Regan Jr, *Alone Together: Law and the Meanings of Marriage* (Oxford University Press, 1999).

[22] S Day Sclater and C Piper, 'The *Family Law Act* 1996 in Context' in S Day Sclater and C Piper (eds), *Undercurrents of Divorce* (Ashgate, 1999), p 6.

[23] C Clulow, 'Supporting Marriage in the Theatre of Divorce', in *No Fault or Flaw*, above n 7, p 20.

[24] The kind of behaviour which amounts to harassment goes beyond violence, or threats of violence. It 'implies some quite deliberate conduct which is aimed at a high degree of harassment of the other party, so as to justify the intervention of the court' (Sir Stephen Brown P in *C v C (Non-molestation Order: Jurisdiction)* [1998] 1 FLR 554).

[25] 'Ouster order' was the terminology used in relation to orders under the *Domestic Violence and Matrimonial Proceedings Act* 1976 and the *Matrimonial Homes Act* 1983. Similar orders made in the

domestic violence, it will be ineffective and arguably dangerous to have merely a non-molestation order without an order which also excludes the other party from the home. Yet there has been a long history, stretching back for over twenty years, in which the courts have debated and disagreed upon the question of whether exclusion should be a matter of 'welfare' or 'justice'.

In a nutshell, the issue has been what to do about a situation in which the living conditions of the mother (usually) and children have become intolerable and might be thought to necessitate an immediate exclusion of the man concerned where it is not possible to point to any violence or obviously adverse conduct on his part. Of course, where we are dealing with actual violence against the mother or a child, the case for exclusion is much more obvious, though enforcement has often proved difficult in practice. The Court of Appeal wrestled unsuccessfully with this question in the late 1970s and early 1980s and two distinct lines of authority—one emphasising welfare and the other emphasising conduct—gave poor guidance to the lower courts who had to deal with the practicalities on a daily basis.[26] Eventually, the House of Lords in *Richards v Richards*[27] handed down a judgment which made it plain that both the welfare of the mother and children and the conduct of the respondent were among the relevant considerations. But the case, in which the wife's allegations were described as 'rubbishy', was widely interpreted as an indication that ouster orders ought not to be made on purely welfare grounds, and that it was necessary to be able to point to at least some adverse conduct of sufficient gravity. Under the legislation then governing the issue,[28] there was no weighting as between the relevant considerations and, unsurprisingly, the suspicion remained that judges would differ with regard to the importance they attached to the competing claims of welfare and justice.

In 1997, a new law governing domestic violence and occupation of the family home came into force following the recommendations of the Law Commission.[29] There is no doubt that the original intentions of the Law Commission were to tilt the balance on this issue more towards protecting the welfare of women and children and, relatively speaking, away from the civil libertarian considerations which militate against the exclusion of a man from his home.

The *Family Law Act* seeks to do this primarily by the enactment of the so-called 'balance of harm test'.[30] Under the statutory test, the court must first ask whether, if the order is not made, the applicant or any relevant child is likely to suffer

magistrates' court were known as 'exclusion orders' under the *Domestic Proceedings and Magistrates Courts Act* 1978. One effect of Part IV of the *Family Law Act* 1996 is to unify the orders made in the various courts under the new terminology of 'occupation orders'.

26 Contrast, for example, *Spindlow v Spindlow* [1979] 1 All ER 169 (in which the Court of Appeal took a largely welfare-based approach) with *Elsworth v Elsworth* (1980) FLR 245 (in which it emphasised the necessity of proving adverse conduct).

27 [1984] AC 174.

28 *Matrimonial Homes Act* 1983, s 1(3).

29 *Family Law Act* 1996, Part IV and Law Commission, *Domestic Violence and Occupation of the Family Home*, Law Com No 207 (1992).

30 S 33(7).

'significant harm' attributable to the respondent's conduct. If the answer to this is 'yes', the court must then make the order unless the harm to the respondent or a child, if the order were to be made, is likely to be as great or greater when balancing one against the other. The statutory test is further complicated in that, in this formulation, it applies only to so-called 'entitled applicants'. Essentially, these are married persons and property owners (or, of course, both in many cases). The test is also relevant to applications by 'non-entitled' applicants, essentially co-habitants and former co-habitants who are not also property owners, but applies in a watered down way in their case.[31] While the court must have regard to the balance of harm test, it is not obliged to make the order, but retains its discretion to do so, where the balance comes down on the side of the applicant. This differential treatment of the married and the unmarried is one of a number of such examples in the Act which are (it is argued, misguidedly) seeking to reinforce marriage as the ideal form of family relationship. Indeed, it might almost be said that those seeking the assistance of the courts are to be held accountable, at least to some extent, for the 'fault' implicit in their failure to give to their partners 'the commitment involved in marriage'.[32]

It is probably still too early to offer a clear view on whether the new legislation will result in greater attention being paid to welfare needs and correspondingly less to fault. But one leading commentator was quick to point out that the statutory test refers directly to the harm being attributable to the conduct of the respondent and thus may be thought to reassert the requirement drawn from *Richards v Richards* that there must be adequate evidence of adverse conduct before an occupation order can be made.[33] Such reported cases as there have been since the implementation of the new provisions would seem to be consistent with this view. Thus the Court of Appeal in *Chalmers v Johns*,[34] the leading case so far, allowed a father's appeal against an occupation order where it could not be said that the mother or child was subject to any real risk of violence from him. It also took the view that the inconvenience involved in a longer journey to school for the child, arising from the mother's decision to move into temporary council accommodation, could not be said to amount to harm.

It certainly seems that it would be premature to conclude that welfare considerations are about to take over completely from fault as the primary determinants of whether or not an occupation order should be made. Occupation of the family home is, on the contrary, likely to remain, at least for the present, as an

[31] S 36(7) and (8).

[32] Under the *Family Law Act*, s 41, in considering applications for orders by cohabitants or former cohabitants, 'where the court is required to consider the nature of the parties' relationship, it is to have regard to the fact that they have not given each other the commitment involved in marriage'.

[33] SM Cretney, *Family Law*, 3rd edn (Sweet & Maxwell, 1997), p 101.

[34] [1999] 1 FLR 393. See also *G v G (Occupation Order: Conduct)* [2000] 2 FLR 36 in which the Court of Appeal held that in principle unintentional conduct could be sufficient to found an occupation order but on the facts found that the conduct of the husband was insufficient to warrant the making of the 'draconian' occupation order which the wife sought.

area in which the debate about the relative claims of justice or welfare in family law will continue as strongly as ever.

Property and Financial Matters

The debate about fault in the United States has to a large extent raged around marital property and alimony awards. Those who argue that fault should play a part in divorce are not usually arguing for restrictions on the right of either spouse to terminate an unsatisfactory marriage, but rather that the no-fault principle ought not to extend to every aspect of the divorce process. Thus, according to Woodhouse:

> Realistic consideration of marital fault would recognize both non-economic and economic harms and provide deterrence and compensation for oppression of women by men (and of men by women).[35]

Such laws are open to criticism on the basis that marital misconduct is essentially non-justiciable. Moreover, allowing fault to influence outcomes may dissociate property allocation and alimony awards from the more important criterion of need and may lead to unpredictability. It is also necessary to bear in mind an important difference between the approach in the United States and that taken by English law. While alimony, or spousal support, evidently still figures strongly in divorce settlements in the United States, in England a combination of the 'clean break' principle and a much more aggressive policy towards the enforcement of child support has marginalised the whole question of spousal support. In the majority of divorces, this will now be limited in time and rehabilitative in nature insofar as it is relevant at all.[36]

It appears that approximately half the states of the United States allow for some consideration of fault in the determination of alimony awards and, to a lesser extent, in allocating property. The fundamental basis of such laws is that consideration of fault is thought to be necessary to achieve justice in the financial consequences of divorce by allowing those aggrieved by marital misconduct to tell their stories and seek compensatory orders.

[35] See n 8, pp 2552–53.

[36] The 'clean break' principle was introduced into English law by the *Matrimonial and Family Proceedings Act* 1984 and is now embodied in the provisions of the *Matrimonial Causes Act* 1973, s 25A. The principles of child support were transformed by the *Child Support Acts* of 1991 and 1995. Further reform will be effected by the *Child Support, Pensions and Social Security Act* 2000. There has, since the 1991 legislation, been an uneasy relationship between the concept of the clean break and the enforcement of child support, but this has reflected the view that there can be no clean break from financial obligations to minor children. It does not detract from the idea that the *adult parties* should as far as possible be able to achieve a clean break as between themselves. It is, of course, conceded that there is a certain artificiality in seeking to draw rigid lines between spousal support and child support since they are in practice undifferentiated in the hands of the recipient, who is usually the mother.

With the introduction of separation grounds for divorce in England in the *Divorce Reform Act* 1969, the emphasis was intended to shift away from the matrimonial offence although, for the reasons discussed above, matrimonial offences remained relevant in divorce law and for a time also in the matrimonial jurisdiction of the magistrates' courts.[37] When the jurisdiction of the divorce court to make orders relating to property and financial matters was also reformed in the early 1970s, the question obviously arose as to the extent to which the matrimonial conduct of the parties should be relevant to the exercise of the court's discretion. Lord Denning gave an early answer to this question in *Wachtel v Wachtel*.[38] No longer would adultery and other common forms of matrimonial failings of themselves be sufficient to lead to a reduction in the financial award which the wife could otherwise have expected. As Lord Denning put it: 'There will be many cases in which a wife (though once considered guilty or blameworthy) will have cared for the home and looked after the family for many years.' It would be 'repugnant to the principles underlying the new legislation' to deprive her of benefits in these circumstances. But he also accepted that there would be 'a residue of cases' where the conduct of one of the parties was both 'obvious and gross'. In those cases, it would be 'repugnant to anyone's sense of justice' to order the other party to support such a person.

The current provision which governs the relevance of conduct in the exercise of the court's discretionary jurisdiction is contained in the *Matrimonial Causes Act* 1925, section 25(2)(g). The court must have regard 'in particular' to a range of factors, including factor (g) which reads:

> the conduct of each of the parties whatever the nature of the conduct and whether it occurred during the marriage or after the separation of the parties or (as the case may be) dissolution or annulment of the marriage, if that conduct is such that it would be inequitable to disregard it.

The question following *Wachtel* (and indeed the one which has continued to exercise the courts up to the present time, despite amendments to the relevant statutory provisions)[39] is what kind of conduct is sufficient to fall within the minority category of cases in which it should influence the property and financial orders made at divorce. While this has continued to be a matter of some

[37] Under the *Domestic Proceedings and Magistrates Courts Act* 1978, s 1, failure to maintain, behaviour and desertion might all found an application for maintenance. The latter two grounds have been largely redundant for years and will disappear altogether when the *Family Law Act* 1996, s 18 is implemented.

[38] [1973] Fam 72.

[39] The inclusion of conduct as an express factor was the result of an amendment to the 1973 Act by *the Matrimonial and Family Proceedings Act* 1984, but this was intended to do no more than give explicit statutory recognition to the existing practice of the courts. The words 'whatever the nature of the conduct and whether it occurred during the marriage or after the separation of the parties or (as the case may be) dissolution or annulment of the marriage' were inserted by the *Family Law Act* 1996. It remains a matter of academic speculation as to whether this amendment was intended to increase, or will have the effect of increasing, the relevance of conduct on these applications.

uncertainty, certain principles do appear to have emerged from the reported cases. The first is that we are looking for some conduct which can be described as quite out of the ordinary and going well beyond what might be expected in the context of marriage breakdown. Firing a shotgun at the husband has qualified,[40] as has inciting others to murder the husband under a contract killing,[41] and assisting the husband with suicide attempts—not on compassionate grounds but to be rid of him and to enable the wife to cohabit with her lover.[42] The second principle is that there must be a clear disparity in the conduct of the two parties—amply illustrated by the facts of *Leadbeater v Leadbeater*,[43] where it could be said with some justification that the husband and wife deserved one another. The wife's propensity for affairs while on holiday was rivalled only by her husband's actions in moving a fifteen-year-old girl into the matrimonial home and having a child with her. In this case, the court thought it would not be inequitable to disregard the wife's conduct. A third principle, which also looks at the question of conduct in the round, is that exemplary conduct by a spouse may occasionally result in a larger than normal award.[44] A final principle (and an important one) is that conduct which directly impacts on the family finances should be relevant.[45] This is perhaps no more than a statement of the obvious—especially where the effect of one spouse's dealings has been to dissipate the family finances and make less available for distribution.[46] The legislation contains provisions which can be utilised in some instances to set aside transactions which have this effect[47] but, alternatively, the court may simply take irresponsible behaviour into account and reduce what it awards accordingly.[48] Yet another approach, which has currently found favour with the courts, is to penalise this kind of financial misbehaviour, especially where it occurs during the course of the proceedings, in costs.[49] The remarkable and comparatively recent case of *Clark v Clark*[50] provides perhaps the best illustration of conduct which combines financial irresponsibility with generally outrageous behaviour and which led to the wife's award being reduced by the Court of Appeal from £552,500 to £175,000. In this case, the parties met at a Christmas party and married when the wife was in her early forties and the husband was nearly eighty. The wife spent a great deal of the husband's

[40] *Armstrong v Armstrong* (1974) 4 Fam Law 156.

[41] *Evans v Evans* [1989] I FLR 35.

[42] *K v K (Financial Provision: Conduct)* [1988] I FLR 469.

[43] [1985] FLR 789.

[44] As in *Kokosinski v Kokosinski* [1980] Fam 72 and *R v R (Financial Provision: Conduct)* (1993) Fam 282.

[45] For examples, see *B v B (Real Property: Assessment of Interests)* [1998] 2 FLR 490; *Beach v Beach* [1995] 2 FLR 160 and *H v H (Financial Relief: Conduct)* [1998] I FLR 971.

[46] This type of 'economic fault' is widely accepted as relevant to marital property distribution and as a factor in alimony awards in the United States. See Woodhouse, n 8, especially p 2538.

[47] The court may make an 'avoidance of disposition order' under the *Matrimonial Causes Act* 1973, s 37.

[48] As in the cases noted above, n 45.

[49] A recent illustration being *Tavoulareas v Tavoulareas* [1998] 2 FLR 418.

[50] [1999] 2 FLR 498.

considerable wealth, refused to consummate the marriage and humiliated him by effectively imprisoning him in a caravan in the garden while she lived with her younger lover in the matrimonial home.

Before leaving the question of the effect of conduct on financial awards, two nullity cases should be mentioned which demonstrate that fraud or misrepresentation at the inception of the 'marriage' may result in a party to a nullity petition either being debarred completely from claiming ancillary relief or, though not debarred as such, being denied anything in the exercise of the court's discretion.[51] Thus, in *Whiston v Whiston*,[52] a bigamist was not allowed to proceed at all with her claim on public policy grounds—that to allow it would be to allow a criminal to profit from her own actions. In *J v S-T (formerly J) (Transsexual: Ancillary Relief)*,[53] a young sexually inexperienced woman 'married' what she thought was an older man who in fact was a female to male transsexual with a plaster of paris penis. Remarkably, she was unaware of the true position and remained unaware of it for seventeen years. When the husband finally sought to have the marriage annulled, his claim for financial relief against his much wealthier 'wife' was refused on the basis of his deception.

Apart from the discretionary jurisdiction on divorce, the courts have a similarly wide jurisdiction to make orders for family provision on death where a range of qualified applicants may claim that the effect of the deceased's will or intestacy or both is 'not such as to make reasonable financial provision' for him or her.[54] In the exercise of this jurisdiction too, questions may arise as to the relevance of conduct by the applicant towards the deceased during his or her life or vice versa. A comparatively recent example is *Espinosa v Burke*.[55] In this case, the judge had refused the claim of an adult daughter on account of her behaviour towards the deceased in the last years of his life. She had been married five times and had a propensity for bringing male partners into her elderly father's home. In the last year of his life, she spent most of her time in Spain with the Spanish fisherman she subsequently married, leaving care of her father to his grandson and a cleaner. The Court of Appeal allowed her appeal on the basis that the judge had attached too much significance to the failure of the daughter to discharge her moral obligation to her father and not enough to her needs or to promises made to her by the deceased. But the Court nevertheless accepted the principle that conduct was a relevant factor to be taken into consideration.

Is fault at all relevant to the question of financial support of minor children? The existence of a mechanical, mathematical, non-discretionary child support

[51] In principle, ancillary relief is available under the *Matrimonial Causes Act* 1973 where a nullity petition is presented—and indeed this is one of the principal reasons why such a petition might be presented in the case of a void marriage.

[52] [1995] Fam 198.

[53] [1997] 1 FLR 402.

[54] Under the *Inheritance (Provision for Family and Dependants) Act* 1975.

[55] [1999] 1 FLR 747.

scheme would surely suggest otherwise.[56] But on a closer examination it becomes clear that fault is indeed relevant and, in some cases at least, it is arguably the basis of liability for child support. Liability arises from the fact of being a 'legal parent'. And, with the exception of the minority situations of children conceived by assisted reproduction or adopted children, legal parenthood flows from the genetic link—or at least the presumed genetic link—arising from marriage.[57] In other words, the legal status of being a parent, the trigger for financial liability, is the result of either intentionally having a child or negligently having a child—as where inadequate precautions are taken with contraception.[58] The issue of liability is very much seen as a matter of personal, individual responsibility, and this is especially argued in the case of men. Perhaps it was a one-night stand—but it is a matter of personal responsibility to ensure that children do not result from one-night stands and, if they do, those at fault must pay with a lifetime of financial responsibility.

It might be argued that the kind of liability which falls on genetic fathers is in nature more akin to criminal or tortious no-fault or strict liability. The argument would be that liability turns on the *responsibility* owed to a child. It is the failure to discharge this responsibility voluntarily *once a child is born* which is the true basis of liability rather than any fault which mayor may not have been implicit in the circumstances of conception. There is some force in this argument but, it is submitted, it is necessary to distinguish between those cases in which pregnancy results from a conscious decision to have a child, in or out of marriage, in the context of a committed relationship and those in which pregnancy results from casual sexual relations. In the case of the former it is reasonable to characterise liability as arising from a voluntary assumption of responsibility for the child which ought to be honoured. In the case of the latter, it would be a distortion to describe the father's position as involving any such assumption, or even recognition, of responsibility. The real foundation for the imposition of liability in these cases is, it is argued, a moral judgment about casual sexual relations which manifests itself on the conception and birth of the resulting child. Thus, while it is true that it is not necessary in law to prove fault as such, the reality is that the moral blameworthiness in being responsible for conception is seen as a sufficient justification for imposing an extensive legal obligation. The argument presented here

[56] Child support is currently governed by the *Child Support Acts* of 1991 and 1995. Although the system will be substantially reformed under legislation introduced by the Labour government, the effect will not be to return to the former discretionary jurisdiction of the courts.

[57] Under the *Child Support Act* 1991, s 1 'each parent of a qualifying child is responsible for maintaining him'. For these purposes, s 54 defines 'parent' as 'any person who is in law the mother or father of the child'.

[58] For a good critique of the essential basis of liability for child support, see H Krause, 'Child Support Reassessed: Limits of Private Responsibility and the Public Interest', in H Kay and S Sugarman (eds), *Divorce Reform at the Crossroads* (Yale University Press, 1990). For a recent collection of essays exploring the debates surrounding child support policy in Europe, Australia and the United States, see J Thomas Oldham and Marygold S Melli, *Child Support: The Next Frontier* (University of Michigan Press, 2000).

(which is reiterated below in relation to adoption and care proceedings) is that fault operates insidiously, as an unrecognised influence or factor, in the determination of legal issues which ostensibly have nothing at all to do with fault.

Might it be argued that the basis of child support is really welfare? The argument would be that parents are liable because the welfare of children dictates that they be properly provided for financially. And so they should, but this misses the point that in the majority of cases which involve the enforcement of child support liability it is the state which is seeking to recoup from the errant father what it has already paid out in social security benefits for the child. In other words, the social security system exists as the prime safety net to ensure a minimum income for mothers and children, and it is this which primarily protects the welfare of those children. The pursuit of the father is not to secure the welfare of the child but to enforce his legal, and what is seen as his moral, responsibility to the child and mother. He is conceptualised as being at fault in not discharging this voluntarily.

The issue of child support leads neatly into the much broader question of the extent to which fault is relevant in determining legal disputes over the welfare and upbringing of children.

Children

The shift away from the notion of the matrimonial offence, which characterised divorce and applications for ancillary relief in the early 1970s, was mirrored by similar developments in the practice of the courts in resolving disputes over children. The landmark case was the decision of the House of Lords in *J v C*,[59] which discredited the former notion that adulterous mothers should be at risk of losing the custody of their children to so-called 'unimpeachable' fathers. Thereafter, it was possible that the wife of an Anglican clergyman could have an affair with the church youth leader without thereby losing her young children in the ensuing custody litigation.[60]

This shift away from fault in determining disputes over residence or upbringing has been reflected in the principle that the child's welfare is the paramount or sole consideration in the court's determination. Although accepted as the most important principle informing the law affecting children, there are signs here too that some believe that the concerns of justice to parents ought not to be wholly ignored in the process.[61] Another way perhaps of expressing the same concern is the view that giving *precedence* to the interests of children does not necessarily involve ignoring the interests of adults. Increasingly, it will be necessary to balance not merely the respective *interests* of children and adults, but also their respective

[59] [1970] AC 668.

[60] *Re K (Minon) (Children: Care and Control)* [1977] Fam 179.

[61] For a damning critique of the principle that children's interests should always be placed first, above those of adults, see Rowthorn, n 17, pp 678–83.

rights which arise, for example, under the European Convention on Human Rights.[62] These approaches might allow for the readmission of fault as a factor in these determinations.

It has remained the case of course that adverse conduct which impacts directly on children themselves (as in the case of their abuse or neglect by a parent),[63] or indirectly (as in the case of violence towards the mother) may result in loss of residence or contact with the child.[64] But where this happens, it is the result of the courts looking to the future, and not to the past, and taking the view that the influence of the parent is harmful to the welfare of the child. It is not, as was formerly the case, a question of penalising the parent for past misdemeanours or of reinforcing moral responsibility. There is perhaps a vestige of this former attitude in the approach of the courts to applications by unmarried fathers for parental responsibility orders.[65] Here the onus is on the father to demonstrate the voluntary assumption of moral responsibility towards the child by showing a genuine interest in the child—though failure to accept financial responsibility has been held not to be fatal to such applications.[66] Again in this context, as with claims for ancillary relief, the reported decisions generally support the proposition that it is only negative conduct of some gravity, such as imprisonment for serious offences, which is likely to result in a father not being awarded parental responsibility[67] or, having once been awarded it, being later deprived of it.[68] It should of course be said that, again in this context, it is not perhaps fanciful to take the view that the concepts of fault and individual responsibility are the underlying rationale for the existence of the rule which withholds parental responsibility from the father in the first place. The father should not have been responsible for a birth out of wedlock and it is necessary to make him pay twice for this—once by requiring him to accept the burdens of parenthood (liability for child support) and once by denying him the benefits of parenthood (a say in upbringing and the right to look after the child).

Elsewhere in the law relating to children, fault continues to play a rather more conspicuous part than might be imagined at first glance. Take, for example, adoption—it is true that Lord Hailsham famously said in *Re W*[69] that unreasonableness was not to be equated with culpability, but many of the courts' decisions on dispensing with parental consent on this ground have come rather close to equating parental inadequacy with unreasonableness.[70] This may be dressed up as

[62] See further Andrew Bainham, 'Children Law at the Millennium', in Stephen Cretney (ed), *Family Law at the Millennium* (Gordans, 2000).

[63] Which could result in prosecution for an offence under the *Children and Young Persons Act* 1933 or an application for a care or supervision order under the *Children Act* 1989, s 31.

[64] For a recent illustration, see *Re* M *(Contact: Violent Parent)* [1999] 2 FLR 321.

[65] The leading case is *Re S (Parental Responsibility)* [1995] 2 FLR 648.

[66] *Re H (Parental Responsibility: Maintenance)* [1996] 1 FLR 867.

[67] As in *Re P (Parental Responsibility)* [1997] 2 FLR 722 and *Re* H *(Parental Responsibility)* [1998] 1 FLR 855.

[68] See *Re P (Terminating Parental Responsibility)* [1995] 1 FLR 1048.

[69] *Re W (An Infant)* [1971] AC 682.

[70] For a particularly good illustration, see the difference of judicial opinion in the Court of Appeal in *Re C (A Minor) (Adoption: Parental Agreement)* [1993] 2 FLR 260.

a process driven by welfare considerations, but parental fault or failings are not usually far below the surface. And we perhaps ought not to forget that most of the other grounds for dispensing with parental consent, though little used today, are still on the statute books and are largely about parental misbehaviour. If persistently failing without reasonable cause to discharge parental responsibility, abandonment and neglect, persistent ill-treatment and serious ill-treatment[71] are not about fault, then what are they about? Interestingly, we have a recent decision which suggests that, conversely, behaviour which is beyond reproach may not be given much weight in the ultimate decision about whether to allow adoption to proceed. In *Re O*,[72] the unmarried father had been unaware of his paternity, the mother having decided not to tell him. No criticism was made of the father who, when he did find out, wished to resist the adoption of the child by foster parents. His consent was nonetheless dispensed with in a decision which manifestly turned on the child's welfare.

In the context of care proceedings, the issue of parental fault is surely central although there has been a marked reluctance to call it that—especially given the emphasis on partnership between parents and the state under the *Children Act*.[73] Nonetheless, the insistence of the House of Lords in *Re H and R*[74] that care orders should never be made on the basis only of suspicion, but on the basis of proof of specific allegations on which the state is relying, looks very much like saying that there must be proof of parental culpability. Of course, this view must now be reassessed in the light of the later decision by the House in *Lancashire County Council v B*.[75] Here the House held that where the child had already been harmed by an unknown perpetrator within the care network, it was not necessary for the local authority to be able to attribute the child's significant harm to any one carer in particular. But this was a case in which one of three carers clearly *was* responsible for the child's injuries and the court took the view that the child should not be denied protection on the basis that it had proved impossible to establish which it was. Moreover, the Court of Appeal had held, on a point which was not appealed, that it was not possible to found a care order on the sole basis of a risk to another child who was in contact with only one of those under suspicion.

We should not leave the question of children and fault without commenting that fault and personal responsibility, whether of the child himself or of his parents, have undergone something of a renaissance in recent years as juvenile justice has taken an increasingly punitive turn under governments of both complexions.[76] The abolition of the *doli incapax* presumption for children over

[71] *Adoption Act* 1976, s 16(2).

[72] *Re O (Adoption: Withholding Agreement)* [1999] 1 FLR 451.

[73] The intention behind the public law regime of the *Children Act* 1989 was that parents should not be stigmatised as failures where their children were looked after by local authorities and that care procedures should be cast in a less threatening and more positive light.

[74] *Re H (Minor) (Sexual Abuse: Standard of Proof)* [1996] AC 563.

[75] [2000] 2 WLR 590.

[76] For an illuminating account of this trend, concentrating on the responsibility of parents for juvenile crime, see L Gelsthorpe, 'Youth Crime and Parental Responsibility', in A Bainham, S Day Sclater and M Richards (eds), *What is a Parent: A Socio-Legal Analysis* (Hart Publishing, 1999), p 217.

ten,[77] the introduction of parenting orders, child safety orders and other complementary measures,[78] and the increased use of custodial options in the case of persistent young offenders,[79] are but the most striking features of what is a general trend away from a welfare and towards a justice model of juvenile justice. Put in the context of this chapter, the central point is that criminal activity by children is seen primarily as a matter of the individual responsibility—indeed fault—of the children themselves and their parents.

We hear so much about the welfare and best interests of children and about the predominance of the welfare principle. Yet the reality is that throughout children law, as elsewhere in family law, we can find plenty of examples of culpability and the concerns of justice having an influence on outcomes. That being the case, the question which now needs to be addressed is the proper role for fault in modern family law and it is that question which I attempt to answer in the following section.

IS THERE A FUTURE ROLE FOR FAULT?

What this brief review reveals is that fault continues to perform a role in family law today which is perhaps more significant than is commonly supposed. But the key questions are exactly what kind of role is it performing and what should be the proper function of fault in family law, if indeed it is to be retained? In attempting to answer these questions, a good starting point is to examine the role of fault in other branches of the law—most obviously criminal law and the law of torts.

Criminal law, with its emphasis on proof of *mens rea*, is self-evidently concerned with establishing fault as a basis of guilt and punishment, though this is qualified by the existence of many offences of strict liability. But the vast majority of *serious* offences may only be committed where there is *mens rea* and this is normally taken to mean intention or recklessness as to consequences.[80] Andrew Ashworth[81] has located the fundamental basis of criminalisation and the requirement of *mens rea* in the principle of *individual autonomy* and *individual responsibility* for actions. This is that liability is in general imposed only on those who may fairly be said to have *chosen* to engage in the behaviour which has resulted in the consequences in question. Yet the principle of individual autonomy, though pervasive, is far from universal and Ashworth also identifies the principle of *welfare* as an alternative basis for criminalisation in some cases. Under the principle of welfare, weight is given to collective social goals such as environmental

[77] *Crime and Disorder Act* 1998, s 34.

[78] Under the *Crime and Disorder Act* 1998, Part I.

[79] Exemplified by the 'secure training order' for persistent young offenders between the ages of twelve and fourteen introduced by the *Criminal Justice and Public Order Act* 1994, s 1(5).

[80] In the case of the majority of serious crimes, advertent recklessness will suffice; but some, of which murder is the most obvious example, are reliant on proof of intention.

[81] A Ashworth, *Principles of Criminal Law*, 3rd edn (Oxford University Press, 1999), p 27 *et seq.*

protection and public safety.[82] While there is an undoubted tension between these two alternative bases of liability, it is not necessarily the case that they are contradictory. But within a system which attaches weight to individual autonomy, there may need to be mechanisms in place which properly accommodate individual rights where social goals are pursued. The principle of autonomy and no liability without fault is also thought to be an important feature in the law of torts. Although there are some examples of outcome-based strict liability in tort, in general, as Cane[83] has put it:

> outcome-based strict liability is in some sense inconsistent with non-legal morality in holding people responsible for outcomes which they did not intend and which they could not have avoided.

The species of fault generally required for tortious liability is intention or negligence and, in contrast to the criminal law, liability will often be imposed for omissions. This basis of liability is particularly germane to family law since the underlying rationale is the existence of a legal duty based on a relationship of proximity between the parties.[84] So too in family law, many of the duties which may be thought to arise and which can give rise to legal consequences if broken depend on the closeness of the relationship between family members. Most obviously, perhaps, parents owe a duty of care towards their children and may be criminally liable for abuse or neglect as well as at risk of having their children removed from them under care procedures. Breach of duty is also clearly the basis of the declining matrimonial offence doctrine. Moreover, as we have seen, one of the primary reasons why a return to fault-based divorce has been advocated, both here and in the United States, has been an attempt to underscore marital obligations and deter marital misconduct. Marriage is a legal status which imposes reciprocal duties on the spouses. Where these duties were not properly discharged, a matrimonial offence might be committed which could found matrimonial relief or which might lead to matrimonial relief being denied.[85] And it is clearly the case that there may be a breach of duty by omission just as there may be by commission. Thus it was that the incorrigibly and inexcusably lazy Mr Gollins[86] could be adjudged guilty of cruelty.[87]

Yet, in tort law too, there is an ongoing debate about how far it should be the purpose of this branch of the law to uphold ethical rules and principles of

[82] *Ibid.*, p 30 *et seq.*

[83] P Cane, *The Anatomy of Tort Law* (Hart Publishing, 1997), p 49.

[84] Enshrined in Lord Atkin's famous 'neighbour principle' in *Donoghue v Stevenson* [1932] AC 562.

[85] Most obviously, this has been so historically in relation to adultery as in *Richmond v Richmond*, see n 5.

[86] *Gollins v Gollins* [1964] AC 644.

[87] In the United States, there has been a comparatively recent emergence of marital torts whereby claims for compensation may be made on the basis of some of the more gross forms of marital misconduct. See Woodhouse, n 8, pp 2538–39. See also Harry D Krause 'On the danger of allowing marital fault to re-emerge in the guise of torts' (1998) 73 *Not. Dame L Rev* 1355.

personal responsibility and how far it is legitimate to pursue other social goals. As Cane continues:[88]

> We could say that giving effect to ethical principles of personal responsibility is only one of the social functions of tort law, and that achieving a socially fair distribution of the burdens of meeting tort liabilities is another. This approach would involve an admission that tort law legitimately serves a number of different social goals which may conflict with one another.

So, to summarise, it is probably fair to say that criminal and tortious liability turn largely on personal responsibility for actions though there are some instances in which the pursuit of wider social goals allows the principle of welfare to take precedence over personal autonomy and liability is accordingly imposed without fault.

Perhaps the most obvious feature which distinguishes family law from these other branches of law is the apparent predominance of the principle of welfare in determining legal outcomes. But it will be suggested that there is plenty of evidence to support the view that the principle of individual responsibility remains relevant to the resolution of many issues and that in many cases it would be artificial to seek to distinguish between the two principles in the way that they operate in the context of the family. This is because the question of the individual responsibility of one member of the family will be directly relevant to the determination of the future welfare needs of another family member.

Here, it is argued, it is necessary to distinguish between adverse conduct or fault which is *backward-looking* and located only in past behaviour and conduct which is *ongoing* and relevant to *future* welfare needs. Family law has developed in such a way that past conduct is now relevant in only a declining number of instances, whereas present and ongoing conduct remains highly significant.

Let us consider first the question of *past* conduct. In general, we can say that the doctrine of the matrimonial offence has had its day (though it will remain the theoretical basis for the majority of divorces) and that where in theory it continues to be utilised it is used not to uphold the obligations inherent in the marriage contract but to facilitate administrative divorce and remarriage. It cannot truly be said that the 'offences' of adultery, behaviour and desertion have much to do with enforcing individual responsibility. In truth, they have more to do with the principle of welfare—it being in the best interests of those who are unhappily married that they be allowed to escape from the situation in a reasonably short timescale. It is, of course, interesting to speculate on the effect which the total abolition of fault-based grounds for divorce might have on the perception of marital obligations and the marriage contract. Leaving religion aside, would the abolition of adultery as a basis for divorce carry the implication that marital fidelity is no longer expected by the law? Some might argue that, even if the reliance on adultery in practice is about getting an early divorce, its removal as a basis for divorce

[88] See n 83, p 28.

would undermine the principle of individual responsibility, and we have seen that this is a concern of the pro-fault lobby both here and in the United States. It has also been argued above that liability for child support, being based on the intention to have a child or the negligence in preventing one, does appear to be support for the principle of individual responsibility of the backward-looking variety. Those cases in which the more extreme forms of adverse conduct have resulted in a reduction in the size of property and financial orders on divorce may also conform with the model of penalising past behaviour and enforcing individual responsibility within marriage. This is certainly a feature of alimony awards in the United States. In the property context, we can also see something of a relic from the past—what we might call the 'disparity principle'. Matrimonial offences could not be relied upon unless the 'injured party' was himself or herself substantially 'innocent', and this is very much the thinking still in those modern cases in which it is sought to argue that the behaviour of one party was so bad that it should have financial consequences.[89] The same may not be said of cases of *financial* irresponsibility which conform much more to the outcome-based or welfare model—the behaviour in question is directly referable to the outcome which the court is seeking to achieve (a fair redistribution of property and financial resources) and, of course, to future welfare needs of a housing or financial nature.

When we consider *present* and *potential* conduct or fault, we can see its immediate relevance to modern family law and the way in which questions of fault can become inextricably linked to questions of welfare. This is most obviously true in children cases. Gone are the days when matrimonial misbehaviour between the adult parties is of itself enough to affect the question of the residence or upbringing of the children, though it has been argued that the personal morality of a parent ought to be relevant in terms of the environment in which it is proposed that the child should be raised.[90] But a propensity for violence or abuse may be highly relevant, not because it is the concern of family law to enforce morally upright behaviour, but because such violence or its potential represents a direct threat to the welfare of the children. Fault is thus relevant, but only because it is relevant to welfare. It is perhaps for this reason that family law fails to uphold the principle in criminal law and the law of torts that, in general, there should be no liability without fault. The concerns of welfare figure so prominently in children cases that it matters not that a parent can boast a record of exemplary behaviour.[91] At the same time, it seems entirely likely that the implementation of the *Human Rights Act* 1998 will lead to challenges to the dominance of the welfare principle if the effect of this is to deny the enforcement of individual rights. The question of parental contact with children seems set to become one key issue around which such claims may be presented. In short, it is likely to be argued that the determination of contact

[89] See nn 40–42.

[90] See Rowthorn, n 17, p 680: 'What matters from this perspective is not simply the love and warmth of the child's home environment, but also the moral character of those who inhabit this environment, for it is these people who will playa crucial role in shaping the child's own moral values.'

[91] As in *Re K*, see n 50 and *Re O*, see n 60.

cannot be *solely* a matter of the child's welfare as it is at present. Individuals who have discharged their responsibilities to the best of their ability should not suffer the liability of losing their *right* of contact without fault on their part.[92]

Elsewhere in family law, the arguments are bound to continue about the relative importance which should be attached to welfare needs and to the claims of justice to individuals. Nowhere will this be more apparent than in relation to the draconian orders which can be made to deal with domestic violence and occupation of the family home, and in relation to what has to be proved against parents before a child may be compulsorily removed from them. Whether family law should be less about welfare and more about enforcing individual family obligations is a question upon which reasonable people may differ. And just as there are many different conceptions of welfare, so there is no obvious consensus on what are now acceptable norms of family behaviour and a good deal of debate about whether the marriage contract itself should be redefined to keep pace with the times. At the same time, it is difficult to escape the feeling that the family justice system should, at least in part, indeed be concerned with justice. One suspects that the uninitiated would expect the courts to make some attempt to adjudicate between 'right and wrong' and not to be preoccupied with acting as welfare agencies. But to achieve anything like an acceptable balance first involves answering the question 'what is family justice?'

[92] These arguments are pursued further by the author in 'Family Rights in the Next Millennium', in *Current Legal Problems* (2000), pp 471–504.

28

Macro Social and Economic Factors in Society which Influence the Success of Financial Rearrangements on Divorce

Alastair Bissett-Johnson*

INTRODUCTION

Factors of general application in society, as opposed to those specific to the parties, may have shaped the success of legislative and judicial solutions to the question of financial provision after marital breakdown.

In the past, these solutions have included quests for 'clean breaks' between the parties such as:

—transfers of the matrimonial home to the parent with care of the child, either in return for a reduced child support obligation by the other parent, or for the owner of the larger occupational pension scheme to be able to retain it;

—equal division of defined matrimonial assets, sometimes (often quite rarely) supplemented by limited periodical payments for a spouse suffering significant financial dependency as a result of marriage or child care. In Canada and Scotland, these schemes typically have provided for an equal division of defined matrimonial assets,[1] supplemented with an additional lump sum or periodical payments to cover specific losses, such as interrupted careers or losses flowing from the breakdown of marriage—for example, a carer's allowance for the parent with whom the child resides. Since then, various attempts have been made to further refine the philosophy of the 'clean break'.

* Professor of Private Law, University of Dundee. The assistance of the British Council with a travel grant to attend the 2000 ISFL conference in Brisbane is acknowledged. The research assistance of Lucia Polanski, a University of Dundee law student, is also acknowledged.

[1] The matrimonial assets usually refer to property acquired during the marriage until breakdown (often defined as the date of separation rather than divorce), but exclude certain assets such as inheritances or gifts from third parties. (For more detail on the Canadian position, see JG McLeod and AA Mamo, *Matrimonial Property Law in Canada* (formerly Bissett-Johnson and Holland); for the Scottish position, see EM Clive, *The Law of Husband and Wife*, 3rd edn (SULI, 1992) and A Bisset-Johnston and C Barton, 'Financial provision on divorce in Scots law—does it need reform?' (2000) *Judicial Review* 265. The English system is much more judicial discretion-based, as exemplified by the *Report to the Lord Chancellor by the Ancillary Relief Advisory Group* (30 July 1998).

These have included, on the capital side, adding extra items for division on divorce such as pensions (and splitting them),[2] or even professional qualifications acquired during the marriage.[3] In an attempt to more fairly share responsibility for child support, ever more complicated algebraic formulae have been devised—but the initial, complicated UK scheme has now been revised in favour of a simple percentage scheme in the new *Child Support, Pensions and Social Security Act* 2000;[4]

—attempts to create a 'clean break'[5] between parties by means of a lump sum payment (sometimes calculated by capitalising periodical payments). The 'clean break' is aimed at enabling each spouse to move on with their life with a minimum of friction and without continued spousal support obligations—though recognising that support for children is a different matter.

The apparent neatness of the 'clean break' obscures the reality that many 'clean breaks' can only be achieved by 'instalment payments' which may be as difficult to enforce as periodical payments and are even more vulnerable in the case of the payer's bankruptcy. Whether the increase in clean breaks represents advice to clients by lawyers in the light of the existing state of the law or a desire by wives to sever links with their former husbands is unclear. If the latter is true, the state surely has an interest in ensuring that the 'clean break' is not achieved by transferring to the state through the social welfare system a burden that might properly be the husband's. In many cases, the claim by the wife has a restitutionary basis, apart from 'need' which can best be dealt by variable orders for periodical payments which can be altered in the light of the way circumstances develop rather than by judicial foresight.

In her controversial study, Weitzman[6] identified some of the unexpected and unintended impact of 'no fault' divorce for women and children when coupled with a desire for a 'clean break'. Weitzman's work has been criticised by Peterson[7]

[2] Post the section on social security.

[3] No definitive position has emerged in the United States; contrast *O'Brien v O'Brien* 498 NYY (2d) 743 (where the professional qualification was treated as a matrimonial asset) with *Re Marriage of Graham* 574 P 2d 752. In general, the Canadian position has been to treat these qualifications as relevant to spousal support (especially restitutionary support where one spouse has benefited professionally from the support of their partner). The one case where a professional qualification was treated as a valuable matrimonial asset was reversed on appeal, *Caratun v Caratun* (1992) 10 O.R. (3d) 385 (Ont CA), leave to appeal to SCC refused (1993) 46 RFL (3d) 7. This avoids the problem of how to value such assets, especially when such a valuation is highly speculative. It was this that led to the decision in *Corless v Corless* (1987) 34 DLR (4th) 598 (Ont UFC) to treat a professional qualification as a matrimonial asset but without value.

[4] For details of the new scheme, see Wikely, 'Child Support—the New Formula (Part 1 and Part 2)' [2000] *Family Law* 820 and 888.

[5] For a discussion of the statistics showing how popular the 'clean break' has become in England, see C Barton and A Bissett-Johnson, 'The Declining Number of Ancillary Relief Orders' [2000] *Family Law* 94.

[6] LJ Weitzman, *The Divorce Revolution: The Unexpected Consequences for Women and Children in America* (Free Press, 1985).

[7] I am grateful to Professor Ira Ellman of the Law School at University of California, Berkeley, for discussions highlighting the best sources on this issue.

and others. When Peterson re-analysed Weitzman's data, he found that the claimed 27 per cent decline in women's standard of living was barely one-third of the figure claimed by Weitzman. Similarly, the men's increase in living standard was only 10 per cent rather than the 42 per cent claimed by Weitzman.[8] Whilst Peterson alleges that Weitzman's work has exaggerated the problem for women,[9] even on Peterson's figures the problem remains substantial.

However, it is not the purpose of this chapter to rake over old ground and past statistics, but rather to see whether the 'clean break theory' has gained momentum in recent years. In this sense, the 'clean break' has not merely been fortified by the changes in family law which promoted it; more importantly, the issue is now whether these adverse implications for women have been compounded by macro changes in society which have left older spouses, and particularly women, vulnerable[10] in the quest for the 'clean break'.

The thesis I wish to explore is whether recent, more general, factors in society have affected the way that various financial provision/matrimonial property regimes on divorce have operated. A subsidiary issue is whether, in times of volatility in society, there is a case for revisiting periodical payments as a better and less crude way of dealing with rearrangement of finances on divorce than the 'clean break' arrangements, which tend to be inflexible and non-variable. We have only just started to devise effective enforcement mechanisms such as the withdrawal of driving licences as a way of enforcing periodical payments. Arguments about the law artificially maintaining women's financial dependency can surely be met by making it easier for husbands to seek a reduction in periodical support or the termination of the order where the wife does not make appropriate efforts to seek employment or get a better job, or to work full time if she is already in employment.

TAX

In some countries (for example, Canada) in the 1980s, there was a reduction in tax rates; this began with President Reagan's efforts in the United States,[11] which

[8] For the debate between Peterson and Weitzman see (1996) 61 *Am Sociological Rev* at pp 528, 537 and 539.

[9] See RR Peterson, 'A Re-evaluation of the Economic Consequences of Divorce' (1996) 61 *Am Sociological Review* 528, in which Peterson's further analysis of Weitzman's conclusions, but based on a bigger sample, failed to replicate them. Whereas Weitzman had claimed that women suffered a 73% decline in women's standard of living after divorce and that men increased their standard of living 43% after divorce, Peterson's figures were that the decline for women was 27% and the increase for men was only 10%. Weitzman's reply to Peterson's analysis seems to be that her computer expert had let her down (see the same volume of the journal, at 537 esp 538).

[10] The (British) Office for National Statistics' *Social Inequalities 2000* report (summarised in *The Times*, 11 May 2000) suggested that in April 1999 men in full-time employment had earnings of £23,000 per annum—42% higher than women.

[11] See, for example, the tax reforms in Canada in 1988.

reduced the attractiveness of 'income splitting'[12] after spouses separated. 'Income splitting' enabled the parties to take advantage of a tax deduction by the payer spouse on a higher marginal rate of tax, and the inclusion of support in the income of the recipient spouse at the lower marginal rate of tax. The greater the difference between the higher and lower marginal rates of tax, the better. More recently, we have seen the abolition of tax advantages for spousal support altogether as in Canada after the decision in *Thibaudeau v Canada.*[13] In Britain, tax relief on maintenance has been phased out over a number of years. People who were divorced before March 1988 were allowed tax relief at the higher rate, if they were subject to it, on payments to wives and children. Thus a husband who was on the 40 per cent higher rate of tax and paid support of £10,000 would get tax relief of £4,000. His wife would add this as income to their salaries if she was in paid work, but if she was not in paid employment she could set it against her income tax personal allowance and those of her children. However, when the tax relief was abolished in April 2000, some 15,000 couples were adversely affected and there were rumours in the *Sunday Times* of a flood of applications to vary the existing orders once the tax relief was abolished.[14] In addition, a further 280,000 people qualifying for lesser tax relief[15] were also affected.[16] The abolition of tax breaks for wealthier husbands/fathers can certainly be urged on the basis of creating a more equal tax regime in which the losses to the state from income splitting could be used to create a minimum guaranteed income or negative income tax or other measures to assure a more adequate income to poorer couples whose marriages had broken down. On the other hand, it was the husbands with

[12] In essence, this allowed the payer of maintenance to deduct spousal or child support payments from (typically) his income only for those same payments to be included in the income of the recipient. If the recipient was on a lower marginal tax rate (say, 50%) than the payer (say, 30%), the difference was met by the taxpayer. Recipients were aware of this saving to the payer and used the tax saving to increase the level of support they would agree to.

[13] (1996) 124 DLR(4th) 449 (SCC). See the amendment in respect of payments made after 1996 to s 56(1)(b) and the abolition of s 56(1)(c) of the Canadian *Income Tax Act* made by SC c 25 s 8(1) and the amendment of s 60(b) and the repeal of s 60(c) by 1997 SC c 25 s 10).

[14] See *Sunday Times*, 26 Mar 2000.

[15] These involved maintenance payments due after 15 Mar 1988. Such payments had to be made:

(a) gross by the payer without deduction of tax;
(b) without a tax liability on the part of the recipient;
(c) any tax relief due to the payer was only due in respect of payments under a court order, child support assessment or written binding agreement;
(d) with no tax relief if direct to children;
(e) and by 1999–2000, the last year of tax relief, the lower of 10% of the married couple's allowance (£1,970) or the payments made in that year.

See A Melville, 'Taxation: *Finance Act* 1999', *Financial Times*/Prentice Hall, 1999).

[16] Typically, these would have been people who were allowed 10% tax relief on £1,970 of child maintenance under (mainly) pre-1988 divorces. This figure was equal to the married couple's allowance and on the abolition of this married person's allowance, the tax benefit for child maintenance was also abolished. The relief was circumscribed by the terms of s 347B of the *Income and Corporation Taxes Act* 1988 as amended by s 36 of the *Finance Act* 1988 (see *Norris (Inspector of Taxes) v Edgson, The Times LR* 30 May 2000.

the greater disposable income who were most likely to be able to afford to pay maintenance.

Inflation, Interest Rates and Life Expectancy

Low inflation rates, and the desire by banks and related institutions to increase their profits by holding down the interest they pay on deposits whilst increasing charges on loans ('the margin or spread'), means that capital sums which at one time might have generated an income on an exhausting fund basis for a dependent spouse after a 'clean break' settlement are no longer large enough to do so. The 'margin' may be a more potent factor than low interest rates since leading economists like Dr Deutsch of the Economic Council of Canada, have opined that the long-term real rate of interest was always around 3.5 per cent, the remaining notional rate of return (interest rate) being accounted for by inflation.[17]

The problem has been further exacerbated by recipients of awards enjoying an extended life expectancy. The life expectancy of a person to some extent varies according to the tables used. For example, Woelke[18] states that tables produced for the pension industry are weighted according to the number of the members of the private scheme involved and are based on the expectation that members of the schemes involved will outlive the life expectancy of comparable members of the general population of England and Wales by about five years.

The recent combination of low interest rates and increasing longevity can have a significant shrinking effect on annuities, which are in some ways an appropriate analogy to lump-sum awards intended to last a middle-aged wife for many years. *Saga Magazine,*[19] a British magazine for senior citizens, suggests that the annuity on £100,000 for the joint life of a sixty-five-year-old man with a wife aged sixty-two had almost halved from £10,871 in 1990 to £5,400 in 1999. The comparable 1999 figure for a sixty-year-old man retiring with a fund of £100,000 is £7,750 per annum, with a further fall to £6,840 when the additional life expectancy has been included. The comparable UK figures for sixty-year-old women are £6,950 shrinking to £6,695. To compensate for this decline, the man would have to save an additional £12,000 and women an additional £4,250 with their capital fund.[20]

[17] For a discussion of this in the context of personal injuries, see *Thornton v Board of School Trustees etc.* [1978] WWR 607 at 640 (SCC). In England, the House of Lords in *Wells v Wells* [1998] 3 All ER 481 (HL) recently decided that recipients of personal injury awards could not be expected to invest their award in investments carrying risk, but must rather be expected to invest them in government stocks carrying about a 3.5% rate of return. In the family law arena, the declining rate of return has led to a recalculation of the interest element in a Duxbury Order by which periodical support is capitalised into a lump sum. See SM Cretney and J Masson, *Principles of Family Law*, 6th edn (Sweet & Maxwell, 1996), pp 444 and 487 for more detail.

[18] 'Is Duxbury the Answer?' [1999] *Family Law* 766.

[19] June 1999 issue, p 110, quoting the Annuity Bureau.

[20] See the *Sunday Times* Money Section, 25 July 1999, front page.

In the context of divorce, the use of 'Duxbury' or similar tables to capitalise income for a woman's interrupted career when calculated at a proper real rate of return produces figures which are so high that, even when paid in instalments carrying interest, few but the 'ultra rich' can afford them. There has been an argument recently about whether the decision of the House of Lords in *Wells v Wells*[21] requires the use of interest rates based on low-risk investments such as index-linked government stocks so as to produce even higher capital sums. Though some authors[22] and judges[23] have doubted the correctness of using low-risk government stock as the basis for a Duxbury calculation, this seems open to question. Why should a middle-aged wife with a possibly limited employment income be expected to take more than limited risks with a capital sum expected to support her over twenty years or so? Although it might be argued that personal injury cases have an element of 'fault' lacking in family cases, the House of Lords did not mention this element in *Wells*. The argument advanced by Lawrence[24] that, had the marriage continued, the parties would have probably taken the risks of the contingencies and vicissitudes of life seems to have been countered by Woelke's argument[25] that the attempt to use the standard of living that the parties would have enjoyed had they continued to be married was abandoned by the *Matrimonial and Family Proceedings Act* 1984. Moreover, the risks that can be shared in a two-partner enterprise (marriage) become less easy to justify for an older wife. The failure to leave divorced women with a sufficient long-term income to care for themselves into retirement runs the risk of adding to social security costs.

EMPLOYMENT

Recent trends in corporate structures in the Western world, such as 'downsizing' by way of early retirement and redundancy, have reduced the opportunities for many people to remain in employment beyond age fifty, particularly after they have lost a job.[26] *The Times*[27] suggested that, for men over fifty, there has been a dramatic drop in employment. According to research commissioned by the employment consultancy Sanders and Sidney, age prejudice in high-technology industries may begin as young as age forty-two. In interviews with 237 candidates

[21] [1998] 3 All ER 481.

[22] 'At a Glance', Family Law Bar Association, and also 'Duxbury—the Future' [1998] *Family Law* 741.

[23] Singer J in *A v A (Financial Provision)* [1998] 2 FLR 833 and Holman J in *F v F (Duxbury Calculation)* 1 FLR 833 have doubted the correctness of the use of low-risk investments such as index-linked government stocks. These decisions ante dated Wells, supra.

[24] 'Duxbury: Is there a Right Rate of Return?' [1996] *Family Law* 560.

[25] [1999] *Family Law* 766.

[26] For example, (1999) 29 *Social Trends*, HMSO Table 4.1 shows a steepening decline in the United Kingdom of men aged between 45 and 54 in the labour force between 1971 and 1997, and the number of men in the workforce aged between sixty and sixty-four has declined by nearly half since 1973: *ibid.*, p 73. See also *Labour Market Trends*, successor to the *Employment Gazette*.

[27] 4 Sept 1999.

over the age of thirty-five seeking professional jobs and 27 employers, 51 per cent aged forty-four and under described cases of age discrimination.[28] Whereas in 1979, some 93 per cent of the over-fifties were in work, the current figure is 68 per cent, with some areas showing even greater falls in employment.[29] However, it is extremely difficult to get accurate figures here. British governments of both persuasions have constantly 'massaged' or 'refined' the ' counting' procedures for establishing who is out of work in order to paint the government in the best possible light[30] or to reduce social security costs such as disability payments.[31] Those who are not 'actively seeking work' are excluded. Yet it may be just those older workers who have been made redundant and then tried repeatedly to get work, or the estranged wife who is seeking work but given up after the first 100 unsuccessful applications, who will be excluded from the unemployed as a person who is 'no longer actively seeking work' in the government's terms.[32] To fit such people into the same category as the 'work shy' seems grossly unreasonable. What is clear is that, in some recent major British mergers, it has been the executives over fifty who have been targeted for retirement. Axa, a major British insurer, pensioned off most executives over fifty and Barclays Bank ran into trouble with the Inland Revenue for trying to retire executives in their forties for whom pensions were not available under the tax rules until they had reached the age of fifty.[33] As a consequence of this, the British government published in April 2000 a document entitled *Winning the Generation Game,* which listed seventy-five recommendations to transform the lives of older people. One key recommendation, starting in 2010, is to raise from age fifty to fifty-five the age at which people could be given early retirement whilst their employers benefited from the tax advantages attaching to private or occupational pension schemes. The government's anxiety is said to originate in its fear that demographic trends such as an increase in longevity will place an increasing burden on the state through the social security system.

[28] See *Sunday Times,* 19 Mar 2000.

[29] According to claims of Don Steele of the Association of the Retired and Persons Over 50, *Sunday Times,* 19 Mar 2000. *The Times,* 25 Apr 2000 claimed that, of the British population aged between fifty and sixty-five, 2.8 million were unemployed.

[30] I am grateful to Professor Ian Walker of the Department of Economics, University of Warwick for suggesting the following accounts of the way in which definitions of the 'unemployed' have changed over time: Atkinson and Micklewright, 'Unemployment Compensation and Labour Market transactions' (1991) 29 *Journal of Economic Literature* 1679, esp at 1683 *et seq.*; and the same authors, 'Turning the Screw: Benefits for the Unemployed 1979–88', in A Dilnot and I Walker (eds), *The Economics of Social Security* (Oxford University Press, 1989), pp 17–51.

[31] In Britain, the social security for those classified as long-term sick or disabled has been higher than the social security available to those merely 'out of work', with the consequence that there has been a tendency for doctors to be asked, and to be willing, to approve applications for sickness or disability benefit, with a consequent risk to the public purse. As a consequence of this, the criteria for qualification for such benefits has recently been tightened.

[32] 'Actively searching for work' is the British government's preferred term in collecting statistics for the unemployed and is the term used in the UK Labour Force Survey. On this basis, the current British unemployment rate for those over fifty seems quite modest.

[33] *Sunday Times,* 19 Mar 2000.

Although the shrinking birth rate in the Western world[34] would apparently suggest a need to continue to employ older, experienced workers, and confirm the folly of 'ageism', the statistics suggest otherwise. Once made redundant, the chances of finding work, even for the well-qualified, decline substantially. The British government has to some extent recognised this by talking of encouraging older people who have lost their jobs to accept lower paid jobs by guaranteeing them a minimum income if they do so,[35] or even guaranteeing older people the right to work until age 70.[36] Such approaches only work, however, if the older workers can find a job. Even if there is difficulty in obtaining accurate statistics about the older unemployed, it is difficult to dispute the conclusions of La Forest J in the Canadian Supreme Court decision in *Richardson v Richardson*,[37] a case in which a forty-six-year-old wife,[38] separated from her husband after eighteen years of marriage and who had virtually never worked since the birth of her second child, found difficulty in finding employment contrary to her expectations. La Forest J found that her job skills had atrophied[39] and continued:

> Mrs Richardson is now in her mid-forties and must find time and energy to care for a child, factors that are by no means negligible in assessing her competitive position against younger people with recent training.[40]

The difficulties of securing employment for the 'middle-aged worker' have an effect on some common solutions to rearranging family finances after divorce. At one time it was common in Canada and the United Kingdom to transfer the

[34] (1999) 29 *Social Trends*, HMSO suggests that there has been a steady decline in the birth rate between 1960 and 1977 when, after a brief spurt in the birth rate, the rate has stabilised (*ibid.*, p 50). At p 29 (*ibid.*) it is suggested that, whereas women born in 1937 had an average of 1.9 children, the corresponding figure for women born in 1967 is 1.3. Both figures suggest that, but for immigration and an increase in life expectancy, the population of the United Kingdom would be falling—it is certainly not operating at replacement level. In addition, there has also been an increase in the number of women who are childless. The predictions are that the 11% of women over forty-five born in 1942 who were childless will rise to 25% for women over forty-five born in 1972.

[35] See *The Times*, 25 Oct 1999 for an indication of the Chancellor of the Exchequer's plans to integrate tax and the benefit system by tax credits for over fifty-year-olds so as to assure those who take low-paid work of an income of £200 per week whilst at the same time limiting the social security bill to the government.

[36] See *Sunday Times*, 28 Nov 1999.

[37] [1987] SCR 857 (SCC).

[38] The case is typical in some ways because married women are increasingly having their children at an older age, which may also affect their ability to re-enter the job market if their marriage subsequently breaks down. In the United Kingdom, the average age at which married women now have their first child has now reached thirty, and women aged between thirty and thirty-four are more likely to give birth than women aged twenty to twenty-four, though they are less likely to do so than women aged between twenty-four and twenty-nine. In medicine, the term 'elderly prima gravida' has risen by ten years within recent memory.

[39] See n 37.

[40] It might be argued that the views of the Canadian Supreme Court in *Moge v Moge* (1992) 43 RFL (3d) 345 and the Full Court of the Australian Supreme Court in *Mitchell and Mitchell* (1995) 19 FLR 44 are more sympathetic to the older wife than the reality of family practice in England. Despite the ostensible willingness of judges in England to award maintenance to such wives, the reality is different. See further C Barton and A Bissett-Johnson, 'The declining number of ancillary relief orders' [2000] *Family Law* 94 and the same authors, 'Financial provision on divorce in English and Scottish law' [2000] *Judicial Review* 265.

husband's share in the matrimonial home to the wife to provide shelter for her and the family. In return, the husband might expect a reduction in the child support that he was to pay in the future or to be able to retain his pension. Both of these options came under attack in the United Kingdom,[41] but more importantly, the assumption which the courts had at one time—that a forty-five-year-old divorced man might be able to buy alternative housing—became questionable for the majority of men who were expected to buy their home on a mortgage. Not merely did finding the sizeable deposit (which a man would need if he were to pay off the mortgage quickly) become difficult, but the monthly repayments became more difficult if the man was in an industry in which layoffs of staff in their early fifties had become usual. To take a common example, the repayment of a mortgage of £100,000 in seven years at a rate of 7 per cent produces a monthly repayment of over £1,500, whereas if the man could have been expected to continue in employment from his divorce at forty-five until retirement at sixty-five, the comparable monthly mortgage repayment figure would be £775.[42] And this at a time in the United Kingdom when tax relief on the interest on mortgage repayments is being run down by government.

SOCIAL SECURITY

At one time in Britain when a marriage broke down it was common for the wife to take over the mortgage on the matrimonial home (and for the husband to transfer his interest in it to her).[43] Provided the interest payments on the home were reasonable, the social security authorities would meet these (but not any capital repayment) as a way of ensuring that the wife and children had a home. In return, the husband/father would reduce his support payments for the wife and children. However, in an attempt to keep the government's social security payments down, the British government made two changes. First—mainly in an attempt to increase the number of people who would have their mortgage payments met by mortgage protection policies if they lost their job—alterations were made to the circumstances in which interest charges on mortgages would be included in housing costs for those in receipt of social security.[44] These had the side effect of covering cases of marital breakdown for which no insurance was

[41] See *Child Support Act* 1991 and 1995 and the decision in *Crozier v C* [1995] *Family Law* 114. For a scathing attack on the UK government's lack of foresight of the problems which emerged with the *Child Support Act*, see Cretney and Masson, n 17, ch 16. The latest of the government's several attempts to reformulate the package is the *Child Support, Pensions and Social Security Act* 2000, which replaces the formula with a simple percentage scheme.

[42] The corresponding figures at 8% are even more graphic—repaying the £100,000 over seven years requires a monthly payment of £1,559, whereas repaying over twenty years requires a monthly payment of £836.

[43] The matter is fully outlined by Priest in her article, 'Capital Settlements and the *Child Support Act*' [1997] *Family Law* 115 and 170.

[44] For more detail, see Wikely, 'Income Support and Mortgage Interest—the New Rules', (1999) 115 *Journal of Social Security Law* 168 and Wikely, 'Income Support and Mortgage Interest—a Further Trap for the Unwary' [1999] *Family Law* 702.

available.[45] Secondly, the *Child Support Acts* of 1991 and 1995 made the transfer of the matrimonial home by a husband to his wife on breakdown of marriage a transaction that could not be used to secure a reduction in child support (though relief was made available for arrangements made before the 1991 *Child Support Act* came into effect).[46] The result of this was to make husbands more reluctant to transfer family homes to their wives on breakdown of marriage, though for a short period when housing prices fell leaving spouses with 'negative equities', husbands/fathers were willing to do this in order to free themselves from liability from their personal obligation under the covenant to repay the capital when they entered into the mortgage. Although full empirical evidence is not yet available, this does demonstrate how a government's desire to reduce public spending can undermine existing family law practice and possibly produce results (eg an increased number of sales of the matrimonial homes on divorce which are contrary to the 'best interest of the child' formula which is central to much family law).

The government has recognised that a disproportionate number of divorced women are dependent on social security. One way of keeping such women off social security during their retirement is to provide for sharing the occupational pension of the richer spouse (usually the husband) with the poorer (usually the wife, as her pension may have been limited by child care or family responsibilities). The *Welfare Reform and Pensions Act* 1999, which came into effect in December 2000, enables courts (or, in Scotland, the parties) to agree to share pensions.[47] The wife (usually) will either become a member of her husband's scheme in her own right (internal transfer) or, in the cases of fully funded schemes, may have the right to seek the transfer of the funds into her own pension by way of an external transfer. Given:

[45] See the Child Poverty Action Group's *Welfare Benefits Handbook 1999–2000* and Mesher and Wood's *CPAG Income Related Benefits: The Legislation* (Sweet & Maxwell, 1999) for more detail. In essence, the delegated legislation—the Income Support (General) Regulations 1987, SI 1987 No 1967 sch 3 para 6 and the Job Seeker's Allowance Regulations, 1996, SI 1996 No 207 sch 2 para 6—changed the old law and created a waiting period of eight weeks before any housing costs could be claimed in respect of mortgages made before 2 Oct 1995; thereafter, for the next eighteen weeks, only half the interest payments could be claimed by way of income support. Finally, the whole interest element of a mortgage relating to a house in which the claimant lived could be claimed provided that the costs were not excessive, and that the rate of interest charged did not exceed a specified interest rate (often lower than the rate actually charged). For new housing costs involving mortgages after 2 Oct 1995, a newer and stricter regime was imposed under para 8 of the Income Support (General Regulations) cited above and para 7 of the Job Seeker's Allowance Regulations cited above. The 26-week waiting period was extended to 39 weeks, although some exceptions were made retaining the lower waiting period—for example, for lone parents claiming income support or a job seeker's allowance. (See, for example, SI 1996/207 para 7(4)(b) and para 6). These changes may have some effect on the case law suggesting that if a 'clean break' left the wife open to future inability to keep up mortgage repayments, the shortfall could be met by state benefits.

[46] See Cretney and Masson, n 17, pp 532 *et seq.* For more detailed discussion, see A Bisset-Johnston 'Changes in pension division on divorce' [2000] *SLT News* 297.

[47] In Scotland, only the part of the pension accruing between marriage and separation is shareable under the normal rules of family law.

—that the valuation of the pension to be shared is under the conservative basis of Cash Equivalent Transfer Value, which may encourage husbands to try to retain their entire pension;
—the fact that the power to share pensions is discretionary rather than obligatory; and
—that many wives will prefer to have the value of the pension in their hands now under an 'off setting' arrangement

The new Act may have less application than the British government hoped.[48]

SUMMARY

Many of the changes referred to have occurred as a result of changes which either the government has no control over—for example, increased longevity—or where the changes have been driven by a desire to control public expenditure in which their effect on the family has been seen as secondary, if it has been recognised at all. At the present time, the responsibility for the family seems dispersed through several government departments. Until the responsibility for the family is seen to be as important as the holding down of public expenditure, continued tensions will exist in devising mechanisms to ensure that women are not left paying too a heavy price for the breakdown of a relationship.

[48] For more detail on the position in Scotland, see A Bissett-Johnson 'Changes in Pension Division on Divorce' [2000] *SLT News* 297. More detail on the English provisions can be found in David Salter 'A Practitioner's Guide to Pension Sharing' [2000] *Family Law* 489 at 543 and 914.

29

De Facto Property Developments in New Zealand: Pressures Impeded Progress

Bill Atkin and Wendy Parker*

THE CONTEXT OF REFORM

In New Zealand, as elsewhere, the pressure to provide property rights after the termination of de facto relationships emanates out of a complex and dynamic set of circumstances. This pressure has finally led New Zealand to pass new property laws which place de facto relationships (including same-sex relationships) on the same basis as marriage.

We can track the trajectory of de facto couples through census information, but only since 1981. Although limited by its self-defining status, the census (a quinquennial event in New Zealand) gives an indication of the rapid rise in popularity of this type of cohabitation. In 1981, a total of 87,960 people considered themselves to be living in a de facto relationship. Ten years later, the figure had nearly doubled to 161,856. The rate of increase continued to climb during the first half of the 1990s, with 247,287 people coming within the category in the 1996 census. If the increase continues at this rate, the 2001 census may well reveal over 10 per cent of the population cohabiting outside of marriage.[1]

As these numbers rise, the New Zealand marriage rate is the lowest it has been for thirty years.[2] The divorce rate remains high, sitting at 12.3 per 1,000 existing marriages in 2000, with the highest rate for women in their late twenties and early thirties.[3] In turn, remarriage has become more popular with two out of five of all marriages in 2000 involving remarriage. De facto relationships are more common among the young, Maori and professional occupations. Four in ten de facto couples have children.[4] The tracking of same-sex de facto rates is hindered by a

* Bill Atkin is a Reader in Law at the Victoria University of Wellington, New Zealand. Wendy Parker is a Policy Consultant, based in Palmerston North, New Zealand.

[1] These figures were due to be released in early 2002 by Statistics New Zealand.

[2] 15.6% per 1,000 people in 2000, as compared with the peak of 45.5 per 1,000 in 1971.

[3] The divorce rate has declined over the last few years and is now moving closer to levels of the early 1990s.

[4] Childbearing patterns reflect changes elsewhere—namely, declining fertility and delayed childbearing. In New Zealand there are significant ethnic differences, with Maori and Pacific Islands women tending towards higher birth rates and younger childbearing ages.

lack of information; however, for the first time the 1996 census included such a question and 6,520 individuals considered themselves part of a same-sex couple.

Where there are relationships, there are relationships that break down, and for some of these there are property disputes. As has occurred elsewhere, the absence of statutory property rights has led to resolution in the courts via the law of trusts. The New Zealand Bench displayed resourcefulness in adapting trust law in this regard and the principles became fairly well settled. Successful claimants are those who can prove that, given their contributions (be they direct or indirect), they could reasonably expect a share in the other parties' property and that a reasonable expectation of property sharing was also the case for the respondent.[5]

While the establishment of fairly clear legal principles was a welcome development, the actual allocation of property often fell well short of 50 per cent, and was often around 20–30 per cent. This was not by any means the only problem. Practitioners reported difficulties in advising clients whether to litigate due to uncertainty of outcome. The word 'lottery' was frequently used to describe chances of success and certainty was certainly not a feature of the common law regime. The cost of litigation, frequently in the High Court, presented a further barrier to accessing justice.[6] Further, we have no idea how many couples resolved their property disputes without access to lawyers or the courts, and what kinds of outcomes were reached in this way. The cumulative effect of these issues was a general perception that the common law remedy, although improved, remained inadequate.

The law of trusts in the de facto property context is set against a backdrop of other legal and social developments. For the last twenty years in New Zealand, we have trod a steady path of including de facto relationships within the Family Court matrix. Notably, this is largely attributable to the growth of child-centred policies. Illegitimacy was banished as a legal status in 1969. In 1986, de facto parents became eligible for familial dispute-resolution procedures, including state-funded relationship counselling to reconcile differences. Domestic violence protection has been available to de facto couples since 1982.[7] The removal of the distinction between de facto and married partners in this context promotes family stability and attempts to minimise the social and economic costs of relationship breakdown to the state. The latter argument holds similar appeal in regard to extending property rights protection to de facto couples. The incremental inclusion of de facto partnerships in a variety of family law left property rights, including inheritance rights, as a visible gap in existing protections.

Matrimonial property law casts a long shadow too. The presumption of equal sharing, in force in New Zealand for twenty-five years, is now an ingrained part

[5] Leading Court of Appeal cases include: *Gillies v Keogh* [1987] 2 NZLR 327, *Phillips v Phillips* [1993] 3 NZLR 159, *Lankow v Rose* [1995] 1 NZLR 277.

[6] The District Court's equitable jurisdiction has a ceiling of NZ$200,000.

[7] In 1995, the *Domestic Violence Act* extended protection beyond a conjugal basis to one of domestic relationship, while at the same time simplifying and strengthening protection orders and including sexual and psychological abuse as grounds for protection.

of the New Zealand experience. Recent law reform attempts are an apposite demonstration of this. The retention of equal sharing, with the use of other compensatory mechanisms to bring about equitable results, provides another example.

The matrimonial property experience has allowed for a layered history of the operation of judicial discretion, developed side by side in the High Court and in the specialist Family Court. The significant shift in the 1976 legislation, which replaced the Act of 1963, was to provide tighter legislative guidance, effectively to steer discretion along socially acceptable lines. The presumption of equal sharing played a key role in this, as did clear direction to treat financial and non-financial contributions on a par and to consider both direct and indirect contributions to the relationship instead of solely to the property. Later we comment on the history of bounded discretion in the light of the new law.

Theoretical influences have also figured. Politicians from both the traditional left and right in New Zealand adopted neo-liberalism with great zeal during the 1980s and 1990s. The current centre-left government marks a departure from these principles to some extent. What might be reasonably loosely termed the 'third way' approach in New Zealand is tasked with delivering social justice in a fiscally responsible manner. Therefore, law reformers during this time were ever mindful of the economic costs of extending property rights to new groups.[8] This in turn impacted on the desirable mix of rules and discretion (in that a lack of certainty is predicted to increase litigation). We pick up on this point later in our paper.

Economic liberalism and moral conservatism often parade hand in hand. Over the last twenty years, and especially since the proliferation of political parties since the introduction of a mixed member proportional electoral system in 1993,[9] the conservative position remains a consistent voice within the chorus for social change. In many ways, the sheer numbers of heterosexual de facto couples have brought social acceptance—albeit begrudgingly in some quarters. As this has occurred, the focus has shifted from whether such relationships are to be discouraged to the issue of whether they are a 'lesser' entity than marriage. According heterosexual de facto couples lesser protection than married couples was a view adopted during the development of the property law reform proposals throughout the 1990s. It was promoted by keeping the statutory regimes separate and distinct from each other via two separate, although linked, Bills. Moreover, the tests for division were different. As we go on to argue, the 1998 de facto

[8] For example, advice to Cabinet in 1997 estimated extending property rights to heterosexual de facto couples would increase fiscal spending by between NZ$1 million and NZ$4 million due to increases in court time and legal aid costs.

[9] This replaced the first past the post system found in many Westminster parliaments. Under MMP, voters have two votes. The constituency vote selects a local MP, and remains a winner-takes-all situation. The party, or list, vote determines the overall makeup of parliament, with each political party gaining seats in the House proportional to their share of the list vote. List seats (usually) top up electorate seats. One impact of MMP has been to increase the number of parties in the House from two or sometimes three, to seven or more.

proposals promoted the use of discretion more broadly than those for previously married couples. Their subsequent incorporation within a single statute alters this.

The convergence of liberal and conservative views also promotes the talisman of 'individual responsibility'. One argument against the inclusion of de facto couples in any statutory scheme is the deliberate shunning of the incidence of marriage by cohabitants. Further, according to this view, if people choose to cohabit and especially to have children, then they are obliged to protect their economic and property affairs and to suffer the consequences of not doing so. It is not the role of the state to interfere in people's lives in this way. Freedom of choice takes precedence over protection, the sanctity of contract must be preserved, and individual property rights must not be eroded by state interference.

Such influences are evident in aspects of the new law. For example, the tightening of judicial ability to override an agreement to contract out of the provisions of the Act signals not only further limits on discretionary power, but an intention to uphold a contract between the parties. Thus individual responsibility is strengthened with the statute a mere safety net under which the test for setting aside a contracting out agreement is a tighter one of 'serious injustice'. Indeed, the general rise of the rules-based approach in New Zealand family law sits happily alongside notions of individual contractual rights and a smaller role for the state, including its judicial branch.

Notions of individual responsibility grate a little, however, against the idea that the property law can and should alleviate economic disparity between ex-partners, and also more widely in terms of gender disparity.[10] This contradiction might be explained by giving the career spouse responsibility to remedy the disparity, rather than the social security system. In other words, the redistribution occurs within the partnership rather than within wider society. Even the more hard-line neo-liberal proponents apply a different set of rules to the weaker members of society—raising again the importance of child-centred approaches in the evolution of property rights laws.

PRESSURES

The changes outlined in this paper indicate a significant shift in family law policy in New Zealand. While we do not suggest that such alterations should ever be a hasty process, the meandering and at times piecemeal approach in this instance suggests pressures against the calls for reform have acted as an effective block to progress.

As we have previously mentioned, the progress of de facto property rights in New Zealand has been closely entwined with matrimonial property. After an

[10] The social objectives of the *Matrimonial Property Act* 1976 have long been lauded—see, for example, *Reid v Reid* [1979] 1 NZLR 572.

initial settling-in period, it became apparent that the social objectives of equality and justice in the *Matrimonial Property Act* 1976 were not being fulfilled. That is, the presumption of equal property division was failing to achieve equitable results. As long ago as 1988, the Royal Commission on Social Policy first raised the themes that resonate still in today's new laws. The Commission, among other suggestions, called for modification of the clean break principle, a prospective approach and a focus on the living standards of children as ways to achieve the ever-elusive equitable result. They also called for de facto property rights protection.[11] Six months later, another eminent and key report—that of the Working Group on Matrimonial Property and Family Protection—also suggested change. Among the proposals put forward by this group was the removal of the section 15 test,[12] leaving one test for the division of all matrimonial property. The working group also suggested better protection of de facto property rights.

Action waned through the late 1980s and the first half of the 1990s. The occasional MP talked to community groups and the Ministry of Women's Affairs embarked on a community consultation process, coming up with a set of guiding principles in 1994. Although dropped from the legislative proposals, and then partially reinstated, their existence has been helpful in providing a framework for discussion of what the law changes are aimed at achieving.

It is sobering to remember that reform proposals for both matrimonial and de facto property have been with the New Zealand Cabinet since 1995. Pre-Cabinet policy development had identified three key deficiencies with the 1976 Act: the lack of equitable outcomes, injustices created by the clean break principle, and lesser protection for marriages ended by the death of one of the parties.[13] Reaching agreement on how these problems were to be overcome resulted in tussles between government officials from the Ministry of Justice and the Ministry of Women's Affairs. This lack of cohesion gave some less enthusiastic Cabinet ministers the opportunity to downgrade the legislative priority several times. Despite these braking pressures, twin Bills eventually emerged from the Parliamentary Counsel's office in February 1998. De facto property rights were finally on the legislative agenda.[14]

The first and second readings proceeded smoothly. The day before the second reading, the inclusion of same-sex couples within the Bill's ambit was proposed via a Supplementary Order Paper put up by the Labour Party, then in opposition. The next example of pressure came with the log-jam that occurred when the Government Administration Select Committee considered the proposals. New

[11] Royal Commission on Social Policy (1988) *The April Report*, vol IV, p 217.

[12] Equal division for common property other than the house and chattels could be departed from by showing a clearly greater contribution to the marriage.

[13] Prior to the reforms passed in 2001, these cases were heard under the *Matrimonial Property Act* 1963, where property was allocated according to monetary and non-monetary contributions traceable to property.

[14] The two bills were the Matrimonial Property Amendment Bill 1998 and the De Facto Relationships (Property) Bill 1998.

Zealand select committees received a shot of adrenaline under MMP, and related procedural changes boosted them, not only in size, but in the diversity of party and personality representation. One can only speculate on the reasons for the arduous eighteen-month trek through select committee territory in this first phase, but we are fairly sure that lack of accord on the issues was one of them. Parliament in fact lost control of the passage of the de facto property rights legislation when the then Minister of Justice halted progress of the issue through the House by calling for public consultation over the inclusion of same-sex relationships across a range of areas. Prompted by the de facto property rights debate, the consultation considered a range of areas including succession, partnership registration and adoption of children. Submissions on the Ministry of Justice discussion paper *Same-sex Couples and the Law* closed on 30 April 2000. Over 4,000 submissions were received. A summary of responses was published in July 2000.[15]

Despite de facto property issues being held in abeyance while the same-sex issues were consulted on, the matrimonial bill was reported back from the select committee, which also released an interim report on the de facto bill. Divergent viewpoints were discernible in the report. The minority Labour Party view signalled the likely direction should (as it subsequently did) this party come to power.

This is not to assert that property rights law presented as a compelling priority for the Labour–Alliance minority government elected in October 1999. It took a back seat to such issues as accident compensation scheme changes and labour law reform. And then, in early April 2000, there was talk of major change to the Bills. At the behest of the Attorney-General and Associate Minister of Justice, Margaret Wilson, Cabinet considered and approved extensive alteration to the proposals, both at the broad policy level and in some of the detail. Official documents again reveal spats between government officials, but this time the Ministry of Women's Affairs' position features more prominently in Cabinet's modifications.

An 82 page Supplementary Order Paper was drafted. However, another pressure appeared and was applied—that of the democratic process. The Green Party, effectively holding the balance of power for the minority coalition government, insisted that change of such magnitude be subject to debate and public input. Supportive of the change in principle, the Greens insisted that process must be adhered to. As a result of this intervention, the Supplementary Order Paper was referred back to select committee—this time to the Justice and Electoral Select Committee.

The new select committee was faced with significant changes to the previous reform proposals, and we go on to outline these shortly. The second round of public submissions brought an increased response, although many were 'form letters'. A large number of petitions concerning the retention of the word 'spouse' to distinguish marriage from de facto relationships were also received by parlia-

[15] *Discussion Paper: Same Sex Couples and the Law, Summary of Responses* (Ministry of Justice, 2000).

ment. As had been the case with the 1998 bills, the select committee report reflected opposing views. This time, however, the views that prevailed were those of the new government which had been in opposition in 1998. Many of these views were quite distinct from what had gone before, and this is visible in the key changes made during 2000 and 2001.

The House agreed to the proposed changes by a majority of four votes, split neatly along party lines although taken as a conscience vote. The proposal to include same-sex couples received a larger majority. The *Property (Relationships) Act* 1976 received the Royal Assent on 3 April 2001. Some contracting out provisions came into effect on 1 August 2001 with the remainder of the Act taking effect on 1 February 2002.

PROGRESS: THE REFORMS

On the assumption that there are good policy reasons to provide a statutory scheme for de facto couples, the next inevitable question concerns the form that should take. As noted above, one of the subsidiary questions relating to this is how distinct the scheme should be from that which governs married couples. In the New Zealand context, this involves yet another fundamental issue—to what extent should the scheme be based on clear rules rather than left to the discretion of the courts? We examine this question in the next section.

The legislation introduced by the previous government was driven by the premise that de facto relationships should be seen as different from marriage. That government was of the centre-right politically and doubtless saw marriage as the preferred model for relationships while grudgingly acknowledging the existence and growing acceptance of other relationships. Thus it was important to the previous government that whatever scheme be applied to de facto couples, it appear in its own separate piece of legislation. Reinforcing this goal, the content of the legislation, while in many respects copying the *Matrimonial Property Act* 1976 and therefore appearing to contain many more set rules than under the law of common law and equity, nevertheless departed from that Act in key respects. The result was a model which contained a greater degree of discretionary provisions than would have applied to married couples. While the home and chattels would be divided according to an equal division rule, other so-called relationship property such as farms, shares, businesses, investments, superannuation and so on were to be divided according to contributions to the relationship. As the latter was to take into account a wide range of both financial and non-financial contributions, the judge's assessment would vary considerably from case to case and the precise outcome in any given situation would be hard to predict. The fact that the test for departure from equal sharing was different from the *Matrimonial Property Act* 1976 also signalled uncertainty.

At the same time as introducing into parliament the De Facto Relationships (Property) Bill, the government also introduced a Bill amending the *Matrimonial*

Property Act. The principal purpose of this Bill was to bring marriages that end with the death of one of the spouses within the ambit of the 1976 Act.[16] Right from 1976, it was thought that there was little policy justification for treating separated and widowed spouses differently. Law reform was therefore finally catching up. The statutory scheme for de facto relationships would also have applied on death, but the previous government was not minded to alter other aspects of inheritance law, such as the rules on intestacy which excluded de facto partners.

The Matrimonial Property Amendment Bill proposed some other changes affecting separated parties, but the underlying mix of rules of equal sharing backed up by elements of discretion was to be left largely unaltered. Perhaps the most significant of the changes was to widen the scope for the court to challenge property disposed of to trusts and companies.

The approach of the centre-left government elected in October 1999 was different. It incorporated provisions on de facto property into the matrimonial property legislation, thus signalling the view that, for legal and policy purposes, there was no essential difference between the nature of the relationships. This of course leaves room for different religious and ideological attitudes, but not so as to impact on the law. Same-sex relationships were also included but not other domestic relationships such as family ones which are covered by legislation in other jurisdictions. This is a little anomalous, given that the focus is now firmly on the law of property, rather than the nature of the relationship, and is illustrated by the change of name from the *Matrimonial Property Act* to the *Relationships (Property) Act.* Logically, other domestic relationships, such as those between family members, could have been brought within the scope of the legislation.

The effect of the law change is to remove the discretionary division of a de facto couple's property other than the home and chattels and, as for married couples, to divide such property prima facie on an equal basis. But, rather more significantly, other changes which will on the one hand tighten the equal division rule and on the other hand introduce a dramatic new element of discretion are now in place.

Under the *Matrimonial Property Act* 1976, equal division of the home and chattels could be defeated only by two narrow exceptions. One was where the marriage was of short duration (normally less than three years), and the other was where there are so-called extraordinary circumstances which rendered equal sharing repugnant to justice. Matrimonial property other than the home and chattels was divided equally unless one party could show that they had made a clearly greater contribution to the marriage partnership, a distinctly softer test than the exceptions for the home and chattels. The new law abandons the contributions exception, with the result that all 'relationship property'—that is, property of married and de facto couples other than 'separate property' (eg gifts and bequests) which is excluded from the scheme—will be divided on the same strict basis that

[16] Surviving spouses could apply under the highly discretionary *Matrimonial Property Act* 1963, which for all other purposes was repealed with the passage of the 1976 Act.

now applies to the home and chattels.[17] This moves the law more in the direction of a rule of equality.

Despite the move just outlined, another major amendment brings back a significant element of judicial discretion.[18] The courts now have a discretion to order one partner to pay a lump sum to the other if the income and living standards of the latter are likely to be significantly lower than those of the other partner because of the division of functions within the relationship. This payment is 'for the purpose of compensating' the less well-off partner and the court must consider the parties' earning capacities and responsibilities to children. Precisely in what circumstances and to what value such orders will be made is hard to predict. While the policy justification for this provision is readily understandable (ie trying to ensure greater equality in practice, not just in theory), a rush to litigate is foreshadowed. The changes bring us closer to the Australian approach, where we note that orders for spousal support continue to be problematic.[19]

Two other points need to be made. First, a de facto relationship is defined as one 'where two people (whether a man and a woman, or a man and a man, or a woman and a woman) are living together as a couple.'[20] This formula, albeit in the slightly altered form of 'two people living together as husband and wife,' is a familiar one in New Zealand legislation, and existing case law will help its application to particular situations.[21] A list of indicative relationship factors is included and these are lifted straight from the *Property (Relationships) Act* 1984 (NSW). But there will doubtless be some grey areas which will need to be tested before the courts. Secondly, the 2001 law changes include some reforms to inheritance law. In particular, widowed de facto partners will come within the intestacy rules and will also be able to apply under the *Family Protection Act* 1955 for a greater share of the deceased's estate.

Overall, then, the law makes major changes to property division for formerly married couples and brings de facto and same-sex couples within the scheme on an equal footing. While the changes appear to strengthen rules at the expense of discretion, as we point out, new discretionary elements of some note have also been introduced.

[17] Strictly speaking, there will be a difference between short-duration marriages and de facto relationships. Such marriages will still come under the Act but property will be divided according to contributions. Short-duration de facto relationships will be outside the Act entirely, unless they fall within an exception: either there has been a child or one party has made a substantial contribution and serious injustice would result if no order were made.

[18] S 15 *Property (Relationships) Act* 1976. S 15A provides the court with a second mechanism to order compensation for 'economic disparity' if it can be shown that the wealthier party's actions led to an increase in that party's 'separate property'.

[19] J Behrens and B Smyth, *Spousal Support in Australia: A Study of Incidence and Attitudes* (Australian Institute of Family Studies, Working Paper 16, Feb 1999).

[20] S 2A(2) *Property (Relationships) Act* 1976.

[21] For example, *Ruka v DSW* [1996] NZFLR 913; *Lichtenstein v Lichtenstein* (1986) 4 NZFLR 25. We note that the old and the new New Zealand definitions follow the New South Wales approach both before and after their 1999 amendments.

RULES VERSUS DISCRETION

One of the ways to judge parliament's decision to bring married and unmarried couples together under the same legislative roof is to explore the advantages and disadvantages of rules- versus discretion-based approaches. If there are good reasons why a discretionary approach better suits those in de facto relationships, then the argument in favour of the previous government's bill is much stronger.[22] In other jurisdictions where matrimonial property is divided on more discretionary principles, this latter question may be less acute.

First, we consider the advantages of discretion. A discretionary approach can reflect the variety of relationships which people enter. Arguably, people who marry buy into a particular kind of social and legal relationship, even though the daily reality may vary. Those who cohabit without getting married have not committed themselves to any particular social structure. The relationship may be casual or permanent, with many shades in between. The relationship may be de facto because the parties are legally unable to marry—for example, because one of them is still married to someone else or because they are of the same gender. The parties may regard their relationship as monogamous or on the contrary may have an open-ended approach to their relationship. A couple might have drifted together without thinking about the implications, or may have quite consciously avoided the trappings of marriage. Of course, these circumstances may also arise in relation to married couples but there is a perception (perhaps unfounded) that they are more likely to occur where parties are unmarried.

We may have a sense that de facto relationships vary much more than married ones, at least with respect to those relationships which are more temporary and casual. We assume that when people marry they see this as a long-term and serious commitment and that marriages which are 'temporary and casual' would be very unusual. But do we really know much about relationships, the level of commitment and the patterns which might distinguish marriages and de facto relationships? In New Zealand, there has been little or no research into these questions, with the result that policy is being developed, at least to a certain extent, blind.

A recent study from Britain suggests that, apart from the aspect of public commitment inherent in marriage, there are few real differences between the attitudes and lifestyles of married and unmarried couples.[23] Further, there is no overwhelming desire that de facto and married couples be treated differently under the law. If such a study were to be replicated in New Zealand with similar results, then the case for a discretionary system for de facto couples standing alongside a

[22] For excellent discussions of the role of rules and discretions in family law, see J Dewar, 'Reducing Discretion in Family Law' (1997) 11 *AJFL* 309; J Dewar, 'Family Law and Its Discontents' (2000) 14 *IJLPF* 59.

[23] J Lewis et al., *Individualism and Commitment in Marriage and Cohabitation* (Lord Chancellor's Department, London, Research Series 8/99, 1999) and J Lewis 'Debates and Issues Regarding Marriage and Cohabitation in the British and American Literature' (2001) 15 *International Journal of Law, Policy and the Family* 159–84. We also note that 40% of de facto couples have children.

more rule-based approach for married persons has little justification in terms of how most people actually live and think.

A second potential advantage in a discretionary system involves the uniquely New Zealand cultural context. In any development of policy in New Zealand, particular attention has to be paid to the perspective of the indigenous Maori people. An unmarried Maori couple may regard themselves as married according to Maori custom, although such customary marriages are not legal marriages under the law. Other Maori couples might see themselves merely as de facto partners. Whatever the understanding, such a couple may have quite different expectations about property rights from those which prevail in contemporary Western thinking. Rules enforcing equal division may be inappropriate, while a discretionary system, depending upon how the law is drafted, may enable the court (although also a Western institution) to take account of Maori attitudes. A similar point can be made with respect to other ethnic groups, especially people from the Pacific Islands, many of whom have now settled in New Zealand.

Under the *Matrimonial Property Act* 1976, what is technically known as 'Maori land' is excluded from the division rules. This prevents the removal of land from the landholding family group. To this extent at least, the law already acknowledges the ways of the indigenous people. But many Maori couples will not have a share in Maori land and are therefore treated the same as other couples. Further, there may be a sense of injustice, especially for Maori women, if they miss out on a share of property which their non-Maori friends are entitled to because of special concessions to traditional Maori values. This point resonated in a Court of Appeal matrimonial case, *Grace v Grace*,[24] where the wife was granted an equitable remedy to overcome the unfairness of the exclusion of Maori land from the *Matrimonial Property Act*. This may suggest that, in the end, the advantages to Maori of a discretionary model may be more apparent than real.

One of the difficulties facing any draftsperson of laws relating to de facto relationships is how to define such relationships. In the absence of a requirement such as registration, it is hard to know at the edges whether a relationship falls inside or outside the scheme.[25] This difficulty is far less acute under a discretionary model, because the judge can, as a matter of discretion, take into account the nature of the particular relationship, the depth of commitment, the actual level of contribution and so on. A rule-based scheme with generous entitlements runs the risk of unfairly benefiting some and denying benefits to others. In New Zealand, in defining a 'de facto relationship', we have adopted the New South Wales model which, while allowing for judicial discretion, provides a certain amount of statutory guidance. The position of marriages is different—on the whole, it is the existence of the marriage and not its quality which is determinative, although under the previous law this was modified somewhat when dealing with property

[24] [1994] NZFLR 961.

[25] There are current proposals forming to introduce a system of registration, but of course the start date of any relationship may precede the registration date.

other than the house and chattels because contributions to the marriage partnership could be taken into account.

The New Zealand statute requires three years of living together as a general rule before the law applies to de facto relationships.[26] This is not so for marriages, although under certain conditions a marriage of short duration will see the property divided otherwise than in accordance with the rule of equality. While there is still uncertainty about the notion of 'living together as a couple', and in particular there will be cases where the exact commencement date of a relationship is uncertain, it is thought that most relationships which satisfy the three year test will be easy to identify. The marginal cases may be few and far between, and the risks of a rule-based approach may therefore be small.

A discretionary régime may be more attractive to those who advocate freedom of choice. If the exercise of discretion is geared towards contributions to the relationship, as it was in the National Party's De Facto Relationships (Property) Bill, the freedom advocates can object less (although some would still prefer a system that people are allowed to 'contract into' rather than one that is imposed). The reason for this is that the law of equitable remedies operates on a contribution basis. Equity, it is true, looks for contributions to assets rather than to the relationship and grants equivocal recognition to non-financial contributions. Nevertheless, a statutory discretionary system is not such a giant step away that it impedes on freedom of association much more than equity does. But herein lies a problem with the discretionary model. If it ends up being only a small change from the current legal position, why bother?

Where there is judicial discretion, a more neutral assessment of what is a fair division of property in all the varying circumstances of a de facto relationship may be possible. Rules pre-determine what is 'fair', as is done to a certain extent by the *Property (Relationships) Act* 1976. Of course, support for a discretionary approach may fluctuate, depending upon how closely an individual's values are akin to those of the judge. Judicial bias has been examined elsewhere.[27]

Clearly, then, there are significant advantages to a discretionary system. But advantages also exist in a more prescriptive framework. A rule-based system—that is, one where the element of judicial discretion is minimised—has greater certainty and predictability. Ideally, it should lead to less litigation and expense because lawyers can advise and people will readily understand what their entitlements are. How true this has been of the rule-based New Zealand domestic property legislation is hard to tell.[28] There is little doubt that the discretionary law prior

[26] Property of shorter relationships can be divided according to the parties' contributions to the relationship. This applies however only if there has been a child or the applicant has made a substantial contribution to the relationship, and there would be serious injustice if an order were not made: s 14A.

[27] C Bridge, 'Reallocation of Property after Marriage Breakdown', in M Henaghan and B Atkin, *Family Law Policy in New Zealand* (Oxford University Press, 1992).

[28] In a small 1987 study, some lawyers said they settled in 90 per cent of cases: J Krauskopf and C Krauskopf, 'Comparable Sharing in Practice: A Pilot Study of Results under the *Matrimonial Property Act* 1976' (1988) 18 *VUWLR* 21 at 23. No recent New Zealand data are available.

to 1976 produced widely differing results,[29] but after the reformed legislation came into force there was a considerable upsurge in litigation. While few contentious areas of interpretation remain and the division of property has become straightforward for broken relationships, there is still a steady stream of cases going before the courts. Given the higher level of breakdown compared with forty years ago, it is hard to determine for sure whether the *Matrimonial Property Act* 1976—now the *Property (Relationships) Act* 1976—saved on litigation. It should be added, however, that many of the cases which are litigated these days are ones where there is substantial property or other uncommon factors such as bankruptcy. Perhaps they would give rise to argument no matter what kind of scheme were adopted.

A rule-based system—especially one which contains a presumption of equal division, as New Zealand's now does in a very strong way—may actually reflect the common contemporary pattern of relationships. Most involve two people who, in their different ways, contribute roughly evenly to the relationship, at least until it breaks down. If this is so, then in today's Western world climate where gender discrimination is generally unacceptable, the notions of partnership and equality are entirely appropriate. Those relationships which do not fit the mould can be dealt with by carefully drafted exceptions and 'contracting out' provisions.

A rule-based system is one which New Zealanders have become used to for matrimonial cases and ought to be understood and accepted naturally by people in de facto relationships. Indeed, for a long time there was a popular myth—probably generated by the inclusion of reference to de facto couples in the original version of the 1976 matrimonial property laws[30]—that after two years of living together a de facto would have their property split evenly. As mentioned above, the discretionary model was abandoned in 1976 because it proved unsatisfactory. To use that model for de facto relationships would be to invite the same criticisms which were heard thirty years ago in relation to marriages. Although this may be mollified somewhat by judges who have been imbued with the operation of the 1976 Act, unpredictability and variation in results would not be unlikely. Given the history of the law in New Zealand, and given the general public acceptance of the main principles of the matrimonial property legislation, a rule-based system for de facto relationships may be more appropriate for New Zealand conditions.

Dividing property according to reasonably clear rules is not inconsistent with also allowing the partners to enter agreements modifying the rules, as was available under the *Matrimonial Property Act* 1976 and now under the *Property (Relationships) Act* 1976. The reason for this is that the agreement will deliver the desired degree of certainty. There is a risk of unfairness if one party concedes benefits unnecessarily to the other party. The New Zealand property legislation deals with this in two ways: first by requiring each party to have independent legal

[29] W Mansell, 'Whither Matrimonial Property?' (1971) 4 *NZULR* 271.

[30] Cls 16 and 49 of the Matrimonial Property Bill 1975.

advice; and secondly by empowering the court to declare an agreement void if the test of 'serious injustice' is met. This is a tighter test than under the previous law and is intended to limit the extent to which contracts can be set aside. In this way, another element of judicial discretion is to be reigned in.

The ability 'to contract out' is a partial answer to those who claim that de facto legislation infringes on de facto partners' freedom of choice. A couple who do not like the imposition of equal sharing can enter into their own agreement. The major qualification on this is, of course, that both parties must agree—there can be no unilateral 'contracting out'. So, where the parties cannot agree, the statutory régime will become the default model.

There are advantages—appreciated more by those used to the Westminster system of government—in parliament's determining the ground rules for division of property, rather than leaving this to be done by the courts. Parliament has the opportunity to hear submissions from experts and members of the public, and parliamentarians usually vote according to popular opinion. The main disadvantages of this are that legislation is harder to change if circumstances change, and popular opinion may not always be the best judge of what is fair and just.

On balance, we consider that the arguments in favour of rules—perhaps with some flexibility at the edges to accommodate the diversity of relationships—rather than discretion prevail. As John Dewar has said: 'One of the most noticeable features of family law legislation since the late 1980s has been the tendency to reduce or eliminate discretion from family law decision-making.'[31] The new power in New Zealand law allowing courts a discretion to compensate for an imbalance in income and standards of living runs counter to this. But the overall treatment in New Zealand of de facto relationships, including same-sex ones, is very much in step with Dewar's thesis. In future, the property division of such relationships will be subject to a rule of equality less easily avoided.

CONCLUSION

In this chapter, we have tracked the volatile history of legislating for de facto relationships within the New Zealand social, political and cultural setting. Our exposition of the various pressures that have impeded progress of law reform in this area resonates with patterns commonly found elsewhere. Other pressures are New Zealand-specific.

Globally, this type of issue is always a political matter. The new law represents a significant policy change. And, while the law is a useful tool of policy implementation, some legal formulations work better than others. Naturally, it is desirable to avoid a system that throws up more legal problems than it solves—for example, cost, uncertainty, inequity of outcome and risk of policy failure. Bringing de facto couples under the more rule-based property system in place in the

[31] J Dewar, 'Family Law and its Discontents' (2000) 14 *IJLPF* 59 at 66.

matrimonial area, and providing rules for succession, is a generally desirable approach. Although there is some tension between competing notions of individuality and state-wide coverage, it appears that freedom of choice may have to give way to social reality and a more coherent legal framework.

30

Politics, Processes and Pressures of Legislating for Children in South Africa

Julia Sloth-Nielsen and Belinda van Heerden*

INTRODUCTION

The last two decades have seen a plethora of laws regulating different aspects of children's lives being introduced in South Africa. In fact, between the passing of the *Child Care Act* (74 of 1983) and the beginning of the new millennium, approximately two dozen different pieces of legislation affecting children and families have been promulgated, regulating *inter alia* such matters as guardianship, domicile, family violence, maintenance, adoption, the position of fathers of natural children vis-à-vis their offspring, education, juvenile whipping, the recognition of customary unions—and so the list continues.[1]

According to the *Year 2000 Statistics* recently published by Statistics SA, nearly 4.4 million children in South Africa (more than 10 per cent of the population) are aged between and birth and four years. Children aged between birth and nineteen years form 45.19 per cent of the overall population.[2] It is evident that the earnings of the approximately 11.5 million employed people in the country,[3] out of a population of over 42 million, together with other sources of tax revenue, have to stretch to provide state resources on social spending in areas such as education, welfare needs and health care. The education budget is in fact the largest at R45.3 billion in 1998/9 (21.9 per cent of government budget), the bulk of this destined for children as the end users. The welfare budget for the same period is R18.61 billion (9.1 per cent) and constitutes the fourth largest budget item of government expenditure.[4] However, 91 per cent of this will be paid out in direct trans-

* Julia Sloth-Nielsen is Associate Professor, Community Law Centre, University of the Western Cape. Belinda van Heerden is a Judge, Cape High Court, South Africa.

1 See generally Julia Sloth-Nielsen and Belinda van Heerden, 'Putting Humpty Dumpty back together again: Towards restructuring families and children's lives in South Africa' (1998) 115 *SALJ* 156.

2 Statistics South Africa, *1998 October Household Survey* (2000).

3 Approximately 9.4 million employed in the formal sector and 2.1 million 'employed' in the informal sector: see Statistics South Africa, *1998 October Household Survey* (2000), pp 42–47.

4 Department of Finance, *Medium Term Budget Policy Statement, 1998* (1998), p 71.

fers, in the main old-age pensions, leaving only 9 per cent available for spending on social services.[5] An amount of R2.7 billion has been projected as the amount that will eventually be expended on the new child support grant when it is fully implemented over the next five years. It is against this fiscal and demographic backdrop that the debate about resources for a new legislative framework for child care and protection is taking place.

BACKGROUND TO THE PROCESS OF CHILD LAW REFORM

As we have previously described elsewhere,[6] the process of amending the existing *Child Care Act* in the period 1994–1996 was characterised by controversy about the nature, scope and import of the intended amendments. The law reform process came amidst two key developments: namely the adoption of first the interim and then the final Constitution, both containing unique clauses on children's rights; and the ratification of the United Nations Convention on the Rights of the Child (1989) in June 1995, which provided an international legal framework for further domestic law reform. It became apparent, too, that the piecemeal approach to tinkering with the existing *Child Care Act* was unsatisfactory. Both international examples and the wording of the Convention itself seemed to indicate that, at the very least, a complete overhaul of South Africa's legislation on child care and protection was called for, given the broad scope of obligations and rights provided for in the Convention.[7]

An important milestone was a conference co-hosted by the Children's Rights Project of the Community Law Centre and the Parliamentary Portfolio Committee on Welfare and Population Development in September 1996.[8] The conference harnessed the expertise of both lawyers and welfare experts from the government and non-governmental sectors, and also involved participants from African countries which are engaged in a similar process of law reform. Both the Deputy Minister of Justice and the Minister for Welfare and Population Development were keynote speakers at the event.

The debates were characterised by a focus on the position of children in difficult circumstances, the fragmentation caused (at least in part) by the lack of integration of legislation and common law, concerns about 'Africanising' South African child law, and the need for an inclusive process of law reform with wide-

[5] Department of Finance, *Medium Term Expenditure Review (Welfare) 1998* (1998).

[6] Julia Sloth-Nielsen and Belinda van Heerden 'Proposed Amendments to the *Child Care Act* and Regulations in the Context of Constitutional and International Law Developments in South Africa' (1996) 12 *SAJHR* 247; and 'The *Child Care Amendment Act* 1996: Does it improve children's rights in South Africa?' (1996) 12 *SAJHR* 649.

[7] South African Law Commission *First Issue Paper on the Review of the Child Care Act,* Issue Paper 13, Project 110 (May 1998), ch 1.

[8] *Towards Redrafting the Child Care Act,* Recommendations of a Conference of the Community Law Centre (University of the Western Cape) and the Portfolio Committee on Welfare and Population Development (September 1996).

scale consultation with stakeholders. Emphasis was placed on the necessity of adopting a realistic approach: crafting legislation which was affordable and indigenous (rather than borrowed from overseas); legislation which focused on existing strengths inherent in our society; and—probably most importantly—legislation with an odds-on chance of actually being implemented both by the executive and at grassroots levels.[9]

The most significant proposal emanating from the conference was the suggestion that the South African Law Commission be requested to undertake the task of drafting recommendations for a review of the *Child Care Act*. In July 1997, at the express recommendation of the Minister for Welfare and Population Development, the Minister of Justice appointed a Project Committee of the Commission for this purpose. Drawing together lawyers, including child rights experts and a children's court commissioner, child welfare experts, social work professionals and representatives from senior echelons within the Department of Welfare, as well as a senior researcher from the commission itself, this committee first set about examining the contours of its initial mandate 'to review the *Child Care Act*'. The consensus of Project Committee members from the outset was that the task facing it was much broader—in fact, that the first Issue Paper would raise the very question as to the appropriate scope of pending law reform in this area.

DETERMINING THE SCOPE OF A NEW CHILDREN'S STATUTE

In May 1998, the Law Commission published an issue paper dealing explicitly with the scope of the proposed law reform endeavour. Asking for responses to exactly 100 questions, the issue paper addressed the challenge of how best to develop a systematic and coherent approach to child law, consistent with South Africa's constitutional and international legal obligations of equity and non-discrimination, concern for the best interests of all children, participation of children in decisions affecting their interests and the protection of children in especially difficult circumstances.[10] For example, the issue paper, after providing a detailed problem statement and situation analysis of the position of children in South African society,[11] attempted to highlight the interface between the heavily interventionist structure underpinning the present *Child Care Act* and emerging policies of family preservation and autonomy.[12] Also, by emphasising the present fragmentation of statutory and other provisions affecting children, the issue paper illustrated the fact that the intersection between common law and statutory law in this sphere can result in conflict and confusion, which can in turn negatively impact upon children's lives.[13]

9 *Ibid.*, p 33ff.
10 *First Issue Paper on the Review of the Child Care Act*, ch 2.
11 *Ibid.*, ch 4.
12 *Ibid.*, ch 7.
13 *Ibid.*, ch 6.

Further, in keeping with the inclusive and holistic approach that the committee was desirous of promoting, the issue paper also reviewed the position of children under customary law and under various religious laws.[14] The diversity of these laws and the imperative of ensuring that the fundamental principles underlying any new children's statute are, on the one hand sensitive to customary and religious norms, yet on the other hand do not violate constitutional protections accorded all children, form the themes running through this part of the issue paper. Threads woven into the fabric of discussion about much of both common and statutory law include the changing definition of the family in modern law, the precise meaning of childhood and when it ends, and dilemmas associated with the fact that the law in South Africa (as elsewhere) has failed to keep abreast of technological change, particularly in the area of assisted reproduction. In the final chapter entitled 'The Way Forward', the issue paper bravely engages with a discourse outside the traditional concern of legal drafters:

> Without detracting in any way from the potential significance and likely benefits to children of a new legislative framework in keeping with constitutional and human rights principles, the reservation has been expressed that (independent of the difficulties associated with the ensuring of the commitment of the resources required to underpin an effective child care and protection system), there are some aspects that legislation alone cannot achieve. For example, it cannot alone produce well-trained, committed and motivated personnel who will bear responsibility for implementation of core provisions of the legislation, nor can it single-handedly change social, religious and cultural attitudes towards children. Social and economic upliftment, too, are ultimately developments which occur outside of the usual domain of legislative drafters, although much can be done in a legislative framework to ensure redress, equity and support for children in the most marginal situations.[15]

The crisp question is whether or not the committee's bold assertion in regard to the role of legislative reform in accomplishing redress, redistribution and support for children is in fact a valid one. Does this necessarily entail a massive injection of financial and human resources which, as we argue later, is unlikely to materialise? Or are there other ways, within a legislative and policy framework, of capturing sufficient fiscal support to achieve the goals set for itself by the committee, and to fulfil community expectations?

The publication of the issue paper was followed by a consultative process without precedent in the law reform approach hitherto adopted by the South African Law Commission. Over and above the wide circulation of the issue paper, and the request for written submissions in response to the document, members of the Project Committee designed and hosted day-long workshops to elicit participation from ordinary people, ranging from school teachers, social workers and child care workers to magistrates, police, academics and representatives from non-governmental organisations. The workshops were presented in all nine provinces,

[14] *First Issue Paper on the Review of the Child Care Act*, chs 8 and 9.
[15] *Ibid.*, para 11.6.

in both large cities and more rural areas, and were characterised by the enormous interest they attracted. A dedicated worksheet, drawn up to facilitate the process of gathering informed responses to the areas raised for discussion, was utilised at the workshops.

With the financial and technical assistance of several foreign children's rights organisations, the views of children themselves were elicited, in an exciting project spanning some thirty groups of children across the country, including children in foster and in residential care, children with disabilities and children with widely differing levels of exposure to the judicial system governing children's lives in South Africa.

The information obtained through these mechanisms was then analysed,[16] and is being incorporated in the next phase of the law reform process. What was particularly striking about the public reaction to the issue paper was the fact that, despite the diversity of participants in the consultative process, the question of 'provisioning' for children and the redistributive potential of the law reform process emerged as perhaps *the* most important concern.

'PROVISIONING' FOR AND 'GOVERNANCE' OF A NEW CHILDREN'S STATUTE?

Time and time again during the consultative process, voices have been heard to the effect that a 'Rolls Royce' statute would make little real difference without the resources to underpin its implementation. But at that same time, it is noteworthy that, as indicated above, the potential and possibilities of the law reform process for better resourcing of structures and institutions for children was clearly grasped by most respondents. The thorny question of provisioning reared its head during 1997 and 1998 in relation to the amount the government was prepared to allocate to the child support grant, which was introduced on 1 April 1998 simultaneously with the beginning of the three-year phasing out of the State Maintenance Grant. Only after forceful lobbying by a broad coalition of non-governmental organisations was the initial derisory amount of R75 per month per child below the age of seven years reluctantly increased to the current level of R100 per month per child. It may seem obvious, but is probably still worth stating, that the determination of a host of important legislative issues in this child law reform process will be informed by resource considerations. So, for example, legislation mandating adequate access to education for children living on the street, the setting up of cluster homes for children infected and affected by HIV/AIDS, the mooted increased role of the children's court as a central feature of child protective mechanisms, and effective support systems for children who are victims of abuse is in reality underpinned by a priori budgetary considerations. In view of the above, it

[16] See *Report on Workshops held Nationwide to Discuss the First Issue Paper on the Review of the Child Care Act*, South African Project Committee on the Review of the *Child Care Act* (1999).

should come as no surprise that provisioning for a new children's statute has already taken centre stage in this legislative drafting process.

A related concern is one which we have termed 'governance'. This notion draws together a range of issues which are potential subjects for coverage in a future children's statute, such as whether or not we need to introduce stronger complaints mechanisms for children whose rights are violated (the idea of a children's ombudsman comes to mind). And linked logically to providing channels for complaints from the ground is the question of monitoring the application of all or aspects of the legislation—for example, through provincial structures, a committee of the Human Rights Commission or a statutory body along the lines of the Medical and Dental Council or the Independent Broadcasting Authority. The consultative process has brought out clearly from grassroots levels the clarion call for legislation that is backed by over-arching control mechanisms—probably a reflection of the present degree of fragmentation (and indeed corruption) experienced by workers in the field.

The conception of the notion of 'governance' does not end at complaints procedures and overall monitoring. Included in its ambit are decision-making and implementation structures at lower levels. Thus, within the welfare sphere, the role of provincial departments in both resource allocation and service delivery appears to be a critical question to be resolved, as the repeated pensions crises (notably in the 'poorer' provinces) have amply demonstrated how differences in provincial approaches can actually subvert national strategies. Conversely, though, the emerging provincial protocols for the management and prevention of child abuse and neglect, which have been favourably received, tend rather to highlight the potential benefits to be derived from tailoring the legislative model to harness regional strengths and accommodate provincial diversity. We must also bear in mind that, since April 1999, local government has had the power to assume a far more prominent role in governance than had formerly been the case.[17] Although the implications of increased responsibilities for this tier of government are still emerging, this development presents the drafters of a new children's statute with yet another variable to be considered in identifying the structures that will form the framework for implementation.

Integrally related to the executive competencies discussed above in relation to governance is the judicial arm of governance in the context of child legislation. Here, numerous representations have been made and submissions received concerning the role of the judiciary in both a decision-making and supervisory capacity. Should the High Court continue to be the so-called 'upper guardian' of children despite its inaccessibility to the vast majority of the South African population? Should the children's court continue to have the relatively limited functions of authorising removal of children in need of care, and of determining

[17] Due to the fact that the transitional arrangements concerning local government ceased to apply on that date, and the powers of local government as contained in ss 151, 155, 156 and 157 of the final Constitution became fully operational (Item 26(1) of sch 6 to the Constitution).

placements of such children, without the concomitant powers of ongoing review of placements, and largely without either the power or the resources to introduce innovation and flexibility? And what of the possibility of moving from an exclusively judicial model to a different model altogether—say, by the introduction of administrative tribunals which include a range of professional voices, or lay panels, such as the widely acclaimed children's panels in Scotland?[18] Even more fundamentally, should a children's statute be weighted in favour of legal or quasi-legal solutions (orders, rulings, interdicts, and so on) to problems concerning parents, families and children, or are there more revolutionary possibilities that might be more appropriate in this part of the world? Something that springs to mind in this regard are current initiatives around family preservation pilot projects,[19] which clearly assume that any intervention is an matter of an ongoing process, rather than of any once-off, rule-based decision. In sum, the responses received indicate that no new children's statute is likely to be successful unless the challenges posed by 'governance' (in both the senses detailed above) are properly considered from the outset.

CHARTING THE FIELD: THE DEVELOPMENT OF A NEW CHILD JUSTICE STATUTE IN SOUTH AFRICA

Setting the Scene

In December 1996, the Minister of Justice appointed a Project Committee of the South African Law Commission to develop proposals for a dedicated juvenile justice statute for South Africa. Until now, children have been tried under ordinary criminal procedural rules, in the same way as adults. Although a few concessions are made to take account of the youth and immaturity of accused children, the legal framework applicable to children does not differ in any material respect from that applicable to adults. This was highlighted during campaigns in the early 1990s, launched by non-governmental organisations, drawing public attention to the plight of children in the criminal justice system, especially those children detained in adult prisons throughout the country.

This Project Committee also commenced its work with the release of an issue paper, setting out the shortcomings of the current system of juvenile justice and calling for proposals for reforms. Wide consultation with the welfare, justice and prisons sectors ensued; in addition, written comment from many individuals and organisations was received. Following upon a detailed analyses of the feedback, a comparative review of foreign examples of juvenile justice legislation, and extensive deliberations within the Project Committee itself, the Law Commission

[18] See, for example, Alison Cleland and Elaine E Sutherland, *Children's Rights in Scotland* (1996), pp 96ff and Lilian Edwards and Anne Griffiths, *Family Law* (1997), ch 8.

[19] The Inter-Ministerial Committee on Young People at Risk, *Report on the Pilot Projects* (Pretoria 1998) 26ff.

released a lengthy discussion paper containing a draft Bill in December 1998. This document too formed the basis of country-wide consultation throughout 1999. The Project Committee has now completed a final report, with an amended draft Bill, which was due to be handed to the Minister of Justice for introduction into the parliamentary process.

In the three and a half years during which the Project Committee on Juvenile Justice has worked, a number of social, economic, political and legislative shifts have taken place in South Africa's emerging democracy. All have had an impact on the final form of the proposed legislation in one way or another. One factor is the increasing public concern about the prevalence of crime in South Africa, especially violent crime. Harsh minimum sentences have been introduced through legislation, new up-to-the minute policing methods debated, and the concern frequently expressed that the human rights enshrined in the South African Constitution have created a criminal justice climate which is too favourable to offenders.

The status of the South African economy, hard hit by globalisation, job losses and shrinking investments in emerging markets, led to the formulation in 1996 of a new macro-economic policy framework (GEAR—Growth Employment and Redistribution Strategy). GEAR replaced the social spending-oriented Reconstruction and Development Program (RDP), which was the original economic platform for the first democratic government of 1994. Hallmarks of the new thinking are restraints on public sector expenditure, cuts to the civil service, and encouraging private sector-led growth. Implications for both a new children's statute and a new juvenile justice system are clear: vast new sums of money are *not* going to be available for the creation or implementation of new services and structures, and the proposed reforms will to a large extent have to rely on existing resources.

Finally, the legislative saga around children in prison has had a sobering effect upon would-be reformists. To cut a long story short, the government adopted legislation in 1994 to free children awaiting trial from adult prisons, following on the earlier campaigns of non-governmental organisations. The implementation of this amending legislation was an unmitigated disaster, as the alternative facilities, run by the Department of Welfare, were either unavailable or unsuitable. Faced with a public outcry when children who were released reoffended with apparent impunity, interim changes to the legislation had to be effected. The new provisions once again provided for awaiting-trial children to be detained in prisons. Intended to be temporary and to apply only until the Welfare Department had provided alternative secure accommodation for awaiting-trial juveniles, this legislation is still in operation, pending the adoption of a new comprehensive juvenile justice statute. And, since 1996 when the interim amendments came into effect, the numbers of children awaiting trial in prison have more than tripled. Although 77 per cent of the original RDP allocation of R33 million has been spent on building and upgrading secure care facilities in all nine provinces, only two such facilities are currently operating (one in Gauteng and the other in the Northern Cape). The lesson that has been learnt from this episode is that, even though South Africa has the most progressive children's rights clause in the world in its Constitution, the current political climate surrounding crime cannot be ignored in the law reform process.

Listening to the Children Themselves

Like its sister project committee, the Project Committee on Juvenile Justice also undertook an ambitious and innovative project aimed at involving children themselves in the process of law reform. This pioneering study—pioneering at least as far as legal drafters are concerned, that is—took the form of the commissioning of a consultative report based on research with children themselves, to include children's perspectives on the shape of the proposed new legislation. The children who were chosen to participate were, save for a control group of senior school children who had had no prior contact with the criminal justice system, all children who had direct experience of juvenile justice. They comprised children undergoing diversion programs, children in various forms of residential care after having been sentenced by courts, and children in prison, both those awaiting trial and those serving sentences.

This strategy of consulting with children was not only intended to give effect, in a practical way, to Article 12 of the Convention on the Rights of the Child, which requires that children's voices be heard in matters affecting them. The committee also suspected that these children's experiences of the present criminal justice system, and the realism of their views, might lend a balance to the harsh sentiments on youth crime that are the media diet of the day!

In the result, the consultation was highly illuminating. Children were asked to respond to questions about chapters of the draft Bill, including police powers, diversion, the proposed introduction of a new inquiry procedure prior to appearance in court, legal representation and sentencing. They were also asked to consider a range of new orders that had been developed by the Project Committee as potential inexpensive diversion options, and to say whether they thought that these orders might be useful additions to the emerging South African system of diversion. Perhaps a few examples will illustrate the valuable insights gained from the children's responses.

Take the issue of sentencing: children were required to comment on what they thought were appropriate sentences for children convicted of serious offences. Apart from a few somewhat anti-human rights ideas (the chopping off of limbs, vigilante action and other similar suggestions), the majority of the children consulted predictably opted for long-term imprisonment. But, in sharp contrast to the recently introduced minimum mandatory sentences of fifteen, twenty, twenty-five years and life imprisonment without parole for certain serious offences, children's perceptions of long-term imprisonment—*for imposition upon children*—were rather different. Most of the children consulted chose a maximum sentence, for the most heinous offences, of between six and fifteen years, as this period, in their perception, is a very long time to be incarcerated. Ninety-eight per cent of the children consulted said that life imprisonment should not be an option for those below the age of eighteen years. They felt that life imprisonment is cruel and inhumane because a child has not experienced enough of life, and can change his or her ways if given the right guidance and support.

As regards the proposal that a minimum age for imprisonment should be set in the future statute, the most common response was that this was desirable, and that the age should be fixed at sixteen years. (In present-day South Africa, the minimum age of criminal capacity is seven years, and children as young as twelve have been sentenced to serve terms in prison.)

The children's views on legal representation were also illuminating. Only half of those in the sample had had legal representation during their own cases, yet many felt that lawyers could positively influence the outcome of a case. Those involved in the consultation expressed substantial support for the novel legislative proposal that children should not be allowed to waive legal representation. This view contrasts strongly with the opinions of traditionalist (adult) lawyers, who in their written submissions on the discussion paper favoured the view that part of the right to legal representation is the right to refuse it.

The children's views have been reflected fully in the final report. Their insights have directly influenced several provisions, and have indirectly influenced many others. As a first for law reformers in this country, an important benchmark towards hearing the voices of children has been set.

Wrestling with the Revenue Realities

Throughout this paper thus far we have alluded to the budgetary implications attached to the process of law writing upon which both project committees have embarked. In an ideal world, law reform would be shaped by a concern for matters of principle, the bedrock of precedent, a desire for internal jurisprudential consistency, adherence to constitutional and international standards and an academic engagement with the niceties of one or another legal solution. Then, having exercised the necessary choices, the law reformers would be able to step aside, leaving matters of implementation and resourcing to the executive. But, as both committees realised from the outset, this ivory tower approach to law reform is an indulgence that they simply could not afford. This realisation has played—and will continue to play—a vital role in the ongoing work of child law reform, both as regards children in trouble with the law and children generally.

Costing the Implementation of the Child Justice Bill—the AFREC Report

The Project Committee on Juvenile Justice was concerned that, in the present economic climate, fiscal considerations could prove a substantial barrier to adoption of a new statute (on the grounds that South Africa cannot afford a new juvenile justice system). Even worse, progressive individual provisions could be scrapped or changed during the parliamentary process as cost-saving devices, or (as has happened with some new laws recently) implementation delayed indefinitely whilst government casts around for the money to put the legislation into operation. Thus projections of the likely cost of the proposed new system were potentially going to be an extremely important consideration when parliament came to deal with the Child Justice Bill.

Also, because of the debacle surrounding the imprisonment of awaiting-trial children, with the Welfare Department still struggling to find (and properly spend) the resources to fund secure-care accommodation as an alternative to prison, the Project Committee wished to put the funding issues squarely on the table. In other words, before government departments leapt in (with the best of intentions) to support a children's rights-oriented juvenile justice statute, the committee wanted a corresponding commitment to provide the resources necessary for its success.

With this in mind, the committee tasked a team of economists from the Applied Fiscal Research Centre of the University of Cape Town to prepare a costing of the juvenile justice system proposed in the discussion paper, and to develop a strategy for its implementation. This was the first time that draft legislation from the Law Commission had been analysed from an economic stance, and it required that a unique interaction between legal drafters and public sector economic policy analysts be established.

The mammoth endeavour involved, first, the preparation (on the basis of limited and sketchy data and statistics) of an economic breakdown of the likely expenditure in the present juvenile justice system. This in turn entailed estimating cross-cutting programs in five national departments (Police, Welfare, Justice, Correctional Services and Education), as well as Police and Welfare Departments at provincial level in each of the nine provinces. Variables included such diverse items as personnel expenditure, court time and police transport, not to mention residential care and the costs of imprisonment. All of this had to be rendered meaningful and relevant without core baseline data, such as the number of children under the age of eighteen years who are arrested each year. This figure had to be assumed on the basis of overall arrest figures, and extracted from the general census statistics which give proportions of children as a percentage of the overall population, for urban, peri-urban and rural areas. A range of further assumptions were developed, such as differential crime rates for urban and rural areas, and the average number of remands in court per case.

Having arrived at the probable baseline cost of the present system of arrest, detention, trial and sentence of children over an annual period, the economists proceeded to plot increased expenditure, as well as potential decreases in expenditure, in the proposed new system. The increased costs to Welfare of diversion programs, which form a central item of the proposed legislative framework, would be countered by decreases in the costs of sentences, predicted the economists. Moreover, the introduction of the pre-trial case conference (termed the 'preliminary inquiry') in the discussion paper might increase the costs to the Department of Justice in respect of magistrates, but would substantially reduce a range of other variables, including police transport, court time, remands and unnecessary detention costs.

In the event, although this was not explicitly part of the brief to the AFREC team, the Project Committee was delighted at the most significant finding of the analysis: that the introduction of the proposed legislative model could bring about savings in the order of R200 million on current government expenditure—and this without taking into account the indirect social and fiscal benefits that could accrue as a result of increased government efficiency, a more child-friendly criminal justice system and, above all, a far more effective and appropriate restorative justice-oriented process for young people who come into conflict with the law.

Drafting a New Comprehensive Children's Statute: Fancy Fiscal Footwork?

The drafters of a new, comprehensive Children's Statute obviously face the same fiscal restraints as those which underpin the AFREC Report. The challenge is therefore to develop strategies to ensure that fiscal considerations do not ultimately torpedo the whole process of developing a new and progressive legislative framework for South Africa's children.

A Bigger Pie?

Given that both human and financial resources are an essential precondition to the success of legislation, the reality is nevertheless that (irrespective of the form of a new children's statute adopted), the overall balance of state spending is *not* going to tilt more in favour of children, whatever the intentions of government. The macro-economic climate set by GEAR clearly abandons state economic intervention and public sector-driven redistribution as the primary mechanisms for the eradication of poverty. As pointed out already, the emphasis falls on stimulation of private sector-led investment, to achieve an enhanced growth rate and improved job creation prospects. Along with this comes fiscal austerity (which suggests no immediate plans for bolstering the overall welfare budget in real terms). GEAR significantly prioritises economic growth and reduction of governmental expenditure and, within this context, there appears to be limited room to capture larger resources to benefit the poorest and most marginalised people in general, and children in particular.[20]

This kind of thinking is not new. In 1996, one of the present authors reviewed the process of constitutionalising rights and, more pertinently, basic social and

[20] See *Public Expenditure on Basic Social Services in South Africa* Financial and Fiscal Commission Report for UNICEF and UNDP (1998), p 21. GEAR targets are not, however, cast in stone, as the deliberations at the Presidential Job Summit held at the end of October 1998 illustrate—see, for example, *Welfare Update* (Dec 1998), p 3.

economic rights for children, and claimed that, in the medium term, the overwhelming political support for the *idea* of children's rights would not necessary translate into measurable gains:

> If a more widespread realisation were to develop that children's rights are not a 'universal good' . . . and that they indeed traverse significant political choices, commitment to potentially controversial long term policies, and thorny questions about the allocation of scarce resources . . . Children's rights issues may no longer be a wise or desirable political horse to back (although the 'we support children' public rhetoric will no doubt continue). Given the incontestable fact that children lack constituency and clout, and considering the mounting evidence of wavering political will, there are surely now substantial obstacles for further general achievements in the field of children's rights.[21]

It is worthy of note that these predictions were made at a time before South Africa adopted what has been termed its self-imposed structural adjustment program (GEAR), and indeed during the honeymoon period when there was still a general expectation that the new government would provide. Shortly after this, these fears were poignantly illustrated when the national NGO campaign to augment the proposed child support grant (by targeting more children, increasing the cut-off ages of beneficiaries, and raising the benefit level) met with limited success as the realisation dawned that more money was simply not going to be forthcoming.

Dividing the Existing Slices More Effectively

A more pragmatic approach would be content with formulating a legislative model that would itself have an effect on resource distribution within the existing 'pie'. This is well illustrated by the example of subsidies to children in institutional care. As the Inter-Ministerial Committee on Young People at Risk reports,[22] the costs of maintaining a child in a residential care institution total at least R75 per day, with the direct subsidy per child amounting to approximately R800 per month. It could be argued that family preservation, rather than institutionalisation, is much more cost-efficient, enabling the same resources to reach a far greater proportion of children in a manner that is certainly more in keeping with the ideal of using removal and institutionalisation as a matter of last resort.[23]

[21] Julia Sloth-Nielsen, 'The Contribution of Children's Rights to the Reconstruction of Society: Some Implications of the Constitutionalisation of Children's Rights in South Africa' (1996) 4 *International Journal of Children's Rights* 323 at 340.

[22] In *Interim Policy Recommendations for the Transformation of the Child and Youth Care System* (Nov 1996), pp 89–90.

[23] Of course, any such shift in resource allocation carries with it the real risk of increasing the cost burden to families and communities—often borne by women as care-givers. Non-governmental organisations have expressed the fear that the introduction of 'developmental social welfare' as a model for welfare service delivery and funding will have this effect. As one author points out: 'It is unacceptable and unsustainable for economic policy to be formed around an assumption that women's work will subsidise cuts in social spending.' (C Sweeting, 'Women and the Family' (1996) 4 *Gender and Development* 5, as cited in Vivienne Bozalek, 'Gender Equality and Welfare Rights in South Africa:

Also, the present amount per child transferred as a direct subsidy to children's homes and other residential care facilities is substantially more than the amount paid out in the form of an old age pension to an indigent person (R520 per month from March 2000). Indeed, it is eight times more than the amount payable to a care-giver caring for a child in his or her home, with the current level of the child support grant pegged at R100 per month. By weighting legislation *against* removal, monies might be freed up within the current expenditure framework to allow for greater emphasis in legislation and in practice for supporting children within their families and communities. However, care would have to be taken to ensure that the funds thus released are *in fact* utilised to provide the appropriate support for family care.

Another example flows from the present system of foster care grants. This grant, payable to a foster parent after a child has been placed in foster care by a children's court order, at present amounts to R374 per month. In 1996/97 alone, the expenditure on these grants was R180 million.[24] Yet no subsidy is payable for the more permanent placement option for children who cannot reside with their family in the long term—namely adoption. In addition, the pending AIDS crisis has raised questions about the appropriateness of this kind of 'foster care' system (attracting a cash subsidy payable to an identified and designated 'foster parent'), where children in villages and townships whose lives will be most affected would benefit more from a broader form of support (with linked financial aid). The more fluid approaches that have been mooted are innovations such as neighbourhood centres offering a broad range of care services, or transfers of available monies to communities and villages as a whole, for the care of their young members as a *community* responsibility.[25] In other words, the question that arises is whether the present level of transfer payments for children can be more equitably shared to accommodate a greater range of child care arrangements.

In October 1999, it was announced that the government was considering cutting individual grants to foster parents and channelling more money to communal child care projects in a bid to cope with the growing number of AIDS orphans (an estimated 2.3 million children—14 per cent of South African children under the age of fifteen years—by the year 2005). This announcement was welcomed by organisations such as Child Welfare, but subject to the proviso that the shift away from individual foster care grants was accompanied by new strategies to cover poor children over the age of seven years who were not eligible for the child support grant.[26]

However, before tackling legislation that attempts to reorganise existing

The Lund Committee on Child and Family Support', *Women & Human Rights Documentation Centre Newsletter* (Apr 1997), p 3 at p 4.

[24] See John Kruger and Shirin Motala, 'Welfare', in Shirley Robinson and Linda Biersteker (eds), *First Call—the South African Children's Budget* (IDASA, 1997), p 85.

[25] See papers presented at the CINDI (Children in Distress) conference on 'Raising the Orphan Generation', Pietermaritzburg, June 1998.

[26] See the *Cape Times*, 25 Oct 1999 ('Money to go to AIDS orphans—foster grants may be cut').

budgetary allocations, a note of caution must be sounded. Rumour has it that when the Lund Committee was briefed to investigate a more equitable and simplified grant system for poor children to replace the pre-existing State Maintenance Grant system, the Sword of Damocles hanging over the committee was the very real risk that this type of grant could be abolished altogether. Aware of this, the committee consciously structured the proposals in such a way as to retain at least the same level of state spending in this area. The Lund Committee experience illustrates the possible danger of tampering too radically with inherited cost allocations, because proposals for change can be used by government as an opportunity to jettison the old without implementing the new. It is a sobering thought that, although the existing State Maintenance Grants have been cut by two-thirds, and new grant applications are no longer being accepted, only 237,000 beneficiaries are allegedly in receipt of the new child support grant, representing a very substantial saving to the state coffers, and providing no clarity about whether the savings thus effected can be rolled over to future years.[27]

The cutting of the State Maintenance Grant has caused enormous hardship, especially to female-headed households in the Western Cape, where 60,000 people (75 per cent being single mothers) are affected. Studies in the Western Cape have revealed that 70 per cent of the children currently benefiting from the State Maintenance Grant will not qualify for the child support grant.[28]

It has been cogently argued that, instead of using R1.7 billion of the revenue generated by higher than expected growth and better than expected revenue collection to reduce the government budget deficit to GDP ratio further, this money could have been used in the National Budget 2000 to provide some income for those poor children not covered by the child support grant. According to recent income poverty estimates, 6.4 million children aged between seven and eighteen years fall outside the CSG 'safety net'—R7 680 million of the R1.7 billion could have been used to give these children R100 per month for the 2000/01 financial year.[29]

Partaking of Someone Else's Slice

In the 1996 publication referred to previously, an attempt was made to identify certain 'support factors' that could assist in sustaining the momentum marking the implementation of children's rights in the initial stages of the reconstruction of South African society. Is it not possible to follow the same approach in the process of conceptualising the economic frontiers of proposed child legislation, in order to bolster the likelihood that such legislation has at least an outside chance of attracting the required fiscal support?

[27] See Judith Streak, 'Poverty Gap between Policy and Spending' (2000) 4 *ChildrenFIRST* 13.

[28] See the *Cape Argus*, 17 Mar 2000 ('60,000 hit by lifelife grant cut'); the *Cape Argus*, 16 Mar 2000 ('Grant cut leaves poor families facing destitution'); and Pia Zain, 'A small process of dying: The impact of the cancellation of the State Maintenance Grant', *NADEL Research Report* No 12 (2000).

[29] Streak, n 27, p 15.

For example, one option open to law reformers might be to exercise choices in such a way as to piggyback on to existing policies and programs with already established public and state support, and therefore a virtually guaranteed source of funding. A case in point is the appropriate role of the children's court in a new statutory dispensation, an issue that has been canvassed above. This is not simply an academic debate, to be viewed in isolation, given the present lack of capacity and low status of the children's court. To a certain extent, the cards are already on the table. The establishment of family courts is more or less a *fait accompli*, and if the proposals of the recent Hoexter Commission,[30] as well as the stated intentions of the Department of Justice,[31] are anything to go by, there is a very realistic prospect of expertise, services and material resources being channelled in the direction of the family courts. As the issues around the likely breadth of jurisdiction of the courts have still to be finally determined, it might be expedient to position a new children's forum within the family court structure, thereby tapping into an existing source of funding, rather than trying to dig a new well altogether.[32]

Similarly, victim empowerment has been endorsed at the highest level of government policy. As a cardinal feature of the National Crime Prevention Strategy (which itself has a generous source of funding through the Reconstruction and Development Program), it has been backed by a vociferous women's lobby. Not only has legislation dealing with family violence been promulgated and put into operation,[33] and a project committee of the Law Commission been tasked with investigating victim empowerment more generally,[34] but at a purely practical level, plans to build and staff community support centres with the express idea of providing services to victims of crime are being implemented.[35] A new legislative framework around reporting and follow-up services in respect of child abuse could perhaps be formulated in such a way as to legitimately exploit this initiative.

Baking a New Pie

Another strategy is to explore the avenue of new sources of funding. Although the room to manoeuvre at the national level seems limited, are there not possibilities of new resources to be accessed with the changes that are taking place in provincial and local government? Some metropolitan councils have already shown an awareness of their role in poverty alleviation and in redressing social inequality.

[30] Commission of Inquiry into the Rationalisation of the Provincial and Local Divisions of the Supreme Court, *Third and Final Report* (Dec 1997), Book 1, Part 2.

[31] See, for example, Department of Justice Family Court Pilot Project, 'Concept document' (Nov 1997).

[32] See Debbie Budlender, 'Doing something with nothing: The family centre pilots', *Issues in Law, Race and Gender* No 7 (Law, Race and Gender Research Unit, University of Cape Town, 2000).

[33] *Domestic Violence Act* 116 of 1998, operative from 15 Dec 1999.

[34] This falls within the ambit of the project on Sentencing (Project 82).

[35] See 'Report of the Portfolio Committee on Welfare on Budget Vote 36: Welfare, dated 15 Mar 1999' *Hansard* (17 Mar 1999), p 249.

For example, Cape Town has launched an initiative on street people (including children)[36] and a similar city-wide endeavour has been started in greater Johannesburg. In Kwa-Zulu Natal, local authorities are engaging in partnerships with the business community to address the plight of children with AIDS.[37] Local government may not be directly involved in some of the types of resource allocation discussed above—grants, subsidies and direct transfers—but there are other possibilities, such as employment of community workers to serve children's needs, provision of capital resources for children's projects, and financial support to civic organisations that can in turn play an important role in implementing the new legislation.[38]

Finally, as the experience of Uganda has shown, it is not impossible that the international community can successfully be mobilised to provide material support for the implementation of new children's legislation, particularly as the extensive children's rights framework enshrined in the Constitution is internationally regarded as something of a beacon to the rest of the developing world. Somewhat cynically, it could be argued that the international children's rights community has a 'moral stake' in assisting us to make these rights a reality.

CONCLUSION

In conclusion, both the Project Committee on Juvenile Justice and the Project Committee tasked with developing a new, comprehensive children's statute have been forced to confront the reality that these law reform processes are not exclusively, or even primarily, *legal* endeavours—on the contrary, they are performances that must be played out on a much larger stage. It would appear that the 'words on paper' are in reality of far less import than the political and economic strategies adopted during the drafting process.[39] We anticipate that the kinds of tactics touched upon above will have an important bearing on the formulation of a new child justice statute and a new children's statute—statutes which are politically acceptable, 'sellable' to the implementers of GEAR, and yet still achieve their primary purpose of protecting and empowering children in accordance with our obligations under the Constitution and the Convention on the Rights of the Child.

[36] Cape Metropolitan Council *Street People: Mission Statement and Recommendations for Local Authorities in the Cape Metropolitan Area* (June 1998).

[37] See Report of the Pietermaritzburg Summit on Children in Distress (July 1996).

[38] Care would have to be taken to ensure some level of equality across the country, given the disparities in revenue collection possibilities that characterise different provincial governments and local authorities: see the *Cape Argus* 24 Feb 2000 ('Stark differences divide provinces').

[39] It is possibly a little unorthodox that this conclusion has been reached by two lawyers who were raised primarily on a diet of weighty legal tomes and voluminous law reports. However, in the interests of successful law reform, we have had to step outside our usual terrain, and engage (albeit as amateurs) with the mysteries of macro-economic strategies.

31

The Introduction and Impact of Joint Custody in Portugal

Maria Clara Sottomayor*

Joint custody was introduced in Portugal in 1995 and was the result of a coalition between feminist and fathers' rights interests. In spite of that, joint custody is not fully accepted by judges with experience in child custody decision-making and has limited popular support. The social reality shows that the division of roles within the family is a traditional one, with women remaining the primary caretakers of children. It is also emphasised that domestic violence and its effects on women and children have emerged as a public issue in Portugal.

This chapter examines three aspects of the development of child custody law: the civil code reform of 1977, which brought about the gender equality principle and the sole custody rule after divorce; the introduction in 1995 of the joint custody rule after divorce as a result of the interaction between the feminist movement and child protection institutions; and the most recent changes to the law, in 1999, which occurred as a result of pressure by fathers' rights groups. The chapter concludes by looking at the consequences of joint custody.

THE PATRIARCHAL FAMILY IN THE CIVIL CODE REFORM OF 1977 AND THE INTRODUCTION OF THE SOLE CUSTODY RULE

The civil code of 1966, before the democratic revolution, postulated a patriarchal and hierarchical conception of the family. In respect of the parent–child relationship, the civil code stipulated that father and mother, if married, were both entitled to paternal power[1] concerning minor children (Article 1879). However, the law differentiated between the entitlement to parental power and its exercise. In accord with the patriarchal and Roman tradition, the father was the only one

* Family Law Assistant at the Portuguese Catholic University, Porto, Portugal.

[1] The contemporary law still uses the patriarchal expression 'paternal power', although it is conceived as a group of parental responsibilities and rights to be exercised in the interest of the children. The feminist language change was not accepted by the legislator, considering that it was difficult in the Portuguese vocabulary to find a new word (although the new dictionaries contain the gender-neutral word 'parental') and because 'paternal power' was the expression used by the legal practice.

legally allowed to represent a minor child, administer her or his property, and take the major decisions concerning the child's support and education, like emancipation, professional instruction and the practise of a job (Article 1881). The mother was entitled to a say about those matters and to collaborate with the father in relation to the child's interests and, where the father was unable to act or was absent, she was authorised to exercise the paternal power (Article 1882). The civil law did not stipulate a solution for the exercise of parental rights and duties after divorce or separation. The law only mentioned that, in the case of divorce, separation or marriage annulment, both parents retained the paternal power, but its exercise was regulated by parental agreement or, in cases of parental conflict, by the Minor Child Court (Article 1902). Mothers usually got custody of children, but the father maintained the power to represent the child, to decide about her or his education, and to administer her or his property. However, according to the opinion of the jurists, in case of divorce or separation, the mother exercised the education role and the father, because of tradition, only performed the function of representation.[2]

Some authors argued that, as family unity was destroyed, the father was not the head of the post-divorce family, and mothers could totally exercise the paternal power.[3] This was the position established by the Civil Code Reform of 1977, which brought family law into harmony with the Constitution of 1976 by introducing the principle of equality between men and women concerning child education and support (Article 36, n 2 of the Portuguese Republic Constitution). This change followed the democratic revolution of April 1974. There had always been a link between political change and family law reforms; as a consequence of this revolution, the civil law abandoned the patriarchal and authoritarian concept of the family. Marriage is now based on the spouses' equality of rights and duties: family life is directed jointly by husband and wife, considering the good of the family and the interests of the spouses (Article 1671)[4] and parents exercise parental responsibility jointly during marriage (Article 1901).

The law relating to custody after divorce did not follow the gender equality trend of the democratic revolution and did not stipulate joint custody after the dissolution of marriage. This was because it was not then known whether parental behaviour after divorce would become more friendly. Until 1977, as a result of traditional family structures, divorce was rare and conflictual.[5] Although divorce was admitted for Catholic marriages in 1975,[6] and mutual consent and no-fault divorce were

[2] J Miranda, 'O poder paternal no Código Civil de 1867 e no novo Código Civil, Breve Confronto' (1967) 2 *Informação Social* 75 at 81.

[3] JCM Almeid, 'O poder paternal no direito moderno' (1969) XV *Scientia Juridica* 77 at 89.

[4] Unless otherwise indicated, the citations to articles are from the Civil Code of 1966.

[5] In 1970, the divorce rate in relation to the number of marriages celebrated was 0.6% and the judicial separation rate was 0.65%: *Estatísticas Demográficas,* Instituto Nacional de Estatística, Portugal, 1970.

[6] See the Additional Pact celebrated in 1975, which amended the original Treaty celebrated in 1940 between the Portuguese State and the Holy See, whose Art 24 originally stated that couples married by the Catholic Church after 1 Aug 1940 renounced the civil right of divorce. Through the Additional Pact it was agreed that spouses married in a Catholic ceremony could be divorced by a civil court.

introduced by Decree no. 261/75, dated 27 May and by Decree 56/76, dated 13 May, the majority of divorces were litigated, and the logic of the divorce-sanction predominated.[7] In 1977, the legislature—although having considered the introduction of joint custody after divorce—decided to be prudent in order to protect the child from parental conflict, and chose sole custody and unilateral exercise of parental rights and responsibilities by the custodial parent (Article 1906, n 1). Parental relationships after divorce were supposed to be inevitably antagonistic, and legislators could not help being mindful of the father's interference in the educative role performed by the mother under the previous legislation.

The law wanted to avoid parental conflicts about the child's life, education and representation as well as the use of the child as a pawn in battles between exspouses. Consequently, the 1977 law decided to concentrate the exercise of parental rights and responsibilities in the hands of the custodial parent. The *ratio legis* of this rule were, on the one hand, psychological grounds—concerning the hostility between ex-spouses after divorce—and, on the other hand, practical reasons.[8] The latter reflect the difficulties created for the custodial parent by the necessity of seeking the consent of the other parent, who might live apart from the child's daily life or even far away from her or him, for each important decision respecting the child's person or property. It is also assumed that the parent who lives with the child is the one more familiar with the child's necessities and personality and because of that is better placed to protect, educate and supervise the child. Sole custody was considered to be the solution which best conformed to the interests of children in providing a stable life and meant that the law wanted to recognise the effective role performed by mothers in children's education after divorce.[9]

Nevertheless, despite the lack of a joint custody provision in the law, case law accepted parental agreements on joint custody if they were in the child's best interest. This outcome was not reflected in the law but was considered to be legally possible if parents agreed to it and if the judge confirmed the agreement, considering that it was in the child's best interest. Under such an agreement, parents

[7] In 1976, mutual consent divorces were 10.6%, in 1977 they were 38.1% and in 1978 they were 47.6%: 'Casamentos e divórcios em Portugal—alguns números sobre a evolução recente' (1983), p 55. Since 1979, the majority of divorces are mutual consent divorces: in 1979, 65%; in 1986, 68.6% and in 1994, 72.7%: see A Torres, *Divórcio em Portugal, Ditos e Interditos, Uma análise sociológica* (Celta Editora, 1996), p 232.

[8] MC Sottomayor, *Exercício do poder paternal relativamente à pessoa do filho após o divórcio ou a separação judicial de pessoas e bens* (Universidade de Coimbra, 1992), pp 168–71.

[9] In fact, the judicial rule about child custody has been maternal preference for children of tender years, up to ten years of age. This was accompanied by other rules like non-separation of siblings, and preference to the parent who has the same sex of the child when he or she is not a child of tender years, and has survived in our judicial decisions until the last decade. Rules of 'experience' and 'the nature of things' were cited by judges to justify maternal preference. Courts used to quote the 6th principle of the Universal Declaration of Children's Rights from the United Nations, that 'the child of tender years must not, except in uncommon circumstances, be separated from her or his mother'. This rule worked like a judicial presumption rebuttable by proof of the mother's incapacity to take care of the child due to her moral behaviour or neglect: Sottomayor, n 8, pp 121–26.

should fix the child's permanent residence and the amount of child support to be paid by the non-residential parent.[10]

THE FEMINIST MOVEMENT AND THE CHANGE IN GENDER ROLES BY LAW

In 1995, the law 84/95, dated 31 August, changed the civil code as it affected custody after divorce. The law specifies that the child's interest means that she or he has the right to maintain a close relationship with the non-custodial parent and allows joint custody where there is parental agreement (Article 1906, n 2). Joint custody is an agreement where parents decide questions affecting the child's life in accordance with the rules applicable during marriage. Major decisions must be decided jointly: in case of disagreement, either parent can go to court to ask for a judicial resolution of the conflict (Article 1901, n 2). Instead of joint custody, parents can decide that certain important matters concerning their children will be decided by both of them (Article 1906, n 3). Portuguese civil law does not stipulate either a legal preference or a presumption for joint custody, at that time maintaining sole custody as the legal rule (Article 1906, n 1).

This law was the result of a proposal prepared by the Portuguese Association of Women Law Professionals and by an institution called Father–Mother–Child, and presented in the parliament by the socialist party.[11] In the Bill, it was argued that the main reason for the introduction of the joint custody provision was the child's interests, particularly their affective and emotional needs. According to the project's arguments, sharing parental responsibility after divorce, and a child's continuing contact with both parents, can make divorce less traumatic for the child and improve her or his psychological development.[12] The feminist case for greater male responsibility in child care was also a reason cited for the change, as it was shown that women after divorce often carry the psychological, social and economic burden of raising children alone. The Portuguese feminist movement intended to fight female discrimination in the labour market and in the public sphere by stimulating fathers' participation in child care in order to avoid women's dependency created by maternity.[13] Joint custody, in spite of being justified from a feminist's viewpoint, also met the demands of fathers for equality in parental rights after divorce. Fathers' rights movements argued that mothers received child custody in 90 per cent of the cases[14] and that the child's relationship with the father

[10] A Leandro, 'Poder paternal: Natureza, conteúdo, exercício e limitações: Algumas reflexões de prática judiciária', in *Temas de Direito da Família* (Coimbra, 1986), pp 113–64, at p 158.

[11] DAR, 5 Jan 1995, II Série-A—N° 11, Projecto de Lei n° 475/VI, pp 124–125.

[12] *Ibid.*, p 125.

[13] The feminist movement is now trying to transform the formal equality principle in a equality of results, obtained through special rules to favour women, like the anticipation of the retiring pension for women who took care of children and a quota for women in parliament.

[14] The official statistics include consensual and litigated cases. Consequently, they do not show the difference between the rates of mother custody in consensual and in litigated cases. In consensual

was diminished. However, considering that child care and domestic work are principally performed by women, even among young people,[15] this fact should not be perceived as discrimination against fathers as a whole, but as the result of the patterns of life followed by couples during marriage.[16] It was also pointed out in the project that social change had made divorce a less conflictual event than in traditional family structures. Nevertheless, the legislator thought that this new attitude towards divorce and the capacity of parents to jointly exercise their parental rights and duties was not the same in all social groups, with better-educated social groups more prepared for joint custody.[17] Among the less favoured groups, divorce is still seen as a sanction against the spouse who breaches their marital duties.[18] As a result, it was decided that joint custody would be applied, considering its social adaptation and in accordance with criteria of reasonableness.[19] It is recognised that the high percentage of mutual consent divorces does not necessarily mean that there is not a high level of conflict between spouses.[20] Mutual consent divorce is not thought to be a divorce without a cause but, rather, a divorce with a cause that the spouses do not choose to reveal to the court.[21] These couples prefer to use divorce by mutual consent because the process is quicker and cheaper than litigation.[22] Consequently, the legislators decided not to expect too much from the joint custody provision and it was only allowed when there was parental agreement.

cases, which represent the majority, fathers are not interested in obtaining child custody. When they want to, they have equal chances of winning. In the 1990s, published decisions indicated that the courts were no longer applying maternal preference. The basis of the decisions is not the old assumptions about motherhood and human nature but the new roles that men and women are supposed to be developing in the family and society with the gradual disappearance of the traditional role of mother, totally dedicated to child care. In consequence, custody has been given to men who have flexible jobs in comparison with full-time working mothers and to men who take care of the child during the period of de facto separation that precedes divorce. However, such decisions often penalise women because they do not perform their traditional housewife role or because they live in a non-marital cohabitation with a man. The relative parental economic situation has also penalised mothers who earn less money than men: MC Sottomayor, *Regulação do exercício do poder paternal nos casos de divórcio* (Almedina, 2000), pp 35–45.

15 A Torres, n 7, pp 46–48.

16 Social inquiries show that less well-educated couples have a rigid division of labour in domestic work and child care, while more educated couples, although having the ideal of sexual equality in sharing work and responsibility in family life, only act according to these values in a smaller number of cases: *ibid.*, p 161.

17 A Leandro, 'Poder paternal: Natureza, Conteúdo, exercício e limitações: Algumas reflexões de prática judiciária', in *Temas de Direito da Família* (Coimbra, 1986), pp 113–64 at p 157. See also DAR, I Série—N° 45, 24 Feb 1995, p 1582; DAR, 24 Feb 1995, II série-A—Número 23 (Report and Opinion of the Fundamental Rights Comission), p 338.

18 A Torres, n 7, pp 84–106.

19 DAR, I Série—N° 45, p 1582.

20 *Ibid.*

21 FMP Coelho, 'Divórcio e separação judicial de pessoas e bens na reforma do Código Civil', in *Reforma do Código Civil* (Ordem dos Advogados, 1981), pp 27–53 at p 29. The divorce rate in 1999 was around 26%. Mutual consent divorces represented 86.9% of the total number of divorces and women filed for 62% of the litigated divorces. See *Portugal 2001, Situação das Mulheres* (2001), p 86.

22 Torres, n 7.

After a brief debate, the final text of the reform was approved unanimously. Apart from minor drafting changes, the initial proposal had two significant alterations. The first was the specific requirement of parental agreement for joint custody, as this point was not clear in the proposal. The second was the omission in the final text, of the alternating residence of the child with both parents, which was recognised in the original proposal as a possible option for parents. Although the final text does not expressly mention this choice, it is arguable that, given the lack of specific prohibition, parents are free to choose their preferred model of joint custody, provided that the judge accepts that this decision is in the child's interest. Anyway, joint physical custody is rarely adopted, as it is practicable neither for parents nor for children, and many judges think that it may endanger the child's sense of stability. Only parents who are particularly concerned about their children and who have support from psychologists have taken this up. Statistics from other countries with experience in joint custody reveal that the prevalent model is joint legal custody with the child's permanent residence being with the mother.[23] We still see the old patterns of family life in the new models—particularly child care as a woman's responsibility. Consequently, joint custody ends up granting rights to fathers without the underlying obligations.

THE FATHERS' RIGHTS GROUPS AND JOINT CUSTODY

The fathers' rights groups which appeared in 1998, and acted as a lobby near the parliament in order to change the child custody laws, were largely responsible for the third step of this evolutionary process.[24] A parental association, Parents Forever, prepared a Bill in which the joint exercise of parental rights should become the legal rule after divorce, refutable only by proof that it was not in the interest of the child. This solution was not supported by empirical studies. The authors of the project only argued with mother–child custody statistics, mixing the litigated cases with the consensual ones and with assumptions not documented in social sciences about changes in gender roles and friendly relationships between parents after divorce.

The project was enacted, but the final text does not go so far as the terms of the project. Joint custody continues to be only legally permitted when there is a parental agreement and where a presumption or legal preference for joint custody was not admitted. The sole custody rule with unilateral exercise of parental rights

[23] EE Maccoby and RH Mnookin, *Dividing the Child: Social and Legal Dilemmas of Custody* (Harvard University Press, 1992), p 268; H Fulchiron, 'Une nouvelle réforme de l'autorité parentale', in *Dalloz* (1993), pp 117–22 at p 121; H Oelkers, H Kasten, and A Oelkers, 'Das gemeinssorgerecht nach scheidung in der Praxis der Amtsgerichts Hamburg—Familiengericht' (1994) 17 *Familien Recht Zeitung* 1980 at 1982.

[24] The Portuguese parliament is characterised by male dominance: in 1999, women represented about 16% of the total number of deputies. This legislature maintains the same trend, at 17.4% women. See *Portugal 2001, Situação das Mulheres*, p 102.

and duties was abolished, and the law states that the judge must try to obtain the agreement of the parents to joint custody. In case of failure, the judge decrees sole custody but must justify the decision. It is a way of improving the idea of joint custody by forcing judges to consider it as an option for parents as father's rights groups complained that judges rejected joint custody. However, I think that, to justify the sole custody decision, it is enough to allege that it was not possible for the judge to obtain the parental agreement. The refusal of one of the parents is considered to be a presumption that parents do not have the necessary capacity of cooperation to make joint custody work.[25]

THE CONSEQUENCES OF JOINT CUSTODY

As joint custody represents a recent change to the law, there are not yet any social scientific studies of its consequences. Speculatively, it seems unlikely to change the present social reality. Joint legal custody will enhance the non-residential parent's self-esteem because the residential parent cannot alone make major decisions about the child. It changes the 'all or nothing' outcome represented by sole custody with unilateral exercise of parental responsibilities and rights. However, it will probably not create meaningful changes in the amount of contact between the non-residential parent and the child.[26] If parents agree on alternating residence, it will increase father–child contact and improve the quality of this relationship, but these cases are likely to be very rare. Besides, joint custody creates the danger of conflicts between parents about child education and the mother's dependency in obtaining the father's consent for important decisions concerning the child.

Recent studies published in Portugal about domestic violence show that divorced and separated women are those more affected by domestic violence.[27] The judicial imposition of, or pressure for, joint custody in domestic violence cases endangers children's well-being, particularly if they witness the violence or are harmed themselves. Requiring the primary caretaker of the child to justify a refusal of joint custody, as the project demanded, would create insecurity, giving the judge a discretionary power to accept or not the reasons alleged by the primary caretaker.

The legal imposition of joint custody can also lead to low child support awards, because of the change in the parents' bargaining power when deciding child custody and support matters. This will further impoverish sole parent families who are already among the poorest in Portugal, since the largest group of divorced

[25] Sottomayor, n 14, pp 136–37.

[26] See the example of the United States where research comparing joint legal custody with sole custody by the mother found no increase in fathers' visitations or involvement in decision-making about the child's life:, CL Albiston EE Maccoby and R Mnookin, 'Does Joint Custody Really Matter?' (1990) 2 *Law and Policy Review* 167.

[27] N Lourenço, M Lisboa and E Pais, *Violência contra as Mulheres* (Cadernos da Condição Feminina n 48, Comissão para a Igualdade e para os Direitos das Mulheres, 1997).

women comprises those who have problems with job instability and low qualifications.[28] To avoid these consequences, courts will effectively need to supervise parental agreements over the amounts of child support, and joint custody must not be applied or suggested in cases of domestic violence or high-conflict parental relationships. To our knowledge, unfortunately, courts usually do not exercise control upon parental agreements due to their heavy caseloads. So the only way to protect children is to maintain the sole custody legal role and to leave joint custody free for parents who really want it and who practise it whatever the law says. I consider that the family is an institution much more determined for human patterns of behaviour observed in social reality than for the law itself. Educational laws, when they are advanced in relation to reality, are just symbolic, and they can inflict adverse effects on women and children.[29] Joint custody is only a statement of principles, but empirical evidence shows that the responsibility for child care is not equally divided between parents. Changes in family behaviour involve a much slower process than legal reforms. Courts cannot help but consider that there is a great distance between the law and social reality in relation to gender roles. Social changes towards gender equality must appear first during marriage if they are to carry weight after divorce in decisions about the allocation of custody and arrangements for their implementation. The aim of the custody rules is not the construction of an egalitarian society, but the protection of the best interests of children.

[28] Torres, n 7, pp 213–15.

[29] For a criticism of the equality reform, which is applicable also to Portuguese divorce, law see MA Fineman, *The Illusion of Equality, The Rhetoric and Reality of Divorce Reform* (University of Chicago Press, 1991).